Aristotle Selected Works

Translations with Commentaries by H. G. Apostle

Aristotle's Metaphysics
Aristotle's Physics
Aristotle's Nicomachean Ethics
Aristotle's Categories and Propositions
Aristotle's Posterior Analytics
Aristotle's On the Soul
Aristotle's Politics (with L. P. Gerson)
Aristotle's Poetics (with E. A. Dobbs, M.A. Parslow)

ARISTOTLE
SELECTED WORKS
Third Edition

Translated by
HIPPOCRATES G. APOSTLE
and
LLOYD P. GERSON

THE PERIPATETIC PRESS
Des Moines, Iowa

© 1983, 1986, 1991 by H. G. Apostle
Published 1983. Second edition 1986. Third edition 1991.

Library of Congress catalog card number: 91-062514

Manufactured in the United States of America

ISBN *cl.* 0-911589-14-7
ISBN *pa.* 0-911589-13-9

Table of Contents

PREFACE

Aristotle's own works are the best introduction to his thought. A serious study of that thought, both comprehensively and in detail, can best be achieved by reading his works in the original Greek. Such study can best reveal his contribution to the understanding of philosophical truths and methods which have become part of our western civilization. But if knowledge of Greek is wanting and a general introduction is desired, the next best source is a scientific and accurate translation. The reason for this is that Aristotle's works are written scientifically, and unscientific translations distort that thought and mislead the reader. Instances of this fact will be given in the *Introduction*. The aim of this book is to serve as a general introduction, whether or not one wishes to continue a serious study of Aristotle.

Within the limits of space there are problems of selection and the manner of presentation. One may include only few works in their entirety, or just parts of many works, or one may take some intermediate position. There are advantages and disadvantages regardless of the choice, for there is a wide variety of interest, preparation, and maturity among the readers. Some are interested in the natural sciences, others in the social sciences, others in the logical works, others in the fine arts, and so on. If only a few works in their entirety are included, the other works will not be available to those who are interested in them. On the other hand, if only parts are included, the unity of a subject as a whole will not be apparent and hence Aristotle's method of treating a subject as a whole will suffer. Again, the young and inexperienced learn better by induction and by starting with what is less abstract, while those with greater maturity would rather start with the more abstract and with demonstrations; and in view of this fact, the selection of subjects and manner of presentation proper to each of these two groups should be made by the instructor.

Perhaps a general introduction to Aristotle should be like a general education given in most of our liberal arts colleges, in which a student gets a general view of many subjects but also majors in a specific field of his interest as a whole. Accordingly, we are including many works (seventeen in all), of which three are in their entirety, most of the rest are more or less half complete, and the remaining are represented by a few chapters. We are including what we consider to be the most important parts of the works which are not given completely, but the unity of some of these is described in the *Introduction*, in which Aristotle's theory of the sciences in general is considered.

I

We have tried to maintain a terminology which is consistent, adequate, familiar, and clear. Key philosophical terms and terms which are proper and important to each of the subjects considered appear in the *Glossary*, and many of them are defined or described or made known in some other way. Terms in italics with initial capital letters signify principles posited by philosophers other than Aristotle. For example, the *One* and the *Dyad* for Plato are the two principles from which all the other things are generated. *Water* for Thales is the material principle from which all other material things are made, and *Intelligence* for Anaxagoras is the cause of order and of goodness in things. Terms in italics but without initial capital letters have meanings which differ somewhat from the same terms without italics but are related to them, and the meanings of such pairs are given in the *Glossary*. Such are the pairs *"substance"* and "substance," *"chance"* and "chance," and *"knowledge"* and "knowledge." Occasionally, expressions in italics are used for emphasis. Expressions appearing in brackets are added for the sake of the reader but are not translations from the Greek.

In the margins of the translations we have inserted the pages and lines of the Bekker text, for this is the standard pagination. The various works of Aristotle along with the Bekker pages containing each of them are listed at the beginning of *References and Notes*, right after the text. Students who wish to acquire the thought of Aristotle accurately should make full use of the *Glossary*, otherwise they may be faced with what appear to be inconsistencies or falsities, which lead to unfair criticism.

In this second edition, a few minor changes have been made, especially in the *Politics* and the *Poetics*.

We are grateful to Professor Daniel W. Graham, who assisted us in making the selection of the various topics; to Professor Gerald V. Lalonde and to Joel F. Wilcox, for clarifying certain points in the *Poetics*, and to Professors Elizabeth A. Dobbs, Morris Parslow, and the late John M. Crossett, who aided us extensively in the translation of the *Poetics;* and to Grinnell College and Hamline University, for help and encouragement in this work.

H. G. Apostle, Grinnell College
and Hamline University
L. P. Gerson, St. Michael's College,
University of Toronto

INTRODUCTION

The Life and Works of Aristotle

I

The earliest source for our knowledge of Aristotle's life is a biography written by the Alexandrian grammarian and librarian, Hermippus of Smyrna, toward the end of the 3rd century B.C. This biography is not extant and its contents are partially preserved in a much later biography written by Diogenes Laertius in the 2nd century A.D. Subsequent biographies rely either on Hermippus or on sources now unknown to us. Although Hermippus and the other biographers undoubtedly drew upon material which goes back to Aristotle's contemporaries, it should be borne in mind that the sources *we* possess go back no further than one hundred years after Aristotle's death. Thus, it is not surprising that there are great gaps in our knowledge of his life or that the source material, encrusted with legends, hearsay, and conjecture, should sometimes present conflicting reports. Still, there is impressive agreement among the biographers about the main lines of a sketch of Aristotle's life.

Aristotle was born in Stagira, a Greek colony on the peninsula of Chalcidice, in 384/3 B.C. Stagira was located close to the border of the Macedonian kingdom. Aristotle's father, a physician named Nicomachus, was employed in the Macedonian royal household, thus affording Aristotle the opportunity to be raised in court circles.

At the age of about 17 Aristotle was sent to Athens to study with Plato in the Academy. There he remained, either until shortly before Plato's death in 347 B.C., or shortly after. Whether it was the death of his teacher or other events that impelled him to leave we do not know.

The next twelve years of Aristotle's life are not well documented. We know that he accepted an invitation from Hermeias, the ruler of Atarneu and Assos in Asia Minor, to join him and a small group of philosophers, some of whom, including apparently Hermeias himself, had been students in the Academy. He remained with Hermeias for 3 years, during which time he married a woman named Pythias who was the niece and adopted daughter of Hermeias. She bore him a daughter, also named Pythias. In 345 or 344 B.C. he moved to Mytilene on the island of Lesbos, again for unknown reasons. There he was joined by Theophrastus, a younger contemporary who would eventually succeed Aristotle in the Lyceum and establish himself as a distinguished philosopher and scientist.

The biographers agree that in 343 or 342 B.C. Aristotle was invited to the court of Philip of Macedon as tutor to his son, Alexander. Unfortunately, we know nothing of what Aristotle taught the man soon to be called Alexander the Great. In 340 B.C. Alexander was appointed regent to his father who was engaged in military activity in Byzantium. Presumably, it was at this time that Aristotle's formal connection with Alexander ended.

There is some doubt about whether Aristotle remained at the court of Philip of Macedon or returned to his home in Stagira during the next five years. In either case, it was in 335 or 334 B.C. that Aristotle returned to Athens where, on the outskirts of the city he rented some land and some buildings which were to be the foundation for his own school, the Lyceum. The name "Lyceum" is taken from one of the epithets of the god Apollo, a temple in whose honor was located close to the school. Tradition has it that the members of the school were called "Peripatetics" because of a covered "walkway" located within the school bounds.

Aristotle was to remain in Athens for the next 11 or 12 years, teaching, writing, and conducting research. Alexander appears to have assisted in his research in natural history by providing numerous specimens from the lands of his empire. We know nothing of any collaboration between the Lyceum and the Academy at this time, although it is likely that relations were not very warm. During this period Aristotle's wife died and he entered into another marriage with a former servant in his household, a native of Stagira, named Herpyllis. She bore him a son, Nicomachus.

In 323 B.C. Alexander died. Anti-Macedonian feelings in Athens flared up with the prospect of the dissolution of the Macedonian empire and the end of their domination over Athens. Those in Athens with Macedonian connections came under suspicion. Aristotle decided, therefore, to leave Athens, for the last time as it happened. He returned to his mother's home town, the Macedonian stronghold of Chalcis, where he owned some property. There he died in 322 B.C., survived by his wife and two children. Aristotle's will is extant, a valuable and moving document, attesting to his close family and personal ties.

The Lyceum continued to exist after Aristotle's death, first under the direction of Theophrastus and then under a succession of lesser figures, down to about 225 B.C. In the minds of Athenians the school seems always to have borne the taint of foreign connections and the Peripatetics never had a hold on Athenian intellectual life to compare with that of the members of the Academy, which existed with some interruptions down to 529 A.D.

II

The above brief account of the life of Aristotle is intended to provide some of the background for the consideration of the exceedingly complex problem of the nature and extent of Aristotle's writings, the so-called *corpus Aristotelicum*. In order to appreciate fully the extent of this problem it will be best to begin with the fascinating and even mysterious story of the transmission of Aristotle's writings, that is, the long passage from the hands of their author into the hands of their first editor some three hundred years later.

When Aristotle left Athens for the last time, copies of his writings or perhaps the originals themselves were left in the library of the Lyceum. Theophrastus, who succeeded Aristotle, apparently had copies of all or some of these books made for his own use. When he died in 287 or 286 B.C. he left these along with his own voluminous writings to his student Neleus who thereafter transported them to his home in Skepsis. Neleus bequeathed the books to his descendents who had no interest in their contents and, as tradition has it, buried them in their basement, presumably for fear of theft. As for the Lyceum books, copies or the originals found their way into the great libraries of Alexandria and Pergamum. It is apparently to these collections that biographers are referring when they give lists of Aristotle's works.

As for the copies held by the family of Neleus, these passed by uncertain means into the hands of one Apellicon of Teos (c.150/140 — 87/86 B.C.), a bookdealer of sorts. The books remained with him until 86 B.C. when the conquering Roman general Sulla entered Athens and seized the books as part of the spoils of war. The books were then removed to Rome and delivered into the hands of a public librarian. They attracted little attention (Cicero appears to have examined them at one point, however) until sometime between 40 and 20 B.C. when a scholar, Andronicus of Rhodes, examined them and resolved to produce an edition of Aristotle's works. With perhaps one exception, that of a work of very dubious authenticity, *The Constitution of Athens,* discovered in the 19th century, Andronicus's edition is exactly the *corpus Aristotelicum* as we know it today.

Our problem begins when we compare the body of Aristotle's works as we know it with the lists of Aristotle's works recorded by the ancient biographers as contained in the great libraries. Our collection contains 46 works, or perhaps more accurately, 46 titles of works (some of these works may themselves be collections of works). The list given by Diogenes Laertius, for example, contains 146 titles. More distressing than the fact that the list of Diogenes Laertius contains titles of works of which we know nothing is the fact that our list contains works which do not appear to be in Diogenes's list, although in some cases this is questionable due to the vagueness of the titles. Thus, it is not only the case that many of Aristotle's works seem to be lost, but there is even some doubt in the minds of some about the attribution of the works we have. The uncertainty would presumably be due to the possibility that Andronicus counted as a work of Aristotle what was really a work of Theophrastus, understandably confused in the mass of material with which he had to work.

We do not know exactly how many of Aristotle's works are missing, for the confusion of his works with the works of others, especially Theophrastus, may even go back to the libraries themselves. It is certain, however, that we are bereft of a great deal of material, including almost all of a score of dialogues of reputedly excellent quality which were left out of Andronicus's edition on the grounds that they were "popular" works easily available. Given the circumstances of the transmission of the works, however, it is remarkable that we have anything at all.

The problems of sorting out (1) what Aristotle wrote and (2) how much of what is attributed to Aristotle and remains is really his seem to be exacerbated by the nature of the works themselves. Many of these works seem to be what we might call "discussion papers" on specific problems or questions within a general area of study. Thus, for example, the *Metaphysics* is a collection of "books" concerning a number of related themes, not all of which seem to display the continuity or development expected of the chapters of one book. They are sometimes repetitive and leave some loose ends, and their collection into the work known as *Metaphysics* may be Andronicus's doing. Similar problems, although generally not as severe, exist for some of the other works. Such remarks about the composition of the works are not intended to discourage the reader about the possibility of getting at the "real" Aristotle. In fact, there is an impressive coherence, a uniform style, and a consistent use of principles in Aristotle's writings considered overall. Still, the reader should be aware that there are many problems in the *corpus*; some of these are interpretive, some concern real or apparent inconsistencies in the works, and some concern gaps in the arguments. Although the circumstances of the composition and transmission of the works cannot be used as a blanket excuse for all of these, it would be fair to say that many matters would be cleared up satisfactorily if we possessed Aristotle's writings in an edition done by him and not by Andronicus.

The very ordering of the works is due to Andronicus and not to Aristotle, and perhaps this alone has had some impact on how Aristotle has been understood ever after. Andronicus ordered the works according to principles set forth by the Stoics. The Stoics divided up the sciences and their curriculum in the following way: (1) logic (in general, the study of *logos* in all its manifestations), which provided the tools for understanding (2) physics or nature as a whole, which prepared one to study (3) ethics, or man's place in the world. Accordingly, Andronicus divided the works in the following way: (1) treatises on logic; (2) treatises on physics or nature (the papers which dealt with matters transcending the physical Andronicus appended to this section and called "metaphysics"); and (3) ethics, including social and political philosophy. To these he appended the *Rhetoric* and *Poetics* which found no precise place in the Stoic schema. Such a schema subtly distorts our perception of Aristotle's ordering of his writings. We have no definite reason to suppose that Aristotle intended the reader of philosophy to begin with the *Categories* and end with the treatise called *Poetics* or that the *Categories* presupposes the least and the *Poetics* the most. One may say of the works we have, however, that their condensed nature and the works by other thinkers which they presuppose suggest that they were written for mature thinkers and not for young beginners.

We shall not take up the vexed problems of whether the corpus shows a development in Aristotle's thinking and if so, precisely what this development was. It would, of course, be very useful to know if, of two apparently conflicting views on an issue, one represents Aristotle's first thoughts on the matter and the other represents his more mature thinking. Unfortunately, theories of development usually tell us more about what the scholar regards as mature and immature thinking than they do about Aristotle. It is perhaps sufficient here to note that it would be exceedingly surprising that in a philosophical career spanning some forty years there was no development or change at all. But what this was is an open question and should be treated as such by the student.

III

Aristotle was primarily a scientist. Almost all of his extant works are scientific treatises. But what is his conception of scientific knowledge? He discusses such knowledge and things related to it at length in his *Posterior Analytics*.

According to his definition, we are said to have scientific knowledge of a thing in an unqualified way when we know (1) the cause of the thing as being the cause of that thing alone and (2) that the thing cannot be other than what it is. The term "cause" here may include more than one cause; and the term "thing" includes also what we call "a fact." In mathematics, for example, we have scientific knowledge of the equality of vertical angles if we can demonstrate that equality. In physics, one who can demonstrate that if an object travels from A to B, there can be no first position through which that object must pass, has scientific knowledge of that fact. There can be scientific knowledge of a thing even without demonstration, if one can give a definition in which the cause of that thing is included. One may define a house, for example, as a structure with a certain form, built with certain materials by an architect, for the purpose of living in it comfortably. Similarly, Aristotle defines anger as a desire, accompanied by pain, to exact revenge because of what appears to be an unjustified belittling of what is due to a man or to those dear to that man. We may add, scientific knowledge of things of a certain kind must be universal to be unqualified and not be knowledge of one or a limited number of individuals, for these are destructible, and their corresponding knowledge is destroyed along with their destruction. To be unqualified, then, knowledge must be of things of a certain kind. Again, scientific knowledge implies conviction concerning what is known, for if one is shaky about a thing or not convinced, one cannot be said to have unqualified scientific knowledge of it.

There can be scientific knowledge in another way also, namely, in a qualified or secondary sense; and in this sense that which is so known exists not of necessity, but for the most part or mostly or as an individual. For example, human behavior may be of such a nature, for occasionally mathematicians make mathematical errors, and generous people do not always act generously; and, in general, the deviation from universality or necessity may be slight or occasional, whether due to the knower or to the thing known or to both, and the error may be one of quantity or of quality or of some other category. Scientific knowledge in modern physics, for example, is mostly of this sort, for quantitative measurements of physical objects are subject to small errors, and such errors are due to the knower or to the nature of the object known or to both. Heisenberg's principle of uncertainty is an example, and such errors are usually present whenever statistical methods are used to acquire principles or demonstrable facts in physics. Scientific knowledge of an individual, on the other hand, is qualified in a different way. John is mortal of necessity, and the cause of this is the fact that he is a composite living thing (for composites are destructible, and, by definition, to be a mortal being is to be a destructible living thing); but he is of necessity mortal only during his lifetime and not universally or always. The unqualified cause of being mortal, on the other hand, is being a composite living thing regardless of time or place, and it is in this sense that every man or every animal is mortal without regard to time or place.

There is still another kind of scientific knowledge in the sciences, whether it be of what is necessarily true or approximately true, and such knowledge is demonstrated knowledge but not through the cause. One may demonstrate that an equiangular triangle is equilateral and think that the cause of being equilateral is the equality of the angles; but this is not true. It can be shown that it is the equality of the sides that causes the equality of the angles, and not the converse. Aristotle uses the following example: it is not the absence of twinkling that causes the planets to be near, but their nearness which causes them not to twinkle. One may call this kind of knowledge, too, "qualified," but in this sense, namely, not through the cause.

Aristotle, of course, is mainly concerned with scientific knowledge which is universal, whether of necessity or approximately, and is acquired through the cause; for it is only such knowledge which uses no irrelevant information as causes and is most general both theoretically as an end in itself and also as a means in its application to *actions* and productions.

Now if one knows a thing scientifically by demonstration through the cause, one knows also the principles which are used to demonstrate that thing. Those principles are (1) indefinable concepts, (2) definitions, (3) hypotheses, and (4) axioms; and the faculty by which those principles can be known or are possessed is called by Aristotle *νοῦς*, which is usually translated as "intellect" or "intuition." It is evident that such a faculty must exist, otherwise no unqualified scientific knowledge is possible; and without that faculty it is even impossible for any clear knowledge other than sensation or imagination to exist; for any other clear knowledge requires the possession of clear concepts, which can be acquired only by that faculty. The premises in a demonstration come from the definitions and the hypotheses; the axioms are used not as premises *with which* one demonstrates conclusions, but as regulative principles, so to say, *by which* conclusions are drawn from premises. In short, both the premises, which require definitions and hypotheses, and the axioms are necessary if scientific conclusions are to be drawn. From these remarks it is evident that, generically taken, the kinds of principles which Aristotle puts forward as necessary for a demonstration hardly differ from the kinds of principles which modern scientists use.

One important principle which Aristotle assumes in a science is the existence of its subject; another related principle is that the premises in a demonstration must be true, whether of necessity or approximately. From these assumptions it follows by logic that the conclusions in a science must be true in the corresponding manner. Problems may arise as to whether straight lines or numbers or ether or ultimate particles of matter or other such objects exist or not, and these problems must be settled, for if such objects do not exist, there can be no science of them.

But are existence and truth necessary in a science? It is generally agreed that they are. Most modern mathematicians, however, take the position that mathematics is not or should not be concerned with the truth or falsity of the principles but only with sets of postulates and the demonstration of theorems from them.

Aristotle's position on this is clear. Man is distinguished from all other animals by having reason, and the best activities of man are those which use reason. Of these activities, the highest are those which are theoretical, that is, those which pursue truth for its own sake, and these activities pursue indemonstrable principles and truths demonstrated from the principles through causes. The other serious activities are neither true nor false, and these are *actions* and productions, but they are best and most effective if they are pursued in accordance with reason, which is true thought. In short, all serious activities of man pursue either reason as such or things in accordance with reason. Now if mathematical activity differs from these, it is either a means to an end or else like the activity of playing games. It cannot be a means to an end, for it is admitted by mathematicians to be theoretical; further, since truth is not assigned to the postulates by them, neither the postulates nor the theorems which follow — if theorems can follow from such postulates at all — can be used with certainty by the other serious activities. Is mathematical activity like that of playing games? But it is to serious activities that dignity and importance is attributed and not to playing games; for games are pursued for relaxation, and relaxation is, in a certain sense, pursued for the sake of serious activity whereas serious activity is never pursued for the sake of relaxation.

What is Aristotle's concept of cause, and how many kinds of causes does he use in a science? When asking a question, one seeks a deeper understanding of a thing, and in answering the question, another uses the word "because," followed by a *reason* or cause or explanation. For example, "Why are vertical angles equal?" "Because they are complements of the same angle, and complements of the same angle are equal." "Why did the chair burn?" "Because it was made of wood, one may say, and all things made of wood are flammable." "Why did John strike Richard?" "Because Richard insulted him, and John is disposed to strike those who insult him." "Why did he ask for $10,000?" "Because he wishes to buy a car." The above answers exemplify the four different kinds of causes according to Aristotle, and they are called, in the order given, "formal," "material," "moving," and "final."

Other examples of a formal cause may be given. Of a house, the formal cause is its form or structure, and this is the manner in which the materials are put together; of a man, the formal cause is the soul; and of a triangle, the formal cause is its form, that is, the manner in which the three sides are put together; and the formal cause in each of these three cases is necessary, for there can be no house without a structure, no man without a soul, and no triangle without the joining of the three sides at their limits. Similarly, there is a material cause in all three; for a man must have a certain kind of body, the house must be made with certain kinds of materials, and the triangle must have a certain kind of plane surface. Again, the moving cause of building the house is the architect or his art, for it is he who gives the orders to the rest of how to put the materials together. In the case of a man, the moving cause is the father according to Aristotle, but both parents according to modern knowledge. But there is no such cause in the triangle, for no mathematician is concerned with such a cause; and, in general, no moving cause is used in the investigation of properties of mathematical objects. Finally, the final cause of a house is its purpose, which is comfortable living. Man's final cause is happiness. But there is no final cause in the case of a triangle, and no mathematician is concerned with such a cause. In fact, mathematical objects are investigated without regard to moving or final causes, for a mathematician has abstracted them from physical objects by leaving out of consideration the causes of motion, i.e., both moving and final causes.

But, one may ask, was not the architect asked by someone else to build the house? Perhaps, and that person may have been a lawyer, or a dentist, or a business man, etc.; but these are indefinite in kind as causes, and none of them participated directly in the construction of the house as such. In other words, they are accidental movers and not definite, whereas the first moving cause of the house as such is definitely and directly the architect. Now science is not concerned with accidental causes, nor can it be concerned with them; for they are indefinite in kind, whereas the causes in a science are definite. It is also evident from the examples that in some cases all the causes are present and so subject to investigation, but that in other cases this is not so.

How is the cause investigated, and when do we know that we have the cause of a thing? Let us turn to the second question first.

An example from mathematics may be used. Why are the angles of a right isosceles triangle equal to two right angles? Not because it is right, for this equality belongs to an isosceles triangle even if it is not right. Similarly, the equality belongs to triangles even if they are not isosceles. Assuming that the next higher genus after 'triangle' is 'polygon,' we can show that the equality does not belong to all polygons. So it appears that the highest genus which is such that the equality belongs to all its members is the genus 'triangle.' We say, then, that two right angles belong to a right isosceles triangle not qua a *right* isosceles triangle (that is, not insofar as it is a *right* isosceles triangle), nor qua an *isosceles* triangle, but qua a triangle. Of the species of polygons, then, triangles and only triangles are such that all its members possess the equality above; and, in a sense, this is another way of saying that the necessary and sufficient conditions for a species of polygons to have the above equality is that it be the species 'triangle.' Similarly, a silver coin sinks in water not qua being silvery or metallic or a coin, but qua having a greater specific gravity than the specific gravity of water, cats take in food qua living things, books are flammable not qua books but qua being made of certain flammable material, and men do certain things qua being desirous of what they think will make them happy.

But one may raise an objection. Triangles are not the only rectilinear figures whose angle bisectors meet at a point, for also regular polygons do. On the other hand, polygons are not subdivided into regular and irregular species, for such subdivision is dichotomous, and dichotomous subdivisions have been shown in *Parts of Animals*, 642b5-4a11, to run into difficulties and impossibilities. Polygons, then, are subdivided according to the number of sides, for it is these that specify the various forms of polygons. Accordingly, it is by accident that the angle bisectors of a quadrilateral or a pentagon or any of the others are concurrent and not qua a quadrilateral or qua a pentagon or etc., since in most cases they do not.

Aristotle's position may be stated universally. Let A be an attribute which belongs to a species S qua G, where G is a genus of S. Then the attribute A is said to be a property of G. Evidently, the genus G appears in the definition of S; so let the definition of S contain the differentiae D, besides G. Since A can be demonstrated as belonging to G without the use of D or any part of it, no part of D contributes to the fact that A belongs to G or to any species of G, including S. So if a man demonstrates that A belongs to S without demonstrating that it belongs to its genus G, he does not know that D does not contribute as a cause or as a part of the cause and is therefore not aware of what the exact cause is. Further, he has not demonstrated the fact that A belongs to the other species of G also, and so his demonstration is not the most universal both as a fact and in its applications. Consequently, he has no unqualified scientific knowledge of the fact. Now it is possible to demonstrate A as belonging to S by using D or a part of it, and such use misleads the demonstrator into thinking that D or a part of it is a part of the cause and hence necessary in the demonstration.

The use of necessary and sufficient conditions, which are often used by mathematicians in their demonstrations, assure the universality of a demonstration, but Aristotle seems to advocate a further requirement; for necessary and sufficient conditions do not distinguish a definition from a property, whereas Aristotle appears to say that there is one and only one unqualified or perfect definition of a definable thing, although he allows qualified definitions of things for certain reasons. Anyway, the use of necessary and sufficient conditions are closest to Aristotle's position with respect to both causality and universality.

We may now turn to the problem of how the cause is investigated in a particular demonstration. One part deals with procedures universally, but we leave this part aside here. The other part has to do with the specific contribution by the investigator, for knowledge of universal procedures alone will not help one to demonstrate a property of a given subject. The reason for this is that the unqualified demonstration that P is a property of a subject S requires specific premises, for, in most cases, both P and S are specific in a science, and so are many or all premises from which P is demonstrated to belong to S; but these premises do not appear in the general procedures and general principles. In an unqualified demonstration, such premises must be immediate, i.e., indemonstrable, and be apprehended by the demonstrator; and it is the ordering of these premises by means of the appropriate axioms which will lead to the required demonstration. For example, the general statement that a straight line parallel to a given straight line may be drawn through any point not on the given line and the premises which arise from this construction do not specify *which* parallel is to be drawn and *what premises* arising from such construction should be taken to demonstrate the equality of the angles of a triangle to two right angles. Such specification of a parallel in a demonstration is a principle which does not appear in the initial axioms and postulates in geometry. But there are many such unmentioned principles, and these are apprehended by what we have called the "intellect" or "intuition."

Indeed, a mark of genius lies greatly in the ability to apprehend without help from others such specific principles and to arrange them in a manner which will lead to the demonstration of a property. The usual expression given by Aristotle to such specific principles is "minor premises," and such premises arise partly because there are a great many species in each science, and their differentiae are themselves principles. Aristotle's statement, that the specific sciences are perhaps infinite, arises from the fact that he considered differentiae to be principles, and such principles to be innumerable.

An important consequence of the above remarks is the difference between Plato and Aristotle with respect to the number of principles of things as well as of scientific knowledge. Plato's first principles as understood by Aristotle are two, the *One* and the *Dyad*, and from these it is stated that the rest follow or are generated. As for scientific knowledge, there is only one science, dialectic, and it is stated that the rest somehow follow from or depend on dialectic; and since that knowledge is only of the unchanging, there can be no scientific knowledge of the physical world and hence no such science as physics. Aristotle regards Plato's principles as too simplistic and the reduction of all things to very few principles as impossible; and by introducing logic as necessary to science, he shows that Plato destroys demonstration and science altogether, even his own science of Ideas.

Finally, how are principles acquired? To say that they are acquired by what we have called "intuition" is not enough. Now principles are universal, and to be a universal concept is to be that which is predicable of many things which have something in common; and he who has acquired such a concept must have apprehended what is common to many and hence must have come in contact, so to say, with many. Further, one cannot have a concept without an image, nor an image without prior sensations. Hence sensations are presupposed by knowledge of principles. To quote Aristotle from the *Posterior Analytics,* "neither can we demonstrate conclusions from universals without prior induction, nor can we acquire universals through induction without sensation," and from *Metaphysics,* "from sensation memory comes into being, . . . from memory experience comes into being, . . . and science and art come to men from experience."

For the sake of clarity, let the term "science" signify collectively the actual or possible principles and theorems concerning a subject which is universally considered, e.g., of mathematical objects or astronomical objects so considered, whether or not the theorems are taken along with their demonstrations. Such definition of science is applicable to most of what we nowadays call "sciences" and allows qualifications whenever these are needed; for we speak of science as being knowledge as just described or as the expressions of such knowledge, be they vocal or written or printed or taped or in some other form. It is also evident that unqualified scientific knowledge of a fact, although not including explicitly knowledge of principles, includes them implicitly; for being knowledge through the cause and hence by means of demonstration, it includes also knowledge of the principles which are posited in that demonstration, and knowledge of principles, as already stated, is intuitive knowledge or intuition.

IV

Let us now turn to Aristotle's classification of the sciences. They are classified in two main ways: (1) according to their subjects and (2) according to their purpose. Sciences differ according to purpose if their aims differ regardless of the subjects pursued, and sciences differ according to subject if their subjects differ regardless of their aims. For example, a mathematician pursues mathematics without regard to its applications to other fields, but an engineer studies mathematics for another reason, to use it in industry or in the construction of a bridge and the like. Both study the same subject but for a different purpose, the mathematician for the sake of truth but the engineer for the sake of production, and for this reason they emphasize different aspects of the same science: the mathematician emphasizes principles and demonstrations, the engineer pays more attention to mathematical facts and conclusions than to principles and the refinements of demonstrations. Again, the activities of both mathematicians and philosophers, generically considered, have the same purpose, and this is the pursuit of truth for its own sake, although their subjects differ; the subject of mathematicians is mathematical objects, that of philosophers is, as Aristotle puts it, "being qua being," that is, the first or most general principles and causes of all things. In short, a scientist studies scientific objects either for the sake of just knowing them or as a means to something else.

A science which is pursued for its own sake is called "theoretical" or "contemplative," and its aim is truth about its objects; a science which is pursued as a means to producing something out of certain materials is called "productive;" and a science which is pursued as a means to *action* for its own sake may be called "practical," for the lack of a better word. The term *"action"* and the corresponding adjective "practical" here are used in a limited sense. An *action* is a human activity but is not theoretical, and it is usually pursued for its own sake. Another term which may describe it is "conduct," if conduct is pursued as an end in itself and not as a means to some other end. Examples of *actions* are those which are generous or temperate or just, playing games, listening to music, enjoying a play, the *actions* of a statesman as such, and the like. Some *actions* are serious, others are relaxations, and some are good, e.g., those which are just or temperate, but others are bad, e.g., those which are unjust or intemperate.

Generically, there are three theoretical sciences: first philosophy, physics, and mathematics. Sometimes Aristotle uses two other Greek words for first philosophy, and these are translated as "wisdom" and "theology," respectively. The word "metaphysics" is an abbreviation from the Greek phrase whose phonetic translation is "meta ta physica," which means *after the physics* and is perhaps the title given by Andronicus of Rhodes. There is no evidence that the *Physics* was written before the *Metaphysics*. In fact, if Aristotle were to be strict in his scientific writings, he would write the *Metaphysics* first; for, according to him, the principles of a subordinate science presuppose principles of the higher science, and metaphysics is the highest science. The cross-references in his works suggest that perhaps there was no definite order in which each treatise was written in its entirety.

Since, of a thing which has a cause, knowledge for its own sake is better than knowledge for the sake of something else, it is evident that knowledge of a fact which has a cause is, at its best, scientific knowledge of that fact; and such knowledge comes under a theoretical science. Further, since man is differentiated from other animals by having reason, activities which require reason most would be the most proper to man; and what is most proper to man is most pleasant. Hence theoretical activities would be the most pleasant to man. Again, such activities are further differentiated according to the dignity of the objects of a science. Hence physics is superior to mathematics; for the objects of physics are physical substances, those of mathematics are quantities, which exist in physical substances, and physical substances are prior to quantities since they are related to them as wholes are to parts. Further, substances themselves are differentiated; for some of them are eternal and divine, but others are destructible. Hence metaphysics, whose objects are eternal and divine, is superior to physics, whose objects are destructible or subject to change. In the order of dignity, then, the three theoretical sciences are metaphysics, physics, and mathematics.

According to Aristotle, metaphysics is concerned with being qua being and the attributes which belong to being as such. But this statement needs clarification. The term "being" has many senses; and in one sense it means a substance but in another it means an attribute of a substance. But since a substance is to an attribute as a whole is to a part of that whole (for an attribute exists in a substance, but not conversely), "being" means primarily a substance but secondarily an attribute. But what is substance? It is discussed in *Metaphysics,* and so are its kinds, its principles, and its attributes. Two inherent principles of physical substances are matter and form, and these are discussed. "Being" means also the attributes of substances, but secondarily, and these are quantity, quality, and the others, and they are considered. There are also attributes of all of the above, e.g., unity, sameness, otherness, priority, cause, and the like; and these are considered. Again, "being" means also potentiality or actuality, and these are discussed. There is also being qua known, and in this sense definition, genus, species, differentia, truth and the like are also discussed. Finally, there is being which exists as form without matter, and the prime mover or God and the other immaterial substances posited by Aristotle are discussed. We may add, the views of Aristotle's predecessors are discussed in almost all his treatises, usually in the first Book of each treatise and later as they are relevant to the particular points under discussion.

We may now turn to Aristotle's *Physics,* which is the science of nature. It is concerned with natural substances qua movable or changeable. First, the principles of other natural philosophers are considered. Then follows a discussion of the principles of motion or of change, which are three: two contraries or opposites and a subject. That which changes is the subject which remains the same during the change, one of the contraries is that from which the subject changes, and the other contrary is that to which the subject changes. Since physics is concerned with natural objects, nature and its senses are made clear and the kinds and number of causes (i.e., explanations of things) are considered, including chance and necessity as causes. Now to understand movable objects one must understand motion; so motion is discussed and defined. And since motion is continuous, is infinitely divisible, requires place, exists in time, and is said by some thinkers to require a void, the *Physics* discusses continuity, infinity, place, time, and void, and considers their existence and definitions.

The three kinds of motion are locomotion, alteration, and quantitative motion, and the other changes are generation and destruction. These and their attributes are discussed. But motion requires a mover; so movers and their relation to the things moved are discussed. Finally, is motion eternal, and is time eternal, and if so, what is the cause? And here the eternal prime mover is proved to exist as a cause.

Aristotle's *Physics* as just described is in one sense very general, but in another sense it includes no mathematics; so it is far different from modern physics. In its generality, it includes as parts the science of inanimate things and that of animate things. Qualitative or nonquantitative chemistry, for example, would come under it, and so would nonquantitative physics, biology in general, zoology, botany, and other special sciences whose objects are subject to change and are treated qua movable but not quantitatively.

We may describe one of the above sciences, that of animate things as a unit. Its title is *On The Soul,* and its objects are living things. At the start, the theories of earlier thinkers are considered and their difficulties are shown. Then the four causes of living things are discussed, namely, form, matter, moving cause, and final cause.

The form of living things is the soul, and its general definition is given. Specifically, that form may be simple or complex, and if complex, its parts are discussed and also their relations. The simplest form is the nutritive soul, which is the form of plants. The next form, that of animals, includes as parts the power of nutrition and the power of sensation, and it is shown that a thing which has a sense (i.e., a power of sensation) must have also the power of nutrition, but not conversely. The two kinds of senses which may exist in animals are proper and common, but the latter presuppose the former. The proper senses are touch, taste, smell, hearing, and vision, and these along with their activities, the objects which cause those activities, and their priorities and other relations are discussed; and similarly with the common sensibles. Imagination and memory presuppose sensation, but sensation does not presuppose imagination or memory. Next comes the discussion of the power of thinking, its activities, and its objects, and also the kinds of thinking and the corresponding objects thought. The material causes of living things depend on the form of those things, and their final causes, which are one by analogy, form a hierarchy in accordance with the hierarchy of the diverse forms. As for moving causes, those of plants are food-taking, assimilating, and growing; those of most animals include also *desire* and that of locomotion; and those of man add also thought and the cause of thought, the latter being the active intellect, the only part in man which is immovable, separable from man, and eternal according to Aristotle.

The third theoretical science is mathematics, which is concerned with quantities as subjects and investigates their properties; and it is concerned with them as motionless objects and not as movable. In fact, as attributes of physical subjects, quantities are not movable, except indirectly or accidentally; but a science is concerned with essential and not accidental attributes. The mathematician, then, abstracts quantities from sensible substances and investigates them qua motionless. Quantities are of two species, discrete and continuous, the former being called "numbers" (i.e., natural numbers greater than 1), the latter being called "magnitudes." Since quantities are abstracted from motion, the moving and final causes do not appear in the investigation. Necessity in mathematics appears in a manner somewhat analogous to that in physics. In physics, if an animal is to be, certain stages must have preceded its existence, and if a house is to be, certain things must have occurred prior to its existence, such as the construction of the foundation and the like. In mathematics, if the definition of a triangle is a three-sided plane figure (and similarly for any other definition), certain properties must simultaneously belong to it. Is there any goodness in the objects of mathematics? Yes, but not directly in their definitions or properties. For order, symmetry, definiteness and the like are species of beauty and kinds of attributes of mathematical objects, and mathematics is in a way concerned with mathematical objects with such attributes even if the term "beauty" does not appear in the investigation.

As already stated, the aim of a productive science is the making of a product. As a science, then, a productive science is concerned with certain truths about its objects; but as productive, it is concerned with the production of its objects according to reason or truths about those objects, and so it uses truth not for their own sake but for the production of those objects. Now production necessitates certain activities by the producer, and if these activities are to lead to the objects as aimed, skills are necessary. For example, medical science is a productive science, and a student first learns the truths about health and things related to it and then as an intern acquires the skills necessary to produce an object, i.e., to make a sick man healthy. Thus the producer takes certain materials and with his skills instills a form upon them. The use of the thing produced may be an end in itself or a means to some other end. The use of a house is comfortable living, which is an end in itself or a part of happiness, and the use of a painting or play produced is the enjoyment of seeing or reading it, respectively. On the other hand, the steel produced from iron ore may be further used to produce another object whose use may be either an end in itself or a means to another end, and if a means to another end, the use of this end itself may be either for its own sake or for the sake of some other end, and so on till a final end is reached. It is evident, then, that an object produced may come either under the fine arts or under such arts as engineering, farming, finance, and the like.

The aim of a practical science is *action* for its own sake. As a science, a practical science is concerned with certain truths about its objects, but as practical, it uses those truths for the sake of *action*, which is an end in itself. Evidently, productive and practical sciences have something in common, for both use truths not for their own sake but for the sake of something else. Ethics and politics are practical sciences, and the end of ethics is the happiness of the individual whereas the end of politics is the happiness of the state as a whole. The unity of ethics may be considered.

Ethics is a practical science whose concern is the ultimate good of man. As a science, it is knowledge of what that ultimate good is; as practical, it is pursued not for its own sake but for the sake of attaining that good. It is generally agreed that the name of that good is "happiness." Hence ethics is a science pursued for the sake of happiness. But there is disagreement as to what exactly happiness is. After going through the theories of other thinkers in his *Nicomachean Ethics,* Aristotle finally arrives at his own definition of happiness, which is: the activity of the soul according to virtue throughout life. This is the first principle of ethics, and the understanding of this principle in depth and the consequent *actions* in accordance with it usually lead to happiness.

The rest of the *Nicomachean Ethics* unfolds the above definition of happiness. The term "virtue" appears in the definition; so its genus and differentia are sought. The genus is 'habit,' which is acquired and not inherited. There are two kinds of virtues, ethical and intellectual. The ethical virtues are considered first, and later the intellectual virtues. The differentia of ethical virtue is 'disposition to pursue pleasure in accordance with the mean,' or 'the golden mean,' as some say. The contrary of virtue is vice, which is an acquired habit disposing man to pursue pleasure in violation of the mean. Since ethical habits are acquired by constant *acting,* and since *actions* by man are voluntary and so presuppose a will, the will as a principle is discussed. Examples of ethical virtues are generosity, bravery, wit, and justice.

There are five intellectual virtues: science, art, wisdom, prudence, and intuition, and these are discussed and defined. There are also dispositions which are mixtures of ethical virtue and vice, and these are considered. Thus, a continent man has the right reason but wrong *desires*, and he is pleased by acting according to reason but pained because his *desires* are not fulfilled. Friendship contributes much to happiness and is discussed at length. Finally, since the activity according to virtue, which is included in the definition of happiness, is pleasant, pleasure is discussed in the last book of *Nicomachean Ethics*. And since the best part of man is the intellect, intellectual activities are superior to ethical activities, and so intellectual pursuits contribute more to man's happiness than ethical pursuits.

Sciences may be either simple or mixed. A simple science is one in which the attributes investigated of a subject belong to that subject qua such a subject, but a mixed science is one in which the attributes investigated of a subject belong to that subject not qua such a subject but are attributes of a subject of another science. Philosophy, physics, and mathematics are simple sciences. For sameness, otherness, contrariety, definition, principle, and other such attributes belong to all or almost all things qua things; action, reaction, direction of movable bodies, time, and place belong to physical bodies qua physical or movable; and parallelism, areas, volumes, functional correspondence, roots, and intersections belong to quantities qua quantities. In every mixed science, then, the subject and the attributes investigated of that subject belong to different sciences, whether those sciences are generically or specifically different. The attributes investigated in a mixed science need not be mathematical; for edible objects may be studied qua marketable or qua politically usable, and the objects of production, such as houses and bridges, may be studied qua endurable or qua objects of beauty.

Now to demonstrate a theorem, a mixed science may borrow either principles or theorems or both from another science; and insofar as it borrows theorems without demonstrating them, it leaves out the cause, i.e., the indemonstrable premises, but uses those theorems in demonstrating an attribute as belonging to its own subject. For example, if the radius of a round table with a plane surface is r, the carpenter borrows and uses the mathematical theorem that the area of a circle of radius r is πr^2 without demonstrating it and then proceeds as follows: πr^2 belongs to the area of a circle of radius r, the area of a circle of radius r belongs to the table's surface area, therefore πr^2 belongs to that area. But $r = 4$ feet; therefore 16π square feet belong to that area, which belongs to the table. Evidently, the subject is a work of art and not a mathematical subject, whether one regards it as a plane circular table of radius 4 or as just a table; but the mathematical theorem that the area of a circle of radius r is πr^2 is not demonstrated, and so the cause of πr^2 as being the area of a circle of radius r is not given by the carpenter. If the carpenter wishes to know that cause, he will have to study it in plane geometry; but then he will be investigating that cause not qua a carpenter but qua a student of geometry.

Universally stated, in a mixed science S, let AM be a theorem in which M is a term signifying a subject of S, and let A be a term signifying an attribute which is proper to another science T. For simplicity, let the immediate premises leading to the demonstration of AM be AB, BC, CD, DE, and EM. Since the terms in AM belong to different sciences, only one of the intermediate premises has terms belonging to the different sciences, and let that premise be CD. Then the terms A, B, and C belong to T while D, E, and M belong to S. A scientist under S need not know the cause B of AC, for the investigation of B belongs to T; but he uses AC as a mediate premise along with CD, DE, and EM to demonstrate AM. As for the premise

CD, in some cases it is produced by art, as in the case of the circular plane surface, but in other cases it belongs to the science S and may be a matter for investigation, like the equality of the angles of incidence and reflection, the index of refraction of a light ray entering a different medium, and the coefficient of friction of wood.

Much if not most of the research done in modern physics and in chemistry, especially quantitative chemistry, is concerned with the investigation of quantitative attributes of the objects of those sciences, and to that extent modern physics, chemistry, and other similar sciences are mixed sciences in Aristotle's terminology. In his *Mechanics,* he states that the subject of that science is physical but the attributes investigated of it are mathematical. Accordingly, he would regard modern physics as being partly a simple and partly a mixed science, and similarly for chemistry and other such sciences. Universally considered, then, the *kinds* of attributes investigated by modern physics were well known to Aristotle, for the attributes of modern physics are either physical but nonquantitative, or quantitative. If they are physical but nonquantitative, they are the kind of attributes which would be investigated in Aristotle's *Physics,* but if they are quantitative, they are attributes which would be investigated in his *Mechanics.* So in speaking of the *Physics,* it would be unfair to say of Aristotle that he made no provision for all the kinds of attributes which modern physics investigates; for this would be arguing about the word "physics," which is used in one sense by Aristotle but in another by modern physicists, and failing to take into account what is said in Aristotle's *Mechanics.*

Modern physics is indeed far advanced in comparison to Aristotle's physics, but this advance should be clearly stated in terms of principles if Aristotle's contribution is to be evaluated. Those principles are (1) the subject, one part of which is (1a) generic and the other parts (1b) specific, (2) the axioms, (3) the definitions, (4) the hypotheses, and (5) the theorems. Modern physics is far advanced with respect to (1b), (2), (3), (4) and (5), but not with respect to (1a), and knowledge of (1a) is prior to and presupposed by all the other principles. Aristotle's first concern is, to put it briefly, "first things first," and (1a) is the first principle of all things within a science; for if the subject generically taken in a generic science is not known, one has no guiding principle to proceed. Moreover, the subject of a science serves also as the unity of that science. If a science is defined in terms of an aim, like strategy, whose aim is victory, or like ethics, whose aim is the happiness of an individual, the aim itself serves in a sense as a subject to which the rest are related. As to scientific methodology, there has been hardly any generic advance since Aristotle, but much advance in specifics.

Can there be a science of history or sociology or anthropology according to Aristotle? It has already been stated that scientific knowledge is universal,

i.e., of things of a certain kind at any time or place, whether those things
exist actually or potentially. If history is defined as an accurate record of
past events, whether all events or events within certain limits or
qualifications, it is not a science since it is limited to a series of individual
actualities along with their accidents, many of which may have great
weight, and such series constitute an individual and not a universal. There
may be methods, universal in character, which lead to greater accuracy
concerning past events, but such accuracy is still limited to individuals qua
individuals and not qua universally considered. As for sociology and
anthropology, each of them has been defined in many ways or described as
including many parts, some of which have universality but others do not.
One may then say that each of them is a science in Aristotle's sense only to
the extent that its statements are universal in character and not limited by
time or place. Further, whether those parts of anthropology or sociology
which lend themselves to universality do or do not come under Aristotle's
definition of politics or psychology or some other science depends on the
definitions given to them, but their discussion is not appropriate here.

Finally, the principles according to which Aristotle divides the sciences
are such as to enable one to tell whether a given statement or problem
belongs to this or that science; but such division, contrary to the opinion of
some critics, does not prevent the qualitative or quantitative growth of the
sciences or the investigation of their relations. In fact, Aristotle's principles
leave the growth of the sciences open. His philosophical statement that
things have unity not only by being the same generically or specifically but
also by being analogous allows analogical things to be investigated in a
unified manner. Logic, for example, is one science by analogy, and so is that
part of mathematics which is considered most universally. Further, the
sciences are perhaps infinite according to Aristotle, as we stated earlier, and
the reason given for this is the indefinitely large number of existing
differentiae and other principles, most of which are still subject to research.
Again, the inclusion of mixed sciences in Aristotle's scheme allows all kinds
of relations among the simple sciences to be considered. Lastly, the
distinctions among the sciences according to subject and also according to
aim, whether theoretical or practical or productive, exhausts the kinds of
possible scientific activities of man.

V

Misconceptions about Aristotle's philosophy are due to many causes, the
primary of which is failure to study all of his major works. For example,
knowledge of what is said in the *Prior Analytics*, which is usually called
"Aristotle's Logic," is not adequate to inform the student of how Aristotle's

Metaphysics, On the Soul, the *Posterior Analytics,* and other major treatises contribute to the understanding of what is said in the *Prior Analytics* and to what some terms in that treatise mean. Other misconceptions are due to failings of other kinds, and a few are due to reading mistranslations. Some misconceptions will be considered.

1. It is said that Aristotle's principles are relative to the stage of scientific knowledge of his time. Another variation goes as follows: Modern science makes Aristotle obsolete.

If Aristotle's principles are obsolete or not true or irrelevant because they are relative to an earlier stage of scientific knowledge, then so are the principles of Newton, Copernicus, Lagrange, Euler, and any thinker who lived before the 20th century, and so will our own scientific principles be at some future date. Further, if the scientific principles advocated in the past become obsolete, all efforts to discover principles for all time will be futile. Moreover, progress will be impossible, for it implies the addition of true principles to past principles which have already been confirmed and are accepted as true. Actually, we have not rejected Aristotle's principle of contradiction, or his four kinds of principles of science listed in Part III, or the temporal order of learning which begins with sensation, and from experience and abstraction and induction and imagination leads to those four principles, or the powers of living things listed in *On the Soul,* or his necessary and sufficient conditions which lead to theorems of maximum generality, or hundreds of others. Finally, if the relativity of all scientific principles to time is accepted as a scientific principle, then that principle itself along with its implications will eventually become obsolete in the future.

2. According to Francis Bacon, who is highly regarded as a philosopher by some modern thinkers, "Aristotle made his natural philosophy (i.e., his *Physics*) completely subservient to his logic" and "corrupted natural philosophy by logic."

Going through the various works of Aristotle, we find no evidence of this at all. For learning according to him proceeds in the following temporal order: sensation, memory, experience, induction and abstraction, science, and art (81a38-b9, 99b34-100b17, 980a27-1a12). Again, Aristotle states that each science except first philosophy has, besides principles which are common to some other sciences, also principles which are proper to itself (75a38-b6, b37-40); and from this it follows that no science can be reduced or be completely subservient to another science. Finally, every theorem in a science consists of terms, at least one of which, the subject or the predicate or the two taken together, is proper to that science (75b7-14); and from this it follows that no theorem in a science can be demonstrated by another science, much less by logic; for, unlike the objects of natural philosophy, those of logic are not physical objects but are limited to terms, premises, and conclusions, all of which exist primarily in the mind and secondarily on paper or in some other such form.

Other variations of Bacon's criticism of Aristotle are the following: "Aristotle's science is non-empirical and is hostile to research or discovery," "Aristotle condemned science or logic for two thousand years," and the like. All of them are similar to that of Bacon and have *no basis at all*.

3. A common misconception is that Aristotle's metaphysics is concerned with the same problems found in what is today called "metaphysics." For example, modern textbooks on metaphysics may deal with problems of space and time, which for Aristotle belong to physics; they may raise problems about free will and determinism, which for Aristotle are logical problems about future contingent propositions; they may raise problems about the immortality of the soul, which for Aristotle is a psychological problem; or they may raise problems about the meaning of proper names and general terms, which for Aristotle are basically logical problems.

Aristotle's metaphysics is also frequently treated as a contribution to discussions about identity or continuity through space and time, and the now commonly used phrase "Aristotelian essentialism" is thought to correspond to Aristotle's own doctrine. In fact, Aristotle's own views on essence are quite far removed from many contemporary views. And though Aristotle certainly does say things in the *Metaphysics* and elsewhere which might be applied to the solution of problems about identity, Aristotle would not accept the manner in which such problems are posed. The main reason for this is that since "being" has many senses, there could not be one general criterion of identity through space and time. In short, the way the term "metaphysics" is used today is not a trustworthy guide to what is to be found in Aristotle's book by that name.

It may be added, in the *Metaphysics* one finds a discussion of such things as principle, necessity, being, unity, potentiality, actuality, definition, and other such subjects, most of which are highly universal and do not come under the genus of spatio-temporal continuants. Even the mathematical objects, discussed in Books M and N of the *Metaphysics*, do not come under that genus; for they are attributes, and as such they have been abstracted from physical objects and are treated as motionless and not subject to time or space, except accidentally or indirectly.

4. Speaking of Aristotle's logic (i.e., *Prior Analytics*), Jan Lukasiweicz says "This purely logical work is entirely exempt from any philosophical contamination," and consequently he is puzzled as to why that logic does not deal with singular terms.

First, Aristotle states in 1005b5-25 of the *Metaphysics* that one of the concerns of metaphysics is to discuss and state the syllogistic principles, and then he proceeds to discuss at length the principle of contradiction. It is evident, then, that the statement "This purely logical work is entirely exempt from any philosophical contamination" is false. Second, to be puzzled why Aristotle's logic does not deal with singular terms is like being puzzled why a mathematician is not dealing with individual triangles, singly taken, or any application of a mathematical object, singly taken. Aristotle's logic, as stated at the start (24a10-13), is the science of demonstration and its object is ultimately demonstration; and as a science, it is concerned with things universally taken, for no science in its primary sense is concerned with singular objects qua singular. Further, syllogisms with singular terms are qualified syllogisms for Aristotle, and knowledge of qualified syllogisms is similar to qualified scientific knowledge of singulars singly taken, as stated earlier. But qualified syllogisms are applications of unqualified syllogisms, which are syllogisms universally taken; and one who has scientific knowledge of unqualified syllogisms can easily apply that knowledge to syllogisms in which singulars appear.

5. It has been said that Aristotle's forms of propositions, i.e., the forms "all A is B," "no A is B," and their denials, are not adequate to take care of all the kinds of propositions.

Most of the time Aristotle uses the forms "B is predicated of all A" and "B belongs to all A," and sometimes the form "all A is B," but all three forms are generically the same, their difference being grammatical. Anyway, the copula "is" in the form "all A is B" can have as many meanings as there are categories (1017a7-b9), and there are ten categories (1b25-2a10). Of an object, then, one may predicate any one of those categories. The predicate "an animal" in "man is an animal" comes under substance, in "man is six feet tall" the predicate comes under quantity, in "John cuts wood" or "John is cutting wood" it comes under action, in "5 is greater than 3" it comes under relation, and similarly with the others. So since a thing can possess or lack something which must come under a category, and since every proposition signifies a possession or the lack of something by something, all possible propositions come under the forms put forward by Aristotle. As for triadic relations and the like, they are qualifications of relations in Aristotle's relational predication. For example, the expression "by 3" in "10 is greater than 7 by 3" qualifies the expression "greater than 7," and this becomes evident if the forms "10 is greater than 7" and "10 is by 3" are considered; for the first has meaning and is true, whereas the second has no meaning and is neither true nor false. Similarly for tetradic and other relations. There are other linguistic forms which give the appearance of not coming under those forms but are reducible to them. For example, "it is raining" is an idiomatic abbreviation of "drops of water from the clouds are falling on the ground," and "if a triangle is equiangular, then it is equilateral" is reducible to "an equiangular triangle is equilateral," and similarly for others. It is a mistake, then, to say that Aristotle's forms do not take care of all propositions and are therefore inadequate.

6. The important problem, of course, is whether Aristotle's logic is adequate for all purposes, especially for demonstration in the sciences. It is generally thought that it is inadequate, but this is based on insufficient knowledge of the principles which Aristotle uses in the sciences.

Many questions arise, especially with the meaning of "demonstration" as used by Aristotle. Now the titles *"Prior Analytics"* and *"Posterior Analytics"* are not those of Aristotle but were introduced by an editor of his works; they do not appear anywhere in the works. Aristotle regards both their contents as parts of one work, which he calls *Analytics* (19b31, 162a11, b32, 165b9, 1005b2-5, 1037b8, 1139b27, 32), and he uses the expression "On the Syllogism" to refer to the *Prior Analytics* (73a14) but the expression "On Demonstration" to refer to the *Posterior Analytics*. He states that the syllogism will be discussed first because it is prior in definition to demonstration (25b26-31). It is evident, then, that in raising the question whether Aristotle's logic is adequate for the sciences, one should include both parts of the *Analytics*; for the first part is general and is presupposed by the second, whereas the second part introduces additional principles for demonstrating theorems in the sciences.

As we stated earlier, the principles used in the demonstration of a theorem are concepts, definitions, hypotheses, and axioms. The axioms, which are regulatory or directive principles, are hardly mentioned in the *Prior Analytics*, although they are used, but they are discussed in the *Posterior Analytics* as being necessary in demonstrating theorems. The terms which Aristotle allows in a demonstration are, for certain reasons, limited to those which are proper to the science in which a theorem is demonstrated; but as for the axioms which he allows, some belong to that science but others are common to other sciences also or are axioms of more universal sciences. Thus in mathematics he would allow many kinds of axioms because, for example, a theorem in solid geometry may use also axioms belonging to lines and surfaces since a solid object may presuppose surfaces or lines and surfaces because a solid object may presuppose surfaces or lines or points in its definition. There are also axioms which concern not the mathematical objects themselves but the premises and statements and syllogisms which signify mathematical objects, and one may *apply* those axioms to them not qua signifying such objects but qua being just premises or statements or syllogisms, respectively.

The inclusion of axioms as the additional principles in a science appears to render Aristotle's *Analytics*, which is his logic in the wide sense as indicated, adequate for demonstrating theorems. A demonstration of a mathematical theorem, that vertical angles are equal, has been given in another work, *Aristotle's Posterior Analytics*, (The Peripatetic Press, 1981, pgs. 250-60, by H. G. Apostle), showing the kinds of principles involved along with some comments.

7. There are many misconceptions due to mistranslation. Two will be considered.

The term whose phonetic translation is "democratia" is translated as "democracy," and from this it follows that, according to Aristotle, democracy is a bad form of government. But this translation, although etymologically sound, is misleading, for it is not in accordance with the meaning given to the Greek term by Aristotle. A careful reading of what the *Politics* states about democratia and its various forms should lead one to translate "democratia" as "mass rule" or "mob rule" or "people's rule" or "ochlocracy," with the understanding that the ruling body under democratia rules not for the sake of all its citizens but for the sake of a certain class — usually the poor — at the expense of the other classes. Our democracy according to the Constitution is certainly not a democratia, for the ruling body is stated in the Constitution as being concerned with the general welfare and not with the interests of one class at the expense of the other classes. Violations, of course, occur in our democracy, but these are contrary to the Constitution and not in accordance with it.

It is generally thought that, according to Aristotle, heavier bodies fall faster than lighter bodies. This is a misconception due to mistranslation of the term βάρος. The two main meanings of this term are (a) total weight of a body and (b) density or specific gravity of a body (217b17-20), and careful readings of the passages in which falling bodies are discussed (215a25-9, 1052b28-9) show that the right translation of that term should be "density" or "specific gravity" and not "weight." Further, Aristotle assumes the existence of a medium which resists falling bodies. From this postulate and the right translation it follows that denser bodies, but not necessarily heavier, fall faster.

8. Some thinkers characterized Aristotle's works (1) as pigeonholing or categorizing things or their knowledge without relating them, and others (2) as forming a system.

Do Aristotle's works form a system? The usual connotations of a system are order as against chaos, dependence or interdependence as against independence, interaction as against freedom from interference, and unity or sameness as against its contrary, which is plurality or distinctness. But what we observe in these works is the inclusion of both contraries and their mixtures. For example, we are told that some things are the same, others are distinct, and the rest are mixtures of sameness and distinctness, and that they may be the same either numerically or specifically or generically or analogically, or distinct in the same manner, or the same in one respect but distinct in another respect. As for interaction and its contrary, we are told that some things can act on others but the rest cannot, that of things which can act on others, some can be affected by other things but the rest cannot, and that of the things which cannot act on others, some can be affected by others but the rest cannot. With respect to dependence or interdependence as against independence, we are told that some things depend on others, either partly or wholly, but other things do not. With respect to order as against chaos, we are told that there is order in science but there can be no order in accidents, and so some things are orderly but others are chaotic. The works of Aristotle as wholes may be viewed in a similar way. Thus some sciences, according to him, depend on other sciences, whether partly or wholly, but others do not so depend. Accordingly, if dependence or interdependence is a necessary condition for any two of Aristotle's works to be parts of a system, then those works do not form a system. If we are to call those works a "system," then, it would be not a *closed* but an *open-ended* system.

As for the assertion that Aristotle pigeonholes or categorizes things without exploring their various relations, it is easily refuted by his inclusion among the categories the term "relation," by the fact that in the *Posterior Analytics* he discusses the ways in which sciences may be related, and by the fact that in the *Metaphysics* he discusses universally the ways in which things may be related to each other with respect to sameness, likeness, analogy, and the like.

CATEGORIES

CONTENTS

Chapter

CATEGORIES

1

Things are named equivocally if only the name applied to them is *1a* common but the expression of the *substance* [i.e., the definition] corresponding to that name is different for each of the things, as in the case of a man and a picture when each is called 'animal'. For only the name is common to these, but the expression of the *substance* corresponding to that name differs for each; for if one were to state what it is to be an animal, he *5* would give a different definition for each of them.

Things are named univocally if both the name applied to them is common and the expression of the *substance* corresponding to that name is the same for each of the things, as in the case of 'animal' when applied to a man and to an ox. For a man and an ox may be called by the common name 'animal', and the expression of the *substance* [corresponding to that *10* name] is the same for both; for if one were to state for each of them what it is to be an animal, he would give the same definition.

Things are derivatively named if they are called by a name which is borrowed from another name but which differs from it in ending. For example, a man may be called 'grammarian', and this name is borrowed from 'grammar'; and he may be called 'brave', and this name is borrowed *15* from 'bravery'.

2

Of expressions, some are composite but others are not composite. For example, 'man runs' and 'man conquers' are composite, but 'man,' 'ox,' 'runs,' and 'conquers' are not composite.

Of things, (1) some are said of a subject but are not present in any subject. *20* For example, man is said of an individual man, which is the subject, but is not present in any subject. (2) Others are present in a subject but are not said of any subject (a thing is said to be present in a subject if, not belonging as a part to that subject, it is incapable of existing apart from the subject in *25* which it is). For example, a particular point of grammar is present in the soul , which is the subject, but is not said of any subject, and a particular whiteness is present in a body (for every color is in a body), which is the subject, but is not said of any subject. (3) Other things, again, are said of a

1b   subject and are also present in a subject. For example, *knowledge* is present
     in the soul, which is the subject, and is said of a subject, e.g., of grammar.
     Finally, (4) there are things which are neither present in a subject nor said
5   of a subject, such as an individual man and an individual horse; for, of things
     such as these, no one is either present in a subject or said of a subject. And
     without qualification, that which is an individual and numerically one is not
     said of any subject, but nothing prevents some of them from being present
     in a subject; for a particular point of grammar is present in a subject but is
     not said of any subject.

3

10   When one thing is predicable of another as of a subject, whatever is said
     of the predicate will be said of the subject also. For example, 'man' is
     predicable of an individual man, and 'animal' of 'man' [or of man];
15   accordingly, 'animal' would be predicable of an individual man also, for an
     individual man is both a man and an animal.
         The differentiae of genera which are different and not subordinate one to
     the other are themselves different in kind, as in the case of 'animal' and
     'science'. For the differentiae of 'animal' are 'terrestrial', 'two-footed',
     'feathered', 'aquatic', etc., and none of these is a differentia of 'science'; for
20   no science differs from another by being two-footed . But if one genus
     comes under another, nothing prevents both genera from having
     differentiae which are the same; for a higher genus is predicable of a genus
     coming under it, and so all the differentiae of the predicate [the higher
     genus] will be differentiae of the subject [the lower genus] also.

4

25   Expressions which are in no way composite signify either a substance, or
     a quantity, or a quality, or a relation, or somewhere, or at some time, or
     being in a position, or possessing [or having], or acting, or being acted upon.
     To speak sketchily, examples of a [name signifying a] substance are 'a man'
     and 'a horse'; of a quantity, 'a line two cubits long' and 'a line three cubits
     long' ; of a quality, 'the white' and 'the grammatical'; of a relation, 'a
2a   double', 'a half', and 'the greater'; of somewhere, 'in the Lyceum' and 'in
     the Agora'; of at some time, 'yesterday' and 'last year'; of being in a position,
     'lies' and 'sits'; of possessing, 'is shod' and 'is armed'; of acting, 'cuts' and
     'burns'; of being acted upon, 'is cut' and 'is burned'.
5   Each of the above, when by itself, is not expressed as an affirmation or a
     denial, but an affirmation or a denial is formed only if such expressions are

combined; for every affirmation and every denial is thought to be either true
or false, whereas no expression which is in no way composite, such as 'a man'   10
or 'white' or 'runs' or 'conquers', is either true or false.

5

A substance, spoken of in the most fundamental, primary, and highest
sense of the word is that which is neither said of a subject nor present in a
subject; e.g., an individual man or an individual horse. Secondary
substances are said to be (a) those to which, as species, belong substances
which are called 'primary', and also (b) the genera of those species. For   15
example, an individual man comes under the species man, and the genus of
this species is animal; so both man and animal are said to be secondary
substances.

It is evident from what has been said that, of things said of a subject, it   20
is necessary for both the name and the definition [corresponding to that
name] to be predicable of that subject. For example, man is said of an
individual man, which is a subject; so the name 'man', too, is predicable [of
the individual man], for one would predicate 'man' of an individual man.
And the definition of man, too, would be predicable of the individual man;   25
for an individual man is a man and also an animal. Thus both the name and
the corresponding definition would be predicable of the subject.

Of things which are present in a subject, in most cases neither the name
nor the definition corresponding to that name is predicable of the subject.
In some cases, however, sometimes nothing prevents the name from being   30
predicable of the subject, but the definition [corresponding to that name]
cannot be predicable of that subject. For example, white is present in a
body, which is the subject, and [the name 'white'] is predicable of that
subject (for that body is called 'white'); but the definition of white will never
be predicable of that body.

Everything except primary substances is either said of a subject which is   35
a primary substance or is present in a subject which is a primary substance;
and this becomes evident if particular cases are taken. For example, 'animal'
is predicable of man, and hence it would be predicable of an individual
man also; for if it were not predicable of any individual man, neither would   2b
it be predicable of man at all. Again, color is present in body, and hence it
would be present in an individual body also; for if it were not present in any
individual body, neither would it be present in body at all. Thus everything
except primary substances is either said of a subject which is a primary   5
substance or is present in a subject which is a primary substance.
Accordingly, if primary substances did not exist, it would be impossible for
any of the others to exist.

Of secondary substances, the species is to a higher degree a substance than a genus of it, for it is closer to a primary substance than a genus of it is. For if one were to state what a given primary substance is, he would give
10   something which is more informative and more appropriate to that substance by stating its species than by stating a genus of it. Of an individual man, for example, he would give more information by calling him 'man' than by calling him 'animal'; for the name 'man' is more proper to the individual man than the name 'animal', whereas the name 'animal' is more common than 'man'. Again, in the case of an individual tree, he will give more information by calling it 'tree' than by calling it 'plant'.
15   Moreover, primary substances are said to be substances in the highest degree because they underlie all the rest and all the rest are either predicable of or present in primary substances. Now the relation of primary substances to all the rest is similar to that of a species [of a primary
20   substance] to a genus of it, since the species underlies the genus; for a genus is predicable of a species of it, whereas a species is not predicable of a genus of it. So in view of this, too, a species [of a primary substance] is a substance to a higher degree than a genus of it. But of the species themselves which are not genera of lower species, no one of them is a substance to a higher degree than another; for you will not give a more appropriate account of the
25   subject by calling an individual man 'man' than by calling an individual horse 'horse'. And in a similar way, of primary substances, no one of them is a substance to a higher degree than another; for an individual man is not a substance to a higher degree than an individual ox.
30   Of all things other than primary substances, it is reasonable that only the species and the genera [of primary substances] should be called 'secondary substances', for of all the predicates these alone [as predicates] indicate a primary substance. For, if one is to state what an individual man is, it is by stating the species or a genus of it that he will say something which is appropriate to him, and he will give more information by saying that he is a man than by saying that he is an animal. Anything else that he might say of him, e.g., that he is white or that he runs or any other such thing, would
35   be remote from him. Thus it is reasonable that, of all things other than primary substances, only the species and the genera [of primary substances] should be called 'substances'.
Moreover, it is because they underlie all other things that primary
3a   substances are called 'substances' in the most fundamental sense. In fact, just as primary substances are [thus] related to all other things, so the species and genera of primary substances are related to all other things [except primary substances], for all these are predicable   of those species and genera. Thus
5   if we call an individual man 'grammatical', this predicate will apply also to [the species] man and to [the genus] animal; and similarly with all other cases.

It is common to all substances that none of them is present in a subject. For a primary substance is neither present in a subject nor said of a subject; and as for secondary substances, it is evident from what follows also that 10 they are not present in a subject. For man is said of an individual man, who is the subject, but is not present in a subject; for man is not present in an individual man. Similarly, animal, too, is said of an individual man, who is the subject, but animal is not present in an individual man. Again, of a 15 thing present in a subject, sometimes nothing prevents the name [of that thing] from being predicable of the subject in which the thing is present, but the corresponding definition of the thing cannot be predicable of that subject. Of a secondary substance, on the other hand, both the name and the definition are predicable of the corresponding subject; for we would predicate of an individual man both the definition of man and that of 20 animal. Thus a substance is not a thing which is present in a subject.

Now this fact is not a property of substances since the differentia [of a substance], too, is not present in a subject; for terrestrial and two-footed are said of man, who is the subject, but are not present in a subject, for they are not present in man. The definition of a differentia, too, is predicable of that 25 of which the differentia is said; for example, if terrestrial is said of man, the definition of terrestrial will be predicable of man also, for man is terrestrial.

Let us not be confused by the thought that the parts of a substance are in the whole substance as if present in a subject and be forced to say that those 30 parts are not substances; for we said earlier[1] that by 'being present in a subject' we do not mean existing as parts which belong to some whole.

It is a mark of substances and [their] differentiae that all things are univocally named from them; for all the predicates corresponding to them 35 are predicable either of individuals or of species. First, since a primary substance is not said of a subject, the corresponding predicate cannot be predicable of anything. As for secondary substances, the species is predicable of the individuals, and the genus is predicable both of the species and of the individuals. The differentiae [of substances], too, are likewise 3b predicable of the species as well as of the individuals. Again, primary substances admit of the definition of their species and the definition of their genera, and a species [of a substance] admits of the definition of its genus; for whatever is said of the predicate will be said of the subject also. 5 Similarly, both the species and the individuals admit of the definition of the differentia. But things were stated to be univocally named if both the name is common and the definition corresponding to that name is the same;[2] hence all things are univocally named from a substance or a differentia [of a substance].

Every substance is thought to indicate a *this*. Now in the case of primary 10 substances there is no dispute, and it is true that a primary substance

indicates a *this;* for what is exhibited is something individual and numerically one. But in the case of a secondary substance, though the manner of naming it appears to signify in a similar way a *this*, as when one
15 uses 'a man' or 'an animal', this is not true, for [such a name] signifies rather a sort of quality; for the subject is not just one [in an unqualified way], as in the case of a primary substance, but man or animal is said of many things. Nevertheless, such a [name] does not signify simply a quality, as 'white'
20 does; for 'white' signifies a quality and nothing more, whereas a species or a genus [of a primary substance] determines the quality of a substance, for it signifies a substance which is qualified in some way. But the determination in the case of a genus is wider in application than that in the case of a species, for he who uses the name 'animal' includes more things than he who uses the name 'man'.
25   Another mark of a substance is that it has no contrary. For what would be the contrary of a primary substance, e.g., of an individual man or of an individual animal? There can be none. Nor can there be a contrary of man or of animal. This mark, however, is not a property of substances but is common to many other things also, for example, to quantities; for there can
30 be no contrary to a line two cubits long or three cubits long, nor to the number ten, nor to any other such thing, though one might say that much is the contrary of little and that great is the contrary of small. But of a definite quantity there can be no contrary.
    Again, no substance is thought to admit of variation of degree. By this
35 I mean not that one [kind of] substance cannot be more of a substance or less of a substance than another (for it has already been stated that this is the case),[3] but that each substance, *as such*, is not said to admit of variation of degree. For example, if that substance is a man, he cannot be more of a man or less of a man, whether he is compared with himself [at different times] or with another man; for one man is not more of a man than another
4a man, unlike one white thing which may be more white, or less white, than another white thing, or one beautiful thing which may be more beautiful, or less beautiful, than another beautiful thing. Now the same thing may admit of variation of degree [but with respect to quality]; a body which is white, for example, may be [truly] said to be more white now than before,
5 and a body which is hot may be [truly] said to be more hot [at one time than at another]. But a substance [*as such*] is never [truly] said to vary in degree; for neither is a man [truly] said to be more of a man now than before, nor is this the case with any of the other [kinds of] substances. Accordingly, a substance [*as such*] does not admit of variation of degree.
10   The mark most proper to a substance is thought to be that, while remaining numerically one and the same, it admits of contraries. In other words, of all things other than [primary] substances, there is no one which, being numerically one [and the same], can be shown to admit of contraries.

A color, for example, being numerically one and the same, cannot be black   15
and white; nor can an *action*, which is numerically one and the same, be
both vicious and virtuous; and similarly with other things which are not
substances. But a substance, being numerically one and the same, admits of
contraries.   An individual man, for example, being [numerically] one and   20
the same, becomes at one time light but at another dark in color, at one time
warm but at another cold, at one time vicious but at another virtuous.

No such thing appears to apply to any of the other things, although one
might object and maintain that a statement or an opinion admits of
contraries. For the same statement is thought to be [sometimes] true and   25
[sometimes] false; for example, if the statement 'that man is sitting' is true,
the same statement will be false after that man gets up. The same applies
to opinions; for if one's opinion that a man is sitting is true, then the same
opinion of the same man will be false after that man gets up. Yet even if we
were to allow this to be so, still the manner in which it happens here differs   30
from that in the other case; for in the other case it is by a change in
themselves that substances admit of contraries, for it is by changing himself
(i.e., by altering) that a man became warm from cold, or dark from light,
or virtuous from vicious. It is likewise with the other substances, for it is by
a change in itself that each of them admits of contraries. But in themselves,   35
statements and opinions keep on being immovable in every way, and they
admit of contraries only when the things [signified by them] have moved;
for the statement 'that man is sitting' keeps on being the same in itself, but   4b
it is said to be first true and then false only when the thing [i.e., that man]
has moved; and the same applies to opinions. Thus, at least in the manner
indicated, only substances have the property of admitting of contraries in   5
virtue of their own change. So if one accepts also these qualifications, then
it would not be true to say that statements and opinions admit of contraries;
for it is not by receiving any contraries in themselves that they are said to
admit of contraries but by the fact that some other things [i.e., substances]
have been affected in this manner, since a statement is now true and later
false not by admitting in itself now one contrary and later another but   10
because what is signified is a fact now but not later.   In fact, neither a
statement nor an opinion can be moved in an unqualified way   by
anything, so they cannot admit of contraries if they cannot be affected. But
as for substances, it is by receiving the contraries in themselves that they are   15
said to admit of contraries; for [animals] become sick and healthy, light and
dark, and they are said to admit of contraries when they themselves receive
them. Accordingly, it is only a substance that, being the same and
numerically one,   has the property of admitting contraries in virtue of its
own change.

Let so much be said concerning substances.

6

20   Of quantities, some are discrete but others are continuous; and some are composed of parts which have relative position to each other, others are composed of parts which do not have relative position to each other. Examples of a discrete quantity are a [whole] number and speech; examples of a continuous quantity are a line, a surface, a body, and, besides these, 25 time and place.

The parts of a number have no common boundary at which they join. For example, five as a part of ten is not joined with the other part, five, at any common boundary, but the two parts are discrete, and three, which is another part of ten, is not joined with the other part, seven, at any common 30 boundary; and in general, it is not at all possible to find any boundary among the parts of a number, for those parts are always discrete. A number, then, is a discrete quantity. Speech is likewise a discrete quantity. Evidently, speech is a quantity, for it is measured by short and long syllables; and by 35 'speech' here I mean vocal speech. Now the parts of speech have no common boundary at which they join, for there is no common boundary at which the syllables are joined; each syllable is separate by itself.

5a   A line, on the other hand, is a continuous quantity, for it is possible to find a common boundary — a point — at which its parts are joined; and in the case of a surface, the boundary is a line, for the parts of a plane are joined at some common boundary. Similarly, it is possible to find a common 5   boundary — a line or a surface — at which the parts of a body are joined. Time and place, too, are quantities like these. For present time is joined with the past and also with the future. Place, too, is continuous, for the parts of 10 a body occupy a place and are thus joined at some common boundary; and so the parts of place, too, which the parts of the body occupy, are joined at the same boundary at which the parts of the body are joined. Hence place, too, would be continuous, for its parts are joined at a common boundary.

15   Again, some quantities are composed of parts which have a relative position to each other, others are composed of parts without having a relative position to each other. For example, the parts of a line have a relative position to each other, for each part lies somewhere, and one could 20 mark off each part and state where it lies in the plane and with which of its other parts it is joined. Similarly, the parts of a plane have a [relative] position, for one could state in a similar way where each part lies and with which of the other parts it is joined. Similar remarks apply to a solid and to place.

25   But in the case of a number, one could not point out how its parts have a relative position to each other or lie somewhere, or which parts are joined with other parts. Nor could one do so in the case of time, for no part of time continues to exist; and how could a thing have position if it cannot continue

to exist? One would rather say that the parts of time have an order in which any one part comes either before or after another. And similarly with numbers, for, in counting, one comes before two, two before three, etc., and in this way there would be an order; but it would not be possible at all to find any position. The same applies to speech also. None of its parts continues to exist, and after it has been pronounced, it no longer exists; and if the parts cannot continue to exist, they can have no position. Accordingly, some quantities are composed of parts having a [relative] position, others are composed of parts having no position.

Quantities in the fundamental sense are only those which we have mentioned; all the others are called 'quantities' indirectly, for we call them so because we have in mind some quantity in the fundamental sense. For example, the white is called 'much' since the surface which is white is much, and an *action* is called 'long' since it takes much time, and a motion is called 'extended' for the same reason; for each of these is so called not in virtue of its nature. In other words, if one were to answer the question 'How long did the *action* take?', he would specify it in terms of time and say that it took one year, or something of the sort; and to the question 'How large is the white?', he would specify the answer in terms of the surface, for he would say that the white has so much surface. Thus quantities in the fundamental sense and in virtue of their own nature are only the ones mentioned; the others are not quantities in virtue of their nature but, if at all, [are called 'quantities'] indirectly.

Again, there can be no contrary to a quantity. In the case of definite quantities it is evident that there can be no contrary, e.g., to a line two or three cubits long or to a surface or to any such quantity; for there is no contrary to any of these, although one might maintain that much is contrary to little and that the great is contrary to the small. But these are relatives and not quantities, for no thing in virtue of its nature is called 'great' or 'small', but only when it is referred to some other thing. For example, a mountain may be called 'small' but a grain 'large', and this is in view of the fact that the latter is greater than others of its kind while the former is smaller than others of its kind. Thus there is a reference to some other thing, for if these were called 'small' or 'large' in view of their own nature [i.e., without being referred to something else], the mountain would not be called 'small' and the grain 'large'. Again, we say that there are many men in the village but few men in Athens, although those in Athens are many times more than those in the village; and we say that there are many people in the house but few in the theatre, although those in the theatre are many more than those in the house. Again, the expressions 'a line two cubits long' and 'a line three cubits long' and others like them signify quantities; 'great' and 'small', on the other hand, signify not quantities but rather relatives, for the great or the small is viewed with reference to something else. So it is evident that these [i.e., 'great', 'small', etc.] are relatives.

30   Again, whether one posits the above as being quantities or not, still no
thing can be contrary to each of them; for how can one [truly] maintain that
there can be a contrary to a thing which is considered not in virtue of its
nature but by being referred to something else?   Again, if the great and the
small were contraries, the same thing would turn out (a) to admit of
35   contraries at the same time and (b) to be contrary to itself. (a) For sometimes
the same thing happens to be great and small at the same time, small in
relation to one thing but great in relation to another; and so the same thing
would turn out to be both great and small at the same time and hence to
6a   admit of contraries at the same time. Yet no thing is thought to admit of
contraries at the same time, as in the case of substances. Although a man,
for example, is thought to admit of contraries, still he cannot be both sick
and healthy at the same time; nor can a body be both white and black at the
same time. In fact, no thing at all admits of contraries at the same time.
5   (b) And the same thing would turn out to be contrary to itself. For if the
great were contrary to the small, since the same thing is both great and small
at the same time, the same thing would be contrary to itself. But it is
impossible for anything to be contrary to itself. Hence neither is the great
10   contrary to the small, nor is much contrary to little. So even if one were to
call these 'quantities' and not 'relations', still they would have no
contraries.
    Contrariety in quantities is thought to belong to place most of all. For
men posit up as being contrary to down, calling 'down' the space at the
15   center of the universe because its distance from the outer limits of the
universe is the greatest. And they seem to apply this terminology to the
definition of contraries for all other things, for they define contraries in a
given genus as things whose distance from each other is the greatest.
20   Quantities do not admit of variation of degree. For example, a line two
cubits long is not more of a line or less of a line than another line two cubits
long; and in the case of numbers, one instance of three is not more three than
another instance of three, and one instance of five is not more five than
another. And of time, too, one instance of it is not more time than another
instance of it. In general, of the kinds of quantities mentioned, no one
instance can be truly said to be more or to be less of what it is than another
25   instance. So quantities, too, do not admit of variation of degree.
    The most proper attribute of quantities is that they are said to be equal
or unequal to each other, for in each of the kinds of quantities mentioned
one quantity is said to be either equal or unequal to another. For example,
one body is either equal or unequal to another, one interval of time is either
30   equal or unequal to another, and similarly for each of the other kinds of
quantities mentioned.   Concerning things other than quantities, no one
would ever think of saying that they are either equal or unequal. A
disposition, for example, is certainly not said to be equal or unequal to

another disposition but rather similar, and one white thing is not said to be equal or unequal to another white thing, but rather similar. So the most proper attribute of a quantity is that it is [truly] said to be either equal or 35 unequal to some other quantity.

7

Things are called 'relative' [or 'relations'] if *as such* they are said to be of something else or to be somehow referred to something else. For example, the greater, *as such*, is said to be of something else, for it is said to be greater than some other thing, and the double, *as such*, is said to be of something else, for it is said to be double of some other thing. It is likewise 6b with all others of this sort. Other examples of relatives are the following: possession, disposition, sensation, *knowledge*, and position ; for each of these, *as such*, is said to be of something else and is not stated in any other way. For a possession is said to be a possession of something, *knowledge* is said to be *knowledge* of something, a position is said to be a position of 5 something, and similarly with all others. Accordingly, relatives are things which, *as such*, are said to be of something else or are referred to something else in some way or other. For example, a mountain is called 'great' when it is related to something, for it is so called by being referred to something; and that which is said to be similar is similar to some other thing, and all 10 others of this sort are said to be relative in the same way. Lying, standing, and sitting, we may add, are positions, and position is a relative. But to lie, to stand, and to be seated are not themselves positions; they are derivatively so expressed from the corresponding positions.

Contraries may exist among relatives. For example, virtue is contrary to 15 vice, and each is a relative; and *knowledge* is contrary to ignorance. But not all relatives have contraries; for there is no contrary to a double, or to a triple, or to any other such thing.

Relatives are thought to admit also of variation of degree. For a thing may 20 be said to be more similar, or less similar, or more dissimilar, or less dissimilar [to something than to something else], or it may be said to be more equal, or less equal, or more unequal, or less unequal [to something than to something else], and each of these is a relative; for the similar is said to be similar to something, and the dissimilar is said to be dissimilar to something. But not all relatives admit of variation of degree; for the double is not said 25 to be more double or less double [to something than to something else], and the same applies to other such things.

All relatives have reciprocal reference to their correlatives. For example, a slave is said to be the slave of a master, and a master is said to be the master 30

of a slave; a double is said to be the double of a half, and a half is said to be the half of a double; and the greater is said to be greater than the less, and the less is said to be less than the greater. It is likewise with the other relatives, except that sometimes the expression requires a different grammatical case. For example, *knowledge* is said to be *knowledge* of the
35 *known*, but the *known* is said to be *known* by *knowledge*; and sensation is said to be sensation of the sensible, but the sensible is said to be sensible by sensation.

Sometimes, however, no reciprocal reference is thought to arise if a relative is not appropriately but mistakenly rendered when referred to [its correlative]. For example, if a wing is stated as being the wing of a bird, no
7a reciprocal reference arises, since a bird is not a bird of the wing; for 'the wing of a bird' is not the appropriate expression since the wing is said to be of a bird not insofar as the latter is a bird but insofar as it is winged, for there are many other things, too, which have wings but are not birds.   Thus if the expression is appropriately rendered, there is a reciprocal reference, e.g., a
5   wing is a wing of the winged, and the winged is winged by the wing.

Sometimes it is perhaps necessary to introduce a new name, if no name exists to which a relative might be appropriately rendered. For example, if a rudder is stated to be of a boat, the statement is not made appropriately, for a rudder is said to be of a boat not insofar as the latter is a boat (for there
10 are boats without rudders, and so there is no reciprocal reference) since a boat is not said to be the boat of [or by, etc.] a rudder. Perhaps the expression would be more appropriately rendered if one were to introduce a word such as 'ruddered', since no name exists, and to say that the rudder is a rudder of the ruddered, or something of this sort; and if the expression is appropriately rendered in this manner, the reference will be reciprocal, for
15 the ruddered is ruddered by the rudder, and the same applies to others of this sort. To take another example, a head would be more appropriately rendered [as a relative] if it were stated to be of the headed rather than of an animal, for it is not insofar as it is an animal that an animal has a head—for many animals have no head—[but insofar as it is headed].

Perhaps the easiest way to grasp relatives which have no names is to posit
20 for them names which come from the correlatives as in the examples already given, e.g., 'winged' from 'wing' and 'ruddered' from 'rudder'. If so, then every relative, if appropriately rendered *as such*, will be stated with reference to its reciprocal correlative, for if it were referred to a chance
25 thing which is not its correlative, there would be no reciprocal reference. I mean that there will be no reciprocal reference even if the thing to which the relative is referred is agreed upon as having a reciprocal reference and as having the corresponding name but the relative is referred to that thing not through the name of its correlative but through the name of some other attribute of the thing. For example, if a slave is stated to be not of a master

but of a man or two-footed or anything of this sort, there will be no 30
reciprocal reference; for that to which the slave is referred is not
appropriately stated. Further, if a relative is appropriately referred to a
thing, and if the thing retains the element to which the reference is
appropriately made, the reference will always be true even if that thing
were to be denied of all its other attributes. Thus if a slave were referred to 35
a master, and if the master were to be denied of all its other attributes, such
as being two-footed and receptive of science and a man, that reference will
always be true if only the master continues being a master,   for it is of a
master that a slave is said to be the slave. But if the reference to its 7b
correlative is not appropriately rendered, and if only that to which the
reference is made is retained but all other things belonging to it are denied,
the reference will no longer be true. For let a slave be said to be of a man
and a wing to be of a bird, and let the attribute of being a master be denied 5
of the man. Then the slave will no longer be [truly] referred to that man, for
if there is no master, neither will there be a slave. Similarly, let the attribute
of being winged be denied of a bird; then a wing will no longer be a relative,
for if the winged does not exist, neither will there be a wing of anything
winged. Accordingly, if a relative is referred to something, the reference 10
should be appropriately rendered. And if a name for the correlative exists,
the reference can be rendered easily, but if no such name exists, perhaps a
name for the correlative should be introduced. And if this is done, then it
is evident that all relatives will be reciprocally referred to correlatives.

Correlatives are thought to exist simultaneously by their nature, and in 15
most cases this is true. For when a double exists, so does the corresponding
half, and when a half exists, so does the corresponding double; and when a
master exists, so does his slave, and when a slave exists, so does his master,
and similarly with others. Moreover, they negate each other simultaneously;
for if no double exists, neither does a half, and if no half exists, neither does 20
a double; and similarly with all others of this sort.

But it is thought that not all correlatives exist simultaneously by their
nature; for the *knowable* might be thought to exist before *knowledge*. Now
in most cases things existed before we acquired the *knowledge* of them, for 25
in few cases or in no cases at all one might observe both the *knowable* and
the corresponding *knowledge* coming into existence at the same time.
Further, when the *knowable* is negated, the corresponding *knowledge*, too,
is negated,   but when that *knowledge* is negated, the *knowable* is not
[necessarily] negated; for if the *knowable* does not exist, neither does the
corresponding *knowledge* (for it would not be the *knowledge* of anything), 30
but if that *knowledge* does not exist, nothing prevents the *knowable* from
existing. For example, in the case of the squaring of the circle, if indeed this
happens to be *knowable*, though there is no *knowledge* of it yet, it is

nevertheless *knowable*.   Moreover, if animals are negated, there will be no
35   *knowledge*, yet many *knowable* things may still exist.
 The situation with sensation is similar, for the sensible object is thought
to exist before the sensation of it exists. For when the sensible object is
negated, the sensation of it is negated also, but the sensible object is not
[necessarily] negated when the corresponding sensation is negated. For
sensations are of bodies and exist in bodies [of animals], and when the
8a   sensibles are negated, the bodies too are negated (for what is sensible is a
body), and when bodies do not exist, neither do sensations; hence if the
sensibles are negated, sensations are negated also. But the negation of
sensations does not necessitate the negation of the sensibles; for when
5   animals are negated, so are sensations, but sensibles, such as bodies and
things which are hot or sweet or bitter and all the other sensibles, [may] still
exist. Again, sensations come into being at the same time as the subject
which can sense, for they come into being when animals are born, but there
are sensible objects which exist even before the sensations of them or
10   animals exist; for fire and water and other such, from which also animals are
composed, exist even before animals at all or their sensations exist. Hence
it would seem that sensibles may exist before the sensations of them do.
 There is the problem whether no substance is said to be a relative, as
15   indeed is thought to be the case, or whether some secondary substances may
be said to be relatives. In the case of primary substances it is true that none
of them are said to be relatives, since neither they as wholes nor their parts
are said to be relatives. For an individual man is not said to be an individual
man of some individual, nor an individual ox to be an individual ox of some
individual.   The same applies to the parts also; for an individual hand is not
said to be an individual hand of [or relative to] someone, though it is said to
20   be *the* hand of someone, and an individual head is not said to be an
individual head of [or relative to] some individual, though it is said to be *the*
head of some individual. The same applies to secondary substances, at least
to most of them. For example, a man is not said to be a man of [or relative
to] someone,   and an ox is not said to be an ox of some individual; and a stick
is said to be not a stick of an individual but *the property* of someone.
25   Evidently, then, things such as these are not relatives; but there is
disagreement concerning some secondary substances. For example, a head
is said to be the head of some animal, and a hand is said to be the hand of
someone, and similarly with others of this sort, so these might be thought to
be relatives.
 Now if the definition of a relative   has been adequately stated, it is very
30   difficult or even impossible to show that no substance is said to be a relative.
If, however, it has not been adequately stated, and if a relative is that whose
being   is the same as being referred to some other thing in some manner,
perhaps something might be said for it. The former definition applies to all

relatives, but being a relative for each of them is not the same as being said,   35
as such, of something else. From these remarks it is clear that, if one
definitely understands something as being a relative, he will definitely
understand also that to which it is said to be referred.

This is evident also from the things themselves. For if one understands
this individual as being a relative, and if to be a relative is the same as to   8b
be referred to some other thing in a certain manner, then he understands
also that to which this individual is referred in that manner; for if he does
not understand at all that to which this individual is referred in that
manner, neither will he understand that it is referred to anything in that
manner. That such is the case becomes clear if we consider individual cases.
For example, if one understands in a definite way that *this* individual is a   5
double, he will immediately understand in a definite way also that of which
it is the double; for if he does not understand that individual as being the
double of any definite thing, he will not understand at all that it is
a double. Similarly, if a man understands *this* individual as being more
beautiful, then for the same *reasons* it is necessary for him to understand
immediately and in a definite way that than which that individual is more
beautiful. He will not just understand in an indefinite way that this   10
individual is more beautiful than something inferior to it, since this will be
an assumption and not *knowledge*; for he would not then understand with
accuracy that the individual is more beautiful than something inferior to it,
since it might so happen that nothing inferior to it existed. Evidently, then,
it is necessary that, if a man is to understand a relative in a definite way, he
will have to understand in a definite way also that to which that relative is   15
said to be related.

Now in the case of a head and a hand and other such things, which are
substances, a man can understand in a definite way what each of them is *as
such*, but it is not necessary for him to understand that to which it is
referred. For one may not understand definitely whose head this head is
or whose hand this hand is. So these would not be relatives; and if they are   20
not relatives, it would be true to say that no substance is a relative.

Perhaps it is difficult to speak firmly about matters such as these without
having examined many cases, but to have gone through the difficulties in
each case would not be without some use.

8

I call 'quality' that in virtue of which some things are said to be such and   25
such. But the name 'quality' is used in many ways.

Qualities of one kind may be called 'habits' and 'dispositions'. Habits
differ from dispositions by being much more lasting and more firmly

30 established, and such are the sciences and the virtues. For a science, even
if moderately acquired, is thought to be firmly established with us and
difficult to displace, unless a great change occurs through disease or some
other such thing. The same may be said of a virtue, e.g., justice or
temperance or any of this sort, for none of these is thought to be easily
35 displaced or easily changed. We call 'dispositions' those qualities, on the
other hand, which are easily displaced or change quickly, e.g., a hot
condition, a chill, sickness, health, and things of this sort; for a man is
disposed in some manner with respect to these qualities but changes
9a quickly, becoming cold after being warm, sick after being healthy, and
similarly with the others, unless any of these qualities happens to become
after a long time so deep-rooted as to be incurable or very difficult to
displace, in which case perhaps it should then be called a 'habit'.
5   It is evident, then, that men intend to call 'habits' those qualities which
last a very long time and are very difficult to displace, for those who have
no firm possession of a science but are easily changeable are not said to have
the habit of that science, though they are disposed in some way with respect
to it, whether better or worse. Thus a habit and a disposition differ in this,
10 that the latter is easily displaced while the former lasts much longer and is
more difficult to displace. But habits are also dispositions, whereas
dispositions are not necessarily habits; for those who have habits are also
disposed in some way according to them, whereas those who are disposed
do not in every case have a habit [corresponding to their disposition].
        Another genus of quality is that according to which we call men, for
15 example, 'natural boxers' or 'natural runners' or 'healthy' or 'sickly', and,
without qualification, those qualities which are named in virtue of some
natural capability or incapability; for these men are said to be such and
such not just by being disposed in some manner but by having a natural
capability or incapability of doing something easily or of not being affected
easily. For example, men are called 'natural boxers' or 'natural runners' not
20 by being disposed in some way but by having a natural capability to do
something easily; and they are called 'healthy' when they have a natural
capability to resist easily being adversely affected by ordinary agents, but
they are called 'sickly' when they have a natural incapability to resist easily
being adversely affected by ordinary agents. The same applies to hardness
25 and softness; for a thing is called 'hard' by having the capability of not being
easily divided, and it is called 'soft' by being incapable of not being easily
divided.
        A third genus of qualities is that of affective qualities and affections. Such
30 are sweetness, bitterness, sourness, and all others which are akin to these;
and we may add also heat, cold, whiteness, and blackness. Evidently, all
these are qualities, for the things which possess them are said to be such and
such with respect to them. For example, honey is called 'sweet' by virtue of

possessing sweetness, and a body is called 'white' by virtue of possessing   35
whiteness; and similarly with the others. Now these qualities are called   9b
'affective' not in the sense that the objects which possess them have been
affected in some way; for it is not by having been affected in some way that
honey is called 'sweet', and likewise with other such objects. Similarly, heat
and cold are called 'affective qualities' not in the sense that the objects which   5
possess them have been affected in any way, but in the sense that each of
those qualities can produce on others a corresponding affection with respect
to sensation; for sweetness can produce an affection with respect to taste,
heat can produce an affection with respect to touch, and similarly with the
others.   10

Paleness and tan and other complexions, on the other hand, are called
'affective qualities' not in the same manner but by being the results of an
affection. Clearly, many changes of color occur because of an affection; for
when a man becomes ashamed, he blushes, when he becomes afraid, he   15
turns pale, and so on. So even if a man has acquired by nature such an
affection arising from some physical coincidence of elements, he is likely to
have a similar complexion; for the bodily disposition of a momentary
constitution of elements arising when one is ashamed would be the same as
that of a natural constitution, so the complexion, too, would by nature be   20
similar in the two cases. Accordingly, all coincidences originating from
certain affections which are difficult to displace and firmly established are
called 'affective qualities'. For pallor and tan are called '[affective] qualities'
(since we are said to be such and such in virtue of them), whether they (a)
come to be in one's constitution according to nature or (b) come to be   25
because of a long illness or scorching and do not easily revert to their original
condition, or even stay with us throughout life; for it is in a similar way that
we are said to be such and such in virtue of them. Those which arise from
[causes] which disappear easily and which soon revert to the original
conditions, on the other hand, are called 'affections' and not 'qualities', for   30
we are not said to be such and such in virtue of them. For neither is the man
who blushes because of shame called 'a blusher', nor is the man who turns
pale because of fear called 'a pale man', but each of them is rather said to
have been affected   in some way. Such things, then, are called 'affections'
and not 'qualities'.

There are some qualities of the soul, too, which are similar to these, and
some of them are called 'affective qualities' while others are called   35
'affections'. For [conditions] which exist right from birth as a result of   10a
certain affections, e.g., insanity and irascibility and the like, are called
'qualities', since we are said to be such and such in virtue of them, e.g., we
are called 'insane' and 'irascible', respectively. Similarly, disorders which
are not natural, but which arise from some other coincidences and are
difficult to get rid of or altogether impossible to remove, are called

5 'qualities', for we are said to be such and such in virtue of them. But we call 'affections' those arising [from coincidences] which quickly revert to the original state. For example, if a man in pain is more irritable [than usual], he is not called 'irascible' by being so irritable when so affected but rather 10 'affected'. So such things are called 'affections' and not 'qualities'.

A fourth genus of qualities is the shape or the *form* of each thing, and we may add to these straightness and curvature and others like them. For a thing, in virtue of each of these, is said to be such and such. For a triangle 15 or a square is said to be such and such, and so does a thing which is straight or curved. And each thing, with repect to its *form*, is said to be such and such.

As for the names 'rare' and 'dense' and 'rough' and 'smooth', one would think that they signify qualities, but they seem to come under a classification which is remote from that of the genus 'quality'; for each of them appears 20 to indicate rather a certain position of the parts. A thing is called 'dense' by having its parts close to each other, but 'rare' by having its parts apart from each other; and it is called 'smooth' in view of the fact that its parts on the surface lie in some way evenly along a straight line, but 'rough' in view of the fact that some of those parts are above such a line while others are below it.

25 Perhaps there are other ways in which qualities might manifest themselves, but those in the most accepted sense of the word are practically the ones we have given.

Qualities, then, are those we have mentioned, and things are called 'such and such' [or 'qualitative'] if they are derivatively named according to quality or are named in some other way from qualities. In most cases or in 30 practically all cases things are derivatively so named; for example, from 'whiteness' a thing is called 'white', from 'grammar' it is called 'grammatical', from 'justice' it is called 'just', and similarly with others. In some cases, however, a thing cannot be derivatively named from a quality because no name exists for that quality. For example, the man who is called 35 'a natural runner' or 'a natural boxer' in virtue of his natural capability is 10b not derivatively so named from any quality; for no name exists for the corresponding capability in virtue of which he is called by that name. And this is unlike the corresponding sciences according to which, as dispositions, men are called 'boxers' or 'wrestlers'; for these two sciences are called 5 'boxing' and 'wrestling', and those who are disposed according to them are derivatively called 'such and such' from them, i.e., 'boxers' and 'wrestlers', respectively. In some cases a name exists for the quality, but that which is called according to that quality is not derivatively so called. For example, from integrity a man is upright, for a man is called 'upright' by having integrity; but 'upright' is not derived from 'integrity'. Such situations, however, do not arise often.

Those things are called 'such and such', then, which are derivatively *10*
called from the qualities mentioned or which are called from those qualities
in some other way.

Contrariety with respect to quality is possible; for example, justice is
contrary to injustice, whiteness is contrary to blackness, and similarly with
others. And things which are named with respect to a quality may be
contrary; for example, the unjust is contrary to the just, and the white is *15*
contrary to the black. But this is not the case with all qualities; for there is
no contrary to red or yellow or other such colors, which are qualities.

Again, if one of two contraries is a quality, so is the other; and this
becomes clear by going over the other categories. For example, justice is *20*
contrary to injustice, and justice is a quality; and so is injustice. Injustice
cannot come under any of the other categories, for it is neither a quantity
nor a relation nor somewhere nor any of the others at all, but only a quality;
and the same applies to other contraries which are named with respect to
a quality.

Things named by a quality admit of variation of degree. One white *25*
thing may be more white or less white than another white thing, and one
just thing may be more just than another. Moreover, a thing with a quality
may admit of that quality to a higher degree, for a white thing may become
more white later. But it is to most things of this sort that this applies, and *30*
not to all. For one might raise the problem whether justice admits of
variation of degree; and similarly with the other dispositions. Some thinkers
disagree about such things, for they say that we should not speak of one
instance of justice as being in any way more justice or less justice than
another instance, and likewise with health, but that one thing may have *35*
more health than another or have more justice than another or have more *11a*
grammatical *knowledge* than another, and similarly with the other
dispositions. Anyway, men do not dispute the fact that at least the things
which are named with respect to a quality admit of variation of degree;
for one man may be said to be more of a grammarian or more healthy or *5*
more just than another, and similarly with other cases. But a triangle or a
square is not thought to admit of variation of degree, nor is any other shape;
for things which admit the definition of a triangle or of a circle are all alike
triangles or circles, respectively, but things which do not admit that
definition cannot be [truly] said to differ in degree [as triangles or circles]. *10*
A square is no more of a circle than an oblong is, for neither of the two
admits the definition of the circle; and without qualification, if two objects
do not admit the definition of a thing proposed, neither of them can be said
to be more of that thing or less of that thing than the other. Accordingly, not
all things named by a quality admit of variation of degree.

Now none of the attributes we have mentioned are properties of qualities, *15*
but things may be said to be like (or similar) or to be unlike each other only

with respect to quality; for one thing may be like another with respect to
quality and nothing else. Thus it is a property of a quality that things are
said to be like or unlike each other with respect to quality.

20   One need not be confused by someone's remark that in our discussion of
qualities we have included also many relatives; for we did say that habits
and dispositions are relatives. Now in almost all such cases the genus is said
to be a relative, but no particular under it is said to be a relative. For, as a
25   genus, *knowledge as such* is said to be of something else (for it is said to be
the *knowledge* of something), but no particular *knowledge, as such,* is said
to be of something else. For example, grammar is not said to be the
grammar of something, nor music to be the music of something; but, if at
all, it is with respect to their genus   that they are said to be relatives. Thus
30   grammar is said to be the *knowledge* of something and not the grammar of
something, and music is said to be the *knowledge* of something and not the
music of something. So each of these [*as such*] is not a relative. In fact, we
are said to be such and such with respect to each of these since it is these that
we possess; for it is by possessing a particular science that a man is said to
35   be a scientist. So it is these particular sciences that would be qualities, and
it is with respect to these that we are sometimes said to be such and such,
and these are not relatives.   Further, if the same thing should happen to be
both a relative and a quality, there would be nothing absurd in listing it
under both genera.

9

11b   Acting and being acted upon, too, admit of contraries and of variation of
degree. Thus heating is contrary to cooling, being heated is contrary to
being cooled, and being pleased is contrary to being pained; so they admit
5   of contraries. And they admit of variation of degree, too; for it is possible to
heat something more, or to heat it less, and also for something to be heated
more, or to be heated less. So acting and being acted upon admit of variation
of degree.

So much, then, may be said concerning these [categories]. We also spoke
concerning being in a position in our account of relatives, saying that it is
10   derivatively named from the corresponding position. As for the rest, i.e., at
some time, somewhere, and possessing, we need not say more than what we
said at the start because they are obvious; thus 'possessing' signifies such
things as being shod and being armed, 'somewhere' signifies such a thing as
in the Lyceum, and so on, as already stated.

10

15   The genera we put forward have been sufficiently discussed. Concerning
opposites, we should state the number of ways in which things are usually

said to be opposed. Things may be opposed in four ways: (a) as a relative
to its correlative, (b) as two contraries to each other, (c) as a privation to the
corresponding possession, and (d) as an affirmation to the corresponding
denial. Typical examples are: the double is opposed to its half as a relative   20
to its correlative, the bad is opposed to the good as one of two contraries to
the other, blindness is opposed to vision as a privation to the corresponding
possession, 'he sits' is opposed to 'he does not sit' as an affirmation to its
denial.

Things opposed as correlatives are said, *as such*, of each other or are   25
referred to each other in some way or other. For example, a double is said,
as such, to be the double of another thing, for it is the double of something.
Also, *knowledge* is opposed to the *known* as a relative to its correlative, and
it is said, *as such*, of the *known*; and the *known* is referred, *as such*, to its   30
opposite, which is *knowledge*, for it is said to be *known* by something, i.e.,
by *knowledge*. Thus things which are opposed as correlatives are said, *as
such*, of each other or are referred, *as such*, to each other in some way or
other.

In the case of opposites which are contraries, though they are said to be
contrary to each other, they are in no way said, *as such*, to be referred to   35
each other; for the good is said to be not the good of the bad but the contrary
of the bad, and the white is said to be not the white of the black but the
contrary of the black. These two kinds of opposition [i.e., correlatives and
contraries], then, differ from each other.

If contraries are such that either one or the other of necessity belongs to   12a
the subject in which it comes to be by its nature or of which it is predicable,
then they have no intermediate; but if there is no necessity for one or the
other of them to belong to the subject, then they always have an
intermediate. For example, disease and health by their nature come to be
in the body of an animal, and it is necessary for one of them, either disease   5
or health, to belong to the body of an animal; and 'odd' and 'even' are
predicable of numbers, and it is necessary for one of them, either oddness
or evenness, to belong to a given number. And between these there can be
no intermediate, neither between disease and health, nor between oddness
and evenness.

But if there is no necessity for any of two contraries to belong to a subject,   10
then there is some intermediate between them. For example, blackness and
whiteness by their nature come to be in a body, and it is not necessary for
either of them to belong to a body; for not every body is either black or
white. Again, the names 'vicious' and 'virtuous' are predicable of men and
of many other subjects, but it is not necessary for either one or the other to   15
belong to the subject of which it might be predicable; for not everyone of
those subjects is either vicious or virtuous. And indeed there is an
intermediate between these contraries, grey or yellow or some other color

between white and black, and between the vicious and the virtuous there is
20   something which is neither vicious nor virtuous. Now in some cases there
are names for the intermediates, e.g., 'grey' or 'yellow' or the name of some
other color between black and white; in other cases, however, there is no
name available, but the intermediate is defined by the negation of both
contraries, e.g., the expression 'neither good nor bad' is used for that which
25   is between good and bad, and 'neither just nor unjust' for that which is
between the just and the unjust.

A possession and its corresponding privation are concerned with the same
[subject], e.g., vision and blindness are concerned with the eye. Universally
speaking, that in which a possession by its nature comes to be is that with
which each of the two is said to be concerned. A subject is said to be
30   deprived of a possession which it is capable of having when that possession
does not belong at all to that subject at the time at which by its nature it
should belong to that subject. Thus we call 'toothless' not any subject which
has no teeth, and 'blind' not any subject which has no vision, but a subject
which does not have teeth or vision at the time at which by its nature it
should have teeth or vision, respectively; for there are some kinds of animals
which from birth have no teeth or no vision, but they are not said to be
toothless or blind, respectively.
35   To be deprived or to have a possession is not a privation or a possession,
respectively. For vision is a possession, and blindness is a privation, but to
have vision is not vision, and to be blind is not blindness; for blindness is a
certain privation, but to be blind is to be deprived of a certain thing and is
40   not a privation. Further, if blindness were the same as to be blind, both
would be predicable of the same subject; but though we say that a certain
12b   man is blind, we never say that he is blindness. But to be deprived and to
have the corresponding possession, too, are thought to be opposed just as a
privation and the corresponding possession are, since the manner of the
opposition is the same; for just as blindness is opposed to vision, so being
5   blind is opposed to having vision.

The object signified by an affirmation or a denial is not itself the
affirmation or the denial, respectively. For an affirmation is an affirmative
statement and a denial is a negative statement, but the objects which are
10   signified by them are not themselves statements. Yet these objects, too, are
said to be opposed to each other as the corresponding affirmation and denial,
since the manner of their opposition is the same; for just as an affirmation
is opposed to its denial, as in the statements 'the man sits' and 'the man does
not sit', so the corresponding facts under them are opposed, i.e., the man
15   when sitting and that man when not sitting.

It is evident, then, that a privation and the corresponding possession are
not opposed as correlatives, since neither, *as such*, is said to be of its opposite;
for vision is not the vision of blindness, nor is it said to be referred to

blindness in any other way. Similarly, we would not say that blindness is of   *20*
vision; what we say is that blindness is *the privation* of vision, not *the*
blindness of vision. Moreover, in all cases correlatives are reciprocally
referred to each other; so if blindness, *as such*, were a relative, its
correlative, too, would be reciprocally referred to it. But there is no
reciprocal reference, for vision is not said to be the vision of blindness.   *25*

That things which are said to be opposed as a possession and the
corresponding privation, too, are not opposed as contraries is clear from
what follows. In the case of contraries between which no intermediate exists,
it is always necessary for one of them to belong to the subject in which it
comes to be by its nature or of which it is predicable; for, as already stated,   *30*
it is between contraries one of which must belong to a subject which can
receive it that no intermediate exists, as in the case of disease and health or
of oddness and evenness. But in the case of contraries which have an
intermediate, there is never a necessity for one of them to belong to every
subject; for it is not necessary for every subject which is receptive of
whiteness or of blackness to be either white or black, or for every subject
which is receptive of heat or cold to be either hot or cold, since nothing   *35*
prevents an intermediate from belonging to that subject. Moreover, we have
already stated that intermediates exist also between contraries neither of
which belongs of necessity to a subject which is receptive of them, unless one
of the contraries belongs to a subject by that subject's nature, as hotness
belongs to fire and whiteness to snow, and to such a subject one of them must
definitely belong, but not either of the two; for fire cannot be cold, and snow   *40*
cannot be black. So there is no necessity for one of two such contraries to   *13a*
belong to every subject which is receptive of them, but only to a subject
which by its nature has one of them, not either of them, but a definite
one.

In the case of a possession and the corresponding privation, neither of the
above is true. First, it is not always necessary for one of them to belong to   *5*
the subject which is receptive of them, for that which has not yet reached
the natural state of having vision is not said to be blind or to have vision; so
possessions and privations are not among such contraries between which
there is no intermediate. Second, neither are they among those contraries
between which there is an intermediate; for either the possession or the
corresponding privation must belong to every subject which is receptive of
them at a certain stage of the subject's existence; for when a man is at the
stage when he can by his nature have vision, then he will be said either to   *10*
have vision or to be blind, not definitely to have vision, nor definitely to be
blind, but either one of the two, since it is neither necessary that he should
have vision nor necessary that he should be blind, but it is necessary that he
should have just one, though either one of them. Again, in the case of
contraries between which there is an intermediate, it was stated that there

is never a necessity for one or the other contrary to belong to the subject
15   [which is receptive of them], except in certain subjects, and to these a
definite contrary belongs. It is clear, then, that a possession and the
corresponding privation are not opposed in any of the ways in which
contraries are opposed.

Moreover, in the case of contraries, unless one of them belongs to a subject
20   by the subject's nature, as hotness belongs to fire, a change in the subject
from one contrary to the other is possible while the subject exists; for it is
possible for that which is healthy to become sick, for that which is light to
become dark, for that which is cold to become hot, for the virtuous to
become vicious, and for the vicious to become virtuous. A vicious man, if
directed to a better way of life and to better arguments, might make some
25   improvement, even a little one; and, once he does this, it is evident that he
might change completely or improve a great deal, for, after an initial
improvement, however small, he changes more easily to virtue and is likely
30   to improve even more. And if he keeps on doing so, he will change
completely to the contrary habit, unless impeded by time. But in the case
of a possession and the corresponding privation, a change in both directions
is impossible; for though a change from a possession to the corresponding
privation is possible, a change from a privation to the corresponding
35   possession is impossible. No man who became blind regained his vision, no
man who became bald regained his hair, and no man who lost his teeth grew
a new set.

Expressions which are opposed as an affirmation to the corresponding
13b   denial are evidently not opposed in any of the ways discussed; for only in
this case is it always necessary for one of the opposites to be true and the
other false. For neither in the case of contraries is it necessary for one of
5   them to be true and the other false, nor in the case of correlatives or of a
possession and the corresponding privation. For example, health and disease
are contraries, but neither of them is true or false. Similarly, the double and
the half are opposed as correlatives, but neither of the two is true or false.
Things which are opposed with respect to privation and possession, too, are
10   not true or false, as in the case of vision and blindness. In general, objects
which are in no way composite expressions cannot be true or false, and the
opposites   which we have given here as examples are not composite
expressions.

One would think that contraries which are stated as composites are most
15   likely to be true or false; for 'Socrates is healthy' is contrary to 'Socrates is
sick'.   But not even of these composites is it always necessary for one to be
true and the other false. For if Socrates exists, one of them will be true and
the other false, but if Socrates does not exist, both will be false; for neither
'Socrates is sick' nor 'Socrates is healthy' is true if Socrates does not exist at
20   all. In the case of a privation and the corresponding possession, if the subject

[which might be receptive of them] does not exist at all, neither statement will be true, and if it exists, it will not always be the case that one statement is true and the other false; for 'Socrates has vision' is opposed to 'Socrates is blind' as a possession to the corresponding privation, and if Socrates exists, it is not necessary for just one of them to be true or to be false (for when Socrates has not yet reached the natural state of having vision, both will be 25 false), but if Socrates does not exist at all, even then both 'Socrates has vision' and 'Socrates is blind' will be false.

In the case of an affirmation and the corresponding denial, on the other hand, it is always the case that one of them will be true and the other false, whether the subject exists or not. For if Socrates exists, it is evident that just 30 one of the statements 'Socrates is sick' and 'Socrates is not sick' will be true or will be false, and similarly if he does not exist. For if he does not exist, 'Socrates is sick' will be false but 'Socrates is not sick' will be true. Thus only expressions which are opposed as an affirmation to its denial have the property that always one will be true and the other false. 35

11

The contrary of a good is of necessity an evil, and this is clear by induction. For example, the contrary of health is disease, and the contrary 14a of bravery is cowardice, and similarly with the others. The contrary of an evil, on the other hand, is in some cases a good but in others an evil. For the contrary of deficiency, which is an evil, is excess, and this is an evil; but the contrary of deficiency or of excess is also moderation, and this is a good. But such double contrariety is observed to exist in a few cases only; in most cases, the contrary of an evil is always a good. 5

Further, in the case of contraries, if one of them exists, it is not necessary for the other to exist also. For if all animals are healthy, health will exist but not disease; and similarly, if all things are white, whiteness will exist but not 10 blackness. Again, if Socrates in health is contrary to Socrates in disease, since both contraries cannot belong to the same subject at the same time, if one of those contraries exists, the other could not exist; for if Socrates in health exists, Socrates in disease cannot exist.

It is clear, too, that contraries come to be by their nature in [subjects] 15 which are the same in species or in genus. For disease and health by their nature come to be in bodies of animals, whiteness and blackness in bodies without any qualification, and justice and injustice in the soul of a man.

It is necessary for any two contraries to be in the same genus, or to be in contrary genera, or to be themselves genera. For whiteness and blackness 20 are in the same genus (for their genus is color), justice and injustice are in contrary genera (for the genus of justice is virtue, that of injustice is vice),

and good and evil are not in any genus but happen to be themselves genera
25   of other things.

12

One thing is said to be prior to another in four ways. (a) In the most
fundamental way, A is said to be prior to B with respect to time, that is, if
A is older than or came before B; for it is in view of a longer time that A
is older than or came before B.
30   (b) In another way, A is said to be prior to B if A's existence follows from
B's existence, but B's existence does not follow from A's existence. For
example, one is prior to two; for if two exists, it follows at once that one
exists, but if one exists, it is not necessary for two to exist, and so the
existence of two does not follow in turn from the existence of one. Thus, A
is thought to be prior in existence to B if A's existence follows from B's, but
35   B's existence does not follow from A's.
(c) In a third way, one thing is said to be prior to another according to
some order, as in the case of the sciences and speeches. For in sciences which
use demonstration there is an order in which one thing comes before
14b   another (for in geometry the elements come before the demonstrations, and
in grammar the letters of the alphabet come before the syllables); and in
speeches likewise, for the introduction comes before the narrative.
There is a fourth sense of 'prior' besides those mentioned. That which is
5   better or more honorable is thought to be prior by its nature. Ordinary men,
too, usually speak of those whom they honor more or love more as having
priority over those whom they honor less or love less. Perhaps this sense of
the word 'prior' is far removed from the other senses.
10   The various senses of 'prior', then, are perhaps those given. It would seem,
however, that besides these there is still another. For, of two things whose
existence follows from each other, it would be reasonable to say that the one
which is in any way the cause of the other is prior by nature to it. That there
are such things is clear from the following. A man's existence and the truth
15   of the statement that he exists follow from each other; for if a man exists,
the statement 'a man exists' is true, and conversely, if that statement is true,
a man exists. But the true statement is in no way the cause of the fact that
20   a man exists, whereas that fact appears to be in some way the cause of the
true statement; for it is by virtue of the existence or nonexistence of that fact
that the statement is true or false, respectively.
There are five ways, then, in which one thing is said to be prior to
another.

13

Things are called 'simultaneous' in an unqualified way and in the most
25   fundamental sense if they come into being at the same time, for none of

them comes into being before or after any of the rest; and such things are said to be simultaneous with respect to time. Two things are called 'simultaneous by nature' if the existence of each follows from that of the other, and if neither is the cause of the existence of the other. In the case of the double and the half, for example, the existence of each of them follows from that of the other (for if the double exists, so does the half, and if the *30* half exists, so does the double), and neither is the cause of the existence of the other.

Immediate divisions under the same genus, too, are called 'simultaneous by nature' [i.e., coordinate], and by 'immediate divisions' I mean [the species] which result by the same division. For example, the feathered *35* [species] is simultaneous by nature with the terrestrial and the aquatic [species], since all these are immediate divisions under the same genus; for the genus animal is immediately divided into the feathered, the terrestrial, and the aquatic [species], and no one of these divisions is prior or posterior [by nature] to another but all three of them are thought to be simultaneous *15a* by nature. Each of these [species] (terrestrial, feathered, aquatic), too, may be further divided into [lower] species, and the species resulting by the same division in each case will be simultaneous by nature. But a genus is always prior [by nature] to each of its species, for the existence of the species does *5* not follow in turn from that of the genus. For example, if an aquatic animal exists, an animal exists, but if an animal exists, it is not necessary for an aquatic animal to exist.

Things are said to be simultaneous by nature, then, (a) if the existence of each follows from that of the other and is in no way the cause of the *10* existence of the other, and (b) if they are immediate divisions under the same genus; and things are said to be simultaneous without qualification if they come into being at the same time.

14

There are six kinds of motion: generation, destruction, increase, diminution, alteration, and change with respect to place [i.e., locomotion].

It is evident that all the motions, except alteration, are distinct from each *15* other; for a generation is not a destruction, an increase or a change with respect to place is not a diminution, and so on. But in the case of alteration there is the problem of whether the altering thing must alter with respect to some one of the other motions. But this is not true. For perhaps we happen *20* to alter with respect to all or most of the affections without partaking of any of the other motions; for it is not necessary for that which is moved with respect to an affection to be increased or be diminished or be moved in any

25   other way, and so alteration would be a motion distinct from the others. For
      if alteration were the same as one of the other motions, then at the same time
      the thing in alteration would have to be increased, or be diminished, or
      undergo some one of the other motions; but this does not necessarily
      happen. Similarly, that which is increased or undergoes some one of the
      other motions should have altered [at the same time]. But there are some
30   things which are increased without being altered. For
      example, when a gnomon is attached to a square in the
      Figure shown, the square has increased but has not altered
      at all, and similarly with others of this kind. Hence the six
      motions would be distinct from each other.
15b   The contrary of motion without qualification is rest ; but the different
      kinds of motion have their own contraries. Destruction is contrary to
      generation, diminution is contrary to increase, and rest with respect to place
      is contrary to change with respect to place. But a change with respect to
5   place seems to be opposed to the change towards the contrary place most of
      all, e.g., the motion upwards is opposed to the motion downwards, and vice
      versa. But of the motion that remains [i.e., of alteration], it is not easy to state
      what its contrary motion is. It seems that there is no contrary to it, unless one
      were to oppose it to rest with respect to quality or to change in the direction
10   of the contrary quality, as in the case of change with respect to place to
      which is opposed rest with respect to place or change towards the contrary
      place; for alteration is change with respect to quality. If so, then to motion
      with respect to quality will be opposed rest with respect to quality, or the
15   change in the direction of the contrary quality (e.g., becoming white will be
      opposed to becoming black), for the changes in the latter case are alterations
      in the direction of contrary qualities.

15

      The expression 'to have' is used in many senses. That which a thing is said
      to have may be (1) a certain habit or a certain disposition or some other
      quality, for we are said to have a certain *knowledge* or a certain virtue; or
20   (2) a quantity, as when one happens to have a certain height, for he is said
      to have a height of three cubits or four cubits; or (3) something he wears,
      such as a coat or a tunic, or something he wears on a part of the body, such
      as a ring on the hand; or (4) a part of the thing, e.g., a man is said to have
      a hand or a foot; or (5) something in a container, e.g., wheat in a vessel or
25   wine in a jar, for the jar is said to have wine, and the vessel is said to have
      wheat, and in all these cases that which is said to have has something as in
      a container; or (6) property, for one is said to have a house or a farm.

In yet another sense, (7) one is said to have a wife, and a wife to have a husband; but this seems to be the most remote sense of 'to have', for by 'having a wife' we mean nothing more than living with a wife.   *30*

Perhaps other senses of 'to have' might appear, but we have listed almost all the usual senses.

ON PROPOSITIONS

CONTENTS

ON PROPOSITIONS

1

16a First we should posit what a noun is and what a verb is; then what each of the following is: a denial, an affirmation, a statement, and a sentence.

Spoken expressions are symbols of mental impressions, and written
5 expressions [are symbols] of spoken expressions. And just as not all men have the same writing, so not all men make the same vocal sounds, but the things of which [all] these are primarily the signs are the same mental impressions for all men, and the things of which these [mental impressions] are likenesses are ultimately the same. These have been discussed in my treatise *On the Soul*, for they belong to a different discipline.

10 Now just as in the soul there are thoughts which are neither true nor false, but also thoughts which must be either true or false, so it is with spoken expressions; for truth and falsity are concerned with combination and separation. Nouns and verbs by themselves (e.g., 'man' and 'the white'), when nothing else is added to them, seem to be thoughts in which nothing
15 is combined or separated, for none of them is as yet true or false. A sign of this is the fact that even the name 'goat-stag', which signifies something, is not yet true or false unless the expression 'to be' or 'not to be' is added to it, either without qualification or with a temporal qualification.

2

20 A noun is a vocal sound which is significant by convention and has no reference to time, and of which no part is significant as [a] separate [part]. For in the name 'Greenfield' the part 'field' does not by itself signify anything, though it would in the expression 'green field'. But composite nouns are not like simple nouns; for in simple nouns a part has no
25 significance at all, whereas in composite nouns the part gives the appearance of having meaning but does not signify anything as [a] separate [part]. For example, in the word 'blackmail' the part 'mail' does not by itself signify a thing. The qualification 'by convention' is added since no noun exists by nature but only when it comes into existence as a symbol. Inarticulate sounds, too, like those of brutes, indicate something, but none of them is a name.

The expression 'not-man' is not a noun, and no name exists by which such   30
an expression is called; for it is neither a sentence nor a denial. But let it be
called 'an indefinite noun', since it may belong [as a predicate] to what exists
as well as to what does not exist. Expressions such as 'of Philo' and 'to Philo',   *16b*
on the other hand, are not nouns but cases of a noun. In other respects, they
have the same definition as nouns, but if 'exists' or 'existed' or 'will exist' is
added to each of them, the resulting expression is neither true nor false,
whereas if it is added to a noun, the resulting expression is always true or
false. For example, 'of Philo exists' and 'of Philo does not exist' are in no way
true or false.   5

3

A verb is [a name] (a) which includes in its meaning also time, (b) of which
no part as [a] separate [part] has any meaning, and (c) which is always a sign
of something said about something else. By 'includes in its meaning also
time' I mean, for example, that while 'recovery' is a noun, 'recovers' is a
verb, for a verb includes in its meaning also time, e.g., present time. In   10
addition, it is always a sign of something said about something else, e.g., of
something said of a subject or present in a subject.

Expressions such as 'is not healthy' and 'is not sick' I do not call 'verbs';
for though they also include time in their meaning and always belong to
something, no name has been posited to indicate their difference from
verbs. Such expressions will be called 'indefinite verbs', and they may   15
belong to what exists as well as to what does not exist. Similarly, 'was
healthy' and 'will be healthy' are not verbs but tenses of a verb; and they
differ from verbs in that verbs include in their meaning present time while
tenses of a verb include time outside the present.

Now verbs stated by themselves are names and signify something (for he   20
who uses them pauses in his thought and the hearer is at ease), but they do
not yet signify that something is or is not the case; for neither are 'to be' and
'not to be' signs of any fact, nor is 'being' a sign of a fact when used by itself
as a participle, for each of these [i.e., 'to be', 'not to be', 'being'] by itself
signifies nothing but a sort of combination which cannot be thought without   25
the [things] which are combined.

4

A sentence is a vocal sound significant by convention, some part of which,
taken by itself, has meaning as an utterance but not as an affirmation or a
denial. I mean, for example, that 'man' signifies something, but not that
something is or is not the case; and it is by the addition of something else   30
[to it] that an affirmation or a denial may be formed. But no syllable of
'virtue' [has any meaning by itself], for the part 'use', too, in the word

'mouse' has no meaning [as a part] but is only a vocal sound. A part of a composite word, on the other hand, may have meaning, as stated earlier, but not taken by itself [as a part].

17a   Every sentence has meaning, not as a natural instrument but, as stated earlier, by convention. Not all sentences are declarative, however, but only those to which truth or falsity belongs. Thus truth or falsity does not belong
5   to all sentences; for example, a prayer is a sentence but is neither true nor false. So let all sentences which are neither true nor false be dismissed here, for their consideration is more appropriate to rhetoric or to poetics.[2] Our present inquiry is about declarative sentences [i.e., propositions].

5

Of propositions, that which is primarily one is an affirmation, the next is
10   a denial; and each of the rest is one by conjunction. Every proposition must have a verb or a tense of a verb [as a part]; for even the definition of man is not yet a proposition, until 'is' or 'was' or 'will be' or something of this sort is added to it. Of course, one may ask why the expression 'two-footed terrestrial animal' is one and not many; for it is one not by the fact that the
15   words are stated together. The discussion of this problem, however, belongs to another discipline. Now a proposition is one either by indicating one [object] or by being one by conjuntion; but we have many propositions if many [objects] are indicated or if the [propositions] are not conjoined.

Let a noun or a verb be called just 'an utterance', since one cannot use such a vocal sound as a statement to indicate something, whether as an
20   answer to a question, or not as an answer but as something he himself intends to state.

Of propositions, those which are simple are statements, i.e., [sentences] in which something is affirmed of something else or is denied of it, and the others, which are composed of statements, are like sentences which are combined. A simple statement is a vocal sound signifying the existence or the nonexistence of something according to one of the divisions of time.

6

25   An affirmation is a statement affirming something of something else; a denial is a statement denying something of something else. Now since it is possible (a) to state of something which exists that it does not exist, and of something which does not exist that it exists, and of something which exists that it exists, and of something which does not exist that it does not exist, and (b) in a similar way to state of something that it exists or does not exist at

a time lying outside the present, then in each of the above cases a man might   *30*
deny what another man has affirmed or affirm what another man has
denied. Clearly, then, to every affirmation there is an opposite denial and
to every denial there is an opposite affirmation. And let an affirmation and
its opposite denial taken together be called 'a contradiction'. By 'opposition'
here I mean the opposition of the same predicate with respect to the same   *35*
subject, without using the subject or the predicate equivocally; and we
include other such qualifications to meet sophistical captiousness.

7

Since some things are universal but others are [predicable of an]
individual (by 'universal' I mean that which by its nature is predicable of   *40*
more than one, and by 'individual' I mean that which is not [so predicable],
e.g., man [or 'man'] is a universal but Callias [or 'Callias'] is [predicable of]   *17b*
an individual), a statement of something as existing or as not existing must
sometimes be stated of a universal and sometimes of an individual.
    If one states universally of a universal [subject] that something is and also
that it is not the case, the two statements will be contrary. By 'stating   *5*
universally of a universal' I mean, for example, 'every man is white' and 'no
man is white.' On the other hand, if one states of a universal [subject], but
not universally, [that something is and also that it is not the case], the two
statements are not contrary, but the things indicated may sometimes be
contrary. By 'stating of a universal, but not universally' I mean, for
example, 'man is white' and 'man is not white' [or 'men are white' and 'men   *10*
are not white']; for though [the subject] 'man' is universal, it is not
universally used in the statement, for the word 'every' signifies not a
universal but something universally taken. But if a predicate which is a
universal is universally taken, then it cannot be truly predicable [of a
subject]; for there can be no true affirmation in which such predicate, taken   *15*
universally, is predicable of a subject. For example, 'every man is every
animal' is false.
    I maintain that an affirmation is opposed to a denial in a contradictory
way if both have the same subject and predicate but one of them [i.e., of the
contradictories] is universally taken while the other is the denial thereof.
For example, 'every man is white' and 'not every man is white' are
contradictories, and so are 'no man is white' and 'some men are white'. But   *20*
if both the affirmation and the denial are universal, [then I maintain that]
the two statements are opposed in a contrary way. For example, 'every man
is white' and 'no man is white' are contraries, and so are 'every man is just'
and 'no man is just'. Hence both members of a pair of contraries here cannot
be true at the same time; but the contradictories of a pair of contraries may

25 sometimes be true of the same subject at the same time, as in the case of 'not
    every man is white' and 'some men are white'.

    Of a pair of contradictory statements with a universal subject universally
    taken,   one of them must be true and the other false; and such is also the
    case if the subject is an individual, as in 'Socrates is white' and 'Socrates is
    not white'.   But of a pair [of contradictory statements]   with a universal
30 subject which is not universally taken, it is not always the case that one of
    them is true and the other false.   For it is possible to state truly that men
    are white and also that men are not white, that men are noble and also that
    men are not noble; for if a man is disgraceful, he is not noble, or if he is
    becoming [noble], still he is not noble.   At first, this fact would seem absurd,
35 because 'men are not white' appears to mean also that no man is white; but
    neither does 'men are not white' mean what 'no man is white' does, nor is
    it necessary [for the two statements to be both true or both false] at the same
    time.

    It is also evident that corresponding to one affirmation there is just one
40 denial; for what a denial should do is to deny the same thing which the
    affirmation affirms, and of the same subject, whether the subject be (a) an
18a individual or (b) a universal, and whether a universal subject is universally
    taken or not. For example, the denial of 'Socrates is white' is 'Socrates is not
    white'. But if the affirmation and the denial have different predicates or
    different subjects,   they are not opposed to each other but are different. The
5   denial of 'every man is white', then, is 'not every man is white'; the denial
    of 'some men are white' is 'no man is white'; and the denial of 'men are
    white' is 'men are not white'.

    We have stated, then, that (a) to one affirmation there is opposed in a
    contradictory manner just one denial and have indicated what those
10 statements are; that (b) contrary statements are different from contradictory
    statements and what these are; and that (c) not every pair of contradictories
    is such that one statement in it is true and the other false, why this is so, and
    when one statement in such a pair must be true and the other false.

    ## 8

    A [statement] is one affirmation or one denial if it signifies [something
    which is] about [a subject which is] one, whether the [subject] is a universal
15 taken universally, or not. Such statements are 'every man is white' and 'not
    every man is white', 'men are white' and 'men are not white', 'no man is
    white' and 'some men are white', provided that the word 'white' has one
    meaning. If in a statement the name posited has two meanings which cannot
    make up something which is one, then the statement is not one affirmation
20 or one denial. For example, if one were to posit the name 'coat' as meaning

a horse and also a man in 'coats are white', this statement would not be one affirmation, nor [would the corresponding denial be] one denial; for the affirmation would not differ from the statement 'men and horses are white', and this itself would not differ from the two statements 'horses are white' and 'men are white'. Accordingly, if these [two statements] signify many [objects] and are many, it is clear that the first [statement], too, signifies   25 many [objects], or else nothing at all (for an individual man is not a horse). So in contradictory statements of this sort, too, it is not necessary for one of the statements to be true and the other false.

9

In the case of that which exists or has occurred, it is necessary for the corresponding affirmation or its denial to be true, or to be false. And in the case of two contradictories with a universal subject universally taken, or   30 with an individual subject, it is always necessary for one of them to be true and the other false, as we stated,[3] but if the subject is a universal without being universally taken, there is no such necessity, and we stated this fact too.[4] Concerning future particulars, on the other hand, the situation is not similar.

First, if every affirmation and every denial is either true or false, then it   35 is necessary for every object, too, either to be or not to be. Accordingly, if one man says that something will be the case while another man denies this, then clearly it is necessary for just one of them to be speaking truly if an affirmation or a denial is either true or false, for in such cases both will not exist at the same time. For if it were true to say that a thing is white (or not   18b white), it would be necessary for the thing to be white (or not white), and if it is white (or not white), then it would be true to affirm that it is (or to deny it); and if the thing is not as stated, the statement is false, and if the statement is false, the thing is not as stated. Accordingly, either the affirmation or the denial must be true, or must be false.   5

If so, [it would appear that] nothing occurs by chance or in either of two ways; nor will it so occur in the future or fail to so occur, but everything [will occur, or will fail to occur,] of necessity and not in either of two ways. For either he who affirms a future event will speak truly or he who denies it; otherwise the event would be just as likely to occur as not to occur, for that which may occur in either of two ways does not occur or will not occur in one way more than in the other.

Again, if a thing is white now, it was true to say earlier that it would be   10 white; so concerning an event which has taken place, it was always true to say 'it is' or 'it will be'. And if it was always true to say 'it is' or 'it will be', the event was not of such a nature as not to be or not to come to be; and if

15

it was not of such a nature as not to occur, it was impossible for it not to occur; and if it was impossible for it not to occur, it was necessary for it to occur. So [it appears that] all future events will occur of necessity. Hence nothing will come to be in either of two ways or by chance, for if it will occur by chance, it will not occur of necessity.

20

Further, one cannot [truly] say of an event that neither the affirmation nor the denial is true, i.e., that the event will neither occur nor fail to occur. Otherwise, if the affirmation is false, the denial [will] not [be] true, and if the denial is false, it turns out that the affirmation [will] not [be] true.   In addition, if it is true to say [of a thing] that it is white and large, both [these attributes] will have to belong [to the thing], and if [it is true to say that] they will belong [to the thing] tomorrow, then they will [have to] belong to it tomorrow.   But if an event will neither occur nor fail to occur tomorrow, there would be no happening [tomorrow] in either of two ways, e.g., a sea fight would neither have to occur nor have to fail to occur tomorrow.

25

30

These and other such absurdities would indeed result, if of every affirmation and its denial, whether with a universal subject taken universally or with an individual subject, it were necessary   for one of the opposites to be true and the other false, and if, of things in the process of becoming, that which would be or which would come to be could not be in either of two ways but of necessity only one of them, in which case there would be no need to deliberate or take *action* with the expectation that, if we act in a certain way, a certain result will come about, but if we do not, it will not come about. For nothing prevents one man from saying now that a certain event will occur ten thousand years hence, and another from saying that the event will not occur; and so that alternative [occurrence or non-occurrence], of which it was at one time true to state that it will come to be, would of necessity come to be [at a later time]. Further, neither would it make any difference whether some men make the contradictory statements or not, for it is clear that things would be such even if neither the affirmation nor the denial were stated; for events would, or would not, occur not because we have affirmed or denied them, and [they would occur, or not occur,] no less if we had said so ten thousand years earlier rather than any other period of time. So if at all times things were such that [a definite] one of two contradictory statements [about the future] would be true, then what that statement says would of necessity come to be, and each [future] occurrence would always be such as to come to be of necessity. For that of which someone stated truly that it will be would not be of such a nature as to fail to occur, and of [such] an occurrence it was always true to say [earlier] that it will be.

35

19a

5

Now these things are impossible; for we observe that principles of things which will occur arise both from deliberations and from *actions*, and that,

in general, objects which do not exist always in *actuality* have alike the 10
potentiality of existing and of not existing; and objects which may be or may
not be may also come to be or may not come to be. It is clear, too, that there
are many objects which have such [a nature]. For example, this coat has the
potentiality of being cut to pieces [at a certain time later] but may wear out
before being so cut. Similarly, it has the potentiality of not being so cut; for 15
if it did not have this potentiality, it could not have the potentiality of
wearing out before. Such is also the case with the other kinds of
generations which are said to possess such potentiality. It is evident, then,
that it is not of necessity that all things exist or are in the process of coming
to be; in some cases a thing may come to be in either of two ways, in which
case the affirmation of each alternative is no more true than the denial of 20
it, whereas in other cases one of the two alternatives is more likely to occur
and in most cases it does occur, but the less likely alternative may still come
to be [*actually*].

Now when a thing exists, it does so of necessity, and when a nonbeing does
not exist, it is of necessity that it does not exist; but it is not of necessity that
every existing thing exists or that every nonbeing does not exist. For it is not 25
the same for a thing to exist of necessity when it exists and for that thing to
exist of necessity without qualification, and similarly with nonbeing. The
same remarks apply to any two contradictories also. Thus everything of
necessity either is or is not, and everything of necessity will either be or not
be; but one cannot [always truly] state that a definite one of the two
alternatives is or will be of necessity. I mean, for example, that a sea fight 30
will of necessity either take place tomorrow or not; but a sea fight will not
necessarily take place tomorrow, nor will it necessarily fail to take place
either, though it will of necessity either take place tomorrow or fail to take
place. So since statements are true in a way which is similar to the
corresponding facts, it is clear that if objects are such that they may turn out
in either of two ways or may admit contraries, the two contradictory 35
statements corresponding to them are of necessity related in a similar
manner. And such indeed is the case with objects which do not always exist
or which are not always nonexistent. For though one of the two
contradictories concerning these objects must be true (or false), it is not
[definitely] the affirmation, nor [definitely] the denial, that will be true but
either one of them; and one of them may be more likely to be true, but not
already true (or already false) at the time [when a man states it]. Clearly,
then, it is not necessary in the case of every affirmation and its opposite 19b
denial [concerning future particulars] that one of them be [definitely] true
and the other [definitely] false; for the situation with objects which do not
exist but have the potentiality of existing and of not existing is not like that
of existing things, but as we have stated.

10

5   Since an affirmation signifies something affirmed of something, and since
the [subject of an affirmation] is a noun or something without a name, and
since in the affirmation both the [predicate] should be one and the subject
should be one (we have already discussed the noun and that which has no
name;[5] for I said that 'not-man' is not a noun but an indefinite noun, since
it, too, signifies in some way something which is one, and in the same way
10   'is not healthy' is not a verb but an indefinite verb), every affirmation and
every denial will be composed of a noun and a verb, each of which may be
definite or indefinite. Thus there can be no affirmation or denial without a
[definite or indefinite] verb; for the expressions 'is', 'will be', 'was', 'is
becoming', and all other such are posited to be verbs, since they also signify
time [in addition to signifying what is said about a subject].
15   Accordingly, the primary affirmation and denial are, to use an example,
'man exists' and 'man does not exist', then 'not-man exists' and 'not-man
does not exist'; and again 'every man exists' and 'not every man exists', and
then 'every not-man exists' and 'not every not-man exists'. And the same
statements may be made for times other than the present.
        When the word 'is' in the statement is added to the predicate as a third
20   element, then the oppositions can be stated in two ways. I mean by this, for
example, that in 'man is just' the word 'is' in that affirmation is a third
element, whether a name or a verb. So because of this fact there arise four
statements, [and in] two of them [the predicates] are related to an affirmation
and its denial as a pair of privations [of 'just'], but [in] the other two [the
25   predicates are related] not [as privations]. By this I mean that the word 'is'
may come before either 'just' or 'not-just', and so may the negation [i.e., 'is
not']; hence four statements arise. The Diagram below will give us an idea
of what we are saying.

   (a) man is just ⟷ (b) man is not just
   (d) man is not not-just ⟷ (c) man is not-just

30   Here the expression 'is' or 'is not' comes before 'just' and also before
'not-just'. Such, then, is the arrangement of these statements, as we stated in
the [*Prior*] *Analytics*.[6] A similar situation arises even if the affirmation has
as a subject a noun which is universally taken, as in the Diagram below.

   (A) every man is just ⟷ (B) not every man is just
35   (D) not every man is not-just ⟷ (C) every man is not-just

But here the statements joined by a diagonal line cannot be both true in the
same manner as in the previous case, though at times both may be true.
        These, then, are two pairs of opposites; but two other pairs arise if to
'not-man' as a subject [a verb or an indefinite verb] is added. Thus:

   not-man is just ⟷ not-man is not just
20a   not-man is not not-just ⟷ not-man is not-just

There can be no other oppositions besides these. The last two pairs form by themselves a group distinct from the previous pairs since they use 'not-man' as a noun.

Whenever the word 'is' does not fit in the statement, e.g., when the verb is 'recovers' or 'walks', the effect of such verb is the same as that when the word 'is' is added: for example, 'every man recovers', 'not every man recovers', 'every not-man recovers', 'not every not-man recovers'. We should not use 'not-every man', but the negation 'not' should be added to 'man'; for the word 'every' signifies not a universal but [a subject] universally taken. This fact becomes clear from the following pairs: 'man recovers' and 'man does not recover', and 'not-man recovers' and 'not-man does not recover'; and these last two pairs differ from the first two pairs in that their subject is not universally taken. Thus the words 'every' and 'no' mean nothing else than that the noun [which is the subject] in an affirmation or a denial is universally taken, but the other parts to be added should remain the same.

Since the contrary of 'every animal is just' is 'no animal is just', it is evident that (a) these two statements cannot be true at the same time and of the same subject but that (b) their opposites [i.e., their contradictories], that is, 'not every animal is just' and 'some animals are just', may sometimes be true [at the same time and of the same subject]. Also, 'no man is just' follows from 'every man is not-just', and the opposite of the latter, which is 'not every man is not-just', follows from 'some men are just', for there must be a just man. It is also evident that if, concerning an individual, a denial is a true answer to a question, then a [related] affirmation is also true concerning that individual. For example, if 'Socrates is not wise' is a true answer to the question 'Is Socrates wise?', then 'Socrates is not-wise' is also true. In universal statements, on the other hand, the corresponding affirmation is not similarly true, but the denial is true. For example, if the statement 'every man is wise' is not true, then the statement 'every man is not-wise' is false but 'not every man is wise' is true; for the latter is the opposite [i.e., the contradictory], whereas the other is the contrary.

Opposites which are indefinite nouns or indefinite verbs, like 'not-man' and 'not-just', might be thought to be like denials without a noun or a verb, but they are not denials; for a denial must always be true or false, but he who says 'not-man' without adding anything else is no closer to saying something true or false than he who says 'man' but is even further away.

The statement 'every not-man is just' does not have the same meaning as any of the above statements, nor does its opposite [i.e., its contradictory], which is 'not every not-man is just'. But the statement 'every not-man is not-just' has the same meaning as 'no not-man is just'.

If nouns and verbs are transposed, the meanings of the resulting statements remain the same, e.g., 'man is white' and 'white is man' have the

same meaning; for if not, there would be many denials of the same thing.
But we have shown[7] that an affirmation has just one denial . For the denial
5   of 'man is white' is 'man is not white'; but if 'white is man' does not mean
what 'man is white' does, its denial would be either 'white is not not-man'
or 'white is not man'.   But the former of the last two statements is the denial
10   of 'white is not-man', whereas the latter is the denial of 'man is white',   and
so there would be two different denials of one statement. Clearly, then, if
the name and the verb are transposed, the meaning of an affirmation or of
a denial remains the same.

11

An expression in which one [thing] is affirmed or denied of many [things],
15   or many [things] are affirmed or denied of one [thing], is not one affirmation
or one denial unless that which is indicated by 'many [things]' is some one
[thing]. By 'one [thing]' I do not mean [things] for which one name is posited
but which do not make up one [thing]. For example, a man is perhaps an
animal and two-footed and tame, and these three make up something which
is one. But whiteness and man and walking do not make up [something
which is] one; so if someone affirms of these something which is one or
20   affirms these of something which is one, though he does so with one vocal
sound, that sound is not one affirmation but many. Accordingly, if a
dialectical question [with many predicates or many subjects which do not
make up one thing] is a request for an answer, whether as a premise or as
one part of a contradiction (and a premise is one of the two parts in a
25   contradiction), there can be no single answer to such a question, even if the
answer were true, for neither is the question single. We have discussed these
matters in the *Topics*.[8] It is also clear that the question 'what is it?' is not
dialectical; for, from a dialectical question, the man who answers should be
given the choice of stating whichever part of a contradiction he wishes. Thus
30   the questioner should specify, for example, whether a man is so-and-so or
not.
Since some things which are predicable [of a subject] separately are
predicable [of it] when combined as if the combination were one predicate,
whereas others cannot be so predicable when combined, what is the
difference [between the two kinds of combined predicates]? For example, it
is true to say of a man separately that he is an animal and that he is
two-footed and also to combine the two into one [and say that he is a
two-footed animal], and likewise to say of a man that he is a man and that
35   he is white, and to combine these two into one [predicate and say that he
is a white man]. But if a man is a shoemaker and also good, we cannot truly
say from these that he is a good shoemaker. For if we were to say, whenever

each predicate is truly said of a subject separately, that the combination of the two should be a predicate of it also, many absurdities would follow. For example, it is true to say of a [white] man that he is a man and also white, and hence that he is a white man; and since he is white and also a white man, it would be true to say of him that he is a white white man, and so on to 40 infinity. Again, if a man is musical and white and walking, these three, too, 21a could be combined many times indefinitely. Again, since 'Socrates' and 'man' are predicable of Socrates, so would 'Socrates Socrates man'; and since 'man' and 'two-footed' are predicable of him, so would 'two-footed man man'.

Clearly, then, many absurdities would follow if one were to say without 5 making any qualification that predicates could be combined. Let us now posit how predicates may be combined.

Of predicates and the subjects of which they happen to be predicable, those which are predicable accidentally, whether of the same subject or of each other, cannot be [combined to form] one [predicate]. For example, if 10 a man is both pale and musical, 'pale' and 'musical' cannot as two words be one [predicate], for both are accidental to the same subject. Neither can the expression 'musical pale' [or 'musically pale'] be one [predicate] if it were true to say that the pale is musical; for it is by accident that the musical is pale, and so 'pale musical' cannot be one predicate. It is in view of this fact that neither can a man, who is a shoemaker and also good, be [truly] called 15 'a good shoemaker' in an unqualified way; but he is truly called 'a two-footed animal', for it is not by accident that he is two-footed and an animal.

Again, predicates which are such that one of them is included in the other cannot combine to form one predicate. In view of this fact, neither can 'pale' be added to itself many times, nor can one call a man 'animal man' or 'two-footed man', for 'animal' and 'two-footed' are included in 'man'. On the other hand, it is true to say of an individual [what he is or happens to be] without qualification, e.g., to call an individual man 'a man', and an 20 individual pale man 'a pale man'. But such cannot always be the case, for when in one of the predicates there is something which is opposed to the other predicate and so leads to a contradiction in the combined predicate, it is not true but false to predicate each predicate of the individual, e.g., it is false to predicate 'man' of a dead man; but if no such opposite exists, it is true to predicate of an individual each of the combined predicates. Or better, when an opposite element is present, it is never true to predicate of 25 an individual each predicate separately, but when no such element is present, it is not always true to predicate each element of an individual. From the statement 'Homer is a poet', for example, does the statement 'Homer is' follow or not? But the word 'is' in the former statement is accidentally predicable of Homer, for it is not the word 'is' by itself that is

30   predicable of Homer but [the verb] 'is a poet'. Accordingly, whenever
      definitions are substituted for the names in a combined predicate which
      contains no contrariety, if the elements are essential and not accidental
      predicates, it would be true to predicate [of the individual] an element [of
      the combined predicate] even without qualification.   But the fact that
      nonbeing is an object of opinion does not make the statement 'nonbeing is'
      true; for the opinion of nonbeing is that it is not, not that it is.

      ## 12

35   Having made these distinctions, we must next consider how denials and
      affirmations concerning what is possible and what is not possible [to be or not
      to be], and what may and what cannot [be or not be], and what is impossible
      and what is necessary [to be or not to be] are related to each other; for some
      difficulties arise.
          Composite expressions with respect to the verbs 'to be' and 'not to be' are
      opposed to each other as contradictories in the following manner. For
21b   example, the denial of 'to be a man' is 'not to be a man' but not 'to be a
      not-man'; and the denial of 'to be a white man' is 'not to be a white man'
      but not 'to be a not-white man' (for if not, since the affirmation or the denial
5   is true in every case, it would be true to say that wood is a not-white man.)
      Since such is the case, the same will be true also of statements which do not
      have the verb 'to be' but some other verbal expression in its place. For
      example, the denial of 'man walks' is not 'not-man walks' but 'man does not
10   walk'; for it makes no difference whether one says 'man walks' or 'man is
      walking.'
          If the preceding argument were true in all other cases, then the denial of
      'possible to be', too, would be 'possible not to be' and not 'not possible to be'.
      But it is thought that the same thing is possible both to be and not to be; for
      everything which is capable of being cut or of walking is also capable of not
      being cut or of not walking, respectively. The reason for this truth is the fact
15   that everything which has such possibility does not always have the
      corresponding *actuality*, and so the negation, too, would belong to that
      thing; for that which is capable of walking is also capable of not walking,
      and that which is capable of being seen is also capable of not being seen. But
      it is impossible for opposite assertions to be truly asserted of the same thing
      [at the same time]; hence the denial of 'possible to be' is not 'possible not to
20   be'. For it follows from what has been said that either (a) the same
      [predicate] can be asserted and denied of the same object at the same time
      or (b) assertions and negations here are formed not by the additions of 'to
      be' and 'not to be', respectively. So if alternative (a) is impossible, alternative
      (b) should be chosen. Thus the denial of 'possible to be' is 'not possible to be'.

The same argument applies to 'may be' also, for the denial of this, too, is   25
'cannot be'. A similar argument applies to the others, too, i.e., to the
necessary and to the impossible. For, just as in the previous cases 'to be' and
'not to be' are the additions determining truth and falsity, whereas the
things underlying them are [subjects such as] 'white' and 'man', so here 'to
be' and 'not to be' become like subjects, while 'it is possible' and 'it may' [and   30
their opposites] become the additions which determine truth or falsity.

The denial of 'possible not to be', then, is not 'possible to be' but 'not
possible not to be', and the denial of 'possible to be' is not 'possible not to be'   35
but 'not possible to be'. It is in view of this, too, that 'possible to be' and
'possible not to be' would be thought to follow each other, for one would
think that the same thing is possible to be as well as possible not to be; for
expressions such as 'possible to be' and 'possible not to be' are not
contradictories. The expressions 'possible to be' and 'not possible to be', on
the other hand, are never true of the same thing at the same time, for they   22a
are opposites; and the expressions 'possible not to be' and 'not possible not
to be' are likewise never true of the same thing at the same time. Similarly,
the denial of 'necessary to be' is not 'necessary not to be' but 'not necessary
to be', and the denial of 'necessary not to be' is 'not necessary not to be'; and   5
the denial of 'impossible to be' is not 'impossible not to be', but 'not
impossible to be', while the denial of 'impossible not to be' is 'not impossible
not to be'.

Universally, then, as we have stated, the expressions 'to be' and 'not to be'
should be posited as subjects, but the others [i.e., 'possible' and 'not possible',
etc.] should be posited as additions to these to produce affirmations and   10
denials; and the following should be regarded as the opposite assertions:

Table I

possible	not possible
may	can not
impossible	not impossible
necessary	not necessary
true	not true

13

If these expressions are posited in this manner, the logical consequences
are as follows. From 'possible to be' follow (a) 'may be', and conversely, and   15
also (b) 'not impossible to be' and 'not necessary to be'; from 'possible not
to be' and 'may not be' follow 'not necessary not to be' and 'not impossible
not to be'; from 'not possible to be' and 'can not be' follow 'necessary not to
be' and 'impossible to be'; and from 'not possible not to be' and 'can not not

20 be' follow 'necessary to be' and 'impossible not to be'. What has been stated
may be viewed from the Table which follows.

Table II

A₁: possible to be	B₁: not possible to be
A₂: may be	B₂: can not be
A₃: not impossible to be	B₃: impossible to be
A₄: not necessary to be	B₄: necessary not to be
C₁: possible not to be	D₁: not possible not to be
C₂: may not be	D₂: can not not be
C₃: not impossible not to be	D₃: impossible not to be
C₄: not necessary not to be	D₄: necessary to be

(Table headers rendered: A, B, C, D subscripts)

Now 'impossible' and 'not impossible' follow from 'may' and 'possible'
and from 'can not' and 'not possible' in a contradictory but converse
35 manner, for the denial of 'impossible [to be]' follows from 'possible to be'
and the affirmation [i.e., 'impossible [to be]'] follows from the denial [i.e.,
from 'not possible to be']; for 'impossible to be' follows from 'not possible to
be' since 'impossible to be' is an affirmation, whereas 'not impossible to be'
is a denial.

We should next consider how statements containing the word 'necessity'
are related. Evidently, they are not related in the manner in which they are
placed; the contraries do follow, but the contradictories are separate. For
22b the denial of 'necessary not to be' is not 'not necessary to be', since both
statements may be true of the same thing [at the same time], for that which
is necessary not to be is not necessary to be. The *reason* that statements
containing the word 'necessity' do not follow in the same way as the other
statements is the fact that the word 'impossible', when added to a contrary
5 subject, amounts to the same thing as the word 'necessary'. For if P is
impossible to be, then P is necessary not to be, but not necessary to be; and
if P is impossible not to be, then P is necessary to be. Thus if the others [i.e.,
'not impossible' and 'impossible'] follow from 'possible' and 'not possible',
respectively, in a manner which is similar, these follow in a contrary
manner since 'necessary' and 'impossible' do not have the same meaning
10 but, as we stated, are inversely related.

But is it not impossible to posit the contradictories of 'it is necessary' in
this manner? For that which is necessary to be is possible to be. For if not,
the denial would follow (since one must either assert or deny something of
something); but if it is not possible to be, it is impossible to be, and so that
which is necessary to be would be impossible to be, a conclusion which is
15 indeed absurd. Moreover, from 'possible to be' follows 'not impossible to
be', and from the latter follows 'not necessary to be'; and so it turns out that
what is necessary to be is not necessary to be, a conclusion which is indeed
absurd. Further, neither 'necessary to be' nor 'necessary not to be' follows

from 'possible to be'; for what is possible to be admits of two alternatives [i.e., it is also possible not to be], whereas if either of the other two statements were true, those two alternatives would not be true. For that which is 20 possible to be is at the same time possible not to be, but if it were necessary to be, or necessary not to be, it would not have the possibility of both alternatives.   What remains, then, is that 'not necessary not to be' follows from 'possible to be'   (for the same is true with respect to 'necessary to be' also),   for this   becomes also the contradictory of that which follows from 'not possible to be'; for from 'not possible to be' follows 'impossible to be' and 25 'necessary not to be', and the denial of the latter is 'not necessary not to be'. Accordingly, these contradictories, too, follow in the manner stated, and nothing impossible happens if they are posited in this way.

One may raise the problem whether 'possible to be' follows from 30 'necessary to be'. For if not, then 'not possible to be' would follow, which is the contradictory [of 'possible to be']; or, if one were to say that 'not possible to be' is not the contradictory, then one must say that 'possible not to be' is the contradictory. But both of these are false of that which is necessary to be. On the other hand, the same thing is thought to have the possibility of being cut and of not being cut, of existing and of not existing, and so that 35 which is necessary to be might not be; and this conclusion, too, is false.

Now it is evident that not everything which is possible to be or to walk has also the possibility of the opposite,   but that there are some things of which [the possibility of the opposite is] not true. Of these, there are those which have a capability but not according to reason, like fire, which has the capability of heating but has a nonrational capability.   Accordingly, some capabilities exist [in persons] with reason and are capabilities leading to 23a many   and also to contrary things; and, of nonrational capabilities, not all [lead to many or to contrary things], as we said. Thus fire does not have the capability of heating and also of not heating, nor do those things which exist always in *actuality*.   But there are also things which have at the same time the possibility of admitting opposites with respect to their nonrational capabilities.   But we are stating this point for the sake of pointing out that 5 not every capability is a capability for opposites, not even those [in some cases] which are said to be capabilities of the same kind.   Some are called 'capabilities' equivocally. For the word 'possible' does not have a single meaning, but in one way 'to be possible' is to be true when the thing signified exists *actually*. For example, we say that a man is capable of walking when he is [*actually*] walking, and, in general, we say 'it is possible to be' when that which is said to be possible is already existing in *actuality*; 10 but we say such things also when the object might come to be *actualized*, e.g., we say 'it is possible for him to walk', meaning that he might walk. The latter capability exists only in things which can be in motion, but the former exists also in immovable things.   It is true to say of each of these that

15

it is not impossible to walk (or to be), that is, of that which is now walking
(or is in *actuality*) and also of that which has the capability of walking [but
is not now walking]. Accordingly, although it is not true to say of that which
is necessary in an unqualified way that it is capable in the latter way, it is
true to say of it that it is capable in the former way.   So since the universal
follows from the particular, that which is of necessity is also possible, but not
possible in every sense of the word 'possible'. And so perhaps the necessary
and that which is not necessary are the principles of what is or is not, and

20

the rest should be regarded as following from these.

It is evident from what has been said that that which exists of necessity
exists in *actuality*; so since eternal things are prior, *actuality* is prior to
potentiality also.   And some things are *actualities* without potentiality,
namely, the first substances,   others are *actualities* with potentiality, and

25

these are prior by nature but posterior in time,   and then there are those
which are never *actualities* but are only potentialities.

14

One may raise the question whether an affirmation is contrary to the
corresponding denial or to a [related] affirmation, and whether the

30

statement 'every man is just' is contrary to 'no man is just' or to 'every man
is unjust'. For example, is 'Callias is just' contrary to 'Callias is not just' or
to 'Callias is unjust'?

Now if spoken expressions follow in accordance with corresponding
thoughts, and if in *thought* a contrary opinion is of a contrary object—for
example, if the opinion 'every man is just' is contrary to the opinion 'every

35

man is unjust'—then a similar relation must exist between spoken
affirmations also. But if, in *thought*, the contrary opinion is not of the
contrary object, then the contrary of an affirmation will be its denial and
not the affirmation of the contrary object. So we must consider which true
opinion is contrary to a false opinion, whether the denial [of the false

40

opinion] or the opinion of the contrary subject. What I mean is the
following. There is a true opinion of a good thing, that it is good, and there

23b

is a false opinion of it, that it is not good, and still another [false] opinion
of it, that it is bad. Which of the last two opinions is contrary to the true
opinion? And if [the last two opinions are numerically] one [opinion], in
virtue of which one is [the true opinion] the contrary?

It is false to think that opinions should be defined as being contrary in
view of the fact that they are opinions of contrary [subjects]. For the opinion

5

of a good thing that it is good and the opinion of a bad thing that it is bad
would be perhaps the same and be true, whether these opinions are more
than one or just one. The [subjects] here are contrary; but opinions are

contrary not by being of contrary [subjects], but rather by being contrary in the manner in which they are related [to the same subject]. So if one opinion of a good thing is that it is good and another that it is not good, and if there are other things which neither belong nor are of such a nature as to belong to a good thing, no opinion of those things should be posited [as being a *10* contrary opinion], whether it be an opinion of that which does not belong to a good thing that it belongs to it or an opinion of that which belongs to a good thing that it does not belong to it (for both kinds of opinions are infinite, those of things which belong when they do not belong and those of things which do not belong when they do belong), but only those in which there is a mistake. Now these are opinions which arise from the generation of things; but generations proceed from opposites, and so do mistakes. *15* Accordingly, since a good thing is both good and not bad, since it is good in virtue of its nature but is not bad in virtue of some attribute (for it is an attribute of a good thing not to be bad), and since an opinion is more true of a thing if it is an opinion of it in virtue of its nature [than if it is an opinion not in virtue of its nature], an opinion will be more false of a thing if it is false in virtue of the nature of that thing [than if it is false not in virtue of the nature of that thing], as in the case of the true opinion.

Now the opinion of a good thing that it is not good is false in view of what belongs to the good thing in virtue of its nature, but the opinion of it that it is bad is false in virtue of an attribute of that thing. Hence the opinion *20* which denies that a good thing is good is more false than the opinion of the contrary [i.e., the opinion of a good thing as being bad]. But the man whose opinion is most false about a thing is he who has a contrary opinion, for contraries are things which differ most concerning the same thing. Accordingly, since only one of these two opinions is the contrary, and since the contradictory opinion is more contrary than the other opinion [i.e., than the opinion that a good thing is bad], it is clear that the contradictory *25* would be the contrary opinion. The opinion that a good thing is bad is composite; for perhaps he who has this opinion must also believe that a good thing is not good. Further, if the situation is to be similar in the other cases also, it would seem that in this way, too, we have given a good solution to the problem; for the contradictory should be the contrary opinion either in all cases or in none. Now in [subjects] which have no contraries, there is a *30* false opinion which is opposed to the true. For example, he who thinks falsely concerning a man is he who thinks that a man is not a man. So if the contrary opinions here are 'a man is a man' and 'a man is not a man', in the other cases, too, the opinions which are contradictory would be contrary.

Again, the opinion of a good thing that it is good is similar to the opinion of a thing which is not good that it is not good; and, we may add, the opinion of a good thing that it is not good is similar to the opinion of a thing which *35*

is not good that it is good.   Then which opinion would be contrary to the
true opinion of a thing which is not good that it is not good? Certainly (a)
not the opinion which thinks that it is bad, for both opinions might
sometimes be true at the same time, and no true opinion is ever contrary to
a true opinion (for [only] some things which are not good are bad, and so the
two opinions might be true at the same time);   nor (b) the opinion that it

40   is not bad, for this opinion, too, might be true, since both 'not good' and 'not
bad' might be predicable of a thing at the same time.   What remains, then,

24a   is that it is the opinion of a thing which is not good that it is good which is
the contrary of the opinion of it that it is not good, for it is this opinion which
is [always] a false opinion. So, too, it is the opinion of a good thing that it is
not good which is the contrary of the opinion of it that it is good.

It is evident that it would make no difference even if we posited the
affirmation to be universal, for in this case the contrary of it would be a
5   universal denial. For example, the contrary of the opinion which thinks that
everything which is good is good is the opinion that nothing which is good
is good. For the opinion of a good thing that it is good, if a good thing is
taken universally, is the same as the opinion that whatever is   good is good,
and the latter opinion does not differ from the opinion that everything
which is   good is good; and similarly with the opinions concerning what is

24b   not good.

So if indeed such is the case with opinions, since spoken affirmations and
denials are symbols of the [corresponding] thoughts in the soul, it is clear that
the contrary of an affirmation concerning something universally taken, too,
is the corresponding denial universally taken; for example, the contraries of
5   'everything good is good' and of 'every man is good' are, respectively,
'nothing good is good' and 'no man is good', but the contradictories are,
respectively, 'not everything good is good' and 'not every man is good'.

It is evident, too, that no true opinion or statement   can be contrary to
a true opinion or statement, respectively. For contrary [opinions or
statements] are of opposites; and whereas the same man may have true
opinions or make true statements concerning two opposites, contraries
cannot belong to the same [subject] at the same time.

PRIOR ANALYTICS

CONTENTS

BOOK I

Chapter

PRIOR ANALYTICS

BOOK I

1

We must first state the subject of our inquiry and the science to which it belongs: the subject is demonstration and belongs to the science of demonstration. We must next define a premise, a term, and a syllogism, and what kind of syllogism is complete and what kind is incomplete; and after these, what is meant by "A is wholly in B" and "A is wholly not in B," and
15 also what is meant by "B is predicated of every A" and "B is predicated of no A."

A premise is a statement affirming or denying something of something else, and it does this universally or partly or indefinitely. By "universally" I mean the statements "A belongs to every B" and "A belongs to no B"; by "partly," the statements "A belongs to some B," "A does not belong to all B", and "A does not belong to some B;" by "indefinitely," the statements "A
20 belongs to B" and "A does not belong to B," without specifying whether it is universally or partly that A belongs or does not belong to B, as in the statements "contraries are subjects of the same science" and "pleasure is not a good."

A demonstrative premise differs from a dialectical premise in that a demonstrative premise is an assertion of one of two contradictory statements (for the demonstrator does not ask for but posits a statement [as being true]),
25 whereas a dialectical premise is any one of two contradictories taken after asking. But a syllogism may be formed, whether the premise is demonstrative or dialectical; for both a demonstrator and he who asks for a statement take a premise stating that something belongs or does not belong to something else and proceed to prove something. So a syllogistic premise without qualification is an affirmation or a denial of something about
30 something else in the manner stated; and it is demonstrative if it is true and
24b taken from the first hypotheses [of a science], but it is dialectical to one who asks for one of two contradictories or to one who proves something by taking what appears [to be true] or generally accepted [as being true], as stated in the *Topics*.[1] For our present needs, then, we have sufficiently defined what

a premise is and stated how syllogistic, demonstrative, and dialectical premises differ from each other; but accurate definitions of them will be   *15* given later.[2]

I call "a term" that into which a premise is resolved, that is, the predicate or that of which the predicate is predicable [i.e., the subject], whether "is" or "is not" is added or removed. A syllogism is a sentence in which, certain things being posited, something other than what is posited follows of necessity from what is posited as being so. By "follows from what   *20* is posited as being so" I mean that it follows because of what is posited as being so, and by "follows because of what is posited as being so" I mean that nothing other than the terms posited is needed to necessitate what follows. By "a perfect syllogism" I mean one which needs nothing outside of what is posited to make evident that which necessarily follows; and by "an imperfect syllogism" I mean one which needs one or more [premises] which   *25* follow necessarily through the terms posited but are not taken through the premises. By "A is wholly in B" and by "B is predicable of every A" I mean the same thing; and by "B is predicable of every A" I mean that there would be no instance of the subject A of which B will not be asserted; and similarly   *30* for "B is predicable of no A."

2

Every premise states that something either exists or necessarily exists or   *25a* may exist, and some of these premises are affirmative while the others are negative in each of the [three] modes [just] stated. Again, affirmative and negative premises may be universal or particular [i.e., belonging partly] or   *5* indefinite. The terms of a universally negative premise are of necessity convertible; e.g., if no pleasure is good, then nothing good is pleasure. The terms of a [universally] affirmative premise, too, are convertible, not universally, but partly; e.g., if every pleasure is good, then some good must be pleasure. The terms of a partly affirmative premise are of necessity   *10* partly convertible; e.g., if some pleasure is good, then some good must be pleasure. The terms of a partly negative premise, however, are not necessarily convertible; e.g., if "man" does not belong to "some animal," it is not necessary for "animal" not to belong to "some man."

First, then, let A and B be the terms of a universally negative premise. Now if A belongs to no B, then B too will not belong to any A; for if B does   *15* belong to some A, say to C, it will not be true [to say] that A belongs to no B, for C is a B. If, however, A belongs to every B, then also B will belong to some A; for if B belongs to no A, then A will belong to no B, contrary to the assumption that A belongs to every B. Similarly, too, if the premise is   *20* particular. For if A belongs to some B, it is also necessary for B to belong to

some A; for if B belongs to no A, A too will belong to no B, [but it was assumed that A belongs to some B]. If, on the other hand, A does not belong to some B, it is not necessary for B not to belong to some A. For example,
25 let B be "animal" and A be "man." Now "man" does not belong to every "animal," but "animal" belongs to every "man."

3

The terms of necessary premises, too, are related in the same manner, that is, a universally negative premise is universally convertible, and each
30 of the affirmative premises is partly convertible. For if A belongs to no B of necessity, then it is also necessary for B to belong to no A [of necessity], for if B may belong to some A, then also A might belong to some B, [contrary to the original assumption]. Again, if A belongs of necessity to every or to some B, it is also necessary for B to belong of necessity to some A; for if it were not necessary, neither would it be necessary for A to belong of
35 necessity to some B. A particular negative premise which is necessary does not convert, and for the same *reason* as the one given before.[3]

Concerning premises of the form "A may be B," since this form has many senses (for we say that A may be B, whenever A is necessarily B, or A is B but not necessarily, or it is possible for A to be B), if the premises are
40 affirmative, conversion of the terms in all cases will be similar to that
25b previously stated.[4] For if A may belong to every or to some B, then also B may belong to some A; for if B could not belong to any A, A too could not belong to any B, as shown previously.[5] The terms in negative premises, on the other hand, are not related in the same way. For in those cases in which
5 "no A may be B" means that of necessity no A is B, or that it is not necessary for any A to be B, the conversion is similar, e.g., if one were to say that no man may be a horse, or that no white [thing] may belong to a garment; for in the first example, it is necessary for no man to be a horse, whereas in the second, there is no necessity for any white thing to belong to a garment, so each premise is converted in a similar manner. Thus if no horse may belong
10 to a man, neither may a man belong to a horse; and if no white [thing] may belong to a garment, neither may a garment belong to a white [thing], for if it is necessary for a garment to belong to some white [thing], it will be necessary for a white [thing] to belong to some garment also, as proved before.[6] Similar remarks apply to particular premises, [i.e., of the form "A may not be some B].[7]

In those cases in which the expression "A may belong to B" means that
15 A belongs to B in most cases or by nature, which is the [main] sense of "may," conversion of negative premises is not similar; for a universally negative premise does not convert, but the partly negative premise converts.

This will be made evident when we discuss things which may be.[8] At present this much is clear, in addition to what has been said: the expression "B may 20 belong to no A, or not to some A" is affirmative in form; for the expression "may be" is regarded like the expression "is," and "is," when added to a predicate, produces always and in every case an affirmation, as in "A is not-good" or "A is not-white" or, without qualification, "A is not-this," and this will be proved later.[9] So the premises in this case, when converted, will 25 be like those in the other cases.

4

Having made the above distinctions, let us now consider with what [premises], when, and how every syllogism is formed. Demonstration will be discussed later.[10] The discussion of syllogisms should precede the discussion of demonstrations because a syllogism is more universal than a demonstration; for a demonstration is a species of a syllogism, but not every syllogism 30 is a demonstration.

Whenever three terms are so related to each other that the last is wholly in the *middle* while the *middle* is wholly in the first or is wholly excluded from the first, there must be a perfect syllogism relating the two extreme terms. By "*middle*" I mean the term which is [wholly or partly or not at all] 35 in another and in which another term is [wholly or partly or not at all]; and in position, too, the *middle* lies between [the other two terms]. By "extreme" I mean that which is [or is not, partly or wholly], in the *middle* or that in which the *middle* is [or is not, partly or wholly].

Thus if A is predicable of every B, and B of every C, it is necessary for A to be predicable of every C; for it was stated earlier[11] how we are using 40 the expression "predicable of every." Similarly, if A is predicable of no B, 26a but B of every C, it is necessary that A be predicable of no C.

If, however, the first term belongs to every B, but B belongs to no C, there can be no syllogism relating the extremes; for nothing follows of necessity from the fact that the terms are so related since the first term may 5 belong to all or to none of the last term, so that neither a particular nor a universal conclusion follows of necessity, and if nothing follows of necessity through these premises, there can be no syllogism. Terms according to which the first belongs universally to the last term are "animal," "man," "horse"; terms according to which the first belongs to none of the last term are "animal," "man," "stone." Nor can there be a syllogism if the first term 10 belongs to none of the *middle* and the *middle* to none of the last. Terms according to which the first belongs to the last term are "science," "line," "medical science"; terms according to which the first belongs to none of the last term are "science," "line," "unit."

If the terms are universally related, then, it is clear in this figure (a)
15   when there can be a syllogism and when there cannot, and that (b) if there
is a syllogism, the terms must be as we stated, and if they are related as we
stated, there will be a syllogism.

If one of the terms is universally related to another and the latter is
partly related to a third, there must be a perfect syllogism whenever
universality is posited to relate the major term with the *middle*, either
20   affirmatively or negatively, and particularity to relate the *middle* with the
minor term. But whenever universality is posited to relate the *middle* with
the minor term or if the terms are related in any other way, no syllogism is
possible. By "major term" I mean that in which the *middle* is [or is not,
wholly or partly], and by "minor term" I mean that which comes under the
middle.

Thus let A belong to every B, and B to some C. Then, if "predicable of
25   every" has the meaning as stated at the beginning,[12] it is necessary that A
belong to some C. Further, if A belongs to no B, and B belongs to some C,
it is necessary that A does not belong to some C; for we have also specified[13]
the meaning of "predicable of, or belonging to none." So there will be a
perfect syllogism [in both cases]. Likewise, there will be a perfect syllogism
even if the relation of B to C is indefinite but affirmative; for the same
30   syllogism is formed whether the minor premise is indefinite or
particular.

If, on the other hand, the universal relation is posited towards the minor
term, either affirmatively or negatively, there will be no syllogism, whether
the relation [of A to B] is affirmative or negative, and whether indefinite or
particular.

Thus if A belongs or does not belong to some B, and B belongs to every
35   C, no syllogism is formed. Let "good," "habit," and "prudence" be the
terms; then A is affirmatively related to C, for all prudence is good. Let
"good," "habit," and "ignorance" be the terms; then no ignorance is good.
Further, let B belong to no C, and let A belong to some B, or not belong to
some B, or not belong to every B; then there can be no syllogism. We may
take the terms "white," "horse," and "swan," or the terms "white," "horse,"
and "raven." The same terms may be taken even if the relation of A to B
26b   is indefinite. Nor is there a syllogism whenever the major premise is
universal, either affirmatively or negatively, but the minor premise is
negative, either particularly or indefinitely, that is, if A belongs to every B,
5   and B does not belong to some or to every C. For, if the *middle* did not
belong to some C, the major term could belong to every or to none of C. For
let the terms be "animal," "man," "white," and then take terms of which
"man" is not predicable, e.g., "swan" and "snow"; then "animal" is
10   predicated of every "swan" but of no "snow," and so there can be no
syllogism. Again, let A belong to no B and B not belong to some C, and let

the terms be "inanimate," "man," "white"; then take instances of "white"
of which "man" is not predicable, e.g., "swan" and "snow." Here the term
"inanimate" is predicable of all "snow" but of no "swan." Further, since "B   *15*
does not belong to some C" is indefinite but true, whether B belongs to no
C or B does not belong to some C, and since no syllogism is formed if terms
are so taken that B belongs to no C (this was stated previously),[14] it is evident
that there can be no syllogism with terms taken in this manner; for what was
stated previously would be true in this case also. Similarly, it can be shown   *20*
[that no syllogism arises] even if [the minor premise] is posited as being
universally negative.

Nor can there be a syllogism if both intervals [i.e., relations of terms in
the major and minor premises] are particular, either both affirmative or
both negative, or one of them affirmative but the other negative, or one of
them indefinite but the other definite, or both of them indefinite. Terms
common to all of these cases are "animal," "white," "horse," and "animal,"   *25*
"white," "stone."

It is evident from what has been said that if there is to be a syllogism in
this figure with a particular [conclusion], the terms must be related as we
have stated and that there can be no syllogism if the terms are related in any
other way. It is also clear that all syllogisms in this figure are perfect, for all   *30*
of them are completed only through the [premises] as posited at first, and
that all problems raised, whether universal or particular, affirmative or
negative, are proved by means of this figure. Such a figure I call "the
first."

5

Whenever the same [term] B belongs to every A but to no C, or to every   *35*
A and every C, or to no A and no C, I call such a figure "the second"; by
"*middle*" in that figure I mean the term [i.e., B] which is predicable
[affirmatively or negatively] of both A and C; by "extremes" I mean the
terms [i.e., A and C] of which B is said; by "major" I mean the extreme
which lies near the *middle*; and by "minor" I mean the extreme which is
further away from the *middle*. The *middle* is placed outside of the extremes
and is first in position. No syllogism in this figure can be perfect; but a   *27a*
syllogism is possible whether the terms are universally related or not.

If the terms are universally related, there can be a syllogism whenever
the *middle* belongs to every instance of one term but to no instance of
the other, regardless of the term to which the *middle* is negatively related;   *5*
otherwise, there can be no syllogism at all.

Thus let B be predicable of no A but of every C. Since the negative
predication is convertible, it follows that A will belong to no B. But it was

stated[15] that B belongs to every C. Hence A belongs to no C, for this was
10   shown earlier. Again, if B belongs to every A but to no C, C will belong to
no A. For if B belongs to no C, C will belong to no B. But it was stated that
B belongs to every A. Hence C will belong to no A, for the first figure has
been formed once more. And since the negative relation is convertible, A
will belong to no C, and so we shall have the same syllogism. These
15   [conclusions] can be proved also by reduction to the impossible.

   It is evident, then, that a syllogism is formed if the terms are related in
the above manner, but the syllogism will not be perfect; for the conclusion
follows of necessity not only from the premises laid down at first but also
from other premises.

   If, however, B is predicable of every A and also of every C, there can
be no syllogism. Terms which exemplify an affirmative relation are
20   "*substance*," "animal," "man"; terms which exemplify a negative relation
are "*substance*," "animal," "number," the *middle* in these is "*substance*."
Further, if B is predicable of no A and also of no C, again no syllogism can
be formed. Terms which exemplify an affirmative relation are "line,"
"animal," "man"; terms which exemplify a negative relation are "line,"
"animal," "stone."

   It is evident, then, that if a syllogism is formed whenever the terms are
25   universally related, the terms must be related as we stated at first, for if they
are [universally] related in any other way nothing follows of necessity.

   If the *middle* is related universally to one of the extremes, then
whenever it is universally related to the major, whether affirmatively or
negatively, but particularly related to the minor and in a way opposed to
universality (by "opposed to universality" I mean, if the universal relation
30   is negative, the particular relation is affirmative, and if the universal
relation is affirmative, the particular relation is negative), a syllogism with
a conclusion which is particular and negative must be formed.

   Thus if B belongs to no A but to some C, it follows that A does not belong
to some C. For since the negative relation is convertible, A will belong to no
35   B, and since B was assumed to belong to some C, it follows that A will not
belong to some C; and so a syllogism in the first figure is formed. Further,
if B belongs to every A but not to some C, it follows that A does not belong
to some C. For if A belongs to every C, then, since B is predicable of every
27b   A, it follows that B will belong to every C, and this contradicts the
assumption that B does not belong to some C. Again, if B belongs to every
A but not to every C, there will be a syllogism of the fact that A does not
belong to every C; and the demonstration will be the same as the one just
given.
5   If, on the other hand, B is predicable of every A but not of every C, there
can be no syllogism. Terms [exemplifying a universally affirmative relation]
are "animal," "substance," "raven," and terms [exemplifying a universally

negative relation] are "animal," "white," "raven." Nor will there be a syllogism if B is predicable of no C but of some A. Terms exemplifying a universally affirmative relation are "animal," "substance," "unit," and terms exemplifying a universally negative relation are "animal," "substance," "science."

Whenever the universal relation is opposed to the particular relation, then, we have stated when there will be a syllogism and when not. But whenever the premises are similar in form, that is, both negative or both affirmative, there can be no syllogism at all.

First, let both premises be negative, and let the universal premise be related to the major term; that is, let B belong to no A and not to some C. Then A may belong to every C or to no C. Terms which exemplify A as belonging to no C are "black," "snow," "animal."

Terms which exemplify A as belonging to every C, however, cannot exist if B belongs to some of A but also not to some of A; for if A belongs to every C and B to no A, B will belong to no C, contrary to the assumption that B belongs to some C. Terms taken in this manner, then, cannot be permitted, so the proof should use the indefiniteness of ["B does not belong to some C"]. For, since "B does not belong to some C" is true even if B belongs to no C, and since, as we stated,[16] no syllogism is formed if [B] belongs to no [C], it is evident that neither can a syllogism be formed by the use of the indefiniteness of ["B does not belong to some C"].

Again, let both premises be affirmative and the universal relation be posited as before, that is, let B belong to every A and to some C. Then A may belong to every C or to no C. Terms exemplifying the negative relation are "white," "swan," "stone"; but terms exemplifying that A belongs to every C cannot be taken for the same *reason* as that stated previously,[17] so a proof should use the indefiniteness of "B belongs to some C." Now if the premise with the minor term is universal, and B belongs to no C and not to some A, A may belong to every C or to no C. Terms exemplifying that A belongs to every C are "white," "animal," "raven;" terms exemplifying that A belongs to no C are "white," "stone," "raven." If the premises are affirmative, terms exemplifying that A belongs to no C are "white," "animal," "snow"; terms exemplifying that A belongs to all C are "white," "animal," "swan."

It is evident, then, that no syllogism can be formed whenever the premises are similar in form [i.e., both affirmative or both negative] but one of them is universal and the other particular. Nor can a syllogism be formed if B belongs to some A and to some C, or not to some A and not to some C, or to some A but not to some C, or not to every A and not to every C, or if it is related to them indefinitely. Terms which are common to all these are "white," "animal," "man," and "white," "animal," "inanimate."

It is evident from the above discussion that if the terms are related to one another in the manner stated, a syllogism is formed necessarily, and that, if

10

15

20

25

30

35

28a

there is to be a syllogism, the terms are necessarily related to one another as stated. It is clear, too, that all the syllogisms in this figure are imperfect
5 (for each of them is made perfect by the addition of some premises which are either necessitated by the terms as laid down or are posited as hypotheses, that is, whenever we give a proof by the use of impossibility [*per impossibile*]), and that no syllogism with an affirmative conclusion can be formed by means of this syllogism but all conclusions, whether universal or particular, are negative.

6

10   If, of two terms, the first belongs to every instance but the second belongs to no instance of a third term, or if both belong to every or to no instance of the third term, I call such a figure "the third." By "*middle*" I mean that of which the two terms are predicable, by "extreme" I mean each of the two predicates, by "major" I mean that which is further from the *middle*, and by "minor" that which is nearer the *middle*. The *middle* is
15 placed outside of the extremes and is last in position. No perfect syllogism can be formed in this figure, but a syllogism is possible whenever the [extreme] terms are or are not universally related to [i.e., belong to] the *middle*.

       If the two terms are universally related to the *middle*, let both A and C belong to every B. Then it is necessary that A belong to some C. For, since
20 an affirmative statement is convertible, B will belong to some C. So since A belongs to every B and B belongs to some C, it is necessary that A belong to some C; for this is a syllogism through the first figure. This can be demonstrated also by the use of impossibility and by exposition; for if both
25 A and C belong to every B, if some instance of B be taken, say M, both A and C will belong to it, and so A will belong to some C.

       Again, if C belongs to every B but A belongs to no B, a syllogism of the fact that A will not belong to some C follows of necessity; for if the premise "C belongs to every B" is converted, the manner of demonstrating that A does not belong to some C is similar to that just given. This conclusion can
30 be proved also by the use of impossibility, as in the previous cases.

       If, however, C belongs to no B but A belongs to every B, there can be no syllogism. Terms which exemplify that A belongs to every C are, A = "animal," C = "man," B = "horse"; terms exemplifying that A belongs to no C are, A = "animal," C = "inanimate," B = "man."

       Nor can there be a syllogism if both A and C belong to no B. Terms exemplifying that A belongs to every C are A = "animal," C = "horse,"
35 B = "inanimate"; terms exemplifying that A belongs to no C are A = "man," C = "horse," B = "inanimate"; the *middle* is "inanimate."

If the terms in this figure are universally related, then, it is evident when there can be a syllogism and when there cannot be. For whenever both extreme terms are affirmatively related to a third term, there will be a syllogism of the fact that one extreme belongs to some of the other extreme; but when both are negatively related to a third term, there will be no syllogism. Further, whenever one premise is negative and the other affirmative, if the premise with the major term is negative and the premise with the minor term is affirmative, there will be a syllogism of the fact that the major term does not belong to some of the minor. But if the first premise is affirmative and the second is negative, there will be no syllogism.

28b

If one term is related universally to the *middle* and the other is partly related to it, whenever both relations are affirmative there must be a syllogism, regardless of which term is universally related to the middle. Thus if C belongs to every B but A to some B, it is necessary that A belong to some C. For since an affirmative premise is convertible, B will belong to some A, so since C belongs to every B and B belongs to some A, C will belong to some A also, and hence A will belong to some C by conversion. Again, if C belongs to some B but A to every B, it is necessary that A belong to some C, for the demonstration proceeds in the same way. The same result can be demonstrated by the use of impossibility and also by exposition, as in the previous cases.

5

10

15

If, however, one extreme is affirmatively related but the other extreme is negatively related to the *middle,* and if the affirmative relation is universal, then whenever the minor term is affirmatively related, there will be a syllogism. Thus if C belongs to every B but A does not belong to some B, it is necessary that A does not belong to some C. For if A belongs to every C, then both A and C will belong to every B; but we assumed that A does not belong to some B. This can be shown also without the use of the impossible, that is, if one takes some of those B's to which A does not belong.

20

Whenever, on the other hand, it is the major which is affirmative, there can be no syllogism; that is, if A belongs to every B but C does not belong to some B. Terms which exemplify the affirmative conclusion are A = "animate," B = "man," C = "animal." No terms can be taken to exemplify a negative conclusion if C does not belong to some of B but belongs to the rest of B. For if A belongs to every B and C belongs to some B, then also A will belong to some C; but it was assumed[18] that A belongs to no C. Consequently, we should proceed as we did before; for, since the expression "C does not belong to some B" is indefinite, it may be taken as true even if C belongs to no B. But if C belongs to no B, it was shown[19] that there can be no syllogism. It is evident, then, that here too there can be no syllogism.

25

30

If, further, the relation of two terms is negative and universal, there may
be a syllogism. For, whenever A belongs to no B but C belongs to some B,
35　A will not belong to some C. Here, again, the first figure will be formed if
the relation of C to B is converted. But if it is the minor term which is
negatively related to the *middle,* there can be no syllogism. Terms
exemplifying an affirmative conclusion are A = "animal," C = "man,"
B = "wild," and terms exemplifying a negative relation are A = "animal,"
C = "science," B = "wild"; the middle in both examples is "wild."

　　　Finally, no syllogism is formed whenever both premises are negative
29a　and one of them is universal but the other particular. Whenever the premise
with the minor term is universal, terms exemplifying a negative relation are
"animal," "science," "wild," and terms exemplifying an affirmative
relation are "animal," "man," "wild." Whenever the premise with the
major term is universal, terms exemplifying a negative relation are "raven,"
"snow," "white." But terms exemplifying an affirmative relation cannot be
5　taken if C belongs to some B but not to the rest of B. For, if A belongs to
every C and C belongs to some B, then A will belong to some B; but it was
assumed that A belongs to no B. Then a proof must be given if the premise
with the minor term is taken as being indefinite.

　　　Nor can a syllogism be formed if both of the extremes belong to some
of the *middle* or both do not belong to some of the *middle,* or one of them
belongs to some but the other does not belong to the rest of the *middle,* or
one of them belongs to some but the other not to all of the *middle,* or if the
premises are indefinite. Terms common to all these cases are "animal,"
10　"man," "white," and "animal," "inanimate," "white."

　　　So in this figure, too, it is evident (a) when there can be a syllogism and
when there cannot, (b) that if the terms are related as stated, a syllogism is
formed necessarily, (c) and that if a syllogism is formed, it is necessary for
15　the terms to be related as stated. It is also evident that all the syllogisms in
this figure are imperfect (for all of them are perfected by additional
premises) and that no universal conclusion, whether affirmative or negative,
can be proved by means of this figure.

　　　7

20　　　It is also clear that whenever no syllogism is formed in each of the three
figures, (a) nothing at all follows of necessity if both terms are affirmatively
or negatively related, but (b) if one term is affirmatively and the other
negatively related and the negative relation is taken universally, there is
always a syllogism which relates the minor to the major term. Thus if A
25　belongs to every or to some B but B belongs to no C, and if both premises

are converted, it is necessary that C does not belong to some A; and similarly in the other figures, for a syllogism is always formed by means of conversion. It is clear, too, that if a particular affirmative is replaced by an indefinite affirmative premise, this will result in the same syllogism in every figure.

Again, it is also evident that all imperfect syllogisms are made perfect   30
by means of the first figure. For all syllogisms come to a conclusion either directly or through impossibility (*per impossibile*), and in both cases the first figure is formed: if they are made perfect directly, they come to a conclusion by means of conversion, which results, as already shown, in the first figure, but if they are proved through impossibility, a syllogism is   35
formed in the first figure when a false statement is posited. In the third figure, for example, if A and C each belongs to every B, then A belongs to some C. For if A belongs to no C, then, since C belongs to every B, A will belong to no B; but it was posited that A belongs to every B. The same applies to the other figures.

Every syllogism can be reduced to a universal syllogism in the first   29b
figure. Evidently, syllogisms in the second figure are made perfect by means of syllogisms in the first figure, but not all of them in the same way; for universal syllogisms are made perfect by conversion of the negative premise, but each particular syllogism is made perfect by reduction to the impossible. Particular syllogisms in the first figure are made perfect by   5
themselves, but they can be reduced to the impossible by means of the second figure. Thus, if A belongs to every B and B belongs to some C, then A belongs to some C; for if A belongs to no C, then, since A belongs to every   10
B, we know by means of the second figure that B will belong to no C, [a contradiction]. A similar demonstration can be given if the syllogism is negative. Thus, if A belongs to no B but B belongs to some C, A will not belong to some C; for if A belongs to every C, then, since A belongs to no B, B will belong to no C by means of the second figure, as already shown.   15
So since the syllogisms in the second figure are reducible to universal syllogisms in the first figure and particular syllogisms in the first figure are reducible to syllogisms in the second figure, it is evident that particular syllogisms, too, will be reduced to universal syllogisms in the first figure. As for syllogisms in the third figure, if their terms are universally related, they   20
are directly made perfect by means of the other figures, but whenever one of the premises is particular, they are made perfect by means of particular syllogisms in the first figure; but these syllogisms, as already stated, are reducible to universal syllogisms in the first figure, so particular syllogisms in the third figure, too, are reducible to universal syllogisms in the first figure. It is evident, then, that all other syllogisms are reducible to universal   25
syllogisms in the first figure.

We have stated, then, how syllogisms which prove that something belongs or does not belong to something else are formed, both those within themselves in the same figure and those which are related to other figures.

8

Since the expressions "A belongs to B," "A necessarily belongs to B," and 30 "A may belong to B" differ in meaning from each other (for some things belong to others but not of necessity, and some neither belong to others of necessity nor belong to them at all but may belong to them), it is clear that there will be syllogisms whose terms in the two premises are similarly related in each of the three cases (e.g., as in the case when A necessarily belongs to B and B necessarily belongs to C, and likewise in the other two cases), and also syllogisms whose terms are not similarly related (i.e., if two of the three relations of belonging, necessarily belonging, and may be belonging appear in the two premises).

13

32a Perhaps enough has been said about syllogisms whose premises state
15 necessary predications, both as to how they are formed and how they differ from syllogisms in which the predications are those of just belonging or not. Concerning syllogisms in which the predications are of that which may be or may not be, let us discuss when and how and through what premises they are formed. By "that which may be" or what it signifies I mean something which is not necessary but which, if posited as existing, does not, because of
20 being so posited, lead to something impossible (that which is necessary, we may add, is equivocally called "that which may be"). That this is what we mean by "that which may be" is evident from the denials and affirmations of its contraries; for "it cannot be" and "it is impossible to be" and "it is necessary not to be" are either the same [in meaning] or [logically] follow
25 one another, and so the opposites of these, i.e., "it may be" and "it is not impossible to be" and "it is not necessary that it not be," respectively, are either the same [in meaning] or [logically] follow one another (for of an object either the affirmation or the denial [is true]). Accordingly, that which may be is not something which exists of necessity, and that which exists not of necessity may be.
30 Now all premises concerning that which may be are convertible into one another [i.e., follow each other]. I mean not that the affirmations follow

their denials [or conversely], but that those whose form is affirmative but with respect to opposites as subjects; that is, "it may be that P is" and "it may be that P is not" follow each other, and so do "it may be that every A is" and "it may be that no A is" and "it may be that not every A is," and also 35 "it may be that some A is B" and "it may be that some A is not B." The same applies to all others. For, since that which may be is not something necessary, and since that which is not necessary admits of not existing, it is evident that (a) if A may belong to B, it may also not belong to B, and (b) if A may belong to every B, it may also belong to no B; and similarly if the 40 premises are particular [e.g., if A may belong to some B], for the demonstration is the same. Such premises, we may add, are affirmative and $32b$ not negative, for "it may be" is used in the same way as "it is," as stated earlier.[20]

Having made these distinctions, let us again state that "A may be" is 5 used in two senses. In one sense, it means that A comes to be in most cases but falls short of coming to be of necessity, as in the case of a man's hair turning gray when becoming old or a man growing [in his early years] or deteriorating with age, or, in general, that which exists by nature (for this has no continuous necessity because, e.g., a particular man does not always exist, although if he does exist, something belongs to him either of necessity 10 or for the most part). In another way, "A may be" means something indefinite, i.e., that it is possible for A to be and also for A not to be, as in the case of an animal walking and not walking, or for an earthquake to occur or not to occur when one is walking, or, in general, that which comes to be by chance; for none of these occurs by nature in one way rather than in a contrary way. Now in both senses each of these [affirmative] premises is convertible with respect to the opposite parts in them, although not in the 15 same way; for that which exists by nature is convertible since its existence is not necessary (for it is in this sense that a man may not turn gray with age), whereas that which is indefinite is convertible since it does not come to be naturally in one way rather than in the opposite way. Scientific knowledge and demonstrative syllogisms do not apply to indefinite things because the middle terms in them are irregular, but such knowledge and such syllogisms 20 do apply to things which exist by nature; and arguments and inquiries are usually about things which may come to be in the latter way. Syllogisms about things which may come to be in the former way can be formed, but usually one does not make such inquiries. These matters will be made more specific later.[21]

POSTERIOR ANALYTICS

CONTENTS

BOOK I

Chapter

POSTERIOR ANALYTICS

BOOK I

1

All teaching and all learning through discourse proceed from previous   *71a*
knowledge. This is evident if we examine all [the kinds of such teaching and
learning]. For such is the way through which the mathematical sciences are
acquired and each of the other arts. And it is likewise with reasonings,   *5*
whether these be through a syllogism or induction, for teaching in each case
proceeds by means of previous knowledge; for a syllogism proceeds from
something [from premises] taken as *understood*, whereas in the case of
induction, the universal is proved because [its truth] is clear in each
particular. Rhetorical arguments, too, produce persuasion in the same way;
for they do so either through examples, in which case there is an induction,   *10*
or through enthymemes, [each of] which, *as such*, is a syllogism.

Previous knowledge must be of two kinds. For, (1) if it is of a fact, one
must have previous belief of it, but (2) if it is of a spoken expression, one
should have an *understanding* of it; and in some cases both (1) and (2) are
required. For instance, (1) it is a fact that in every case it is true either to
affirm or to deny something of something else, but (2) concerning the term
"triangle", [one should *understand*] that it means so-and-so; and in the case   *15*
of a unit, one must both *understand* what the term "unit" means and know
the fact that a unit exists; for each of these is not made known to us in the
same way.

Now what one need know to acquire new knowledge may be (*a*) that of
which he has prior knowledge or (*b*) that which he learns while acquiring
new knowledge, i.e., that which happens to come under the universal
whose knowledge he [already] has; for one had previous knowledge of the   *20*
fact that every triangle has the sum of its angles equal to two right angles,
but as to the fact that the thing drawn in the semicircle is a triangle, this he
was led on to learn at the time [he was acquiring new knowledge]. Thus,
of some things, learning takes place in this manner, and it is not through a
middle term that the last term is made known; and such are the things
which happen to be particulars and are not [predicable of or do not belong   *25*
to] a subject. Before the learner is led on to a thing or acquires syllogistic
knowledge, however, perhaps it should be said that in a certain manner he
knows but in another manner he does not. For if he does not know that the
thing simply exists, how can he know in an unqualified way that its angles
are equal to two right angles? So it is clear that it is in a certain sense that
he *knows*, namely, he *knows* universally, but not without qualification;

30   otherwise, one will be faced with the dilemma in the *Meno*: a man will learn
either nothing at all or what he already knows.   For surely we should not
speak in the manner in which some try to disprove this. They ask: "Do you
know or not that every dyad is even?" When the answerer says he does, they
bring forward a dyad of whose existence and hence of whose evenness they
expect him not to know. They offer a disproof by asserting that what people
know to be even is not every dyad but only those which they know to be
71b dyads.   What people essentially know, however, is that of which, *as such*,
they possess and have acquired a demonstration,   and they have acquired
a demonstration not of every instance which they know to be a triangle or
to be a number, but of every number or of every triangle without any
5   qualification.   For no posited premise is taken in a form such as this: "every
number which you know [to exist is such-and-such]" or "every rectilinear
figure which you know [to exist is such-and-such]"; it is taken thus: "every
thing [universally taken is such-and-such]". But (I think that) nothing
prevents one who is learning something to *know* it in one sense but to be
ignorant of it in another; for what is absurd is not that there is a sense in
which one knows that which he is learning, but that he knows it in this sense,
namely, *insofar as* and *in the manner in which* he is learning it.

            2

10   We think that we *know* each [thing] without qualification, but not in the
sophistical manner with respect to an attribute, when we think that (a) we
know the cause through which the thing exists as being the cause of that
thing and that (b) the thing cannot be other than what it is. That *knowing*
is something of this sort is clear from the fact that both those who do not
know and those who *know* think that *knowing* is of this sort, but the former
15   [only] think that they are disposed in this manner whereas the latter are so
disposed but also *know;* so it is impossible for that of which there is
unqualified *knowledge* to be other than what it is.
     Now we shall consider later[2] whether there is still another way of
knowing; but we speak also of knowing through demonstration. By "a
demonstration" I mean a scientific syllogism, and by "a scientific syllogism"
I mean a syllogism in virtue of which, by possessing, we *know*
[something].
20   If, then, to *know* is such as we have posited it to be, it is also necessary for
demonstrated *knowledge* to proceed from [principles   which are] (1) true,
(2) primary, (3) immediate, and also (4) more known than, (5) prior to, and
(6) causes of the conclusion; for it is in this way that the principles will also
be appropriate to what is proved. Now there may be a syllogism even
25   without these, but such syllogism will not be a demonstration, for it will not
produce *knowledge*.

The [principles] should be true,   since nonbeing cannot be *known*; for instance, it cannot be *known* that a diagonal of a square is commensurable [with a side of that square].

Demonstrated *knowledge* must be acquired from primary [premises], which are indemonstrable; otherwise one who has no demonstration of them [i.e., of demonstrable premises] will not *know*.   For to *know* that of which there is a demonstration not with respect to an attribute is to have a demonstration of it.

[The premises] should be the causes of, more known than, and prior [to   *30* the conclusion]. They must be the causes of [the conclusion], since we *know* a thing [only] when we know the cause of it;   they must be prior by nature to the conclusion, if they, *as such*, are its causes;   and they must be previously known, not only in the other manner, i.e., by being *understood*, but also by being known that they are.   Now each of the terms "prior" and "more known" has two meanings; for that which is prior by its nature is not the same as that which is prior relative *to us*, and that which is more known   *72a* [by its nature] is not the same as that which is more known *to us*. By "prior and more known relative *to us*" I mean those things which are nearer to sensation, but by "prior and more known without qualification" I mean those things which are further from sensation; and those things which are furthest from sensation are the most universal, but those things which are nearest to sensation are the individuals, and these two kinds are opposed to   *5* each other.

To say that *knowledge* comes from something primary is to say that it comes from principles which are appropriate [to the thing *known*]; for by "primary" and "a principle" I mean the same thing. Now a principle of a demonstration is an immediate premise,   and a premise is said to be immediate if there is no other premise prior   to it. A premise is one part of a statement, [in which] one [predicate is affirmed or denied] of one [subject]; and it is dialectical   if it is any one part of a statement taken   *10* indifferently, but it is demonstrative   if it is definitely that part which is true.   A statement is either part of a contradiction [i.e., of two contradictories]; and a contradiction is an opposition in virtue of which there is nothing between [its two parts].   An affirmation is that part of a contradiction in which something is affirmed of something, and a denial is that part in which something is denied of something.   I call an immediate   *15* syllogistic principle "a thesis" if it cannot be proved and if it is not necessary for a learner to possess in order to learn something;   but I call it "an axiom" if the learner must possess it to learn anything (for there are some things of this sort, and it is this name that is mostly used for such things).   If a thesis takes the form of either part of a statement (I mean, for example, if it states   *20* that something is the case, or that it is not the case), it is a hypothesis,   but if this is not so, it is a *definition*   (for a *definition* is a thesis, e.g., the arithmetician posits the expression "a unit is that which is indivisible with respect to quantity", and this is not a hypothesis; for what a unit is, and that a unit exists, are not the same).

25   Since we should have conviction and knowledge of a fact by having such a syllogism of it which we call "a demonstration", and since this syllogism proceeds from certain [principles] which are [or are true], it is necessary not only to know the primary [principles], whether all or some, prior [to the fact or conclusion], but also to know them to a higher degree [than the fact or conclusion]; for that [i.e., the cause] because of which a thing exists always

30   exists to a higher degree than the thing, e.g., that because of which we like a thing is liked more than the thing.   So if indeed we know and also have conviction [of a fact or conclusion] through the primary [principles], then we know and are convinced of these even more [than of the fact or conclusion] since it is through these that we also know and are convinced of what follows. One cannot have more conviction of (*a*) things he does not happen to know, or of (*b*) things towards which he is not better disposed to know,

35   than of things which he knows.   And this will be the case if one has no prior knowledge of things of which there is conviction through demonstration; for it is necessary for one to be convinced more of the principles, whether of all or of some of them, than of the conclusion.   And if one is to have *knowledge* through demonstration, not only should he know and be convinced of the

72*b* principles more than of what is proved, but, relative to the statements opposed to these principles, from which [statements] there can be a syllogism of a contrary mistake, there should be nothing other than these principles of which he is more convinced and knows to a higher degree, if a *knower* without qualification, *as such* a *knower*, is to be unchangeable in his conviction.

3

5   Some are of the opinion that there is no *knowledge* because of the requirement of *knowing* the primary [principles], while others think that there is *knowledge* but that there is a demonstration of everything. Neither of these [beliefs], however, is either true or necessary.

Those who make the assumption that there is no *knowing* at all maintain that (*a*) one is led to an infinite regress since one cannot *know* what follows from what is prior if there is nothing first (and in saying this they speak

10   rightly, for it is impossible to traverse an infinite number of things), and that (*b*) if there is a stop and there are principles, these will be unknowable since there can be no demonstration of them, for they assert that *knowing as such* is knowing by demonstration only. So if it is not possible to know the first [principles], neither will it be possible to *know* without qualification

or in the fundamental sense what follows from these, unless it be by   15
hypothesis, namely, if the [premises or principles] are [known].

The latter thinkers agree with the former in thinking that one can *know*
only through demonstration, but [they think that] nothing prevents all
[statements] from being demonstrable since a demonstration may be
circular or reciprocal.

We on the other hand maintain that (1) not all *knowledge* is
demonstrable but that (2) *knowledge* of immediate premises is indemonstr·   20
able.   And it is evident that this [i.e., (2)] is necessary; for if it is necessary
to *know* the prior [premises] from which a demonstration proceeds, and if
these [premises] eventually stop when they are immediate, they must be
indemonstrable. Such then is our position, and we also maintain that there
is not only *knowledge*,   but also (3) a principle of *knowledge* because of
which we know the terms   [of that *knowledge*].

Clearly, it is impossible to have unqualified demonstration of statements   25
in a circular manner, if a demonstration *as such* is to proceed from
statements which are prior and more known;   for it is impossible for one
statement to be at the same time prior and posterior to another, unless it be
in different ways, that is, prior *to us* but posterior in an unqualified way,
which is indeed the manner in which induction makes things known to us.
But if such is the case, the expression "unqualified understanding" would   30
not be defined well but would have two meanings, or else the other
demonstration which proceeds from what is more known *to us* would not
be unqualified.

Those who say that a demonstration may be circular are faced not only
with the difficulty just stated but also with saying none other than that P is
if P is;   but in such a case it is easy to prove everything. This becomes clear   35
if we posit three terms;   for we maintain that it makes no difference
whether a return [to the original premise] occurs through many rather than
through few [syllogisms], or through few rather than through only two.
Now if, whenever P is, also Q must be, and whenever Q is, also R must be,   73a
it follows that whenever P is, also R must be. So if in fact, whenever P is,
also Q must be, and whenever Q is, also P must be (for to be a circular proof
is to be just this), let P here be R. Then to say "whenever Q is, also P must
be" is to say "whenever Q is, also R must be", and this leads to "whenever
P is, also R must be". But R is the same as P; hence those who maintain that
a circular demonstration exists turn out to be saying nothing else but "if P   5
is, then P is," an easy way of proving everything.

What is more, the above [proof] is not even possible, except with terms
which follow from each other, as in the case of properties.   Now it has been
shown[3] that if [only] one thing is laid down, there is never a necessity for
something else to be   (by "one thing" I mean one term or one thesis), but   10
from at least two primary theses something may be, if indeed there is to be

a syllogism. So if A follows both from B and from C, and if these [B and C]
follow from each other as well as from A, then in this way one may prove
in the first figure all the premises initially posited, as shown in the treatise
15   *Concerning Syllogisms.* [4] But it was also shown that in the other figures
either no syllogism is formed or no syllogism is formed of the things initially
posited; [5] and there can never be a circular proof of that [i.e., a premise or
a statement] whose terms are not predicable of each other.   So since there
are only few such [premises whose terms are predicable of each other] in
demonstrations, it is evidently fruitless and impossible to say [truly] that
there is a demonstration [of premises or statements] from each other and
20   that because of this there may be a demonstration of every [premise or
statement].

           4

     Since that of which there is unqualified *knowledge* cannot be other than
it is, the *known* [fact] by way of demonstrated *knowledge* will have to be
necessary. Now demonstrated [*knowledge*] is that [*knowledge*] which we
possess by having a demonstration [of it]; hence a demonstration is a
syllogism which proceeds from necessary [premises]. We must consider,
25   then, from what [premises] and what kinds [of premises] demonstrations
proceed. But first, we will specify what we mean by "[belongs] to every
[instance of a subject]", "[belongs] essentially", and "[belongs]
universally".
     By "[belongs] to every [instance of a subject]", I do not mean that which
[belongs] to some [instances of a subject] but not to others, nor that which
[belongs to every instance] sometimes but not at other times, [but that which
belongs to every instance of the subject and always]. For instance, in saying
30   that animal [belongs] to every man, [I mean that] if it is true to call this thing
"man", then it is also true to call it "animal", and if it is true to call it "man"
now, then it is also true to call it "animal" now; and it is likewise with "a
point [belongs] to every line". A sign of this is the fact that we bring an
objection against those who assert that something, say B, [belongs] to every
[instance of a subject] by pointing out that B does not [belong] to some
[instances] or that sometimes it does not [belong to every instance].
35   By "essential" I mean (1) those [elements] which belong to the whatness
of a thing, e.g., a line belongs to a triangle and a point belongs to a [straight]
line (for the *substance* of each thing mentioned is composed of [elements
such as] these, and these [elements] are included in the thing's expression
which states the whatness of that thing), or (2) that [attribute] in whose
expression, which states its whatness, the thing to which the attribute
belongs is included. For example, straightness belongs [only] to a line, and

so does circularity; and to numbers belong oddness and evenness, and also   *40*
the prime, the composite, the equilateral [i.e., the square], and the oblong;   *73b*
and in the expressions for these [attributes] there is included a line in the case
of straightness and of curvature, and a number in the case of the others.
In other cases, too, [attributes] such as these which belong to their subjects
in a similar manner I call "essential"; but [attributes] which belong to
subjects in neither of these ways I call "accidents", and such are musical   *5*
[knowledge] and whiteness in animals.

Again, there are things which are not said of other subjects. For instance,
the walking [thing], being a thing other than [just walking, i.e., being a
subject of that walk], is [also] walking or is white, but a substance and
whatever indicates a *this* is not some other thing but is, *as such*, just what
it is. So (3) things which are not said of other subjects I call "essential", but
things which are said of other subjects I call "attributes".

In still another way, (4) if P belongs to a thing because of P itself, it is   *10*
said to be essential [to that thing], but if P belongs to the thing not because
of P itself, it is said to be an accident [of that thing]; for instance, if there
was lightning while a man was walking, lightning was an accident [of
walking], for lightning occurred not because he was walking but we say that
it just happened to occur during the walk.   But if P belongs to a thing
because of P itself, then [we say that] it belongs to the thing essentially;   for   *15*
instance, if an animal died because it was decapitated, it died in virtue of
its decapitation, since it died through its decapitation, but it did not, when
decapitated, just happen to die by accident.   So a thing, P, which is said to
be essential to what is *knowable* without qualification, whether it be such
that the subject of which it is predicable is included in it [in the predicate]
or such that it belongs to the subject, exists causally and also belongs [to the
subject] necessarily; for it cannot fail to belong to the subject, whether
without qualification or in the sense that it or its opposite belongs to that
subject.   For instance, to a line must belong either straightness or   *20*
curvature,   and to a number must belong either oddness or evenness, for a
contrary is either a privation or the contradictory within the same genus,
e.g., evenness in a number qua number follows from the fact that the
number is not odd;   so if it is necessary to either affirm or deny   [a predicate
of a subject], it is also necessary for essential predicates to belong to their
subjects.

Let the meaning of "[to belong] to every [instance of a subject]" and of   *25*
"essential", then, be such as stated above.

By "[belonging] *universally* [to a subject]" I mean that which belongs to
every instance [of that subject] and which belongs to it essentially and qua
that subject.   Hence it is evident that that which belongs *universally* [to a
subject] belongs to it necessarily.   Now that which belongs essentially [to a
subject] is the same   as that which belongs to the subject qua that subject;

30 for example, a point and straightness belong essentially to a line, for they
also belong to it qua line, and two right angles belong to a triangle qua
triangle, for the equality of the angles to two right angles is also essential to
the triangle. Thus a thing belongs *universally* to a subject when it can be
proved to belong to any chance instance of it and to belong to it
primarily. For instance, (1) the equality of the sum of the angles of a
triangle to two right angles does not belong *universally* to a figure, for
35 although it is possible to prove that some [species of] figure   has its angles
equal to two right angles, it is not possible to prove it for any chance figure,
and he who proves this equality to two right angles does not use any chance
figure. For a square too is a figure, but the sum of its angles is not equal to
two right angles, and although the sum of the angles of any chance isosceles
triangle is equal to two right angles, the isosceles triangle   is not the first
figure [having this attribute] since the triangle is prior [to the isosceles
triangle in having this attribute]; so if the equality of the angles to two right
40 angles or any other [such attribute] is proved to belong to any chance
instance of a thing and to belong primarily to that thing, then it is said to
74a belong to this first thing *universally*, and the demonstration of the [attribute]
which belongs essentially to that subject is [said to be] *universal*. But the
demonstration [of the attribute] in the case of the other subject [of a figure]
is in some sense not essential, (2) nor is the demonstration *universal* in the
case of the isosceles triangle since the [attribute] belongs to other figures
also.

5

5   We should not be unaware that we often happen to be in error when [an
attribute] which is to be proved *universally* of a subject, although it is
thought to be proved *universally* of the subject qua first, does not belong
to it as first. We make this mistake thus: (1) when no [subject] can be taken
which is higher [i.e., more universal] than each [subject] or each of the
[subjects considered]; or (2) when a [subject] can be taken which is higher
than a number of things differing in species but no name exists for it; or (3)
10 when there happens to be [a higher subject] but one gives a proof for a part
of a whole, for there can be a demonstration for each part, and [the
attribute] will belong to every instance of each part, yet the demonstration
will not be universal of this part as first (by "a demonstration of this part as
first qua first" I mean a demonstration which is *universal* of this part when
taken as first).

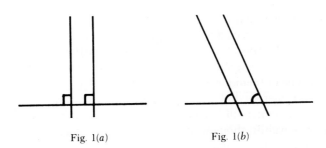

Fig. 1(a)   Fig. 1(b)

As an instance of (3), if one were to prove that perpendiculars to a straight line do not intersect, as in Fig. 1(a), the demonstration might be thought to be [*universal*] of this [subject, i.e., of those perpendiculars] because non-intersection belongs to every pair of perpendiculars to a straight line; but the demonstration is not *universal*, if indeed non-intersection occurs not by the fact that the corresponding angles are equal in this manner [i.e., by being right angles], but insofar as they are just equal, as in Fig. 1(b). Again, (1) if no triangle other than the isosceles existed, the equality of the angles to two right angles might be thought to belong to an isosceles triangle qua isosceles triangle. Finally, (2) the alternation of proportionals [i.e., if A:B :: C:D, then A:C :: B:D] might be thought to belong to numbers qua numbers, to lines qua lines, to solids qua solids, to time intervals qua time intervals, [etc.,] as in the separate proofs which were given formerly, although such alternation may be proved for all of them by a single demonstration. But a theorem was given separately for each because there was no one name for numbers, lines, time intervals, solids, [etc.,] which differ from each other in kind. Nowadays, however, the theorem is proved *universally*; for alternation belongs to these not qua lines or qua numbers or etc., but qua being this [thing], and it is to this [thing] that alternation is now assumed to belong *universally*. It is because of this that even if a man were to prove separately for each [species] of triangles (equilateral, scalene, isosceles), whether by one [kind of] demonstration or by different demonstrations, that the sum of the angles is equal to two right angles, he would not yet know *universally*, except in a sophistical manner, that the triangle has its angles equal to two right angles, even if no other [species] of triangles exists besides those three; for (a) neither would he know that the equality belongs to each species of triangle qua triangle, (b) nor would he know, except by enumeration, that it belongs to every [species of the triangle] with respect to form, even if there is no species of triangles which he does not know. When then does he know *universally* or when does he know without qualification? Clearly, he knows [*universally* or without qualification] if the essence of a triangle and that of equilateral triangles, whether of each or of all [of the latter], are the same. If, however, the essences are not the

35   same but different, and if the equality to two right angles belongs to the
angles of an isosceles triangle qua triangle, then he does not know [without
qualification or *universally*].   But does [the attribute] belong [to the subject]
qua triangle or qua isosceles triangle? And [if the attribute belongs to the
subject qua one of them,] when does it belong [to that subject] primarily in
virtue of that one? And of what subject is the demonstration *universal*?
Clearly, [an attribute will belong] primarily [to that subject which results]
after the removal [in thought of certain elements or principles from the
original subject]. For example, to a bronze isosceles triangle belongs the
equality of the sum of its angles to two right angles; and [that equality] still

74b [belongs] to what remains if we remove [in thought] the bronze and the
equality of the two sides,   but not [if we remove in thought] its figure or its
limit.   Yet [each of these last two is] not the first [by whose removal the
equality does not remain].   Which then is the first? If this [essential part] be
the triangle, then it is in virtue of this [part] that the equality belongs to the
others   also, and a demonstration [of the equality of the angles to two right
angles] is *universal* in virtue of [the fact that the subject is a] triangle.

6

5   Now since demonstrable *knowledge* proceeds from necessary principles
(for it is impossible for that which one *knows* to be other than it is),   and
since essential [elements or attributes] belong to their subjects
necessarily—(for (*a*) some of them belong to the whatness [of their subjects],
while (*b*) the others are such that in their whatness belong the subjects of
which they are predicable, and either they or their opposites necessarily

10   belong to those subjects) —it is evident that a demonstrative syllogism
would proceed from [principles or premises] such as these, for every thing
[predicable of a subject] belongs to that subject either in this manner or as
an accident, but accidents belong [to their subjects] not of necessity.
We should either (*a*) state the case in this manner, or else (*b*) posit as a
principle that a demonstration is [of the] necessary, and if [a conclusion] is

15   demonstrated, it cannot be other than it is. Hence the syllogism should
proceed from necessary [premises]; for from true [premises] one may prove
[a conclusion] and still not demonstrate it, but from necessary [premises]
one cannot but demonstrate it since the result of a demonstration is now this
[i.e., something necessary]. A sign of the fact that a demonstration proceeds
from necessary [premises] is also the manner in which we raise objections

20   against those who think that they have demonstrated [a conclusion], for we
say that [what is concluded] is not necessary, whether we (*a*) think that,
taken as a whole, it may be other than it is, or (*b*) raise the objection just for
the sake of argument. It is also clear from these remarks that those who think
that they are positing the principles properly, when the premises they
choose are generally accepted and   true, are simple-minded, as in the case

of the sophists who maintain that to *know* is to have *knowledge*.⁶ For that
which is a principle [in a science] is not that which is or is not generally
accepted, but that which is primary in its genus,   about which something   25
is proved; and further, not every truth is appropriate   to a given genus.
   That the syllogism [of a demonstrated conclusion] should proceed from
necessary [premises] is evident also from the following. If a man who has no
argument of the *why* of a fact (assuming a demonstration of it to be possible)
is not a *knower*, and if A belongs necessarily to C, but the middle term B
through which this was demonstrated is connected to A and C but not of   30
necessity, then the man will not know the *why* of the connection since this
necessary connection is not caused by the middle term; for the middle term
may not be [connected with A and C], whereas the conclusion is [true] of
necessity.   Again, if a man who is still living, without having lost his
memory and without a change in the fact, retains the argument but does not
understand the fact now, neither did he understand the fact previously; but
if the middle term is not necessary, it may have been destroyed. [And if it   35
was,] then although the man still lives and retains the argument and there
has been no change in the fact, he does not understand the fact now. Hence,
neither did he understand it before.   And if the middle term has not been
destroyed but may be destroyed, the result would be possible and might
happen. But it is impossible for one to have understanding [of a fact] under
these circumstances.
   If the conclusion is necessary, then, nothing prevents the middle term,   75a
through which the conclusion was proved, from not being necessary; for it
is possible for the necessary to be proved also from what is not necessary,
just as it is possible for what is true to be proved also from premises which
are not true.   But when the middle term is necessary, the conclusion too is   5
necessary, just as from true premises a true conclusion is proved always.
For let A be necessarily [predicable] of B, and this [likewise] of C; then it is
also necessary for A to belong to C [of necessity]. But if the conclusion is not
necessary, the middle term, too, is not of such a nature as to be necessary.
For let A belong to C but not of necessity, and let A belong to B [of necessity]   10
and B belong to C of necessity; then A will belong to C also of necessity. But
A was posited [to belong to C not of necessity]. Accordingly, since that which
one *knows* by a demonstration should be necessary, it is clear that he should
have a demonstration of it through a necessary middle term also; otherwise
he will not *know* either the *reason* why it is so   or the fact that it is
necessary,   but either he will think that he *knows* a thing when in fact he   15
has no understanding of it, if he believes that which is not necessary to be
necessary, or he will not think [that he knows it] in a similar manner,
whether he understands the fact through middle terms or the *reason* for that
fact and through immediate premises.
   If the term "essential" be such as we defined it earlier,   then there can

be no demonstrated *knowledge* of attributes which are not essential [to
20   their subjects], for it is not possible to prove the conclusion as being
necessary; for a [nonessential] attribute may not belong [to its subject], and
it is of such an attribute that I am speaking here. But perhaps one might
raise the problem as to why one should be asking for premises concerning
those attributes if the conclusion is not necessary; for to do so does not differ
25   from asking for any chance premises and then stating the conclusion. One
should ask for them, however, not in order to draw a necessary conclusion
through the premises obtained, but in order to force the opponent who
grants the premises to grant also the conclusion, and to grant the conclusion
as true if the premises are granted as true.

Since a thing which belongs essentially to its subject and qua that subject
30   in each genus does so of necessity, it is evident that scientific
demonstrations (*a*) are about things which belong essentially to their
subjects and (*b*) proceed from such things. For accidents are not things
which belong to their subjects of necessity, and so, of necessity, a man has
no understanding of the *reasons* for the conclusion; and this is the case
even if the conclusion were always true, but not in virtue of [the cause], as
in the case of syllogisms through signs, for one will not *know* [that which
belongs] essentially [to the subject] as belonging in virtue of [that subject],
35   nor [will he *know*] the *reason* for it.   But to *know* the *reason* is to *know*
through the cause; hence the middle term should belong to the third term
through it [i.e., the third term], and the first term should belong to the
middle term through it [i.e., the middle term].

7

As a consequence, it is not possible to prove something in one genus by
passing over from another genus; for example, one cannot demonstrate a
geometrical theorem by arithmetic. For there are three things in
40   demonstrations: (*a*) that which is demonstrated [in] the conclusion, i.e., an
essential [attribute] as belonging to some genus; (*b*) the axioms, and axioms
are [things] *from which* a demonstration proceeds; and (*c*) the genus, which
75b is the subject whose *attributes* and essential attributes are made known by
a demonstration. Accordingly, things *from which* a demonstration
proceeds may be the same [in different sciences]. But if two sciences are
concerned with different genera, [a demonstration in one science cannot be
used to investigate the essential attributes of the genus of the other science].
5   For instance, one cannot apply an arithmetical demonstration to the
[essential] attributes belonging to magnitudes, unless magnitudes are
numbers;[7] and the manner in which one may [make such application] in
some cases will be discussed later.[8] Thus an arithmetical demonstration is

always concerned with its own genus, and similarly for demonstrations in other sciences. So it is necessary that either (*a*) the genus be the same without qualification, or (*b*) the genera be the same in some respect, if a demonstration is to pass over from one genus to another. That it is otherwise 10 impossible is clear from the fact that [in the same science] the end terms [i.e., major and minor terms] and the middle terms must come under the same genus; for if [the attributes are] not essential [to a subject], they will be accidental. It is because of this that one cannot prove in geometry that there is one science of contraries or that the product of two cubes is a cube; and, in general, one cannot prove [a theorem] in one science by using another science unless things in the first science come under those in the second, as 15 in the case of those under optics in relation to geometry, and those under harmonics in relation to arithmetic. Nor [does it belong to geometry] to prove an [attribute] of lines if this [attribute] belongs to lines not qua lines or not qua proceeding from the proper principles of geometry. For instance, if the straight line is the most beautiful of all [species of] lines, or if it is contrary to the circular line, [geometry cannot prove this], for these [attributes, i.e., being most beautiful and being contraries] belong to those lines not qua coming under the proper genus of geometry, but qua being 20 common to other [genera also].

8

It is also evident that, if the premises from which the syllogism proceeds are universal, also the conclusion of such a demonstration and, we may add, of an unqualified demonstration is of necessity eternal. Hence there can be no unqualified demonstration and no unqualified *knowledge* of destructible things, but there may be [a syllogism concerning them] as if in an accidental 25 manner, namely, not universally but at a certain time or in a qualified manner. And whenever there is [such a syllogism], one of the premises must be destructible and not universal; it must be destructible in view of the fact that it is [only] by being destructible that also the conclusion will be destructible, and it must not be universal since it will be true of whatever is said under certain circumstances but not under others, and so one will prove a conclusion not universally but only of something existing at this or 30 that moment. It is likewise with *definitions*, since a *definition* is either a principle of demonstration, or [like] a demonstration which differs [from a demonstration] in the position of its terms, or else [like] a conclusion of a demonstration. As for demonstrations and sciences of things which happen frequently, e.g., of an eclipse of the Moon, it is clear that qua being of such and such a kind, they are always [true], but qua not always existing, they are 35

[true] under certain circumstances. As in the case of the eclipse, so it is in other such cases.

9

Since it is evident that each conclusion, say, "A is C", cannot be demonstrated except from the principles of the subject A, whenever the attribute C is proved to belong to A qua A, then to *know* that conclusion is not just to have a proof of it from premises which are [merely] true and indemonstrable and immediate. For it is possible to have proofs in the manner in which Bryson squares the circle, but such arguments prove [a conclusion] by the use of something which is [more] common and which belongs also to another subject; and in view of this the arguments would apply also to other subjects which are not of the same genus. But then one would not *know* that C belongs to a subject A qua A, except accidentally [or as an attribute], for otherwise the demonstration would not be applicable to another genus also.

Now we *know* each [fact] in a nonaccidental way when we know (*a*) that [an attribute] belongs [to the subject] in virtue of that [subject] and (*b*) that it belongs to it from the principles of that subject qua that subject, e.g., when we know that the equality of the angles to two right angles belongs to a subject in virtue of that subject and from the principles of that subject. And so if C belongs to A essentially, it is necessary for the middle term B to be in the same generic line [as A]; or else [the things *known* must be] like the objects of harmonics [which are proved] through arithmetic. Now such [objects, as in harmonics,] are proved in the same manner, but there is a difference; for the fact [proved] belongs to another science (since the subject comes under a different genus), but the *reason* for the fact belongs to the higher science within which the *attributes* are essential. So from these remarks, too, it is evident that one cannot demonstrate something in an unqualified way except from the principles of each subject. But the principles of these [two sciences] have something in common.

If this is evident, it is also evident that it is not possible to demonstrate the principles proper to each subject, for those other principles [from which the proper principles might be demonstrated] would be the principles of all, and the science having those principles would be fundamental to all [the other sciences]. For he who understands a fact from higher causes also *knows* it to a higher degree, since he understands it from prior causes when he understands it from causes which are not caused; so if he understands the fact to a higher degree or in the highest degree, the corresponding *knowledge* too would be [*knowledge*] to a higher degree or in the highest degree, respectively. But a demonstration [in one genus] is not applicable to another genus, except in the manner already stated, namely, in the manner in which geometrical demonstrations are applicable to those in mechanics and in optics, and arithmetical demonstrations to those in harmonics.

It is difficult to know whether one understands [a fact in the primary sense] or not, for it is difficult to know whether one understands [a fact] from its own principles or not; for understanding *as such* [in the primary sense] is this, [namely, knowing a fact through its own principles]. We think that we *know* [a fact] if we have a syllogism of it from [premises which are merely] true and primary; but this is not the case, for [the conclusion] must be in the same generic line as the primary [premises].

10

By "the principles in each genus" I mean those whose existence cannot be proved. Now the meaning of both the primary [terms] and those [which are formed] from them is taken [as *understood*]; but as for the existence [of the things signified], it must be posited for the principles but proved for the others. For example, the meaning of "a unit" or "straightness" and of "a triangle" [must be taken as *understood*]; but whereas the existence of a unit and of a magnitude must be posited, that of the rest must be proved.

Of the [principles] used in demonstrative sciences, some are proper to each science but others are common to many sciences, and the latter [principles] are common by analogy since they are used as far as the genus of things under each science extends. For example, a proper principle is "a line is such-and-such [a magnitude]", and [likewise for] straightness; but a common principle is "if equals are subtracted from equals, the remainders are equal", and this is sufficient when used only for one genus, for it would have the same effect even if it were assumed [by the geometer to apply] not to all [quantities] but to magnitudes only, and by the arithmetician to numbers only. Proper [principles] are also those whose existence is posited and whose essential [attributes] are investigated by a given science, e.g., units in the case of arithmetic, and points and lines in the case of geometry. A science posits that each of these exists and that it is so-and-so. As for the essential *attributes* of these, what each of the corresponding terms means is posited, e.g., what "oddness" or "evenness" or "square" or "cube" means is posited by arithmetic, and what "incommensurable" or "to be broken" or "to be inclined" means is posited by geometry, but that each essential *attribute* exists is proved through the common [principles or axioms] and from what has been demonstrated. Astronomy, too, proceeds in the same manner. For every demonstrative science is concerned with three things: (*a*) those which it posits to exist (and these are [things under] the genus whose

essential *attributes* it investigates), (*b*) the so-called "common axioms",
15   *from which* it demonstrates as from first   [principles], and (*c*) the *attributes*,
the meaning of whose [corresponding terms] it posits.

Nothing prevents some sciences, however, from omitting some of these,
like the hypothesis that the genus exists, if it is evident that the genus exists
(for it is not clear in the same way that a number exists and that heat and
coldness exist),   or like the meaning of [the terms which signify] *attributes*
20   if [those terms] are clear, just as nothing prevents [the mathematical
sciences] from assuming the meaning of the common [principles or axioms]
which are familiar, such as "equals from equals yield equal remainders."
Nevertheless these [principles] are by nature   three in kind, (*a*) that [i.e., the
genus] concerning which something is proved, (*b*) those [i.e., the *attributes*]
which are proved [of the genus], and [the common axioms] *from which*
[something is proved].

That   which is necessarily so through itself and is thought to be so of
necessity is neither a hypothesis nor a petition; for a demonstration, being
25   a syllogism, is directed not to the verbal expression of it but to [the *thought*]
in the soul.   For it is always possible to object to a verbal expression, but it
is not always possible to object to a [*thought*] in the soul.   Accordingly,
whenever something which can be proved is assumed but is not proved by
the teacher, then (*a*) if it is thought to be the case by the learner, it is a
30   hypothesis, not an unqualified hypothesis but relative to the learner only,
but (*b*) if there is no opinion or even a contrary opinion   in the [soul of the]
learner, then it is taken as a petition. And this is the difference between a
hypothesis and a petition; for a petition is that which goes against the
opinion   of the learner or that which, being demonstrable, is taken and used
without proof.

35   Terms   are not hypotheses (for they do not state that something is or is
not the case), but it is in premises that hypotheses [exist]. Terms   need only
to be *understood*; and [*understanding*] is not a hypothesis, unless one were
to maintain that listening is a hypothesis also. Thus a conclusion arises [only]
if something is the case whenever something else is the case. Nor does the
40   geometer lay down something false, as some have maintained by saying that
one should not use a falsehood but that the geometer speaks falsely when he
says that the line drawn is a foot long when this is not the case, or that the
77a   line is straight when this is not the case. For the geometer draws conclusions
not from the fact that the [particular] line drawn   of which he is speaking
is so-and-so, but through what the things drawn stand for.   Again, every
petition or hypothesis is [a statement] taken either universally or partly,
whereas a term   is neither the one nor the other.

11

If there is to be a demonstration, there is no necessity for the Forms or for   5
the one to exist apart from the many. But it is of necessity true to say that
the one [as something which is said] about the many exists; for if this [i.e.,
the one] did not exist, the universal would not exist, and if the universal did
not exist, the middle term would not exist, and so a demonstration too would
not be [possible]. So there should be something which is one and the same
and which, without being equivocal, is said about many things.

As for the principle "one cannot simultaneously affirm and deny   10
something [truly] . . . ," no demonstration assumes it [as a premise], unless
the conclusion too is to be proved in this manner. And [in the latter case]
the conclusion is proved if the first [i.e., major] term is taken as being truly
affirmed and not truly denied of the middle term. But it makes no difference
whether we take the middle term as being and not being, and likewise for
the minor term. For if we grant that it is true to say of that which is a man   15
that it is an animal and not not-animal, even if it be also true to say of that
which is not-man [that it is an animal and not not-animal], still it will be true
to say of that alone which is a man that it is an animal and not not-animal;
for it will be true to say that Callias, even if it be true to say that also
not-Callias, is an animal and not not-animal. The cause of this is the fact that
the major term is affirmed not only of the middle term but also of other
middle terms, because it is predicable of many terms; so it makes no   20
difference to the conclusion whether both the middle term and a term other
than it comes under the major term.

The principle "every [predicate] must be either affirmed or denied [of a
subject]" is assumed by a demonstration through impossibility; and it is
used not always universally but only to the extent it is required, and [in a
given science] it is required for its genus. By "for its genus" I mean the
genus in which one carries out a demonstration, as already stated   25
previously.[9]

All sciences have some things in common, and these are the common
[axioms]. By "common [axioms]" I mean those [principles] which the
sciences use [as principles] *from which* they demonstrate [conclusions]; and
those [principles] are not the [subjects] about which they prove [something]
nor the [*attributes*] which they prove [as belonging to a subject].   Dialectics
too [is common] to all [sciences];   and so is any other [discipline] which tries
to prove universally the common [axioms], e.g., that everything must be   30
either affirmed or denied, or that if equals are taken from equals the
remainders are equal, or other such [common axioms]. But dialectics is not
concerned with anything definite or with any one genus, for it would not be
asking questions; for he who demonstrates would not ask questions because
he cannot prove the same [conclusion] from opposite things.   This has been
shown in the treatise *Concerning the Syllogism.*[10]   35

13

Knowing a fact differs from *knowing* a *reasoned* fact. First, it differs from it within the same science, and in two ways: (*a*) whenever the corresponding syllogism does not proceed through immediate premises (for
25   then it is not the first cause that is taken, but *knowledge* of the *reasoned* fact is [*knowledge*] according to the first cause), and (*b*) whenever the corresponding syllogism proceeds through immediate [premises], yet not through the cause but through the more known [*to us*] of two convertible [terms]. For, of two terms which are reciprocal predicates of each other, sometimes nothing prevents the one which is not the cause from being more
30   known [*to us*], in which case the demonstration would proceed from this [term as the middle term].

For example, in the demonstration of the fact that the planets are near because they do not twinkle, let C be "planets", B be "not twinkling", and A be "near". Now it is true to affirm B of C, for the planets do not twinkle. And it is also true to affirm A of B, for that which does not twinkle is near;
35   and this fact may be taken as being so by induction or through sensation. Then it is necessary for A to belong to C, and in this way it has been demonstrated that the planets are near. This syllogism, however, is not of the *reasoned* fact but of the fact; for it is not because of their not twinkling that the planets are near, but because of their nearness that they do not twinkle. Now one may prove "not-twinkling" of ["planets"] through
40   "being near", and then the demonstration will be of the *reasoned* fact.
78b   Thus, let C be "planets", B be "being near", and A be "not-twinkling." Then B belongs to C, and A (i.e., "not-twinkling") belongs to B; hence A belongs to C. And this is a syllogism of the *reasoned* fact; for the term taken [as the middle] is the first cause.

5   Again, some thinkers prove that the Moon is spherical through its [manner of] waxing; for, [they say,] since that which waxes in such a manner is spherical, and since the Moon waxes [in such a manner], it is evident that the Moon is spherical. Now a syllogism formed in this manner is of the fact. But if the major and middle terms are interchanged, the resulting syllogism is of the *reasoned* fact; for it is not because of its [manner of] waxing that the
10   Moon is spherical, but it is because of its being spherical that the Moon waxes in such a manner. Here, let C be "the Moon", B be "sphericity", and A be "waxing [in such a manner]."

In cases in which the middle term is not convertible [with the major] and in which that which is not the cause is more known [*to us*], what is proved is the fact, not the *reasoned* fact. Again, in cases in which the middle term is posited outside, here again, the demonstration is of the fact and not of the
15   *reasoned* fact, for what is stated is not the cause. For example, why does a wall not breathe? In view of the fact that it is not an animal, [one might say]. Now if not being an animal were the cause of not breathing, then being

an animal would have to be the cause of breathing (for if the denial [of something] is the cause of A's not belonging to B, the affirmation [of it] is the cause of A's belonging to B),   just as if the wrong proportion of the hot and cold is the cause of not being healthy, the right proportion of the hot and   20
cold is the cause of being healthy. Similarly, if the affirmation [of something is the cause] of belonging, the denial [of it is the cause] of not belonging. From examples such as the above, then, it does not follow that the things stated [as causes are the causes]; for not every animal breathes. A syllogism with such a cause   is formed in the second figure. Thus, let A be "animal", B be "breathing", and C be "wall". Then A belongs to every B (for every   25
breathing thing is an animal) but to no C, and so B belongs to no C; hence, no wall is breathing. Such causes   are like those which are stretched too far, and this amounts to giving as a middle term that which is far [from being a primary cause], like the statement by Anacharsis: "There are no flute   30
players in Scythia, for there are no vines there."

   These, then, are the differences between a syllogism of a fact and a syllogism of a *reasoned* fact within the same science and with respect to the position of the middle term.

   But a *reasoned* fact differs from a fact in another way also, namely, when   35
each is investigated by a different science. Such are those [facts and *reasoned* facts] which are so related that the [investigation of the] former comes under   the [science of the] latter, as in the case of optical [facts] in relation to geometry, mechanical [facts] in relation to solid geometry, those of harmonics in relation to arithmetic, and [celestial] phenomena in relation to astronomy.   Some of these sciences bear almost the same name, e.g.,   40
mathematical and nautical astronomy,   also mathematical and acoustical   79a
harmonics.   For in [nautical astronomy and acoustical harmonics] it belongs to [the scientist] who uses the faculty of sensation to know the fact, but it belongs to the mathematical scientist to know the *reasoned* fact; for it is the latter who possesses the demonstration through the cause, although he is often unaware of the fact (for he is like those who investigate objects   5
universally but who are often unaware of some individual cases because they did not attend to them).   The objects [of such mathematical sciences], though different in *substance*, use forms.   For mathematics is concerned with forms, and these are not [predicable] of underlying subjects;   for even if geometrical objects are [predicable] of [other] subjects, still they are investigated not qua being [predicable] of those subjects.   Now as optics is   10
related to geometry, so some other science (e.g., the science of the rainbow) is related to optics;   for it belongs to the physicist   to know the fact, but it belongs to the optical scientist to know the *reasoned* fact, whether in an unqualified manner or with respect to mathematics.   There are many sciences which are related in this manner even if one science does not come under another, as in the case of the medical science in relation to geometry;

15   for here it belongs to the physician to know that circular wounds heal more
slowly [than other kinds], but it belongs to the geometer to know the
reasoned fact.

14

Of the syllogistic figures, the most scientific is the first. For the
20   mathematical sciences (e.g., arithmetic and geometry and optics) carry out
their demonstrations by means of this figure, and, in short, nearly all those
sciences which investigate the *reasoned* fact; for it is in this figure that the
syllogism of the *reasoned* fact is formed, either altogether or in most cases
or in most [of those sciences]. So because of this, too, this figure would be
the most scientific; for the most fundamental thing in understanding [a fact]
is the contemplation of the *reason* for it. Again, it is only through this figure
25   that we investigate the *knowledge* of the whatness of a thing. For in the
second figure the syllogism formed is not affirmative, whereas the
knowledge of the whatness of a thing is affirmative; and in the third figure
an affirmative syllogism is possible but is not universal, whereas the
whatness of a thing is universal (for it is not in some cases only that men are
30   two-footed animals). Finally, this figure does not need the others at all,
whereas it is through this figure that the other figures are completed and
increased until immediate premises are reached. It is evident, then, that the
most fundamental figure in *knowing* is the first.

18

It is also evident that if a faculty of sensation is absent from the start, some
corresponding science must be lacking, seeing that a science cannot be
40   acquired if indeed we learn either by induction or by demonstration. Now
81b   a demonstration proceeds from universals , whereas an induction proceeds
from particulars. But universals cannot be investigated except through
induction (and even the so-called "things by abstraction", although not
separable [from substances], are made known to us by induction since some
5   of them belong to each genus insofar as each thing in that genus is
such-and-such [a quantity]), and it is impossible to learn by induction
without having the power of sensation. For of individuals [there can be
only] sensation, and no *knowledge* of them can be acquired; and neither can
we demonstrate conclusions from universals without induction, nor can we
acquire universals through induction without sensation.

27

One science is more accurate than and prior [by nature] to another (*a*) if
it is the same science both of the fact and of the *reasoned* fact, but not of
the fact apart from the *reasoned* fact, or (*b*) if it is not about a subject rather
than if it is about a subject, as in the case of arithmetic when contrasted

with harmonics, or (*c*) if it proceeds from fewer rather than from additional   35
principles, as in the case of arithmetic when contrasted with geometry. By
"additional" I mean, for example, [a point relative to a unit is a principle
by addition, for] a unit is a *substance* without position, but a point is a
substance with position, and [I call] the latter [a principle] by addition.

28

A science is one if it is of one genus of things, [and these are] all those
[things] which are composed of the primary [elements] or are parts or are
essential *attributes* of these [composites or parts]. But one science is   40
different from another if neither the principles of both come from the same
[elements] nor those of either [science] come from those of the other science.   87*b*
We have a sign of this when we go back to the indemonstrables; for these
must be in the same genus as the things demonstrated. And a sign of this is
the fact that the things proved through them are in the same genus or are
generically related.

30

There can be no *knowledge* of that which [exists or comes to be] by
chance; for that which [exists or comes to be] by chance occurs neither   20
necessarily nor in most cases but in a manner which is different from these,
while a demonstration is concerned with one or the other of these [i.e., it is
of the necessary or of that which occurs in most cases]. For every syllogism
proceeds through premises which are either necessary or [true] in most cases;
and if they are necessary, the conclusion too is necessary, but if they are
[true] in most cases, the conclusion too is such. Thus, if that [which exists or   25
comes to be] by chance does so neither of necessity nor in most cases, no
demonstration of it would be possible.

31

Nor can one *know* [a thing] through sensation. For even if sensation is
of the such and not of a *this*, still that which one senses must be a *this* and   30
must exist somewhere and now. But that which is universal and belongs to
all [of a kind] cannot be sensed; for it is neither a *this* nor existing [only]
now, otherwise it would not be universal (for we call "universal" that which
exists always and everywhere). So since demonstrations are universal, and
since these [i.e., universals, or what is universally predicable or considered]
cannot be sensed, it is evident that we cannot *know* individuals through   35
sensation. Besides, even if it were possible to sense the fact that an
[individual] triangle has its angles equal to two right angles, it is clear that
we would still be seeking a demonstration and would not, as some say,'' be
having *knowledge* of that fact; for what we are sensing is of necessity an
individual, whereas it is by knowing universally that we can possess

40   *knowledge.* In view of this, even if we were on the Moon and were
     observing the Earth shutting out the Sun's light, still we would not
88a understand the cause of the eclipse; for what we would be sensing is the fact
     that there is an eclipse at that moment but not the *reason* for that fact,
     universally taken, since that sensation, as stated before, would not be of the
     universal. Of course, from many observations of a fact we might, after the
     search for the universal, possess a demonstration; for from many individual
5   cases the *universal* [might be made] clear. Now the *universal* is an object
     of honor, since it reveals the cause. So concerning such [individuals] whose
     cause is distinct from them, *universal* [knowledge of them] is more
     honorable than the sensation and the mere thinking [about them]. As for the
     primary [principles], this is another matter.[12]
10   It is evident, then, that it is impossible for one to *know* a demonstrable
     thing by sensing it, unless by "sensing" one means possessing *knowledge*
     through demonstration. In some problems, however, reference may be
     made to lack of sensation; for we might not have made inquiries if we had
     the corresponding observations, not that we would have understood
     [universally the fact] *by* observation, but that *from* observation we would
     have gained possession of the universal. For example, if we had observed
15   that the burning glass had holes in it and that the light was passing through
     them, also the cause of burning might have been clear to us from the
     observation of each instance separately and the immediate thought of the
     fact that such is the case in every instance.

         ## 32

         It is impossible for all syllogisms to have the same principles. First, we
     shall examine this fact logically.
20   Now some syllogisms are true, but others are false. For although it is
     possible to prove a truth from false premises, this occurs in just one way, i.e.,
     when A is truly affirmed of C, but the middle term B is false; for [then]
     neither A belongs to B, nor B to C. And if middle terms were taken [to prove
25   these, i.e., AB and BC], there would be false [premises or syllogisms] because
     every false conclusion proceeds from false premises; but from true premises
     proceed true conclusions, and what is false is different from what is
     true.
         Again, not all falsities are proved from the same principles. For there are
     falsities which are at the same time contrary to each other or impossible; for
30   example, "justice is injustice or cowardice", "a man is a horse or an ox", "the
     equal is greater or less."
         Again, even from what is laid down [as true], not all truths are proved
     from the same principles; for the principles of many things are generically
     different and are not applicable to each other. For example, units are not

applicable to points, for the latter have position whereas the former have no position. But terms must be placed either between other terms or above 35 them or below them, or else, some must be placed between terms while others must be placed outside of them.

Nor can any set of common principles, such as "a proposition must either 88b be affirmed or denied", be such that all else can be proved from them. For the genera of things are different, and some [principles] belong only to quantities while others only to qualities, and it is along with these [principles] that a proof through common principles is possible.

Again, the principles are not much fewer than the conclusions; for the [immediate] premises are the principles, and [for a new conclusion] a [new] 5 premise is [added] either by an outside addition or by the insertion of a new term. Again, the conclusions [are] indefinite, but the terms [among common principles] are finite in number. Finally, some principles are necessary, others are possible.

If we examine the situation in the above manner, then, we see that it is impossible for the principles to be the same or finite when the conclusions 10 are indefinite.

If, on the other hand, a man were to speak in a different manner and say, for example, that one set of principles belongs to geometry, another to reasoning, a third to medical science, etc., would he be saying anything other than that each of the sciences has [its own] principles? It would be ridiculous, too, to say that they are the same in view of the fact that each [principle, or set of principles] is the same with itself, for in this manner everything turns out to be the same. Moreover, to require that the 15 principles be the same for each conclusion cannot mean that any conclusion is proved from all those principles, for this argument is rather weak. Neither does this occur in the mathematical sciences as known to us, nor is this possible by analysis; for the immediate premises are principles, and a new conclusion is proved only by taking a new immediate premise. Again, if 20 one were to say that it is the first immediate premises which are the principles, there would be one [immediate premise] in each genus.

If neither every conclusion requires for its proof all the principles nor are the principles different in such a manner that those of one science are different from those of another, then it remains to consider whether the principles of all [the sciences] are generically related but that from one set of principles follows one set of conclusions but from another set follows 25 another set. But it is evident that this too cannot be the case; for it was shown that the principles of things which differ in genus are different in genus. For principles are of two kinds: (a) those *from which* and (b) those *about which*; and whereas those *from which* are common, those *about which* are proper, as in the case of a number and a magnitude.

POSTERIOR ANALYTICS

BOOK II

1

The [kinds of] things we inquire about are equal in number to those we *know*, and they are four: (1) a fact, (2) the *reason* for a fact, (3) if an object
25 exists, (4) what a thing is.

Now when we inquire (1) whether this is the case or that is the case, positing our inquiry in the form of a number, e.g., whether the Sun is being eclipsed or not, we are inquiring about a fact. A sign of this is the following: when we find that the Sun is being eclipsed, we cease inquiring; and if we know from the start that the Sun is being eclipsed, we do not inquire whether it is being eclipsed or not. When we know the fact, however, we
30 inquire into (2) the *reason* for it, e.g., knowing that the Sun is being eclipsed or that the Earth is shaking [i.e., there is an earthquake], we inquire into the *reason* for the Sun's eclipse or for the Earth's shaking. This, then, is the manner in which we inquire about (1) and (2); but our inquiry about some things proceeds in another manner. For example, we inquire (3) whether a centaur or God exists or not; and by "whether an object exists or not" I mean whether the object simply exists, not whether it is white or not. And knowing the fact that an object [simply] exists, we ask (4) "What is it?", e.g.,
35 "What is God?" or "What is a man?"

2

The kinds and number of things which we seek and which we know after discovery, then, are those just listed above. Now when we inquire whether something is or is not a fact or whether an object simply exists or not, we inquire whether it has a *middle* or not. And when we further inquire, after knowing that something is a fact or that an object exists (i.e., whether
90a partially or simply), into the *why* of it or the whatness of it, then we ask "What is its *middle*?". By "partially or simply" as applied to a fact or to the existence of an object, respectively, I mean the following. If one asks "Is the Moon being eclipsed?" or "Is the Moon waxing?", he is inquiring about a partial existence, for it is in such questions that we inquire whether a subject is some qualified thing or not; but if one asks "Does a Moon exist or not?"
5 or "Does night exist or not?", he is inquiring about a simple existence. It follows, then, that in all our inquiries we inquire either (*a*) whether there is a *middle* or (*b*) what the *middle* is; for the cause is a *middle*, and in all cases it is this that is sought. Thus, in asking, "Is [the Moon] being eclipsed?", we inquire whether there is some cause or not; and when we

know that there is some cause, we further ask "What is that cause?" For the
reason that a *substance* simply exists but not that it is this or that, or that   10
a *substance* has something which is essential or accidental to it but not that
it simply exists, is the *middle*. By "simply [exists]" I mean just the subject,
e.g., the Moon or the Earth or the Sun or a triangle, and by "something
[which the subject is]" I mean equality or inequality [to two right angles],
or an eclipse, if there is something in the middle or not. For it is evident
that in all these the whatness and the *why* are the same. Thus, to the   15
question "What is an eclipse?", one may answer "It is the privation of light
from the Moon, [caused] by the Earth's interposition"; and to the question
"Why is there an eclipse?" or "Why is the Moon being eclipsed?", one may
answer "Because its light disappears when the Earth is interposed between
the Sun and the Moon". Again, to the question "What is harmony?", one
may answer "It is a ratio of [small] numbers in a high and a low note"; and
to the question "Why is the high note in harmony with the low note?", one   20
may answer "Because the high and the low notes have a ratio of [small]
numbers". Thus we have two questions, "Is there a harmony of the high
and the low notes?" and "Is the ratio of these high and low notes in [small]
numbers?"; and when we grant the fact [that there is such a ratio], we
further ask "What is that ratio?".

That the inquiry is about the *middle* is clearly indicated by cases in which
the *middle* is sensible. For we inquire when we have not sensed [it], as in the   25
case of the eclipse, whether there is or there is not [a *middle* of it]. If we were
on the Moon, however, we would not have inquired either if [an eclipse]
occurs or why [it occurs], since both these would have been plain at the same
time; for from sensation we would have understood the universal also. For
we would then have sensed that the Earth was obstructing the light, and at
the same time it would have been plain that the Moon was being eclipsed;   30
and from these the universal would be formed.

As is our manner of saying, then, to understand the whatness of a thing
is the same as to understand the *why* of it; and this is either of a thing simply
taken and not of something belonging to it,   or of something belonging to
it, e.g., of the equality of the angles of a triangle to two right angles (or else
[of those angles as being] greater or less [than two right angles]).

3

It is clear, then, that in all these inquiries a *middle* is sought. Next, let us   35
discuss how the whatness of a thing is proved, in what manner it is referred
[to a demonstration], what a *definition* is, and of what things there is a
definition; but first, let us go over the difficulties concerning these
problems. Let the starting-point of what we have to say be that which is   90b
most appropriate to the arguments which follow.

One might raise this question: "Is it possible to know the same thing and in the same respect both by *definition* and by demonstration, or is this impossible?" For (*a*) a *definition* is thought to be of the whatness of a thing,

5   and the whatness of a thing is in every case universal and affirmative, but some syllogisms are negative and some are not universal, e.g., all syllogisms in the second figure are negative, and no syllogism in the third figure is universal. Moreover, (*b*) there is not even a *definition* of everything which is affirmatively concluded in a syllogism in the first figure, e.g., of the fact that every triangle has its angles equal to two right angles. The argument

10   for this is as follows. To *know* that which is demonstrable is to have a demonstration of it, so if *knowledge* of such things is had [only] by a demonstration, it is also clear that neither can there be a *definition* of them; for otherwise a man might also *know* them by a *definition* but without having a demonstration of them, since nothing prevents a man from not having at the same time a demonstration of them. (*c*) We may be convinced

15   sufficiently of this from induction also; for we never came to know by defining something which either belongs essentially to a thing or is an accident of it. (*d*) Finally, if a *definition* [of a thing] is a certain knowledge of the *substance* [of it], it is evident that things of this sort [i.e., essential attributes and accidents] are not even *substances* [of things to which they belong].

It is clear, then, that there is no *definition* of everything of which, *as such*, there is also a demonstration. But is there a demonstration of everything of

20   which there is a *definition*, or not? (*a*) Concerning this problem, too, one argument is the same [as that given above]. For of one thing, insofar as a thing is one, there can be but unique *knowledge*. So if to *know* a demonstrable thing *as such* is to have a demonstration of it, something impossible will follow; for he who has a *definition* without a demonstration [of that thing] will also *know* [it without a demonstration]. (*b*) Moreover, the

25   principles of demonstrations are *definitions*, and it was shown earlier[13] that of these there can be no demonstration. For either the principles will be demonstrable and so there will be other principles of these principles, in which case this will proceed to infinity, or the first [premises] will be indemonstrable *definitions*.

But if not everything definable is demonstrable and not everything demonstrable is definable, still are there some things which are both definable and demonstrable, or is this impossible? (*a*) But there is no

30   demonstration of that of which there is a *definition*. For a *definition* is of the whatness or of the *substance* [of a thing], whereas all demonstrations appear to assume and to posit the whatness of a thing; for example, the mathematical sciences [assume and posit] what a unit is and what oddness is, and the other sciences do likewise. (*b*) Again, every demonstration proves something about something else, e.g., that something is or is not the case; but

in a *definition* no one [term or element] is predicable of another. For 35
example, we do not predicate "animal" of "biped" or "biped" of "animal";
nor do we predicate "figure" of "plane", for planeness is not a figure, and
a figure is not [necessarily] plane. (*c*) Again, showing the whatness of a thing
is different from showing a fact about it. Accordingly, a *definition* makes 91a
known the whatness of a thing, whereas a demonstration makes known that
something either is or is not predicable of something else. And two
demonstrations differ if they are not related as a part to a whole. What I
mean is the following. It is proved that an isosceles triangle has its angles
equal to two right angles if it is proved that every triangle has this attribute;
for [the isosceles triangle is] a part while [the triangle is] a whole. But these, 5
i.e., a fact about a thing and the whatness of it, are not related to each other
in this manner; for neither is a part of the other.

It thus appears that there is no demonstration of everything of which
there is a *definition*, nor a *definition* of everything of which there is a
demonstration; nor in general can the same thing be both definable and
demonstrable. Clearly, then, neither could a *definition* be the same as a 10
demonstration, nor could one of them be under the other; otherwise. the
subjects which are signified by them would be related to each other in a
similar manner.

4

Let so much, then, be the discussion of the above difficulties. But is there
a syllogism or a demonstration of the whatness of a thing, or is this not the
case (as the preceding argument assumed)? Now a syllogism proves
something about something else through a middle term, whereas the 15
whatness [of a thing] is proper [to that thing] and is predicable [of it] in [the
statement of] what the thing is. Now these [a thing, its whatness, the middle
term] must be convertible [if whatness is to be demonstrable]. For if A is
proper to C, then clearly it is also proper to B and B is proper to C, and so
all of them are proper to each other. Moreover, if A belongs to every B as
the whatness of B and if B is stated universally of every C as the whatness 20
of C, then also A must be stated [universally] of C as the whatness of C. But
if one does not grant both [predications] in such a manner (that is, if A is
[stated universally] of B as the whatness of B but B is [stated] not as the
whatness of whatever [it is predicable]), it is not necessary for A to be
[universally] predicable of C as the whatness of C. Both these [predications],
then, will have to be [predications] of whatness, and so B, too, which is 25
[predicable] of C, will have to be the whatness [of it]. But if [a thing] has
both a·whatness and an essence, the essence will be prior as the *middle*.
And, in general, in proving the whatness of a man, let C be a man, and let

A be the whatness of a man (whether this be a biped animal or something
else). Accordingly, if one were to give a proof [of AC], it would be necessary
30   for him to predicate A of every B [as a middle term]. But this [i.e., B] will
be another formula, and so this [formula] too will be the whatness of a man.
So one grants that which he is to prove; for B too will be the whatness of a
man.

[This problem] should be examined with [only] two premises which are
primary and immediate, for [only then] that which has been said becomes
35   most evident. Thus, those who prove the whatness of a soul or of a man or
of any other thing through convertible terms are begging the question. For
example, if one were to assert that a soul is that which causes its own life and
that this is a number which moves itself, he would be begging the question
91b   [in concluding that] a soul is, *as such*, a number which moves itself, in the
sense that the two are the same thing. For if A follows B and B follows C,
A will not [necessarily] be the essence of C, but what will be true to say is
only this, [that A follows C, or that C is A]; and if A is, *as such*, a [genus of
B] and is predicable of every B, still [it does not follow that A is the whatness
5   of B, or of C]. For the essence of animal too is predicable of the essence
of man (for every essence of man is an essence of animal just as every man
is an animal), but not in such a way that the two are one. Accordingly, if
one does not make such a concession [i.e., that the two are one], he will not
prove that A is the essence or *substance* of C; and if he makes such a
10   concession, he will have already granted B as being the essence of C, and
so he does not demonstrate since he begs the question.

5

Again, as we have stated in our analysis of figures, no syllogism [of the
whatness or essence of a thing] is possible through the method of division;
for in no way does it become necessary for a thing to be so-and-so from the
15   [mere] fact that this is the case and that is the case, just as in no way does
one demonstrate by using an induction. For a conclusion should neither be
asked for by the questioner nor follow if the answerer grants it; it should
follow from the fact that [the premises] as posited are so-and-so, even if the
answerer denies it. For example, the definer asks, "Is a man an animal or
lifeless?" Then he posits the answer "a man is an animal", but he has not
proved it. Then he asks "Is every animal terrestrial or aquatic?", and again
20   he posits the answer "an animal is terrestrial". And finally he posits that a
man is the combined whole, namely, a terrestrial animal; but this does not
necessarily follow from what he himself has said. It makes no difference
whether [the divisions] made are few or many; the result is the same. So the
use of division by those who proceed in this manner ends neither in a

syllogism nor even in a conclusion of what may be drawn from a syllogism. For what prevents a combination of things from being truly affirmed of a   *25* man without revealing to us either the whatness of a man or his essence? Moreover, what prevents such division from adding something superfluous to the *substance* of a thing, or omitting something, or passing over something?

Although these difficulties are admitted, one may still offer a solution by including everything in the whatness of a thing and choosing by division [the parts of the whatness] in [the proper] succession, positing the first by   *30* questioning, and [by this process] omitting nothing. Now this [procedure] is necessary, if everything is to fall within the division and nothing is to be omitted; and [what follows, i.e., the whatness,] must now be *indivisible* [in species]. Nevertheless [this method] contains no syllogism [of whatness] but, if at all, makes [whatness] known to us in some other way. And there is nothing absurd in this; for perhaps he who uses an induction, too, does not   *35* demonstrate, yet he indicates something. Thus he who reaches a *definition* by means of division does not use a syllogism. For just as in the case of conclusions, which are given without middle terms but are affirmed to follow of necessity from certain things which are laid down, one may ask for the *reason*, so it is in the case of definitions which are affirmed by means of division. For example, to the question "What is a man?", one may answer   *92a* "An animal, mortal, footed, biped, wingless". Why? [He will answer] by adding one thing after another; for he will say, and by division think that he will prove, that everything is either mortal or immortal. But such formulation, taken in its entirety, is not a *definition*. So even if one were to try to demonstrate by means of division, still the process of arriving at a   *5* *definition* does not become a syllogism.

6

Can we nevertheless demonstrate the whatness of a thing with respect to its *substance*, but hypothetically, by forming the essence from the [elements] proper to its whatness, if these are the only [elements] in the whatness and constitute, when taken together, something proper to the thing? For the result will be the essence of the thing. But, as before, do we   *10* not assume the essence in this case also, since the proof must proceed through a *middle*? Moreover, just as in a syllogism we do not posit what syllogizing is (for each of the premises from which a syllogism is formed is always a whole or a part), so the term "essence" should not appear in the syllogism but should be something apart from what is posited; and to one   *15* who raises a doubt as to whether there has been a syllogism or not, the answer should be in the affirmative, for what a syllogism was posited to be was just this. And to one who denies that the conclusion of the syllogism is the essence, one must answer by affirming that it is; for the essence was posited as being just that. So the conclusion of a syllogism follows of necessity even without a statement of what a syllogism or an essence is.

20   One might give a proof hypothetically, too, as in the following example: if the essence of badness is the essence of divisibility, and if the essence of [one] contrary is the essence of the contrary [of the other contrary] for things which have contraries, since goodness is contrary to badness and indivisibility is contrary to divisibility, it follows that the essence of goodness is the essence of indivisibility. But here, as before, one has assumed an

25   essence in the proof; and he has assumed it in order to prove an essence. But [he assumed a] different [essence, one may retort, and] let us grant this. [Our position, however, still stands], for even in demonstrations, in which A is affirmed of B, A and B [may be] convertible; yet neither [A and B] nor their definitions are the same.

The same dilemma arises, however, against both those who prove [essence] by division and those who use a syllogism such as the one just given.

30   Why will a man be a two-footed terrestrial animal but not an animal and terrestrial [and two-footed]? For, from what is assumed, the predicates do not necessarily become one; they would be like the musical and the grammatical, as in the case of a man who is both musical and grammatical.

7

By what method, then, will one who is defining [a thing] prove its

35   *substance* or its whatness? He will not reveal it either (*a*) as a demonstrator does from [premises] which are agreed upon, in the sense that when something [the premises] is the case something else [the conclusion] of necessity follows, since this will be a demonstration, or (*b*) as one who makes an induction through the fact that the particulars are clear, in the sense that every [particular] is such-and-such and not otherwise, for [induction] proves

92b   not the whatness but that something is or is not the case. What other method is there left? Certainly, he will not prove it by means of sensation or by pointing his finger to it.

5   Again, how will he prove whatness? For he who knows the whatness of a man (or of any other thing) must also know that a man exists, and no one knows that nonbeing exists; for although one [may know] what an expression or a name signifies, as when one uses the name "goat-stag," he cannot know what a goat-stag is. Moreover, if one were to prove both the whatness and the existence of an object, how would he do it with the same argument?

10   For a *definition* signifies one thing, and so does a demonstration; but the whatness of a man is different from the fact that he exists.

Again, we also say that it is by a demonstration that we must prove of each thing that it exists, if it is not a *substance*. But existence is not the *substance* of anything, for being is not a genus. So it is a demonstration [which will

prove] that something exists; and indeed this is what the sciences are now   15
doing. For the geometer has assumed the meaning of the term "a triangle",
but that a triangle exists is something which he proves. So what will one
prove if he is defining whatness? [The whatness of] a triangle? Then while
knowing by a *definition* the whatness [of a triangle], he will not know
whether [a triangle] exists. But this is impossible.

It is also evident that those who define objects nowadays, in view of the   20
manner in which they present the definitions, do not prove that the objects
exist. For even if there exists something [e.g., a circumference] which is
equidistant from a center, one may still ask for the *reason* why the object
exists. Moreover, why is this a circle? One might equally say that it [the
object defined] is made of copper. For such definitions do not make known
also the fact that the objects stated are possible or the fact that they are
definitions of the objects of which these thinkers are speaking. But it is
always possible to ask for the *why*.   25

If, then, he who defines [an object] proves either the whatness of the object
or what the name means, and if [what is given as a] *definition* is not of the
whatness in any way, then it will be an expression having the same meaning
as the name. But this would be absurd. For, in the first place, there would
be *definitions* of *nonsubstances* and of nonbeings also, since nonbeings too   30
can be signified. Second, all expressions would be *definitions*; for it would
be possible to posit a name for any kind of expression, and so all discussions
would be in terms of definitions, and even the *Iliad* would be a *definition*.
Third, no science would demonstrate that this name reveals that [object];
so neither do *definitions* include this in what they reveal.

It appears from the above, then, that neither is a syllogism the same as a   35
definition, nor are they of the same object, and, in addition, that neither
does a *definition* demonstrate or prove anything, nor is it possible to know
the whatness [of a thing] by a *definition* or a demonstration.

8

We should consider once more which of the above [arguments] are stated   93a
well and which are not stated well, what a *definition* is, and whether there
is in some sense a demonstration and a *definition* of the whatness [of a thing]
or not.

As we stated previously, to understand what a thing is is the same as to
understand the cause of its existence; and an argument for this is the fact   5
that there is a cause, which is either the same or different, and if different,
then [the whatness of the thing is] either demonstrable or indemonstrable.
Accordingly, if [the cause is] different and [whatness] can be demonstrated,
it is necessary for the cause to be a middle term and for the proof to be in

the first figure (for what is proved is both universal and affirmative). One
10   way [of proving whatness], then, would be the one just examined, namely,
proving the whatness [of a thing] through something else; for, in the proof
of the whatness of a thing it is necessary that the middle term (*a*) be a
whatness and [being between two things proper to each other] (*b*) be proper
[to them] also. So, [in such a proof,] one will prove one of the essences of the
same thing but not the other.

We have stated earlier that this method could not be a demonstration [of
15   the whatness of a thing]; but it may be a logical syllogism of the whatness.
So let us start once more and discuss a method by which there may be [a
demonstration of whatness].

Now just as we seek the *reason* for a fact when we have the fact (and
sometimes both are revealed at the same time, but certainly the *reason*
cannot be known before the fact), so similarly it is clear that [we seek] the
20   essence of an object not without having the fact that the object exists; for it
is impossible to understand what an object is if we are ignorant that the
object exists.   Of an object's existence, however, sometimes we have
accidental knowledge, but sometimes we have knowledge of a part   of it.
Of thunder, for example, we know that it is a certain sound in the clouds;
of an eclipse, that it is a certain privation of light; of a man, that he is a
certain kind of animal; and of the soul, that it is a [certain] thing which
25   moves itself.   Now whenever we have [only] accidental knowledge that an
object exists, then of necessity we have nothing of the object which
contributes to the whatness of it,   for neither do we know that the object
exists; and to seek what an object is without having knowledge that it exists
is to seek nothing. But whenever we have some [knowledge] that the object
exists, then it is easier [to proceed]. Thus, the manner in which we have
30   something of a thing towards the whatness of it is similar to the manner in
which we have of its existence.

Of things of whose whatness we have something, then, let the following
be the first example. Let A be an eclipse, C be the Moon, and B be Earth's
interposition.   Now to inquire whether the Moon is being eclipsed or not is
to inquire whether B exists or not. This differs in no way from inquiring
whether there exists a reason   for it [i.e., for the eclipse]; and if there is, then
we say that that other thing [i.e., A] also exists.   Again, we may ask: "Which
35   part of the contradiction is the reason, that of having the angles [of a
triangle] equal or that of not having them equal to two right angles?" When
we discover the answer, if this be through the *middles*, we know at the same
time both the fact and the *reason* for that fact; if, on the other hand, [the
answer is] not [through a *middle* or *middles*], then we know the fact but not
the *reason* for it. Thus let C be the Moon, A an eclipse, and M the inability
of the Moon when full to cause moonlight when there is no visible object
between us and the Moon. Then if M (the inability to cause moonlight when

there is no [visible] object between us and the Moon) belongs to C, and A (an $93b$
eclipse) belongs to M, the fact that the Moon is being eclipsed is clear, but
the *reason* for it is not yet clear, and we know that an eclipse exists, but we
do not know what an eclipse is. So although it is clear that A belongs to C,
to inquire why it does is to inquire what B is, whether an interposition or 5
a rotation or a quenching of the Moon; and this [B] is the reason for the other
end term, i.e., for A in the example given, for an eclipse is an interposition
by the Earth. Again, what is thunder? It is the quenching of fire in a cloud.
Why does it thunder? Because the fire in a cloud is quenched. Let C be
"cloud", A be "thunder", and B be "quenching of fire". Then B belongs to 10
C (to "cloud"), for the fire is quenched in it [i.e., in the cloud], and A (i.e.,
"sound") belongs to this [to B]; and here B is the formula of A, the major
term. And if of this, too, there be another middle term, it will be from the
formulae left out.

We have stated, then, the manner in which the whatness of a thing is 15
arrived at and becomes known; so neither a syllogism nor a demonstration
of whatness can be formed, yet whatness is revealed through a syllogism
and a demonstration. Thus, of a thing, neither is it possible to know
without demonstration its whatness, if this has another cause, nor can there
be a demonstration of whatness, as we stated also in our discussion of the 20
difficulties.[14]

9

In some cases, the cause of a thing is different [from that thing], in others,
this is not the case; so it is clear that, in some cases, the whatness of a thing,
too, is immediate [i.e., without a *middle*] and a principle, and both the
existence and the whatness of such a thing should be laid down or made
evident in some other way. This is indeed what the arithmetician does; for
he lays down both what a unit is and the fact that it exists. But in the case 25
of a thing which has a *middle* and the cause of whose *substance* is different,
the whatness of it can be revealed through a demonstration, as we already
said, but it cannot be demonstrated.

10

Since a *definition* is said to be a formula of the whatness of a thing, it is 30
evident that there will be a formula which gives the meaning of a name or
a name-like expression, as in the case of the whatness signified by
"triangle" qua "triangle". And it is when we know that the object [signified
by the name] exists that we seek the *reason* through which it exists. It is
difficult in this manner, however, to acquire [a whatness of] an object if we

do not know that the object exists; and the cause of the difficulty, as stated
before,[15] is the fact that we may not know whether the object exists or not,
35   except by way of an accident. Further, a formula may be one in two ways,
(*a*) by a conjunction, like the *Iliad,* or (*b*) by virtue of the fact that [the
formula] indicates one thing about one thing but not by way of an
accident.
     The above, then, is one [kind of a] definition of a definition. Another
[kind of a] definition is a formula which reveals the *reason* through which
94a the thing exists. Thus the former [definition] signifies [an object] but does not
prove [that the object exists], whereas the latter is evidently like a
demonstration of the whatness of the thing but differs from a demonstration
in the manner in which the terms are posited; for there is a difference
between stating why it thunders and stating what thunder is. In the first
5   case, one will say "because fire is quenched in the clouds", but in stating
what thunder is, one will say "sound in the clouds due to the quenching of
fire". Thus the same formula is stated in different ways; and in one way it
is a continuous demonstration, but in another it is a *definition*. But "sound
in the clouds", too, is a definition of thunder; and this is the conclusion of
the demonstration of the whatness of thunder. As for the *definition* of a
10   thing without a *middle*, it is an indemonstrable thesis of the whatness of the
thing.
     So one [kind of] *definition* is (*a*) an indemonstrable formula of the
whatness [of a thing]; another is (*b*) a syllogism of the whatness but differs
from a demonstration in grammatical form; a third is (*c*) the conclusion of
a demonstration of the whatness of a thing.
15   It is evident from the above statements, then, (1) in what way a
demonstration of the whatness of a thing is possible and in what way it is
not possible; (2) of what [things a demonstration of whatness] is possible and
of what [things] it is not; (3) how many meanings the term *"definition"* has;
(4) how a [*definition*] proves the whatness of a thing and how it does not;
(5) of what objects there is [a *definition*] and of what objects there is not; (6)
how a [*definition*] is related to a demonstration; (7) and how there can be
[both a *definition* and a demonstration] of the same thing and how there
cannot be.

11

20   Since we think that we *know* a thing when we know its cause, and since
the causes are four—(1) the essence, (2) the things whose existence
necessitates the existence of something else, (3) the first thing which caused
motion, and (4) the final cause [or, that for the sake of which]—all these
causes are shown through a *middle*.

The [things] whose existence necessitates the existence of something else cannot be [shown] when only one premise is granted, since at least two 25 [premises] are needed, and it is [shown with two premises] when these have a common middle term; so the conclusion necessarily follows when one middle term is granted. This is clear also from the following example. Why [or through what] is the angle inscribed in a semicircle a right angle? Or, putting it in another way, from what [fact or facts or middle term does it follow that] it is a right angle? Let A be a right angle, B be half of two right angles, and C be the angle in a semicircle. Then B is the cause of the fact that A (a right angle) belongs to C (the angle in a semicircle); for B is equal to A, and C is equal to B (for C 35 is half of two right angles). Thus A belongs to C by virtue of B (half of two right angles); and this is what it is to be a right angle in a semicircle. And this is the same as the essence [of a right angle in a semicircle], since it is this that is signified by the formula. Moreover, the middle term has also been shown to be the cause of the essence.

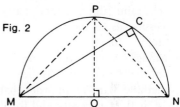

Fig. 2

Again, why was the war against the Athenians declared by the Persians? Or, putting it in another way, what is the cause of the war which was waged against the Athenians? It is the fact that the Athenians along with the 94b Eretrians had raided Sardis; for this was the first moving cause. Let A be war [against], B be prior raiders, and C be the Athenians. Now B (i.e., prior raiders) belongs to C (i.e., to the Athenians), and A belongs to B (for war is declared against those who *acted* unjustly earlier); so A belongs to B (i.e., 5 war is declared against prior raiders), and B belongs to C (for the Athenians are prior raiders). Hence here, too, the cause as the first mover is the *middle*.

Lastly, there is the final cause [or, that for the sake of which]. Why does a man walk? In order to be healthy. Why does a shed come to be? For the 10 sake of preserving the implements. In the first case, [walking is] for the sake of being healthy; in the second, [a shed comes to be] for the sake of the preservation [of the implements]. And there is no difference between the questions "Why should a man walk after supper?" and "For the sake of what should a man walk after supper?". Let C be a walk after supper, B be the prevention of the rise of food, and A be being healthy. Also, to a walk after supper let there belong the prevention of the rise of food to the orifice 15 of the stomach, and let this prevention be healthy; for it is thought that B (the prevention of the rise of food) belongs to C (a walk) and that A (being healthy) belongs to B. What, then, is the cause through which A, the final cause, belongs to C? It is B, the prevention of the rise of food. Now B is as it were the formula of A, for it is in this way that A will be rendered. Why 20 does B exist in C? In view of the fact that to be healthy is to be this, namely, to be in such a state. One should then transpose the formulas, and in this way things will be more evident.   But the sequence of becoming in this case is the reverse of that in the case of causes according to motion. For in the latter

25   case it is the *middle* which must have occurred first, whereas in the former it is C, the last term; and the final cause [must come to be] last.

The same [thing or fact] may exist both for the sake of something and of necessity, as in the case of light which passes through [the pores of] a lantern;   for that [i.e., light] whose parts are smaller passes through

30   openings which are larger both (*a*) of necessity, if indeed light at a distance from the source arises by traversing that distance, and (*b*) for the sake of something, namely, in order that we may not stumble. But if a thing may exist [both of necessity and for the sake of something], can it also come to be [of necessity and for the sake of something]? For example, when fire is extinguished [in the clouds], does thunder (*a*) necessitate a hiss and a sound and also (*b*) occur (as the Pythagoreans say) for the sake of threatening and

35   terrifying those who lie in Tartarus?   There exist a great many examples like this, especially in things which are composed or cause others to be composed according to nature;   for, in one sense, nature acts for the sake of something, in another, it acts by necessity.   Necessity, of course, is of two

95a   kinds: (*a*) that according to nature and tendency, and (*b*) that by force; the latter being contrary to tendency. For example, a stone may go down but also up, but not by the same kind of necessity.

As for things [which come to be] from *thought*, some (e.g., a house or a

5   statue) never come to be by chance or by necessity but for the sake of something, but others (e.g., health or safety) come to be also by luck. And what comes to be for the sake of something does so most of all,   whether by nature or by art, among things which may exist now in one way and now in another, whenever the generation proceeds not by luck and so the end is good;   but by luck   no thing comes to be for the sake of something.

12

10   The cause of a thing which is coming to be or which came to be or which will come to be is the same as that of the thing which exists now; for that cause is the middle term [or *middle*], except that it exists when the thing exists, it is coming to be when the thing is coming to be, it came to be when the thing came to be, and it will be when the thing will be. For example, why did the eclipse [of the Moon] occur? Because the Earth came to be

15   between [the Sun and the Moon]. [In a similar manner, the eclipse] is coming to be because [the Earth] is coming to be [between the Sun and the Moon], it will occur because [the Earth] will go between, and there is [an

eclipse now] because [the Earth] now is [between]. Again, what is ice? Let it be granted that it is congealed water; and let C be water, A be congealment, and the cause B, which is total absence of heat, be the *middle*. Now to C belongs B, and to B belongs A (i.e., congealment). Then ice is   20
being formed when B is being formed, ice has been formed when B has been formed, and ice will be formed when B will be formed. So such a cause is coming to be at the same time as that [i.e., the effect] of which it is the cause, and it exists at the same time as that of which it is the cause; and similarly if the effect is in the past or in the future.

But in the case of [things] which do not [exist or come to be] simultaneously, is it possible, as it is thought by us, for some of them to be   25
the causes of others in a continuous time, [i.e., for the cause] of a thing that occurred to be another thing that occurred [before it], of a thing in the future to be another thing [prior to it], and of a thing which is now occurring to be another thing which occurred before?

Now a syllogism proceeds from the outcome [i.e., the end of a process], which comes later; and in this case, too, the starting point is the [later] outcome. In view of this, similar remarks apply to things which are coming to be. But from a thing which is prior [as an outcome or a process] there is   30
no [syllogism], e.g., [there is no syllogism of the fact that] since a thing came to be, another thing will come to be later; and it is likewise with things in the future. For, whether the interval [between two outcomes] be indefinite or definite, it would not be true to say that, since the [earlier] has come to be, also the later [outcome] will come to be; for in the interval between the two outcomes, when one of them [i.e, the earlier] has already come to be,   35
it will be false to say this. The same argument applies to the future also. Nor is it true to say that since this came to be in the past, the other will come to be in the future; for the middle term must be contemporaneous, [that is,] it must be in the past if the two things came to be in the past, it must be in the future if they will be in the future, it must be [in the process of] coming to be if they are [in the process of] coming to be, and it must be existing if they are existing, whereas no two such things can be contemporaneous if one of them is in the past and the other is in the future. Moreover, the time   40
interval between the two can be neither indefinite nor definite; for within   95b
this interval it will be false to say this. But it is worth examining what in a thing makes events continuous in such a way that after the outcome of one of them there is a coming to be of another. It is clear, however, that a thing in the process of coming to be is not consecutive to an outcome; for neither is one outcome consecutive to another, seeing that these are limits and   5
indivisible. Hence just as points are not consecutive to each other, so in the case of outcomes, for in both cases they are indivisible. Nor, for the same *reason*, is that which is [in the process of] coming to be [consecutive to] a past outcome; for that which is [in the process of] coming to be is divisible,   10

whereas an outcome is indivisible. Thus just as a line is related to a point, so is that which is [in the process of] coming to be to an outcome; for that which is [in the process of] coming to be includes an infinity of outcomes.

These facts should become more evident when a universal discussion of motion is considered.[16]

Concerning the manner in which the middle term figures as a cause in generations which are successive, let so much be granted; for in these cases,
15   too, the middle and major [terms] must be immediate. For example, if B came to be, then A came to be; but B came to be later, while A came to be earlier.   Now B is the starting point because it is nearer to the present moment, which is the starting point of time. Again, B came to be if C came to be [later]. So A came to be of necessity [before B] if C came to be, and
20   the cause is B; for if C came to be, then B came to be of necessity [earlier], and if B came to be, then A came to be of necessity earlier.   If these are granted in this manner, will the middle term stop with an immediate [premise] or will there be always [a term] between because of the infinite? For no outcome is consecutive to another outcome, as we have [already]
25   stated.   Still   we must start from a middle term and something which is first from the present moment.

The argument for future [generations] is similar. For if it be true to say that C will be, it must be true to say that A will be before [C will be]. And the cause of this will be B; for if C will be, then B will be before [C], and if B will be, then A will be before [B]. And the division in such a case will
30   be infinite in a similar way, for future [outcomes] are not consecutive. But here, too, the starting point must be taken as immediate.

Such indeed is the case in things which are produced. Thus, if a house came to be, then stones must have been quarried and shaped. Why this? In view of the fact that a foundation must have come to be, if indeed a house
35   came to be; and if a foundation came to be, then before it stones must have been shaped. Again, if a house is to be in the future, then in a similar manner stones will have to be shaped before. And this is similarly proved through a middle term, for a foundation has to be built before [the house].

Since we observe that among some of the things which come to be there exists a circular generation, this may occur if indeed the middle and
40   extreme terms follow each other, for in these cases conversion is possible.
96a Now this has been proved[17] in the first part [of this work], since the conclusion is convertible; and, in this case, the proof is circular.   In occurences the following appears to be the case. When the earth is moistened, water vapor
5   must be formed; and when this is formed, a cloud [must be formed]; and when this is formed, water must be formed; and when this is formed, the earth must be moistened; but this was the starting point, so a circular process has occurred, for when anyone of these exists another will exist, and when this exists then another will exist, etc., till the starting point is reached.

Now some things that come to be do so universally (for they exist or come
to be in this manner always and in every case); others are not coming to be
always but do so in most cases, e.g., not every man grows a beard but most   *10*
men do. In such cases the middle term, too, must exist in most cases. For if
A is predicable of B universally and B is predicable of C universally, then
it is necessary that also A be predicable of C always and in every case (for   *15*
to be universal is just this, to be [predicable] in every case and always). But
it was assumed [that A is predicable of C] in most cases; so the middle term
B, too, must exist in most cases. Accordingly, there will be also immediate
principles which are [true] in most cases, [and these will be of] things which
exist or come to be in most cases.

16

Concerning a cause and its effect, one might raise a problem. (*a*) When   *35*
there is an effect, is there a cause also? For example, if there is a shedding
of leaves or an eclipse, is there also a cause of the shedding of the leaves or
of the eclipse, e.g., the possession of broad leaves in the first case and the   *98b*
interposition of the Earth in the second case? For if these are not [their
causes], some other things will be their causes. Also, (*b*) if there is a cause,
is there simultaneously an effect also? For example, if the Earth is between
[the Moon and the Sun], is there an eclipse [also], or if [a plant] has broad
leaves, is there a shedding of [its] leaves [also]?

But if in such cases [i.e., (*a*) and (*b*)] one answers affirmatively, there   *5*
would be simultenously both a cause and its effect, and there would be a
proof of each of them through the other. For, let A be the shedding of
leaves, B be possession of broad leaves, and C be a vine. Then since A
belongs to B (for whatever has broad leaves sheds its leaves) and B belongs
to C (for every vine has broad leaves), A belongs to C; and so every vine   *10*
sheds its leaves. The cause here is B, which is the *middle*. But it is also
possible to demonstrate the fact that a vine has broad leaves through the
shedding of its leaves. For let D be the possession of broad leaves, E be the
shedding of leaves, and F be a vine. Then E belongs to F (for every vine   *15*
sheds its leaves) and D belongs to E (for whatever sheds its leaves has broad
leaves); so every vine has broad leaves, and the cause is the shedding of its
leaves. If, on the other hand, it is not possible for each of the two [i.e., of A
and B, or, of D and E] to be the cause of the other (for the cause is prior to
the effect) , and if it is the interposition of the Earth which is the cause of
the eclipse [of the Moon], then the eclipse is not the cause of the interposition
of the Earth. Accordingly, since a demonstration through the cause is   *20*
through the *why* [of a fact], whereas a demonstration not through the cause
is [merely] of the fact, one [who knows the interposition of the Earth
through the eclipse] knows the fact but not the *reason* for the fact.
Evidently, the eclipse is not the cause of the Earth's interposition, but the

latter is the cause of the eclipse; for the interposition of the Earth is included in the formula of the eclipse, and so it is clear that it is through the former [the interposition] that the latter [the eclipse] is known, but the former is not known through the latter.

25   But is it not possible for one [effect] to have more than one cause? For, one might say, if it is possible for the same thing to be predicable of many things primarily [i.e., immediately], let A belong to B primarily and also to C primarily, and let these [B and C] belong to D and E, respectively. Then A will belong to D and also to E; and B will be the cause of A's belonging to D but C will be the cause of A's belonging to E. So the existence of a cause

30   necessitates the existence of the thing [i.e., the effect], whereas the existence of the thing [i.e., the effect] necessitates the existence not of whatever is a cause but of some one cause and not of all of them.

On the other hand, if the problem is always *universal* and the cause is a whole, the effect, too, will be *universal*. For example, the shedding of leaves [belongs] to some determinate whole, even if this [whole] has species; and it is *universally* that it belongs to these [taken together], whether these

35   be all plants or plants of a certain kind. So the *middle*, too, should be coextensive with these [taken together] and also with the effect, and the [*middle* and the effect] should be convertible. For example, why are the trees shedding their leaves? If this be because of the coagulation of sap, then if a tree is shedding its leaves, its sap is coagulating, and if the sap (not of anything but of [any] tree) is coagulating, then the tree is shedding its leaves.

17

99a   Can the same [effect] which belongs to every [subject] have different causes and not the same cause, or not? But if [the effect] has been demonstrated essentially and not by means of a sign or an accident, then it cannot be such [as to have different causes], for the major term's formula is the *middle*; but if such is not the case, then the same effect can [have

5   different causes]. Now it is possible to consider [as causes] things which are accidental to the effects or to the subjects, but [such cases] are not thought to be [scientific] problems. But if [causes] are not [so considered], the middle term will be similarly related [to the extreme terms]; [that is,] if [the subjects are] equivocally named [by the effect], the middle term will be equivocally named [also], but if [the subjects are taken] as under a genus, [the middle term] will be similarly related [to them].

For example, why are proportionals also proportional by alternation? The cause [taken] in lines [may be] different from that in numbers, but [it may

10   be] the same also; for it is different [if lines are taken] qua lines [and numbers

are taken qua numbers], but it is the same [if lines and numbers are taken] qua having such-and-such an increase. Such is the case in every instance. On the other hand, the similarity of one color to another color and the similarity of one figure to another figure have different [causes], for the term "similarity" is equivocally used in the two cases; in the first case [it means] perhaps the possession of proportional sides and equal angles, but in the case of colors [it means] oneness in senation or some other such thing. In the case 15 of things which are the same by analogy, the middle terms, too, will be [the same] by analogy.

The cause, the effect, and the [subject] to which [these belong] follow each other in the following manner. Relative to each [species of the subject] which one may take, the effect is wider. For example, the equality of the exterior angles to four right angles [as an attribute of a subject] is wider than all the triangles, or all the squares, but it is coextensive with all [polygons] 20 taken together; for all the [plane rectilinear figures] which have their exterior angles equal to four right angles have in a similar manner a [coextensive] *middle*. Now the *middle* is the formula for the major term; and it is in view of this that in every case scientific knowledge is acquired through a definition. For example, the shedding of leaves belongs to [all] vines and is wider, and it belongs to all fig trees and is wider, etc. However, it is not wider than all of them taken together but equal in extent. So if you 25 take the middle term next [to the shedding of leaves], this will be the formula for the shedding of leaves; for, first there will be a middle term which applies to all [of them together and which indicates] the fact that all of them are such-and-such [i.e., have broad leaves], then another middle term between this [and the shedding of leaves], namely, the coagulation of sap or some other such thing. Finally, what is the shedding of leaves? It is the coagulation of the sap at the junction of the leaf-stalk and the stem.

Now if one inquires, in the case of a cause and its effect, how the fact that 30 one of them follows from the other should be presented by means of syllogistic figures, the following may be said. Let A belong to every B, and B belong to each of the D's, but be wider. B will then belong universally to the D's (for by "belonging universally" [here] I mean that the predication is not convertible, whereas by "belonging universally in a primary way" I mean that the predication, though not convertible with each [subject], is convertible with all [the subjects] taken together and is 35 coextensive with them). Thus B [will be] the cause of A's belonging to the D's. A, then, should extend beyond B, otherwise why should this be a cause rather than that? Now if A belongs to all the E's, then these will be some one thing other than B; for, if not, how will it be possible to [truly] say that A belongs to whatever E belongs but E does not belong to all of that to 99b which A belongs? For why should there be no cause [of A's belonging to the E's] as there is in the case of A's belonging to all the D's? So the E's, too,

will be some one thing. This [cause] should be looked for; and let it be C. Then the same [effect] may have more than one cause, but not in [subjects]
5   which are the same in kind. For example, the cause of longevity in quadrupeds is the absence of bile, but in birds it is their leanness or some other thing. Thus if [the subjects] do not proceed immediately to something which is *indivisible* but there are many middle terms and not just one, the causes too will be many.

19

15   Concerning a syllogism and a demonstration, it is now evident what each of them is and how it is formed; and it is at the same time evident what demonstrative *knowledge* is, for it is the same. As for the principles, how they come to be known and what is the knowing habit of them, this will be made clear if we first raise some preliminary problems.
20   We have stated earlier[18] that one cannot *know* through demonstration without knowing the immediate primary principles. Concerning the knowledge of immediate [premises], and whether it is the same [knowing habit as that through demonstration] or not, one might discuss some difficulties, [i.e.,] both (1) whether [the habit in each case] is *knowledge* or
25   not, but if not, whether it is *knowledge* in one case but some genus other [than *knowledge*] in the other, and (2) whether those habits do not exist in [the soul from the start] but come to be in it, or exist in it [from the start] but we are unaware of them.
    Now it is absurd [to assume] that we possess them [from the start], for it would then follow that we possess knowledge which is more accurate than demonstration without being aware [of that knowledge]. If, on the other hand, we acquire them without previously possessing them, how would we come to know them or learn them without previously existing knowledge?
30   For this would be impossible, just as in the case of demonstration which was discussed previously.[19]
    It is evident, then, that we are not of such a nature as to possess them [from the start] or to acquire them without the possession of any knowledge or any habit. So we must have some kind of power, but not such which is more honorable in accuracy. Now this appears to be the case in all animals,
35   for they have an innate discriminating power called "the power of sensation". And when sensations occur, some animals retain sense impressions while others do not. Animals which do not retain sense impressions, either not at all or not those which they cannot retain, have no knowledge besides the corresponding sensations; but animals which, after
100a the occurrence of sensations, retain the sense impressions have something in the soul besides [sensations]. When many such [sense impressions] have accumulated, another difference now arises between those animals which can form a formula from the retention of such [sense impressions] and those

which cannot.   Accordingly, from a sensation there arises a memory, in the manner we have stated, and from many memories of the same thing there arises [one] experience (for many memories [of the same individual] are a single experience).   Again, from experience[s] or   from every universal which is now stabilized in the soul and which, being one besides the many, would be one and the same in all of them, [there arises] a principle of art or of science, of art if it is a principle about generation, but of science if it is a principle about being.²⁰ So neither are these habits [i.e., principles of science and of art] present in the soul [from the start] in any determinate way, nor do they come into being from other more known habits. [They arise] from sensation, like a reversal in battle brought about when one man makes a stand, then another, then a third, till a principle   is attained; and the soul is of such a nature as to be capable of being affected in this way.

Let us state once more what has just been said but not clearly. When one of the [things] without differences has made a stand, [there is formed] in the soul the first universal (for though one senses an individual, [the power of] sensation is of the universal, e.g., of man, not of the man Callias),   and then again another [universal] among these makes a stand, [and the process goes on] till a universal which has no parts makes a stand; for example, "such-and-such an animal" [makes a stand], and this proceeds till "animal" [makes a stand], and in the latter case similarly. Clearly, then, we must come to know the primary [universals] by induction;   for it is in this way that [the power of] sensation, too, produces in us the universal.

Since of the *thinking* habits by which we *think* truly some are always true while others (e.g., opinion and judgment) may be also false; since scientific knowledge and intuition are always true and no genus [of knowledge] exists which is more accurate than scientific knowledge except intuition; since the principles of demonstration are [by nature] more known than [what is demonstrated], and all scientific knowledge is knowledge by means of reasoning whereas there could be no scientific knowledge of the principles;   and since nothing can be more true than scientific knowledge except intuition; it follows from a consideration of these facts that intuition would be [the habit or faculty] of principles, and that a principle of a demonstration could not be a demonstration and so [the principles] of scientific knowledge could not be scientific knowledge. Accordingly, if we have no genus of a true [habit] other than scientific knowledge, intuition would be the principle [or starting point] of scientific knowledge. Moreover, a principle would be about a principle, and every [other kind of knowledge] is similarly related to the corresponding fact.

TOPICS

CONTENTS

BOOK I

Chapter

16. Distinguishing the differences between things within the same or in different genera.

17. Apprehending likenesses of things under the same or in different genera.

18. Special uses of knowing meanings of a term, distinguishing differences in things, and apprehending likenesses in things.

TOPICS

BOOK I

1

The purpose of this treatise is to devise a method whereby we shall be   *100a*
able, from generally accepted opinions, (a) to give a proof of every problem
proposed and (b) to avoid being inconsistent when defending a thesis. First,   *20*
then, we should state what a syllogism is and what its different kinds are,
so that the dialectical syllogism may be understood, for it is this that we seek
in the treatise before us.

A syllogism is an expression in which, certain things being laid down,   *25*
something other than these results necessarily because of what is laid
down.

A demonstration is a syllogism (a) whenever the premises are true and
primary (i.e., indemonstrable), or (b) whenever our knowledge of the
premises comes originally from true and primary premises.

A dialectical syllogism is a syllogism which reasons from generally   *30*
accepted opinions as premises. Premises are true and primary if one is   *100b*
convinced of them because of themselves and not because of other premises;
for one should not seek *reasons* for the principles in a science but should be   *20*
convinced of [the truth of] each principle in virtue of that principle
itself.

Generally accepted opinions are opinions which are accepted by all
people, or by most, or by the wise, and if by the wise, then by all of them,
or by most, or by those who are most known and held in esteem.

An eristic syllogism is (a) a syllogism which proceeds from what appear
to be generally accepted opinions but are not, or (b) what appears to be a   *25*
syllogism proceeding from generally accepted opinions or from what
appear to be generally accepted opinions without being so, but is not. For
not every opinion which appears to be generally accepted is really a

generally accepted opinion. Indeed none of the opinions which are called "generally accepted" makes an entirely superficial impression, as the principles of contentious arguments happen to do; for the nature of the
30   falsity in these [principles] is immediately and for the most part quite clear
101a even to those with little power of comprehension. Now let the first kind of eristic syllogisms, too, be called "syllogisms," but the second kind which we called "eristic syllogism" is really not a syllogism at all, since it appears to prove something but does not.
5   Further, besides all the 'syllogisms' we have mentioned, there are the fallacies which start from premises appropriate to certain sciences, as happens in geometry and sciences related to geometry. This form of argument seems to differ from the syllogisms already mentioned; for a man
10   who draws a figure falsely proves something neither from true nor from primary premises nor from opinions which are generally accepted. Indeed he does not come under the definition [of a dialectician or an eristic person], for he does not use as premises opinions which are generally accepted (a) by all people or most or the wise, or (b) by all or most or the most eminent of the wise, but, using false premises having terms appropriate to a science,
15   proceeds to form a syllogism; for he commits a fallacy either by not describing semicircles as he should, or by drawing certain lines not as they should be drawn.
        Let the kinds of syllogisms, then, taken in outline, be those mentioned
20   above. In general, concerning all we have said and what we shall say from now on we will be specific only up to a certain extent, because our intention is not to give an accurate account of any of these matters but to go over them in outline as much as is required, regarding it quite adequate, in view of the kind of inquiry before us, to be able to recognize each of them in some way or other.

                              2

25   Following upon what has been said we should state for how many and what kinds of things this discipline is useful. They are three: for intellectual training, for ordinary conversations, and for sciences considered philosophically. That it is useful for intellectual training is quite evident; for
30   when we have a method of inquiry we can more easily deal with a subject proposed. It is useful for arguments with others in general because when we have collected the opinions of many people we will be able to deal with those before us by using, not opinions held by others, but their own, shifting their opinions when these appear to us to be badly stated. It is useful for the
35   sciences philosophically considered, for if we can go over the difficulties on both sides of a philosophic issue in a science we can detect more easily what

is true and what is false about each side. In addition, it is useful for the first
[presuppositions] leading to the principles of each science. For to say
anything about principles by the use of principles appropriate to each
science is impossible, since the latter are principles of that science, but each   *101b*
of these principles must be discussed by means of generally accepted
opinions. But this [kind of discussion] is proper or most appropriate to
dialectic, for dialectic, being exploratory, is the path to the principles of
every inquiry.

3

We shall be in perfect possession of this method if we are disposed in a   *5*
way similar to that when we possess rhetoric or medical science or any such
faculty, and this is when we have the ability to do what we choose to do by
using what is possible. For neither will a rhetorician use every means to
persuade, nor will a doctor do so to heal; but if he omits none of the means
which are possible, we can then say that he has adequate possession of his   *10*
science.

4

First, then, we should consider the parts of which our inquiry consists.
Now if, concerning arguments, we were to grasp the number and kinds of
things they are used for and the materials out of which they are made, and
how we can be well supplied with them, we would be adequately prepared
to meet an issue before us. The materials from which arguments proceed are
the same and equal in number to the things with which syllogisms are   *15*
concerned. For arguments are constructed out of premises, and syllogisms
are concerned with problems; and every premise and every problem
indicates either a genus [in a wide sense] or a property [in a wide sense] or
an accident (for the differentia, too, should be ranked together with the
genus [in its main sense]). But since a property of a thing may signify either
its essence or not, let it be divided into those two parts; and let the part   *20*
which signifies the essence be called "definition," but the other part be
called "property" [in the narrow sense], which is the name usually given to
it.

It is clear from what has been said, then, that according to the present
division, the parts turn out to be four: property, definition, genus, and   *25*
accident. No one should suppose us as saying, however, that each of these
as stated is in itself either a proposition or a problem; what we are saying
is that propositions or problems are formed from these. Now things

proposed differ from problems in the manner in which they are expressed.
30 For if an expression is put thus: " 'A man is a two-footed animal' is the
definition of man, is it not?", it becomes a thing proposed, and so does the
expression " 'Animal' is the genus of man, is it not?"; but if an expression is
put thus: "But is 'two-footed terrestrial animal' the definition of man, or
not?", or "But is 'animal' the genus of man, or not?", it becomes a problem.
35 Similarly, too, in other cases. So there is good reason for the propositions and
the problems to be equal in number; for you can make a problem out of a
proposition by changing the manner of expression, [and conversely].

5

Let us now state what each of the following is: a definition, a property,
a genus, and an accident.

A definition is an expression which signifies the essence of a thing. It is
102a stated either as a phrase in place of a name, or as a phrase in place of a
[shorter] phrase, for it is possible to define even some things signified by
parts of a phrase. Those who put forward as a definition only a name in
whatever form clearly do not give a definition of a thing, since every
5   definition is a phrase [with more than one name]. Let also a thing such as
this [i.e., a name put forward as the definition of another name], however,
be posited as being definitional [i.e., as coming under the part concerned
with definitions]. The statement "the decorous is the noble" would be an
example, and similarly for the problem "Is sensation the same as *knowledge*,
or not?"; for most of the time in arguments about definitions, too, is spent
in deciding whether a certain thing is the same as or different from another
thing. Without qualification, then, let all matters coming under the inquiry
10 into definitions be called "definitional." Clearly, from the examples we just
gave, they are of such a kind [i.e., definitional]; for if we can argue that two
things are the same as or different from each other, we shall be supplied in
the same manner with the means of dealing with definitions. Thus, having
shown that A is not the same as B, we will have destroyed a definition [based
on the sameness of A and B]. The converse of what we have said, however,
15 does not follow. To show that A is the same as B is not sufficient to establish
a *definition*; but to show that A is not the same as B is sufficient to
overthrow that *definition*.

A property of a thing is [an attribute] which does not reveal the essence
of that thing but belongs only to that thing and is convertible with it as a
20 predicate. For example, a property of man is being capable of learning
grammar; thus if M is a man, then he is capable of learning grammar, and
if M is capable of learning grammar, then he is a man. For no one calls P
a property of Q if P can belong to something other than Q. For example,

to be sleeping is not a property of man, even if it happens that during a certain time, T, sleeping belongs only to man. But even if one were to call 25 a thing such as this [i.e., sleeping belongs only to man during T] "a property," he would have to say that it is a property not without qualification but during a certain time, or in relation to some other thing, etc. Thus being on the right side of B may be a temporary property of A, and being two-footed may be a property of A if A happens to be compared with C, e.g., two-footed is a property of man if compared with a horse and a dog. It is clear, then, that if B may belong to some other thing besides A, A and B cannot be convertible [without qualification] as predicates of each other; for example, if something is asleep, there is no necessity for it to be 30 a man.

A genus is that which, being in the whatness [or definition] of things which differ in species, is predicable of each of those things. By "predicates in the whatness of A" I mean such predicates which are appropriate to call A when one is asked "What is A?". For example, if one is asked, "What is a man?", it is appropriate to say "an animal." The problem whether A and 35 B come under the same genus or under different genera, too, is generic [i.e., pertaining to genus], for it, too, comes under the inquiry about the genus. For, having argued that "animal" is the genus of man, and similarly the genus of ox, we shall have argued that man and ox come under the same 102b genus; and if we can show that G is the genus of A but not of B, we can argue that A and B do not come under the same genus [G].

An accident of a thing, A, is (1) that which, being none of the above (i.e., neither a definition nor a property nor a genus of A), belongs to A, or (2) that 5 which may or may not belong to any one and the same thing, like sitting, which may or may not belong to one and the same thing, or like whiteness, for nothing prevents the same thing from being at one time white but at another not white. Of the *definitions* of accident the second is better; for, 10 if the first is stated, one who is to understand it must have prior knowledge of what a definition and a genus and a property are, whereas the second definition is by itself sufficient to let one know the thing which is signified by that definition. Under the inquiry concerning accidents may be placed also all other comparisons of things which involve an accident in any way, 15 such as the problem whether the noble or the expedient is preferable, the problem whether or not a life according to virtue is more pleasant than a life of indulgence, and any other problem which happens to be stated in a manner such as these; for in all such problems one asks: "To which one of 20 the two subjects does the predicate belong more than to the other?" It is clear from the examples given that nothing prevents an accident from becoming a property of a subject at a certain time or relative to another subject or other subjects. Sitting, for example, which is an accident of a man will be a property of that man whenever he alone is sitting; and if he is not

the only one who is sitting, sitting is still a property of him relative to those
25 who are not sitting. Thus nothing prevents an accident of a subject from
becoming a property of that subject at a certain time or relative to certain
persons or things in general, but then it will not be a property without
qualification.

6

One should keep in mind that all the arguments which may be used
against a given property or genus or accident may be likewise used also
against a given definition. For, having shown that (a) the definition given
30 of a thing does not belong only to that thing, as we do also in the case of a
property, or (b) that what is given as a genus in the definition is not really
the genus of the thing defined, or (c) that a thing included in the definition
given does not belong to the thing defined (something which one would use
in the case of accidents also), we will have refuted that definition; so,
according to our previous statement, all the listed arguments [i.e., those
against a given property or genus or accident] are in a certain sense
35 definitional. But because of this fact we should not seek a single method
applicable universally to all [kinds of] problems; for it is not easy to find one,
and if one were to be found, it would lack clarity and be difficult to use for
the treatise before us. If, on the other hand, a special inquiry for each of the
103a genera of problems is made, then from the [principles] appropriate to each
genus the way to the solution of each problem becomes easier. So, as stated
before, we should (1) sketch the division of this treatise and (2) assign each
of the other problems [i.e., those which may come under more than one
division] to its most appropriate division by calling them, for example,
"definitional" or "generic." Thus the [problems] mentioned are practically
5 assigned to each division.

7

First of all we should specify the number of senses of the term "the same."
It would seem that, sketchily taken, "the same" is used in three senses; for
we usually say that things are the same either numerically or in species or
in genus. We say things are numerically the same if many names are used
10 for something which is one thing, e.g., when we call something "a covering"
and also "a cloak." Things are said to be the same in species which, though
many [numerically], do not differ in species, e.g., two men are the same in
species, and so are two horses; for when things such as these come under the
same species, they are said to be the same in species. Similarly, things which

come under the same genus are said to be the same in genus, as in the case of a man and a horse [for both are animals]. It would appear that the sense 15
in which water from the same spring is called "the same" is in some way different from the senses already mentioned. But this sense, too, should come under that in which things are said to be the same in species in some way or other, seeing that all such things seem to be akin and closely related to each other. For every instance of water is said to be the same in species 20
as every other instance because of a certain likeness, and instances of water from the same spring differ in no way other than that they are very similar; and for this reason we do not distinguish instances of water from instances of other things which are called "the same in species" in one way or another. The sense of the term "the same" most agreed upon by all men is that in which things are said to be numerically one. But this sense, too, is usually 25
employed in many ways: (a) in the main and primary sense, whenever the same thing is called by different names or definitions, e.g., by the names "a covering" and "a cloak," or by "a man" and "a two-footed terrestrial animal"; (b) second, whenever the same thing is called also by one of its properties, e.g., by "a man" and "that which can acquire *knowledge*," or by "fire" and "that which by its nature goes up," and (c) third, whenever the 30
same thing is called also by an accident, e.g., by "Socrates" and "the man who sits there" or "that musical man"; for in each of these examples one wishes to signify a thing which is numerically one. That what has just been said is true may best be perceived if one substitutes the alternative expression in each case. For we often order a person to call one of those who are sitting by mentioning just his name; but if the person ordered happens 35
not to understand who is to be called, then, by using some accident instead so that the person ordered might better understand, we tell him "that man there who is sitting" or "that man there who is talking," clearly supposing ourselves to be signifying the same man by name or by accident.

8

Let the name "the same," then, as we said, be used in three distinct senses. 103b
Now one way of being convinced that arguments proceed from the elements mentioned and through these and towards these is by induction; for if one were to examine each of the things proposed or each of the 5
problems, it would be apparent to him that it is formed either from the definition of a thing or from a property or a genus or an accident of it. Another way of being convinced is by means of a syllogism. For every predicate of a thing [as a subject] must be either convertible with that subject or not. If it is convertible [with respect to predication], it would be either a definition or a property; for if it signifies the thing's essence, it is 10

a definition, but if not, it is a property (for a property is just this: that which is convertible with its subject but does not signify its essence). But if it is not convertible with the thing, it is either in the definition as a part said of the subject or not. If it is a part in the definition, it would be a genus or a differentia, since a definition is composed of a genus and differentiae; but if it is not a part of the definition, then clearly it would be an accident, for it was stated that an accident of a thing is that which is neither a definition nor a genus nor a property but belongs to that thing.

9

Next, we should specify the genera of predicates in which the four topics listed above are found. They are ten in number: whatness, quantity, quality, relation, somewhere, at some time, being in position, possessing [or having], acting, and being acted upon [or being affected]. For an accident or a genus or a property or a *definition* will always come under one of these categories, seeing that every thing proposed through some one of these topics signifies either a whatness or a quality or a quantity or some one of the other categories. It is clear from the [statements] themselves that a statement which signifies the whatness of a thing signifies sometimes a *substance* of it, sometimes a quality of it, sometimes some other category. For whenever the object before a person is a man and that person says "this object is a man" or "this object is an animal," that person states the object's whatness, and the predicate signifies a substance; and whenever that object is whiteness, which is a color, and that person says "this object is whiteness" or "this object is a color," he [still] states the object's whatness, and the predicate signifies a quality. Similarly, if the object before a man is a magnitude of one cubit and he says "this object is a magnitude of one cubit," he states that object's whatness, and the predicate signifies a quantity. It is likewise with each of the other cases; for in each of them, if one states [exactly] what the object before him is or states a genus of it, the predicate of his statement signifies the whatness of that object. But whenever the predicate states something else about the thing, it signifies not the whatness of it but a quantity of it or a quality of it or something under some other category. So the kinds of things from which arguments proceed and about which they deal are, in nature and in number, those stated above. We should discuss next how we will acquire them and through what means we will be well supplied with them.

10

First, then, we should specify what a dialectical proposition is and what a dialectical problem is. Not every proposition or problem should be posited 5 as being dialectical; for no one in his right mind would propose something which is not accepted by anyone or regard as a problem something which is evident to all or to most, since in the latter case no doubt exists, and in the former one just does not posit what everyone denies. A dialectical proposition, then, is a question [for an assent to] something generally accepted by all or most of the people or by the wise, and if by the wise, either by all or by most or by those who are most known; but it is not 10 contrary to general opinion, for one might posit something which is thought to be true by the wise, provided that it is not contrary to the opinions of most men. Dialectical propositions include also (a) propositions which resemble generally held opinions, (b) the contradictories of contraries of generally accepted opinions, and (c) all opinions in accordance with the established 15 arts. For (a) if it is generally accepted that the same science deals with contraries, it is likewise accepted that the same power of sensation senses contraries, and if it appears that grammar is generally accepted as being a single science, then it appears that flute-playing, too, is generally accepted as being a single science, but if many, then many; for all these examples seem to be similar and akin to each other. Similarly, too, (b) propositions 20 which are the contradictories of contraries of generally accepted opinions would appear to be generally accepted; for if it is generally accepted that one should treat friends well, it would be also generally accepted that one should not treat friends badly. Here, "one should treat friends badly" is a contrary of "one should treat friends well," and the contradictory of that 25 contrary is "one should not treat friends badly." Similarly, if one should treat friends well, one should not treat enemies well; for "one should treat enemies well," too, is the contradictory of a contrary of "one should treat friends well." Here, a contrary of "one should treat friends well" is "one should treat enemies well." It is likewise with others of this sort. By comparison, too, if, the contrary of a generally accepted opinion is predicated of the contrary of the subject, such predication will appear to be generally accepted. For example, if one should treat friends well, he should 30 also treat enemies badly. Here, it would appear that treating friends well is contrary to treating enemies badly; but whether this, too, is truly the case or not will be taken up in our discussion concerning contraries. It is clear that opinions which are in accordance with the arts, too, are dialectical propositions; for one would posit that which is thought to be the case by 35 artists who have studied their subjects; for example, concerning matters within the medical art or geometry, the dialectician would posit what is thought by the physician or the mathematician, respectively, to be the case, and similarly in other arts or sciences.

11

104b   A dialectical problem is a [statement] (1) which is to be investigated for
its choice or rejection or its truth and knowledge, either for itself, or as an
aid to some other choice or rejection or truth and knowledge, and (2) about
which (a) there is no opinion in one way or another, or (b) most people have
5   opinions contrary to those of the wise, or the wise have opinions contrary to
those of most people, or there are contrary opinions among the wise or
among most people. For it is useful to know (a) some problems with a view
to choice or avoidance, (e.g., whether one should choose pleasure or not),
others with a view to knowledge alone (e.g., whether the universe is eternal
or not), still others not with a view to choice or avoidance or just for their
10   knowledge but as an aid to some of these (for there are many things we wish
to know, not for themselves, but for the sake of other things, in order to
know something else by means of them. There are also problems for which
there are syllogisms leading to contrary conclusions (for one is faced with a
15   difficulty whether so-and-so is the case or not because there are convincing
arguments for and against a position), and also great problems for which we
have no arguments since we find it difficult to give *reasons*, e.g., the
problem whether the universe is eternal or not (for one might make
inquiries into such problems also). Let propositions and problems, then, be
specified as we stated.
20   A thesis is (1) a paradoxical belief contrary to general opinion but held by
some eminent philosopher (e.g., the statement "one cannot state a
contradiction," as Antisthenes said, or "all things are in motion," as
Heraclitus said, or "being is one," as Melissus said), for to pay attention to
any chance person's statements which are contrary to general opinions
would be silly; or, it may be (2) a belief based on an argument which is
25   contrary to general opinion (e.g., the belief, held by sophists, that not all
things either were generated or are eternal, for a musician who is a
grammarian is a grammarian neither by having become so nor by being
eternally so), for even if such belief is not accepted by someone, it might be
accepted because of the argument for it.
30   Now a thesis is also a problem; but not every problem is a thesis since some
problems are such that we have no opinion about them either way. It is clear
that a thesis is a problem; for it follows from what has been said that either
most people disagree with the philosophers about a thesis, or there is
disagreement among the philosophers or among most people, seeing that a
35   thesis is a belief which is contrary to general opinion. Nowadays, practically
every dialectical problem is called "a thesis." It makes no difference,
however, regardless of how these are called; for we distinguished theses in
105a   this manner not for the sake of introducing names but in order that their
differences will not escape us.

Not every problem or thesis need be considered for examination but only those for which one who is perplexed needs an argument, not punishment or evidence by sensation; for those who raise the problem whether or not one 5 should honor the gods or love his parents deserves punishment, while those who raise the problem whether snow is white or not need sensation. Nor, again, should one consider a problem or a thesis whose solution is close to a demonstration or too far removed from it; for the former is not difficult, while the latter is too difficult to be handled by the art.

12

With the above things settled, we should distinguish the number of 10 species of dialectical arguments. One of them is induction, the other is a syllogism. We stated earlier what a syllogism is; as for induction, it is the passage from particulars to universals, e.g., if the most effective pilot is the one who has *knowledge*, and likewise for the most effective charioteer, then 15 the best in each [of the arts] is he who has *knowledge*. Now an induction is more persuasive and clearer and more known [than a syllogism] according to the senses and is common to most people, but a syllogism is more forceful and more obvious to those who are contentious.

13

Let the genera of things with which arguments are concerned and from 20 which arguments are formed be specified as stated earlier. As for the kinds of means by which we will be well supplied with syllogisms and inductions, they are four: (1) the acquiring of propositions, (2) the ability to distinguish the number of senses of each expression, (3) the discovery of the differences 25 of things, and (4) the inquiry into likenesses of things. The last three of these, too, are in a certain sense propositions; for it is possible to make a proposition from each of them. For example, "the term 'choiceworthy' may mean the noble or the pleasurable or the expedient," "sensation differs from *knowledge* in that *knowledge* may be acquired again after having been lost, whereas sensation cannot," and "the relation of the healthy to health is like 30 the relation of that which can cause a good bodily disposition to the good bodily disposition itself."

The first of these arises from the ability to make distinctions, the second from finding differences, and the third from the inquiry into likenesses of things.

14

One should select propositions in as many ways as there are distinctions
35   among propositions, i.e., by having available opinions held by all or by most
men, or by all or most or the most eminent of the wise, or opinions contrary
105b to those which appear to be so, and also those which are in accord with the
arts. One should form also the contradictories of opinions which are
contrary to what appear to be generally accepted opinions, as already
stated. It is useful, too, to form propositions by selecting not only those
5   which are generally held, but also those which are similar to these, e.g., like
the proposition "contrary sensible objects are sensed by the same power of
sensation," for it is the same science that deals with contrary intelligible
objects also, and the proposition "we see by receiving something into
ourselves and not by emitting something from ourselves," for it is in this
manner that the other kinds of sensations occur, since we hear by receiving
something from outside and not by emitting, and we taste something in a
10   similar manner; and similarly in the other cases. Again, we should take as
principles or as theses which are generally accepted those which appear to
be true in all or in most cases, for they are posited by those who do not
observe exceptions to them. We should select also propositions from written
works and make separate lists under each genus of things, e.g., "On Good,"
15   "On Animals," "On Each Kind of Good," starting with the category of
whatness. We should take note also of opinions held by each eminent
thinker, e.g., "Empedocles said that the elements of bodies are four"; for
one might accept an opinion made by an eminent thinker.
20   Sketchily considered, propositions and problems may be divided into
three parts; for some propositions are ethical, some are about objects of
physics, and some are logical. Ethical propositions are such as "Whether one
should obey his parents rather than the laws, if these disagree," logical are
such as "whether it is the same science that deals with contraries, or not,"
25   and those about objects of physics are such as "whether the universe is
eternal or not"; and similarly for problems. Each of these kinds cannot be
easily rendered by a *definition*, but we should try to recognize each of them
by habit gained through induction, examining them by making use of the
examples given above.
30   For purposes of philosophy, we should study propositions and problems
as instruments for truth, but dialectically, we should employ them to impart
opinion. Every proposition should be taken in its most universal form, and
then it should be made into many; e.g., the universal expression "it is the
same science that investigates opposites" should then be made into "it is the
same science that investigates contraries," "it is the same science that
35   investigates relatives," etc. In the same manner, each of these should be
further divided, as far as this is possible, e.g., "it is the same science that

investigates good and evil," "it is the same science that investigates white and black," "it is the same science that investigates hot and cold," etc., and similarly with other statements taken in their most universal form.

15

Concerning propositions, then, let the above remarks be sufficient. *106a* Concerning the number of senses of a term, we should deal not only with the number of senses in which it is used but also try to give a formula of each of them; of the term "good," for example, we should say not only that in one way it means justice or bravery or etc., and in another the healthy or the 5 productive-of-good-bodily-condition or etc., but also that in the first case it means the things stated as being in themselves qualities of a certain kind but in the second case it means the things stated as being not qualities in themselves but things which can bring about (in the examples given) health or a good bodily condition. Similarly also in other cases.

Whether a term has only one meaning in species or many should be 10 considered by the following means. First, one should examine if its contrary is stated in many ways, whether these differ in species or in name, for in some cases a difference in names indicates at once a difference in the things signified. For example, the contrary of "sharp" in musical notes is "flat," but in solid edges it is "dull." Clearly, then, the contrary of "sharp" has many senses; accordingly, the term "sharp" has many senses also, for the 15 contraries of "flat" and of "dull," both of which are called "sharp," differ in meaning. For the term "sharp," though contrary to both "flat" and "dull," is not the same in meaning when it is contrary to "flat" as when it is contrary to "dull." Again, the contrary of the term βαρύ (= "flat," also "dull," and "heavy," and "dense") in the case of voice is "sharp," but in the case of a solid mass it is "heavy"; so the term βαρύ has many senses, since the contrary of it, too, has many senses. Similarly, the contrary of the term 20 καλός (= "beautiful," also "fine," and "noble") is "ugly" in the case of an animal but "poor" in the case of a house; so the term καλός is equivocal.

In some cases there is no difference in the name of the contrary of a thing but it is at once obvious that the meanings of that name differ in kind, as in the case of "clear" and "obscure"; for voice is called "clear" or "obscure," 25 but so is color. So the names do not differ when applied to both cases, but the difference of their meanings in kind is at once obvious; for color is not called "clear" in a sense in which voice is so called. This is clear also by sensation; for things of the same kind are sensed by the same faculty of 30 sensation, but that which is called "clear" in voice and also in color is not judged by the same faculty: it is judged by vision in the latter case but by the faculty of hearing in the former case. It is likewise with that which is called "sharp" or "dull" in flavors and also in solid edges; for in the latter case it is judged by touch but in the former case by taste. So here, too,

35 neither one nor the other of the two contraries differs in name in each of the two cases, for "dull" is used for both just as "sharp" is.

Further, if a name when applied to one thing has a contrary but when applied to another has no contrary at all, it has more than one meaning, as in the case of the name "pleasure"; for the contrary of what is called "pleasure" when one is drinking is what is called "pain" when one is thirsty, but there is no contrary and so no name to the pleasure of beholding that

106b the diagonal of a square is incommensurable with the side. And love which accompanies the *thought* of someone has hate as its contrary, but love as a bodily activity has no contrary at all; so it is clear that the name "love" is equivocal. Again, two contraries as names may have intermediates in some

5 cases but none in others, or they may have intermediates which do not mean the same thing. Thus "light" and "dark" as applied to colors have "gray" as an intermediate but as applied to beer they have no contrary at all, or else they have the name "medium," which differs in meaning from "gray." So "light" and "dark" are equivocal terms. Once more, we should see if two

10 contraries have many intermediates for some cases but only one in other cases, as in λευκόν (= "clear," and also "white") and μέλαν (= "black," and also "obscure"); for in the case of colors there are many intermediates, whereas in the case of sounds there is only one, namely "soft."

Again, one should examine and see if the term which is opposed as the

15 contradictory of another term has many meanings; for if it does, then the original term has many meanings also. For example, the expression "not seeing" is used in many senses, namely, it may mean (a) not having vision and also (b) not actually using one's vision. This being so, it follows that "seeing," too, has many senses, for one of them is opposed to "having no

20 vision" and the other to "not using one's vision."

Again, terms which signify privation and possession should be examined; for if one of the two has many meanings so does the other. For example, if "sensing" means (a) an affection with respect to the soul and also (b) an

25 affection with respect to the body, then "not sensing," too, means the contrary of (a) and also of (b). Clearly, the two terms just mentioned are opposed with respect to privation and possession, for animals have by nature two faculties, one with respect to the soul and another with respect to the body.

30 Again, one should examine inflected forms of terms. Thus if "justly" has more than one meaning, then "just," too, will have more than one meaning; for corresponding to each meaning of "justly" there will be a meaning of "just." For example, if "justly" means according to one's *judgment* and also with the right judgment, then, similarly, the term "just" will have the corresponding meanings. Likewise, if "healthy" has more than one

meaning, "healthily" too will have more than one meaning. Now "healthy"   35
means (a) that which produces health, (b) that which preserves health, and
(c) that which is a sign of health; so "healthily," too, means: in such a way
as to produce or to preserve or to be a sign of health, respectively. Similarly
with the others: whenever a term has more than one meaning, an inflection   *107a*
of it, too, will have more than one meaning; and whenever an inflection of
a term has more than one meaning, the term itself will have more than one
meaning also.

We should examine also the genera of categories coming under a name
and see if the name is predicable of things under the same category; for if
not, then clearly the name is equivocal. For example, in the case of food, the   5
term "good" means that which can produce pleasure, in the medical art, it
means that which can produce health, when applied to the soul, it means a
soul of a certain quality, e.g., temperate or brave or just, and similarly if it
is applied to man. Occasionally it applies to a certain time, e.g., the right or   10
proper time, and often to a certain quantity, e.g., the proper amount, for the
proper amount, too, is called "good." Consequently, the term "good" is
equivocal. In a similar way, the term "clear" means transparent when
applied to water, but when applied to voice it means easy to hear. The term
"sharp," too, like the term "clear," is applied to things in about the same
manner, for it is not predicable of all things in the same way; for a sharp   15
voice is a swift voice, as experts in harmonic numbers tell us, a sharp angle
is an angle less than 90° (i.e., an acute angle), and a sharp knife is a knife
with a very sharp angle.

We should examine, too, the genera of things under the same term to see
if they are distinct without any of them coming under another, as in the case
of the term "man" when applied to a man and a picture of a man; for the   20
definitions of these two corresponding to the term "man" are distinct
(without one of them coming under the other). For "man" when applied to
a man means an animal of a certain kind, but when applied to the picture
it means a work of art of a certain kind (and neither is a man a work of art
nor is a work of art a man). But if one of the two genera comes under the
other, the definitions corresponding to the same name applied to the two
things need not be different. For example, the term "animal" is a genus of
a raven, and so is the term "bird"; and when we call a raven "a bird," we
also mean that it is an animal of a certain kind, so both genera are predicable   25
of the same thing, the raven. And, similarly, whenever we call a raven "a
flying biped animal," we also mean that it is a bird; so even if the two genera
are considered in this manner, both of them are predicable of the raven, and
so are their definitions. But if no one genus comes under another, this does
not take place; for whenever we call a picture of an animal "an animal" we   30
do not mean that it is an animal, as something alive, and whenever we call
an animal "animal" we do not mean that it is a picture.

We should examine not only if the genera to which a given term is applicable are distinct without any of them coming under another, but also the contrary of that term in the same manner; for if the contrary of that term has many meanings, so does the term itself.

35

It is also useful to take a look at definitions of the terms formed when the term in question is combined with other terms, as in the case of "clear water" and "clear voice"; for if the added parts—here, the parts "water" and "voice"—are taken away from the two definitions, the resulting parts in the definitions should be the same (that is, if the term in question is to have the same meaning). This does not happen if the term in question is equivocal, as in the example given here. For the definition corresponding to the first composite will be "water with a transparent quality" but the definition corresponding to the second composite will be "a voice which is easily heard." And when the terms "water" and "a voice" are taken away from the corresponding definitions, the two expressions left are not the same. But they should be, if indeed the term "clear" is to have the same meaning when applied to water and to voice.

107b

5

Equivocation often occurs unawares in the definitions of terms, too, and for this one should examine the definitions also. For example, if one says that being a sign of health or being productive of health is defined as "being symmetrically related to health," one should not let it go at that but examine what "symmetrically" means in each case; for, if in one case it means a thing which is such as to produce health, but in the other, a thing which is such that it indicates a certain kind of disposition, then "symmetrically" is equivocal.

10

Again, one should examine if the terms are not comparable with respect to degree or likeness. For example, we say that this water is clear and that voice is clear, but water and voice are not clear in the same sense, for an instance of water can be neither more clear than nor just as clear as an instance of a voice; and similarly with the term "sharp," when we call both a flavor and a sound "sharp." Hence each of the terms "clear" and "sharp" is equivocal; for some instances to which it is applicable cannot be compared with respect to likeness or degree. But if all instances to which a term is applicable were so comparable, the term would be univocal.

15

Now of genera which are different without any of them coming under any other, their differentiae too are different in kind, as in the case of "animal" and "science" (for their differentiae are different). So we should examine if the differentiae of things coming under genera such as those just mentioned are called by the same name. For example, "sharp" is a differentia of voice and also of a solid material, for sharpness may differentiate one voice from another, and similarly one solid material from another. So "sharp" when applied to voice and solid materials is equivocally used, for it is the differentia of genera which are different and neither of which comes under the other.

20

25

Again, we should examine things called by the same name and see if their differentiae are different, e.g., we say that bodies have color and also that tunes have color. But the differentiae of "color" when applied to bodies are "vision-piercing" and "vision-compressing," whereas the differentiae of 30 tunes are not the same as these. So the term "color" is equivocal, for differentiae which are the same apply only to things which are generically the same.

Again, since a species is not a differentia of anything, we should examine to see if one of two things called by the same name is a species but the other is a differentia. For example, the term "radical" in "a radical citizen" 35 signifies a differentia in politics, but "$\sqrt{2}$" in the expression "$\sqrt{2}$ is a radical" signifies a species. Hence "radical" is equivocally used in the two cases.

16

The investigation of the number of senses which a term may have, then, should proceed through the above and other such similar means. As for the differences among things, they should be investigated (a) within the same genus under which they may fall, as in the problems "What is the difference 108a between justice and bravery?" and "What is the difference between prudence and temperance?" (for all differences such as these come under the same genus, or (b) from different genera, if these do not differ very much, as in the problem "What is the difference between sensation and *knowledge*?"; for differences of things whose genera are far apart are quite 5 obvious.

17

Likeness should be examined among things which come under different genera, and as follows: (a) "A is to B, as C is to D," e.g., "*knowledge* is to the *known*, as sensation is to the sensible"; "A is in B, as C is in D," e.g., 10 "vision exists in the eye, as intellect exists in the soul" and "calm exists in the sea, as stillness exists in air." We should train ourselves most of all in things whose genera are very far apart, for then we shall be more easily able to perceive at a glance likenesses in the other cases. We should also examine things coming under the same genus to see if there is something which is the 15 same in all (species), e.g., in a man and a horse and a dog; for insofar as there is something which is the same in them, to this extent they are alike.

18

It is useful to have examined the various senses of a term for the sake of clarity (for if the various senses of a term have been made apparent to a
20   man, he would be in a better position to know what exactly he is positing) and for the sake of forming syllogisms in accordance with the facts themselves and not just by the use of names. For if the senses of a term used are not clear, the answerer and the questioner may not be directing their *thoughts* to the same sense of a term; but once the senses of a term are made
25   apparent and the answerer posits the particular sense of the term he has in mind, the questioner would appear ridiculous if his argument is directed not against this sense of the term. Knowing the various senses of a term is useful also in guarding against committing fallacies and in misleading others by means of fallacies. For, knowing the senses of a term, (a) we will not only avoid committing fallacies but also know if the questioner argues not against
30   the sense of the term we have in mind, and (b) we ourselves, when questioning others, will be able to mislead others by means of fallacies, if they do not happen to know the various senses of a term. This, however, is not possible in all cases of terms which have many senses, but only in those in which the answer to a question is true for some of the senses of a term but false for the other senses. This way of arguing, however, is not appropriate to dialectics; and for this reason dialecticians should avoid
35   altogether using such verbal arguments, unless an opponent is unable to discuss a subject before him in any other way.

The discovery of differences among things is useful both for forming
108b syllogisms concerning sameness and otherness among things and for gaining knowledge of what a thing is. Clearly, it is useful for syllogisms concerning sameness and otherness; for, having discovered any kind of difference between two things, we will have shown that those things are not the same. And it is useful in knowing what a thing is, because we usually determine
5   the formula which is proper to the *substance* of a thing by the differentiae appropriate to that thing.

The investigation of likeness in things is useful (a) for inductive arguments, (b) for hypothetical syllogisms, and (c) for the rendering of definitions.
10   (a) It is useful for inductive arguments, because we claim that it is by induction from similar individuals that we are lead to the universal; for it is not easy to induce universals without knowledge of likenesses among things.

(b) It is useful for hypothetical syllogisms because it is generally accepted that, among things which are like, what is true of one is true of the others
15   also. So if we are well supplied with cases of similars for discussion, we shall have prior admission that whatever is true in those cases is also true in the

case which is at issue before us. Then having shown that something is true in those cases, we shall have shown by hypothesis a similar truth in the case before us; for, with the hypothesis that whatever is true in those cases is also true in the case before us, we shall have demonstrated our point in the case before us.

(c) It is useful for the rendering of definitions because, if we are able to *20* perceive what is the same in each of a number of particulars, we shall be at no loss in placing the thing under the right genus when we are defining it; for the most common predicate in a definition of a number of particulars which states what those particulars are is their genus. Likewise, the investigation of likeness is useful also for definitions of things which are far different. For example, calm at sea is the same as stillness in air (for calm *25* and stillness are instances of tranquility), and a point on the end of a line is the same as a unit in a number (for a point and a unit are instances of beginnings or principles). So having stated the genus common to all particulars, we regard this manner of defining as not inappropriate. Those who define things in this manner usually state their definitions in about the same way; for they say that a unit is the beginning of a number, and a point *30* is the beginning of a line. Clearly, then, they place both a number and a line under a genus common to both, i.e., under "beginning."

The means by which syllogisms are formed, then, are those we have given; the common rules for which those means are useful are as follows.

SOPHISTICAL REFUTATIONS

CONTENTS

Chapter

SOPHISTICAL REFUTATIONS

1

164a 20   Let us discuss sophistical refutations and also what appear to be refutations but are fallacies and not refutations, starting from things which are first according to nature.

Evidently, there are syllogisms, but also arguments which are thought to
25   be but are not syllogisms. For, just as in other fields what is thought to be because of some likeness is not really the case, so it happens with arguments. Among men, too, there are those who are in good physical condition but also those who, like tribesmen, only appear to be so by puffing up and dressing
164b 20   up themselves, and there are those who are beautiful because of their beauty but also those who only appear to be so by embellishing themselves. So, too, with inanimate things; for, of these, some are truly silver and others are truly gold, but there are also those which are not and yet appear to be so to our senses, like certain stones and compounds of tin which appear silvery and
25   also certain yellow-colored metals which appear to be gold. In the same way, there are syllogisms and refutations; and there are also arguments which appear to be syllogisms and refutations because of inexperience but are not, for inexperienced people view such arguments as if from a great
165a   distance. Now a syllogism consists of expressions so posited that through these something else of necessity is asserted, and a refutation is a syllogism whose conclusion contradicts another conclusion; but there are arguments which do not conclude or contradict anything but are thought to do so for
5   many reasons, the most natural and most commonly used being the argument by means of names. For since it is not possible to discuss these things by bringing forward the things themselves, we use names as symbols of the things, and so we think that what follows for the names [as symbols]
10   follows for the things themselves also, as with counters when used to count objects. But the two cases are not similar; for the names are finite in number and so are the arguments, whereas the things symbolized by those names are limitless in number, and hence the same expression or a single name of necessity signifies many things. Accordingly, just as those without skill in

counting are taken in by the experts, so those without the experience to use   *15*
names effectively in arguments commit fallacies or are taken in when others
do so. For this reason, then, and for others to be stated later, there exist what
appear to be syllogisms and refutations but are not.

Since for some people it is more convenient to be thought to be wise than   *20*
to be wise without being so thought (for sophistry appears to be wisdom
without being so, and a sophist is one who makes money by appearing to
possess wisdom without really possessing it), it is clear, too, that such people
must rather so behave as to be thought to philosophize than actually
philosophize without being thought to do so. The function of a person who   *25*
has knowledge, then, if taken in relation to each of two ways of knowing,
so to say, is (a) to avoid speaking falsely about the things he knows and (b)
to be able to show up the person who speaks falsely about those things; and
acting according to (a) depends on the ability to give [right] answers, but
according to (b) on the ability to secure [right] answers. Those who would
be sophists, then, must make an inquiry into the genus of arguments already   *30*
stated, for this would suit them; for a faculty of this kind will make them
appear to be wise, since this is their intention.

It is clear, then, that there is such a genus of arguments, and that the aim
of those whom we call "sophists" is to possess such a faculty. Let us now
discuss the number of species of sophistical arguments, the number of things   *35*
of which this faculty consists, the number of parts of this discipline, and all
other things which contribute to this art.

2

There are four genera of arguments which may enter into a discussion:
didactic, dialectical, investigative, and eristic. Didactive arguments proceed   *165b*
to prove something from the appropriate principles of each subject and not
from the opinions of the answerer (for he who learns should be convinced
of what he is learning); dialectical arguments proceed from generally
accepted opinions and prove contradictories of opinions held by the
opponents; investigative arguments proceed from what is thought to be true   *5*
by the answerer or from what a man who claims to have scientific
knowledge must know (we have discussed elsewhere in what manner he
must know); contentious arguments (a) proceed from what appear to be but
are not generally accepted opinions or (b) appear to prove something
without actually doing so. Arguments which are demonstrative have been
discussed in the [*Posterior*] *Analytics*, those which are dialectical or   *10*
investigative have been discussed elsewhere. Let us now discuss those which
are contentious and eristic.

3

We must first take note of the number of things aimed at by those who compete in arguments or like to win them. They are five in number: refutation, falsity, paradox (e.g., the contrary of a generally accepted opinion), solecism, and babbling (the last of these being to force the opponent to say the same thing many times); or, if not these, then what is aimed at is what appears to be each of these. Men intend to give the appearance of refuting their opponents most of all; second, to show that the opponent said something false; third, to lead the opponent into stating a paradox; fourth, to lead the opponent to make a solecism, that is, to force the answerer, from what he says, to use inappropriate language; lastly, to force the opponent to repeat something unnecessarily. . . .

34

As to (a) the number and kinds of sources from which fallacies are committed between opponents in arguments, (b) how we can show that an opponent is stating something false and also make him state things contrary to generally accepted opinions, (c) the materials used to form syllogisms, (d) how we should ask questions and what order we should use in asking them, (e) what things all such arguments are used for, (f) how the answerer should respond both in general and to each particular case, and (g) how one should refute arguments and syllogisms, let the above discussion suffice for all. It remains now to recall our original proposal and bring our discussion to an end with a few words.

Our intention was to find a syllogistic faculty which, starting from the most generally accepted opinions, deals with problems before us; for this is the essential function of the dialectical and of the investigative arts. But since, on account of its nearness to the art of sophistry, this faculty seeks means which can be used not only for dialectical purposes but also as a pretense to knowledge, for this *reason* we laid down for our treatise not only the function of being able to grasp an argument but also the function of being able, in a similar way when opposing an argument, to defend a thesis by means of the most generally accepted opinions. We have stated[1] the *reason* for this; and it is because of this, too, that Socrates was asking questions but giving no answers, for he admitted that he did not know. Now we have made clear in our earlier discussion the number of things to which and the number of materials from which this will come about, and the sources from which we shall be well supplied with materials; also, how we should ask questions and arrange all our questioning, and how we should answer and refute syllogisms. We have made clear also other arguments which come under the same *inquiry*. In addition to these, we have gone through the subject of fallacies, as already stated earlier.[2] So it is evident that the things we intended to discuss have been completed adequately. We must not, however, fail to notice the outcome of this discipline. For of all things discovered, those which had resulted from earlier labors were advanced part by part by those to whom they were handed down. New discoveries usually advance but little at first, yet such advance is far more useful than the development which follows later. For perhaps, as people say, "the beginning is the greatest part of the whole," and it is for this reason that it is the most difficult. For it is the smallest in magnitude to the same extent as it is the greatest in power, and so it is the most difficult to be seen; but once discovered, it is easier to add to it and develop the rest. And indeed this is what happened to rhetorical theories (and to practically all the other arts); for those who discovered the principles of this art advanced it very little, but those who are highly thought of nowadays, being as if heirs to a succession of many who have contributed little by little, advanced the art considerably. Thus Tisias came after the first founders, then Thrasymachus followed Tisias, then Theodorus after Thrasymachus, and likewise many others added many parts to rhetoric; so indeed it is no wonder that at present this art has a multitude of parts. Now of this discipline it is not true that one part was thoroughly done but another was not; in fact, nothing existed at all. Even the teaching of contentious arguments by paid instructors was conducted in a manner similar to that of Gorgias; for what students were given to learn by heart were speeches, some rhetorical and others in the form of question and answer, in which each of the two sides thought that most of the arguments were placed. For this reason, the teaching of rhetoric from instructors to students was quick but without art; for these instructors assumed that educating students in rhetoric is making them learn not that art but the products of that art, as if one were to say that teaching a man the science of preventing painful walking is not teaching him the art of shoe-making or the sources from which he can acquire a thing of this sort, but presenting him with many kinds of varieties of shoes; for such a teacher will be of help to what the man needs, but he will not impart the art of making shoes. Concerning rhetorical matters, too, there is much that has been stated long ago, but up to now nothing at all of a syllogistic nature, except a great deal of time spent in artless inquiries. If, then, it appears to you, after considering this *inquiry* from its beginnings, that it has been adequately treated when compared with the other disciplines which have been developed by tradition, there would remain for all of you, or you who are our students, the task of pardoning us for what is left yet to be done, but of showing much gratitude for the discoveries we added.

PHYSICS

CONTENTS

BOOK I

Chapter

PHYSICS

BOOK I

1

Since understanding and *knowing* in every *inquiry* concerned with things having principles or causes or elements results from the knowledge of these (for we think that we know each thing when we know the first causes and the first principles and have reached the elements), clearly, in the science of nature too we should first try to determine what is the case with regard to the principles.

The natural way to proceed is from what is more known and *clearer* to us to what is by nature *clearer* and more known; for what is known to us and what is known without qualification are not the same. So we should proceed in this manner, namely, from what is less *clear* by nature, though *clearer* to us, to what is by its nature *clearer* and more known. Now the things that are at first plain and *clear* to us are rather mingled, and it is later that their elements and principles become known to those who distinguish them. Consequently, in the case of each thing, we should proceed from its entirety to each of its constituents, for it is the whole that is more known by sensation; and a thing in its entirety, since it includes many constituents as parts, is a kind of a whole. In a sense, a name is related to its formula in the same way, for a name signifies some whole without distinguishing its parts, as in the case of "a circle"; but its definition analyzes the whole into its constituents. Children, too, at first call every *man* "papa" and every woman "mama", but later on they distinguish each of them.

5

All thinkers posit contraries as principles, e.g., (a) those who say that the universe is one and motionless (even Parmenides posits the *Hot* and the *Cold* as principles and calls them "*Fire*" and "*Earth*") and (b) those who speak of the *Rare* and the *Dense* and (c) Democritus, who posits the *Solid* and the *Void*, calling them "*Being*" and "*Nonbeing*", respectively, and who uses [as differentiae] *Position, Shape,* and *Order* as

184*a* 10

15

20

25

184*b* 10

188*a*

20

genera of contraries (for example, in the case of position, these are *up*
25   and *down,* and also *in front* and *behind;* but in the case of shape, they
are the *angular* and the *non-angular,* and also the *straight* and the *circular*).

It is clear, then, that in a sense all thinkers posit contraries as principles, and with good reason; for (a) neither must one principle be composed of another principle, (b) nor should they be composed of other
things but the other things should be composed of them. Now the primary contraries possess both these attributes: (b) They are not com-
30   posed of other things because they are primary, and (a) neither of them
is composed of the other because they are contraries. However, we
should attend to an argument as well in order to see how this turns out
to be the case.

First we must grant that no thing by nature acts on, or is acted on
by, any other chance thing, nor does any thing come to be from any
other [chance] thing, unless one grants that this takes place in virtue of
35   of an attribute. For how could the white come to be from the musical
unless the musical were an accident of the not-white or the black? But
the white does come to be from the nonwhite, not from any nonwhite
188*b*   but from black or some intermediate color; and the musical comes to be
from the nonmusical, not from any nonmusical but from the unmusical
or something between the musical and the unmusical, if there is such.

Nor again does any thing, when destroyed, change into any chance
thing. For example, the white is destroyed not into the musical, unless
5   it be in virtue of an attribute, but into the nonwhite, not into any chance
nonwhite but into black or some other intermediate color; and the musical is similarly destroyed into the nonmusical, not into any chance nonmusical but into the unmusical or some intermediate between the two,
if there is such.

It is likewise with all other cases, since the same formula applies even
10   to things which are not simple but composite; but we fail to notice this
happening because no names have been given to the opposite dispositions. For the harmonious must come to be from the inharmonious, and
the inharmonious, from the harmonious; and the harmonious must be
destroyed into something which is not harmonious, not into any chance
15   thing but into that which is opposed   to the harmonious. It makes no
difference whether we speak of harmony or of order or of composition,
for evidently it is the same formula which applies to them. Again, the
generation of a house and of a statue and of any other thing takes place
in a similar way. For a house is generated from objects which exist not
in composition but are divided in a certain way, and likewise for a statue
20   or anything that has been shaped from shapelessness;   and what results
in each of these are order in one case and a composition in the other.

If, then, all this is true, every thing that is generated or destroyed is so from or to a contrary or an intermediate. As for the intermediates, they are composed of contraries; the other colors, for example, are composed of white and black. Thus every thing which is generated by nature is a   25 contrary or composed of contraries.

Up to this point most of the other thinkers were quite close in following this line of thinking, as we said before[1]; for they all said that the elements, also called "principles" by them, are contraries, as if compelled by truth itself even if they gave no reason. However, they differed from each   30 other thus: Some of them used prior   contraries, while others used posterior, and some used contraries more known in formula, while others used contraries more known according to sensation; for some posited as causes of generation the *Hot* and the *Cold*, others, the *Moist* and the *Dry,* while others posited the *Odd* and the *Even,* and still others, *Strife* and *Friendship;* and these differ from each other in the way stated. So   35 the principles which they used are in one way the same but in another distinct. They are distinct in the manner in which most thinkers took them to be; but they are the same insofar as they are analogous, for they   189*a* are taken from the same two sets of contraries[2] some of them being wider while others narrower in extent.   In this way, then, they spoke of them in the same and also in a distinct manner, some in a worse and others in a better way, and, as we said, some posited them as more known according to formula while others as more known according to   5 sensation. For the universal is known according to formula but the individual according to sensation, since the formula is of the universal but sensation is of the part; for example, contrary principles according to formula are the *Great* and the *Small,* those according to sensation are the *Dense* and the *Rare.*

It is evident, then, that the principles should be contraries.   10

6

Next, we should consider whether the principles are two or three or more than three.

There cannot be just one principle, since there cannot be just one contrary, nor can the principles be infinite, since otherwise being will not be *knowable.* Also, in every genus there is just one contrariety, and "substance" is one genus. Besides, it is possible for things to be generated from a finite number of principles; and it is better if they come to be   15 from a finite number, as Empedocles says, than from an infinite number (for Empedocles thinks that from his finite principles he can give an account of all that Anaxagoras can from his infinite principles). Again,

some contraries are prior to others, and some come to be from others, as
in the case of the sweet and bitter and of the white and black, but the
20   principles must always remain. So it is clear from all these arguments
that the principles are neither one nor infinite.

Since the principles, then, are finite, there is some reason in positing
them to be not only two; for one might raise the problem as to how
density can by nature act on rarity, or rarity on density, so as to produce
something. The problem is similar in the case of any pair of contraries;
25   for it is not *Strife* that *Friendship* brings together and makes something
out of, nor does *Strife* make something out of *Friendship*, but both act
on a third and distinct object. Some thinkers use even more such objects
from which they construct the nature of things.

In addition to the above, if no nature distinct from the contraries is
assumed, one might also raise another *difficulty*, for among things, we
30   observe no contrary as being a substance. Now a principle should not
be a predicate of any subject, since there would then be a principle of a
principle; for the subject is a principle and is thought to be prior to what
is a predicate of it. Moreover, we maintain that no substance is contrary to a substance. So how can there be a substance which is composed of nonsubstances? Or, how can a nonsubstance be prior to a substance?

35   In view of all this, if we were to grant as true both the previous state-
189b   ment   and this [argument],[3] then, to preserve both, it would be necessary for us to assume a third [principle], like the one held by those
who say that the universe is of one nature, i.e., of water or fire   or an
intermediate between them. This principle seems to be rather an inter-
5   mediate; for fire and earth and air and water are already composites
with contraries. And on account of this, those who posit as an underlying subject something distinct from these four elements do so not without good reason. Other thinkers choose air from the four elements; for of
these, air has sensible differences to the least degree. Then water comes
next. Yet all these thinkers regard this one principle [or, the *One*] as tak-
10   ing on a shape by means of contraries, i.e., by *Density* and *Rarity*, and in
varying degrees. Now such contraries, considered universally, are
clearly excess and deficiency, as stated previously.[4] And the doctrine
that the *One*   and *Excess* and *Deficiency* are principles of things, we
may add, seems to be an old one, except that it is not stated in the same
manner; for the early thinkers said that the two [contraries] act but the
15   *One* is acted upon, whereas some of the later thinkers   stated rather the
contrary, namely, that the *One* acts while the two [contraries] are acted
upon.

From a consideration of these and other such arguments, then, it
would seem that there is some reason in maintaining that the elements

are three, as we said before; but there is no reason in maintaining that they are more than three, for one element is sufficient [as a subject] to be acted upon. If with four [elements] there are two contrarieties, a dis- 20 tinct intermediate nature will be needed for each contrariety; and if, being two, they can generate from each other, one of the two contrarieties will be superfluous. And along with this, the primary contrarieties cannot be many; for "substance" is a single genus of being, so the principles can differ in priority and posteriority and not in genus (for 25 in a single genus there can be only one contrariety, and all other contrarieties [in that genus] are thought to be referred to one).

It is evident, then, that there can be neither only one nor more than two or three elements; but, as we said before, there is much *difficulty* as to whether there are two or three.

7

We shall now give our own account by first going over generation 30 universally, for in proceeding according to nature we should first investigate what is common and then what is proper in each case.

We say that something comes to be from something else or that some one thing is coming to be from some other thing by speaking either of simple or of composite things. By this I mean the following: (a) A man becomes musical or the not-musical becomes musical, and (b) the not- 35 musical man becomes a musical man. In (a), I call "simple" the man or 190a the not-musical, which is becoming something else, and also the musical, which is what the former [the man or the musical] becomes; and in (b), when we say that the not-musical man becomes a musical man, we call "composite" both the thing generated and that which is in the 5 process of becoming.

Now of these, in some cases we say not only "A becomes B" but also "B comes to be from A", as in "the musical comes to be from the notmusical"; but we do not speak likewise in all cases, for we do not say "the musical came to be from the man" but "the man became musical".

Of simple things that come to be something, some of them persist 10 throughout the generation but others do not. For when a man becomes musical, he persists during the generation and is still a man [at the end of it], but the not-musical or the unmusical does not so persist, whether as a simple thing or when combined with the subject.

With these distinctions granted, then from all things which are being generated one may gather this, if he is to attend carefully to the manner of our statement—that there must always be something which underlies 15 that which is in the process of becoming and that this, even if numerically one, in kind at least is not one (and by "in kind" I mean the same thing as by "in formula", for "to be a man" and "to be unmusical" do not have the same meaning). And one part of that which is being generated persists but the other does not, that is, what is not an opposite persists (for the man persists) but the musical or the unmusical does not,

20   and neither does the composite persist, i.e., the unmusical man.

We say "B comes to be from A" rather than "A becomes B" of things which do not persist, i.e., we say "the musical is generated from the unmusical" but not "the musical is generated from the man"; but occasion-

25   ally we do likewise also of things which persist, for we say "a statue comes to be from bronze" but not "bronze becomes a statue".   As for the generation from the opposite which does not persist, it is stated in both ways: We say both "B comes to be from A" and "A becomes B", for we say both "the musical comes to be from the unmusical" and "the unmusical becomes musical"; and in view of this, we do likewise in the

30   case of the composite, for we say both "from being an unmusical man he becomes musical" and "the unmusical man becomes musical".

Now "becoming" has many senses: (a) In certain cases a thing is said to become a *this* in a qualified sense, while (b) a becoming without qualification exists only of substances.   And it is evident that in the former cases something underlies that which is in the process of generation; for

35   in the generation of some quantity or some quality or some relation or sometime or somewhere, there is some underlying subject, because only a substance is not said of [predicated of] some other underlying subject

190b whereas all others are said of substances. However, it will become evident on further examination that also substances and all other unqualified beings are generated from some underlying subject, for there is always some underlying subject from which the thing generated

5   comes to be, e.g., plants and animals from seeds.

Things in the process of generation without qualification may be generated by the changing of shape, as a statue from bronze; or by addition, like things which increase; or by the removal of something, like the statue *Hermes* from stone; or by composition, like a house; or by alteration, like things which alter with respect to their matter. It is evident that

10   all things which are being generated in this manner are generated from an underlying subject. So it is clear from what has been said that the thing in generation is always a composite, and there is that [say, A] which is generated, and what comes to be that [i.e., A] is something else, and this in two senses, either the subject or the opposite. By "the opposite" I mean, for example, the unmusical; by "the subject" I mean the

15   man; and the shapelessness and the formlessness and the disorder are opposites, while the bronze and the stone and the gold are underlying subjects.

Thus if, of things by nature, there are causes or principles   of which those things are composed primarily and from which they come to be not accidentally, but come to be what each of them is called according to its *substance,* then everything which is generated is generated from a   20 subject and a *form;* for the musical man is composed, in a sense, of a man and the musical, since one would be analyzing the formula [of the musical man]   by giving a formula of each of these two. Clearly, then, things in generation come to be from these [causes or principles].

Now the subject is in number one but in kind two;   for a man or gold   25 or matter in general can be numbered, for it is rather this [the subject] which is a *this,* and it is not as from an attribute that the thing in generation comes to be from this, but what is an attribute is the privation or the contrary; and the form is one, as in the case of order or music or some other such predicate. So in a sense the principles may be spoken of as being two, but in another sense as being three;   and they may also   30 be spoken of as being the contraries,   for example, if one were to say that they are the musical and the unmusical or the hot and the cold or the harmonious and the inharmonious; but in another sense they may not be so spoken of, for the contraries cannot be acted upon by each other. And this problem   is solved because there is a subject which is distinct [from the contraries], for it is not a contrary. So in some sense   35 the principles are not more than the contraries but are two in number, so to speak; yet on the other hand, they are not entirely two but are three   191*a* because in each of them there is a distinction in essence;   for the essence of a man is distinct from the essence of the unmusical,   and the essence of the unshaped is distinct from that of bronze.

We have stated, then, the number of the principles concerning the generation of physical objects and how they are so many, and it is clear that there must be something which underlies the contraries and that   5 the contraries are two. Yet in another sense this is not necessary, for one of the contraries is sufficient to produce the change by its absence or presence.

As for the underlying nature,   it is *knowable* by analogy. Thus, as bronze is to the statue or the wood is to the bed or the matter or the *formless* object prior to receiving a *form* is to that which has a *form,*   10 so is this [underlying nature] to a substance or to a *this* or to being. This then is one of the principles, though it is not one nor a being in the manner of a *this;* another [principle] is the formula; then there is the contrary of the latter, and this is the privation.

In what sense these [principles] are two and in what sense more than   15 two has been stated above. First it was stated that only the contraries are principles, then it was stated that there must be something else, an underlying subject, and so the principles must be three. From the pre-

ceding statements it is evident how the contraries differ, how the principles are related to each other, and what the underlying subject is. As
20   to whether it is the form or the underlying subject that is a substance,
this is not yet clear.[5] But that the principles are three and how they
are three and what their manner of existence is, this is clear.

Concerning the number of the principles and what they are, then, let
the above be our investigation.

                        8

We will now proceed to state that the *difficulty* of the early thinkers,
too, is solved only in this manner.

In seeking the truth and the nature of things from the philosophical
25   point of view, the first thinkers, as if led astray by inexperience, were
misled into another way of thinking by maintaining the following: No
thing can be generated or be destroyed because a thing must be generated either from being or from nonbeing; but both of these are impos-
30   sible, for being cannot become something since it already exists, and a
thing generated cannot come to be from nonbeing since there must be
some underlying subject [from which it is to be generated]. And
exaggerating the consequences in this manner, they concluded by saying
that there is no plurality of things, but that only *Being* itself exists. This
is the doctrine they adopted, then, and for the *reasons* stated.

Our position, however, is that, in one way, the expressions "to be
35   generated from being or from nonbeing" or "nonbeing or being acts upon
or is acted upon by something, or becomes a *this*, whatever this may
191b   be" do not differ from "a doctor acts upon or is acted upon by something"
or "from a doctor something else is or comes to be"; hence, since each of
these expressions has two senses, it is clear that also each of the expressions "from being [or nonbeing]" and "being [or nonbeing] acts upon
or is acted upon" has two senses. Thus, the doctor builds [a house] not
5   qua a doctor but qua a builder, and he becomes grey-haired not qua a
doctor but qua black-haired; but he heals or becomes a nondoctor qua
a doctor. So since, in saying "a doctor acts or is acted upon by something,
or from a doctor he becomes something else", we do so mainly when it
is qua a doctor that he acts upon or is acted upon by something or that
he becomes something else, it is clear that also "to become something
10   from nonbeing" means this, namely, to become something qua not-
being.

It is the failure to make this distinction that led those thinkers astray,
and through their ignorance of this they added so much more as to
think that nothing else is generated or exists [besides *Being*], thus doing
away with every [kind of] generation. Now we too maintain, as they do,

that nothing is generated from unqualified nonbeing, yet we do maintain that generation from nonbeing in a qualified sense exists, namely,
with respect to an attribute; for from the privation, which in itself is a 15
not-being, something which did not exist is generated. Such generation
from nonbeing, of course, is surprising and is thought to be impossible.
In the same way, we maintain that being is not generated from being,
except with respect to an attribute; so this generation too takes place in
the same manner, as if an animal were to be generated from an animal, 20
or an animal of one kind from an animal of another kind, i.e., if a dog
were to come to be from a horse. For the dog would then come to be not
only from an animal of another kind, but also from an animal, but not
qua an animal since this is already there. But if an object is to become
an animal not with respect to an attribute, then it will do so not from
an animal, and if it is to become a being, then it will do so not from
being, nor from nonbeing, since we have stated⁶that "from nonbeing" 25
means qua not-being. And we may add here that [by this] we do not
reject the truth of "everything either is or is not".

This then is one way [of solving the difficulty]; but there is another,
in view of the fact that we may speak of things with respect to their
potentiality as well as with respect to their *actuality*, and we have settled
this elsewhere with greater accuracy.⁷

As we said, then, the difficulties through which some thinkers are com- 30
pelled to reject some of the things which we maintain are now solved;
for it was because of these [*difficulties*] that earlier thinkers also deviated
so much from the path which leads to the belief in generation, destruction, and change in general. If they had perceived this [underlying]
nature, this would have released them from all their ignorance.

9

Other thinkers,⁸ too, have perceived this nature, but not adequately. 35
For, in the first place, they agree that there is unqualified generation
from nonbeing, thus granting the statement of Parmenides as being 192*a*
right;⁹ secondly, it appears to them that if this nature is numerically one,
then it must be also one potentially, and this makes the greatest difference.

Now we maintain that matter is distinct from privation and that one
of these, matter, is nonbeing with respect to an attribute but privation is 5
nonbeing in itself, and also that matter is in some way near to a substance but privation is in no way such.

These thinkers, on the other hand, maintain that the *Great* and the
Small are alike nonbeing, whether these two are taken together as one

or each is taken separately. And so they posit their triad in a manner
10   which is entirely distinct from ours. Thus, they have gone so far as to
perceive the need of some underlying nature, but they posit this as being
one; for even if someone [Plato] posits the *Dyad,* calling it "the *Great*
and Small", he nevertheless does the same since he overlooks the other
[nature].[10]

Now in things which are being generated, one of these [two natures]
is an underlying joint cause with a *form,* being like a mother, so to
15   speak;[11] but the other part of the contrariety might often be imagined,
by one who would belittle it, as not existing at all. For, as there exists an
object   which is divine and good and something to strive after, we
maintain that one of the principles is contrary to it, but that the other
[principle],   in virtue of its nature, by nature strives after and desires
that object. According to the doctrine of these thinkers, on the other
20   hand, what results is that the contrary desires its own destruction. Yet
neither would the form strive after itself, because it does not lack it, nor
does it strive after the contrary, for contraries are destructive of each
other. Now this [principle] is matter, and it is like the female which desires the male and the ugly which desires the beautiful, but it is not by
25   itself that the ugly or the female does this,   since these are only attributes.

In one way, this [principle] is destroyed or is generated, but in another way it is not. For, as that   which is in something [in the matter],
it is this which in itself is being destroyed, since it is the privation in it
[in the matter] that is being destroyed; but as that which exists in virtue
of its potentiality,   this is not being destroyed in itself but is necessarily
indestructible and ungenerable.   For (a) if the latter were to be generated, it would have to be generated from something else which is
30   present and must be a primary underlying subject; yet its nature is to
be just this, so it would then be existing prior to its generation   (for by
"matter" here we mean the primary underlying subject in a thing, from
which [matter], as something present but not as an attribute, something
else is generated). And (b) if it were to be destroyed, it would ultimately
arrive at this very thing, so it would then be destroyed prior to its
destruction.
35   Concerning the principle with respect to form, whether it is one or
many and what it is or what they are, its accurate determination is a
192b   task belonging to first philosophy[12] and will be laid aside till then;   but
as regards the natural and destructible forms, we shall consider them in
this treatise later.

That there are principles, what these are, and how many they are, let
the above as given so far be our account of them. Next, let us proceed
from another starting-point.

BOOK II

1

Of things, some exist by nature, others through other causes. Animals
and their parts exist by nature, and so do plants and the simple bodies,
for example, earth, fire, air, and water; for we say that these and other
such exist by nature. Now all the things mentioned appear to differ
from things which are composed not by nature. All things existing by
nature appear to have in themselves a principle of motion and of standstill, whether with respect to place or increase or decrease or alteration. But a bed or a garment or a thing in some other similar genus,
insofar as each of them is called by a similar predicate and in virtue of
existing by art, has no natural tendency in itself for changing; but
insofar as it happens to be made of stone or earth or to be a composite
of these, it has such a tendency and only to that extent. So nature is a
principle and a cause of being moved or of rest in the thing to which it
belongs primarily and in virtue of that thing, but not accidentally. I
say "not accidentally" in view of the fact that the same man may cause
himself to become healthy by being a doctor; however, it is not in virtue
of becoming healthy that he has the medical art, but it is an accident
that the same man is both a doctor and becoming healthy, and on account of this, the one is at times separate from the other. Similarly, each
of the other things produced has in itself no principle of producing, but
in certain cases [in most cases] such a principle is in another thing or is
outside of the thing produced, as in the case of a house and other manufactured products, while in the remaining cases it is in the thing itself
but not in virtue of that thing, that is, whenever it is an accident in the
thing that causes the production in it.

We have stated, then, what nature is. Things which have such a
principle are said to have a nature; and they are all substances, for
each of them is a subject, and nature exists always in a subject. And
they and whatever essentially belongs to them are said to exist according to nature, as, for example, the upward locomotion of fire; for this

192*b*
10

15

20

25

30

35

193a [locomotion] is not nature, nor does it have a nature, but it exists by nature or according to nature.

We have stated, then, what nature is and what exists by nature and according to nature. As far as trying to prove that nature exists, this would be ridiculous, for it is evident that there are many such things;

5 and to try to prove what is evident through what is not evident is a mark of a man who cannot *judge* what is known through itself from what is known not through itself.   That this can take place is clear; for a man born blind may form syllogisms concerning colors, but such a man must be using mere names without conceiving the corresponding things.

10 Some think that the nature or *substance* of a thing existing by nature is the first   constituent which is in the thing and which in itself is without shape, like wood in the case of a bed or bronze in a bronze statue. (According to Antiphon, a sign of this is the fact that if one plants a bed and the moistened wood acquires the power of sending up

15 a shoot, what will result is not a bed but wood, thus showing that the arrangement of the parts according to custom or art belongs to the object planted by accident, but that the substance is that which persists while it is acted upon continuously.) And if each of these is also related to another object in the same way, say bronze and gold to water, bones

20 and wood to earth, and similarly with any others, then it is that other object which is the nature and the *substance* of those things. It is in view of this that some say that the nature   of all things is earth; others, that it is fire; others, air; others, water; others, some of these; and others, all of them. For whatever each thinker believed to be of this sort, whether only one object or more than one,   he posited this or these as

25 being all that is substance, but all other things as being affections or possessions or dispositions of substances, and also this or these as being eternal (for they said that there is no change from one of them to something else), but the other things [he posited] as being in generation and destruction a countless number of times.

In one way, then, nature is said to be the first underlying matter in

30 things which have in themselves a principle of motion or of change, but in another it is said to be the *shape* or form according to formula;   for just as we call "art" that   which exists in virtue of art   and is artistic, so we call "nature" that which exists in virtue of nature and is natural. Neither in the former case would we say that a thing has something in virtue of art   or that there is art   if the thing is only potentially a bed

35 but has not yet the form of a bed, nor is it so in things which are *com-*

193b *posites* by nature; for that which is potentially flesh or bone has not yet its nature   or does not yet exist by nature until it acquires the form according to the formula by which [form] we state what flesh or bone is when we define it. Thus, in another way, the nature of things which

have in themselves a principle of motion would be the *shape* or form,
which does not exist separately from the thing except according to 5
formula.   As for the *composite* of the two, e.g., a man, this is not nature,
but [we say] it exists by nature.

Indeed, the form is a nature to a higher degree than the matter; for
each thing receives a name when it exists in actuality rather than when
it exists potentially.   Moreover, it is from a man that a man is generated, but a bed is not generated from a bed (and in view of this they
say that nature is not the shape but the wood, since, if it buds, what is 10
generated is wood and not a bed); so if in the latter case it is the art,
in the former too it is the form that should be nature, for it is from a
man that a man is generated.   Again, when we speak of nature as
being a generation, this is a process toward nature [as a form]; for the
term "nature" as signifying a process is not like the term "doctoring".
The latter term signifies a process toward health, not toward the art of
doctoring, for doctoring which begins from the art of doctoring cannot 15
be a process toward the art of doctoring; but nature [as a process] is
not related to nature [as a form] in the same way, for from something
the growing object proceeds to something or grows into something. Into
what does it grow? Not into that from which it begins but into that
toward which it proceeds. Thus it is the *form* that is nature.   "*Form*"
or "nature", it may be added, has two senses, for privation, too, is in a 20
way a form;   but whether there is a privation or a contrary in an
unqualified generation or not must be considered later.[13]

2

Having distinguished the various senses of "nature", we should next
investigate how the mathematician and the physicist differ with respect
to their objects, for physical bodies have also surfaces and solids and
lengths and points, and these are the concern of the mathematician. 25
Moreover, is astronomy a distinct science or a part of physics? For it
is absurd that the physicist should understand what the Sun or the
Moon is but not what their essential attributes are, not to mention the
fact that those who are concerned with nature appear to be discussing
the shape of the Moon and of the Sun and to be raising the problem of 30
whether the Earth and the universe are spherical or not.

Now the mathematician, too, is concerned with these, but not insofar
as each is a limit of a physical body; nor does he investigate attributes
qua existing in such bodies. That is why he separates them, for in
thought they are separable from motion; and it makes no difference, nor 35
does any falsity occur in separating them [in thought].   Those who

posit Ideas, too, are doing the same but are unaware of it; for they are
separating the physical objects [from motion], although these are less
separable than the mathematical objects. This becomes clear if one tries
to state the definitions in each [science], both of the subjects and of
their attributes. For oddness and evenness and straightness and curvature, and also a number and a line and a figure, will each be defined
without reference to motion; but not so in the case of flesh and bone
and a man, for these are defined like a snub nose and not like curvature. This is also clear in those parts of mathematics which are more
physical, such as optics and harmonics and astronomy, for these are
related to geometry in a somewhat converse manner. On the one hand,
geometry is concerned with physical lines but not qua physical; on
the other, optics is concerned with mathematical lines not qua mathematical but qua physical.

Since we speak of nature in two ways, as form as well as matter, we
should investigate the whatness [of the objects of physics] as we would
the whatness of snubness. Such objects, then, should be investigated
neither without matter nor with respect to matter [alone]. With regard
to this we might also raise another problem. Since there are two natures,
with which of them should the physicist be concerned? Or should he be
concerned with that which has both natures? Of course, if with both
natures, then also with each of the two natures. So should the same
science be concerned with both natures, or one science with one and
another with the other?

If we turn our attention to the ancients, physics would seem to be
concerned with matter, for even Empedocles and Democritus touched
upon form or essence only slightly. But if art imitates nature and the
same science should understand the form and the matter to some extent
(for example, the doctor should understand health, and also bile and
phlegm in which health exists; the builder should likewise understand
the form of the house, and also the matter, namely, bricks and wooden
materials; and similarly in each of the other arts), it should be the concern of physics, too, to know both natures.

Moreover, it belongs to the same science to be concerned with the
final cause or the end and also with whatever is needed for the sake of
the final cause or the end. But nature is [also] an end and a final cause;
for if, in that which is in continuous motion, there is some end of that
motion, this [end] is the last and the final cause. And it is in view of
this that the poet was carried away when he made the ridiculous statement "he has an end [death], for the sake of which he was born". For
not every last thing tends to be an end, but only the best, seeing that in
the case of the arts, too, some of them just make the matter but others

make it serviceable and that we use things as if they exist all for our   35
own sake (since in a certain sense, we too are an end, for "final cause"
has two senses, as we stated in *"On Philosophy"*[14]). Indeed, there are   194*b*
two arts which rule over matter and have knowledge of it—the art
which is concerned with the use of it and the art which directs the production of it. Thus the art which uses matter is also in a sense directive,
but as directive it differs from the other insofar as it knows the form,
while the art which directs the production knows the matter; for the   5
steersman knows what kind of form the rudder should have and orders
its production, but the engineer knows from what kind of wood it
should be produced and how it should move.   Now in objects produced
according to art, it is we who produce the matter for the sake of some
function,   but in natural objects it is there all along.

Again, matter is relative to some thing, for distinct forms require
distinct matter.

To what extent should the physicist understand the form or the what-   10
ness? Up to a point, just as the doctor understands sinews and the smith
understands bronze, for each of them [sinews and bronze] is for the
sake of something, and the physicist is concerned with what is separable
in kind but exists in matter; for both man and the Sun beget man.   As
for a separate form, how it exists and what it is, this is a task to be
settled by first philosophy.   15

3

Having made these distinctions, we should next examine the causes,
their kinds and number. Since our *inquiry* is for the sake of understanding, and we think that we do not understand a thing until we have
acquired the *why* of it (and this is to acquire the first cause), clearly   20
we should do this as regards generation and destruction and every
physical change so that, with an understanding of their principles, we
may try to refer to them each of the things we seek.

In one sense, "a cause" means (1) that from which, as a constituent,
something is generated; for example, the bronze is a cause of the statue,   25
and the silver, of the cup, and the genera of these [are also causes].

In another, it means (2) the form or the pattern, this being the formula of the essence, and also the genera of this; for example, in the
case of the octave, the ratio 2:1, and, in general, a number and the parts
in the formula.

In another, it means (3) that from which change or coming to rest   30
first begins; for example, the adviser is a cause, and the father is the

cause of the baby, and, in general, that which acts is a cause of that
which is acted upon, and that which brings about a change is a cause of
that which is being changed.

Finally, it means (4) the end, and this is the final cause [that for the
sake of which]; for example, walking is for the sake of health. Why
does he walk? We answer, "In order to be healthy"; and having spoken
thus, we think that we have given the cause. And those things which,
after that which started the motion, lie between the beginning and the
end, such as reducing weight or purging or drugs or instruments in
the case of health, all of them are for the sake of the end; and they
differ in this, that some of them are operations while others are
instruments.

The term "cause", then, has about so many senses. And since they
[the causes] are spoken of in many ways, there may be many nonaccidental causes of the same thing; for example, in the case of a statue,
not with respect to something else but qua a statue, both the art of
sculpture and the bronze are causes of it, though not in the same manner, but the bronze as matter and the art as the source of motion. There
may be also causes of each other; for example, exercise is a cause of
good physical condition, and good physical condition is a cause of
exercise, although not in the same manner, but good physical condition
as an end, while exercise as a principle of motion. Again, the same
thing may be a cause of contraries, for if one thing, when present, is
the cause of another, then the first, when absent, is sometimes also said
to be the cause of the contrary of the second; for example, we say that
the absence of the pilot was the cause of the capsizing, while his
presence was the cause of safety.

All of the causes just mentioned fall into four most evident types. For,
the letters of the syllables, the matter of manufactured articles, fire and
all such in the case of bodies, the parts of the whole, the hypotheses
of the conclusion —in all of these there are causes in the sense that they
are *that of which* the latter consists; and in these, those first mentioned in each case are causes in the sense that they are the underlying
subject, as in the case of the parts, but each of the others is a cause
in the sense of essence, and this is the whole or the composition or the
form. As for the seed and the doctor and the adviser and, in general,
that which acts, all these are causes in the sense of the source of change
or of standstill or of motion. Finally, each of the rest is a cause as the
end or the good of the others; for that for the sake of which the others
exist or are done tends to be the best or their end. Let there be no
difference here between calling this "the good" or "the apparent good".

These, then, are the causes and their number in kind; but their modes
are numerically many, although when summarized they too are fewer.

For causes are spoken of in many ways, and even within the same kind
one cause may be prior or posterior to another; for example, the cause 30
of health is the doctor or the artist, and the cause of the octave is
the ratio 2:1 or a number, and whatever includes each is always a
cause. Again, there are accidental causes and their genera; for example,
Polyclitus as a cause of a statue is distinct from a sculptor as a cause,
since the sculptor is by accident Polyclitus. Also, whatever includes 35
the accident would be a cause; for example, a man, or, in general, an 195*b*
animal, would be a cause of the statue. Even of accidents, some are
more remote or more near than others; for example, this would be the
case if the white or the musical were to be called "a cause" of the
statue.

Of all causes, both those said to be *proper* and those said to be
accidental, some are said to be causes in the sense of being in potentiality, others in *actuality;* for example, the cause of the house to be 5
built is the builder and of the house that is being built the builder
who is building. Similar remarks will apply to the things caused by the
causes already listed; for example, the cause may be a cause of this
statue or of a statue or of a portrait in general, and it may be a cause of
this bronze or of bronze or of matter in general. Similar remarks may
be made in the case of accidents. Again, both accidental and *proper* 10
causes and also the objects caused may be spoken of in combination;
for example, not Polyclitus, nor the sculptor, but Polyclitus the sculptor.

However, all these are six in number, and each is spoken of in two
ways. For as a cause or an object caused each may be stated as a particular or as a genus of a particular; as an accident or as a genus of an 15
accident; in combination or singly taken; and in each of these either in
actuality or in virtue of its potentiality. And there is this difference, that
causes which are in *actuality* and are taken as individuals exist, or do
not exist, at the same time as the things of which they are the causes, for
example, as in the case of this doctor who is healing and this man who
is being healed, and this builder who is building and that building 20
which is being built. But with respect to potentiality this is not always
so; for the house is not destroyed at the same time as the builder.

We should always seek the ultimate cause of each thing, as in other
cases; for example, a man builds in view of the fact that he is a builder,
and a builder builds in virtue of his art of building; accordingly, this
latter is the prior cause. It is likewise with all other cases. Moreover, 25
causes generically given should be stated of effects generically given,
and particular causes, of particular effects; for example, a sculptor
[in general] of a statue [in general], and this sculptor of this statue.
Also potential causes should be stated of potential effects, and causes in
actuality of effects in *actuality*.

Let this, then, be a sufficient description of the number of causes and
30   the manner in which they are causes.

        4

Luck and *chance*, too, are said to be causes, and many things are said
to exist and to come to be through luck or *chance*. Accordingly, we must
inquire (a) in what manner luck and *chance* are causes among those
35   given, (b) whether luck and *chance* are the same or distinct, and, as a
whole, (c) what luck is and what *chance* is.

Some thinkers[15] even raise the problem of whether luck and *chance*
196a   exist or not; for they say that nothing comes by luck, but that in every
case in which we say that a thing comes to be by *chance* or luck there
is a definite cause. For example, if a man came to the market and met
by luck someone whom he wished but did not expect to meet, the cause
5   of this meeting is the wish to come and buy something. Similarly, in the
other cases which are said to happen by luck there is always a [definite]
cause, and this is not luck; for it would indeed appear strange if luck
were something, and one might even raise the question as to why not
even one of the ancient wise men, in speaking of the causes of genera-
10   tion and of destruction, said anything definite about luck. So it seems
that they, too, thought that nothing could exist by luck. Yet this too is
surprising: Many things come to be and exist by luck or by *chance*.
And although we know that each of these can be referred to some
15   [definite] cause, like the old argument which eliminated luck, nevertheless all speak of some of these things as being by luck and others as
being not by luck; and on this account, this fact should have been
touched upon by them in some way or other.

Now none of the ancient thinkers thought that luck was some thing,
such as *Friendship* or *Strife* or *Intelligence* or *Fire* or some other such
thing. And this is certainly strange, whether they believed that luck
20   does not exist or thought that it does but neglected to discuss it; for they
sometimes used it, as in the case of Empedocles, who said that air is not
always separated in the highest region but wherever it might chance.
Anyway, he did say in his cosmology "it happened to run to that region
at that time, but it often ran otherwise"; and he also said that most of
the parts of animals came to be by luck.
25   There are some[16] who say that chance is a cause both of this heaven
and of everything that is in the ordered universe; for they say that the
vortex came to be by chance, and so did the motion which separated the
parts and caused the present order of the universe. And this is very
surprising; for they say, on the one hand, that animals and plants neither

exist nor are generated by luck but that the cause is nature or intellect   30
or some other such thing (for it is not any chance thing that is generated
from a given seed, but an olive tree from this kind and a man from that
kind), and, on the other, that the heavens and the most divine of the
visible objects were generated by *chance*, which cause is not such as   35
any of those in the case of animals or plants. Yet if such is the case, it
deserves attention, and it is right that something should be said about it.   196*b*
For, besides the fact that the statement is absurd in other ways, it is
more absurd to speak thus when they observe nothing generated by
chance in the heavens but many things happening by luck among things
which [according to them] neither exist nor are generated by luck, even
if probability would have it the other way around.   5

There are also others[17] who seem to think that chance is a cause but is
not revealed to human *thought*, that it is something divine and rather
godlike.

Let us inquire, then, what chance is and what luck is, whether they
are the same or distinct, and how they fit into the causes already
described.

5

To begin, then, since we observe that some things come to be always   10
in the same way and others [come to be] for the most part, it is evident
that luck as a cause and what comes to be by luck are none of those
things, neither of what is necessary or eternal nor of what is for the most
part. But since of things that come to be there exist, besides these, also
others, which all say exist by luck, it is evident that luck or chance does   15
exist; for we grant that such things do come to be by luck and that
things which come to be by luck are of such a kind.

Of things that come to be, some do so for the sake of something [else]
but others do not; and of the former, some come to be according to
choice and others not so, but both these are for the sake of something;
so it is clear that, besides things which exist necessarily or for the most   20
part, there are also others to which final cause may belong. Things to
which final cause belongs may be done by *thought* or by nature. Now
when such things come to be by accident, we say that they do so by
luck; for just as being exists either essentially or by accident, so may a   25
cause exist. In the case of a house, for example, a cause which is essential is the art of building, but one that is accidental is the white or the
musical. Thus the essential cause of something is definite, but the accidental cause is indefinite,   for a great many accidents may belong to a
thing.

30   As it was stated, then, when this happens in things for the sake of
which there is generation, then it is said to happen by *chance*   or by
luck. The difference between these two will be specified later,[18] but for
the present it is evident that both belong to things for the sake of something. For example, a man engaged in collecting contributions would
have gone to a certain place for the sake of getting the money,   had
35   he known; but he went there not for the sake of this, and it is by accident that he got the money when he went there; and this happened
197a   neither for the most part whenever he went there, nor of necessity. And
the end, which is getting the money, is not a cause present in him,   but
it is something done by *choice* or by *thought*, and he is then said to
have gone there by luck;   but if he had gone there by *choice* and for
the sake of this, whether he was getting the money always or for the
5   most part, then he would have done so not by luck.

It is clear, then, that luck is an accidental cause of things done according to *choice* and for the sake of something; and so both *thought*
and luck are concerned with the same thing,   for *choice* is not without
thought.

Now the causes of things which might come to be by luck are of
10   necessity indefinite. In view of all this, (a) luck seems to be something
indefinite or not revealed to man,   and (b) there is a sense in which
nothing would seem to come to be by luck;   for both these opinions are
right, since there is a good reason for them. For what comes to be by
luck does so in a qualified sense, namely, in virtue of an accident, and
it is as an accident that luck is a cause; but as a cause without qualification, it is a cause of no thing.   For example, of a house the builder is
15   the cause, but accidentally it is the flute player; and in going to a place
and getting the money, but not doing so for the sake of getting the
money, the accidental causes might be a great many, such as wishing
to see someone or following someone or avoiding someone or going to
see a play. And it is right to say that luck is contrary to reason; for
20   reason   is of what is always or for the most part, while luck is present
in events which are outside of these. So, since such causes are indefinite,
luck too is indefinite.

In some cases, however, one might raise the problem of whether a
cause as luck may not be any chance thing whatever, as in the case of
health, for example, whether the wind or the heat from the sun is such
25   a cause but not the purge;   for, of accidental causes, some are nearer
[to the effects] than others.

Luck is called "good" when the result is good, but "bad" when the
result is bad; and it is called "good fortune" and "misfortune" when its
goodness and badness, respectively, are of considerable magnitude. In
view of this, even if great goodness or badness is missed by a little, we

are said to have been fortunate or unfortunate; for the small difference
seems negligible, and so *thought* regards good fortune or misfortune as 30
if attained. Further, it is with good reason that good fortune has no
certainty, for luck has no certainy; for what comes to be by luck does so
neither always nor for the most part.

As we stated, both luck and *chance* are causes, but accidental; and
they are among things   which come to be neither without qualification
nor for the most part, and for the sake of something. 35

6

The term "chance" differs from "luck" by being a wider predicate; for
every effect by luck is also an effect by chance, but not every effect by
chance is an effect by luck. Luck and an effect by luck belong also to 197*b*
whatever good fortune and *action* in general belong. It is for this reason, too, that luck is necessarily a cause of what may result by *action*. A
sign of this is the fact that good fortune seems to be either the same as
happiness or close to it; and happiness is a kind of *action,* for it is a good 5
action. Hence, whatever is incapable of *acting* is also incapable of doing
anything by luck. And it is because of this that inanimate things and
brutes and children, having no *choice,* cannot do anything by luck;
and neither good nor ill fortune can belong to them, except in virtue of
some similarity, as in Protarchus' statement that the stones of which 10
altars are made are fortunate, for they are honored, while those leading
to the altar are walked upon. Of course, even these things are affected
by luck, but in a sense, that is, when one *acts* on them by luck, but in no
other way.

As for chance, it exists also in the other animals and in many inanimate things. For example, we say that the horse who came is a chance 15
[cause], that is, his coming saved him, but he did not come for the
sake of being saved; and the tripod which fell [on its feet] is a chance
[cause], for though its being on its feet is for the sake of being sat on, it
did not fall for the sake of being sat on.

Thus it is evident that in things which come to be without qualification for the sake of something, when the effects, whose causes are
outside of them, do not come to be for their own sake, then we say that 20
they come to be by chance; and of these, those *chosen* by those who
have *choice* are said to come to be by luck. A sign of this is the use of
the phrase "in vain" when that for the sake of which something is done
does not result, as in walking which is for the sake of bowel movement;
if the movement does not result after one has walked, we say that he 25
has walked in vain and that the walking was futile, thus regarding as

futile that which was by nature for the sake of something that did not result, although by nature it does result (for it would be ridiculous to say that a man had bathed in vain if as a consequence the Sun was not eclipsed, seeing that the bathing was not for the sake of the Sun's
30   eclipse). So chance, as its name also indicates, exists when something occurs in vain, so to speak, for the stone that fell did so not for the sake of striking the man, but by chance, seeing that it might have been thrown by someone for the sake of striking the man.

Things occurring by *chance* are most distinct from those occurring by luck in things generated by nature; for when something has been gen-
35   erated contrary to nature, then we say that it did so not by luck but rather by *chance*. And there is another distinction, for in the one case the cause is outside, in the other it is inside.
198a   We have stated, then, what chance is, what luck is, and in what they differ from each other. As for the manner in which they are causes, each of them is a source which begins motion; for each is always a cause of what results either by nature or by *thought,* and each of them
5   as a cause may vary indefinitely in number.

Now, since *chance* and luck are causes of effects caused either by the intellect or by nature, when each of them comes to be an accidental cause of such an effect, then it is clear that, since nothing that is acci- dental is prior to what is essential, no accidental cause is prior to an
10   essential cause. Thus *chance* and luck are posterior to intellect and nature.   Hence, however true it may be that chance is the cause of the heavens,   intellect or nature is of necessity a prior cause of many other things and of this [whole] universe.

7

It is clear, then, that there are causes and that there are as many
15   [in kind] as we have stated; for the *why* of things includes just so many [in kind]. For the *why* is referred either (a) ultimately to the whatness in the case of what is immovable, as in mathematics (for it is ultimately referred to the definition of a straight line or of commensurability or of something else), or (b) to the first mover —for example: Why did they
20   declare war? Because they were raided—or (c) to a final cause: [in declaring war] for the sake of ruling the enemy, or (d) to matter, as in things generated. Evidently, then, the causes are those stated and are as many in number.

Since the causes are four, it is the task of the physicist to understand all of them; and as a physicist he should state the *why* by referring it to all of them—the matter, the form, the mover, and the final cause. The

last three often amount to one; for both the whatness and the final cause   25
are one, and the first source of motion is the same in kind as these
(for man begets man), and, in general, this is so in the case of a movable
mover. But a mover that is not movable is not a cause within physics,
for it moves without having in itself motion or a principle of motion but
is immovable. Accordingly, there are three disciplines: one concerning   30
immovable things, a second concerning things which are in motion but
are indestructible, and a third concerning destructible things.

The *why,* then, is given by being referred to matter, to the whatness,
and to the first mover, for in generations causes are sought mostly in
this manner: "What comes after what?", "What was the first thing   35
that acted or was acted upon?", and at each step always in this way.
Now the principles that cause physical motion are two: One of these
is not physical, for it has no principle of motion in itself, and such is   198*b*
that which moves another without itself being moved, as in the case of
that which is completely immovable and primary among all; and
such is also the whatness or the *form,* for this is the end or final cause.
So, since nature is a final cause, we should also understand this [cause].
So the *why* must be given in all [four] ways, namely, (1) that this must   5
follow from that (the phrase "this from that" to be taken either without
qualification or for the most part); (2) that if this is to be, then that
will be (as in the case of premises, from which conclusions follow); (3)
that this was the essence; and (4) because it is better in this way (not
without qualification, but relative to the *substance* of each thing).

8

We must discuss first (a) why nature is a cause for the sake of some-   10
thing; then (b) how necessity exists in physical things, for all thinkers
make reference to this cause by saying, for example, that since the hot
and the cold and each of such things are by nature of such-and-such a
kind, certain other things must exist or come to be (for even if they   15
mention some other cause—one of them mentions *Friendship* and
Strife, another[20] mentions *Intelligence* —they just touch upon it and let
it go at that).

The following question arises: What prevents nature from acting, not
for the sake of something or for what is better, but by necessity, as in
the case of rain, which does not fall in order that wheat may grow. For,
one may say, what goes up must be cooled, and the resulting cold water   20
must come down, and when this takes place, the growth of corn just
happens; similarly, if a man's wheat is spoiled on the threshing floor,
rain did not fall for the sake of spoiling the wheat, but this just hap-

pened. So what should prevent the parts in nature, too, from coming
to be of necessity in this manner, for example, the front teeth of neces-
25 sity coming out sharp and so fit for tearing but the molars broad and
useful for grinding food, not however for the sake of this but by coincidence? A similar question arises with the other parts in which final
cause seems to exist. If so, then whenever all the parts came together
30 as if generated for the sake of something, the wholes which by *chance*
were fitfully composed survived, but those which came together not in
this manner, like the man-faced offspring of oxen mentioned by Empedocles, perished and still do so.

This is the argument, then, or any other such, that might cause a
difficulty. Yet it is impossible for things to come to be in this manner;
35 for the examples cited and all things by nature come to be either always
or for the most part, but none of those by luck or *chance* do so like-
199a wise. It is not during the winter that frequent rain is thought to occur
by luck or by coincidence, but during the summer, nor frequent heat
during the summer, but during the winter. So if these be thought to
occur either by coincidence or for the sake of something and if they
5 cannot occur by coincidence or by chance, then they occur for the sake
of something. Besides, those who use the preceding arguments, too,
would admit that all such things exist by nature. There is, then, final
cause in things which come to be or exist by nature.

Moreover, in that which has an end, a prior stage and the stages that
follow are done for the sake of that end. Accordingly, these are done in
10 the manner in which the nature of the thing disposes them to be done;
and the nature of the thing disposes them to be done in the manner in
which they are done at each stage, if nothing obstructs. But they are
done for the sake of something; so they are by nature disposed to be
done for the sake of something. For example, if a house were a thing
generated by nature, it would have been generated in a way similar to
that in which it is now generated by art. So if things by nature were
to be generated not only by nature but also by art, they would have
15 been generated just as they are by nature disposed to be generated. So
one stage is for the sake of the next. In general, in some cases art com-
pletes what nature cannot carry out to an end, in others, it imitates
nature. Thus, if things done according to art are for the sake of something, clearly also those according to nature are done for the sake of
something; for the later stages are similarly related to the earlier stages
in those according to art and those according to nature.
20 This is most evident in those of the other animals which make things
neither by art nor by having inquired or deliberated about them; and
from this latter fact arise discussions by some thinkers about the problem of whether spiders and ants and other such animals work by intel-

lect or by some other power. If we go a little further in this direction, we observe that in plants, too, parts appear to be generated which con- 25 tribute to an end, for example, leaves for the sake of protecting the fruit. So if it is both by nature and for the sake of something that the swallow makes its nest and the spider its web and that plants grow leaves for the sake of fruit and send their roots not up but down for the sake of food, it is evident that there exists such a cause in things which come 30 to be or exist by nature. And since nature may be either matter or *form*, and it is the latter that may be an end while all the rest are for the sake of an end, it is *form* that would be a cause in the sense of a final cause.

Now error occurs even with respect to things produced according to art; for example, a grammarian did not write correctly and a doctor did not give the right medicine; so clearly this may occur also in things that 35 come to be according to nature. If then there are (a) things produced 199*b* according to art in which there is a right final cause and (b) also things done erroneously when the final cause has been aimed at but failed, a similar situation would exist also in natural things, and monstrosities in these would be failures of final causes. So too must have been the case 5 in the original formation of the offspring of oxen, if they could not attain a certain limit or end; for there must have been some corruption in the source from which their generation started, like that in the seed nowa- days. We might add, too, that the seed must have come into being first and not the animals all at once, and the expression "first the whole- natured"[21] meant the seed. And final cause exists also in plants, though 10 it is less capable of being articulated. So did olive-headed offspring of vines come into being just as man-faced offspring did from oxen, or not? It would seem absurd; but they must have, if indeed this was also the case in animals. Again, any chance thing might otherwise be generated from a seed.

In general, he who asserts this rejects things existing by nature as well 15 as nature itself. For what exists by nature is a thing which, having started from some principle in itself, finally arrives by a continuous mo- tion at a certain end; and neither is the end the same from every princi- ple, nor does any chance end come to be from a given principle, but from the same principle the same end comes to be, if nothing obstructs. As for the final cause or what acts for the sake of the final cause, it might take place by luck. (For example, we say "the stranger came by luck 20 and departed after paying the ransom" if he would have come for the sake of doing this [had he known], not that he came for the sake of this; and this happened by accident, for luck is an accidental cause, as we stated earlier.[22]) But if it takes place always or for the most part, it is not 25 an accident nor does it come to be by luck; and in natural things it takes place always, if nothing obstructs.

It is absurd to think that nothing comes to be for the sake of something if the moving cause is not observed deliberating (and we may add, even art does not deliberate); and if the ship-building art were in the wood, it would have produced results similar to those produced by na-
30 ture. So if there is a final cause in art, so also in nature. This is most clearly seen in a doctor who heals himself; nature is like that.

It is evident, then, that nature is a cause and that it is a cause also in this manner, namely, for the sake of something.

9

35 As for that which is necessary, does it exist by hypothesis or also
200a simply? Nowadays it is thought that what exists by necessity does so in generation, as if one were to consider the wall as having been constructed by necessity, since what is heavy travels down by its nature and what is light travels up by its nature, and so the stones and the foundations are down, then earth right above because it is lighter, and finally
5 wood at the very top since it is the lightest. However, although a wall is not constructed without these, still it is constructed not because of these (except in the sense that they are causes as matter) but for the sake of sheltering or preserving certain things. Similarly, in all other cases in which there is a final cause, although what is generated could not have been generated without a nature which is necessary for it, still
10 it is not because of what is necessary (except as a material cause) but for the sake of something. For example, why is a saw such-and-such? So that this may come to be or for the sake of this. But this final cause cannot come to be unless the saw is made of iron. So if there is to be a saw capable of doing this work, it is necessary that it be made of iron. What is necessary, then, exists by hypothesis and not as an end; for
15 it exists in matter, while final cause is in the formula.

The necessary in mathematics is in some way parallel to that in things generated according to nature. Since this is what a straight line is, it is necessary for a triangle to have its angles equal to two right angles, but the converse is not the case; but if the angles of a triangle were not equal to two right angles, neither would a straight line be what it is said to be. In things generated for the sake of something, this parallelism proceeds
20 in a reverse manner. If the end will exist or exists, what precedes it also will exist or exists; but if what precedes the end will not or does not exist, then, just as in the other case the starting-point is not what it is posited to be if the conclusion is not true, so here, the end or final cause will not or does not exist if what precedes it will not or does not exist. The final cause here, we may add, is also a starting-point, not of *action*,

but of reasoning; but in the other case [e.g., in mathematics], it is the whatness that is the starting-point of reasoning, for no *actions* exist there. Thus, if there is to be a house, certain things must be made or be 25 available or exist (or the matter in general, which is for the sake of something, such as bricks and stones in the case of a house); but the end does not exist because of these things, except in the sense that they are a cause as matter, nor will the house come to be because of these. In general, then, if there are no stones, there can be no house, and if there is no iron, there can be no saw; whereas in mathematics, if the angles of the 30 triangle are not equal to two right angles, the principles from which the equality to two right angles follows cannot be such as are posited.

It is evident, then, that the necessary in natural things is what we call "matter" and also the motions of matter. We may also add that both causes must be stated by the physicist, and the final cause more so than the cause as matter, for it is the former which is the cause of the latter, not the latter, of the end; and we may also add that the end is the final cause and that the starting-point is the definition or the formula, as in 35 the case of things produced according to art. For example, if a house is 200*b* such-and-such a thing, such other things must be produced or be available; and so in the case of a man: If he is such-and-such, then such other things must be or come to be, and if these, then such others likewise. Perhaps the necessary exists also in the formula; for, if one has defined 5 the operation of sawing as being such-and-such an act of division, then this cannot take place unless the saw has teeth of such-and-such a kind, and these cannot be of such-and-such a kind unless they are made of iron. Indeed, even in formulas there are some parts which are parts as if they were the matter of these formulas.

BOOK III

1

200*b*   Since nature is a principle of motion or of change and our *inquiry*
is about nature, we should not neglect to inquire what a motion is; for
15   if we are ignorant of what a motion is, we are of necessity ignorant of
what nature is. When we have explained motion, then we shall try in
the same manner to take up what follows.

Now a motion is thought to be one of those things which are continuous, and it is in the continuous that the infinite first appears; and for
this reason, it often happens that those who define the continuous use
20   the formula of the infinite, that is, they say that the continuous is that
which is infinitely divisible. Again, a motion is thought to be impossible
without place and void and time. Clearly, then, because of all this and
because of the fact that these are common and belong universally to
all the others, we must first undertake to inquire about each of these;
25   for the investigation of what is specific should come after that of what
is common.

As we said, then, our first inquiry is about motion. To begin, there is
(a) that which exists in actuality only and also (b) that which exists
both potentially and in actuality,   and this may be a *this* or a *so-much*
or a *such* or, likewise, any of the other categories of being. As for that
which is relative to something, it may be stated with respect to excess
30   or deficiency or with respect to its being able to act or be acted upon or,
in general, with respect to its being able to move or be moved;   for
that which is able to move is able to move that which can be moved, and
that which can be moved can be moved by that which can move.

Now no motion exists apart from things; for that which changes always does so either with respect to substance or with respect to quantity
35   or with respect to quality or with respect to place, and there can be no
thing common to these which is not, as is our manner of speaking, a *this*
201*a*   or a quantity or a quality or some one of the other categories.   Thus

neither a motion nor a change can exist apart from these [categories] if nothing else exists but these.

In all cases, each of these [categories] may exist in two ways; for example, with respect to a *this,* it may be the *form* or the privation of that *form,* with respect to quality it may be whiteness or blackness, and 5 with respect to quantity it may be the complete or the incomplete. Similarly, with respect to locomotion the thing may be up or down or it may be heavy or light. Thus there are as many kinds of motion or of change as there are kinds of being. In view of this distinction between 10 the actual and the potential in each genus, a motion is [defined as] the actuality of the potentially existing qua existing potentially. For example, the actuality of the alterable qua alterable is an alteration, the actuality of what can be increased or (its opposite) what can be decreased [qua such] is an increase or decrease (no name exists which is a common predicate of both), the actuality of the generable or destructible [qua such] is a generation or a destruction, and the actuality 15 of the movable with respect to place [qua such] is a locomotion.

That a motion is what we have stated it to be is clear from the following. When the buildable, insofar as it is said to be such, exists in actuality, it is then [in the process of] being built, and this is [the process of] building; and similarly in the case of learning, healing, rolling, leaping, ripening, and aging.

Since, in some cases, the same things exist both potentially and ac- 20 tually, but not at the same time nor with respect to the same thing (as in the case of that which is potentially hot but actually cold), many of them will eventually both act and be acted upon by each other; for each of them has the potentiality both of acting and of being acted upon. Consequently, that which causes a motion physically is also movable, for every such thing which causes a motion is itself moved. There are some 25 who think that every thing that moves another is itself moved; now what the situation is with respect to this will be made clear from other arguments[23] (for there exists also something which causes a motion but is itself immovable), but as for a motion, it is the actuality of that which exists potentially when it is in *actuality* not qua itself but qua movable.

By "qua" I mean the following. Bronze is potentially a statue, yet it is 30 not qua bronze that the actuality of bronze is a motion; for to be bronze and to be movable by something are not the same, since if they were the same without qualification or according to formula, the actuality of bronze qua bronze would be a motion. So they are not the same, as stated. This is clear in the case of contraries; for to be capable of being 35 healthy and to be capable of being sick are distinct, for otherwise being 201*b* sick and being healthy would be the same. It is the underlying subject,

be it moisture or blood, which is one and the same, whether in health or
in sickness.   Since, then, to be bronze and to be potentially something
else are not the same, just as to be a color and to be visible are not the
5   same,   evidently it is the actuality of the potential qua potential that
is a motion.

It is clear, then, that this is what a motion is and that an object happens to be in motion just when this actuality exists, and neither before
nor after. For each [such] thing may be sometimes in *actuality* and
sometimes not, as in the case of the buildable, and it is qua buildable
10   that the *actuality* of the buildable is [the process of] building. For this
actuality is either [the process of] building or the house. But when the
house exists, it is no longer buildable; and it is the buildable that is being built. This *actuality*, then, must be [the process of] building, and
[the process of] building is a [kind of] motion. Moreover, the same ar-
15   gument applies to the other motions.

2

That we have stated the facts well is also clear from (a) what the
other thinkers are saying about motion and from (b) the fact that it is
not easy to describe it in another way. For (b) one could not place
motion or change in some other genus; and (a) an examination of the
20   way in which some thinkers posit motion clearly shows them to be
saying that it is otherness or inequality or nonbeing,[24] none of which
(whether that which is other or that which is unequal or that which is
nonbeing) need be in motion, and besides, a change is no more into
these or from these than into or from their opposites.

The cause of positing motion as being some one of these is the fact
25   that motion is thought to be something indefinite; and the principles in
one of the two columns of contraries are indefinite because they are
privative, for none of them is a *this* or a *such* or any of the other categories. And a motion is thought to be indefinite because of the fact that
it cannot be placed in an unqualified way either under the potentiality
30   or under the *actuality* of things; for neither that which is potentially a
quantity nor that which is *actually* a quantity is necessarily moved. And
although a motion is thought to be an *actuality* of a sort, yet it is incomplete; and the cause of this is the fact that the potential, of which this is
the *actuality*, is incomplete. And it is indeed because of this that it is
difficult to grasp its whatness; for it must be placed either under priva-
35   tion or under potentiality or under unqualified *actuality*, but none of
202a   these alternatives appears possible. What remains, then, is the manner

in which we described it, namely, that a motion is a sort of an *actuality* —an *actuality* such as we have stated, difficult to grasp but capable of existing.

The mover too is movable, as has been stated, that is, every mover which is potentially movable and whose absence of motion is rest; for the absence of motion in that which may be in motion is [said to be] rest. For to act on the movable qua such is precisely to move it. But it 5 [i.e., the mover] acts on it by contact; so it is at the same time acted upon. Thus it is of the movable qua movable that a motion is the actuality; and this happens by contact with that which can move, so the latter too is at the same time acted upon. And the mover always has a form, whether a *this* or a *such* or a *so-much*, which is a principle and 10 a cause of motion when the mover moves [something]; for example, a man in actuality begets a man from what is potentially a man.

3

Moreover, the solution to the problem raised concerning a motion is now evident: A motion is in a movable [object], for it is of the movable that it [motion] is the actuality, and it [motion] is caused by that which can move [the movable]. And the *actuality* of that which can cause a 15 motion is not distinct, for there must be one actuality in both; for a thing can cause a motion by its potency, and it [the thing] causes a motion by *actualizing* that potency. But this *actuality* is in the movable, so it is alike one *actuality* [numerically] in both, just as it is the same interval from one to two and from two to one and the same interval from A going up to B and from B coming down to A. For these [two] 20 intervals are [numerically] one, although their formula is not one; and similarly with the mover and that which is moved.

However, there is a logical *difficulty*. Perhaps it is necessary for the *actuality* of that which can act to be distinct from the *actuality* of that which can be affected; in the one, it is [the process of] acting, in the other, it is [the process of] being affected, and the function or end of the first is an action, but that of the second is an affection. Now if both 25 [*actualities*] are motions, in what [subject or subjects] do they exist if they are distinct? Either (a) both are in that which is affected or is moved, or (b) [the process of] acting is in that which acts and [the process of] being affected is in that which is being affected; and if the latter motion, too, were to be called "an acting", then it would be equivocally so called.

Now, if (b), then the motion will be in the mover, for the same argu-

30   ment applies to the mover and to the object moved; so either every
     mover will be moved, or, having motion, it will not be moved. But in
     (a), if both motions are in the object which is being moved or is being
     affected, that is, both [the process of] acting and [the process of] being
     affected (for example, if both teaching and learning, which are two, are
     in the learner), then, first, the *actuality* of each will not be in each, and
     second, it will be absurd for that object to have two motions at the same
35   time (for what will be the two alterations of that which is proceeding
     toward one form?).   But this is impossible; so there will be one *actu-*
202b *ality.* But it would be unreasonable for two [motions] which are distinct
     in kind to be one and the same *actuality;* for if indeed teaching and
     learning (and in general, acting and being affected) were the same, then
     also to teach and to learn (and in general, to act and to be affected)
5   would be the same, and so it would be necessary for the teacher to learn
     everything that he teaches (and in general, for that which acts to be
     affected by every affection it causes).
         Nevertheless, neither is it absurd for the *actuality* of one thing to be
     in another thing (for teaching is the activity of a man who can teach
     but it is an activity *upon another man;* it is not cut off but is an activity
     of A upon B), nor can anything prevent one *actuality* from being the
     same for two things —not in the sense that the essence is the same for
10   both, but in the sense in which potential being is related to being in
     actuality.   So it is not necessary for the teacher to learn, even if to act
     and to be affected are the same, not however in the sense that the
     formula which states the essence is one (as in the case of the formula
     of clothing and of garment), but in the sense that the road from
     Thebes to Athens and that from Athens to Thebes is the same, as it
15   was stated before;[25] for things are in every way the same not if they
     are the same in any way whatsoever, but only if to be each [i.e., if their
     essence] is the same.   Nor is to learn the same as to teach, if teaching
     and learning are [numerically] the same, just as the direction from A
     to B is not one and the same as that from B to A, if the distance connect-
20   ing A and B is one.   In general, however, neither are teaching and learn-
     ing the same in the main sense,   nor are acting and being affected, but
     that to which they belong, which is motion, is the same;   for to be an
     actuality of A upon B and to be an *actuality* of B by A are distinct in
     formula.
         What motion is has been stated both universally and with respect to
25   its parts, for it is not unclear how each of its species will be defined; for
     example, alteration is the actuality of the alterable qua alterable, or, in
     more known terms, it is the actuality of that which can act or that which
     can be affected qua such, whether without qualification or in each par-
     ticular case   (as in [the process of] building and in [the process of]
     healing). Each of the other motions will be defined in the same manner.

BOOK IV

10

Next to what has been said comes the discussion of time. Concern- 30
ing time, we would do well, by using the common arguments also, to
go over the *difficulties* (a) as to whether it is a being or a nonbeing and
(b) as to what its nature is.

That time is either altogether nonexistent, or that it exists but hardly
or obscurely, might be suspected from the following: One part of it has
come to be but no longer exists; the other part will be but does not yet
exist; and it is of these two parts that infinite time, or any time one might   218a
take, is composed. But it is thought that what is composed of nonbeings
cannot participate in *substance*.

In addition, if any thing with parts is to exist, then, when it exists, all
or some of its parts must exist. But, although time is divisible, some   5
parts of it have been and the others will be, and no part of it exists. And
as for a moment, it is no part of time; for a part measures the whole,
and the whole must be composed of the parts, but it is thought that time
is not composed of moments.

Again, it is not easy to see whether the moment which appears to
divide the past and the future (1) always remains one and the same or   10
(2) is always distinct.

(2) If it is always distinct, while no two distinct parts of time exist
simultaneously unless one part contains while the other is contained (as
the smaller interval of time is contained by the greater), and if a moment
which does not exist but existed before must have been destroyed sometime, then two moments cannot exist simultaneously, but always the   15
prior moment must have been destroyed. Now the prior moment cannot have been destroyed in itself because it existed then. And it cannot
have been destroyed in some later moment. For let us posit that moments, like points on a line, are not consecutive to each other; then if
indeed it was not destroyed in a succeeding moment but in another, it   20
would have existed simultaneously with the infinitely many moments
between itself and that other, and this is impossible.

(1) Moreover, neither is it possible for the same moment to remain always the same; for no finite and divisible thing, whether continuous in one or in many dimensions, has just one limit, and the moment is a limit,
25   and it is possible to cut off a finite time. In addition, if to be simultaneous, but not prior or posterior, with respect to time is to be in the same thing, which in this case is the moment, and so if both the prior and the posterior   were to be in this moment,   things which happened ten thousand years ago would exist simultaneously with those happening today, and no one event would be either prior or posterior to another event.
30   Let this, then, be the discussion of *difficulties* faced in connection with what belongs to time.

As to the whatness or the nature of time, it is as unclear from the accounts handed down to us as it is from the *difficulties* just discussed.
218*b*   Some say that time is the motion of the whole;   others say that it is the sphere itself.   But then a part of a revolution will be time, and it [i.e., that part] is certainly not a revolution; for what we have here taken is a part of a revolution, not a revolution. Moreover, if there were more than one heaven,   the motion of any one of them, like that of any other,
5   would be time in a similar way, and so a plurality of times would exist simultaneously. As for those who said that time is the sphere of the whole, they thought so in view of the fact that all things are in time and also in the whole sphere; but this is too superficial [a doctrine] to require an examination of its impossible consequences.
10   However, since time is thought to be most of all a sort of motion or of change, we should look into this. Now a change or motion of each thing exists only in the thing which is changing or wherever it happens to be moving or changing; but time exists alike both everywhere and with all
15   things. Moreover, every change is faster or slower, but time is not; for the slow and the fast are defined in terms of time (the fast is that which moves much [distance] in a short [time], and the slow is that which moves a little [distance] in a long [time]), but time is not defined in terms of time, whether taken as being quantitative or as being qualitative.   Thus it is evident that time is not a motion; and it makes no difference at present whether we use the term "motion" or the term
20   "change."

11

On the other hand, time cannot exist without change; for when there is no change at all in our *thought* or when we do not notice any change, we do not think that time has elapsed, just like the legendary sleeping

characters in Sardinia who, on awakening from a long sleep in the pres- 25
ence of heroes, connect the earlier with the later moment into one
moment, thus leaving out the time between the two moments because
of their unconsciousness. Accordingly, just as there would be no intermediate time if the moment were one and the same, so people think that
there is no intermediate time if no distinct moments are noticed. So if
thinking that no time has elapsed happens to us when we specify no 30
limits of a change at all but the soul appears to *rest* in something which
is one and indivisible, but we think that time has elapsed when sensation has occurred and limits of a change have been specified, evidently
time does not exist without a motion or change.

It is evident, then, that neither is time a motion nor can it exist with- 219a
out a motion.

Since we are inquiring into the whatness of time, we should begin by
considering how time belongs to a motion. Now together with a motion
we sense time also. For even if it is dark and we are not being affected 5
through the body but some motion exists in the soul, we think without
hesitation that along with that motion also time has elapsed; and further,
when some time is thought to have elapsed, it appears that also some
motion has occurred simultaneously. Thus time is either a motion or
something belonging to a motion; and since it is not a motion, it must
be something belonging to a motion. 10

Since a thing in motion is moved from something to something else
and every magnitude is continuous, a motion follows a magnitude; for
a motion is continuous because a magnitude is continuous, and time is
continuous because a motion is continuous (for the time elapsed is always thought to be as much as the corresponding motion which took
place). Now the prior or the posterior are attributes primarily of a 15
place, and in virtue of position. So since the prior and the posterior exist
in magnitudes, they must also exist in motions and be analogous to those
in magnitudes; and further, the prior and the posterior exist also in time
because time always follows a motion. Now the prior and the posterior 20
exist in a motion whenever a motion exists, but the essence of each of
them is distinct [from a motion] and is not a motion. Moreover, we also
know the time when we limit a motion by specifying in it a prior and a
posterior as its limits; and it is then that we say that time has elapsed,
that is, when we perceive the prior and the posterior in a motion. And 25
we limit it [the time] by believing that they are two distinct things and
that there is something else between them; for when we conceive the
extremes as being distinct from what is intermediate and the soul says
that there are two moments, the one prior and the other posterior, it is
then that we also say that this is time, for what is limited by moments
is thought to be time, and let this be assumed. So when we perceive the 30

moment as being one, and not as prior and again as posterior in a motion, or as being the same thing, but as prior to something and as posterior to something else,   then no time is thought to have elapsed since
219b   neither was there a motion. But when we perceive it now as prior and
later as posterior, then we say that time has elapsed. For time is just
this: The number of a motion with respect to the prior and the posterior.
So time is not a motion, but a motion has time qua the number of it.
A sign of this is the following: We *judge* the greater and the less by a
5   number, and we *judge* a motion as being greater or less by time;   so
time is a sort of number.

Now since "a number" has two senses (for both that which is numbered or is numerable is a number, and also that by which   we number), time is that which is numbered   and not that by which we number
(that by which   we number is distinct from that which is numbered);
10   and just as a motion is always distinct, so is time.   But taken simultaneously every time is the same, for the moment whenever existing is
the same, though in essence it is distinct;   and, qua being prior and
posterior, it measures time.   The moment is in one way the same and
in another not the same; for, qua being now in one [subject] and now in
another, it is distinct (this is the essence of its being that moment), but
15   qua a being whenever it exists, it is the same.   For, as stated before,
and in our manner of saying, a motion follows a magnitude, and time
follows a motion. And a travelling object, by which we know the motion and both the prior and the posterior in it [the motion], follows a
point   in a similar way. And whatever this   may be (whether a point
20   or a stone or some other such thing), it is the same,   but in formula it is
distinct   (just as the sophists regard Coriscus in the Lyceum as being
distinct from Coriscus in the Agora); and it is distinct by being now in
one place and now in another. A moment follows a body in locomotion
just as time follows a motion, for it is by the body in locomotion that we
25   know the prior and the posterior in that motion;   and qua being numerable, the moment exists as prior or posterior.   So in these, too, when
existing as a being, the moment is the same (for what is prior or posterior
is the [same] body in motion),   but in essence it is distinct,   for it is
qua numerable that the moment is prior and posterior. And it is this
30   that is most knowable, for a motion too is known because of the body in
motion; and a locomotion is known because of the body in locomotion,
since it is the body in locomotion that is a *this* and not the motion. In
one way, then, that which is called "a moment" is always the same, but
in another it is not; for so it is in the case of the body in locomotion.

It is also evident that neither would a moment exist if time did not
220a   exist, nor would time exist if a moment did not exist; for just as an object
in locomotion and that locomotion are together, so the number   of an

object in locomotion and the number of that locomotion are together. For the number of a locomotion is time, and a moment is like an object in locomotion, as if a unit of a number. Moreover, time is also contin- 5 uous by means of a moment, and it is divisible with respect to a moment; for this too follows from the corresponding locomotion and the object in that motion, since (a) the motion or locomotion is one with the object which is in locomotion, seeing that this [object] is one, not as a being when existing (for it might also stand still) but in formula, and (b) the object in locomotion determines the prior and the posterior motion. And an object in locomotion follows in a way a point; for a point 10 both maintains the continuity and serves as a limit of a line, since it is the beginning of one and the end of another line. But if a point is so taken that it is used as two, a stop is necessary, if the same point is to be a beginning as well as an end. As for the moment, it is always distinct because the body in locomotion is always in motion; hence time is a 15 number not as in the case of the same point when this is both a beginning and an end, but rather as the extremities of the same object, and not as if these were parts, both because of what was said (for the intermediate point will be used as two, and so there will be rest) and because it is evident that neither is a moment a part of time nor is a division a part of a motion, just as points are not parts of a line. However, two 20 lines are parts of a line. Accordingly, qua being a limit, a moment is not time but an attribute [of it], but qua numbering, it is a number; for the limits belong only to that of which they are the limits, but the number of [say] these horses, e. g., ten, belongs also elsewhere.

It is evident, then, that time is a number of motion with respect to the 25 prior and the posterior and that it is also continuous (for it is of something which is continuous).

12

The smallest number, taken without qualification, is two. But if the number is qualified, in one sense there is a smallest, but in another there is not. For example, in the case of lines, the smallest number in plurality is two or one; but as a magnitude there is no smallest, for 30 every line is always divisible. So it is likewise with time; for, with respect to number, the smallest is one or two, but there is no smallest with respect to magnitude.

It is also evident that we do not speak of time as being fast or slow, 220*b* but we speak of it as being much or little and long or short. For qua continuous, it is long or short, but qua a number, it is much or little. But it is not fast or slow, just as no number by which we number things is fast or slow. Also, time everywhere is simultaneously the same; but 5 time existing before is not the same as time existing after, since a change, taken at present as one, is distinct from a change in the past and from one in the future.

Time as a number is not that by which we count but that which is
10 counted, and, occurring before and after, it is always distinct, for the moments are distinct. The number of one hundred horses and of one hundred men is one and the same, but the things of which it is the number are distinct: Horses are distinct from men. Also, just as a motion may be one and the same again and again, so can time also, as a year or a spring or an autumn.
15   Not only do we measure a motion by time, but also time by a motion, because they limit each other; for an interval of time limits a motion by being the number of that motion, and a motion limits the time. And we say that the time taken is much or little by measuring by a motion just as we speak of a number by measuring by the numerable, as for example
20 by one horse in the case of the number of horses. For we know a plurality of horses by its number, and again, we know the number of horses itself by one horse. And it is likewise with time and motion; for we measure a motion by time, and time by a motion. And this happens
25 with good reason, for a motion follows a magnitude and time follows a motion, since they are all quantitative and continuous and divisible; for a motion has these attributes because the corresponding magnitude is such-and-such a thing, and time has them because of the motion. And we measure both a magnitude by the corresponding motion, and the
30 motion by the magnitude; for we say that the road is of great distance if the journey is great, and the journey is great if the road is of great distance, and also that the time is much if the motion is, and the motion is much if the time is.
221a   Since time is a measure of motion and of being moved, it measures a given motion when some one motion is specified which will measure the whole motion (like a foot length which measures a given length, and this is done when some one magnitude is specified which will measure the whole [magnitude]). And for a motion to be in time is for both the
5 motion and the being of the motion to be measurable by time (for that time will simultaneously measure both the motion and the being of that motion); and for a motion to be in time is just this, that its being be measurable. It is clear that for other things, too, to be in time is just this, that the being of each of them be measurable by time; for "to be in time"
10 [for each thing] means one of the following two: (1) to exist when time exists, and (2) as we speak of some things, to be in a number, either (a) as a part or an *attribute* of a number, and in general, as something belonging to a number or (b) in the sense that there is a number of the thing in question.

Since time is a number, the moment and the prior and all such are in   15
time just as the unit and the odd and the even are in numbers (for each
of the latter is something belonging to a number, while each of the
former to time), but things are in time as in a number.   If so, they are
contained by time just as things in place are contained by place.   So
it is also evident that to be in time is not to exist when time exists, just   20
as to be in motion or in place is not to exist, respectively, when a motion
or a place exists. For if to be in something were to be in it in this manner, all things would be in any chance thing, and so the heaven would
be in a grain, for when the grain exists also the heaven exists. But this
is an accident, while in the other case one thing necessarily follows another; so a thing in time is followed by time when the thing exists also,   25
and a thing in motion is followed by a motion when the thing exists.

Since that which is in time is in a sense as in a number, corresponding
to any thing which is in time, a greater time than that time may be taken.
So all things in time are contained by time just like all other things which
are in something, like the things in a place which are contained by a   30
place. And a thing is somewhat affected by time, as in the usual saying
that *time wastes things away,* and things grow old by time, and people
forget by lapse of time, but they have not learned or become young or   221*b*
beautiful; for time in virtue of itself is a cause rather of destruction
since it is a number of motion, and what a motion does is to make a thing
depart from what it is.

It is evident, then, that eternal things, qua existing always, are not in
time; for neither are they contained by time, nor is their existence mea-   5
surable by time.   A sign of this is the fact that they are not affected at
all by time, which indicates that they are not in time.

Since time is a measure of motion, it would also be, as an attribute,
a measure of rest, for every state of rest is in time. For, although a thing
in motion has necessarily moved, it does not follow that a thing in time   10
moved also; for time is not a motion but a number of motion, and what
is at rest may also be in a number of motion. However, not everything
which is motionless may be at rest but only that which is deprived of
motion but can by nature be moved, as it was stated earlier.

To be in a number is to be a thing (a) of which there is a number and   15
(b) whose existence is measurable by the number in which it is; and so
if a thing is in time, it is measurable by time.   So time will measure
both a thing in motion and a thing at rest, the one qua in motion and the
other qua at rest; for it will measure the quantity of motion of the first
and the quantity of rest of the other.   So a thing in motion will be measurable qua a quantity   by time not without qualification, but insofar as   20
its motion is a quantity. Thus no thing can be in time if it can be neither

in motion nor at rest; for to be in time is to be measurable by time, and time is a measure of motion as well as of rest.

It is evident, then, that not every nonbeing can be in time, as in the
25 case of things which cannot be otherwise, like the nonbeing of a diagonal of a square commensurate with the side. In general, if time in virtue of itself is a measure of a motion, but a measure of the others as an attribute, it is clear that the things whose existence is measurable by time must exist by being at rest or in motion. Accordingly, things which are destructible and generable and, in general, things which at
30 one time exist and at another do not, all of them must be in time; for there exists a greater time which will surpass their existence and the measure of their *substance*. Of objects which do not exist but are con-
222a tained by time, some of them existed (e.g., Homer sometime existed) and others will exist (e.g., something in the future), depending on the direction in which time contains them, and if time contains them in both directions, then they both existed and will exist; but if time does not contain them at all, then they neither existed nor exist nor will exist. Such are those nonbeings whose opposites always exist. For example,
5 the diagonal of a square is always incommensurable with the side, and this is not in time; accordingly, a diagonal commensurate with the side does not exist in time, and so it always does not exist, seeing that it is the contrary of a thing which always exists. As for objects whose contraries are not eternal, it is possible for them to be and not to be, and generation and destruction of them is possible.

13

10 The [present] moment is a continuity of time, as it was stated, for it makes the past and the future continuous; and it is a limit of time, for it is the beginning of the one [the future] and the end of the other [the past]. But this is not evident as it is with the point, which persists. The
15 moment divides potentially, and, qua such, it is always distinct, but, qua connecting, it is always the same, as in the case of mathematical lines. For, in thought, a point is not always one; for if the parts [of a line] are divided, it [the point] is distinct, but qua one, the point is in every way the same. So too with the moment: In one way, it is potentially a division of time; in another, it is the limit and the unity of both
20 [parts]. Both the division and the union are the same and with respect to the same, but in essence they are not the same.

This is one way, then, in which the term "moment" [or "now"] is used, but in another, it means a moment which is near the moment in the first sense. We say "he will arrive now," meaning by this that he will arrive today; and we say "he arrived now," meaning that he came today. But what is narrated in the *Iliad* did not take place now, nor did the flood; for though the time from the present moment to these is continuous, their time is not near the present moment.

The expression "sometime" means a time definitely related to the 25 moment taken in the first sense. For example, we say "Troy was captured sometime [ago]" and also "a flood will take place sometime [from now]"; for these [events] are determined in relation to the present moment. Thus there will be a certain quantity of time from now to the latter event, and there was a certain quantity of time from now to the former event; and if there is no time which is not sometime, every [interval of] time will be finite.   But will time come to an end? Cer- 30 tainly not, if indeed a motion always exists.   Is time then distinct or does the same time occur again and again? Clearly, as it is with motion, so it is with time. For if it is one and the same motion   that occurs at some time, then also the time will be one and the same, but if not, then not.

Since the present moment is both an end and a beginning of time, 222*b* though not of the same time, but the end of what has passed and the beginning of the future, just as a circle has its convexity and its concavity in the same thing in some way, so is time always at a beginning and at an end;   and because of this, time is thought to be always distinct. For 5 it is not of the same thing that the moment is both a beginning and an end, since if it were, it would be two opposites simultaneously and in the same respect.   And time will certainly not come to an end, for there is always a beginning of it.

The term "presently" signifies a part of future time which is near the present and indivisible moment, and "already" signifies a part of past time not far from that moment.   When will you walk? We say "pres- 10 ently", since we intend to do so in the near future, or we say "I already walked". But we do not use the expression "Troy has already been captured" since the time of the event is too far from now. Also, "recently" signifies a part of the past which is near the present moment. When did you come?   We say "recently", if the time of this event is near the present moment. But we say "long ago", if a past event is far from now. A 15 thing is said to depart from its condition *suddenly* if it does so in a time interval which is imperceptible because of its shortness; and every change is by nature a departure from an existing condition.

All things which are generated or destroyed are so in time; and for this reason some called time "the wisest of things", but Paron the Pythagorean, speaking more rightly, called it "the stupidest", in view of the fact

that we also forget in it.   It is clear then that time in virtue of itself
20   is a cause rather of destruction than of generation, as stated also earlier
(for a change in virtue of itself is a departure from an existing condition),
but that it is accidentally a cause of generation and of being. An adequate sign of this is the fact that no thing is generated   without itself
being somehow in motion or acting, but a thing may be destroyed even
25   if it is not in motion. And it is this [change] most of all that is usually
said to be a destruction by time. However, it is not time that causes this
either, but this change happens to come to be in time.

We have stated, then, that time exists, what it is, the number of
senses of "moment", and what the terms "sometime", "recently", "already", "presently", "long ago", and "suddenly" mean.

14

30   With these distinctions thus laid down, it is evident that every change
or every thing in motion is in time; for the faster or slower exists with
respect to every change, since it appears to be so in every change. By
223a   "the faster in motion" I mean that which, being in uniform motion and
over the same interval, changes into a subject before another does so,
for example, in locomotion, if both things move along the circumference
of a circle or both along a straight line, and similarly in the other cases.
5   But what exists prior to another exists in time, for things are said to be
prior or posterior in virtue of their time interval from the present moment, which is the boundary of the past and the future; so since the
moments are in time, also the prior and the posterior will be in time, for
that in which the moments exist is also that in which the time intervals
between the moments exist. But the term "prior" with reference to the
10   past is used in a manner contrary to that with reference to the future;
for, with reference to the past, we call "prior" that which is further from
the present moment, and we call "posterior" that which is nearer, while
with reference to the future, we call "prior" that which is nearer to the
present moment, and we call "posterior" that which is further. So since
the prior is in time and every motion must have a prior, it is evident that
15   every change and every motion is in time.

It is also worth inquiring how time is related to the soul and why time
is thought to exist in everything, on the earth and on the sea and in the
heaven. Is it not in view of the fact that it is an *attribute* or a possession
of a motion, by being a number (of a motion), and the fact that all these
20   things are movable? For all of them are in a place, and time is simultaneous with a motion, whether with respect to potentiality or with
respect to *actuality*.

One might also raise the problem of whether time would exist or not if no soul existed; for, if no one can exist to do the numbering, no thing can be numbered and so clearly no number can exist, for a number is that which has been numbered or that which can be numbered. So if 25 nothing can do the numbering except a soul or the intellect of a soul, no time can exist without the existence of a soul, unless it be that which when existing, time exists, that is, if a motion can exist without a soul. As for the prior and the posterior, they exist in a motion; and they are time qua being numerable.

One might also raise this question: Of what kind of motion is time the 30 number? Is it of any kind? For things are generated and are destroyed and increase in time, and they also alter and travel in time. Accordingly, insofar as each of these [changes] is a motion, in that respect there is a number of each motion. On this account, it is of a continuous motion taken without qualification that there is a number, but not of a specific 223*b* motion. But, as it is, other things may also be in motion, and there may be a number of each of those motions. Is there a distinct time for each of them, then, and will there be two equal times simultaneously, or is this not the case? Now there is one and the same time alike and simultaneously, though in species also those times which are not simultaneous are one and the same; for if there were to exist dogs and also horses, 5 seven in each case, their number would be the same. Likewise, the time of motions with simultaneous limits would be the same, although one motion might be fast and another not, or, one of them might be a loco-motion and the other an alteration; yet their time would be the same, if indeed their number is equal and if they are also simultaneous, for example, in the case of an alteration and of a locomotion. And it is 10 because of this that, although the motions may be distinct or separate, their time is everywhere the same, seeing that the number of equal and simultaneous things is everywhere one and the same.

Since locomotions exist, and of these a circular locomotion also exists, and since the numerable is numbered by something which is of the same kind (e.g., units by a unit, horses by a horse, etc.), in the same way time is measured by some definite time. And it is measured as we said, 15 time by a motion and also a motion by time; and this is so in view of the fact that the quantity of both a motion and of a time interval is measured by a motion definite in time. Accordingly, if of all things under the same genus it is the primary that is their measure, a uniform circular motion is a measure most of all since its number is most 20 known. Neither an alteration nor an increase nor a generation can be uniform, but a locomotion can.

On account of this, it is thought that also time is the motion of the sphere, for the other motions are measured by it and also time is mea-

sured by this motion. And because of this there arises also the common
25   saying that human affairs and all other things which have a natural
motion or generation or destruction are circles; and this is in view of
the fact that all these are *judged* by time and that they end and begin
as if according to some cycle, for also time itself is thought to be a
30   circle; and this again is thought to be so because it is of such locomotion
that time is the measure and is itself measured by such motion.   Thus,
to say that things which come into being are circles is to say that there
is a circle of time, this being so in view of the fact that time is measured
by a circular locomotion; for that which is measured appears to be
224a   nothing else besides the measure, unless the whole be taken as a
plurality of measures.

   It is rightly said, too, that the number of sheep and that of dogs is the
same if they are equal; but they are neither the same ten nor the same
5   ten things, just as the equilateral and the scalene are not the same triangles although, being both triangles, they are the same figure; for
things are said to be the same if their differentiae do not differ, but not
so if their differentiae do differ.   For example, if the differentia of one
triangle differs from that of another, then the two triangles are distinct;
but as figures the two triangles come under one and the same differentia, and so they are not distinct figures. For one species of "a figure"
10   is "a circle", another is "a triangle", and of triangles, one species is "an
equilateral", another is "a scalene"; accordingly, also the latter [triangle]
is the same figure [as the former] for it too is a triangle, but it is not the
same triangle. So, too, the numbers mentioned are the same, for one of
them does not differ from the other by a differentia of "a number"; but
they are not the same ten, for the things of which "ten" is a predicate
15   differ: They are dogs in one case, but horses in the other.

   Concerning time, then, both about time itself and whatever is pertinent to its inquiry,   let this be our discussion.

BOOK V

1

Every thing that is changing does so either   224*a*

(a) accidentally, as when we say that the musical is walking, when in fact what is walking is that of which musicality is an attribute; or

(b) simply, i.e., when some part in it is changing, for we say that the   25
body is being healed when in fact it is just the eye or the chest that is being healed, and these are parts of the whole body; or

(c) if it is in motion neither accidentally nor in the sense that only something in it is in motion, but by being primarily itself in motion, and it is this that is essentially movable. Now one movable thing is distinguished from another in virtue of a distinct motion, as in the case of the alterable, and even within alteration the healable is distinct   30
from that which can be heated.

It is likewise with the mover, for (a) it may move another accidentally, or (b) it may do so in virtue of a part in it, or (c) it may do so primarily and essentially; for example, it is the doctor who heals [something], although it is the hand that strikes [something].

There are then (a) the primary mover and (b) that which is in motion   35
and also (c) the time in which [a motion occurs], and besides these (d) that from which and (e) that to which [a motion proceeds]. For   224*b*
every motion proceeds from something and to something; and the primary object which is in motion and that from which it is moved and that to which it is moved are all distinct, as in the case of the wood and the hot and the cold which are, in the order given, that which is in motion, that to which the motion proceeds, and that from which the motion proceeds. Clearly, then, the motion is in the wood and not in   5
the form; for what causes a motion or is moved is not the form or the place or the so-much [a quantity], but there are a mover, that which is in motion, and that to which the thing in motion proceeds. (For a change is named after that to which a thing is moved rather

that that from which it is moved; thus a destruction too is a change
10   to nonbeing, even if that which is being destroyed is changing from
being, and a generation is a change to being, even if from nonbeing.)

We have stated earlier[26] what a motion is.   As to the forms and the
affections and the place to which things in motion are moved, these are
immovable,   like science and heat. However, one might raise the question of whether affections (like whiteness, which is an affection) are
15   motions,   for then there will be a change toward a motion. But perhaps
it is not whiteness that is a motion, but whitening.   And in these,   too,
a change may be (a) accidental or (b) in virtue of a part or of something
else or (c) primary and not in virtue of something else; for example,
that which is being whitened changes (1) to that which is being thought
20   accidentally (for to be thought is an accident of a color), (2) to a color
in view of the fact that the white is a part of a color, and (3) to Europe
in view of the fact that Athens is a part of Europe, but [it is changed]
to a white color essentially.

It has been made clear, then, how a thing, whether a mover or a thing
in motion, moves essentially or accidentally, or with respect to some-
25   thing else or primarily;   and it is also clear that a motion is not in the
form but in the thing in motion or in the movable when in *actuality*
[qua movable].

Accidental change will be omitted from discussion, for it exists in all,
and always, and is a change for all things;   but nonaccidental change
does not exist in all, but only in contraries, in intermediates, and in con-
30   tradictories.   We may be convinced of this by induction. Change proceeds also from an intermediate,   for this [the intermediate], being in
some sense an extreme, serves as a contrary relative to each of the two
contraries. On account of this, when an intermediate is related to a
contrary or a contrary to an intermediate, both are said to be contraries
in some sense; for example, the middle note is low relative to the high
35   but high relative to the low, and grey is white relative to black but black
relative to white.

225a   Since every change is from something to something, as even the name
μεταβολή [= "change"] makes clear (for the word μετά indicates something after something else, and one of these comes before while the
other comes after), that which is changing would be limited to four
alternatives: either from a subject to a subject or from a subject to a
5   nonsubject or from a nonsubject to a subject or from a nonsubject to a
nonsubject; and by "a subject" I mean something signified by an affirmative term.   From what has been said, then, there must be only three
[kinds of] changes: (a) that from a subject to a subject,   (b) that from a

subject to a nonsubject, and (c) that from a nonsubject to a subject; 10
for there is no change from a nonsubject to a nonsubject because there
is no opposition, whether between contraries or between contradictories.

Now a change from a nonsubject to a subject with respect to contradiction is a generation, and it is an unqualified generation if the
change is unqualified, but a qualified generation if the change is qualified. For example, a change from non-white to white is a qualified 15
generation; but that from an unqualified not-being to a substance is
an unqualified generation, in virtue of which we say that a thing is
generated in an unqualified and not in a qualified way.

A change from a subject to a nonsubject is a destruction, and it is an
unqualified destruction if it is a change from a substance to not-being,
but a qualified destruction if it is a change from a qualified being to the
opposed negative, as we said in the case of a generation. 20

Now if "nonbeing" has many meanings and there can be a motion
neither of nonbeing according to composition or division nor of potential nonbeing, which is the opposite of unqualified *actual* being (for
the not-white or not-good may nevertheless be accidentally in motion,
since the not-white might be a man, but the unqualified not-*this* can in 25
no way be in motion), nonbeing can in no way be in motion; and if
this is so, then neither can a generation be a motion, for it is nonbeing
that becomes [something]. For, however true it may be that something is generated with respect to an accident, it is still true to say that
nonbeing belongs to that which is becoming [something] without qualification. Likewise, nonbeing cannot be at rest. These difficulties, 30
then, arise if nonbeing is taken to be in motion; and, we may add, if
every thing in motion is in a place, nonbeing would have to be somewhere, but it cannot be in a place. A destruction, too, cannot be a motion; for the contrary of a motion is a motion or rest, but a destruction
is the contrary of a generation.

Since every motion is a kind of change, and there are three kinds of 35
change as stated before, and changes with respect to generation and
destruction are not motions but are changes with respect to contradic- 225*b*
tion, only a change from a subject to a subject must be a motion. As for
the subjects, they are contraries or intermediates; for a privation also is
posited here as a contrary, and it is indicated by an affirmation, as in the
case of "naked", "toothless", and "black". Hence, since the categories 5
are distinguished as being of substance, quality, whereness, whenness,
relation, quantity, acting, and being affected, there must be three [kinds
of] motions, namely, those of quality, those of quantity, and those with
respect to place.

2

10   There is no motion with respect to a substance because no thing is
contrary to a substance. Nor is there a motion with respect to a relation; for, when one of the relatives is changing, the other may not be
truly related to the first even if it is not changing, and so their motion
is accidental. Nor is there a motion of a thing which acts or is affected,
15   or of a thing in motion, or of a mover, for there is no motion of a
motion, no generation of a generation, and in general, no change of a
change.
      Now there may be a motion of a motion in two ways, either (1) when
a motion is taken as a subject, as when a man [as a subject] is moved
if he changes from light to dark (and in this sense, [we may ask] is a
20   motion, too, really heated or cooled or changing place or increasing or
decreasing? This is impossible; for a change is not a subject.), or (2)
when some other subject changes from one kind of change to another,
as when a man changes from sickness to health. But this too is not possible except accidentally, for this motion is a change from one kind to
25   another (and likewise with a generation and a destruction, except that
the latter are changes into opposites in a certain way, while a motion
is a change but not in a similar way). Accordingly, a man will be changing from health to sickness and at the same time from this change to
another change. So it is clear that if he becomes sick, he will have
changed into some other kind of change (of course, he may also be rest-
30   ing), but not always into a chance change; and this change, too, will be
from something to something else. And so this opposite change will be
that of becoming healthy. But this [change] will be by accident; for
example, in changing from recollection to forgetfulness, it is that to
which these belong that changes now towards *knowledge* and now
towards ignorance.
      Moreover, this will go on to infinity, if there is a change of a change
35   or a generation of a generation; for if there is of the latter, so must there
226a   be of the former. For example, if an unqualified generation was being
generated at some time, then also the thing in unqualified generation
was being generated, and so it [that thing] was not yet a thing in unqualified generation but was in a qualified generation during this time;
and again this, too, was something in the process of generation, and so
it was not yet in the process of generation. And since in an infinite
5   series there is no first, there will be no first [here] either, and thus no
thing that succeeds it. Accordingly, none of them can be generated or
be in motion or be changing.
      Moreover, the same subject may have also a contrary motion and a
coming to rest and a generation and a destruction. So when a thing in

generation becomes a thing in generation, it is then being destroyed;   10
for neither at the end of the process nor after the process is it a thing
in generation, for what is [in the process of] being destroyed must
exist.

Again, there must be matter which underlies both that which is being
generated and that which changes. What matter would this be which
would become a motion or a generation in the manner in which a body
or a soul changes with respect to quality? And, in addition, into what
will they be moving? For there must be something whose motion proceeds from something to something else, but this something is not a
motion [as a subject] or a generation. And how can this be? For there   15
is no learning of learning, and so no generation of a generation, and no
specific generation of itself. Finally, since there are three kinds of motion
[locomotion, alteration, increase or decrease], then the underlying nature, as well as that to which it proceeds, must be one of these; for example, a locomotion must be altering or moving locally.

In general, since a thing may be in motion in three ways, either
accidentally or in virtue of a part of it or in virtue of itself, a change may   20
change only accidentally, as when he who is being healed is also running or learning. However, we decided earlier to omit the discussion of
accidental change.[27]

Since, then, there can be no motion of a substance or of a relation or of
acting or of being affected, it remains that there can be a motion only
with respect to quality or quantity or place, for there is a contrariety in   25
each of these. Accordingly, let a motion with respect to quality be called
"alteration", for this is the name commonly attached to this motion. By
"a quality" I do not mean that which is in the *substance* of a thing (for a
differentia, too, is called "a quality"), but an affective quality in virtue
of which a thing is said to be affected or to be incapable of being
affected. As for a motion with respect to quantity, there is no general   30
name for it, but "increase" and "decrease" are the names for the two
kinds respectively: an increase is a motion toward a complete magnitude; a decrease is a motion away from a complete magnitude. Finally,
a motion with respect to place has neither a general name nor a specific
name for any of its kinds; so let "locomotion" be the general name,
although this term in its main sense is applied only to things which do   35
not by themselves stop when changing place and to things whose mo-   226*b*
tion with respect to place is not caused by themselves.

A change within the same kind but with respect to the more and the
less is an alteration; for a change from a contrary or to a contrary is a
motion, whether unqualified or qualified, and when toward the less,

5   it will be said to be a change to a contrary [of a quality], but when
     toward the more, it will be as if from a contrary to [the quality] itself.
     It makes no difference whether the change be qualified or unqualified,
     except that the contraries in the first case must belong to the thing in a
     qualified way; as for "the more" or "the less", they apply to the thing
     which has or has not more or less of the contrary. From what has been
     said, then, it is clear that these are the only three motions that exist.
10   A thing is said to be motionless [or immovable] (a) if it cannot be
     moved at all, like a sound, which is [said to be] invisible; (b) if after
     much time a thing is moved with difficulty or its motion begins slowly,
     and in this case we say that it is hardly movable; (c) if a thing has a
     nature so as to be moved and can be moved, but it is not in motion when,
     where, and in the manner in which it is its nature to be in motion, and
15   of things called "motionless" only this is called "resting", for rest is the
     contrary of motion and so it would be the privation of motion in that
     which can be in motion.
         It is evident from what has been said, then, what motion is, what rest
     is, how many changes there are, and what the kinds of motions are.

BOOK VII

1

Every thing in motion is necessarily being moved by some thing.
Now if it does not have the source of motion in itself, it is evident that 25
it is being moved by some other thing; but if it has it in itself, let AC
be that which is moved but not in the sense that some part of it [i.e., of
AC] is moved.

For one thing, the belief that AC is moved by itself because the
whole of it is moved and is moved by nothing external is similar to the 30
belief that DEF is moved by itself when DE moves EF and is itself in
motion, because one does not perceive which is moved by which,
whether DE by EF or EF by DE. For another, a thing which is being
moved by itself would never cease being in motion by virtue of the fact 242*a*
that some other thing stops being in motion. So if a thing in motion
ceases to be so by virtue of the fact that some other thing stops, then it
is being moved by another thing. This having been made evident, every
thing in motion is necessarily being moved by some thing.

To return, since AC is taken as being in motion, it must be divisible; 5
for, as already shown, every thing in motion is divisible. So let it be
divided at B. Then when BC is resting, also AC must be resting; for if
not, let it be in motion. Then while BC is resting, AB might be in motion,
and then AC would not be in motion essentially. But it was assumed
that it [i.e., AC] is in motion essentially and primarily. It is clear, then, 10
that when BC is resting, also AC will be resting, and it is then that it
[i.e., AC] ceases to be in motion. But if a thing stops or ceases to be in
motion by the fact that something else rests, then it is being moved by
another.

It is evident, then, that every thing in motion is being moved by some
thing; for every thing in motion is divisible, and if a part of it is resting, 15
then also the whole will be resting.

Since every thing in motion is being moved by some thing, every
thing whose motion is in place   must also be moved by another; and

also the mover is being moved by another, that is, if it too is in motion,
and also that other mover is [likewise] being moved by another. Now
20   this does not go on to infinity but stops at some point, and there is something which is the first cause of being moved.   If this is not the case
but the process goes on to infinity, let A be moved by B, B by C, C by D,
and let this proceed in this manner infinitely. Then since that which
causes motion is itself in motion at the same time, it is clear that both
25   A and B will be in motion at the same time; for when B is in motion also
A is in motion, and when B is in motion also C is,   and when C, also D
is. Accordingly, the motion of A, B, C, and the rest will be simultaneous.
We may also consider each of these motions by itself; for even if each
30   of these things is moved by one of the others, nevertheless its motion is
numerically one and is not infinite with respect to its limits,   if indeed
every thing in motion proceeds from something to something, for the
motion is either numerically the same, or generically, or in species.
By "numerically the same motion" I mean one that starts from numerically the same limit and proceeds to numerically the same other
242b limit during the same numerical time, for example, from this whiteness,
which is one numerically, to that blackness [which is one numerically]
during this time, which is one numerically, for if during another time
[also], the motion is no longer numerically one but is one in species. A
5   motion is generically the same if it is in the same category of *substance*
or genus; and it is the same in species if that from which it proceeds is
the same in species and that to which it proceeds is the same in species—
for example, the motion from whiteness to blackness or that from goodness to badness. These have been discussed also previously.[28]
To return, let the motion of A be E, that of B be F, that of C and D be
10   G and H, respectively, and let T be the time during which A is moved.
If the motion of A is definite, so will its time be, and so T will not be
infinite.   But A and B and each of the others were taken as being in
motion at the same time. So it turns out that the motion EFGH,   which
15   is infinite, occurs in a definite time T; for the objects succeeding A,
being infinite, were taken as being in motion during the [same] time in
which A is in motion. So all are in motion during the same time. And
whether the motion of A be taken as being equal to or greater than that
of B, it makes no difference;   for in every case, an infinite motion will
occur in a finite time, which is impossible.
20   It would thus seem that what we set out to show has been shown,
but it has not quite been shown, because nothing absurd follows; for in
a finite time there may be an infinite motion, not the same motion, but
one motion here and another there and so motions of many or of an
infinite number of objects, and in this situation such indeed is the case.
25   But if that which is moved primarily with respect to place and with a

corporeal motion must be in contact or continuous with the mover, as we observe this happening in all cases, there will be of all of them [i.e., of movers and things moved] something which is one or is continuous. So since this may be the case, let it be granted, and let the [resulting] magnitude or the continuous thing be ABCD and its motion be EFGH. Whether it is finite or infinite makes no difference; for it will be in mo- 30 tion in the finite time T just the same, whether it is infinite or finite. Yet each of the two alternatives is impossible. So it is evident that the series must stop somewhere and it will not proceed to infinity, and one thing will not always be moved by another but there will be a first thing which is moved. The fact that a hypothesis was introduced to 243*a* show this result, of course, makes no difference; for the positing of something which might be should not have resulted in anything absurd.

2

The primary mover, not as a final cause but as a source of motion, exists together with the thing which is being moved. I say "together" because there is nothing between the two, for this is common in every 5 case of a thing in motion and its mover. Since the motions are three [in kind]—one with respect to place, another with respect to quality, and a third with respect to quantity—the things in motion too must be three [in kind]. Now a motion with respect to place is a locomotion, one with respect to quality is an alteration, and one with respect to quantity is an increase or decrease; we shall discuss first locomotion, for this is the 10 primary of [the kinds of] motions.

Every thing in locomotion is moved either by itself or by another thing. In the case of those things which are moved by themselves, it is evident that the thing moved and the thing causing it to be moved are together; for it is in the things themselves that the primary mover exists, so there is nothing between them. 15

As for those things which are moved by other things, this must take place in four ways; for locomotions caused by other things are four in kind (pulling, pushing, carrying, and turning), since all other motions with respect to place are referred to these [four]. Thus pushing along is a kind of pushing, namely, one in which the mover, in pushing the thing away from itself [i.e., from the mover], continues to do so behind it; 20 pushing away, on the other hand, is a pushing in which the mover does not follow the thing which it causes to be in motion. As for throwing, this happens when the mover causes a thing to move from itself [i.e., from 243*b* the mover] with a motion which is greater than the natural locomotion, and then the thing continues to travel as far as its motion holds. Again,

pushing apart and bringing together are, respectively, [kinds of]
pushing away and pulling; for pushing apart is a [kind of] pushing
5   away (for it is a pushing away either from itself or from another),
whereas bringing together is a [kind of] pulling (for it is a pulling [a
thing] toward itself or toward another). And such is the case with the
species of these, e.g., packing and combing, for the one is a [species of]
bringing together, the other a species of pushing apart. It is likewise
with the other combinations and separations, for all will turn out to be
[kinds of] pushing apart or bringing together, with the exception of
10   those which take place in generation and destruction. At the same
time it is evident that there is no other genus of motion besides combination and separation; for all [the species of motions] are distributed within the ones mentioned. We may also add that inhaling is a [kind of]
pulling and exhaling is a [kind of] pushing. It is likewise with spitting
and all other motions occurring through the body by which something
15   is taken in or is given out, for some of them are pullings and the others
are pushings away. The other motions with respect to place, too, should
be referred [to the four genera], for they all come under them.

Again, of these four, carrying and turning are referred to pulling and
pushing. Carrying may take place in three ways, for that which is
20   carried is moved accidentally in view of the fact that it is in or on a
thing in motion, and that which carries it does so either by being pulled
244a   or by being pushed or by being turned; and so carrying is common to
all three. As for turning, it is a composite of pulling and pushing; for
that which causes turning must be pulling one part of the thing and
pushing another part since it forces one part away from itself and another part toward itself.

5   Thus, if that which pushes and that which pulls are together, respectively, with that which is pushed and that which is pulled, it is evident
that in locomotion there is nothing between that which is being moved
and that which causes motion.

Moreover, this is evident also from the definitions; for pushing is a
motion from the thing itself [which pushes] or from another to another,
and pulling is a motion from another to the thing [which causes it] or
10   to another when the motion of that which pulls is faster than the motion
which would separate continuous things from each other, for it is in this
way that one part is pulled along [with that which pulls]. It might be
thought that pulling exists also in another way, for it is not in this way
that wood pulls [i.e., attracts] fire. But it makes no difference whether
that which pulls is in motion or at *rest* when it is pulling, for in the
latter case its pulling is from where it is and in the former it is from
15   where it was. Now a mover cannot cause a thing to be moved, whether
244b   it does so from itself to another or from another to itself, unless it is in

contact with it; so it is evident that in locomotion there is nothing between the thing in motion and its mover.

Nor   is there anything between that which is being altered and that
which is causing it to alter. This is clear by induction, for, in every
case, the last thing which causes alteration is together with the [first]   5
thing   which is being altered by the corresponding [mover], and these
are affections coming under quality; for we say that a thing is being altered when it is being heated or being sweetened or getting dense or
getting dry or getting white [etc.]. And this applies to inanimate and
animate bodies alike and, in the case of animate things, to the parts
without the power of sensation as well as to the powers of sensation   10
themselves; for the latter are somewhat altered, since a sensation in
actuality is a motion through the body, and during that [motion] the
power of sensation is somewhat being affected. Thus an animate thing
can be altered by every alteration by which an inanimate thing can, but
an inanimate thing cannot be altered by every alteration by which an
animate thing can;   for an inanimate thing cannot be altered with re-   15
spect to a power of sensation, and further, an inanimate thing is not
aware of being affected but an animate is aware.   Of course, nothing   245*a*
prevents an animate thing too from being unaware when the alteration
takes place not with respect to the powers of sensation. Accordingly, if
indeed the thing which is being altered is altered by a sensible,   it is evident that in every case the last thing which causes alteration is together   5
with the first thing which is being altered. For example, the air is continuous with the thing [causing alteration], and the body [which is being
affected] is continuous with air; and a color is continuous with light, and
light with sight.   It is in the same way with hearing and smelling, for the
primary mover   relative to that which is moved is air; and similarly with
taste, for the flavor is together with the sense of taste. It is likewise with   10
inanimate things and those without the power of sensation. So there can
be nothing between that which is being altered and that which is
causing alteration.

Nor again can there be anything between that which is being increased and that which is causing the increase; for the first thing that is
causing the increase attaches itself to that which is being increased in
such a way that the whole becomes one. Again, that which is causing
decrease does so when some part is detached from that which is being
decreased. So that which is causing increase or decrease is continuous   15
[respectively with that which is being increased or decreased], and there
is nothing between [two] things which are continuous [with each
other].

It is evident, then, that no intermediate exists between that which is
being moved and the mover which is primary   or last in relation to   245*b*
the thing which is being moved.

3

It will be seen from what follows that all things which are altered are altered by the sensibles and that alteration exists only in things which 5 in virtue of themselves are said to be affected by the sensibles. For in other things one might come to the belief that alteration exists in shapes and *forms* and habits or the processes of acquiring or of losing these; yet alteration exists in none of these. For when the thing in the process 10 of being shaped or arranged has been completed, we do not call it by the name of that out of which it is made (e.g., we do not call the statue "bronze", or the candle "wax", or the bed "wood", but we use derivative terms and call them "brazen", "waxen", and "wooden", respectively). But when a thing has been affected or altered, we still call it by the [original] name; for we say that it is the bronze or the wax that is hot 15 or hard, and not only so, but we also say that the wet or the hot is 246a bronze, thus naming the matter in a manner similar to that of the affection. So, if with respect to the shape or *form* the thing generated and in which the shape exists is not [so] named, but with respect to the affections or the alterations it is [so] named, it is evident that those generations cannot be alterations.

Again, it would also seem absurd to speak in such a manner and to 5 say, for example, of a man or of a house or of any other thing that has been generated that it has been altered. But when a thing is being generated, perhaps there must be something which is being altered, for example, the matter may be condensing or becoming rarefied or becoming hot or cold; yet the things which are being generated are not [only] altering, nor is their generation [just] an alteration.

10   Further, neither the habits of the body nor those of the soul are alterations. For, of the habits, some are virtues and the others are vices, and neither a virtue nor a vice is an alteration; but a virtue is a kind of perfection (for when each thing acquires its own virtue, it is then said 15 to be perfect; for a thing exists in the highest degree according to nature when, to use an example, like a perfect circle, it has become a circle in the highest sense and the best circle), while a vice is the destruction of or the departure from it [i.e., from that perfection]. Accordingly, just as we do not call the completion of a house "an alteration" (for it is absurd to say that the coping or the roofing with tiles is an alteration or that 20 the house is being altered when it is being coped or roofed but not that 246b it is being completed), so it is in the case of virtues and vices and of those who have them or are acquiring them; for some are perfections while the others are departures, in which case none of them is an alteration.

Further, we also speak of virtues as coming under things which are such that they are somehow related to something. For we take the vir-

tues of the body, such as health and good physical condition, to be mix-   5
tures and right proportions of hot and cold, in relation either to one
another or to the surroundings; and it is likewise with physical beauty
and strength and the other virtues and vices, for the being of each is
such that it is somehow related to something, and that which has it is
well or badly disposed towards the *proper* affections (and by "*proper*   10
affections" I mean those by which it [i.e., the virtue or vice] is being
generated or destroyed). Thus, since neither the relations themselves
are alterations, nor can any of them be altered or generated or, in general, change, it is evident that neither a habit nor the losing or acquiring of a habit is an alteration; but perhaps when these are generated
or destroyed some other things must be altered, as is also the case with   15
forms or *shapes,* as, for example, those which are present in things hot
or cold or dry or wet or in things in which they happen to exist primarily. For we say that a vice or a virtue has to do with those things by
which the possessor of it is by nature altered; for a virtue makes one
be either unaffected or affected in a manner in which he ought to be,   20
while a vice makes him be affected or unaffected in the contrary manner.

It is likewise with the habits of the soul, for the being of each of them,   247a
too, is such that it is somehow related to something; and the virtues [of
the soul] are perfections, while the vices are departures. Again, a virtue is well disposed toward its *proper* affection, while a vice is badly
disposed. Thus neither these [habits] nor the processes of losing or of
acquiring them could be alterations. And while they are being gener-   5
ated, the sensitive part of the soul is of necessity being altered, and it
is being altered by sensible objects. For every ethical virtue is about
bodily pleasures and pains, and these exist in *action* or in remembering
or in expecting; and in *action* they [pleasures and pains] occur by way   10
of sensation and so they are moved by some sensible objects, while
in remembering and in expecting they come from sensation, for people
are pleased either by remembering what affected them or by expecting
what they will be affected by. Thus all such pleasures are produced by
sensible objects. Since along with pleasures and pains in a man virtues   15
and vices also arise (for these are concerned with pleasures and pains)
and since pleasures and pains are alterations of the sensible part of the
soul, it is evident that losing or acquiring them [virtues and vices] also
must take place when something else is being altered. Hence their
generation is accompanied by alteration, but they themselves are not
alterations.

Moreover, neither are the habits of the thinking part of the soul altera-   247b
tions, nor is there a generation of them. For one thing, we speak of
those [habits] of the *knowing* part very much more than of any of the
others as being among things which are somehow related to some-

thing. Moreover, it is also evident that of these there is no generation;
5   for the potentially *knowing* becomes *knowing* not by having itself being moved at all but by the fact that something else existed; for when
that which exists with respect to a part comes into being, then it is
[only] in a sense that one *knows* by the universal that which exists in
part. Then again, there is no generation of the use or of the activity
[of something], unless one thinks that there is a generation also of see-
10   ing or of touching, and being in activity is similar to these. As for the
acquisition of *knowledge,* when this first occurs, it is not a generation;
for we speak of *knowing* and of thinking wisely when *thought* has come
to a rest or to a stop, and there is no generation toward a state of rest,
for, as previously stated, there is no generation at all of any becoming.
Again, just as we do not say that a man has become once more a scientist when from being drunk or asleep or sick he reverts to the contrary
15   state (even if just before this [sober] state he could not use [his]
science), so it is when at first he acquires the habit; for he comes to be
thinking wisely and *knowing* when the soul has settled down from its
natural restlessness. And on account of this, children can neither learn
248*a*   nor discriminate through sensation as adults do, for [in their soul] there
is much restlessness and motion. And for some things the soul settles
down and comes to a rest by nature itself, while for others it does so by
other things, but in both cases this occurs when certain things are
5   altered in the body, as in the case of the use and the activity [of thought]
when a man becomes sober or is awakened.

From what has been said, then, it is evident that being altered and
alteration occur in sensible things and in the sensitive part of the soul,
and in no other things except accidentally.

BOOK VIII

1

Was motion ever generated without having existed before, and is it 250*b* being destroyed in such a way that nothing will be in motion, or neither was it generated nor is it being destroyed, but it always existed and it will always exist, being (a) everlasting and (b) without the possibility of ceasing in what exists and (c) as if a sort of life belonging to things 15 which are formed by nature?

All thinkers who say something about nature declare that motion exists because they posit an ordered universe; and all of them speculate about generation and destruction, and this speculation is not possible if motion does not exist. Now those who say that there is an infinity of universes, some of them in the process of generation and others in the process of destruction, declare that motion always exists (for the gen- 20 eration and destruction of the universes must take place with motion); but those who say that there is just one universe, whether existing always or not, make assumptions also concerning motion as reason requires. If, however, it is possible that at some time no thing be in motion, this must happen in two ways: either (a) as Anaxagoras declares (for he says that all things were together and at rest for an infinite inter- 25 val of time but that *Intelligence* caused motion in things and separated them) or (b) as Empedocles does (according to whom things are now in motion and now at rest, in motion when *Friendship* is causing the *Many* to become *One* or when *Strife* is causing the *Many* from the *One*, but at rest during the time intervals which separate these processes), when he speaks thus:

> Once more do they achieve plurality 30
> From scattered oneness, and thus far they come
> To being, with no permanent existence;
> And in so far as they continuously 251*a*
> Never cease interchanging, just so far
> Their cycle is unmovable forever.

5   For we must take him to be saying: "but since the motions alternate
     from one kind to the other". So we must examine these alternatives
     and see what the situation is, for the truth will be of use not only
     to the investigation of nature but also to the *inquiry* into the first
     principle.
          Let us begin with what we laid down earlier in the *Discourses on*
10   *Nature*.³⁰ We have stated that motion is the actuality of the movable
     qua movable. So the things capable of having each kind of motion must
     exist. And even apart from the definition of motion, everyone would
     agree that, for each kind of motion, it is the object capable of that
     motion which has that motion (for example, what is being altered is
15   the alterable, and what travels is that which can change with respect
     to place), so that there must be a burnable object before there is a
     process of being burned, and an object which can burn another object
     before a process of burning that object. Certainly, these [objects]
     too must either (a) have been generated at some particular time before
     which they did not exist, or (b) be eternal.
          Now if each kind of movable object was generated, then before its
     kind of motion there must have occurred some other change or motion
20   by which the object, capable of being moved or able of causing motion,
     was generated. But if such objects always preexisted without motion,
     this appears to be in itself unreasonable, and it must appear even more
     unreasonable as we consider the matter further. For if, when there
     exist things which can be moved and things which can cause motion,
     at one time there is a first thing that causes motion and also one that is
25   being moved, but at another [i.e., prior] time there is no such thing but
     there is only rest, then this   must have changed before;   for there must
     have been some cause of rest, since rest is the privation of motion. Thus
     there would be a change before the first change. For some things cause
     motion in one way only, while others can cause contrary motions; for
30   example, fire burns but does not cool, but it is thought that there is just
     one science   of contraries. Even in things of the former type   there
     appears to be some similarity; for cold causes heat if it changes direction
     somehow or departs,   just as a scientist voluntarily commits an error
251b when he uses his science in the contrary manner. Things, then, which
     have the potentiality of acting or of being acted upon, or else of causing
     motion or of being moved, have it not in every way but [only] when
     they are disposed in a certain way and approach one another. Thus it
     is when there is an approach   of two things that one of them causes a
     motion and the other is moved, and when disposed to act in a certain
5   way   that the one can cause motion and the other can be moved.
     Accordingly, if motion did not always exist, it is clear that no two things
     would be so disposed as to have the potentiality of being moved and of

causing motion, respectively, but it is necessary for [at least] one of them to change; for in things which are related this must take place; for example, if A is double of B now but was not double of B before, then at least one of them, if not both, must have changed. Hence, prior to the first change there would be another change. 10

Moreover, how can there be a before and an after if time does not exist? Or, how can time exist if motion does not exist? So if time is a number of motion or a sort of motion, then if indeed time always exists, motion too must be eternal.

Now all thinkers, with one exception, appear to agree concerning 15 time, for they say that time is ungenerable. And it is at least because of this that Democritus shows that it is impossible for all things to have been generated, for he considers time to be ungenerable. Plato alone says that time was generated; for he says that both time and the heaven came into existence simultaneously [31] (the heaven was generated, according to him). So if it is impossible for time to exist or to be conceived 20 without moments and a moment is a sort of middle serving both as a beginning and an end, the beginning of future time but the end of past time, then time must always exist; for the extremity of any last part of an interval of time that may be taken will have to be in some one of the moments, since nothing of time is present to us except a moment. 25 Thus, since the moment is both a beginning and an end, there must always be time on both sides of it. And if there is [always] time, it is evident that there must [always] be motion too, if indeed time is an *attribute* of motion.

The same may be said concerning the indestructibility of motion. For just as in positing the generation of a first motion it was shown that a 30 change prior to that motion existed, so in positing a last motion [it can be shown that a change later than that motion will exist]; for that which ceases to be in motion does not at the same time cease to be movable (for example, that which ceases being burned does not at the same time cease being burnable, since a thing may be burnable without being in the process of being burned) and that which stops causing a motion 252a does not at the same time [necessarily] stop being able to cause a motion. And when the destructive destroys something, it [the destructive] too will have to be destroyed, and that which will destroy this will also have to be destroyed later; for a destruction too is a kind of change. So if the consequences are impossible, it is clear that motion is eternal and does not at one time exist and at another cease to exist; and indeed, the manner in which these thinkers speak seems rather that 5 of fiction.

Similar remarks apply also to the statement that such is the case by nature and that this should be regarded as a principle; and this would

seem to be the statement of Empedocles, who says that to rule and cause motion alternately, at one time by *Friendship* and at another by *Strife*, is something which belongs to things of necessity and that things
10   are at rest during the intervals separating these states. Perhaps also those who posit one principle, like Anaxagoras would speak in the same manner.   Yet none of the things formed by nature or according to nature is disorderly, for nature is a cause of order in each thing;   and the relation of the infinite to the infinite has no formula,   while every order is a formula. Nor indeed is it the work of nature that things should
15   be at rest for an infinite time, then in motion at some later time, with no more difference in the latter time than in the former and no order of any sort. For a thing by nature is either disposed in a simple way and not in one way at one time but in another at another time (for example, by nature fire travels up, and it is not the case that at one time it travels up but at another it does not), or it has a pattern if it is not simple.
20   Hence, it would be better to say that things are at rest and in motion alternately, as Empedocles or any other thinker who may have spoken in this manner does, for there is order in such a state of affairs.   Yet even he who asserts this should not only state it but also state its cause, and he should neither avoid positing something nor posit an unreason-
25   able axiom but should use an induction or a demonstration;   for these hypotheses are not causes, nor is the essence of *Friendship* or of *Strife* to be these, but the essence of *Friendship* is to unite and that of *Strife* is to separate.   And if he says that each of these [i.e., *Friendship* or *Strife*] acts on some things only, he should mention those things for each case, as in the case of men (in whom there is something which brings them
30   together, and this is friendship, while enemies avoid each other); but he assumes this to be the case in the whole universe, for [according to him] it appears to be so in some cases. Also, some argument is needed to show that each of the two principles rules alternately for an equal interval of time.

It is not a right belief to regard universally as an adequate principle the following, that it is always so or it always happens to be so, which is
35   what Democritus does in referring the causes of nature to this, that
252b   things were happening in the same way before. He does not think that one should seek a principle of that which is or happens always, and he is right in some cases but not in all cases; for the triangle too has its angles equal to two right angles always, yet there is some other cause
5   of this eternality, although of principles which are eternal there are no other causes.

Let these be our remarks concerning the fact that there was no time when motion did not exist and that there will be no time when motion will not exist.

6

Since motion must always exist without interruption, there exists 10
necessarily something first which causes motion, and this may be one
or many; and a first mover must be immovable. The problem of whether
each immovable mover is eternal is not relevant to the present argument; but the fact that there must exist something which is immovable
and exempt from all external change, both unqualified and accidental, 15
and which can move another, is clear from the following considerations.

If one wishes, let it be possible for some things to exist sometime and
then not to exist, but without being in the process of generation or
destruction; for, if any thing without parts exists at one time and does
not exist at another, perhaps it is necessary for it to be at one time and
not at another without being in the process of changing. And let also 20
this be possible, namely, that some principles which are immovable but
can cause motion be now existing and now not existing. Still, not all of
them [i.e., the principles] can be so; for clearly there is something that
causes things which move themselves to be at one time and not to be
at another. For although every thing that moves itself must have a 25
magnitude, that is, if no thing without parts can be moved, still from
what has been said this is not necessary for a mover.

Now no one of the things which are immovable but not alway existing can be the cause of [all] the things that are continuously being generated and destroyed, nor yet can any of those which always move certain things while others [always] move others. For neither each of them
nor all of them can be the cause of a process which exists always and 30
is continuous, for that process is eternal and exists of necessity whereas
all those [movers] are infinite and do not exist at the same time. So it
is clear that, even if (a) countless times some principles which are im- 259*a*
movable movers and many of those which move themselves are being
destroyed while others are coming into being and (b) one immovable
mover moves one thing while another moves another, nevertheless,
there is something which contains and exists apart from each of them
and which is the cause of the existence of some of them and the non- 5
existence of the others and also of the continuous change; and this is a
cause of these [movers], while these are the causes of the motion in
other things. So if motion is indeed eternal, the primary mover too will
be eternal, if it is just one; but if there are many [primary movers],
there will be many eternal [movers]. We should regard them to be one
rather than many, or finite rather than infinite; for if the consequences
are the same, we should always posit a finite number [of causes], since 10
in things existing by nature what is finite and better should exist to a
higher degree, if this is possible. It is sufficient even if it [i.e., the mover]

is just one, which, being first among the immovable [movers] and also eternal, would be the principle of motion in all the rest.

It is evident also from the following that there must be some one
15   mover which is eternal. Now we have shown[32] that there must always be a motion, and if always, it must also be continuous;   for also that which exists always may also be continuous, but what is in succession is not [necessarily] continuous. Further, if [a motion is] continuous, it is one. And it is one if both the mover is one and the thing in motion is one; for if now one thing causes it to move and now another, the whole motion
20   will be not continuous but in succession.

One might be led to the belief that there exists a first immovable mover, both from the arguments just given and by attending to the principles   of movers. Evidently there are some things which are sometimes moved but sometimes at rest, and because of this it was made clear that neither all things are moved or all are at rest, nor that some of
25   them are always at rest and the others are always moved; for this is shown by those things which have the double potentiality of being sometimes moved and sometimes at rest.   So since such things are clear to all and since we also wish to show the nature of each of the other two (namely, that there are things which are always immovable
30   and also others which are always in motion), having proceeded in this direction and posited[33] that (a) every thing in motion is moved by something which is either immovable or in motion and (b) a thing in motion is always moved either by itself or by another, we arrived at the position that of things in motion there is a first; and this is (a) a self-mover if
259b   [only] things in motion are considered but (b) immovable if all are considered.[34] And evidently we do observe such things which move themselves, for example, living things or the genus of animals.[35] Indeed, these [e.g., animals] even helped create the opinion   that in a thing a motion which did not exist at all [before] may arise, because we ob-
5   serve this happening in them; for it seems that at one time they are without motion but later they are moved.

This must be granted, then, that such things do cause in themselves one [kind of] motion,[36] but that they do not cause it independently; for the cause is not from them, but there are other natural motions which animals have but not through themselves, such as increase,   decrease,
10   and respiration, and each animal has these motions while it is at rest and is not being moved by itself.[37] The cause of these [motions] is the surrounding objects [e.g., air] and many things which enter the animal, such as food in some [motions]; for while this is being digested, it sleeps, and when the food is distributed, the animal wakes up and moves itself, but the first source [of these motions] comes from the outside. On ac-
15   count of this, animals are not moved by themselves continuously; for

what causes the motion is something else, which is itself in motion and is changing in relation to each thing that can move itself.

Now in all these the first mover and the cause of that which moves itself is [also] moved by itself, but accidentally, for it is the body that changes its place; and so what is in the body also moves itself as if by   20
a lever. From these arguments one may be convinced that if there is an immovable mover that is itself in motion but accidentally, then that mover cannot cause a continuous motion. So if indeed a motion must exist continuously, then there should be some first mover which cannot be moved even accidentally, if, as we have said,[38] there is to be in   25
things an unceasing and everlasting motion and if being itself is to *rest* [always] in itself and be in the same [state]; for if the principle stays [always] the same, then the whole too must stay the same and be continuous in its relation to the principle. Now to be moved accidentally by itself is not the same as to be moved accidentally by another; for to be moved by another belongs also to some principles in the   30
heavens, those which have many locomotions,[39] whereas the former belongs only to destructible things. Further, if there is something which is eternally of this kind, causing something to be moved but being itself immovable and eternal, then the first thing that is moved by it must   260a
also be eternal. This is clear also from the fact that there would otherwise be no generation or destruction or change in the other things unless there were something which would cause motion while being in motion. For the immovable [mover] will always cause one and the same motion and in the same manner inasmuch as it itself in no way changes in rela-   5
tion to the thing moved; and as for that which is moved by something[40] whose motion is directly caused by the immovable [mover], because of the fact that it is related to things [which it moves] now in one way and now in another, it is a cause but not of the same motion. And so, because of the fact that it is in contrary places or forms [at different times], it imparts motion to each thing in contrary ways and so makes   10
it be [for example] now at rest and now in motion. From what has been said, then, the problem which was first raised[41]—why it is that not all things are in motion or at rest or why some are not always in motion and the others not always at rest, but some of them are now in motion and now at rest—has now become evident, for the cause of it is now clear: It is the fact that some things are moved by an eternal immovable mover,   15
and so they are always changing; others are moved by an object in motion, which [object] is changing, and so they too must change; and as for the immovable [mover], as already stated, inasmuch as it remains [always] simple and in the same manner and in the same [state], it causes [always] one and a simple motion.

10

10   Let us now discuss the fact that the primary mover must have no parts
and no magnitude, after having first determined some prior facts in
connection with it.

One of these is the fact that nothing which is finite can cause a
motion for an infinite time. Now there are three things, the mover, the
object in motion, and the time during which the motion occurs; and
15   either all of these are infinite, or all are finite, or [only] some (i.e., one or
two) are finite. Let A be the mover, B the object in motion, and T the
infinite time. Now let A_1 [a part of A] move B_1, which is a part of B.
Then the time taken to do this is not equal to T, for it takes more time
to move a greater object. Hence, the time T_1 taken [for A_1 to move
B_1] is not infinite. Now by adding to A_1 [equal parts from A], I shall
20   use up all A, and by doing likewise to B_1, I shall use up all B; but I
shall not use up the time T by always subtracting a part which is equal
[to T_1], for T is infinite. So the entire A will move the whole of B in a
finite part of T. Consequently, no object can be given an infinite motion
by that which is finite. Evidently, then, nothing which is finite can
cause a motion for an infinite time.
25   In general, it will be made clear from what follows that it is not
possible for an infinite power to be in a finite magnitude. Let a greater
power be that which always effects an equal result in less time, for
example, as in heating or in sweetening or in throwing or, in general, in
causing a motion. If so, then that which can be affected must also be
30   affected by that which is finite but has infinite power, and more by this
than by another, for an infinite power is greater [than a finite power].
But this cannot take place in an interval of time. For if T be the time
in which an infinite power has heated or pushed something and S be
266b   that [time] in which a finite [power] did so, then when I increase the
latter power by adding to it repeatedly one finite power after another,
I shall eventually reach a finite [power] which will cause the motion
[the heating or pushing] performed in time T [by the infinite power];
for by always adding to a finite [quantity an equal quantity] I shall
eventually exceed any finite [quantity], and likewise by always subtracting [an equal quantity] I shall eventually arrive at one which is
less [than any given finite quantity]. But then, a finite power [will be
reached which] in an equal time will cause the motion caused by the
5   infinite power, and this is impossible. Consequently, no thing which is
finite [in magnitude] can have an infinite power.

Moreover, nor can a finite [power] be in an infinite [magnitude]. In
fact, though in a smaller magnitude [of one kind of body] there may be
a greater power [than in a greater magnitude of another kind], still a
greater power will be in some greater [magnitude of the second kind].

Let AZ be an infinite [magnitude]. Now [a finite magnitude] AB has a certain power which, let us say, will move M [over a certain interval] 10 in time T. If I take a magnitude twice as great as AB, this will move M in half the time T (for let this be the proportion), and so it will move M in T/2. Now if I continue increasing the magnitude in a similar way, I shall never exhaust AZ, but the time required for the increasing magnitude to move M will eventually be less than any given time. So the power [in AZ] will be infinite, for it will surpass any finite power. 15 But for a given finite power the time taken [to move M] must also be finite; for if power P_1 moves M in time T_1, a greater power P_2 will move M in a lesser but a definite time T_2 in inverse proportion [that is, $P_1:P_2 :: T_2:T_1$]. And like a plurality and a magnitude, a force is infinite if 20 it exceeds every definite force.

This result may also be shown in this way, namely, by taking a power, which is generically the same as that in the infinite magnitude but which is in a finite magnitude, and then measuring by it the finite power which is [assumed to be] in the infinite [magnitude].

It is clear from the above arguments, then, that neither can an infinite 25 power be in a finite magnitude, nor a finite power in an infinite magnitude.

At this point, it is well to discuss first a problem concerning objects in locomotion. If every thing in motion but not moved by itself is caused to be moved by another, how is it that some of them, like things thrown, are continuously in motion when the mover is not touching 30 them? If the mover moves at the same time something else also, e.g., air, and if it is this [air] which causes the motion while being in motion, it is likewise impossible for this [air] to be in motion when the first mover neither touches it nor causes it to be in motion, so all of them should be simultaneously in motion, or they should all cease simul- 267a taneously when the first mover ceases even if, like a stone, it [the first mover] makes that which it causes to be moved to act like a mover.

We must then say this, that the first mover causes air or water or some other such object, which by nature can move another and be moved by another, to be like a mover. But this object does not simul- 5 taneously cease being a mover and an object moved. It ceases simultaneously being moved when the mover ceases causing it to be moved, but it may still be a mover; and in view of this, it may cause some other consecutive object to be moved (and the same may be said of this other object). But an object begins to cease [being a mover] when the power to cause motion which is transmitted to the consecutive object is lessened; and the object finally ceases [being a mover] when the preceding mover transmits to it no power to cause motion but only 10 causes it to be in motion. These must cease simultaneously, i.e., the

one being a mover and the other being in motion, and so must the whole
motion.   Now this [kind of] motion occurs in things which may sometimes be in motion and sometimes at rest, and the motion is not
continuous   though it appears to be so; for it is a motion of objects
15 which are either in succession or in contact, since there is not [just]
one mover but the objects are consecutive with each other.   And in
view of this, such motion, which some call "circular displacement",
takes place also in air and in water. Now the problem raised cannot be
solved in a way other than that just stated.   In a circular displacement
all objects are movers and in motion at the same time, and so they cease
20 at the same time. But it appears that there is [just] one object continuously in motion. If so, by what is it moved? Certainly, not by itself.

Since in things there must exist a continuous motion,   which is one,
this one motion must be of some magnitude (for that which has no
magnitude cannot be in motion) which is also one and is moved by one
[mover]; otherwise, there will be not a continuous motion but a number
25 of consecutive and divided motions. As for the mover that causes the
motion, if one, either it is a mover in motion or it is immovable. If in
motion, then it will have to be following along   and be changing
267b and also be moved by another object;   so this series will stop and end
with a motion caused by something immovable. Now the latter of
necessity does not change   along with the object moved, but it will
always have the power to cause motion (for to cause motion in this
way occurs without effort); and this motion alone, or more than any
5   other, is regular,   since the mover does not change at all.   And if
the motion is to be similar, the object in motion, too, should not be
changing in relation to it [the mover].   Now this [the mover] must be
either in the middle or at the circumference [of the sphere],   for these
are the principles [of the sphere].   But things whose motions are
fastest are nearest the mover, and such [i.e., fastest] is the motion of the
circumference;   so the mover is there.
10   A problem arises, namely, whether it is possible for a thing in motion
to cause motion continuously,   but not like that which pushes again and
again and so does something continuously by doing successively; for
either the thing itself pushes or pulls or does both, or else this is passed
on from one thing to another, as it was stated earlier in the case of
things thrown,   in which the air or the water causes motion in the
15   sense that it is one part after another that is moved. In either case, it
cannot be one motion; it is a number of consecutive motions. So the
only continuous motion is that which the immovable mover causes; for,
being in a similar state, that mover will be similarly disposed towards
the object moved and be continuously so.

With these things settled, it is evident that the first and immovable mover cannot have a magnitude. For if it has a magnitude, this must be either finite or infinite. Now it was shown earlier in our discussions on 20 nature that no infinite magnitude can exist [actually]; and it was just shown that a finite [magnitude] cannot have an infinite power and that an object cannot be moved by a finite [magnitude] for an infinite time. But the prime mover causes eternal motion and for an infinite 25 time. Hence, it is evident that He [the prime mover] is indivisible and without parts and has no magnitude at all.

GENERATION AND DESTRUCTION

CONTENTS

BOOK II

GENERATION AND DESTRUCTION

BOOK II

1

328b   We have discussed how blending, touching, acting, and being affected belong to things which change according to their nature; and as for unqualified generation and unqualified destruction, we have stated to what things they belong, how they belong to them, and the cause for their

30   belonging to them. Concerning alteration, too, we discussed in a similar way what is altering and in what respect it differs from generation and destruction.

We have still to investigate the so-called "elements of bodies"; for generation and destruction of all composite natural substances cannot take place without sensible bodies. Some say that the underlying matter of these

35   bodies is one in kind, e.g., *Air* or *Fire* or something between these but still

329a   a body and separable; others say that it is more than one, some positing *Fire* and *Earth*, others adding to these two also *Air* as a third element, and others, e.g., Empedocles, include also *Water* as a fourth element, and they say that generation and destruction of things occur by the combination or separation

5   or alteration of these elements.

Let us take it as agreed that those things from whose change (whether this be combination or separation or some other change) generation and destruction occur, are well said to be principles and elements. But those who posit, besides the bodies mentioned, only one kind of matter which is also

10   corporeal and separable, are mistaken; for this [matter or] 'body,' being sensible, cannot exist without a contrary, since this indefinite 'body,' which some call "the principle," must be either light or heavy or cold or hot. As it is described in Plato's *Timaeus*,[1] it has no definiteness at all; for Plato did

15   not state clearly whether his '*Receptacle*' is separate or separable from the elements. Nor does he use it at all, when he says that it is a sort of subject

which underlies the elements and is prior to them, like gold in things which are made of gold; and even this manner of expressing the situation is not well put, for although in a thing altered the underlying subject — gold, in the comparison — remains, a thing generated or destroyed cannot be named after the material from which it has been generated or destroyed [e.g., when water changes to air, air is not called "watery"]. Yet Plato says that to call a [golden] thing "gold" is by far the truest way of describing it;[2] and, although the corporeal elements are solid, in making an analysis of them he ends up with planes.[3] But it is impossible for the "nurse"[4] and the primary matter to be planes.

We maintain that,[5] although there is matter in sensible bodies, this matter, from which the so-called "elements" are generated [from each other, i.e., earth, water, fire, air], cannot exist separately by itself but always has a contrary [e.g., hardness or softness or heat, etc., is predicated of it]. We have given a more accurate account of these matters elsewhere. Since, however, it is in this manner that the primary bodies are made of matter, we should give an account of them also, regarding matter as a primary principle and inseparable but underlying contraries; for the hot is not the matter for the cold, nor is the cold the matter for the hot, but it is matter that underlies the hot or the cold. First, then, the potential body, which is sensible, is a principle; second, the contraries are principles, e.g., heat and coldness; and third, there is now fire and water and other such, but these change into each other and are not such as Empedocles and others say (otherwise there would be no alteration), whereas the contraries do not [themselves] change. Nonetheless, the number and kinds of these [contraries] as principles of a body should be stated; but the other thinkers assume and use them without stating why they are these and why they are so many.

20

25

30

35
329b

5

2

Since we seek the principles of sensible bodies, which are tangible, and since a tangible body is one the sensation of which is touching, it is evident that not all contrarieties make up the kinds and principles of bodies but only those with respect to touch; for bodies differ with respect to contraries, and these are contrarieties with respect to touch. For this reason, neither whiteness and blackness, nor sweetness and bitterness, and similarly none of the other sensible contrarieties make up an element [of a body]. Yet vision is prior to touch, and so its underlying object, too, is prior to that of touch; but [this object, i.e., color] is an affection of a tangible body not qua tangible but with respect to something else, even if that happens to be prior by nature [to the object of touch].

10

15

Now we should specify first which of the differentiae and contrarieties of tangible things are primary. The contrarieties with respect to touch are the following: the hot and cold [i.e., heat and cold as attributes and similarly for
20 the rest], the dry and moist, the heavy and light, the hard and soft, the viscous and brittle, the rough and smooth, and the course and fine. Of these, the heavy or the light can neither act on nor be affected by other things; for it is not by acting on or by being affected by other things that bodies are called "heavy" or "light." But the elements should be capable of acting on or of being affected by each other, for they blend with each other and
25 change into each other. But things are called "hot" and "cold" and "moist" and "dry" in virtue of the fact that some of them can act on and the rest can be affected by others. The hot is that which brings together things of the same kind (for separating things from each other, which *Fire* does according to some thinkers, is really bringing things of the same kind together, since things which differ in kind are taken apart from each other); the cold is that
30 which draws or brings together things of the same kind or of different kinds alike; that which is moist, having no definite boundaries of its own, is easily adaptable to the boundaries of other [containing] things; that which is dry can have definite boundaries of its own but is not easily adaptable to other [tangible] boundaries. As for the coarse and the fine and the viscous and the brittle and the hard and the soft and the other differentiae, they are derived from the dry and the moist. For since that which can fill up something is
35 derived from the moist, because the moist has no boundaries of its own but
330a is easily adaptable and assumes the boundary of that which it touches, and since that which is fine can fill up something (for what has fine or small parts can fill up something, since each part of what fills up something is wholly touched by what surrounds it, and what is fine is such a thing most of all), it is evident that what is fine is derived from the moist, and what is
5 course is derived from the dry. Again, the viscous is derived from the moist (for the viscous is the moist which has been somewhat affected, e.g., oil), while the brittle is derived from the dry; for the brittle is completely dry, and so it has been solidified because of lack of moisture. Again, the soft is derived from the moist (for the soft yields into itself but, unlike the moist,
10 does not entirely change shape, and for this reason the moist is not soft although softness belongs to the moist), and the hard is derived from the dry (for the hard is the solidified, and the solidified is the dry).

Each of the terms "dry" and "moist," to be sure, has more than one meaning, for the moist and the wet are opposed to the dry and, again, the
15 dry and the solidified are opposed to the moist; but all these are derived from the primary dry and the primary moist mentioned above.[6] For since the dry is opposed to the wet, and since the wet has foreign moisture on the surface whereas the sodden is deeply penetrated with moisture but the dry is deprived of such moisture, it is evident that the wet is derived from the

moist, but the dry which is opposed to it is derived from the primary dry. *20*
Once more, the moist and the solidified are likewise related; for the moist
is that which has its own moisture whereas the sodden has foreign moisture
deeply penetrated into itself, but the solidified is deprived of moisture. So
these, too, are derived from the [primary] dry and wet, respectively.

It is clear, then, that the other differentiae are reduced to the primary *25*
four differentiae but that these are not reduced to fewer primary
differentiae; for neither the hot as such is moist or dry, nor the moist as such
is hot or cold, nor again do the cold and the dry come under each other [or
any of them under the other] or under the hot or the moist. Hence the
differentiae must be four only.

3

Since the elements [as differentiae] are four, which combined with each *30*
other yield six pairs, and since contraries by their nature cannot coexist in
combination (for it is impossible for the same thing to be both hot and cold
or both dry and moist at the same time), it is evident that the pairs that can
coexist must be only four: hot with dry, hot with moist, cold with moist, and *330b*
cold with dry. And these four pairs are attributed according to reason to the
four bodies which appear to be simple: fire, air, water, and earth; for fire
is hot and dry, air is hot and moist (for air is like water vapor), water is cold *5*
and moist, and earth is cold and dry. So it is with good reason that the
differentiae [in pairs] are distributed among the primary bodies, and the
number of these is fixed according to reason.

Of all those who maintain that the elements are simple bodies, too, some
posit only one kind, others two kinds, still others three, and the rest four.
Those who assert that the elements are only one in kind and say that the rest *10*
of the bodies are generated by condensation and rarefaction happen to posit
[actually] two principles [as attributes], the *Rare* and the *Dense*, or the *Hot*
and the *Cold*, for it is these which make possible all other intermediate
bodies, while the one element which underlies all these is like matter. Those
who start with two elements (e.g., Parmenides posits *Fire* and *Earth*) say
that the intermediate bodies, (e.g., air and water) are blends formed from *15*
the two elements. Those who say that the elements are three (e.g., Plato adds
also a blend between two elements in his *Divisions*) speak likewise. Indeed,
those who posit two and those who posit three elements say practically the
same thing, except that the former divide the intermediate bodies into two
kinds whereas the latter regard them as one in kind. Still others, like
Empedocles, posit from the start four elements; but he, too, reduces them *20*
to two, for he says that *Fire* is opposed to the other three.

Now what we call "fire" and "air" and each of the others are not simple but blended. The simple elements are such as these but not the same as these. Thus that which is similar to fire is fiery but not fire, what is similar to air is airy but not air, and similarly for the others. Fire is the excess of heat and ice is the excess of coldness; for freezing and boiling are excesses of coldness and heat, respectively. If, then, ice is the freezing of the moist and the cold, fire too will be the boiling of the dry and the hot. In view of this, nothing comes to be from ice alone or from fire alone.

Since the simple bodies are four, those in each pair will exist in the corresponding places. For fire and air move towards the outer boundaries but earth and water towards the center; and fire and earth are extremes and most pure, but water and air are intermediates and more like blends. And they form two contrarieties; for water is contrary to fire, and earth is contrary to air; for, in each contrariety, the attributes of one contrary are contrary to those of the other. But each of the four elements is simply characterized by one attribute: earth by dryness rather than cold, water by cold rather than moisture, air by moisture rather than heat, and fire by heat rather than dryness.

25

30

331a

5

4

Since it was determined earlier[7] that there is a reciprocal generation of simple bodies from each other, and this appears to occur also for sensation (for otherwise there would have been no alteration, which occurs by way of tangible attributes), we should discuss (a) the manner in which this reciprocal change occurs and (b) whether each simple body can be generated from any of the others or from some but not from others.

Now it is evident that each of them can by its nature change to any of the others; for generation takes place from a contrary to a contrary, and any two [corporeal] elements are contrary to each other because they have contrary differentiae. For the two differentiae of some elements are contrary, respectively, to the two differentiae of some other elements, as in fire and water (fire is hot and dry, water is moist and cold), whereas in other cases only one differentia of one element is contrary to a differentia of another element, as in air and water (air is moist and hot, water is moist and cold). Universally, then, each simple body can by its nature be generated from any other simple body; and it is certainly not difficult to see how this can be done for every pair of differing elements, for each can be changed to any of the others, although some can do so faster than others or easier than others.

Now those elements which have a differentia in common change into each other quickly, but those which have nothing in common do so slowly;

10

15

20

25

and this is the case because it is easier to change one than to change many attributes. For example, the change from fire to air is easy (for fire is hot and dry, and air is hot and moist, so if the dry is overcome by the moist, the result is air), and so is the change from air to water (for air is hot and moist, and water is cold and moist, so if the hot is overcome by the cold, the result is water). The change from water to earth occurs in the same way, and so does the change from earth to fire, for in each of the two cases there is a differentia in common; for water is moist and cold, but earth is cold and dry, so if the moist is overcome by the dry, the result is earth. Again, since fire is dry and hot, but earth is cold and dry, if the cold is destroyed [by the hot], earth will become fire. So it is evident that generation of simple bodies from each other can be cyclical, and that the manner of change just described is the easiest because, in each case, that which changes and that into which it changes have a common differentia.

But the changes from fire to water and from air to earth, and again from water and earth to fire and air, respectively, can occur but with greater difficulty, because each of these changes necessitates a change of more than one attribute in the element that changes; for if the change is to be from water to fire, both the cold and the moist must be destroyed, and again, if the change is to be from earth to air, both the cold and dryness must be destroyed. In the same way, if the change is to be from fire to water, or from air to earth, both attributes of fire, or of air, must change. So each of these generations takes a longer time.

If, on the other hand, in each case only one of two contraries is destroyed, the change is easier than that when both contraries are destroyed but the two changes are not reciprocal. Thus fire changes to earth while water changes to air, and air changes to fire while earth changes to water. For whenever the cold in water or the dry in fire is destroyed, the result will be air (for the hot in fire and the moist in water will remain), and whenever the hot in fire or the moist in water is destroyed, the result will be earth because the dry in fire or the cold in water will remain. And similarly, air changes to water and earth to fire. For whenever the hot in air or the dry in earth are destroyed, the result is water (for the moist in air and cold in earth will remain), and whenever the moist in air and the cold in earth are destroyed, the result will be fire because the hot in air and the dry in earth will remain, and the hot and the dry belong to fire, as stated earlier. The generation of fire is also in agreement with what we sense; for flame is fire most of all, and it is burning smoke, which consists of air and earth.

If, in consecutive simple bodies, an element is destroyed [either the identical element, or the other two], no transformation into another body can be made because what is left in each is either the same identical element or a pair of contraries; but no body can be formed with identical or contrary elements. For example, if dryness of fire and moistness of air were to be

30

35

331b

5

10

15

20

25

30

destroyed, the hot alone would be left, and if the hot were to be destroyed, the moist and the dry, which are contraries, would be left. Similarly with any other consecutive pair, for in such a pair there is one identical element
35   and the other two elements are contraries. Hence, it is at the same time clear that some transformations from one simple body into another require a destruction of just one element, others require two such successive destructions.
332a   We have stated, then, (a) that every simple body is generated from some other simple body, and (b) the manner in which a transformation is made.

7

334a   Concerning the elements out of which bodies are composed, those who think that (a) the elements have something in common or (b) the elements can change into each other must accept also (b) if they posit (a), or also (a) if they posit (b). But those who posit no reciprocal generation nor allow any
20   one of them to come from any other, except in the sense in which bricks come from a wall, are faced with the problem of how flesh or bones or any of the like can be generated from elements. This problem is faced also by those who say that elements are generated from each other; for how can something other than the elements be generated from them? What I mean is this: water is generated from fire, and fire from water; for there is something which is common to the two, and this is the underlying subject.
25   Now flesh, too, is generated from them, and also marrow; but how can these be generated from them? For, according to those thinkers who speak as Empedocles does, in what manner can flesh and marrow and the like be generated from the elements? Such 'generation' must be a composition, like that of a wall from bricks and stones; and such 'blend' must be a mixture of
30   very small elements which retain their nature and are juxtaposed to each other. So such indeed is the manner in which flesh and the others will have to be generated from the elements. But if so, it turns out that fire or water cannot come out of *any* part of flesh in the way in which a sphere could be formed from this part of wax and a pyramid from some other part; for a sphere or a pyramid might be formed from either of the two parts of wax.
35   It is indeed in this manner that fire and water would have to be generated
334b   from *any part of flesh*; but this cannot be done in accordance with the principles of those thinkers, except in the manner in which a stone and a brick come from a wall, i.e., each of them from a different place or part of the wall. A similar difficulty is faced also by those who posit one kind of matter for their elements, namely, how something can be generated from both the elements, e.g., from the cold and the hot, or from fire and earth.

For if flesh comes from both elements and is neither of them nor a 5
composition in which each of them preserves its nature, what else can that
composition be if not just matter? For the destruction of either element will
produce either the other element or just matter.

One might say, however, that since a thing may be more or less hot or
cold, whenever it is simply one of these in actuality, it is the other only 10
potentially. But whenever it is not one of them entirely but exists as hot-cold
or as cold-hot because blends destroy the excesses of hot and cold, then it is
neither matter nor actually existing as simply one or simply the other
contrary but exists as an intermediate; and as such, being potentially more
hot than cold (or vice versa), it may be twice as hot as cold, or thrice, or 15
related to it according to some other such ratio. Then all other things will
be blends of contraries or of elements, and the elements will come from
them potentially in some way, not as their matter, but in the way we stated;
and, taken in this way, the thing generated is a blend, but in the other, it 20
would be matter. And since contraries are also affected by each other, as
specified in the first part of this treatise[8] (for that which is *actually* hot is
potentially cold and that which is *actually* cold is potentially hot), if the hot
and the cold are not equally strong, the weaker changes to the stronger side;
and similarly with other contraries. First, then, it is in this sense that 25
elements are changing, and then there arise changes in flesh and bones and
the like, the hot becoming cold and the cold hot, whenever they are being
brought to the mean; for here nothing happens, and the mean is of
considerable extent and not indivisible. Similarly, it is in virtue of a mean
that the dry and the moist and the like cause the generation of flesh and 30
bones and others of this sort.

8

All blended bodies — those whose place is near the center of the universe
— are composed of all the simple bodies. Earth is present in all of them,
because each of them exists in the highest degree and mostly in its
appropriate place. Water, too, is present, because a composite body must 35
possess a boundary, and, of the simple bodies, water alone is easily adaptable
in shape; and, besides, earth cannot keep its parts together without moisture. 335a
In fact, it is moisture that does this; for if all moisture is taken away, the
parts fall apart.

Earth and water, then, are present in compounds for the *reasons* just
stated, but air and fire are present in view of the fact that they are contrary 5
to earth and water, respectively; for earth is contrary to air and water is
contrary to fire, that is, in the manner in which one substance may be
contrary to another [i.e., in virtue of contrary attributes]. So since

generations proceed from contraries, and since in bodies there may be present extremes of two kinds of contraries (i.e., those in earth and in water), there may be present in those bodies also the other extremes of those contraries; hence in every composite body all simple bodies will be present.

10   This seems to be confirmed also by the food each composite takes; for all of them are nourished by the same kinds of bodies of which they are composed, and all of them are nourished by many kinds of simple bodies. For even plants, which are thought to be nourished by one kind only, i.e., by water, are really nourished by many kinds, for here earth is mixed with water. For this reason, too, farmers water plants after mixing [earth with water].

15   Now since food is akin to matter but that which is fed is a *shape* or form along with matter, it is reasonable from these facts that, of the simple bodies which are generated from each other, fire alone should be the one which is nourished, as our predecessors too maintained; for fire alone of the simple

20   bodies is most akin to form because by its nature it travels towards the boundary (of the universe). In fact, each body by its nature travels towards its own place, and the *shape* or form of each of them is at its boundaries.

We have explained, then, the fact that all bodies (near the center of the universe) are composed of the simple bodies.

9

Since some things are generable and destructible and their generation

25   happens to be in the region about the center of the universe, we should discuss all generations collectively and likewise state what their principles are and how many there are; for it is easier for us to investigate each of these specifically after we have first understood them universally.

The principles of generation are equal in number and the same

30   generically as those which exist among eternal and primary things; for one of them exists as matter, another as *form*. But there should also be a third present, for these two are not sufficient to effect a generation, as already stated in our introduction [to the *Physics*]. Now it is the cause as matter in generable things which can at one time be and at another not be. For (a) some objects exist of necessity, i.e., those which are eternal, (b) others of

35   necessity do not exist (it is impossible for those in (a) not to be and those in
335b   (b) to be, and this is because objects coming under what is necessary cannot occur in any other way); but there are some which are possible to both be and not be, and it is these that are generable and destructible, for at one time they exist but at another they do not. Consequently, generation or

5   destruction must be of that which is possible to be and also not to be, and for this reason it is this object that is the cause as matter in generable things,

while the cause as that-for-the-sake-of-which (i.e., as final cause) is the *form* or form, which is the formula of the *substance* (of each generable thing).

But there should be a third principle also, one that our predecessors dreamed of but made no mention of at all; for some of them thought that the nature of Forms was an adequate cause of the generation of things. Thus   *10* in Plato's *Phaedo*,[9] Socrates raises an objection against others who said nothing [about the cause of generation] but makes the hypothesis that some things are Forms but the others exist by participating in those forms, and that each of the latter is said to exist in virtue of the Form by which it is named but to be generated or to be destroyed by acquiring or losing, respectively, the participation in that Form; and he thinks that, if these   *15* hypotheses are true, the Forms are causes of generation and of destruction.[10] Other thinkers, however, think that matter itself is the cause of generation or destruction; for, according to them, motion proceeds from matter.

But none of the above thinkers speaks well. For if the Forms are the causes of generation and of destruction, then, with the hypothesis that the Forms and the things participating in them always exist, why do those Forms generate and destroy things intermittently and not continuously?   *20* Moreover, what we observe in some cases is that the cause of generation is something other than a Form; for it is the doctor who makes a man healthy and a scientist who teaches others science, in spite of the existence of Health-Itself and Science-Itself as Forms and of things which participate in those Forms. Similar remarks apply to other things which are done in virtue of a power. Now if one were to say that it is matter that generates things because of its motion, he would be speaking more as a physicist than as the   *25* above thinkers; for that which causes alteration and changes the form of things is more of a cause in generating things than the Forms are, and whenever we speak of that which causes things to change, by nature and by art alike, we are accustomed in every case to say that the cause is a mover of this sort. But this way of speaking, too, is not right; for matter is something   *30* which can be affected or be moved, whereas causing motion or acting belongs to another kind of power. This is clear in things which are generated by art and by nature. It is not water itself that produces from itself an animal, and what makes a bed out of wood is not the wood itself, but art. So, because of this, these thinkers too do not speak rightly; they omit the   *35* main cause, for they do away with essence or *form* of things. In addition,   *336a* by eliminating the cause as form, they attribute to bodies the powers through which things are generated in a very instrumental manner. For, they say, since by nature the *Hot* separates things whereas the *Cold* brings them together, and since each of the other things either acts or is acted upon,   *5* it is from these [the *Hot* and the *Cold*] and because of these that all other things are generated and destroyed. Yet it appears that even fire itself is moved and is affected. Moreover, what they say is about the same as if one

were to say that it is the saw or each instrument that causes a thing to be
10   produced, since the wood must be sawed if it is to be divided and must be
planed if it is to be smoothed, and similarly with the others. But however
true it may be that fire produces things or causes them to be moved, these
thinkers fail to observe that fire is inferior to instruments in the manner in
which it causes them to be moved. We, on the other hand, have given a
general account of the various causes earlier,[11] and here[12] we have spoken
specifically about matter and *form* as causes.

10

15   Further, since locomotion has been shown to be eternal,[13] it is necessary
from the above discussion that generation, too, be continuous; for
locomotion will produce a continual generation because the generator[14]
always alternates by coming nearer to and then going farther from that
which can generate [its kind]. It is at the same time clear that what we stated
earlier,[15] too, was right, i.e., that the change which is primary [in existence]
20   is locomotion and not generation; for it is far more reasonable for that which
causes being to become nonbeing to be an existent thing than for that which
causes being to exist to be a nonexistent thing. Now that which travels exists,
but that which is in the process of coming to be does not [yet] exist; and it
is for this reason that locomotion is prior [in existence] to generation.
         Now since it is assumed and has been shown[16] that generation and
25   destruction of things are continuous, and since we maintain that it is
locomotion which causes becoming, it is evident that, if there exists only one
[kind of eternal] locomotion, both [generation and destruction] cannot exist
because they are contraries; for that which remains always in the same
condition produces by its nature always the same thing, and hence there will
30   be always either generation or destruction. But motions should be many and
contrary, whether with respect to locomotion or by being irregular; for
contraries are produced by contrary causes. And it is for this reason that the
cause of generation and of destruction is not the primary [i.e., circular] but
the elliptic motion;[17] for such locomotion has both continuity and two kinds
of motion. For, if generation and destruction are to be continuous and exist
336b always, (a) there must be something which is always in motion, so that these
two changes may not terminate, and (b) there must be motions of two kinds,
if not only one of those changes is to occur. Now the cause of continuity is
the locomotion of the whole [universe], but the cause of coming nearer and
going away is the inclined [i.e., elliptic] motion, for in this motion the body
5   alternates by coming nearer to and going further from [the center of the
universe, i.e., of the Earth]. And since the distances of this body [from the
Earth] are unequal, its motion, too, will be irregular. So if by approaching

and being near the Earth this body causes generation, then by retreating and being further from the Earth it causes destruction, and if by approaching many times it generates many times, it likewise causes destruction by retreating many times; for contrary changes are brought about by contrary causes. And destructions and generations according to nature occur during equal intervals of time; and it is for this reason that the time intervals and the lives of living things have a number and are specified by a number, for there is an order in all things and every life and time interval is measured by a period, not all things by the same period but some by a shorter and others by a longer one. Thus for some the unit of measure is the time-length of a year, for some it is greater than that, and for others it is less than a year. *10* *15*

What we sense, too, appears to be in agreement with what we are saying; for we observe that there is generation as the Sun approaches but destruction as it retreats from the Earth, and that the time-intervals of the two changes are equal; for the durations of destruction and generation according to the nature of these are equal. It often happens, however, that things are destroyed in a shorter time [than usual] because they interfere with each other. For, since matter lacks uniformity and is not everywhere the same, generations too must lack uniformity and be quicker in some cases but slower in others; so the lack of unformity in generations causes a lack of uniformity in corresponding destructions. *20*

As we stated,[18] however, generation and destruction are always continuous, and they will never fail because of what we said. And this happens with good reason. For, since the nature of each thing always 'desires,' as we maintain, that which is better, and since to be is better than not to be (we have discussed elsewhere the various senses of "to be"), and since being cannot belong to everything since each of these is far removed from the principle of existence, God perfected the universe by using the remaining alternative, namely, a never-ending generation; for in this way existence would be most highly connected, because a never-ending coming-to-be or an eternal generation is closest to substance [which is being in the highest sense]. The cause of this, as we have said many times,[19] is the circular motion [of the universe]; for it alone is continuous. It is for this reason that all those other things which change to each other with respect to their affections and their powers, e.g., the simple bodies, imitate circular motion; for, whenever water becomes air, air becomes fire, and fire becomes water again, we say that the generation has completed a circle because it came back to its starting-point. So it is by imitating a circular locomotion that a rectilinear locomotion, too, is continuous. From these remarks it is at the same time clear why the various bodies, which travel to their appropriate places, have not yet separated in place from one another in the infinite lapse of time; for this is a problem which many thinkers raise. *25* *30* *337a* *5* *10*

The cause of this is the fact that bodies are transformed into each other; for if each body stayed in its own place and did not change by a neighboring body, it would have been separated in place from the other bodies long ago. So, first, bodies change because of the [Sun's] dual motion [i.e., approaching and retreating from the Earth]; second, because of that change, no body can
15 remain [always] in any definite place. It is evident from the above discussion, then, why generations and destructions exist, and through what cause, and what the generable and destructible bodies are.

If there is to be motion, there must be a mover, as already stated elsewhere,[20] and if there is to be motion always, there should always be something which causes it; and if motion is to be continuous, there must be
20 a mover, one and the same, which is immovable, ungenerable, and unalterable. But if there are to be many circular motions, the movers must be many but all of them must come in a certain manner under a single principle [a mover]. Since time is continuous, it is necessary for motion to be continuous also, if time as such cannot exist without motion. Thus time is a
25 number of something which is continuous, i.e., of a circular motion, as specified in the discussion at the start.[21] But is motion continuous by virtue of the fact that the moving body is continuous or by virtue of the fact that that (whether this be place or [some] other *attribute*) with respect to which the body moves is continuous? Clearly, it is by virtue of the moving body; for how can an *attribute* be continuous if not by virtue of the fact that it belongs to a thing [a body] which is continuous? But if motion, too, is continuous by virtue of an *attribute* with respect to which it occurs,
30 continuity will belong to place alone, for place has a certain sort of magnitude; so it is of this [i.e., place] alone that there is circular continuity, and hence it is place that is always continuous with itself. Consequently, that which produces a continuous motion is a body whose motion is circular, and this motion makes time continuous.

11

Since among things which move continuously with respect to generation
35 or alteration or any change in general we observe some which succeed or are
337b generated one after another without an end, we should investigate whether some of them will do so of necessity or none of them will so do but each of them is such that it may not come to be. It is clear that some of them [may not come to be]; and, because of this, "it will be" and "it is likely to be" are
5 distinct [in meaning]; for if it is true to say now that P will be, it will be true sometime in the future to say "P is"; but if it is true to say now that P is likely to be, nothing prevents P from not [ever] coming to be; for example, a man who is likely to walk might not walk. In general, then, since some things now existing may not exist [in the future], it is clear that things which are now

coming to be, too, will not necessarily be in the process of coming to be [in the future].

But are all things [in the process of coming to be] such that no one of them [will always be in the process of coming to be] or not, but that some of them are necessarily and without qualification coming to be [i.e., again and again without stopping], and that just as some existing things cannot cease to be but others can, so some things in the process of coming to be never cease but others do? For example, the solstices of the Sun are of necessity coming to be and it is impossible for them ever to stop doing so.

Now that which is prior must have come to be, if that which is posterior will come to be, e.g., if a house is to come to be, the foundation must have come to be, and if this is to come to be, clay must have come to be; but if the foundation came to be, is it also necessary for the house to come to be? Not at all, unless it is necessary without qualification for the house to come to be; and if this be the case, then it is necessary for the house, too, to come to be after the foundation came to be. For then the prior, as already stated, will be so related to the posterior that if the former is to be, it is necessary for the latter, too, to come to be. Accordingly, if it is necessary for the posterior to come to be, it is necessary for the prior, too, to come to be; and if it is necessary for the prior to come to be, it is likewise necessary for the posterior to come to be, not because it is necessary for the prior to come to be but by the fact that the posterior was posited to come to be [without qualification] of necessity. Thus it is for a sequence in which the posterior will exist of necessity that the necessity of each [i.e., the posterior or the prior] implies the necessity of the other, and if the prior is coming to be, the posterior must always come to be also.

If, however, the parts of a sequence proceed infinitely downwards,[22] there will be no unqualified necessity for the posterior to come to be [after the prior], not even a hypothetical necessity; for it will then be necessary for the prior, through which the posterior must come to be, to be always different. So if there is no principle [i.e., a beginning, or an end] in the infinite, neither will there be a first part because of which it is necessary [for all the other parts] to come to be. Neither will it be true to say, in things in which there are limits [as ends], that there is an unqualified necessity of coming to be, e.g., to be a house, whenever a foundation has come to be; for whenever a foundation has come to be, if it is not necessary for it to come to be always, it will turn out for that, which may not always come to be, always to [come to] be. But if its coming to be is necessary, it should always be coming to be; for to be of necessity and to be always coincide, since that which is necessary cannot [ever] not-be. Thus if something exists of necessity, it exists eternally, and if eternally, then of necessity; and if its coming to be occurs of necessity, it exists eternally, and if eternally, also of necessity. Hence if the coming to be of something occurs necessarily without

10

15

20

25

30

35

338a

5   qualification, it must be cyclical and return upon itself; for it must either
have a limit or not, and if not, it must either be rectilinear or cyclical. But
if indeed it is eternal, it cannot be rectilinear because it can in no way have
a principle, whether downwards (as in future events) or upwards (as in past
10   events). But there must be a principle, if it is not limited, and also be eternal.
For this reason, it must be cyclical. Hence [the parts] necessitate each other,
that is, if part B comes to be of necessity, so does the prior part A, and if A,
so does B; and this necessity continues eternally, for it makes no difference
whether the sequence of events has two parts, A and B, or more than two
parts, A, B, C, . . . N.

15   That which comes to be of unqualified necessity, then, does so in a
cyclical motion; and if in a cyclical motion, then each part is coming to be
and also has come to be [earlier], and if this happens of necessity, the coming
to be of the parts is cyclical.

The things stated above are indeed reasonable, seeing that cyclical motion
which is eternal has manifested itself both in the revolution of the heavens
and in other ways,[23] and these motions occur and will occur of necessity,
338b   both they and those which occur because of them; for if that which is in
cyclical motion always moves some other thing, the motion of the latter
which is moved, too, must be cyclical. For example, since there is an upper
revolution [of the heavens], the Sun moves cyclically in such-and-such a
way, and since the Sun so moves, the seasons come to be cyclically and
5   return upon themselves, and since these do so, again other things under
them do so likewise.

One may ask why some things appear to come to be cyclically (e.g., rain
and air come to be cyclically, so if there are clouds, rain must follow, and
if there is rain, clouds must follow), but men and [other] animals do not
return upon themselves in such a way that the same individual comes to be.
10   For there is no necessity for you to come to be, if your father came to be;
but if you came to be, your father must have come to be. This process of
coming to be seems to proceed in a rectilinear manner.

The starting-point of the above problem is the following: whether all
cyclical instances of coming to be return upon themselves in a similar way
or not, or some of them do while remaining numerically the same but others
do by being in kind the same only. Now moving things whose *substance* is
15   indestructible will evidently remain numerically and also specifically the
same (for motion will [always] follow [numerically] the same thing), but
[movable] things whose *substance* is destructible must return upon
themselves specifically and not numerically the same. For this reason, in the
cyclical coming to be of water from air, air from water, water from air
again, etc., water and air do not remain numerically the same but are
specifically the same. But even if in such cases some of them remain
numerically the same, still their *substance* is not such as not to be capable
of nonexisting.

ON THE SOUL

CONTENTS

BOOK I

ON THE SOUL
BOOK I

1

We regard knowing to be noble and honorable, and one kind of it to be *402a*
more so than another either by virtue of its accuracy or because its objects
are better and more wonderful; and for both these *reasons* it is reasonable
that we should give a primary place to the inquiry concerning the soul. It
is thought, too, that the knowledge of the soul contributes greatly to every 5
kind of truth, and especially to [that about] nature; for the soul is as it were
the principle of animals.

Now we seek to investigate and to know, first, both the nature and the
substance of the soul and, secondly, its attributes, some of which are
thought to be proper *attributes* of the soul while others are thought to 10
belong through the soul to animals¹ also. But to attain any conviction concerning the soul is in every way one of the most difficult things. For although
the inquiry here is common to that in many other [sciences] also, I mean
the inquiry into the *substance* and the whatness of the subject, one might
think that there is some one method applicable to every subject whose
substance we wish to know, as in the case of proper attributes, which are 15
known [by the method] of demonstration. If so, one should inquire what
that method is. But if there is not some one and a common method of
coming to know the whatness of things, the matter becomes even more
difficult; for we would then have to determine the manner [of inquiry] to
be used for each subject. And even if it were evident what that manner is,
whether a demonstration or a division or some other method, we are still 20
faced with many problems and uncertainties as to what we should use as
starting-points in the inquiry; for different sciences proceed from different
principles, as in the case of numbers and of planes.

First, perhaps it is necessary to determine the genus under which the soul
falls and the whatness of the soul, that is, whether it is a *this* and a substance,
or a quality, or a quantity, or falls under some other of the categories 25
already distinguished;   and further, whether it is one of those things which
exist potentially or is rather an actuality, for this makes no small difference.

Again, we should consider if the soul is divisible into parts or has no *402b*
parts,   and whether every [kind of] soul is homogeneous or not, and if not
homogeneous, whether souls differ in species or in genus;   for those who
nowadays discuss and make inquiries about the soul seem to limit their
investigations to the human soul.   We should be careful, too, not to overlook 5

the problem of whether there is a single definition for the soul, such as the soul of an animal, or a different definition for each (e.g., for a horse, a dog, a man, and a god) wherein an animal, taken universally, is either nonexistent or posterior;   and similarly for anything which might have a common predicate. Again, if there are not many souls   but only parts [of a soul in
10   each thing], there is the problem of whether the inquiry into the whole soul should precede or follow that into the parts of it.   And with regard to the parts, too, it is difficult to determine which of them are by their nature distinct from one another.   There is also the problem of whether the inquiry into the parts should precede or follow that into their functions, e.g., whether the inquiry into the intellect should precede or follow that into thinking [as an activity], whether the inquiry into the sentient part should precede or follow that into sensing [as an activity], and similarly in the case of the other parts. And if the inquiry into the functions should precede that
15   into the parts, one might still raise the problem whether the inquiry into the objects to which those functions   are directed should precede that of the corresponding parts, e.g., whether the sensible object should be sought before the sentient part of the soul,   and whether the object of thought should be sought before the thinking [part].

It seems that not only is the knowledge of a *substance's* whatness useful to the investigation of the causes of the attributes of that *substance* (as in mathematics, in which knowledge of the whatness of straightness and cur-
20   vature and a line and a plane are useful in perceiving the number of right angles to which the sum of the triangle's angles is equal), but, conversely, [knowledge of] the attributes [of the *substance* of a thing] contributes a considerable part to the knowledge of the whatness [of that *substance*]; for whenever we can give an account of all or most of the obvious attributes
25   of a thing, we are in the best position to formulate its *substance*. For the starting point of every demonstration is the whatness of a thing; so if a
403a   *definition* fails to make us know by inference those attributes or even facilitate a conjecture about them, then clearly it is in every case so stated as to be dialectical or empty.

The *attributes* of the soul, too, give rise to a problem. Are they *attributes* of that   which has the soul also, or is there any one of them which is proper
5   to the soul?   This problem must be settled, but it is not easy.

Now in most cases it appears that [such *attributes*] cannot exist unless the body is being affected or is acting, as in anger, courage, *desire*, and sensation in general. Thinking, most of all, seems to be proper to the soul; but if this, too, is a species of imagination   or incapable of existing without imagina-
10   tion,   then it, too, could not exist without a body. Accordingly, if there is any function or affection of the soul proper to the soul, the soul can be separated [from the body], but if no function or [affection] is proper to the soul, the soul could not be separated from the body but would be just like

the straight. The straight qua straight has many attributes, e.g., it touches a bronze sphere at a point; but the straight as something separated [in existence from a body] cannot so touch it, for it is inseparable [from a body]   *15* since it exists always with a body.

Now it seems that all the *attributes* of the soul, e.g., temper, good temper, fear, pity, courage, also gladness and love and hate, exist with the body; for the body is being affected simultaneously with these. This is indicated by the fact that sometimes when strong or striking affections occur, we are   *20* not at the same time irritated or afraid, but at times when the affections are weak or obscure, we are moved, and the body is agitated in a manner similar to that when we are angry. Again, a more evident example is the fact that we become afraid even if there is no [external] cause of fear.

If such be the case, it is clear that the *attributes* of the soul are things   *25* whose formulae include matter. So the corresponding definitions will be as follows: anger, for instance, is a certain motion of such a body or bodily part or faculty of that body, caused by such and such a mover for the sake of such and such an end. And because of these facts, it becomes evident that it belongs to the physicist to investigate the soul, either every [kind of] soul or such [which is inseparable from a body]. Accordingly, a physicist and a dialectician would define each [*attribute* of such a soul] in a different   *30* way. For instance, in stating what anger is, the dialectician would say that it is a desire to retaliate by causing pain, or something of this sort, whereas a physicist would say that it is the rise in temperature of the blood or heat round the heart. Thus the latter would state the matter, the former would   *403b* state the form and formula; for the formula is the form of the thing, but that form must be in such and such a matter if it is to exist. It is like the case of a house. Its formula is such as this: a covering which tends to prevent its contents from being destroyed by wind or rain or scorching heat, but   *5* another would speak of it as being stones and bricks and timber; still another would speak of it as being the form in these materials for the sake of such and such an end.

Which of the above three [definitions] will the physicist give? Is it the one concerned with the matter but overlooks the formula, or the one concerned with the formula only? Is it not rather the one which includes both [the matter and the formula]? Then what should we call each of the other two [thinkers]? Should we not say (1) that there is no [scientist] who is concerned [only] with the *attributes* of matter which are inseparable and is concerned   *10* with them qua separable, (2) but that it is the physicist who is concerned with all [the attributes] which are functions or *attributes* of such and such a body or matter; and, of the things which are investigated not qua such attributes, (3) that it is the artist who is concerned with some [*attributes*], e.g., the carpenter or the physician, if those things happen to be [works of art], (4) that it is the mathematician who is concerned with inseparable   *15 attributes* but by abstraction and not qua *attributes* of such and such a body,   and (5) that it is the first philosopher who is concerned with [things] insofar as they are separate?

But let us return to the point from which we digressed. We were saying that the *attributes* of the soul qua such [*attributes*], as in the case of temper and fear, are inseparable from the physical matter of animals and are not like a line or a plane.

2

20   In our inquiry into the soul we must, while going over the difficulties which should precede their solution, consider also the doctrines of those before us who had something to say concerning the soul in order that we may accept whatever was stated well, but guard ourselves against anything which was not stated well. The starting-point of our inquiry is to lay down
25   before us those things which are particularly thought to belong to the soul by virtue of its nature.

Now that which is animate is thought to differ most of all from that which is inanimate in two ways, by having [self]-motion and by sensing. From our predecessors, too, these two are mainly the things about the soul which were handed down to us. Some declared that soul is particularly and primarily
30   that which causes motion; and thinking that no thing which is not itself in motion can cause another thing to be in motion, they came to the belief
404a   that soul is a thing in motion. In view of this, Democritus asserted that soul is a sort of fire and hot. For, of the infinite [kinds of] shapes and atoms, those which are spherical he called "fire" and "soul", these being like the so-called "motes" in the air which appear in the sunbeams entering through windows. And he said that all these seeds [i.e., shapes and atoms] are the
5   elements of the whole of nature (Leucippus, too, speaks similarly) but that those of them which are spherical are souls because elements of such shape are most capable of passing through openings and moving all other things by being themselves in motion. These thinkers regard soul to be that which furnishes animals with motion; and, in view of this, they regard breathing
10   as being the definition of living. For, they think, after the surrounding air presses upon the bodies [of animals] and forces out [atomic] shapes which furnish the animals with motion, because those shapes are never at rest, other such shapes from outside come to the aid by entering the body during respiration, and these prevent the escape of the shapes already in the bodies
15   by compression and solidification; and animals live as long as they are able to do this.

What the Pythagoreans have said, too, seems to amount to the same *thought;* for some of them identified the soul with the motes in the air, others with that which moves these motes. And these motes were referred
20   to because they appear to be continuously in motion, even when the air is completely calm.

   The *thinking* of those who say that the soul is that which moves itself,
too, amounts to the same thing. For these thinkers seem to believe that
motion is most appropriate to the soul, and that, while all other things are
moved by the soul, the soul is moved by itself; and it does so because they
observe nothing moving something else which is not itself in motion.   *25*
   Similarly, Anaxagoras and all others who declare that *Intelligence* caused
the universe to be in motion say that it is the soul which moves other things;
but Anaxagoras does not speak altogether like Democritus. The latter declares that the soul and the intellect are simply the same, for, according to
him, what is true is [the same as] what appears to be; and for this reason
he regards Homer's phrase "Hector lay thinking other thoughts"[2] as well put.   *30*
He does not, however, treat the intellect as a certain faculty concerned with
truth but says [merely] that the soul and the intellect are the same. Anax-   *404b*
agoras speaks less clearly about these matters. In many places he says that
Intelligence is the cause of beauty and rightness; in other places he says that
it is the soul, for it exists in all animals, great and small, worthy of honor
and less honorable. But the so-called "intellect", when spoken of with   *5*
respect to prudence, does not appear to belong alike to all animals, not even
to all men.
   Those, then, who considered the soul from the point of view of the motion
of animate things regarded it as being the most capable of causing motion;
but those who considered it from the point of view of knowledge or sensation of things placed it among the principles, some positing these to be   *10*
many, but others only one, [the soul itself]. Thus Empedocles regarded the
soul as being composed of all the [kinds of] elements and each of these as
being a soul. He says:

        By Earth we see Earth, by Water Water,
        By Ether Ether divine, by Fire destructive Fire,
        By Love Love, and Strife by bitter Strife.[3]   *15*

   In the same manner Plato, in the *Timaeus*, constructs the soul out of
elements; for, according to him, like is known by like, and things are
composed of principles. In [my] treatise *On Philosophy*, too, a similar
description [of Plato's views] is given: Animal Itself is composed of the Idea *20*
of *One Itself* and of the primary Length, the primary Breadth,[4] and the
primary Depth;[5] and the rest are composed in a similar manner. In still
another way, he regards the *Intellect* as the *One, Knowledge* as Two (for
this is [arrived at] in one way only), Opinion as the Number of the Plane,
and Sensation as the Number of the Solid. For Numbers, according to him,
are the Forms themselves and the principles [of other things], and they are   *25*
composed of elements; and things are apprehended, some by the intellect,
others by *knowledge*, others by opinion, and others by sensation; and the

above Numbers are the Forms of things.   And since the soul was thought
to be capable of causing motion and of knowing, some thinkers   combined
30   these two and declared that the soul is a number moving itself.

But thinkers differ as to what the principles of the soul are and how many
of them there are, especially between those who posit them as being corpo-
405a   real and those who posit them as being incorporeal; and these differ from
those who combine these two and declare that the principles are of two
kinds. And there are differences as to the number of principles also; for some
speak of only one, others of many. The accounts they give of the soul, too,
follow from the positions they take [with respect to the principles]; for they
regard, not without good reason, the thing whose nature is to cause motion
5   as being among the primary.   Thus some are of the opinion that the soul
is fire, for fire, too, is [thought to be] composed of the finest particles and
[to be] the most incorporeal of the elements; besides, it is in the primary
sense both in motion and that which moves other things [according to these
thinkers].

Democritus speaks even more precisely than the others by stating the
cause of each of the two [traits of the soul just mentioned];   for he says that
10   the soul is the same as the intellect, that it is [composed]   of the primary
and indivisible bodies, that it can cause motion because of the smallness and
the shape [of the particles] and of the fact that of the various shapes the
spherical is the most easily moved, and that such is both the intellect and
fire.[6]

Anaxagoras seems to speak of the soul and *Intelligence* as being different,
15   as we have already stated. But he treats them as if they were of one nature,
except that he posits *Intelligence* as being the highest principle of all things;
at any rate, he says that, of all things, *Intelligence* alone is simple, unblended, and pure. Yet in saying that *Intelligence* set the universe in motion he
attributes both knowing and moving other things to the same principle.

Thales, too, judging from the anecdotes related of him, seems to have
20   regarded the soul as something which can cause motion, if indeed he said
that the loadstone possesses soul, for it moves iron.

Diogenes, like some others, thinking that [air] is composed of the finest
particles and is a principle,   [regards the soul as being] air, and for this
reason he thinks that the soul both knows and causes motion; for he thinks
that insofar as it is first [i.e., a principle] and the other things are composed
25   of it, it knows, but that insofar as its particles are the most fine, it can cause
motion.

Heraclitus asserts that the principle is soul, if indeed it is an exhalation
from which the other things are composed, that it is the most incorporeal
and always in a state of flux, and that what is in motion is known by a thing
in motion.   Both he and many other thinkers think that [all] things are in
30   motion. Alcmaion, too, seems to regard the soul in about the same way as

these thinkers, for he asserts that soul is immortal because it seems to be like immortal things, and that it possesses immortality by being always in motion; for, according to him, all divine things, the Moon, the Sun, the stars, *405b* and the whole heaven are in a continuous motion.

Of the rather crude thinkers, like Hippo, some went as far as to declare that the soul is water. They seem to have been persuaded by the fact that the seed of all [animals] is moist; for Hippo refutes those who assert that the soul is blood by pointing out that the seed is not blood but is the primary 5 soul. Others, like Critias, regarding sensation to be most appropriate to the soul, declared that soul is blood and that [sensation] occurs because of the nature of blood.

Thus each of the elements found its advocate except earth; and no one declared the soul to be earth, unless it be anyone who said that the soul is composed of all the elements or that every element is a soul. 10

Now all thinkers define the soul by three things, so to say: motion, sensation, and incorporeality; and each of these is referred to the principles. It is in view of this that even those who, using about the same language, define it as knowing, posit it to be, with one exception, either an element or composed of elements; for they say that like is known by like 15 and that, since the soul knows all things, it consists of all the principles. Accordingly, those who assert that there is only one cause or one element, such as fire or air, posit the soul, too, to be one; but those who assert that the principles are many posit the soul, too, to be many. Anaxagoras alone 20 says that *Intelligence* cannot be affected and that it has nothing in common with any of the other things. But how *Intelligence*, if it is such, will know and through what cause, he did not say anything, nor is it evident from his writings. Again, those who posit contraries among the principles say that the soul, too, consists of contraries, and, similarly, those who posit one of 25 two contraries, such as the *Hot* or the *Cold* or some other such thing, posit the soul to be that contrary; and, in view of this, these thinkers appeal to language for support of their views. Thus those who posit the *Hot* say that it is because of this principle [and the word ζέω (= "boil")] that the word ζῆν (= "living") is used, and those who posit the *Cold* say that it is because of inhaling and the word κατάψυξις (= "cooling") that the word ψυχή (= "soul") is used.

The above, then, are the doctrines concerning the soul which were hand- 30 ed down to us and the *reasons* for which they were so held . . .

BOOK II

1

The doctrines concerning the soul handed down to us by our predecessors have been sufficiently discussed. Let us then turn to another starting point,

5   as it were, and try to determine what the soul is and what would be its most common formula.

Now one genus of things we call "substance", but (1) one kind under this we regard as matter, which taken by itself is not a *this*, (2) another as *shape* and form, in virtue of which something is directly called "a *this*", (3) and a third, the composite of the above two kinds. Matter exists as potentiality;

10   form exists as actuality, but in two senses: e.g., (a) as *knowledge*, and (b) as the exercise of *knowledge*.

Bodies are thought to be substances most of all, especially natural bodies; for the latter are the principles of all the rest. Of natural bodies, some possess life but others do not; and by "life" we mean self-nourishment and

15   growth and deterioration of that body. So every natural body which partakes of life would be a substance of the composite kind. And since there exists such a kind of body (for it has life), the soul would not be a body; for a body is not something which belongs to a subject but exists rather as

20   a subject or as matter. Accordingly, the soul must be a substance as the form of a natural body potential with life, and [such] substance is an actuality. So the soul is the actuality of such a body.

But actuality is spoken of in two ways, as in the case of *knowledge* and as in the case of the exercise of *knowledge*. Evidently, the soul is an actuality as in the case of *knowledge*; for sleeping and being awake depend on the

25   existence of soul, and being awake is analogous to the exercise of *knowledge*, whereas sleeping is analogous to having [*knowledge*] but not exercising it. Now in the same individual the *knowledge* of a thing is prior in generation to the exercise of that *knowledge*. In view of this, the soul is the first actuality of a natural body with the potentiality of having life; and a body

412b   of this kind would be one which has organs. The parts of plants, too, are organs, but they are entirely simple; e.g., the leaf shelters the rind and the rind shelters the fruit, and the roots are analogous to the mouth, for both of these take in food. If, then, there is something common to be said about

5   every [kind of] soul, this would be: "the first actuality of a natural body which has organs". And in view of this, one should not inquire whether the soul and the body are one or not, just as one should not ask whether the wax and its shape or, in general, the matter of each thing and that of which it is the matter are one or not; for, although the terms "one" and "being" have many senses, the dominant sense is that of actuality.

We have now stated universally what the soul is: with respect to its 10
formula, it is a *substance*, and this is the essence in such and such a body,
as in the case of instruments. For example, if an axe were a natural body,
its *substance* would be its essence, and this would be its soul; and if that
essence were removed, there would no longer be an axe, except by equivocation. Now [the essence with the body], here, is an axe; but the soul is the 15
essence and the formula not of such a body, but of such a natural body
which has in itself the principle of moving and of stopping.

What has just been said should be observed in the parts [of a living body]
also. If the eye were an animal, its vision would be its soul; for vision is the
eye's *substance* with respect to [the eye's] formula. The eye itself is the 20
matter for vision; and if [vision] departs, there is no eye any longer, except
equivocally, as in the case of the eye in a statue or a painting. What was
stated of the part [the eye] should be taken to apply to the whole living body,
for there is an analogy; this part is to that part [in the case of the eye] as the
sentient power as a whole is to the whole sentient body qua such. Thus, 25
that which is potentially living is not that which has lost the soul but that
which possesses it. As for the seed or the fruit, it is potentially such and
such a body. Now being awake as an actuality is like seeing or cutting, but 413a
the soul as [a first] actuality is like vision and the power of the instrument
[i.e., of the axe]; and the body is that which exists as potentiality. And
just as the eye is its vision with its pupil, so the animal is its soul with its
body.

It is not unclear, then, that the soul, or parts of it if by its nature it has
parts, cannot be separated from the body; for the actualities in some [living 5
things] are those of the parts themselves. But nothing prevents some actualities from being separable, because they are not actualities of any body.
Further, it is not clear whether the soul as the actuality of the body is like
the sailor of the boat.

In outline, then, let the above distinctions and sketch concerning the soul 10
suffice for the present.

2

Since what is clear and more known with respect to formula arises from
what is unclear but more evident [to us], let us try, by the use of such
[method], to go over the soul once more; for the formula which defines the
soul should not only make us know the fact, as most definitions do, but also 15
include and make evident the cause. Formulae which are given as definitions nowadays are like conclusions. For instance, what is squaring [of an
oblong rectangle]? It is the [construction of an] equilateral rectangle which
is equal in area to an oblong rectangle. Now such a definition is a formula
of the conclusion. But if a definition states that squaring an oblong rectangle
is finding the mean proportional of the sides of that rectangle, it states the 20
cause of the thing.

As a starting-point of our inquiry, then, let us state that an animate thing is distinguished from an inanimate thing by living. The term "living" has many senses; but let us say that a thing is living even if it has in itself only one of the following: the intellect, the power of sensation, the power of producing motion and of stopping with respect to place, the power of
25   moving with respect to nutrition, that of deterioration, and that of growth. Thus all plants, too, are thought to be living; for they appear to possess in themselves such a power and a principle through which they grow and deteriorate in contrary directions, for those which are constantly nourished and continue to live grow [and deteriorate] not only upwards without doing
30   so downwards, but alike in both directions, indeed in every direction, and they do so as long as they are able to take in food.

Now the power of nutrition can exist apart from the other powers, but in mortal beings none of the other powers can exist apart from this power. This fact is evident in plants; for no power other than that of nutrition
413b   belongs to them. Accordingly, living belongs to [all] living things because of this principle, but it belongs to animals primarily because of the power of sensation; for even those beings which have no power to be in motion or go to another place but have the power of sensation are called "animals"
5   and not only "living things". Of the sentient powers, that of touch is primary; and just as the nutritive power can exist apart from that of touch or any other power of sensation, so the power of touch can exist apart from any of the other powers of sensation. By "power of nutrition" we mean such part of the soul of which plants partake also; all animals, however, are
10   observed to have the power of touch. As for the cause of each of these facts, it will be discussed later.[7]

At present let us say only so much, that the soul is the principle of the [functions] already stated and that it is defined by the power of nutrition or of sensation or of *thinking* or of producing motion. Whether each of these powers is a soul or a part of a soul, and, if a part, whether it is such
15   as to be separable only in definition or also in place, are problems to be faced. In the case of certain powers the solution is not difficult to perceive; in the case of some others, there are difficulties. For just as in the case of some plants, when each is divided and the parts are separated, each part appears to continue to live, as if the soul of each such plant is actually one
20   but potentially many, so in the case of some insects, when cut into parts, other kinds of soul are observed to continue to live. For each part has both the power of sensation and that of locomotion, and if the power of sensation, it has also the powers of imagination and of desire; for whenever there is sensation, there is also pleasure and pain, and whenever these exist, *desire*
25   too must exist. With regard to the intellect or the speculative faculty, it is not yet evident; but this seems to be a different genus of soul, and [perhaps] it alone can be separated [from the body], just as that which is eternal [can

be separated] from that which is destructible.   As for the other parts of the soul, it is evident from what we have said that they are not separable,   in spite of what some thinkers say.   But it is evident that they are distinct in definition; for the essence of a sentient power is distinct from the essence   *30* of a power of forming opinions, if indeed sensing and forming opinions are distinct, and similarly with each of the other powers mentioned.   Further, some animals have all the powers mentioned and some have only some of them, but some [living things] have only one power; and it is from this fact that the differentiae of animals arise.   As for the cause of this fact, it will   *414a* be considered later.⁸ Almost the same remarks apply to the powers of sensation; for some animals have all of them, others have some of them, and certain animals have only the one most necessary, and this is the power of touch.

Now the expression "that by which we live or sense" has two meanings, just like the expression "that by which we *know*" (in which the word "that"   *5* may mean either *knowledge* or the soul, for we speak of *knowing* by one or by the other) and similarly for the expression "that by which we are healthy" (in which "that"   may mean either health or a part of the body, or even the whole body). Further, of these meanings, *knowledge* or health is a *form* or a form of some kind or a formula and, as it were, the *actuality*   *10* of the receptive subject, which is the subject which *knows* [in the case of *knowing*] but the subject which is healthy in the case of health (for the *actuality* of that which can act is thought to be in the subject which is affected or is [so] disposed). Accordingly, since the soul is primarily that by which we live or sense or *think*, it would be the formula or the form but not the matter or the subject [of the living thing]. For, as we have already stated, the term "substance" has three meanings, i.e., form, matter, and the   *15* composite of these two; and of these three, matter is potentiality, but form is actuality. So since the living thing is the composite of the two, it is not the body that is the actuality of the soul, but the soul that is the actuality of the body, and of a certain [kind of] body.   And, because of this, those who think that the soul does not exist without a body or is not a body of any   *20* sort have the right belief. For the soul is not a body but something of   a body, and, because of this, it exists in a body. But it exists in such and such a body and not as the earlier thinkers thought; they fitted it to a body without further specifying what that body is or what kind of a body it is, although there is no evidence that any chance body can receive any chance   *25* soul.   According to reason, too, the case is such as the following: each thing's actuality by its nature can exist [only] with the [kind of] potentiality which belongs to that thing or with its appropriate matter.

It is evident from the above remarks, then, that the soul is a certain actuality or formula of that which has the potentiality of being such and such a thing.

3

30   Of the soul's powers mentioned above,[10] namely, those of nutrition, desire,
sensation, locomotion, and *thinking,* some living things possess all, as we
said,[11] others some, and others only one.   Plants possess the power of nutrition
414b   only, other living things possess this and also the power of sensation. Those
which possess the power of sensation have the appetitive power also. For
the species of desire are *desire* and temper and wish, and all animals have
at least one power of sensation, that of touch; but that which has sensation
5   has also pleasure and pain and is affected by pleasurable and painful objects, and, if so, it has *desire* also, since *desire* is a desire for the pleasurable.
Further, [all animals] have the power of sensing food. Food is sensed by
touch, since all animals are nourished by dry and moist and hot and cold
objects, all of which are sensed by touch; but the other sensible objects are
10   sensed by touch only indirectly;   for sounds and colors and odors contribute
nothing to food, whereas flavors are a species of tangible [qualities]. Hunger
and thirst are *desires,* hunger being a *desire* for dry and hot objects, and
thirst for cold and moist objects; and flavor is a sort of seasoning of these
objects. These facts will be made clear later,[12] but at present let us say so
15   much, that those animals which have [the power of] touch have [the power
of] desire also. As for imagination, it is not clear; but it will be examined
later.[13] Some animals possess also the power of locomotion, and others, i.e.,
men and perhaps beings such as men or even more honorable than men,
possess also the power of *thinking* and an intellect.
20   It is clear [from the above discussion], then, that a single formula for a
soul could be given in the same manner as for a figure;   for neither does
a figure exist apart from the triangle [and the quadrilateral] and the rest [of
the species of figures], nor does a soul exist apart from the [kinds of] souls
listed above.   A common formula for a figure, too, can be given which will
fit all [kinds of] figures, but it will not be proper to any [one kind]; and
25   similarly in the case of the [kinds of] soul mentioned above.   In view of this,
it is ridiculous to seek a common formula which will apply to these or other
such cases but fail to be proper to things or appropriate to each ultimate
species, but not seek one which is proper to a thing or appropriate to each
species.
There is a parallelism in the [kinds of] figures and in the [kinds of] soul;
30   for in both figures and animate things there is a succession in which that
which is prior exists always potentially in that which is posterior. For
instance, the triangle exists [potentially] in the quadrilateral, and the nutritive power exists [potentially] in the sentient power,   and so one must seek
the whatness of each kind. For instance, "What is the soul of a plant?",
"What is the soul of man?", "What is the soul of a nonrational animal?".
415a   The *reason*   why [the powers of the soul] are related in such succession is
a matter which requires consideration;[14] for the sentient power cannot exist

without the nutritive power, but the latter power can exist without the former, as it does in plants. Again, without the sense of touch none of the other senses can exist; but the sense of touch can exist without any of the other senses, for there are many animals which have neither vision nor a 5 sense of hearing nor a sense of smell at all. Again, of living things which have the power of sensation, some have the power of locomotion but others do not. Finally, some living things — very few — have [also] the power of judging and of *thinking;* for, of mortal beings, those which have the power of judging have all the other powers also, but those which have one of the 10 latter powers do not all have the power of judging, and, of the latter, some do not even have imagination while others live only by imagination. Concerning the speculative intellect, its discussion is of another kind. [15]

It is clear, then, that the formula most appropriate to each of these [powers] is also the formula of each [kind of] soul.

4

One who intends to make an inquiry into the kinds of soul must first grasp 15 the whatness of each kind and then proceed to what follows or what other things should be sought. On the other hand, if one is to state what each of these is, e.g., what the thinking or the sentient or the nutritive power is, prior to this he should state what thinking or sensing [or taking in food] is; for activities or *actions* are prior in formula to the corresponding powers. If so, 20 then, again, since the objects to which the activities are directed should be investigated before the activities, for the same *reason* those objects (e.g., food, sensible object, object of thought) would have to be determined first.

First, then, we should discuss food and reproduction; for the nutritive soul exists in the other kinds of soul and is the primary and most common power 25 of souls, and it is in virtue of this [power] that living belongs to all living things. The function of this soul is to reproduce and to use food. For the most natural function of living things which are perfect and neither defective nor generated by chance is to produce another thing like itself (e.g., an animal produces an animal [of the same kind], and a plant likewise a plant) in order that they may partake of the eternal and the divine as far as they can; for 415b all [living things] 'desire' [the eternal and the divine], and it is for the sake of this that those which *act* according to nature do so. The expression "that for the sake of which", of course, has two senses: (a) that which is done, and (b) that for which it is done. Accordingly, since [such] living things cannot share in the eternal and the divine continuously (because no destructible thing, which is the same and numerically one, can last forever), they partake 5 of the eternal and the divine only as far as they can, some sharing in these more, others doing so less; and what lasts forever is not that which is [numerically one and] the same, but something like it, i.e., something which is one not numerically but in species.

The soul is the cause and the principle of a living body. Now the terms "cause" and "principle" have many senses, and, similarly, the soul is a cause
10 in the three specified senses of "cause"; for it is a cause as a source of motion, and as a final cause, and as the *substance* of an animate body.

Clearly, it is a cause as the *substance* [of an animate body]; for the cause of the existence of each thing is the *substance* of that thing, existence in living things is life, and the cause and principle [in living things] is the soul.
15 Further, the formula of that which exists potentially is its actuality.

It is evident that the soul is a cause as final cause also. For just as the intellect acts for the sake of something, so does nature, and nature's end is a final cause. Such [end] in animals is the soul and [is an end] according to their nature; for all natural bodies are instruments of the soul, and, as in the
20 case of animals, so in the case of plants, [natural bodies] exist for the sake of their soul.   And, [as already stated], "that for the sake of which" has two senses: (a) that which is done, and (b) that for which it is done.

Finally, the soul is also a cause as a source of motion with respect to place, but such power does not exist in all living things. Alteration and growth, too, exist [in living things] by virtue of their soul; for sensation is thought to be
25 a species of alteration, and no thing without soul can have sensations. Similar remarks apply to growth and deterioration; for no thing can by its nature grow or deteriorate without taking in food, and no thing can be nourished unless it shares in life.

416a   Empedocles did not speak rightly when he added that the roots of plants grow downwards because the earth [in them] according to its nature travels downwards, and that the [branches] grow upwards because fire [in them according to its nature] travels upwards. First, he did not grasp the terms "up" and "down" rightly, for up and down are not the same for all things as they are for the universe; if the organs of the body are to be called "the
5 same" or "different" according to their functions, then heads are to animals as roots are to trees.   Further, what is it that holds together the earth and the fire [in an animal] which tend to travel in contrary directions? They would part from each other, unless there were something to prevent separation; but if there is something, this would be the soul and [also] the cause of growing and of taking in food.

10   Some   are of the opinion that fire's nature is without qualification the cause of food and of growth; for, according to them, fire alone of all the bodies or elements appears to nourish itself and to grow. And in view of this, one might come to the belief that it is fire that performs the function of causing growth and nourishment in both plants and animals. Now fire is in some way a joint cause; however, it is not the cause without qualification.
15 It is rather the soul which is the cause. For the growth of fire proceeds indefinitely, as long as there is fuel to be burned; but a thing which is composed by nature of all [the elements] has a limit and a [certain] ratio [of

elements] with respect to both size and growth, and these [i.e., limit and ratio] belong to the soul and not to fire, and to the formula rather than to the matter of that thing.

Since it is the same power of the soul that is both nutritive and reproductive, we must specify first what food is; for this power is distinguished from the others by its function of taking in food. Now it is thought that food is a contrary of [another] contrary, though not of every [kind of] contrary, but of that which is generated and also increased in size from its contrary; for, in many cases, one contrary is generated from its contrary, but not all of them are quantities, as in the case of a healthy man from a sick man. But not even the above-mentioned contraries appear to be food to each other in the same way; for water is food to fire, but fire does not nourish water. So it is in simple bodies most of all that one of two contraries is thought to be food and the other to be that which is nourished.

Yet there is a difficulty. For some of these thinkers say that like is nourished by like, just as it grows by like; but, as already stated, others have the opposite opinion, namely, that it is a contrary which is nourished by its contrary, since (a) like is not affected by like and food must change and be digested, and (b) change in every case proceeds to that which is opposite or intermediate. Again, food is acted upon in a certain way by that which is nourished; but the latter is not acted upon by food, just as the carpenter is not acted upon by his materials; for it is the materials that are acted upon by the carpenter, whereas he himself changes only from inactivity to activity. Now it makes a difference whether food is that which is finally taken or that which is initially taken into the body. If it is food in both cases, the first being undigested but the second digested, then the term "food" would have two meanings; for insofar as food is undigested, it is *contrary* to that which is nourished, but insofar as it is digested, it is *like* that which is nourished. So it is evident that each of the two views is in one sense right but in another sense wrong.

Since no thing is nourished unless it partakes of life, that which is nourished would be an animate body qua animate; so food, too, is relative to an animate body and not [just] an accident of it. But to be food and to be a thing which can cause growth are distinct. For insofar as the animate body is a quantity, that which nourishes can cause the body [merely] to grow; but insofar as that body is a certain *this* and a substance, that which nourishes is food, for it preserves the *substance* [of that body], and [that body] continues to exist as long as it can be nourished. And food can also act in the generation not of that which is nourished (for the *substance* of that which is nourished already exists, and a thing which exists preserves itself but does not reproduce itself), but of another [substance] like that which is nourished. So such a principle of the soul is a power of such a nature as to preserve that which has it and to preserve it qua such, while food

20   provides [the material necessary] for the activity [of that power]. For this
     reason, an [animate thing] cannot exist if it is deprived of food.
         There are three things [in nutrition]: (a) that which is nourished, (b) that
     with which a thing is nourished, and (c) that which acts in nourishing. That
     which acts is the primary soul,   that which is nourished is the body which
     has that soul, and that with which [the body] is nourished is food. So since
     it is just to name things after the ends [they aim at] , and since the end [of
25   an animate thing] is to reproduce another thing like itself,   the primary soul
     would be the soul which can reproduce a thing like itself. Now the phrase
     "that with which it is nourished" has two meanings, like the phrase "that
     with which one steers"; for the latter may mean either the hand or the
     rudder, one of which is both a mover and a thing moved, but the other only
     a mover. Thus all food must be capable of being digested, and that whose
     activity causes digestion is heat.   For this reason, every animate thing has
     heat.
30   We have now given an outline of what food is; further clarification will
     be taken up later in a treatise   appropriate to that subject.

         5

         Having made the above distinctions, let us discuss what is common to all
     the kinds of sensation. Now sensation depends on being moved and being
35   affected, as already stated,[16] for it is thought to be a species of alteration. But
417a some thinkers say that also like is acted upon by like. How this is possible
     or impossible has already been discussed in our general treatise on acting
     and being acted upon.[17] There is the problem, however, as to why there can
     be no sensation of the sensations themselves as well, and why [the sense
     organs] do not themselves produce sensations without the external objects,
5   although there exist in [those organs] fire and earth and the other elements,
     which are objects of sensation, whether directly or indirectly through their
     attributes.
         Now it is clear that the sentient [soul or part] exists not in activity but only
     potentially. Thus it is like fuel, which does not itself burn by being fuel,
     unless there is something to cause it to burn; otherwise it would cause itself
10   to burn and would have no need of actual fire to set it afire. Then since "to
     sense" has two meanings (for (1) that which has the capacity to hear or to
     see is said to hear or to see, even if it happens to be asleep, but also (2) that
     which is *actually* hearing or seeing), the term "sensation", too, would have
     two meanings; it may mean either sensation as potentiality or sensation
     when in activity. Similarly, the term "to sense", too, may mean either to
     have the potentiality of sensing or to be *actually* sensing.
15   First, let us state that being acted upon and being moved and being in
     activity are the same; for motion, too, is an activity, but incomplete, as
     stated elsewhere.[18] Now everything which is acted upon or moved is acted

upon or moved by that which can act and *actually* does so. For this reason, a thing is acted upon in one sense by what is like it but in another sense by what is unlike it, as already stated;[19] for what is acted upon is unlike [the   *20* agent], but after it has been acted upon, it is like [the agent].

We must distinguish also the senses of "potentiality" and of "actuality", for up to now we have been using them without qualifying the senses of each. We call something "a *knower*" (a) in the sense in which we might say that a man is a *knower*, since he can be a *knower* or have *knowledge*, but also (b) in the sense in which a man already has *knowledge*, e.g., grammati-   *25* cal *knowledge*. Each of these two men is capable [of *knowing*], but not in the same manner; the first is capable in view of the fact that his kind and his matter are of a certain sort,   the second in the sense that he can exercise the *knowledge* [he already has], if he wishes, provided that no external agent prevents him. But (c) in a third and dominant sense we call a man "a *knower*" if he is actually exercising his *knowledge* when contemplating a given fact. The first two men are *knowers* in virtue of a potentiality; but whereas the one   *30* has the potentiality of altering by learning and often by changing from a contrary habit,   the other has the potentiality [of changing] in another way, e.g., from the inactive possession of sense   or of grammar to the exercise of   *417b* that possession.

The term "to be acted upon", too, does not have a single meaning. In one sense, it means a kind of destruction by a contrary, in another, it means rather a preservation of a thing which exists potentially by a similar thing which exists actually in a manner in which potentiality is related to actuali-   *5* ty; for that which possesses *knowledge* becomes that which exercises that *knowledge*, and this becoming, as such, either is not an alteration (for the progress is towards itself and in its actuality) or is an alteration of a different kind.   In view of this, it is not right to say that a prudent man is changed in quality when he is judging rightly, just as it is not right to say that a builder is changed in quality when he is building a house.   Accordingly, it is just to say that that which changes a thing from being potential to the   *10* actuality of that potentiality with respect to thinking or judging rightly is not teaching but should have some other name, and that which, from being potential, learns or acquires *knowledge* by that which actually [*knows*] and can teach, either (a) should not be called "being acted upon," as already stated, or (b), [if called "an alteration"], this term should be taken in two senses: (i) as a change to a privative disposition, and (ii) as a change to a   *15* [positive] habit and to the nature [of the thing learned].

In the case of the sentient soul, the first change occurs by that which gives birth to [the animal with that soul]. When born, the animal now possesses sensing in a way in which one possesses *knowledge;* and we speak of the *actual* [sensing by that being] in the same way as we speak of the exercise of *knowledge*.   But there is a difference. [In the case of sensation], that   *20* which acts in producing *actual* sensation is external to the thing which senses it, and this is the visible or the audible or any of the other sensible objects; and the cause of this is the fact that sensation, when *actual*, is of an individual object.   *Knowledge*, on the other hand, is of things universally taken, and these   exist in the soul in a certain manner. It is in view of this that thinking depends upon a man whenever he wishes to think; but

25   sensing does not depend on him [alone], for a sensible object must be present.   Similar remarks apply to *knowledge* of sensibles,   and for the same *reason*, for sensible objects are individuals and are external to man.

Further clarification of the above matters will be made later at the appropriate time.   At present, it is sufficient to make the following distinc-

30   tions: just as "to be potentially" has more than one sense, one of them being the sense in which we might say that a boy can lead an army, the other being the sense in which an adult [who is a general] can lead an army, so it is with

418a   "the sentient soul". Since there are no names to bring out these differences, but since we pointed out the fact that things which exist potentially may differ and also the manner in which they may differ, we must use "to be acted upon" and "to be altered" as if they were basic names for the two differences;   but the sentient soul exists potentially in a way like the sensible object when this already exists in actuality, as already stated.[20] Accordingly,

5   while this soul is being acted upon, it is unlike that object; but after it has been acted upon, it is a likeness of that object and exists in a way like that object.

6

In dealing with each power of sensation, we should first discuss the corresponding sensible object. The term "sensible object" has three senses, in two of which we say that the object is sensed directly [or essentially or in itself], while in the third we say that the object is sensed [accidentally or]

10   indirectly. In one of the first two senses, the object is proper to one sense, but in the other, it is common to all the senses. By "proper" I mean a sensible object (a) which cannot be sensed by any of the other senses and (b) about which the corresponding sense cannot be mistaken. For example, vision is of color, the sense of hearing is of sound, and the sense of taste is of flavor. In the case of the sense of touch there are a number of differences,

15   yet each sense discriminates the corresponding objects and is not mistaken about those objects. Thus vision is not mistaken about the colors it senses, nor the sense of hearing about the sounds; but each sense may be mistaken as to what the [substance] which has color is, or where it is, or what the [substance] which is sounding is, or where it is. Sensible objects such as these, then, are said to be proper to the corresponding senses.

The things which are called "common sensibles" are motion, rest, number, shape, and magnitude, for each of them is not proper to any one sense

but is common to all; for motion can be sensed by touch, and by vision, 20
[etc.].

Sensible objects which are said to be sensed indirectly [or accidentally]
are, for example, the son of Diares, if he is white, since it is by way of an
attribute [i.e., whiteness] that man senses him [as a substance]; for what he
senses [directly] is [the attribute] whiteness, which belongs to the son of
Diares. For this reason, vision is not even affected by the sensible object qua
being such a thing [i.e., a substance].

Of the direct sensibles, those which are proper are sensible in the basic
sense, and it is to them that the *substance* of each sense [or sensation] is by 25
its nature related.

7

That to which vision is related is the visible object; and the visible object
is (a) color and (b) an object which may be expressed by a formula but
happens to be nameless. This will become clear as we proceed. Now the
visible object is color, and this exists on that [i.e., the surface] which is visible 30
in virtue of itself; and by "in virtue of itself" I mean not by its formula but
by the fact that it has in itself the cause of being visible.

Now every color can set in motion a transparent medium which exists in 418b
activity, and this is the nature of color. It is indeed for this reason that no
[color] is visible without light, but every color of a thing is visible in light.
So we should discuss first what light is.

There is something which is transparent; and by "transparent" I mean
that which is visible, not visible in itself, simply speaking, but visible because 5
of a color belonging to another kind of object. Such a thing is air, water,
and many solid bodies; for water or air is transparent not qua water or qua
air, respectively, but by the fact that there is a nature in them which is the
same in both and also in the eternal body of the uppermost region of the
universe. Now light is the activity of what is transparent qua being trans- 10
parent; and darkness, too, exists in it [the transparent medium], but potentially. Light, then, is as it were the color of the transparent medium when
the latter is caused to exist in actuality by fire or a thing such as a celestial
body, for this [body], too, has something which is one and the same [as that
which fire has].

We have stated what the transparent is and what light is. Light is neither
fire, nor a body at all, nor yet something which emanates from a body 15
(for, if so, it too would be a body), but the presence in a transparent medium
of something which comes from fire or from some other such thing; for
two bodies cannot exist at the same time in the same place. Now light is
thought to be contrary to darkness; darkness, however, is the privation of
such disposition in the transparent (body), so it is clear that the presence of 20
that disposition is light. So Empedocles, or any one whose doctrine is

similar to his, is not right in saying that light travels and that at some
moment it is somewhere between the Earth and that which surrounds it but
escapes our notice; for this doctrine is contrary both to truth [which follows]
25   from argument and to what is observed. For if the interval traversed were
short, light [so taken] might escape our notice, but that it does so from East
to West is too big a claim to accept.

   That which can receive color is [itself] without color, and that which can
receive sound is [itself] without sound.   That which is without color is (a)
the transparent and (b) the invisible or the hardly visible (such as is thought
30   to be dark); and such is the transparent, but when it exists potentially and
not in actuality, for it is the same nature which is at one time darkness but
419a   at another time light.   However, not everything which is visible is visible
in light, but only the appropriate color of each thing; for some things are
not visible in light but produce sensation in darkness, that is, those which
5   appear fiery or luminous (there is no single name for these), e.g., fungi, flesh,
and the heads, scales, and eyes of fishes; but in none of these is the appropriate color seen. A discussion of the *reason* why these things are thus seen
belongs elsewhere.   At present this much is evident, that what is seen in
light is color, and for this reason no color is seen without light; for, as already
10   stated, to be a color is to be that which causes motion in that which is
transparent when in activity,   and light is the actuality of that which is
transparent. This is evident from the following sign. If a colored object is
placed in contact with the eyes, its color will not be seen; but [if the object
is placed at a distance], the color moves the transparent medium, e.g., the
15   air, and this, being continuously in motion [up to the eye], moves this sense
organ.

   Democritus, then, does not speak rightly when he thinks that, if the
intervening space were to become void, one would see an ant distinctly even
if it were in the sky; for this is impossible. Seeing takes place when the
[organ] of sense is affected in a certain way, but the [organ] of sense cannot
be affected [directly] by what is seen, the color itself; what remains, then,
20   is that it is affected only by what is between the color and the eye, and so
there must be some [medium] between [the eye and the color]. If, on the
other hand, the intervening space were void, it would be true to say, not
that the color will be seen distinctly, but that the color will not be seen at
all.

   We have stated, then, the *reason* why color must be seen in light. As for
fire, it can be seen in darkness as well as in light, and this fact is necessary;
25   for [in darkness] the [potentially] transparent becomes [actually] transparent
by the action of fire.

   The same arguments apply to sound and to odor, too, for neither of these
produces sensation when in contact with the corresponding sense organ. So
it is the intervening medium that is moved by odor and sound, and it is by

the intervening medium that the corresponding sense organ is moved. And
whenever the object which produces sound or odor is placed in contact with
the corresponding sense organ, it produces no sensation. Similar remarks   *30*
apply to touch and taste, although this does not appear to be the case; but
the *reason* for the [apparent difference] will become clear later.[21] The
intervening medium in the case of sound is air. But in the case of odor the
medium has no name; for here there is an *attribute* which is common to
air and water, and this *attribute* is related to that which has odor as trans-   *35*
parency is related to [that which has] color. For aquatic animals, too, appear
to have the power of sensing odors; but men and other terrestrial animals   *419b*
which breathe cannot sense odors without breathing air in.   The *reason* for
this, too, will be discussed later.[22]

12

Universally speaking, we should bear in mind that every sense is receptive   *424a*
of the forms of sensible objects without their matter, and in a sort of way
in which wax receives the impression of a signet-ring without the iron or   *20*
gold, for the wax receives the impression of the golden or bronze [ring] not
qua gold or qua bronze. Similarly, a sense too is affected by a thing which
has color or flavor or sound, not insofar as that thing is signified by its name,
but insofar as it is such-and-such [i.e., colored or flavored or sounding] and
according to the corresponding formula. Now the primary sense organ is   *25*
that in which such a power [i.e., sense] resides, and it is the same [numerical-
ly as the power] but the essence of each of them is different; for that which
senses would be a certain magnitude. However, neither the essence of a
sense nor the corresponding sensation is a magnitude; they are, respectively,
the power [of the sense organ] and a certain formula [in that organ].

From the above discussion it is also evident why objects which are exceedingly sensible destroy the sense organs; for if the motion [of the medium]   *30*
is stronger than [what] the sense organ [can stand], the formula — and this,
as we saw, is the sense — [of the sense organ] is ruined, like the harmony
and the pitch of instruments when the strings are struck hard. And it is also
evident why plants never have any sensations, although they have some part
as soul and are somewhat affected by tangible objects; for they become cold
or warm. The cause of this is the fact that they have no mean [with respect   *424b*
to sensible contraries], nor any such principle which can receive the forms
of sensible objects; but they are affected by things along with the matter of
those things.

One might raise the problem whether a thing which cannot smell could
be affected in any way by odors, or whether a thing which cannot see could   *5*
be affected at all by colors; and similarly in the other cases. But since the
object of smell is odor, if anything produces a sensation of smell, it is odor;
so a thing which cannot smell is not of such a nature as to be affected by

odors (and similarly if the thing lacks any of the other senses), and if it has
a sense, it can be affected by those and only those sensible objects which
10   correspond to that sense. This is clear from the following also. That which
acts upon a body is not light or darkness or sound or odor but the [medium]
in which each of these exists; for instance, what splits the timber is the air
along with its thunderbolt.   On the other hand, tangible and flavorous
objects do act [upon bodies]; for, if not, by what would inanimate bodies be
affected or altered?   If so, will the other sensible objects, too, act [upon
15   bodies]?   Is it not the case that not every body can be affected by odor or
sound, and that those which are affected are indeterminate and do not
remain [so affected], as in the case of air? For air is odorous as if it has been
affected in some way. Then what is smelling if it is not an affection of some
kind? But smelling is also sensing, whereas air, when affected [by odor],
immediately becomes [merely] sensible.

BOOK III

1

That there is no sense other than the five already listed — those of seeing, hearing, smelling, tasting, and touching — one might be convinced by the following arguments.

Let the following assumptions be made. We do possess the sense of everything which can be sensed by touch (for all the *attributes* of tangible objects qua tangible are sensed by us through the sense of touch); and, if indeed we lack any sense, we must lack the corresponding sense organ also; and things which we sense by touching can be sensed by the sense of touch, which we happen to possess, but things which we sense through an intervening medium and not by touching can be sensed by means of simple elements (e.g., air or water) in the following manner. It is a fact that if sensible things which differ in genus can be sensed through a single medium, the possessor of the corresponding sense organ must be capable of sensing both kinds of sensible objects (e.g., this would be the case if the sense organ were made of air, and if air were the medium for sound and color); but if there are many media for the same sensible object, e.g., if color can be sensed through air and water (for both these are transparent), then the possessor of only one [sense organ, which is composed either of air or water] will still be capable of sensing the things which are sensible through either of the two media. Now each sense organ is composed of only one of the two simple elements (air or water), for the pupil is made of water, [the organ of] hearing is made of air, and [the organ of] smell is made out of one of these two; fire is either in none of the [organs] or in all of them (for no animal can sense without heat), and earth is either in none or, if at all, is blended in [the organ of] touch most of all in a special way. It would remain, then, that there can be no sense organ [which is made of something] other than water or air; and some animals do possess [organs made of air or water]. Consequently, all senses are possessed by animals which are neither incomplete nor maimed; for even the mole appears to have eyes beneath its skin. So if there is no other [kind of] body [besides the four elements] and no *attribute* other than those of these bodies, no sense could be lacking [in a complete animal].

Further, it is not possible for there to be an organ proper to the common sensibles, i.e., to motion, rest, shape, magnitude, number, and unity, which we sense indirectly by each sense; for we sense all these by motion. For instance, a magnitude is sensed by motion, and hence shape too is so sensed, for shape is a king of magnitude; rest in a thing is sensed by the absence of motion in it; and a number is sensed by the negation of continuity and by the special [senses], for each of these senses a unity. So it is clear that there can be no proper sense for any of these objects, e.g., for motion; for, if there were, we would be sensing them in a way in which we are now sensing a sweet object by vision.   But we do this [i.e., we sense a sweet object by vision] by the fact that we happen to possess a sense for each of them [sweetness and color], and in view of this fact we recognize them when they happen to be together;   or else, we would not be sensing them at all, except

25   indirectly, as in the case of Cleon's son, whom we sense not as Cleon's son but as white, for this white happens to be Cleon's son.

Now we do have a common [faculty of] sensation   of the common sensibles which senses them not indirectly, so there is no proper faculty which senses them; for otherwise   we would not be sensing them at all,

30   except in the manner in which we see Cleon's son, as it was stated before. As for the proper senses, they sense each other's objects indirectly; and it

425b   is not qua themselves, but qua one sense   when it senses simultaneously [two or more] sensibles in the same [substance], e.g., [when it senses] the bile as being bitter and yellow.   For neither one nor the other of the [proper] senses [vision, sense of taste] can state that both [the bitter object and the yellow object] are one object;   and for this reason one may be mistaken in thinking, for example, that if the object is yellow, it is bile.

5   One might inquire why we have many senses and not only one. Is it not in order that the [attributes] which accompany [the proper sensibles] and are common, e.g., motion and magnitude and number, be less likely to escape our notice? For if vision were our only sense and whiteness its [only] object, the [common sensibles] would be more likely to escape our notice and all [sensibles] would be thought to be the same thing because, for example, colors and magnitudes accompany each other. As it is, the fact that common

10   sensibles exist also in other [proper] sensibles reveals [to us] that each of the common sensibles is distinct from the others.

2

Since we sense the fact that we are seeing or hearing [or etc.], we must do so either by vision or by some other sense. Then the same sense would be sensing both vision and its object, which is color; so either there would

15   be two senses of the same object, or [vision] would be sensing itself. Further, if the sense which senses vision were different from vision, either the senses would be infinite in number or some one of those senses would be sensing itself. So we should assume that it is the first sense [i.e., vision] which senses itself.

But there is a difficulty; for if to sense by vision is to see, and if that which is seen is color or that which has color, then if a man were to see that which

20   is seeing, that which primarily sees too would have color. It is evident, then, that the expression "to sense by vision" does not have only one meaning; for, even when we do not see, it is by vision that we discriminate both

darkness and light, although not in the same manner. Further, that which sees, too, is in a certain sense colored; for each sense organ is receptive of its sensible object but without the matter of that object. It is in view of this that sensations and imaginings of those objects exist in the sense organs even 25 when those objects are gone.

Now the activity of the sensible object and the activity of the sensation [of it] are one and the same, but the essence of each of them is not the same. I mean, for example, that *actual* sound and the *actual* hearing [of it are one and the same]; for a man may have hearing [potentially] and not be [*actually*] hearing, and that which has sound [potentially] is not always sounding. But when that which can hear is *actually* hearing and that 30 which can sound is [*actually*] sounding, then *actual* hearing and [the corresponding] *actual* sounding occur simultaneously; and one might say that 426a these two are *hearing* and *sounding*, respectively. So if a motion and an action and an affection are in that which is acted upon, then both the *actual* sound and the *actual* hearing [of it] must be in that which has the power [of hearing]; for the activity of that which can act and cause motion comes 5 to be in that which is being affected. In view of this, it is not necessary for that which causes motion to be moved. Accordingly, the activity of that which can sound is sound or *sounding*, and the activity of that which can hear is hearing or *hearing*; for "hearing" has two meanings, and so does "sound". The same account may be given of the other senses and their sensible objects. For just as action and [*actual*] affection are in that which 10 is being affected and not in that which is acting, so the activity of the sensible object and of that which can sense is in that which can sense.

Now in some cases the activities have names, e.g., "*sounding*" and "*hearing*", but in others there is no name for one or the other; for the activity of vision is called "seeing", but that of the color has no name, and the activity of the sense of taste is called "*tasting*", but that of flavor has no 15 name. And since the activity of a sensible object and of the corresponding sense is one, although the essence of each of the two [activities] is different, it is necessary for hearing and sound, taken as activities, to cease to exist or to continue to exist simultaneously; and similarly with flavor and taste and the others. But if they are taken as potentialities, there is no such necessity.

The earlier natural philosophers, thinking that neither whiteness nor 20 blackness can exist without vision, nor flavor without the sense of taste, did not state the facts well; for in one sense they were right, but in another wrong. For, since each of the terms "sensation" and "sensible objects" has two meanings, they were right if the terms mean *actual* sensation and sensible object in activity, respectively, but they were wrong if the terms 25 mean potential sensation and sensible object in potency, respectively. But these thinkers were using terms which have more than one meaning without distinguishing the two meanings.

If harmony is a vocal sound, and if voice and hearing are one and the same in one sense, although not so in another, and if harmony is a formula, then hearing too must be a formula of some sort. And it is because of this fact that excessive pitch, whether high or low, destroys the sense of hearing; and similarly, excessive flavors destroy the sense of taste, extremely bright or dusky colors destroy vision, and strong odors, whether sweet or bitter, destroy the sense of smell, and these facts indicate that each of the senses is a formula. And it is in view of this, too, that sensible objects which are pure and unblended, e.g., the acid or the sweet or the salty, are pleasurable whenever they are brought into a [proper] proportion; for then they are pleasurable. In general, however, that which is a blend [or a] harmony is more [pleasurable] than a high or a low tone, and, in the case of touch, that which can be heated or cooled [is more pleasant than the hot or cold; for] each sense is a formula, and [a sensible object] in excess causes pain or destroys [the corresponding sense].

Now each sense is relative to its own sensible object, it exists in a sense organ qua such organ, and it discriminates the differences in that object; thus vision discriminates whiteness and blackness, the sense of taste discriminates sweetness and bitterness, and similarly in the other cases. But since we discriminate also between whiteness and bitterness and [in general] between a sensible object of one kind and a sensible object of another kind, by what [power] do we sense also the fact that the two sensible objects differ?

We must do so by a sense; for both objects are sensible. From this fact it is also clear that flesh cannot be the ultimate sense organ; for, if it were, it would be necessary for that which discriminates [any two sensible objects] to do so by contact [with those objects]. Nor again can we judge that sweetness is distinct from whiteness [by each of the two corresponding organs or senses] separately, but both these objects should be made known to a single [faculty]; for, otherwise, it would be as if my sensing one object and your sensing an object [of a different kind] could make it clear [to you, or to me] that the two objects are distinct from each other. Only a single [faculty], then, should assert that the two objects are distinct; for sweetness is distinct from whiteness. So it is the same [faculty] that asserts this; and just as it asserts [this distinction], so it thinks it or senses it.

It is clear, then, that it is not possible to judge separately by separate [faculties] the fact that [sensible objects of different senses are different]; and from what follows it is also clear that it is not possible to discriminate such difference at separate times. For just as it is the same [faculty] which asserts that goodness is distinct from evil, so when [that power] asserts that A differs from B it asserts also that B differs from A, and the time [when A and B are asserted to be different] is not accidental as it is, for example, if I now assert that A differs from B, but not that it now differs from B. It

asserts the difference both (a) now and (b) as being a difference now; and
so [it asserts that it is] at the same time [that A is distinct from B]. Hence
it is an inseparable [faculty that distinguishes A from B], and it [asserts that
the distinction exists] at an indivisible time.

On the other hand, [one may say that] it is impossible for the same thing,
qua undivided, to have contrary motions in an undivided time. For if [a   *30*
sensible object] is sweet, it moves the sense or thinking in one way, if it is   *427a*
bitter, it moves it in the contrary way, and if it is white, it moves it in a
[generically] different way. Then is the discriminating sense, which is indivisible numerically and inseparable, at the same time divided in essence?
In one sense, it is the divisible which senses divided objects, but in another
sense [it does so] qua indivisible; for in essence [that which senses] is divisible,   *5*
but locally and numerically [that which does this] is indivisible.

Is not this impossible? For, although the same indivisible thing may be
potentially both contraries, in essence it cannot be [these contraries]; it is
when in *actuality* that it is divisible [into these contraries]. An object, for
example, cannot be both white and black at the same time; so if the corresponding sensing or thinking is a thing such as that object, it cannot be acted
upon by the forms of these [i.e., of black and white at the same time]. But   *10*
the [discriminating sense] is like the so-called "point", which may be taken
either qua one or [qua] two; and this is the manner in which [this sense] is
divisible. So qua indivisible, the discriminating sense is one and judges
simultaneously; but qua existing as divisible, it uses the same point of
reference twice at the same time. Accordingly, insofar as it uses the limit
twice, it makes two separate judgments as if of two separate things; but
insofar as it uses it only once, it [judges it] by one [judgment] and at one
time.

Concerning the principle by means of which we speak of animals as being   *15*
capable of sensing, let the above distinctions suffice.

3

The principal differentiae by which thinkers define the soul are two, (a)
motion with respect to place and (b) thinking and discriminating and sensing. Both thinking and judging rightly are thought to be like a sort of   *20*
sensing, for [according to these thinkers] in each of these two cases the soul
discriminates something and knows things; and the ancient thinkers, too,
went as far as to assert that judging rightly and sensing are the same. Thus
Empedocles said "For thought in men increases with what is before them",
and elsewhere, "whence it befalls them ever to change their right judgments
too"; and Homer, too, had in mind the same thing when he said "such is   *25*
the nature of man's thought".[23] For all these thinkers believed that thinking,
like sensing, is corporeal, and that like is sensed or judged rightly by like,
as we explained at the beginning of this treatise.[24] But these thinkers should

427b have discussed at the same time the fact that errors occur; for errors are
more appropriate to animals, and their souls are subject to error the greater
part of their existence. So either all appearances must be true, as some
thinkers assert, or an error must be an apprehension of what is unlike, for
5 such apprehension is contrary to knowledge of like by like; but it is thought
that it is the same science that knows two contraries and the same disposition
that is erroneously disposed to those contraries.

Now it is evident that sensing and judging rightly are not the same thing;
for all animals share in the former, but only few of them in the latter.
Thinking, too, which may be right or wrong (right thinking is prudence or
10 science or true opinion, but wrong thinking is the contrary of each of these)
is not the same as sensing; for sensation of the proper sensibles is always true,
and it exists in all animals, but *thinking* may be also false, and it belongs
to no animal which has no power of reasoning. Imagination, too, differs
15 from sensation and from *thought;* but without sensation there can be no
imagination, and without imagination there can be no belief.

Evidently, thinking is not the same as believing. For this affection [i.e.,
thinking] is within our power, whenever we wish to be thinking (for we can
bring it about before our eyes, as those do who use mnemonic devices and
20 form images); but forming opinions is not up to us, for an opinion must be
either true or false. Again, whenever we are faced with the opinion that
something is dangerous or fearful, we are also affected immediately, and
we do so likewise whenever something inspires courage; but whenever we
imagine these, we are disposed towards them like spectators looking at
25 dangerous or encouraging objects in paintings. Belief itself, too, has differentiae; the species of belief are *knowledge*, [true] opinion, prudence, and the
contraries of these, but the discussion of their differences belongs to another
treatise.²ʳ As for thinking, since it differs from sensing, and since one [spe-
cies] of it is thought to be imagination and the other to be belief, we must
discuss belief after having specified what imagination is.

428a If imagination is that in virtue of which an image is formed in us, but
not something spoken of in a metaphorical way, it [may be] some power
or habit by which we discriminate, whether truly or falsely; and such are
5 [the powers or habits of] sensation, opinion, *knowledge*, and intellect.

That it is not sensation is clear from the following. Sensation is either
a faculty, like vision, or an activity, like seeing; but images may be formed
even if neither the one nor the other is present, as in sleep. Again, sensation is always present [in animals], but not imagination. And if *actual*
10 sensation were the same as imagination, the latter would exist in all the
nonrational animals; but it is thought not to exist in all of them, e.g., not in
ants or bees or worms. Again, sensations [of proper sensibles] are always true,
but most imaginations turn out to be false. Once again, when we are
sensing a sensible object accurately, we do not say, for example, that it

appears to us to be a man; we do so rather when we are not sensing the object distinctly, and it is only then [that our statement may be] true or false. Finally, as we said earlier, visual impressions appear to occur even when our eyes are closed. 15

Further, imagination is none of those [powers or habits] which are always true, such as *knowledge* or the intellect; for imagination may be also false.

It remains, then, to see if imagination is opinion; for an opinion may be true or false. But opinion is attended by conviction (for a man cannot have an opinion of objects if he is thought not to be convinced of them); and, although most nonrational animals have imagination, none of them has conviction. And, we may add, every opinion is accompanied by conviction, which follows when one has been convinced, and that which causes a man to be convinced is reason; but although some nonrational animals have imagination, none of them has reason. It is evident, then, that imagination cannot be opinion aided by sensation, nor opinion through sensation, nor yet a combination of opinion and sensation, both because of the above arguments and clearly in view of the fact that opinion is of nothing but of the object which is also sensed (and by "a combination" here I mean, for example, an imagination which is a combination of the opinion concerning the white and the sensation of the white, certainly not a combination of the opinion concerning the good and the sensation of the white). Now to appear to be is to have an opinion of that which is sensed as such but not indirectly. But one may have also false appearances of things of which he has at the same time true belief; for instance, the Sun appears to be a foot in diameter, but one may be convinced that it is greater than the inhabited world. So it turns out that, while a thing remains unchanged, (a) a man, without having forgotten or having changed his conviction, has abandoned his true opinion which he had of that thing, or else, (b) if he still has that opinion, his [opinion of that thing] is both true and false. But a [true opinion] would become false only when the thing would change to its contrary without being noticed. So imagination is neither one of these [opinion, sensation] nor a combination of them. 20 25 30 428b 5

Now (1) since it is possible, when one thing has moved, for another thing to be moved by the first, and (2) since imagination is thought to be a species of a motion, to occur not without sense but in sentient beings, and to be of objects which can be sensed, and (3) since motion can be produced by the activity of a sense and must be, if so produced, similar to a [corresponding] sensation, such motion could neither occur without sensation nor exist in beings which are not sentient; and, according to such motion, (a) the possessors of it do and are affected by many things, and (b) that motion may be true or false [of what it denotes] and occurs for the following *reasons*. 10 15

First, the sensation of proper sensible objects is true or has the least possible falsity. Second, there is the sensation of the objects of which these 20

[proper sensibles] are attributes, and in this case one may now *think* falsely; for, as to [the sensation of] the whiteness of an object, there is no falsity, but as to whether the [substance which is sensed as being] white is this thing or some other thing, there may be falsity. Third, there is the sensation of the common sensibles (e.g., of motion and of magnitude) that accompany the [substances] which are accidental to (the proper sensibles) and to which the
25 proper sensibles belong; and it is about these [the common sensibles] most of all that sensation may be mistaken.

Now the motion brought about by the activity [of sense] differs from the three kinds of sensations listed above.   The first kind is true whenever the [corresponding] sensation is present;   but the other [two] kinds, whether [the sensation is] present or absent, may be false, and especially when the sensible object is at some distance from the sentient being. Accordingly, if no thing
429a other than imagination has the things stated above,   then imagination would be a motion produced by the activity of sense. The name φαντασία (imagination), too, is derived from φάος (light); for vision is the sense in the highest degree, and without light it is not possible to see. And
5 because imaginations persist in us and are similar to the corresponding sensations, animals do many things according to them, some (i.e., nonrational animals) because they possess no intellect, and others (i.e., men) because their intellect is sometimes clouded by passion or disease or sleep.

Concerning imagination, what it is and why it exists, let the above discussion suffice.

4

10 Concerning the part of the soul with which the soul knows and judges rightly, whether it is separable with respect to magnitude or not so separable but [only] with respect to definition, we should consider what its differentia is and how thinking takes place.

If thinking is indeed like sensing, then it would either be a process of
15 being affected in some way by the object of thought or be some other thing such as this. So [the thinking part of the soul] should be incapable of being affected but capable of receiving the form [of the object of thought] and be potentially such as that [form] but not the [form] itself; and the intellect should be related to the object of thought in a manner similar to that in which a sense is related to its sensible object. And, since the intellect [can] think every [object of thought], it must exist without being blended [with something else] in order that, as Anaxagoras says, "it may rule", that is, in
20 order that it may know. For, if it appears along [with some other thing], the [latter will] prevent or obstruct [the knowledge of] another kind [of thing]; hence it is necessary for [the intellect] to be of no nature other than that of [mere] potentiality. So the part of the soul which is called "intellect" (by "intellect" I mean that [part] by which the soul [can] *think* and believe) is

actually none of the things prior to thinking. In view of this, it is not even
reasonable that it should be blended with the body, for it might then acquire   *25*
some quality, e.g., coldness or heat, or there might be even an organ [for
it], as there is for the sentient power; but, as it is, there is no [such organ].
So those who say that the soul is a place of forms speak well, except that it
is not the whole soul but only the thinking part of it, and that [that part]
is not actually but potentially the forms [of things].

It is evident from the sense organs and the corresponding sensations that   *30*
the impassivity of the sentient [soul] is not similar to that of the thinking
[soul]. For a sense loses its power of sensing immediately after [it is acted   *429b*
upon by] a very strong sensible object, e.g., it cannot hear sound immediately after very loud sounds, it cannot see immediately after very bright colors,
and it cannot smell immediately after very strong odors. The intellect, on
the other hand, immediately after having thought a very highly intelligible
object, can think objects which are less intelligible not less but even more;
for the sentient soul cannot exist without a body, whereas the intellect is   *5*
separable.   And whenever the intellect becomes each particular [intelligi-
ble object] in the sense in which we speak of a scientist when he is *actually*
a scientist (and this occurs when a scientist can exercise [his *knowledge*] by
himself), even then it exists somehow potentially and in a similar manner,
although not in a manner like that prior to having learned or discovered [the
object it knows];   and it is [only] then that it is capable of thinking of itself.

Since there is a difference between magnitude   and the essence of a   *10*
magnitude, between water   and the essence of water, and so too in many
other cases, but not in all (for in some cases [a thing and its essence] are the
same), the [soul] discriminates flesh and the essence of flesh either by
different [powers] or [by the same power] but differently disposed towards
them;   for flesh   exists not without matter   but as *this* snubness in *this*
[nose]. Accordingly, it is by the sentient power that the [soul] discriminates   *15*
the hot and the cold and the things whose formula is flesh; but it is by a
different power, one which is either separate   or related to it as a bent line
when straightened out to the bent line itself,   that the soul discriminates
the essence of flesh. Again, of things which exist by abstraction, the straight
is like the snub, for it exists with that which is continuous; but its essence,
if it is different from the straight, [is discriminated] by a [power] different   *20*
[from that which discriminates the straight]. For let [that essence] of the
straight be duality. Then [the soul discriminates duality] by a different
[power] or else by the same [power which discriminates the straight] but
when this power is differently disposed. In general, then, as [certain] things
are separable from matter, so are those concerning the intellect.

One might raise this question: if the intellect is simple and not capable
of being affected and has nothing in common with anything else, as Anaxagoras says, how will it think, if thinking is a species of being acted upon?   *25*

For it is thought that it is insofar as two things have something in common that one of them acts and the other is acted upon. Again, [one may raise the problem] whether the intellect itself, too, is intelligible. For, if the intellect is intelligible not with respect to something else and if what is intelligible is one in kind, then either it will belong to the other things [also] or it will be blended with something which makes the intellect intelligible as it does the other things.

30   But we stated earlier²⁶ when we distinguished the [two] senses of "to be acted upon in virtue of something common" that the intellect, prior to thinking, is in a certain way potentially the intelligible objects but is none of them actually; and it should [be regarded potentially] as [being] in a
430a tablet which has no actual writing. This is indeed the case with the intellect. Moreover, the intellect itself is intelligible like the [other] intelligible objects. For, in the case of objects without matter, that which thinks and that which is being thought are the same, for theoretical *knowledge* and
5   its *knowable* object are the same; and as for the *reason* why [the intellect] does not think always, this matter should be examined.²⁷ But in the case of objects which have matter, each of them is potentially intelligible. Consequently, intellect will not belong to the latter objects (for it is a potentiality of such things but without [their] matter); but it will belong to an intelligible object.

5

10   Since in each genus of things there is something, e.g., matter, as in every case of [things by] nature (and matter is that which is potentially each of these things), and also something else which, by producing those things, is the cause and is capable of acting, as in the case of art in relation to its material, these different [principles] must belong to the soul also. And one
15   [principle] is an intellect of the sort that can become all things, but the other is such that, like a sort of disposition, it can make all things, as in the case of light; for in a certain sense light, too, makes potential colors be *actual* colors. And the latter intellect is separable and cannot be affected by or be blended with anything, and in *substance* it exists as an *actuality;* for that which acts is always more honorable than that which is acted upon, and the principle [of a thing which has matter is always more honorable] than the matter [of that thing].
20   *Actual knowledge* is the same as the thing [*known*]; potential *knowledge,* however, is prior in time [to *actual knowledge*] in an [individual], but, as a whole, it is not [prior] in time. But the [active intellect] is not at one time thinking and at another not thinking. When separated [from the body], it is *as such* just that [i.e., intellect], and only this [part of the soul] is immortal and eternal. But we do not remember in view of the fact that, although this [part of the soul] cannot be affected, the intellect which can be affected
25   is destructible, and without it [it] cannot think.

6

The thinking of indivisibles is among things concerning which there can be no falsity; but objects to which truth or falsity may belong are combinations of concepts already formed, like unities of things, and as Empedocles said: "where sprang into being many neckless heads", which were then put together by *Friendship*. These separate [concepts], too, are combined in the same way, as in the case of "incommensurability" and "the diagonal [of a square]". If [thinking] is of past or future objects, it includes also time in the combination. Now falsity exists always in a composite; and even if one [says] "the white is not-white", he has combined "not-white" [with "the white"]. One may, however, state every composite as being a division also. At any rate, truth or falsity belongs not only, for example, to the [thought] "Cleon is white", but also to "Cleon was white" and "Cleon will be white". As for that which produces a unity [of concepts] in each case, it is the intellect.

Since things may be indivisible in two ways, potentially or *actually*, nothing prevents [the intellect] from thinking the indivisible when, for example, it thinks a length; for [a length] is *actually* indivisible and [is thought] in an indivisible time, since time is divisible or indivisible in a way similar to that in which a length is. Accordingly, it is not possible to state in each half of that time what [part of the length] it is thinking; for if [the length] is not divided, it does not exist [*actually* as many], but only potential-ly. But if [the intellect] thinks each half [of the length] separately, then it divides the time [along with the length] also; and in this case [the two parts] are as it were [two *actual*] lengths. And if [the intellect thinks the length] as being composed of two parts, then [it does this], too, in the time taken [to so think] the two parts. As for the indivisible not in quantity but in kind, the intellect thinks it in an indivisible time and by an indivisible [thought or act] of the soul. But [it does so] indirectly, not insofar as these (i.e., the object thought and the time taken) are divisible, but insofar as they are indivisible; for in these, too, there is something indivisible which, being perhaps not separable, makes each of them (e.g., the length [thought] and the time [taken]) one. And this exists similarly in everything continuous, whether this be time or length. As for a point or any division or whatever is indivisible in this manner, it comes to be known just as a privation is known; and similarly for others [of this sort]. For instance, how does one know evil or black? In a sense, he knows each by its contrary. But that which [so] knows [each of these] should exist potentially and should be included in that [i.e., in its contrary]. If, however, there is among causes a thing in which there can be no contrary, then [this thing] knows itself and exists in *actuality* and is separate.

An assertion, like an affirmation, is of something about something else, and in every case it is [either] true or false. But the intellect is not in every

30

430b

5

10

15

20

25

case [of this sort]. If it is of whatness with respect to essence, it is [always]
true, and it is not [a thought of] something about something else; and just
30   as seeing a proper [sensible] is [always] true, whereas [believing] that the
white thing seen is a man (or is not a man) is not always true, so it is with
things which are without matter.

7

431a   *Actual Knowledge* is the same as the object [of *knowledge*]; potential
knowledge, however, is prior in time in any single [individual], but, as a
whole, it is not [prior] in time, for all things which come into existence do
so from things which exist actually.
5   Now it is evident that the sensible object causes the faculty of sensation
when existing potentially to become *actual;* for [this faculty] is neither
affected nor altered. In view of this, [its *actuality*] is a different kind of
motion; for, as stated elsewhere,[28] motion [in the usual sense] is the *actuality*
of that which is incomplete, but the *actuality* of what is complete, being
unqualified, is distinct [from such motion]. Accordingly, sensing is like
mere naming or [mere] conceiving; but whenever [the sensible object] is
10   pleasant or painful, [the soul], as if affirming or denying, pursues or avoids;
and to be pleased or pained [for the soul] is to be in activity with the sentient
mean towards the good or the bad, respectively, qua such; and *actual*
aversion and *actual* desire are, respectively, just that. And the parts [of the
soul] which can desire and can avoid are not different from each other or
from the sentient part, except in essence.
15   Images are to the *thinking* soul like sense impressions. But when the
[*thinking* soul] affirms or denies them as good or bad, it pursues or avoids,
respectively, and for this reason the soul never thinks without images; [they
are] like the air which affects the eye in a certain way, while the eye in turn
[affects] something else, and similarly in the case of hearing. And the last
20   thing [to be affected] is a single thing and a single mean, but it is many in
essence.
We have stated earlier[29] what it is that judges the difference between the
sweet and the hot; here, too, let us discuss this matter as follows. There is
a single [*thinking* faculty which judges], and [it exists] in a manner like a
boundary. And the [images of the sweet and the hot], too, being one by
analogy and numerically, are to each other as the others [the sensations of
the white and the black] are to each other. For what is the difference
between asking how [the soul] discriminates things not   in the same genus
25   and how it discriminates contraries, such as [the sensation of] whiteness and
the [sensation of] blackness. So let C and D be related to each other as A,
[the sensation of] whiteness, and B, [the sensation of] blackness, are related
to each other. Then, by alternation, it follows that [A:C :: B:D]. Now if
C and D are to belong to a single [subject], then this subject, like the subject

to which A and B belong, will be one and the same numerically but not in essence. The same may be said if A were to be sweet and B were to be white.   *431b*

The thinking part, then, thinks the forms in the images;   and just as what is to be pursued and what is to be avoided [when sensible objects are present] is determined for it   by the corresponding [sensations], so it is moved when images are before it and there is no sensation. For example, sensing a beacon   5 as being fire, it knows by the common faculty of sensation that the enemy is approaching when it sees the beacon in motion.   At other times, it forms judgments and deliberates about future objects relative to present objects by means of images or thoughts   as if it were seeing these objects; and whenever it asserts that [certain objects imagined] are pleasurable or pain- ful, it pursues or avoids [those objects] as it does when it senses objects;   and   10 it does so in *actions* in general.

Objects which are outside of the sphere of *action,* too, i.e., the true and the false, come under the same genus, namely, that of good and evil; they differ, however, [by being good or evil] either without qualification or in a qualified way.

As for the so-called "objects by abstraction",   the [thinking faculty] thinks them as if it were thinking of the snub-nosed;   for in thinking of the snub-nosed qua snub-nosed, it does so not as something separated [from matter], but in thinking it qua concave, if it were to *actually* so think it, it would think it apart from the flesh in which concavity is present.   So   15 whenever the [thinking faculty] is thinking [physical objects], it thinks the mathematical objects [in them] as if they were separate objects, although they are inseparable [from physical objects or from physical matter].

In general, then, the intellect when in *actuality* is the objects   which it thinks. But whether the intellect, which is not separate from magnitude, can or cannot think any separate object is a matter to be considered later.

8

We may now sum up the main points concerning the soul under one   20 heading and state once more that the soul is all things, but in a certain sense; for things are either sensible or intelligible, and in a certain sense, *knowl- edge* is the objects *known* while sensation is the sensible objects. We should inquire, then, in what sense this is the case.

Knowledge and sensation may be so marked off as to correspond to things; and if [*knowledge* and sensation] exist potentially, [they correspond]   25 to things existing potentially, but if actually, to things existing actually. The *knowing* and sentient [powers] of the soul are potentially these things, namely, the *knowable* and sensible objects, respectively; and they must either be those things themselves or [their] forms. Certainly, they cannot be the things themselves; for it is not the stone [itself] which is in the soul but the form of the stone. The soul, then, is like the arm of a man; for just   *432a* as the arm is an instrument of instruments, so the intellect is a form of forms and the faculty of sensation is a form of sensible objects.

Now since, as it is thought, no thing exists apart from sensible magni-
5   tudes, then intelligible objects, both those which are said to exist by abstraction and the dispositions and *attributes* of sensible objects, [must] exist in
the forms of sensible objects. And it is because of this that (a) no one can
ever learn or *understand* anything without sensing anything, and that (b),
when speculating, one must do so along with an image; for images are like
10 sense impressions, except that they are without matter. Imagination, however, is different from assertion and from denial; for truth or falsity is a
combination of concepts. In what way, then, will the primary concepts
differ from images? Surely neither they nor the other [kinds of thoughts] are
images, although they cannot exist without images.

9

15 The soul of animals has been defined by two powers, (A) that of discriminating, whose function is *thought* and sensation, and also (B) that of
causing motion with respect to place. The power of sensation and the
intellect have been sufficiently specified by the above discussions. Let us
now consider what it is in the soul that causes motion, whether it is some
20 one part of the soul and is separable, in magnitude or in definition, or the
whole soul; and if it is a part, whether it is some special part distinct from
the ones usually discussed or those enumerated, or some one of these.

An immediate problem may be raised here as to the manner in which we
should speak of parts of the soul and the number of such parts, for in some
sense there appear to be an indefinite number of them and not only (1) the
25 estimative part and the parts concerned with temper and *desire*, as some
thinkers[30] specify, or (2) the part which has reason and the irrational part,
as other thinkers specify; for, according to the differentiae by means of
which these thinkers separate these parts, there will appear also other parts,
already mentioned, which are much further apart from each other than
these. For instance, such will be: (a) the nutritive part, which belongs to
30 plants as well as to all animals; also (b) the sentient part, which one could
not easily posit as being nonrational or as having reason; again, (c) the
432b imaginative part, which is distinct in essence from all the other parts but
presents much difficulty as to whether it is the same as or distinct from any
of them, if one were to posit separate parts of the soul; lastly, (d) the
appetitive part, which would be thought to be distinct from all the others
5   both in definition and in what it can do. It is indeed absurd, too, to tear the
last-mentioned part away from the other parts, for wish occurs in the
estimative part, and both *desire* and temper come under the nonrational
part; and if the soul is [divided into] three parts [as in (1)], there will be
desire in each of those parts.

Returning to the subject concerning which our present discussion arose, let us inquire what it is that causes an animal to move from one place to another. Now one would think that growth and deterioration, which are motions belonging to all [living things], are caused by the reproductive and nutritive parts, which exist in all [those things]; and as for inhaling and exhaling and sleep and waking, they will be examined later,[31] for these too present considerable difficulty. As for the part concerned with locomotion, let us consider what the mover is which causes an animal to travel.

Clearly, it cannot be the nutritive power. For this motion occurs always for the sake of something and is accompanied either by imagination or by desire; for, if not forced, no animal moves [with respect to place] unless it desires or avoids something. Besides, plants too would be capable of causing [loco] motion and so would have organic parts to bring about such motion.

Similarly, it cannot be the sentient part [of the soul]; for there are many [kinds of] animals which have the faculty of sensation but are stationary and motionless till the end of their lives. So since nature does nothing in vain and leaves out nothing which is necessary [for an end], except in cases of defect or incompleteness, such [i.e., the stationary] animals are complete and not defective, as confirmed by the fact that they can reproduce and reach maturity and deteriorate, and so they would have possessed also organic parts for travelling.

Nor again can that mover be the estimative part or the part which is called "intellect". For the speculative part does not think of anything which is to be *acted* upon and does not assert anything about what should be avoided or pursued, whereas [loco] motion exists in that which avoids or pursues something; and when this part speculates about a matter [to be *acted* upon], even then it does not directly bid avoidance or pursuit. For instance, many times it *thinks* of something fearful or pleasurable, but it does not bid us to be afraid; it is the heart which is moved [if the object is fearful], or some other part if the object is pleasurable.

Again, [a man] is not [necessarily] moved even if the intellect gives the order and *thought* asserts that something should be avoided or pursued, as in the case of the incontinent man who *acts* according to *desire*. And, in general, we observe that the possessor of medical science does not [necessarily] cure, and this shows that the authoritative [moving principle] which causes action in accordance with *knowledge* is some other [part of the soul] and not the part which has *knowledge*.

Finally, desire too is not the authoritative [principle] which produces this kind of motion; for continent men have desires and *desire* certain things, but they follow the intellect and do not *act* to attain the objects of their desire.

10

There appear, then, to be at least two [possible] movers here, desire and
10   the intellect, provided that one were to posit imagination as being a kind
of thinking. For many [*actions*] which are against *knowledge* follow imagination; and in the other animals there is neither thinking nor judgment, but
[only] imagination. So both of these — intellect and desire — [appear to]
have the power of causing locomotion.

Now the intellect [meant here] is that which judges for the sake of
15   something and is practical; and it differs from the speculative intellect with
respect to the end in view. Every desire, too, is for the sake of something;
for it is for the object of desire which is the starting-point of the practical
intellect, and the last [step reached by the practical intellect] is the beginning of *action*. So it is with good reason that these two — desire and
practical *thought* — appear to be the moving causes; for what causes motion
20   is the appetitive [soul], and it is through this that *thought* causes motion,
for the starting-point of [this] *thought* is the appetitive [soul]. Imagination,
too, when it causes motion, does so not without desire. One thing which
causes motion, then, is the appetitive [soul]; for if there were two, the
intellect and desire, they would cause motion according to some common
form. As it is, the intellect does not appear to cause motion without desire;
for wish is a [species of] desire, and whenever a man is moved according
25   to judgment, he is moved according to wish also. But desire [may] cause
motion in violation of judgment [also]; for *desire* is a [species of] desire.

Now the intellect [is] in every case right; but desire or imagination [may
be] right and [may be] wrong. In view of these facts, what always causes
motion is the object of desire; but this object may be either the good or
the apparent good, although not every [kind] but that which is practicable,
30   and what is practicable may exist now in one way and now in another. It
is evident, then, that the power of the soul which causes [loco]motion is that
which is called "desire".

433b   As for those who distinguish the parts of the soul, if they are to distinguish
them or separate them according to powers, a great many parts will arise:
the nutritive, the sentient, the thinking, the deliberative, and also the appetitive part; for these differ from one another more than the *desiring* part does
from the part concerned with temper.

5   Now since desires may arise which are contrary to each other, and this
takes place whenever reason and *desire* are contrary to each other and
arise in [animals which] have a sense of time (for the intellect bids us to
resist for the sake of the future but *desire* [bids us to pursue] for the sake
of the present, and what is pleasurable now may appear to be pleasurable
10   without qualification and good without qualification because one may not
look to the future), there can be [only] one mover in kind, the appetitive
[part] qua appetitive, while the first mover in all cases is the object of desire

(for this causes motion by being thought or imagined and is not in motion), but numerically [there can be] many movers.

Now in motion there are three things [which may be distinguished]: (1) the mover, (2) that by which it moves, and (3) that which is moved; and a mover may be either (a) that which is immovable, or (b) that which causes 15 motion but is also moved. The immovable mover here is the practicable good, the mover which is also moved is the appetitive part (for that which is in motion is moved qua desiring, and its [kind of] motion is a species of desire taken as an activity), and that which is in motion [only] is the animal. The instrument with which desire causes motion is at this point corporeal; and, for this reason, its study comes under the treatise which 20 investigates the functions common to body and soul. [32] At present, we may briefly say that the mover which causes motion instrumentally lies where a beginning and an end coincide, as in a ball-and-socket joint; for here the convex and concave sides [coincide], the one being an end and the other a beginning. For this reason, one of them is at rest but the other is in motion; and they are different in definition but not separate in magnitude, for all 25 things are moved by being pushed or pulled. Thus, something should remain fixed, as in a [rotating] wheel, and it is from this thing that motion should begin.

In general, then, as already stated, an animal causes its own motion qua being appetitive, and it cannot be appetitive without imagination. Now imagination may be either with judgment or [merely] sentient; and [not only 30 man but] all the other animals partake of sentient imagination.

11

We must consider also what the mover is in imperfect animals, [i.e.,] those 434a which have only the sense of touch, [and] whether imagination and *desire* can belong to them or not. Now it appears that they can be pained or pleased; and, if so, they must also have *desire*. But how can imagination be in them? Must we not say that, just as their motions are indefinite, so these 5 [*desire* and imagination] exist in them but in an indefinite way?

Sentient imagination, as we have stated, exists in all other animals also, but deliberative imagination exists [only] in animals which use reason in practical matters. For, in the latter case, whether one will *act* in this or that manner is a function of judgment; and a man must make the measurement by a single [principle], for he pursues the greater [good]. Consequently, one must be able to produce a unity out of many images. And this is the *reason* 10 why it is thought that [sense imagination] has no opinion, seeing that it does not have [the power] to connect [images], whereas [opinion] includes imagination. In view of this, desire does not have the power to deliberate. Now sometimes desire [i.e., *desire*] overpowers and displaces wish, and this happens whenever incontinence prevails; at other times, however, it is the

[wish] that does this to [*desire*]. Thus each [kind of] desire [overpowers and displaces] in turn the other, as one sphere [does to another]). By its nature,
15 however, the higher [desire, i.e., the wish] is always the higher principle, and it prevails [over the lower, i.e., over *desire*]; hence there arise three kinds of locomotion. As for the [part of the soul] that *knows*, it is not moved but remains still. So since one belief or statement is universal but the other is of a particular (for the former [merely] asserts that such a kind of man should do such a kind of thing, whereas the latter asserts that this thing before me is of such a kind and I am such a kind of man), it is the latter
20 opinion which causes the motion and not the universal; or else, it is both, but the universal is rather at rest whereas the other is not.

12

Now everything which is living and has a soul from the time it is generated till it is destroyed must, as such, possess the nutritive soul, for that which is generated must grow and reach maturity and deteriorate, and these are impossible without food; so it is necessary for the nutritive power
25 to exist in everything which grows and deteriorates. But it is not necessary for the power of sensation to exist in all living things. For a thing whose body is simple cannot have the sense of touch, and an animal cannot exist without
30 this sense; and things incapable of receiving forms without matter cannot [have this sense].
    Animals, on the other hand, must have a sense, if nature does nothing in vain; for all things existing by nature are for the sake of something, or else they will be coincidences of [things which are] for the sake of something. Accordingly, if every body which can travel from one place to another did
434b not have a power of sensing, it would be destroyed and would not attain its end, which is [its] nature's function. For how will it be nourished? Stationary [living things] take nourishment from the source at which they have grown; but a body which is not stationary and has been generated with a soul or an intellect capable of judgment cannot [be nourished] without the
5 faculty of sensation. (As for [a body] which is ungenerable, it cannot have [the power of sensation]. For, why should it have it? [Perhaps because it would be] better for its body or for its soul. But, as it is, this cannot be the case; for neither will its [soul] think any more [by having sensation], nor will its body, [being ungenerable], exist more because of [sensation]). No [generable] body which is not stationary, then, can have a soul without the power of sensation.
    Further, if a thing has the power of sensation, it must be either simple
10 or a blend. It cannot be simple; for then it will not have the sense of touch, which is necessary [for sensation]. This is clear from the following. Since an animal is an animate body and every body is tangible, and since a tangible body is sensible by the sense of touch, the body of an animal must

be capable of sensing by touch [other bodies] if the animal is to save itself.
For the other senses (i.e., sense of smell, vision, sense of hearing) are sensing   15
[their objects] through other [external media], whereas if [the body of an
animal] touches an object but has no power of sensing it, it will not be able
to avoid some tangible objects and accept others, and in such a case the
animal cannot save itself. It is in view of this, too, that tasting is a sort of
touching, for it is of food, and food is a tangible body; but sounds and colors   20
and odors do not nourish [the body of an animal], nor do they make it grow
or deteriorate. So the sense of taste too must be a species of touch, because
it is a sense of tangible and nourishing objects. Accordingly, these two senses
[of touch and of taste] are necessary for an animal, and it is evident that no
animal can exist without the sense of touch.

   As for the other senses, they exist also for the sake of living well,   and,
we may add, they must exist not in any chance species of animals but in   25
certain species, i.e., those which can travel from place to place. For if these
are to save themselves, they should sense not only objects which they can
touch but also objects at a distance;   and sensation of objects at a distance
is possible if sensation through an intervening medium can take place when
that medium is acted upon by the sensible object and the sense is acted upon
by that medium. For just as the mover of an object in locomotion acts till   30
the change is made (as when A pushes B and causes it to push C and so a
motion through an intermediate object is produced, in which case the first
mover pushes without being pushed, the last object C is pushed without
pushing another, but the intermediate object B both pushes and is pushed,
and [there may be] many intermediates), so it is in the case of alteration,   435a
except that the [mover] causes alteration while remaining in the same
place.   Thus, if one were to dip an object into wax, motion would occur just
so far as the object is dipped; [if one tries to dip the object into] a stone, there
will be no motion at all; [if in water], the water will be moved far [beyond
the object dipped]; [and if in air], the air will be moved the furthest and will   5
both act and be acted upon, if it remains unified.   It is in view of this that
in reflection, too, instead of saying that vision proceeds [i.e., travels] from
the eye out and is reflected, it is better to say that the air is acted upon by
the shape and color [of the object seen], while remaining unified as far as
it proceeds. Now the air remains unified after [striking] a smooth surface,
and so upon returning it moves one's vision;   and this is as if   the impression in the wax had penetrated through to the other side [of the wax].   10

13

   It is evident, then, that the body of an animal cannot be simple; I mean,
for instance, that it cannot be made of fire alone or of air alone. For, without
the sense of touch, an animal cannot have any other sense since, as already
stated,[33] every animate body [of an animal] has a sense of touch. Now the

15 other elements, with the exception of earth, might become sense organs, but
    each of them produces sensation through something else, an intervening
    medium; but the sense of touch [produces sensation] by the direct touching
    [of its objects], and it is in view of this that it has [received] its name. And
    although the other organs, too, sense by touch, they do so through something
    else; but only the sense of touch is thought to sense [its objects] through
20 itself. Consequently, no body of an animal is made of [only one of] those
    other elements [fire, air, water].

    Nor can such body be made of earth [alone]. For the sense of touch is
    like a mean between all tangible objects, and its organ can receive not only
    all the differentiae of earth, but also those of hot and cold and the other
25 tangible objects. So it is because of this that we cannot sense by our bones
435b or hair or such parts of the body, for these are made of earth; and it is
    because of this that plants, too, have no sense, for they are made of earth,
    and without the sense of touch no other sense can exist.

    The organ of touch, then, is not made of earth [alone] or of any other
 5 single element. Hence it is evident that animals which are deprived of this
    one sense must die; for neither a thing which is not an animal can have this
    sense, nor is it necessary for an animal, which must have this sense, to have
    any of the other senses. It is because of this fact, too, that the excesses of
    the other sensible objects, e.g., of colors and sounds and odors, destroy only
10 the corresponding sense organs and not the animal, except indirectly, e.g.,
    when an [excessive] sound is accompanied by a thrust or a blow, or when
    [excessive] odors or objects of sight set other things in motion which in turn
    destroy the sense of touch. Flavors, too, destroy the sense of touch in this
    manner, i.e., insofar as they happen to act excessively as objects of touch.
    But the excesses of tangible objects [qua tangible], e.g., of hot or cold or hard
15 objects, destroy the animal; for the excess of every sensible object destroys
    the corresponding sense organ, and so such object of touch too destroys the
    sense of touch, in virtue of which living [for an animal] is defined, since it
    was shown that an animal cannot exist without the sense of touch. It is in
    view of this that the excess of tangible objects destroys not only the organ
    of touch but also the animal, since [the sense of touch] is the only sense which
    an animal must have [if it is to live].

20 An animal possesses the senses other than that of touch not for the sake
    of existing but for the sake of living well, as already stated.[34] For instance,
    it has vision so that it may see [objects at a distance], for [it lives] in air or
    water or, in general, in a transparent medium; it has the sense of taste
    because of what is pleasant or painful to taste, so that it may sense [the
    pleasant] in food, *desire* it, and move itself [towards it]; but it has the sense
    of hearing, so that it may be informed [by others through sound]; and it has
25 a tongue, so that it may convey information to others.

HISTORY OF ANIMALS

CONTENTS

HISTORY OF ANIMALS

BOOK I

1

486a5   Some parts of animals are incomposite, that is, those which are divisible into homogeneous parts, like flesh, which is divisible into flesh; others are composite, that is, those which are divisible into nonhomogeneous parts, like a hand, which is not divisible into hands, nor a face into faces.

Some parts such as the above are called not only "parts" but also "limbs,"
10   and such parts are those which, although being wholes, have in themselves parts which are distinct from each other, like a head, a leg, a hand, a whole arm, and a chest; for each of these parts is [in itself] a whole and also has parts which are distinct from each other. All nonhomogeneous [parts], however, are composed of homogeneous parts; e.g., a hand is composed of flesh, sinews, and bones.

15   Of animals, some are such that the parts of one member are the same [in kind] as the corresponding parts of the other members; others are such that the corresponding parts are not the same. In the case of men, the corresponding parts which are the same in kind are their noses and eyes, and also their flesh and bones, and the same applies to horses or to any group of
20   animals which are called "the same in species"; for, in each group, one whole member is to another whole member as each part of the first is to the corresponding part of the second. Other animals, although the same, differ with respect to excess and defect, and such are those which are of the same genus; and by "genus" I mean, for example, that of birds, or that of fish, for in each of these groups there is a differentiation with respect to genus into
25   many species, i.e., those of fish and those of birds.

Almost all the parts within each genus of animals, however, differ (a), by
486b5   having contrary attributes or differing in degree within the same contrariety, e.g., they differ in color or in shape, or (b), by differing with

respect to number or magnitude, and, in general, with respect to excess and
defect. For some have soft but others hard flesh, some have a long bill but   *10*
others a short one, and some have many but others few feathers. But there
are even further distinctions in their parts, for some have spurs but others
not, and some have crests but others not. But, one may say, most [animals]
and the parts which make up their bulk either are the same or differ within   *15*
a contrariety and with respect to excess or defect, for one might posit the
more and the less in quality as coming under excess and defect,
respectively.

Some animals have parts which neither have the same form nor differ
with respect to excess and defect but are the same by analogy; e.g., the bone
is analogous to the backbone of a fish, and so is the nail to the hoof, and the   *20*
hand to the claw, and the scale of fish to the feather; for feathers are to a
bird as scales are to a fish.

The parts which various animals have, then, are either the same [in form
or by analogy] or different, but they may differ also in position; for many
animals have the same parts but these are not located in the same way. For   *25*
example, some have their teats in the breast but others near the thighs.   *487a*

Of homogeneous [parts], some are soft and moist, others are dry and solid.
Those which are moist either remain so in general or only so long as they
perform their natural function; e.g., blood, serum, fat, suet, marrow, sperm,
gall, milk in animals which have it, flesh, and other parts analogous to these,   *5*
and also, but in a different way, excretions, e.g., phlegm and the contents
of the intestines and the bladder. Parts which are dry and solid are such as
sinews, skin, veins, hair, bones, cartilage, nails, horns (a term equivocally
used for the whole in virtue of the shape and for a part of it), and such other
parts which are analogous to these.   *10*

Animals differ also with respect to their ways of life and *actions* and
character, as well as their parts. Concerning these differences we shall first
speak sketchily but later we shall speak of each genus in greater depth.

Differences with respect to ways of life and character and *actions* are   *15*
such as the following. Some animals are aquatic and others are terrestrial.
Of the aquatic, some live and feed in water, take in and give out water, and
cannot live unless they are in water, as in the case of most fish. Others feed
and spend their time in water but breathe air and not water, and they bring   *20*
forth their offspring out of water; and many such animals walk also on land,
e.g., the otter, the beaver, the crocodile, others have wings, e.g., the diver
and the grebe, and others are without feet, e.g., the water snake. Some
animals get their food in water and cannot live outside the water, but they   *25*
do not take in water or air, e.g., the sea-nettle and the oyster. Of water
animals, some live in the sea, some in rivers, some in lakes, and some in
marshes, e.g., the frog and the water-newt.

30   Of land animals, some take in and give out air, also called "inhaling" and "exhaling," e.g., man and all land animals which have lungs; others do not take in air but live and get their food on land, e.g., the wasp, the bee, and the other insects. I call "insects" all those which have nicks on their bodies, either on their bellies or on both their bellies and backs.

387b   Of land animals, many, as already stated, get their food from the water. But of water animals in the sea not one gets its food from land.

Some animals live first in water and then change into another shape and
5   live out of water, e.g., the larva of the gadfly, which later becomes a gadfly. Again, some animals are stationary, others travel from place to place. Stationary animals live in water, but no land animals are stationary.

Of animals in water many by nature adhere to other objects, e.g., many kinds of shellfish. We may add that the sponge, too, is thought to have some
10   sort of sensation; and a sign of this is the fact that, as it is said, it is rather difficult to detach it unless the motion to do so is stealthily made. Other [water animals] attach themselves to other objects but also detach themselves from them, e.g., the genus of the so-called "sea-nettle"; for some of them detach themselves at night to seek food. Other [water animals] are
15   unattached but motionless, e.g., oysters and the so-called "holothuria." Other [water animals] swim, e.g., fishes and mollusks and also crustacea, like the crawfish. Others walk, e.g., the genus of crabs; for these are water animals but move by walking.

Of land animals some have wings, e.g., birds and bees, and these differ
20   from each other in their manner of flying; others are terrestrial [i.e., travel on land]. Of those which are terrestrial some walk, some crawl, and some wriggle. But, unlike the fish which can only swim, no animal can move only by flying; for even leather-winged animals walk — the bat has feet, and the
25   seal has imperfect feet. Some birds, too, have useless feet, and because of this they are called "footless"; and these birds, small in size, are well-supplied with wings. Practically all the birds which are similar to these have excellent wings and useless feet, e.g., the swallow and the [sickle-like] drepanis; for all of them resemble each other in their habits and plummage, and in appearance they differ very little. The so-called "footless" bird is seen at all
30   seasons; but the drepanis only after the rains in the summer, for it is during this time that it is seen and captured, but usually this bird is hardly seen. There are many animals which walk as well as swim.

Other differences among animals with respect to their ways of life and
488a   actions are such as the following. Some of them are gregarious, some are solitary, whether terrestrial or winged or those which swim, and some play both roles; and of those which are gregarious and pastoral, some associate with each other but others are scattered here and there. Gregarious animals
5   among birds are such as pigeons, cranes, and swans (none of those which have crooked talons are gregarious), those among water animals are many

kinds of fish, e.g., the so-called "migrants," "tunny-fish," "pelanys" and "bonitoes." Men play both roles: [they are gregarious or pastoral]. By "associating with each other" I mean those which work together for a common end — a thing which not all gregarious animals do. Social animals are such as men, bees, wasps, ants, and cranes; and some of these come *10* under leadership but others associate without leadership. Thus cranes and the genus of bees come under a leader, but ants and a great many other animals associate without a leader.

Again, some gregarious and some solitary animals stay in the same locality, others of these roam from one place to another. And some are *15* carnivorous, others herbivorous, others omnivorous. And some eat a particular kind of food, e.g., the genus of bees and that of spiders; for the bees use honey and certain other sweets, the spiders live by catching flies, and certain others live on fish. And some get their food by hunting; others *20* by storing it up, while others do not.

Again, some use dwellings, others do not; some of the first kind are moles, mice, ants, and bees, some of the second kind are many kinds of insects and quadrupeds. Further, some live underground, e.g., lizards and snakes, others on the ground, e.g., horses and dogs. And some make holes for *25* themselves, others do not. And some are nocturnal, e.g., owls and bats, others live in daylight.

Again, some are tame, others are wild; and some are always tame, others are always wild. Thus men and mules are always tame, but leopards and wolves are always wild. And some can be tamed quickly, e.g., elephants. And those kinds which are tamed exist also in a wild state, e.g., horses, oxen, *30* sheep, goats, and dogs.

Again, some make sounds, others do not; and still others make vocal sounds; and of the latter some make articulate sounds, others do not. And some twitter but others are silent; and some are musical but others are not. What is common to all of them is that they sing or chatter most in *488b* connection with intercourse.

Again, some live in the fields, e.g., the ringdove, some on the mountains, e.g., the hoopoe, and some near men, e.g., the pigeon.

Again, some are lustful, e.g., the partridge and the cock along with its kind, while others have a tendency to chastity, e.g., the genus of crows, for *5* the latter rarely have intercourse.

Of sea animals, some live in open seas, some near shores, and some among rocks.

Again, some are combative but others guard themselves; by "combative" I mean those which are aggressive or retaliate when treated unjustly, and by *10* "guarding themselves" I mean those which have the means of evading attack.

With respect to character, animals differ as follows. Some are good-tempered, lacking spirit, and not given to retaliate, e.g., the ox; others
15 are hot-tempered, tending to retaliate, and unteachable, e.g., the wild boar; others are prudent and timid, e.g., the stag and the hare; others are mean and treacherous, e.g., the snake; others are free-spirited and brave and highbred, e.g., the lion; others are thorough-bred, wild, and treacherous, e.g., the wolf. By "highbred" I mean coming from good stock, and by
20 "thoroughbred" I mean not departing from its own [specific] nature."

Again, some are unscrupulous and malevolent, e.g., the fox; and others are spirited, affectionate, and disposed to fawn, e.g., the dog; others are good-tempered and easy to tame, e.g., the elephant; others are bashful and tend to guard themselves, e.g., the goose; others are envious and fond of elegance, e.g., the peacock.
25 Of all animals, man alone has the ability to deliberate. Many animals participate in memory and are capable of instruction, but none but man can recall the past.

A more accurate account concerning the character and way of life of each genus of animals will be given later.

BOOK VIII

1

We have discussed, then, the other [i.e., material] nature and the manner of generation of animals. Their *actions* and ways of life differ with respect to their character and their diet.

Now in most animals [other than men] there are traces of psychical traits
20 whose differences are more evident in man. For, just as the parts of other animals have similarities to the parts of man, as we stated earlier, so the psychical traits in most animals resemble such traits in man as tameness and ferocity, good temper and harshness, bravery and cowardice, fear and courage, and temper and unscrupulousness and, with respect to thinking,
25 good intelligence. For, with respect to some of these, some animals differ from man in degree, and, with respect to others, man likewise differs from many animals in degree (for some of the above traits exist in men to a higher

degree, others exist in animals to a higher degree), but, with respect to still others, the difference is one of analogy; for just as art and wisdom and intelligence exist in men, so [by analogy] certain natural powers exist in 30 some animals. Such a situation becomes most evident at the stage of childhood; for in children one may see the traces and seeds of what will at a later stage be habits, since the soul of children at that stage hardly differs, 588b so to say, from the soul of brutes. Hence there is nothing unreasonable in saying that some traits are the same in men and in some other animals, others are close, and others are analogous. Thus nature proceeds from inanimate things to animals in small stages, so that, in the continuity of 5 things, the boundary between two stages and the right placement of a stage between two others escape us.

Now the first genus of things after the inanimate objects is the genus of plants, and plants differ from each other in that some are thought to partake of life to a greater degree than others; and the whole genus of plants appears to be animate relative to the other [i.e., inanimate] bodies but inanimate 10 relative to the genus of animals. As we just now stated, the transition from plants to animals is continuous. One would indeed find it difficult to say whether certain [living things] in the sea are animals or plants; for they are by nature attached to other things, and many of them perish if they are separated from those things; thus the pinna is so attached, and the razor shell 15 cannot survive if it is detached. In general, the entire genus of testaceans resemble plants more than they resemble animals which move from place to place.

As for sensation, some [living things] give no indication that they have it, others do but feebly. The nature of the body of some of them is fleshlike, as in the so-called "tethya" [i.e., ascidians] and the genus of acalephae; but 20 the sponge is in every way like a plant. Thus in the scale of living things there is a sequence in which those at each stage always appear to have more life and motion than those at the preceding stage.

The same applies to the *actions* in life. For the function of a plant which comes from seed appears to be no other than to reproduce another thing like 25 itself, and, similarly, some animals have no other function. And it is indeed for this reason that such *actions* are common to all [living things]. But if living things have also sensation, their ways of life now differ because of the pleasure in intercourse and their ways of bringing forth their offspring and 30 of rearing them. Some [animals], just like plants, simply give birth to their own kind at definite seasons; others also seek food for their young, and when they have accomplished this, their young take off and the association comes 589a to an end; others which are more intelligent and have memory go even further and keep their association with their offspring. One part of the life [of these animals], then, takes the form of *actions* in procreation, another takes the form of *actions* in getting food; for these two forms constitute the 5 whole concern and way of life [of these animals]. The [kinds of] food taken differ with respect to the [kinds of] materials out of which [these animals] are made. For growth of each kind of animal occurs according to the nature of the materials out of which these animals consist. That which occurs according to the nature [of each animal] is pleasant; and each [kind of animal] pursues that which is pleasant according to its own nature.

PARTS OF ANIMALS

CONTENTS

BOOK I

Chapter

ON PARTS OF ANIMALS

BOOK I

1

639a   In every investigation or systematic inquiry, whether of the humbler or the nobler sort, the knowledge which may be acquired of the subject appears to be of two sorts: one is properly called "scientific knowledge" and
5   the other is a sort of educated judgment. In a way, it is a mark of an educated man to be able to judge successfully what is well stated and what is badly stated by a speaker. Indeed, we think that a man is completely educated if he is of this sort [about all subjects] and that a man has received a well-rounded education if he is able to do this. But we consider this man
10   to be unique in his ability to judge almost all subjects, whereas a man may be limited in his judgment only to things of one nature; for there may be a man who is so disposed only to a part of a whole.

It is clear, then, that in the inquiry concerning nature there should be certain rules by reference to which one shall be able to display good judgment concerning things presented to him, regardless of whether the
15   statements made are true or false. I mean, for example, the problem whether one should begin (a) with the *substance* of each [species under a genus], e.g., with the nature of man, a lion, an ox, or the like, taking each separately, and then proceed with what follows, or rather (b) with what is common to them [i.e., with the *substance* of their genus] and then proceed to the attributes which are common [to all the species under that genus].
20   Now there are many attributes, such as sleep, respiration, growth, decay, and death, and, in addition, other such affections and dispositions not yet clear or definite to be stated at present, which are common to many genera of animals which differ from each other. But it is evident that, if we consider each species of animals separately, we shall often be repeating the
25   same discussion; for example, each of the attributes listed above belongs to horses and to dogs and to men, so if one were to discuss each species separately, he would necessarily repeat the same things when he comes to
30   each of the common attributes. Perhaps some of those attributes, although
639b   called [univocally] by the same name, have further specific differences for

different species, as in the case of animal locomotion, which does not appear
to be one in species; for flying, swimming, walking, and creeping are called
"travelling" but differ specifically from each other. For this reason, one
should not overlook how the investigation should proceed, that is, whether
he should start first with the generic attributes and then proceed to the   5
specific, or rather start immediately with those of each species. We have at
present said nothing specific about this matter, nor yet about another matter
which requires the following consideration: whether the investigator of
nature should, like the mathematicians who give proof of astronomical
objects, start first with the observed attributes belonging to each species of
animals separately and to their parts, and then proceed to state the why,   10
i.e., their causes, or follow some other method. Moreover, since there
are many causes of generation in nature, e.g., a final cause and also a
moving cause, we should specify which of these is by nature first and which
is second. It appears that the one called "that for the sake of which" comes
first; for this is the reason, and the reason is the starting-point alike in works 15
of art and in things which have been composed by nature. For once a
physician has defined health and a housebuilder a house, whether by
thought or by sensation, they go on to make statements and give causes of
each of the things they do and also the *reasons* why the things should be
done in a certain manner. Now the final cause and the noble exist in the   20
works of nature more than in the works of art; but that which is a necessary
condition, to which almost all thinkers try to refer to [causes] of things
without distinguishing the number of meanings of the term "necessity,"
does not exist alike in things which exist according to nature. For things
which exist of necessity without qualification belong to eternal things,
whereas things which exist of necessity by hypothesis, like things of art, as 25
in the case of a house and the like, belong also to all things which are
generated [by nature]. Thus such-and-such matter [as a material cause] will
of necessity preexist, *if* a house or some other such end is to come to be; and
such-and-such generation or motion should be completed first, and after this
something else, and in the same way each of the others in succession should
come to be or exist until the end and final cause is reached. The same applies 30
also to things which are generated by nature.

But the manner of demonstration and of necessity in physics is not the   *640a*
same as that in the [other] theoretical sciences, and this has been discussed
elsewhere.[1] For the starting-point in [those theoretical sciences] is that which
exists, while in [physics] it is that which will be. Thus, if A, e.g., health or
a man, is such-and-such, it is necessary for something else, say B, to exist or   5
to have been generated; but if B exists or has been generated, it is not
necessary for A to exist or to come to be. It is not possible to associate the
necessity of the latter demonstration to that of what is eternal, so as to say:
if B exists, also A exists. These matters, too, have been specified elsewhere,

and also the kinds of things in which A and B are convertible and the *reason* for the convertibility.

10 Another matter which should not be neglected but discussed, as the earlier thinkers have done, is in what way each thing comes to be generated by nature rather than in what way it exists; for the difference between these two ways is not small. It seems that we should start, as we have stated earlier,
15 first by grasping the phenomena concerning each genus of things, then discuss the causes [of those things], and finally proceed with the generation [of those things]; for this turns out to be the case (even more so) in the construction of a house. For if such is the form of a house (or if a house is [defined as] such-and-such), then it is constructed in such [sequence]. For a generation occurs for the sake of the *substance* [i.e., the form of the thing generated], but the *substance* of that thing does not exist for the sake of its
20 generation. For this reason, Empedocles was wrong when he said that many things exist in animals because it was an accident that their generation was such, e.g., the backbone is so divided into vertebrae because it happened to break by contortion during the development. But he was not aware (a) that the seed, when formed, should exist in such a way as to have such-and-such a power of developing, and (b) that the parent who produced the seed was
25 prior in existence [with a similar backbone] and in definition; for it is man that begets man, and so it is because the begetter has such a form that the thing begotten happens to have the same kind of form. Similar remarks apply to things which are thought to be generated by chance, too, as in works of art also; for some things which come to be by art do so also by
30 chance, as in the case of health. The mover which produces works of art, of course, is similar to and exists before the work of art, and such is the art of a sculptor; for, here, a statue is not produced by chance. Art in this case is the formula of the work of art which may be produced and it exists [in the artist] without matter. But [some] things produced by art may result in a similar manner also by chance; for they are produced as they would be by art [as in the case of health].

For the above reasons, the best way of stating the case is to say: since such is the essence [i.e., the form] of man, 1(a) he must have such [parts] because
35 of that essence, for he cannot exist without those parts, or what is very close to this, namely, 1(b) it is altogether impossible for him to exist in any other
640b way, or at least to exist well as a man. Then the existence of those parts will follow. Further, since such is the case, (2) it is necessary for the generation of man to develop in such-and-such a manner, and in view of this, such a part develops first, then such other part, and so on. And, similarly, all other things which are composed by nature are generated in the same manner.
5 Now the ancients, who were the first to philosophize about nature, considered the material principle and attended only to this kind of cause.

They inquired what this principle is, what kind of thing it is, how the whole
of a thing is generated from this and by what mover, e.g., whether by *Strife*
or *Friendship* or *Intelligence* or accident, assuming that the underlying
matter must have such a nature, e.g., that of necessity fire is hot but earth   10
is cold, and that the former is light but the latter is heavy. For this is the
manner in which they regarded the universe, too, as having been
constructed. They spoke of animals and plants, too, in a similar manner. For
instance, they said that the belly and the other receptacles of food or of
excretions were formed by the current of the water in the body; that the   15
rush of the air from the body caused the formation of the nostrils; that air
and water are the materials of bodies; and that, according to all of them,
nature consists of such bodies.

But if men and animals and their parts exist by nature, [these thinkers]
should have spoken about flesh and bones and blood and all homogeneous
bodies, and similarly about nonhomogeneous bodies, e.g., face and hand and   20
foot, both insofar as each of them is a thing of a certain kind and also with
respect to its power [or function]. For it is not enough to consider [only] the
materials out of which each is formed, e.g., out of fire or out of earth, just
as, if we are to speak of a bed or of some other such thing, we should try to
describe its form rather than its matter, e.g., rather than [say that it consists   25
of] bronze or wood, or else, we should include the *composite* [of form and
matter], for a bed is this [form] in that [matter] or this [matter] with that
[form]; so we should speak also of its form and the manner in which it is
constructed, for its nature with respect to *shape* is more important than its
nature with respect to matter.

Now if each animal and each of its parts were to exist by virtue of its   30
shape and its color, what Democritus says would be right, and such appears
to be his belief. At any rate, he says that it is clear to everyone that a man
is a thing such as his *shape*, seeing that he is recognized by his shape and his
color. But the *form* of a dead man, too, has the same shape, and yet a dead   35
man is not a man. Again, [what appears to be a hand] is not a hand regardless
of its disposition; e.g., a bronze or wooden hand is not a hand, unless the   641a
term "hand" is equivocally used, just as a physician in a drawing or a flute
made of marble is not a physician or a flute, respectively; for such a hand
cannot perform its function, just as such a flute or a physician cannot
perform the function proper to a [real] flute or physician, respectively.
Similarly, no part of a dead man, such as what one might call "an eye" or
"a hand," can perform the function of what is really an eye or a hand,   5
respectively. These thinkers, then, spoke without making any qualifications,
and in the same way in which a carver might call a wooden hand "a
hand."

The natural philosophers, too, spoke in the same way when they discussed

generations of things and the causes of shapes. But by what powers were
these things and shapes fashioned? Perhaps a carpenter will say by the axe
10   or by the auger, whereas a natural philosopher, by air or by earth, and in
this case, the carpenter's answer will be better than that of the natural
philosopher; yet to say even such a thing, e.g., that the surface was made
concave here and plane there by such a stroke of the tool here and such
there, is not enough. But if he were to say that he himself did [with his tool]
so-and-so here and so-and-so there so as to produce such a *form* and for a
15   certain purpose, he would be giving the [full] cause. It is clear, then, that
those natural philosophers did not speak rightly; and in speaking of such an
animal, and of a [hand], one should state what it is and what kind of thing
it is, just as one speaks of the form of a bed, and similarly with each of the
parts [of an animal]. If indeed this [i.e., an animal] is its soul or a part of the
soul or something which includes the soul (at any rate, when the soul
20   departs, what is left is no longer an animal and no part of the animal remains
the same, except in shape only, like the animals which turned into stone in
the fable), it would be the function of the physicist to discuss and understand
the soul, or if not the whole soul, then that part with respect to which an
animal is of such-and-such a kind, and also what the soul or a part of [an
25   animal] is, and likewise for the attributes which belong to such a substance.
This is especially so since the term "nature" has two meanings, one of them
being matter and the other *substance* [i.e., form or essence]. And this
substance functions also as a moving cause and as a final cause; and such a
part of the animal is either the whole soul or a part of the soul. So from this
30   point of view, too, he who investigates nature should discuss the soul [of an
animal] more than the matter, and to the extent that that matter is a nature
existing for the sake of the soul and not conversely. In fact, wood too is a bed
or a tripod, but only potentially.

Keeping in mind what has been said, one might raise the problem
whether the function of physics is to discuss the whole soul or a part of that
35   soul. If it be the whole soul, there would be no philosophy other than natural
science. For the intellect [which is a part of the soul] is an intelligible object,
641b   and so knowledge of physics would include all things. For it belongs to the
same science to investigate both the intellect and its intelligible object, if
indeed the discussion of these two, which are correlatives, as in every case
of correlatives, would come under the same [scientific] investigation (as in
that of sensation and sensible objects). Or else, not every soul or part of the
5   soul is a source of motion, but the principle of growth is the same as that in
plants, the source of alteration is the sentient part [as in animals], whereas
the source of locomotion is a distinct part and not the thinking part, for
although locomotion exists in the other animals, *thought* exists in no animal
[except man]. Clearly, then, we should not discuss the whole soul; for not

every part of the soul is a nature but only some, whether one or more than 10
one. Again, no objects reached by abstraction [i.e., no mathematical objects]
come under theoretical physics [i.e., science of nature], for nature [as form
and source of motion] does everything for a purpose; for it appears that, just
as in works of art the [source and cause of motion] is art, so in the [natural]
things themselves there is a kind of source and cause [of motion] such as heat
and cold which comes to us from the universe. For this reason, it is probable 15
that the heavens, more than the mortal animals, were originated by such a
cause, if they were originated; for, at any rate, order and definiteness
appear in heavenly objects much more than in us, whereas change and luck 20
exist rather in mortal things. Yet some thinkers say that every animal was
generated and exists by nature, but that the heavens, in which nothing
appears to be by chance or in disorder, were formed by luck or by chance.
But, whenever there appears to be some end towards which motion, if not
obstructed, is directed and finally terminates, we say that *this* is [always and 25
definitely] for the sake of *that*. So there appears to be such a thing which
we call "nature." For indeed it is not from any chance seed that a certain
kind of living thing is generated, nor any chance seed from a certain kind
of living thing. Each kind of seed, then, is a principle which develops into
a definite kind of living thing; for it exists by [a certain kind of form] as a 30
nature, or, at any rate, it develops from it. Moreover, that from which the
seed comes is prior [as a mover, as form, and as final cause] to the seed itself;
for the seed is the starting-point of a generation, whereas its end [or
perfection] is the substance [generated]. But there is something prior [in
existence] to both the seed and that into which the seed develops, and that
is [the perfect living substance] from which the seed comes. For a seed may
be viewed in two ways: (a) from its [source], and (b) from what it finally
becomes; for it is a seed from where it came, e.g., from a horse, and a seed 35
from which something else, e.g., a mule [or a horse] will develop, so it is a
seed related to a horse and a mule [or another horse] not in the same way,
but as stated. Further, the seed exists as potentiality [for something], and we 642a
already know how potentiality is related to actuality.

There are, then, two causes: final cause and necessity; for many things
occur by being necessary [for other things as ends]. Perhaps one may ask:
what kind of necessity is this necessity, when we speak of it here? For it
can be neither of the two kinds which are specified in our treatise on 5
Philosophy.[2] There is, however, a third kind in things which are generated;
for we say that food is a necessary thing, not in either of the first two ways,
but in view of the fact that [a living thing] cannot exist without this
[necessary] thing. This kind of necessity is like the hypothetical necessity, as
in the following: since an axe is made to cut wood, it is necessary that it be 10
hard; if so, it is necessary that it be made of bronze or iron. Similarly, since

a [living] body is an organ (for each of its parts exists for a certain purpose, and so does the whole body), it is necessary that it be of such a kind and composed of such parts, if it is to fulfill its purpose.

It is clear, then, that there are two ways in which causes exist, that those
15 who speak of causes [in things by nature] should, in the first place, take into account causes in both ways, or if not, at least try to do so, and that those who fail to mention them say nothing about nature; for nature [as final cause or form] is more of a principle than matter. In fact, even Empedocles, guided by truth itself, happens to hit upon this fact in some of his passages and finds it necessary to speak of the *substance* or nature [of certain things]
20 as being their ratio, e.g., when he is giving an account of what bone is; for he says that it is not one or two or three or all [four] of its elements but a [certain] ratio of their blend. Clearly, then, flesh too exists in the same manner, and so do each of the other parts [of a living thing].

25 The *reason* why our early predecessors did not come upon [the two causes mentioned above] is the fact that they were not aware of the essence of things or of the definition of their *substance*. The first who touched upon [this cause] was Democritus, not regarding it as necessary in the investigation of nature but yielding to it by the facts themselves; but in the time of Socrates, the concern for this cause increased, and, although the
30 inquiry into nature came to an end, philosophers turned their attention to the instrumental [i.e., practical] virtues and to political science.

To take an example, the method of showing [the two causes] is as follows: breathing exists for the sake of, say, [living], and breathing occurs necessarily because of, say, A. Now "necessary" sometimes means that, if the final cause, [living], is to come to be, then such things are necessarily so-and-so; but sometimes it means that things are so-and-so and by nature.
35 For it is necessary for the hot to be breathed out and, when it resists, for an inflow of air to be breathed in again; and these are now necessary [for
642b living]; but the alternation of inhaling and exhaling of air when the hot air within resists the cold air outside is a necessity of the other kind.

We have stated above, then, the way in which our *inquiry* should proceed and how the causes of the things under investigation should be understood.

2

5   To arrive at [a definition of] each thing, some thinkers use a bipartition [i.e., a division of a genus into only two differentiae]. But this method is sometimes not easy, at other times impossible. For in some cases there will be only one differentia but the rest of the parts superfluous, as in (a) "footed,

cloven-footed, two-footed" and (b) "footless." The main differentia in (a) is "two-footed," while the parts "footed" and "cloven-footed" are superfluous, otherwise, the same part, "footed," will necessarily be repeated many times. Further, one ought not to break up a genus, e.g., of birds, in   *10* such a way that some come under water animals but others under some other genus, as is done in published dichotomies. In this dichotomy into similars the name "bird" appears, in another, the name "fish"; but other   *15* genera are not named, e.g., those of sanguineous and bloodless animals for no name for each of these two genera appears in the dichotomy. So if indeed animals under one genus ought not to be broken as stated, a dichotomous division would be useless, since it divides and breaks up a genus; for some many-footed animals would come under terrestrial but others under water animals.   *20*

3

   Again, a dichotomy must introduce a privative term [as one of the two differentiae], and those who divide by a dichotomy do use such a term. But a privation qua privation has no differentiae, for it is nonbeing, and nonbeing can have no species under it. For instance, there are differentiae of "footed" and also of "winged," but not of "without feet" or of "without wings." But a differentia which is universal must have particular species   *25* under it, for, if not, why would it be universal and not particular? Now there exist universal differentiae, and they have species. Of "winged," for instance, one species is "unsplit" and the other is "split," and of "footed," one species is "many cleft," another is "two cleft," as in animals which are cloven-hoofed, a third is "uncleft" or "undivided," like animals with solid   *30* hoofs. Now it is difficult even to use such differentiae, e.g., "winged" and "without wings," so as to include each [kind] of animals under only one of the resulting species (ants, glowworms, and some other animals, for instance, fall under both "winged animals" and "wingless animals"); and it is most difficult or impossible to do so under "bloodless animals." For each   *35* differentia [of the dichotomy] must include only some animals [of a certain kind], and so must its opposite differentia. So if the *substance* of animals   *643a* which differ in kind could not come under one and indivisible species·but will have distinct differentiae, like that of birds and men (for two-footedness is distinct in each of them, [but men are wingless while birds are winged]), and if both are sanguineous, their blood will differ also, or else blood will not be a part of the *substance* [of men or of birds]. If such were the case,   *5* then, one differentia would belong to both. Clearly, then, it is impossible under these conditions for a privation to be a differentia.

Now the differentiae will be equal in number to the indivisible kinds of animals, if indeed animals are indivisible and the [ultimate] differentiae are indivisible and if no differentia is common to more than one kind of animal.
10   So if no differentia can exist which is both common and also indivisible, it is clear that many kinds of animals would come under a differentia which is common. Then if the differentia under which each kind of animal falls is proper, no differentia can be common [to more than one kind of animal], otherwise different kinds would come under the same differentia. Hence, neither should the same indivisible [kind of animal] fall under different
15   differentiae, nor different indivisible kinds fall under the same [indivisible differentia], and every kind of animal should fall under some one differentia. Accordingly, it is evident that it is not possible to place the various indivisible kinds of animals, or the kinds of things of any other genus, under differentiae by the use of bifurcate division. Indeed, those [Plato and followers] who advocated [a bifurcate division into differentiae] themselves [say] that the number of ultimate differentiae must be equal to
20   the number of all indivisible kinds of animals. But if the first differentiae of a given genus were "white" [and "black"] and the differentiae of each of these also two, and so on until the [last and] indivisible differentiae [are reached], all the last differentiae would be 4 or 2^n, where n is greater than 2, and such would be the number of [indivisible] species.
25   Now a differentia is a form in a [certain] matter, for no part of an animal exists without matter, nor does it exist only as matter; for it is not a body of any kind that is an animal, as we stated many times, and the same applies to a part of an animal's body. Further, a subdivision [of a genus] should be made by means of elements in the *substance* of a thing and not by means of essential attributes [which can be demonstrated to belong to it]. For example, in subdividing a [plane rectilinear] figure, one should not use "equality of its angles to two right angles" and "equality of its angles to
30   more than two right angles" as differentiae, for the equality to two right angles is an attribute of a triangle.
Again, a subdivision should be made in terms of opposites [e.g., contraries within a genus], for the [resulting species] are opposed to each other in virtue of such opposites; e.g., in terms of whiteness and blackness in the case of color and in terms of straightness and curvature in the case of lines. Accordingly, if a genus has different species, the differentiae should be two opposites and not a color as one of the differentiae and travel by swimming
35   as the other. Moreover, living things [should not be subdivided] in terms of
643b functions common to the body and soul, e.g., in terms of travel by land and by flying (just mentioned); for in some kinds of animals both such differences exist, e.g., some ants [have wings and] fly but others are wingless [and travel by land]. Nor, again, should animals be subdivided into those

which are wild and those which are tame; for one might think that a subdivision of the same [ultimate] species is made. For, one may say, every species which has tame members happens to have also wild members, as in 5 the species of men, horses, oxen, dogs in India, pigs, goats, and sheep; for if the members of each of these are equivocally called by one name, a further subdivision would have been made, but if each of those groups is one [i.e., indivisible] in species, then wildness and tameness cannot be differentiae [of its species]. In general, this must occur if any such differentiation [into species] is made by a single subdivision. We should try, however, to use as 10 genera of animals those names which most men have usually used who described them [for example], as "the genus of birds," "the genus of fish" [etc.], each of which is defined by many differentiae and not by a single dichotomy. The method of dichotomy either fails altogether, since the same species will fall under many subdivisions and contrary [species] will fall 15 under the same subdivision), or else there will be either only one simple differentia or a combination of differentiae. And if a subdivision is made not with respect to a differentia, the definition formed will necessarily have unity by [mere] juxtaposition [and will not be a unity of matter and form], and the sequence of dichotomies will in the same way lead to a definition by such juxtaposition. This happens, for example, to those who bifurcate 20 [animals] into winged and wingless, and then bifurcate the winged into tame and wild or into white and black; for neither tameness nor whiteness is a differentia of wingedness [qua wingedness] but each is a differentia of another [differentia as a] starting-point and both are [merely] accidents of wingedness. For this reason we should divide from the start each differentia into many differentiae, as we said; for [certain] privations may become differentiae even by a division made in this manner but not by a 25 dichotomy.

The impossibility of reaching [the definition of] each of the [last] species by dichotomous division of a genus, as some think, becomes evident also from the following.

It is impossible for every species of a subdivision to have a single differentia, whether this differentia be simple or composite. (By "simple" 30 I mean one taken without other differentiae, like "cloven-footed"; by "composite" I mean one taken along with other [differentiae], e.g., "many-toed-cloven-footed" along with "cloven-footed." For, starting with a genus, it is such successive divisions into differentiae which tend to make a composite differentia be a unified whole [i.e., tend to signify a species as a unity]. Linguistically, however, only the last differentia is thought to be 35 *the* differentia [of the species], e.g., only "many-toed-cloven-footed" or "biped," for "footed" and "many-footed" are superfluous). But clearly, *644a* many such [differentiae] are impossible; for, when one proceeds [by dichotomy], one arrives at an ultimate but not at the last [differentia] and [the essence of] the species. In the case of man, the differentia by division

5   is either "cleft-footed" or, if taken along with the [prior differentiae], the composite which includes also "footed" and "biped." Now if man were only a cleft-footed [animal], this ["cleft-footed"] alone would be its differentia. But since this is not the case, [man's] differentiae must be many, and these cannot come under a single division. At any rate, it is not [always] possible for the same [species] to be [reached] by a single dichotomy, since one [of the two differentiae of that dichotomy, being a privation and so incapable of

10   further differentiae, 642b21-2,] is an ultimate differentia [but not the last differentia of a species].

It is impossible, then, to reach [all the differentiae of] each species by dichotomous divisions.

4

One may raise the question of why men did not use as a higher genus a

15   name to include under it both aquatic and winged animals; for there are some *attributes* common to these as there are to the other animals also. Nevertheless, they were right in specifying by names the animals as they did. Animals which differ with respect to excess or in degree are brought under a single genus, but those which differ by being analogous are brought under separate genera. I mean, for example, that birds of one kind differ

20   from birds of another in degree or with respect to excess (some have long wings, others have short wings), but fish differ from birds with respect to analogy (feathers are to birds as scales are to fish); so it is not easy to bring all [animals under one genus], for the majority of animals are the same by analogy.

Since the *substances* of things are their ultimate species, and since things

25   under an ultimate species do not differ in kind (e.g., Socrates and Coriscus are the same in species or kind), one must either first discuss the things which belong universally to all animals, or else repeat the same thing [for things which belong to all animals] many times, as we have said;[3] for what is universal is common, and by "a universal" we mean that which belongs to many.

There is a difficulty, however, as to what kinds of things one should undertake to discuss. For insofar as that which is indivisible in species is the

30   *substance* [of a group of things], it would be best, if one could, to investigate separately the things coming under each of the indivisible [i.e., ultimate] species, as in that of men, and in the genus of birds, which has many [ultimate] species, to proceed in the same way with each of those species,

e.g., the ostrich, or the crane, or any other such. On the other hand, insofar as one would be repeating the same things about an *attribute* because it belongs to many [species], such repetition would be rather absurd and [needlessly] lengthy. So perhaps it is right (a) to discuss those things which are common to a genus of animals (e.g., to birds or fish or some other unnamed genus with species like those of birds and fish), which are well specified by men, and which have one common nature and belong to species which do not differ from each other much, but (b) to discuss individually things which are not common as in (a) and belong, for example, [only] to men [e.g., thinking and the intellect] or to any other such [species].

Almost every genus is marked out by the shape of the parts of the body or of the whole body of each of its members, if these are similar, as in the case of the birds, the fishes, the cephalopoda, and the testacea. For the parts of the members of each of these genera differ, not by being similar by analogy, as bone of a man differs from the spine of fish, but rather with respect to their bodily *attributes*, such as size, softness or hardness, smoothness or roughness, and the like, or, in general, with respect to degree.

We have stated, then, the manner in which we should accept from others the *inquiry* into nature, the way in which the investigation of animals would best proceed, and, with regard to the division [of the subject], the possible way which one should use to grasp the [whole] subject, and the *reason* why the method of dichotomy is in one sense impossible and in another empty. With these matters established, let us proceed to the following and make a fresh start.

5

Of substances which are composed by nature, some are ungenerable and indestructible throughout eternity, while others partake of generation and destruction. The former are honorable and divine but less subject to investigation by man (for there is very little evidence from sensation which we can use to make inquiries about those things which we aspire to understand); but concerning plants and animals, which are destructible, there is much more information to use for knowledge because they are all around us. For one may learn many things about each of these two genera [the indestructible and the destructible] provided one wishes to exert oneself sufficiently. Each of them holds its own delight.

Now the knowledge we may attain of the former substances [i.e., the eternal], even if it be but little, is still, because of its value, more pleasant than all other knowledge of the things around us, just as, with people in love,

35   getting a glimpse of any small part of their beloved is more pleasant than
645a   seeing with accuracy many other things, however great. On the other hand,
        the knowledge of terrestrial things exceeds that of divine substances because
        of its greater accuracy and scope, and it balances the philosophy of divine
        objects if we add as a *reason* the nearness of the things known and their
5   relevance to our life. Having already treated the divine objects to the extent
        that they appear to us, we now proceed to discuss the nature of animals,
        without leaving out, as far as possible, any of them, whether honorable or
        not. For even in the case of those which do not delight our senses,
        nevertheless the nature which designed them gives inconceivable pleasures
10   to those of us who are by nature philosophers and are able to gain theoretical
        knowledge of causes. Indeed, it would be strange and contrary to reason if
        we enjoy beholding representations of them by attending to the artistic skill
        of the painter or the sculptor but show no more love for beholding the
15   natural formation of those animals, at least when we are able to perceive the
        causes of that formation. For this reason, we should show no childish dislike
        for the investigation of the humbler animals, for there is something
        marvellous in all natural objects. And, just as Heraclitus is reported to have
        said to strangers who wished to meet him but, seeing him warming himself
20   by the furnace, hesitated to enter (he bade them not to be afraid to enter,
        saying "there are gods even in this kitchen), so one should approach the
        inquiry into every kind of animal without trepidation, seeing that there is
        something natural and noble in each one of them. Indeed, things which are
        formed not by chance but for the sake of something exist in the works of
25   nature most of all, and the end for whose sake a thing is formed or came to
        be has the rank of nobility.

        Now if anyone regards the investigation of the other animals as being
        unworthy, he ought to show the same regard for the investigation of himself
        also; for one cannot witness without much dislike the [material] parts of
30   which man consists, e.g., blood, flesh, bones, veins, and others of this sort.
        Similarly, when one is discussing any [material] part or implement, he
        should be expected (a) not to mention only its material, and (b) to regard the
        object of the discussion as being not the materials but the whole *form*, e.g.,
        not bricks or clay or wood but the house, and, in a discussion about nature,
35   not those [parts] which sometimes exist apart from a [material] substance but
        the *composite* or the whole substance.
645b   First, then, one should distinguish the attributes of each genus, [i.e.,] those
        which are essential to all animals, and afterwards try to state their causes.
        Now as we·stated earlier,[4] there are many things which are common to
5   many animals, some of them being common without qualification, e.g.,
        feet, wings, scales, and also *attributes* in the same way but others being
        common by analogy. By "analogy" I mean, for example, that some animals
        have lungs, others have no lungs but something else which corresponds to

lungs; and some animals have blood, others have no blood but something
which is analogous to blood and has the same function as blood. To discuss   *10*
each of the [common things] separately for each [species of animals] when
treating all that belongs [to a species] would be, as we stated earlier, to say
the same thing many times; for many things which are the same belong to
many animals. Enough, then, of things [common to many animals].

Since every instrument exists for the sake of something else and every   *15*
part of the body of an animal has a purpose, which is some *action*, it is
evident that the composite body of an animal is formed for the sake of some
full *action*. For sawing was not made for the sake of the saw but the saw for
the sake of sawing; for sawing is a certain kind of use of the saw. So the body
of an animal, too, is somehow formed for the sake of the soul, and each part   *20*
of that body has a function for which it has been formed by nature.

First, then, we should discuss (a) the *actions* which are common to all
animals, (b) those which are common to each genus of animals, and (c) those
which are common to each species. By "common to all" I mean those which
belong to all animals; by "common to each genus," those whose differences
between them are observed to be in degree, as in the genus of birds; and by   *25*
"common to each species," as in the case of the species of men, every *action*
whose definition, universally taken, admits of no differentiae. *Actions* of the
type (a) are common by analogy, those of type (b) are common generically,
and those of type (c) are common specifically. Now things for the sake of
which *actions* are performed clearly vary in the same way in which
corresponding *actions* do; and, similarly, *actions* which happen to be prior   *30*
to and ends of other *actions* [vary] in the same way in which the [material]
parts which perform the latter *actions* do. Thirdly, things whose existence
necessitates the existence of other things belonging to them [vary in the
same manner in which the latter things do, and conversely]. By "affections"
and *"actions"* I mean reproduction, growth, copulation, waking, sleeping,
travelling, and all other such attributes which belong to animals; and by   *35*
"parts" I mean nose, eye, the whole face, and each of those things which are
called "limbs." Similarly with all other things.   *646a*

Concerning the manner of our *inquiry*, then, let the above discussion
suffice. As for the causes, let us try to discuss both those which are common
and those which are proper, beginning first, as we have specified, with what
is primary [by nature].

GENERATION OF ANIMALS

CONTENTS

BOOK I

Chapter

GENERATION OF ANIMALS

BOOK I

1

We have now discussed the other parts of animals, both with respect to what is common to all of them and separately what is proper to each genus, and the manner in which each part exists on account of such a cause — I mean the final cause. For there are four causes: (1) the final cause, (2) the formula of the *substance* (and those two should be assumed as being practically one), (3) the cause as matter, and (4) the principle of motion [or mover]. We have discussed the other three causes (for both the formula [of the *substance*] and the final cause as an end are the same, and the parts of animals are their matter, those of the whole animal are nonhomogeneous, those of each of the nonhomogeneous are homogeneous, and those of each of the latter are the so-called "elements of bodies").

It remains now to speak of (a) the parts which contribute to the generation of animals and of which nothing definite has been stated before, and of (b) the nature of the moving cause. The inquiry into this cause is in some way the same as that into the generation of each [animal]; and it is for this reason that the two inquiries are brought together last and are so arranged that the inquiry into the parts of animals is followed by the inquiry into the principle of the generation of animals.

Some animals come into being from the union of male and female, that is, among those genera of animals in which both male and female exist, for such generation occurs not in all genera. It occurs in all but few of the blooded animals which mature into male and female; it occurs also among those bloodless animals which have both sexes and so give birth to offspring of the same species, but other bloodless animals give birth to offspring which are not of the same species, and such are those which are generated not by the union of male and female but from decayed earth and excretions. To

speak in general of animals which possess locomotion, whether by
swimming or flying or using their bodies on land, in some of them the entire
genus has both male and female, not only in those which are blooded, but
also in some which are bloodless; and in the [latter], this applies to the whole   *30*
genus in some cases, e.g., to all cephalopoda and crustacea, but in other cases   *715b*
to most of the genus, e.g., to most insects. Of these, those which come to be
by the union of animals of the same genus give birth to offpsring of the same
genus also. Those, however, which come to be not from animals but from
decayed matter do in fact generate, but the offspring are of another genus   *5*
and are neither male nor female, and such are some of the insects; and this
happens with good reason. For if those which are generated not by animals
were themselves to give birth to offspring by uniting, then the offspring, if
(1) of the same kind, should have come from parents whose birth occurred   *10*
by the same principle [i.e., union of male and female]. We maintain that this
is a reasonable axiom to posit; for this is what happens with the other
animals. But if (2) the offspring are unlike [not of the same genus] and are
capable of uniting to generate, the nature of their offspring would again be
different [from that of the parents], and the nature of what this offspring
would generate would again be different from their parents, and this would
proceed to infinity. But nature avoids the infinite; for the infinite is   *15*
imperfect, whereas nature always seeks an end.

Animals which do not travel, like the testacea and those which live by
being naturally attached to something else, are not male or female because
of the closeness of their *substance* to the *substance* of plants; for just as
plants are neither male nor female, so are these animals, and they are called   *20*
["male and female"] in virtue of a similarity or analogy to plants since they
differ in this respect but little from them. Thus, there are cases among trees
of the same kind, too, in which some bear fruit but others do not but
contribute to the ripening of the fruit of those which bear, as in the fig-tree   *25*
and the caprifig.

The same happens in the case of plants also. Some come to be from seed,
but others as if by chance brought about by nature; for they come to be from
the decay of earth or of some parts of plants, for some of them are formed
not by themselves separately but in trees, like the mistletoe. Plants, however,
should be investigated as such separately. [Chapters 2-20 omitted.]

21

Let so much be said concerning these matters. At the same time, the
things which are to be considered next are evident from the above
discussion, namely, how the male contributes to the generation of offspring
and how the seed from the male causes that which is generated. Does it exist

immediately as a part of the embryo, blended with the matter from the
5   female, or is the body of the sperm no part of the embryo but its power or
its motion is? For it is that [power or its motion] which acts, whereas that
which is formed and receives the *form* is a remnant of the residue in the
female. Indeed, such appears to be the case both according to reason and
10   from facts. For, universally considered, no single thing which comes to be
from that which can be acted upon and that which can act appears to have
present in itself [as matter] that which can act, nor, in general, if it comes
to be from that which is moved and that which causes motion. Moreover,
the female qua female is at any rate that which can be acted upon, whereas
the male qua male is that which can act and has a principle which initiates
motion. So if the ultimate predicates of these [male and female] are taken,
15   the one [the male] qua that which can act or a mover and the other [the
female] qua that which can be acted upon or a thing moved, that which is
generated from them is not one except in the sense in which the bed which
comes from the carpenter and the wood is one or in the sense in which the
ball which comes from the wax and the [spherical] form is one. It is clear,
then, that it is not necessary that something should be detached from the
20   male, or, if something is, that it should be, because of this, present in the
thing generated [as a material part], unless it be something done by the
mover or something as form, like health by the medical art in a man who
has been cured.

      The argument just stated is in agreement with reason as well as with facts.
For it is because of [this argument] that the male among some animals, e.g.,
some insects, although uniting with the female, does not appear to insert
25   anything of itself into the female, but on the contrary the female does this
into the male. For that which the semen in the female accomplishes [among
animals in which the male inserts a part of itself into the female] is that
which the heat or power of the male does when the female inserts into the
male the receptive part of her secretion. And it is for this *reason* that such
30   animals remain united for a long time but give birth to their offspring soon
after they separate. Accordingly, they remain united until [the heat or
power of the male] has accomplished its function [just as the semen does],
and, after they separate, the female soon brings forth the embryo; for what
is born is imperfect, and all such animals breed larvae. The most convincing
sign of what happens in birds and in the genus of oviparous fishes is the fact
35   that neither does the semen come from all the parts of the male nor does the
730a   male emit such a part which exists within the things generated; it makes a
living thing only by its power in its semen, as we said in the case of insects
in which the female inserts a part of herself into the male. For even if a
5   female bird happens to be in the process of producing a wind-egg but is
united with a male before the egg has begun to turn completely white from
being pale-yellow, the egg becomes fertile instead of a wind-egg; and if she

is united with another male while the egg is still pale-yellow, the whole
brood that is born turns out to be like that male. It is for this reason that some
of those who take an interest in rearing a steady stock of fine birds proceed   *10*
as follows: they change the males for the first and second mating, since they
do not suppose that the semen is mingled with the egg and exists as a part
in it, or that it comes from all the parts of the male, for then it would have
come from both males and so the chick would have those parts twice; they
make the change so that the power of the male's semen may cause the
matter and food in the female to become of a certain kind, for this can occur   *15*
by the added heat and mellowing from the second semen, since the egg is
receiving food while it is growing. The same thing also happens in the
generation of oviparous fishes. When the female has laid her eggs, the male
sprinkles its semen over them, and the eggs which have been contacted by   *20*
it are fertilized, but those which have not been contacted remain
unfertilized; and this fact indicates that the contribution of the male to the
embryo is not quantitative but qualitative.

22

From what has been said, then, it is clear that neither does the seed of an   *25*
animal come from all the parts of the [male's] body, nor does the female
make such contribution to the formation of what is generated as the male
does, but that the male contributes the principle which causes motion but
the female contributes the matter; and it is because of these facts, too, that
the female does not by herself give birth to what is generated, for she
requires a principle as a mover and as that which will determine [the form   *30*
of what is generated]. In at least some animals, however, e.g., in birds, that
nature [of the female] can generate [i.e., eggs] up to a certain extent; for the
female generates something, but this is incomplete and is called "a
wind-egg." Further, the development of that which is generated takes place
in the female and not in the male; for, again, neither does the male emit that
which is fertilized nor the female, but both contribute their part to it in the   *35*
female because the matter of that which is to be generated exists in the   *730b*
female. Further, not only must the matter from which the embryo is formed
be there, but also additional matter required for the growth of the embryo
must be available there. Hence the birth must take place in the female.
Surely the carpenter must work *on the wood* and the potter *on the clay* and,   *5*
in general, all workmanship and the last motion must be applied *to the
material* [which is being worked], e.g., the process of building is *in the house
which is being built.* From these examples one will perhaps understand how
the male contributes to generation. For not every male emits semen; and   *10*
[the semen] of those which do is no [material] part of the embryo which is

formed. This is like the case of the carpenter, from whom no [material] part goes into the wood and no part of his art becomes a [material] part of what
15 is produced, but it is the *shape* or form which, by his motion on the wood, is informed into the thing produced; and his soul has the form and the *knowledge* which cause the hands or some other part [of the body] to produce a certain kind of motion (the same if the objects produced are the same, but different if the objects produced are different), while the hands and the instruments act on the matter. In a similar way, the nature in the
20 male which emits semen uses the semen as an instrument with a [certain kind of] *actual* motion, like the motion of the instruments used to make a work of art, for the motion by art is in a certain way in the [wood which becomes a work of art]. Those males which emit semen, then, contribute to the generation in the above manner. On the other hand, the case of animals
25 which do not emit semen but the female inserts part of herself into the male is similar to the case of one who would bring the materials to the workman. For, because of the weakness of such males, nature is not such as to act by other means but sits watching motions which are hardly strong and
30 resemble those made by men working on soft materials and not by carpenters; for nature uses no other means [like art and instruments] to work on what is produced but, so to say, its own parts.

METAPHYSICS

CONTENTS

BOOK VI

1. Generically, the three theoretical sciences are first philosophy, physics, and mathematics.

2. There is no science of accidental being or accidents.

BOOK VII

1. The primary investigation of being is that of substance.

2. The objects that are thought by other thinkers to be substances.

3. The kinds of those objects are essence, universal, genus, and subject.

4. Essence belongs primarily to substances.

5. Difficulties in attributing essence to attributes.

6. A thing and its essence are the same.

13. Universals are not substances. Hence Ideas cannot exist.

16. The parts of sensible substances are not substances.

17. Form as the cause of unity and existence of a sensible substance.

BOOK VIII

1. Substance as matter which underlies change in sensible objects.

6. The differentia as cause of unity in a definition, and the genus as matter.

BOOK IX

1. Active and passive potencies in motion.

2. Rational and nonrational potencies in the soul.

3. The Megaric School fails to distinguish potency from actuality.

4. The view that everything is possible is necessarily false.

5. The conditions for actualization of rational and nonrational potencies.

6. Analogous nature of potentialities and actualities.

7. When is P potentially Q? How is Q named?

8. Actuality is prior to potentiality in formula, in substance, and in time in a sense.

METAPHYSICS

BOOK I (=A)

1

All men by nature desire understanding. A sign of this is their liking of sensations; for, even apart from the need of these for other things, they are liked for their own sake, and of all sensations those received by means of the eyes are liked most. For, not only for the sake of doing something else, but even if we are not going to do anything else, we prefer, as one might say, seeing to the other sensations. The cause of this is the fact that, of all the sensations, seeing makes us know in the highest degree and makes clear many differences in things.

By nature, animals are born with the power of sensation, and from sensation memory comes into being in some of them but not in others. Because of this, animals which can remember are more prudent or more teachable than animals which cannot remember. Of the former, those which cannot hear sounds are prudent but cannot be taught, such as the bee or any other species of animals like it, but those which can hear can also be taught.

All animals, except men, live with the aid of appearances and memory, and they participate but little in experience; but the race of men lives also by art and judgment. In men, experience comes into being from memory; for many memories of the same thing result in the capacity for one experience. And experience seems to be almost similar to science and art, but science and art come to men through experience; for, as Polus rightly says, "experience made art, but inexperience, luck."

Now art comes into being when out of many notions   from experience we form one universal belief concerning similar facts. For, to have a belief that when Callias was having this disease this benefited him, and similarly with Socrates and many other individuals, is a matter of experience; but to have a belief that this benefited all persons of a certain kind who were having this sickness, such as the phlegmatic or the bilious or those burning with high fever, is a matter of art.

Experience does not seem to differ from art where something is to be done; in fact, we observe that men of experience succeed more than men who have the theory but have no experience. The cause of this is that experience is knowledge of individuals but art is universal knowledge, and all *actions* and productions deal with individuals. The doctor does not cure 'a man' universally taken, except accidentally, but Callias or Socrates or someone else to whom also the essence of man happens to belong. If, then, someone without experience has the theory and knows the universal but is ignorant of the individual included under this universal, he will often fail to cure; for it is rather the individual that is curable. Nevertheless, we regard understanding and comprehension as belonging to art more than to experience, and we believe that artists are wiser than men of experience; and this indicates that wisdom is attributed to men in virtue of their understanding rather than their experience, inasmuch as men of understanding know the cause but men of experience do not. For men of experience know the fact but not the *why* of it; but men of art know the *why* of it or the cause. It is because of this that we regard also the master-artists of a given craft as more honorable, as possessing understanding to a higher degree, and as wiser than the manual workers, since the former know the causes of the things produced, but the latter are like certain inanimate things which act but do so without understanding that action, as in the case of fire which burns. Inanimate things bring about the effects of their actions by some nature, while manual workers do so through habit which results by practicing. Thus, master-artists are considered wiser not in virtue of their ability to do something but in virtue of having the theory and knowing the causes. And in general, a sign of a man who understands is the ability to teach, and because of this we regard art more than experience to be science; for those who have the art can teach, but those who do not have it cannot teach. Again, we do not consider any of the sensations to be wisdom, although these are the most authoritative in the knowledge of individuals; but they do not tell us the *why* of anything, as for example why fire is hot, but only the fact that it is hot.

The first who arrived at any art that went beyond the ordinary sensations was probably admired by men, not only because there was some usefulness in the objects arrived at, but also as being wise and superior to others. As more arts were arrived at, some for the necessities of life and others as the only ends of *activity*, those who arrived at the arts for the latter purpose were always believed to be wiser than those who did so for the former because their sciences were not instrumental to something else. Now when all such arts were already developed, the sciences concerned neither with giving pleasure to others nor with the

15

20

25

30

981b

5

10

15

20

necessities of life were discovered, and first in such places where men
had leisure. Accordingly, it was in Egypt that the mathematical arts were
25   first formed, for there the priestly class was allowed leisure.

In the *Ethics*[2] we have stated the difference between art and science
and the others which come under the same genus.   But the purpose of
our present discussion is to bring out this: all men believe that what is
called "wisdom" is concerned with the first causes and principles; so
30   that, as stated before, a man of experience seems to be wiser than a man
who has any of the sensations, a man of art wiser than a man of experi-
982a   ence, a master-artist wiser than a manual worker, and theoretical sciences
to be wisdom to a higher degree than productive sciences.   Clearly,
then, wisdom is a science of certain causes and principles.

2

5   Since this is the science we are seeking, we must inquire what are the
kinds of causes and principles whose science is wisdom. If we were to
go over the beliefs which we have about the wise man, this might perhaps make the answer more evident. We believe (a) first, that the wise
man *knows* all things in a manner in which this is possible, not, however,
10   *knowing* them individually; (b) second, that a wise man can acquire
knowledge of what is hard and not easy for any man to know (ability to
have sensations is common to all, and therefore easy, but not a mark of
wisdom); (c) third, that he who is more accurate and more able to teach
the causes in each science is wiser; (d) fourth, that of the sciences, the
15   one pursued for its own sake and for the sake of understanding is wisdom
to a higher degree than the one pursued for the sake of what results
from it; (e) fifth, that the superior science is wisdom to a higher degree
than the subordinate science, for the wise man must not be placed in
rank by another but must set the ordering, and he must not obey another but must be obeyed by the less wise.

20   These, then, are the beliefs in kind and in number which we have
concerning wisdom and wise men. Of the attributes listed, that of *knowing* all things must belong to him who has universal *knowledge* in the
highest degree; for he understands in a sense all the underlying subjects.
And the most universal things are on the whole the hardest for men to
25   know, for they are most removed from sensations. Also, the most accurate of the sciences are those which are concerned mostly with the
first causes, for the sciences with fewer principles are more accurate
than those which use additional principles; for example, arithmetic is
more accurate than geometry. Moreover, the science which investigates
causes is more capable of teaching than the one which does not; for

those who teach are those who state the causes of each thing. Further, 30
to understand things or *know* them for their own sake belongs in the
highest degree to the science of that which is *known* in the highest degree; for he who pursues *knowing* for its own sake will pursue most of all
the science taken in the highest degree, and such is the science of that 982b
which is *knowable* in the highest degree; and that which is *knowable* in
the highest degree is that which is first or the causes, for it is because of
these and from these that the other things are known, and not these
because of the underlying subjects. Finally, the supreme science, and
superior to any subordinate science, is the one which knows that for the 5
sake of which each thing must be done, and this is the good in each case,
and, in general, the highest good in the whole of nature.

From all that has been said, then, it is evident that the name which is
sought applies to the same science; for it is this science which must investigate the first principles and causes, and the good or final cause is 10
one of the causes.

That it is not a productive science is also clear from those who began
to philosophize, for it is because of wondering that men began to philosophize and do so now. First, they wondered at the *difficulties* close at
hand; then, advancing little by little, they discussed *difficulties* also 15
about greater matters, for example, about the changing attributes of the
Moon and of the Sun and of the stars, and about the generation of the
universe. Now a man who is perplexed and wonders considers himself
ignorant (whence a lover of myth, too, is in a sense a philosopher, for a
myth is composed of wonders), so if indeed they philosophized in order
to avoid ignorance, it is evident that they pursued science in order to 20
understand and not in order to use it for something else. This is confirmed by what happened; for it was when almost all the necessities
of life were supplied, both for comfort and leisure, that such thinking
began to be sought. Clearly, then, we do not seek this science for any 25
other need; but just as a man is said to be free if he exists for his own
sake and not for the sake of somebody else, so this alone of all the
sciences is free, for only this science exists for its own sake.

Accordingly, the possession of this science might justly be regarded
as not befitting man; for human nature is servile in many ways, and so, 30
as Simonides says, "God alone should have this prerogative," and it
would be unworthy of a *man* not to seek the science proper to his nature.
If, then, there is something in what the poets say and the Deity is by
nature jealous, he would most probably be so in this case, and all men 983a
of intellectual eminence would be unfortunate. But neither is it possible
for the Deity to be jealous (nay, according to the proverb, "bards tell
many a lie"), nor need we suppose that there is a science more honorable

5   than this one. For the most divine science is the most honorable, and a
    science would be most divine in only two ways: if God above all would
    have it, or if it were a science of divine objects. This science alone
    happens to be divine in both ways; for God is thought by all to be one
10 of the causes and a principle, and God alone or in the highest degree
    would possess such a science. Accordingly, all the other sciences are
    more instrumental   than this, but none is better.

    However, the acquisition of this science must in a sense bring us to
    a state which is contrary to that when we began our inquiries. For all
    men begin, as we said, by wondering that things are as they are when
    the cause has not been investigated, as in the case of marionettes or of
15 the solstices or of the incommensurability of the diagonal of a square
    with respect to its side; for all seem to wonder at the fact that no least
    unit of magnitude exists which can measure both the side and the diag-
    onal of a square. But we must end with the contrary and, according to
    the proverb, the better state, as is also the case in these instances when
    one has learned the cause; for nothing would make a geometrician
20 wonder so much as this, namely, if a diagonal were to be commensurable
    with the side of a square.

    We have stated, then, the nature of the science we are seeking, and
    the aim of our concern and of our entire *inquiry*.

3

    It is evident, then, that we must acquire *knowledge* of the first causes
25 (for we say that we understand each thing when we think that we know
    its first cause), and causes are spoken of in four senses. In one sense, we
    say that *the substance* or the essence is a cause (for the *why* leads us
    back to the ultimate formula, and the first *why* is a cause and a prin-
30 ciple); in another, it is the matter or the underlying subject; in a third,
    the source which begins motion; and in a fourth, the cause opposite to
    the previous, namely, the final cause or the good (for this is the end of
    every generation and every motion). We have investigated these causes
983b sufficiently in the *Physics;*[3] however, let us examine the contributions of
    others before us who attempted the investigation of being and philos-
    ophized about truth. For clearly they, too, speak of certain principles
    and causes, and so there will be some profit in our present *inquiry* if we
5   go over what they say; for either we shall discover some other genus
    of cause, or we shall be more convinced of those we just stated.

    Most of those who first philosophized regarded the material kinds of
    principles as the principles of all things; for that of which things consist,

and the first from which things come to be and into which they are finally resolved after destruction (this being the persisting *substance* of 10 the thing, while the thing changes in its affections), this they say is the element and the principle of things; and because of this they think that nothing is generated and nothing perishes, since such a nature is always preserved. Just as in the case of Socrates when he becomes noble or musical, we do not say that he is generated in the full sense, nor that he 15 perishes in the full sense if he loses these habits, because Socrates himself as an underlying subject still persists, so it is in the other cases; for there must be some nature, either one or more than one, which is preserved and from which the others are generated.

However, these thinkers do not all agree as to the number and kinds of such principles. Thales, the founder of such philosophy, says that this 20 principle is *Water* (and on account of this he also declared that the earth rests on water), perhaps coming to this belief by observing that all food is moist and that heat itself is generated from the moist and is kept alive by it (and that from which things are generated is the principle of 25 all); and he came to this belief both because of this fact and because the seeds of all things have a moist nature, and water is the principle of the nature of moist things.

Some[4] think that even the ancients, who lived long before the present generation and were first to speculate about divine things, had similar beliefs about nature, for they represented Ocean and Tethys as fathers 30 of generation,[5] and the oath of the Gods as being by *Water* or *Styx* (as the poets called it);[6] for that which is most ancient is most honorable, and that which is most honorable is that by which one swears. Perhaps 984a it may not be clear whether this doctrine about nature happens to be primitive and ancient; at any rate, Thales is said to have spoken out in this manner concerning the first cause. As for Hippo, one would not consider him worthy of being included among these thinkers because of the shallowness of his *thought*. 5

Anaximenes and Diogenes posit *Air* as being prior to *Water* and as being in the highest degree a principle of simple bodies; but Hippasus of Metapontium and Heraclitus of Ephesus posited *Fire* as the principle. Empedocles posited four principles, adding to the principles already stated a fourth, *Earth;* for he says that these always persist and are not generated but combine into a unity or are separated out of a unity in 10 varying numbers of parts.

Anaxagoras of Clazomenae, older than Empedocles but later in philosophical works, says that the principles are infinite; for he says that almost all homogeneous things (as in the case of water and fire) are generated and perish only in this sense, namely, by combination and 15 separation, and neither are they generated nor do they perish in any other sense but stay eternally the same.

From what has been said one might think that the only cause is the kind which is called "material". But as philosophers progressed in this manner, the facts themselves opened the way for them and contributed
20   in forcing them to make further inquiries. However true it may be that every generation and destruction proceeds from some one principle, or even more than one, why does this happen and what is the cause? For, indeed, the underlying subject itself does not cause itself to change. What I mean, for example, is this: neither the wood nor the bronze causes itself to change; the wood does not make a bed, nor the bronze a
25   statue, but some other thing is the cause of the change. Now to seek this is to seek another principle, namely, as we might say, the source which begins motion.

Now those who were the very first to take up this kind of *inquiry* and to say that the underlying subject is one were not dissatisfied with them-
30   selves; but some of those who say that the underlying subject is one,[7] as if defeated by this inquiry,   say that the *One*[8] and the whole of nature is immovable not only with respect to generation and destruction (for this was an old belief and agreed upon by all) but also with respect to every other change, and this belief is peculiar to them. Of those who
984b   said that the universe is one, then, none happened to discern also a cause of this kind, except perhaps Parmenides, and to this extent, that he
5   posits not only one cause but in some sense two causes.   But those who posit more than one,[9] such as the *Hot* and the *Cold*, or *Fire* and *Earth*, are more able to state the second cause; for they regard *Fire* as having a nature which can move things, but *Water* and *Earth* and such things as having a contrary nature.

Following these thinkers and their principles, since such principles were not sufficient to generate the nature   of things, later thinkers,
10   forced once more by truth itself as we said,[10] sought the next principle. For it is perhaps unlikely that *Fire* or *Earth* or any other such should cause things to be or become good or noble   or that those thinkers should have thought so; nor again was it right to entrust a matter of such
15   importance to *chance* or to luck.   When someone[11] said that *Intelligence* exists in nature, as in animals, and that He is the cause of the arrangement and of every kind of order in nature, he appeared like a sober man in contrast to his predecessors who talked erratically. We know that Anaxagoras openly made these statements, but Hermotimus of Clazo-
20   menae is credited with having made them earlier. Those who had such beliefs, then, posited as principles of things both the cause of what is noble and the moving cause.

4

One might suspect that Hesiod was the first to seek such a cause, or someone else who posited *Love* or *Desire* as a principle in things, as 25 Parmenides does also; for the latter says, in describing the generation of the universe,

> Love first of all the Gods she planned.

And Hesiod says,

> First of all was Chaos made,
> And then broad-breasted Earth
> And Love 'mid all the Gods supreme.

And these suggest that there must be in things some cause which will 30 move them and bring them together. As to how we are to assign priority to these thinkers concerning these beliefs, let this await later *judgment*.[12]

Now since in nature there appeared to exist also the contraries of good things, not only order and what is noble but also disorder and what 985a is base, and bad things appear to be greater in number than good things, and base than noble things, accordingly, another thinker introduced *Friendship* and *Strife*, each as the cause of each of the two genera of things, respectively. For if one were to follow up and attend to the *thought* intended rather than to the vague expression of Empedocles, he 5 would find *Friendship* as the cause of good things and *Strife* as the cause of bad things. Thus, if we were to say that in a sense Empedocles both mentions and is the first to mention *Badness* and *Goodness* as principles, we might perhaps be right, if indeed the cause of all good things is *Goodness* itself and of all bad things *Badness* itself. 10

As we said, then, the thinkers up to the time of Empedocles appear to have touched upon two of the causes which we distinguished in the *Physics*,[13] the material cause and the moving cause, but lightly and not at all clearly, as untrained men box in fights; for, also these go around 15 their opponents and often strike fine blows, but neither do these box scientifically, nor do the above thinkers seem to understand what they are saying, for they appear to use the two causes occasionally and to a small extent. For Anaxagoras uses *Intelligence* as an artificial device for the arrangement of the universe, and when faced with the problem of giving the cause for the necessary existence of something, then he drags 20 in *Intelligence*; and in other things which are generated he uses as a cause any other thing rather than *Intelligence*.[14]

As for Empedocles, although he uses the causes more frequently than Anaxagoras, he does so neither adequately nor consistently. At any

25 rate, he often makes *Friendship* separate the elements and *Strife* combine them. For when the elements in the universe are separated by
Strife, the parts of fire combine into one unity, and so do the parts of
each of the other elements; and again when the elements are brought
together into one unity by *Friendship*, the parts of each element are
of necessity separated from their corresponding unity. Now, in contrast
30 with his predecessors, Empedocles was the first to introduce this cause
with further differentiation, positing not one but distinct and contrary
principles of motion. Moreover, he was the first to speak of the four so-
985b called material elements, not using them as four, however, but only as
two, *Fire* by itself, and the elements opposed to it (*Earth, Air,* and *Water*)
as of one nature. One may gather this by studying his verses. This, then,
is our version of this thinker concerning the manner of his expression
and the number of principles he posited.
5   Leucippus and his associate Democritus declare that the *Full* and the
Void are the elements, calling the one "being" and the other "nonbeing",
that is, the *Full* or the *Solid* is being but the *Void* or *Rare* is nonbeing
(hence, they say that being exists no more than nonbeing, inasmuch as
a body exists no more than void), and that these are the material causes
10 of things. And just as those thinkers, who posit one underlying substance, generate all other things by its *attributes*, positing the *Rare* and
the *Dense* as the principles of all other changing attributes, so these
thinkers say that the differentiae are the causes of all other differences
15 in things. These differentiae are three: *Shape, Order,* and *Position*.
For they say that things differ only in contour, arrangement, and turning; and of these, contour is shape, arrangement is order, and turning is
position. For A differs from N in shape, AN from NA in order, and Z from
N in position. As for motion, what its source is or how it belongs to
20 things, they casually neglected as the other thinkers did. Such, then, I
say, seems to be the extent of the inquiries which the earlier thinkers
made into the two causes.

5

Contemporaneously with these thinkers, and even before them, the
so-called Pythagoreans, who were engaged in the study of mathematical
25 objects, were the first to advance this study, and having been brought
up in it, they regarded the principles of mathematical objects as the
principles of all things. Since of mathematical objects numbers are by
nature first, and (a) they seemed to observe in numbers, rather than
in fire or earth or water, many likenesses to things, both existing and
in generation (and so they regarded such and such an attribute of num-

bers as justice, such other as soul or intellect, another as opportunity, 30
and similarly with almost all of the others), and (b) they also observed
numerical *attributes* and ratios in the objects of harmonics; since, then,
all other things appeared in their nature to be likenesses of numbers, and
numbers to be first in the whole of nature, they came to the belief that 986a
the elements of numbers are the elements of all things and that the
whole heaven is a harmony and a number. And whatever facts in numbers and harmonies could be shown to be consistent with the *attributes*, 5
the parts, and the whole arrangement of the heaven, these they collected
and fitted into a system; and if there was a gap somewhere, they readily
made additions in order to make their whole system connected. I mean,
for example, that since ten is considered to be complete and to include
every nature in numbers, they said that the bodies which travel in 10
the heavens are also ten; and since the visible bodies are nine, they
added the so-called "Counter-Earth" as the tenth body.

We have discussed these matters more accurately elsewhere;[15] but
we are going over them here in order to learn from these thinkers what
principles they posit and how these principles fall under the causes we
have named. Indeed, these thinkers appear to consider numbers as 15
principles of things, and in two senses: as matter and also as affections
or possessions of things. The elements of a number are the *Even* and the
Odd, the *Odd* being finite and the *Even* being infinite; the *One* is composed of both of these (for it is both even and odd); a number comes 20
from the *One;* and, as we said, the whole heaven is numbers.

Other members of the same school declare that the principles are ten,
that is, ten pairs arranged in two columns, opposite against opposite:

Finite-Infinite	Resting-Moving
Odd-Even	Straight-Curved
One-Many	Light-Darkness
Right-Left	Good-Bad
Male-Female	Square-Rectangular

25

Alcmaion of Croton seems to have come to such belief, and either he got
it from them or they got it from him. For Alcmaion was in the prime of 30
life when Pythagoras was old, and he expressed himself just about as
they did; for he says that a great many things relating to men come to
two, meaning any chance contraries (not a specific list like that given
by the others), for example, white and black, sweet and bitter, good
and bad, great and small, etc. Thus, Alcmaion gave indefinite hints
about the rest, but the Pythagoreans stated both how many and which 986b
are the contrarieties.

From both of these schools, then, we can gather this much, that the
principles of things are the contraries, and from the Pythagoreans we

5   are told how many and which the contraries are. But these schools have
not been clearly articulate as to how their principles can be grouped and
related to our list of causes;   however, they seem to place the elements
under the material kind of cause; for they say that substances consist
of or are fashioned out of these elements as out of constituents.

10   This account, then, is sufficient to give us a view of the *thought* of
those early thinkers who declared the elements of nature to be more
than one. There are some, however, who spoke of the universe as if it
were of one nature; but not all of them were alike, either in expressing
themselves well,   or in speaking in accordance with the nature of
things.   Our discussion of them, then, is in no way relevant to the
present inquiry into the causes; for, unlike some natural philosophers

15 who assume being to be one   and yet generate things from it as from
matter, these thinkers speak in another way. For the former posit also
motion (at any rate, they generate the universe), but these say that the
universe is immovable. However, this much is pertinent to our present
inquiry. Parmenides seems to conceive the *One* with respect to formula

20 but Melissus conceives it with respect to matter; hence, the former says
that it is finite but the latter says that it is infinite. Xenophanes, who was
the first among these to speak of the *One* (Parmenides is said to have
become his disciple), said nothing clearly, nor does he seem to have
touched upon the nature of the *One* in any of these two senses; but
gazing at the whole heaven, he said, "the *One* is God."

25   As we said, these thinkers need not be considered in our present
inquiry. Two of them, Xenophanes and Melissus, may be completely
ignored as being somewhat immature; but Parmenides, being more
observant, seems to be saying something. For, claiming that nonbeing,
in contrast to *Being*, does not exist, he thinks it is necessary that *Being*

30 be one and that nothing else be (we spoke more clearly about this in the
Physics).[16] But being forced to conform to phenomena, and believing
that these are one according to formula but many according to sensation, he now posits two causes or two principles, the *Hot* and the *Cold*,

987a as if speaking of fire and earth; and he classifies the *Hot* as the principle
with respect to being but the *Cold* as the principle with respect to nonbeing.

From what has been said, then, and from the wise men whose account
concerning these matters has by now been considered, we gather this

5   much: the first philosophers posit a corporeal principle (for water and
fire and such things are bodies), some of them using only one corporeal
principle and the others more than one, but both place these principles
under one kind, the material principle; other philosophers, however,
posit as a cause both the material principle and the source of motion,
and the latter cause is regarded as one by some but as two by others.

Down to the Italian school,   then, and apart from them, philosophers   *10*
expressed themselves rather weakly concerning the causes of things,
except that, as we said, they have in fact used two kinds of causes, one
of which, the source of motion, was regarded as one by some but as
two by others. The Pythagoreans, however, spoke of two principles in
the same manner   but added this much (which is peculiar to them),   *15*
that the *Finite* and the *Infinite* and the *One* are not to be regarded as
being other natures, such as fire or earth or some other thing of this sort,
but that the *Infinite* itself and the *One* itself are the *substances* of the
things of which they are predicated, and hence that numbers are the
substances of all things. Concerning principles, then, they spoke in this   *20*
manner, and concerning the whatness of a thing, they began to discuss
and give definitions but gave too simple a treatment. For they were defining superficially and thought that the *substance* of what is defined
is the *substance* of the first   thing to which the definition belongs, as
if one were to think that the double is the same as two, because two is   *25*
the first thing which is double of some other thing. But to be double and
to be two are not equally the same; otherwise, one thing will be many,
and this was indeed happening with these thinkers.   This much, then,
may be gathered from the earlier philosophers and the ones that
followed.

6

After the philosophies named came the system of Plato, which fol-   *30*
lowed these philosophies in many respects but also had its own pe-
culiarities distinguishing it from the philosophy of the Italians. For,
having in his youth become familiar first with Cratylus and the Heracli-
tean doctrines (that all sensible things are always in a state of flux and
that no science of them exists), he continued to believe these even in
his later years. Now Socrates was engaged in the study of ethical matters,   *987b*
but not at all in the study of nature as a whole, yet in ethical matters he
sought the universal and was the first to fix his *thought* on definitions.
Plato, on the other hand, taking into account the *thought* of Socrates,
came to the belief that, because sensible things are always in a state of   *5*
flux, such inquiries were concerned with other things and not with the
sensibles; for there can be no common definition of sensible things when
these are always changing. He called things of this other sort "Ideas"
and believed that sensible things exist apart from Ideas and are named
according to Ideas. For the many sensibles which have the same name
exist by participating in the corresponding Forms. The only change   *10*
he made was to use the name "participation"; for the Pythagoreans say

that things exist by imitating numbers, but Plato, changing the name, says that things exist by participating in the Forms. As to what this imitation of or participation in the Forms might be, they left this an open question.

15   Further, he says that besides the sensible things and the Forms, and between these, there exist the Mathematical Objects, differing from the sensible things in being eternal and immovable, and from the Forms in that there are many alike whereas the Form itself corresponding to these is only one.

Since the Forms are the causes of all other things, he thought the 20   elements of the Forms are the elements of all things. As matter, the *Great* and the *Small* are the principles; as *substance*, it is the *One*. For from the *Great* and the *Small* and by participation in the *One* come the Forms, and these are Numbers.

In saying that the *One* is a substance, and not that it is something else of which "one" is predicated, he spoke like the Pythagoreans, and like them he believed that the Numbers are the causes of the *substance* of 25   all other things. But he was unlike the Pythagoreans, (a) in making the *Infinite* not one principle but a *Dyad*, consisting of the *Great* and the *Small*, (b) in saying that the Numbers exist apart from the sensible things and not that these are numbers, and (c) in positing the Mathematical Objects between the Numbers and the sensible things; and this is peculiar to him. Now Plato, unlike the Pythagoreans, posited 30   the *One* and the Numbers as existing apart from things and introduced the Forms because he was making logical inquiries (for earlier thinkers had no knowledge of dialectics), and he made the other nature a *Dyad* because the Numbers, except those which are first, could be generated 988a   with natural ease from it as from some plastic material. Yet what really happens is the contrary; for this sort of generation is not reasonable. For these thinkers make many things out of the matter, and the Form generates only once; but what we observe is that from one piece of matter one table is made, while he who puts the form upon the matter, 5   although he is one, makes many tables. The relation of the male to the female is similar, for the female is impregnated by one copulation, while the male impregnates many females. But these are imitations of those principles.

This, then, is how Plato described the causes we are seeking. It is evident from what has been said that he uses only two causes, the cause 10   of the whatness and the cause according to matter (for the Forms are causes of the whatness of the other things, and the cause of the whatness of the Forms is the *One*). It is also evident what the underlying matter is, in virtue of which the Forms are predicated of the sensible things, and the *One* is predicated of the Forms; this is the *Dyad*, or the *Great*

and the *Small*. Further, he assigned the cause of goodness and the
cause of evil to the elements, one to each of them, just as some of the   *15*
earlier philosophers (for example, Empedocles and Anaxagoras) sought
to do.

7

We have given a concise and summary account of those who spoke
and the manner in which they spoke concerning the principles and the   *20*
truth; yet we have gathered only this much from them, that not one of
those who spoke of a principle or a cause mentioned any other than
those we described in the *Physics*,[18] but all appear to have touched upon
them in some sense, although lightly.

Some speak of the principle as being matter, whether they assume it
to be one or many, and whether they posit it to be a body or incorporeal;   *25*
for example, Plato speaks of the *Great* and the *Small*, the Italians of
the *Infinite*, Empedocles of *Fire* and *Earth* and *Water* and *Air*, Anaxagoras of the infinitude of homogeneous things. All these thinkers did
touch upon this kind of cause, and so did those who spoke of *Air*, or of   *30*
Fire, or of *Water*, or of something denser than fire but thinner than air
(for some spoke of the first element as being of this kind). The latter
thinkers touched upon this cause only; others, however, touched upon
the source which begins motion, as for example those who posited
Friendship and *Strife* or *Intelligence* or *Love* as a principle.

As for the essence or the *substance*, no one expressed it *clearly*, but   *35*
those who posit the Forms speak of it more than anyone else; for, it is   *988b*
not as matter that they posit the Forms as causes of the sensible things,
and the *One* as a cause of the Forms, nor do they believe that the Forms
and the *One* are causes in the sense of a source which begins motion (for
they are rather causes of motionlessness and of rest, so they say), but the
Forms furnish the essence in each of the other things, and the *One* fur-   *5*
nishes the essence in each of the Forms.

As for that for the sake of which *actions* and changes and motions take
place, they speak of it as a cause in some sense, but not as it is stated
here or in the sense in which it is in its nature a cause. For, those who
speak of *Intelligence* or of *Friendship*, although they posit each of these
causes as a good in a sense, do not nevertheless do so in the sense that
some things exist or are generated for the sake of these but speak as if   *10*
motions proceed from these. In a similar way, those who say that the
One or *Being* is of such a nature say that it is the cause of the *substance*
of other things but not that those things exist or are generated for the
sake of the *One* or of *Being*. So the fact is that in one sense they speak

15 of the good as a cause but in another sense they do not; for they speak
of it not essentially but accidentally.

All these thinkers, then, being unable to touch upon another cause,
seem to confirm the fact that we have described the number and kinds
of causes rightly. Moreover, it is clear that, if we are to seek the causes,
we must either seek all of them in the ways stated or seek them in some
20 of the ways stated. Let us next go over the possible *difficulties* with
regard to the way in which each of these thinkers has spoken and also
state what the situation is concerning the principles.

8

Those who say that the universe is one and posit as matter some one
nature which is corporeal and has magnitude clearly err in many ways;
25 for they posit the elements of bodies only, but not of incorporeal things,
even though incorporeal things exist. Also, in trying to state the causes
of generation and destruction, although they speak as natural philosophers about all things, they leave out the cause of motion. Moreover,
they do not posit the *substance* or the whatness as a cause of anything;
30 and besides, they easily call any of the simple bodies, except earth, a
principle without examining how these are generated from each other
(I mean fire, water, earth, and air). For things are generated from each
other by combination, or by separation, and it makes the greatest difference as to which of these is prior and which is posterior. For, (1) on the
35 one hand, the most elementary of all would seem to be the first things
989a out of which the others are generated by combination, and of the bodies
such would be the ones which have the smallest parts and which are
most fine. Hence, those who posit fire as the principle would be most
consistent with this statement. Each of the other thinkers, too, agrees
5 that the element of bodies is of this sort. At any rate, none of those who
posited only one element claimed that earth is that element, clearly
because its parts are great, but each of the other three elements has
found an advocate; for some say that fire is that element, others water,
still others air. (But why do they not ever name earth, as common people
10 do? For these say that all things are earth. Hesiod, too, says that of the
bodies earth was generated first; so, this happened to be an old and a
popular belief.) According to this argument, then, he who says that
the element is any one of the simple bodies other than fire, or posits
that it is denser than air but finer than water, would not be speaking
15 rightly. But, (2) on the other hand, if that which is posterior in generation is prior in nature, and that which is concocted or made into a com-
pound is posterior in generation, the contrary would be the case: water

would be prior to air, and earth would be prior to water. Let this, then, be our account of those who posited one cause such as we have stated.

The same might be said even if one posits more than one element; for example, Empedocles speaks of matter as being the four bodies. For he too is faced with consequences, some of which are the same as those we have just given, while others are peculiar to him. For we observe that these bodies are generated from each other, and in this way no one of them, such as fire or earth, stays always the same body (we spoke about these matters in the *Physics*);[19] and as for the cause of things in motion, whether one or two should be posited, he must be thought to have spoken neither altogether rightly, nor altogether reasonably. In general, those who speak in this manner are of necessity discarding alteration; for cold will not come from heat, nor heat from cold. For how can the contraries themselves be affected, and what single nature would become now fire and now water? Empedocles says there is no such single nature.

If we were to believe that Anaxagoras spoke of two elements, we would most certainly do so from his statements, which he himself did not articulate, but which he would have accepted of necessity as indicating two elements if one were to induce him to see this. To say that the principle was a blend of all things is absurd not only in many other respects, but also (a) because it follows that they must not have been blended before, (b) because no chance thing can by nature be blended with any chance thing, and (c) in view of the fact that *attributes* and accidents would be separable from substances (for it is the same things that can be blended and be separated); however, if one were to follow him up by putting together closely what he intends to say, perhaps he would appear to be more modern in his statements. For when nothing was separated, clearly nothing could be truly asserted of that substance; I mean, for example, that it was neither white, nor black, nor grey, nor otherwise colored, but necessarily without color, for otherwise it would have had one of these colors. Similarly and by the same argument, it would have been without taste and without any other similar attribute. Thus, it could have neither any quality, nor any quantity, nor be an instance of a *this*, otherwise, some one thing expressed by a species would have belonged to it. But this would be impossible if indeed all were blended together, for otherwise a thing of some one species would have been separated from the other species; but he said that all were blended except *Intelligence*, and that this alone is unblended and pure. From these statements, then, it follows that he was speaking of two principles, the *One* (for this is simple and unblended) and the *Other*, which we posited as being indefinite before it becomes definite and participates in some form. Thus, while he spoke neither rightly nor clearly, he meant

20

25

30

989b

5

10

15

20   to say something like what later thinkers were saying and what now
      appears more and more to be the case.
          But these thinkers happen to be at home only with discussions regard-
      ing generation and destruction and motion; for it is almost of substances
      of this kind alone that they seek the principles and causes. However,
25   those who investigate all things, positing some of them to be sensible
      and others nonsensible, are clearly examining both genera; consequently,
      we should dwell on them at greater length and gather what they say
      well and what not well with reference to our present inquiry.
30   The so-called Pythagoreans use principles and elements which are
      more foreign than those which the natural philosophers use. The cause
      of this is that it was not from sensible things that they took them; for the
      mathematical objects, with the exception of those of astronomy, are
      without motion.   Yet all their discussions and studies are concerned
990a with nature; for they generate the heavens,   retain the facts as regards
      the parts, *attributes*, and operations within the heavens, and use up the
      principles and the causes for these facts, as if agreeing with the other
      natural philosophers that being is just this, namely, that which is sensible
5   and is contained in the so-called heavens. But, as we said, they claim
      that the causes and the principles are sufficient to rise up to the higher
      of beings,   and that they are more suited to these than to the discus-
      sions about physics. However, these thinkers say nothing as to how there
      can be motion if only the *Limit* and the *Unlimited* or the *Odd* and the
10   *Even* are assumed,   or how, without motion and change, there can be
      generation and destruction and the operations of the bodies which are
      carried   within the heavens.
          Moreover, whether it is granted to them that a magnitude is com-
      posed of these principles or this is shown to be so, still, we may ask,
      how will some bodies be light and others heavy?   If we consider what
15   they assume and say, they are speaking no more of mathematical bodies
      than of physical bodies;   and this accounts for the fact that they have
      said nothing whatever about fire or earth or the other bodies of this
      sort, just as they have nothing to say, I suppose, which is peculiar to
      sensible bodies.
          Further, how are we to accept, on the one hand, that the *attributes*
20   of numbers and the numbers themselves are the causes of what exists
      and is generated in the heavens both in the beginning and now, and
      on the other, that no numbers exist other than the ones of which the
      universe consists? For, when they say that opinion and opportunity lie
      in a certain region and injustice and separation (or blend) a little above
25   or below, stating that a demonstration of this is the fact that each of
      them is a number, but it then turns out that already a plurality of mag-
      nitudes exists together in this place because these *attributes* follow the

corresponding places, we may then ask: Are these numbers the same as the numbers in the heaven which must be accepted as being these things, or are they distinct from them? Plato at least says that they are 30 distinct from them, although he, too, regards all of them as numbers, both these things and their causes, but the latter as intelligible while the former as sensible numbers.

9

Let us leave the Pythagoreans for the present, for to have touched upon them as much as we did is sufficient. Those who posited the Ideas as causes, first, in seeking to find the causes of the things about us, 990b introduced other things equal in number to these, as if a man who wished to count but, thinking that he could not do so with the few things at hand, created more. In seeking the causes of these things, they proceeded from these to the Forms, which are about equal to or not less than these; for, there exists a Form having the same name as that which 5 is predicated of many sensibles, of substances as well as of non-substances, and of these things as well as of eternal things.

Yet none of the ways which are used to show that the Forms exist appears convincing; for, from what is laid down, in some cases a syllogism 10 is not necessarily formed, and in others it follows that there will be Forms even of things of which we think that no Forms exist. For, according to the arguments from the sciences there will be Forms of all things of which there are sciences; according to the "one predicated of many" argument there will be Forms even of denials; and according to the argument, that we can think of something which has been destroyed, there will be Forms of destructible things, for an image of what has been 15 destroyed can exist.

Again, of the most accurate statements, some posit Ideas of relations, yet we deny that a genus of relations exists by itself, and others speak of the *third man*. And in general, the statements concerning the Forms discard those things whose existence we prefer to the existence of the Ideas; for what follows is that Number is first and not the *Dyad*, 20 that the relative is prior to that which exists by itself, and all other conclusions which, drawn by some believers in the doctrine of Ideas, are contrary to the principles of that doctrine.

Again, according to the belief in virtue of which we say that Ideas exist, there will be Forms not only of substances but also of many other things (for not only of a substance is a concept one but also of any 25 other thing, and not only of substances are there sciences but also of other things; and a countless number of other such difficulties follow).

According to what necessarily follows and the doctrine of Forms,
30   if Forms can be shared, only of substances must there be Ideas; for Ideas
are not shared as attributes, but each Idea must be shared in this sense,
namely, qua not being said of a subject.   I mean, for example, that if a
double participates in Double Itself, it does so also in eternity, but as
in an attribute, for eternity is an attribute of the Double.   Accordingly,
991a   the Forms will be of substances;   and the same names signify substances whether applied to these things or to the Ideas, otherwise, what
will be the meaning of saying that there exists something apart from the
many things here, the one over the many? And if each Idea and the
things that participate in it have the same form, there will be something
common to all; for, why should the form of two be one and the same in
5   the perishable two's and the many eternal Two's   any more than in
Two Itself and any perishable two? But if that form is not the same for
all, they would be equivocally named, and this would be similar to
calling both Callias and a piece of wood "a man", although we observe
nothing common in them.
Above all, one might go over the difficulties raised by this question:
10   What do the Forms contribute to the eternal things among the sensibles   or to those which are generated and destroyed? For, they are not
the causes of motion or of any other change in them. And they do not in
any way help either towards the *knowledge* of the other things   (for,
they are not the *substances* of them, otherwise they would be in them)
or towards their existence   (for they are not constituents of the things
15   which share in them). It might perhaps seem that they are causes in the
way in which whiteness is a cause when it is blended in the white thing.
But this argument, first used by Anaxagoras and then by Eudoxus and
some others, can easily be upset;   for it is easy to collect many statements contradicting such a doctrine. Moreover, all other things do not
20   come to be from the Forms in any of the usual senses of "from". And
to say that the Forms are patterns and that the other things participate
in them is to use empty words and poetic metaphors. For, if we look
up to the Ideas, what will their function be? Any chance thing may be
or become like another thing even without being copied   from it, so
25   that, whether Socrates exists or not, a man like Socrates might be born.
Likewise, it is clear that this might be the case even if there were to be
an eternal Socrates.   Moreover, there will have to be many patterns of
the same thing, and so many Forms; of a man, for example, there will
be Animal, Two-footed, and at the same time Man Himself.   Also,
30   Forms will be patterns not only of sensible things but also of other
Forms; for example, this is how the genus will be related to a species of
it among the Forms. Thus, the same Form will be both a pattern and
991b   a copy.

Again, it would seem impossible for a *substance* to exist apart from that of which it is the *substance*. Accordingly, how could the Ideas, being the *substances* of things, exist apart from them? In the *Phaedo*[20] this is stated in this manner: The Forms are the causes of the existence as well as of the generation of things. But even if the Forms do exist, still   5 no thing which participates in something is generated unless there is a mover. And many other things are generated, such as a house or a ring, of which we[21] say no Forms exist. Clearly, then, also the rest may be generated by such causes as the ones which produce the two things just mentioned.

Again, if the Forms are Numbers, how will they be causes? Is it in   10 view of this, that the things themselves are other numbers, for example, that one man is this number, Socrates is that number, and Callias is another?   Why then are the Numbers causes of the latter? If the former are eternal but the latter are not, this difference too would not account for it at all.   On the other hand, if it is in view of this, that the things about us are ratios   of numbers, like a harmony, clearly there is still some one thing in each of the numbers which form that ratio. If this thing then is the matter, it is evident that the Numbers themselves will   15 be certain ratios of something to something else.   I mean, for example, that if Callias is a numerical ratio of fire and earth and water and air, his Idea too will be a Number of certain underlying things; and Man Himself, whether it is a Number of a sort or not,   will still be a numerical Ratio and not just a Number. Because of all this, then, none of   20 these will be just a Number.

Again, from many numbers one number is formed, but how can one Form be formed from many Forms?   And if it is not from them   but from the Units in them that a Number is formed, such as 10,000 for example, how are the Units related to each other in the Number formed? Many absurdities will follow whether the Units (a) are all alike in kind, or (b) are not alike in kind, either in the sense that, prior to the forma-   25 tion of this Number, the Units of each Number are alike in kind but not alike in kind with those of any other Number, or in the sense that no one Unit is alike in kind with any other Unit. For, having no attributes,   with respect to what will the Units differ? These alternatives are neither reasonable nor in agreement with our thinking.

Again, these thinkers must set up another genus of number as the subject of arithmetic, and also other genera, all of which are simply called "Intermediate Objects" by some of them. But how is this to be done, and from what principles will these objects come?   Or, why   30 will these be between the things about us and the Ideas? Again, each of the Units in Two is generated from a prior *Dyad*, although this is   992a impossible.   Again, why is a Number, taken as a whole, one?

Again, in addition to what has been said, if the Units are different, these thinkers should have spoken like those who say that the elements are four or two, for each of those thinkers does not call the elements by a common name, such as "body", but calls them "fire" and "earth", whether body is common to both fire and earth or not; but as it is, these thinkers speak of the *One* as if it were homogeneous, like fire, or like water. But if this is so, the Numbers will not be substances; but it is clear that, if there is a *One Itself* and this is a principle, the term "one" is used in many senses, for no other way is possible.

When we wish to reduce substances to their principles, we posit lengths as being formed from the *Long* and *Short* (a sort of species of the *Great* and *Small*), planes from the *Wide* and *Narrow*, and bodies from the *Deep* and *Shallow*. But then, how will a plane have a line, or a solid have a line and a plane? The *Wide* and *Narrow* is a genus distinct from the *Deep* and *Shallow*. Accordingly, just as a number does not belong to these, in view of the fact that the *Many* and *Few* is distinct from them, so it is clear that none of the higher will belong to any of the lower. Nor yet is the *Wide* a genus of the *Deep*, for then the body would have been a species of the plane. Further, from what principles are the points, which are present in magnitudes, generated? Even Plato was struggling against this genus of things as being geometrical suppositions, and he called the point "principle of a line"; however, he often posited the indivisible lines as this genus, although such lines must have limits. Thus, if from an argument the existence of a line follows, from the same argument follows also the existence of a point.

In general, although philosophy seeks the cause of visible things, we have left out such a cause (for we say nothing about the cause which begins change), and thinking that we state the *substances* of these things, we assert the existence of other *substances*; but as to how the latter are *substances* of the former, our statements say nothing, for "participation", as we said,[22] means nothing. Nor do the Forms touch upon that which we observe in the sciences to be indeed the cause, for whose sake each intellect and each nature acts, and which we claim to be one of the principles; but philosophy has become mathematics for modern thinkers, although they say that mathematics should be studied for the sake of other things.[23]

Moreover, one would come to the belief that the underlying substance as matter is too mathematical, and that it is a predicate and a differentia of a substance and of matter rather than matter, that is, I am speaking of the *Great* and the *Small*; and this is like the *Rare* and the *Dense*, of which the natural philosophers speak as being the first differentiae of the underlying subject, for these are species of *Excess* and *Deficiency*. As for motion, if the *Great* and the *Small* are motion, it is clear that the Forms will be moved; if not, whence did motion come? Indeed, the whole inquiry into nature is discarded.

Also, what seems to be easy is not done, namely, to show that all 10 things are one; for, if we grant all their assumptions, what follows from the examples they use is not that all things are one but that there is a *One Itself.* And even this is not shown, unless we grant that the universal is a genus; but this is impossible in some cases.

Nor are there any arguments to show how Lengths and Planes and Solids, which come after the Numbers, exist or will exist, or what 15 power they have; for these can neither be Forms (for they are not Numbers), nor Intermediates (for these are Mathematical Objects), nor yet destructible, but they appear to be another and a fourth genus of objects.

In general, the search for the elements of all beings, without distinguishing the many senses of the term "being", makes discovery impossible, especially if the manner of proceeding is by seeking the kinds 20 of elements out of which things are composed. For it is indeed impossible to find the elements out of which acting, being acted upon, or straightness are composed, but if at all, those of substances alone can be found; consequently, it is not true to think that one is seeking or has found the elements of all things. And how would one be taught the elements of all things? Clearly, it is not possible for him to start 25 with previous knowledge of them. For, just as a man who is learning geometry, although he may have previous understanding of other things, has no previous knowledge at all of what that science is concerned with and what he is about to learn, so it is also in other cases; so if there is a science of all things, as some say, he who is learning it could have no 30 previous knowledge of it at all, although all instruction received proceeds by means of previous knowledge of some or all of the elements, whether by means of demonstration or by means of definition; for one must have prior understanding of the elements from which a definition is to be formed and these must be known; and learning by induction proceeds similarly. But if, on the other hand, the science under con- 993a sideration happens to be innate, it is strange that we are not aware of possessing the best of all sciences.

Again, how will one know in that science the elements out of which its objects are composed, and how will this be made clear? This, too, presents a *difficulty,* for there might be disagreement, as there is about certain syllables; for some say that *za* is composed of *s, th*, and *a,* but 5 others say that it is a distinct sound and is none of those which are known. Moreover, how could one come to know the objects of sensation without the corresponding power of sensation? But if indeed the

elements of which things are composed are the same for all, one should
be able to do so, as one does in the case of the composite sounds which
10   have elements proper to sound.

10

It is clear, then, also from what has been said before, that all thinkers
seemed to seek the causes named in *Physics*,[24] and that besides these
we have no other that might be named. But they talked about these
15   vaguely; and in one sense they stated them all, but in another they did
not state them at all. For philosophy about all things at the start seems
to falter, inasmuch as it is at first both new and just beginning. For example, this is how Empedocles speaks of bone, as existing by virtue of a
ratio, and this would be the essence or the *substance* of a thing. But
20   then, it is likewise necessary that flesh and each of the others have a
ratio, or else none at all; and it is because of this ratio that also flesh
and bone and each of the others will exist, and not because of the matter
(which he calls "fire" and "earth" and "water" and "air"). But while he
would have necessarily agreed if someone had pointed this out to him,
he himself did not state it *clearly*.
25   These matters were pointed out before. But let us return to them
once more and list the problems that might be raised;[25] for these might
perhaps help us somewhat in solving some of the later problems.

BOOK II (= α)

1

30   The investigation of truth is in one sense difficult, in another easy. A
993b sign of this is the fact that neither can one attain it adequately, nor do
all fail, but each says something about the nature of things; and while
each of us contributes nothing or little to the truth, a considerable
amount of it results from all our contributions. Thus, if the truth seems
5   to be like the door in the proverb "Who would miss it?", in this sense
it would be easy; but to have some of the whole truth and not be able
to attain the part we are aiming at, this indicates that it is difficult.
Perhaps the cause of this difficulty, which may exist in two ways, is in
10   us and not in the facts. For as the eyes of bats are to the light of day, so
is the intellect of our soul to the objects which in their nature are most
evident of all.

It is just to be grateful not only to those with whose opinions we might agree, but also to those who have expressed rather superficial opinions; for the latter, too, have contributed something, namely, they have handed down for us the habit of thinking. If there had been no Timo- *15* theus, we would not have much lyric poetry; and if there had been no Phrynis, there would have been no Timotheus. The same may be said of those who spoke about the truth; for some of them handed down to us certain doctrines, but there were others before who caused them to be what they were.

It is also right for philosophy to be called "a science of truth". For the *20* end of a theoretical science is truth, but the end of a practical science is performance; for even if practical scientists examine how things are, they investigate what is relative to something else and what exists at the moment, and not what is eternal. Now we do not understand a truth without its cause; also, of things to which the same predicate belongs, the one to which it belongs in the highest degree is that in virtue of which it belongs also to the others. For example, fire is the *25* hottest of whatever is truly called "hot", for fire is the cause of hotness in the others. Likewise, therefore, that is most true which is the cause of truth in whatever is posterior to it. Accordingly, the principles of eternal things are of necessity always the most true; for they are true not merely sometimes, nor is there anything which is the cause of their existence, but they are the cause of the existence of the other things; *30* accordingly, as each thing is related to its existence, so is it related to its truth.

2

But clearly there is a beginning, and the causes of things are not in- *994a* finite, either as a series or in kind. For neither can one thing come from something else as from matter ad infinitum (for example, flesh from earth, earth from water, water from fire, and so on without an end), nor *5* can the source which begins motion (for example, a man is moved by air, air by the sun, the sun by *Strife*, and so on without limit) be such. Similarly, the final cause cannot proceed to infinity; for example, walk- ing for the sake of health, health for the sake of happiness, happiness for the sake of something else, and in this manner always one thing *10* being for the sake of another. And the case of the essence is similar. For of the intermediates, of which there is a last and also a prior, the prior must be the cause of the posterior. For if we had to say which of the

three is the cause, we should say the first; certainly not the last, for this
15   is the cause of none, nor yet the middle, for it is the cause of only one
(and it makes no difference whether it is one or many, or whether infinite or finite in number). But of things which are infinite in this
manner (and of the infinite in general) all the parts are alike intermediate, except the last; so that if there is no first, there is no cause at all.
20   Nor can the process go on to infinity in the downward direction, with
a beginning at the top, so that from fire should come water, from water,
earth, and in this manner always a coming to be of something in another
genus. For something comes to be from something else in two ways
(excluding the sense in which "from" means after, as in "the Olympic
games come from the Isthmian games"), either as a *man* comes to be
25   from a boy by a change in the latter, or as air from water. By "a *man*
comes to be from a boy" we mean, in general, that which has come to
be from that which is coming to be, or the completed thing from that
which is in the process of being completed; for there is always something between, as in the case of generation, which is between existence
and nonexistence, so in the case of that which is being generated, which
is between being and nonbeing. Now a learner is a man who is coming
30   to be a scientist, and this is the meaning of saying "from a learner he
is becoming a scientist". On the other hand, when we say "water comes
to be from air", in this case the air is destroyed. On this account, in the
former case the process is not reversible, and the boy does not come to
994b   be from the *man;* for from the generation it is not that which is in the
process of becoming that is coming to be, but that which exists after that
generation. It is in this way, too, that the day comes to be from the morning, namely, that it comes after the morning; on this account, the morning does not come from the day either. But in the other case the process
is reversible. In both cases, however, the number cannot go on to
5   infinity. For in the one case, those which are between must have an end;
in the other, things change back and forth, for the destruction of either
one is the generation of the other. At the same time, what is first,
being eternal, cannot be destroyed; for since generation does not proceed upwards to infinity, it is necessary, when something is generated
with the destruction of something else, that that which is first, in the
sense *that from which*, should be eternal.
         Moreover, the final cause is an end, and as such it does not exist for
10   the sake of something else but others exist for its sake. Thus, if there is
to be such one which is last, the process will not be infinite; but if there
is no such, there will be no final cause. But those who introduce an infinite series are unaware of the fact that they are eliminating the nature
of the good, although no one would try to do anything if he did not

intend to come to a limit. Nor would there be intellect in the world; for, 15
at any rate, he who has an intellect always *acts* for the sake of something,
and this is a limit, for the end is a limit.

But the essence, too, cannot always be reduced to another definition
longer than the preceding one. First, if such reduction were possible,
each definition in the resulting series would be a definition to a higher
degree than the one which precedes it; but if there is no final definition
which is first, neither will any of the others be such as stated.   Second, 20
those who speak in this manner eliminate *knowing;* for it is not possible
for us to understand unless we come to the indivisibles.   Nor is it possible to know   a thing; for how can we think of an infinite number of
parts in this sense?   For the situation here is not similar to that with the
line which, being divisible without a stop, cannot be conceived unless
we stop   (for here, one who is to traverse the infinite line   will not 25
count the sections). But the matter in a moving object must also be
conceived.   Moreover, no object can be infinite;   and if it is, at least
the essence of infinity is not infinite.[26] Again, if the kinds of causes were
infinitely many, knowing   would still be impossible; for we think we
have understanding when we know the causes, but the infinite by addi- 30
tion cannot be gone through in a finite time.

3

The way we receive a lecture depends on our custom; for we expect 995a
a lecturer to use the language we are accustomed to, and any other
language appears not agreeable but rather unknown and strange because we are not accustomed to it; for the customary is more known. The
power of custom is clearly seen in the laws, in which the mythical and
childish beliefs prevail over our knowledge about them because of cus- 5
tom. Some people do not accept statements unless they are expressed
mathematically; others, unless they are expressed by way of examples;
and there are some who demand that a poet be quoted as a witness.
Again, some demand accuracy in everything, while others are annoyed
by it, either because they are unable to follow connections or because 10
they regard it as petty. For accuracy is sometimes petty, and as in business transactions, so in discussions it seems mean to some people.

Therefore, one should already be trained in how to accept statements,
for it is absurd to be seeking science and at the same time the way of
acquiring science; and neither of them can be acquired easily. The 15
accuracy which exists in mathematical statements should not be de-
manded in everything but only in whatever has no matter. Accordingly,

the manner of proceeding in such cases is not that of physics; for perhaps all nature has matter. (Hence, we should first inquire what nature is; for in this way, too, it will become clear what the objects of physics are, and in addition, whether one science or more than one should investi-
20   gate causes and principles.)

BOOK III (=B)

1

With regard to the science which is the subject of our inquiry, we
25   must first state the problems which should be discussed first. They are concerned with matters about which some thinkers expressed different beliefs, and besides them, with some other matters which may happen to have been overlooked. Now those who wish to succeed in arriving at answers will find it profitable to go over the *difficulties* well; for answers successfully arrived at are solutions to *difficulties* previously discussed,
30   and one cannot untie a knot if he is ignorant of it. The *difficulties* raised by *thought* about its object reveal this fact: insofar as *thought* is in *difficulties*, it is like those who are bound; and in both cases one cannot go forward. Accordingly, one should first study all the difficulties both
35   for the purposes stated and because those who inquire without first going over the *difficulties* are like those who are ignorant of where they
995b   must go; besides, such persons do not even know whether they have found or not what they are seeking, for the end is not clear to them, but it is clear to those who have first gone over the *difficulties*. Further, one who has heard all the arguments, like one who has heard both parties in a lawsuit or both sides in a dispute, is necessarily in a better position to *judge* truly.
5   The first problem, which is concerned with the objects discussed in our introduction, is (1) whether it belongs to one or to many sciences to investigate the causes, and (2) whether that science should attend only to the first principles of substances or also to the principles from which all men proceed to prove something, for example, whether it is
10   possible at the same time to assert and deny one and the same thing or not, and other such principles; and (3) if that science is about sub-stances, whether it is one science that deals with all substances or more than one, and if more, whether all are of the same rank or some of them should be called "wisdom" and the others something else. And we must
15   also inquire into this, (4) whether sensible substances alone should be

said to exist or besides these also others, and if others also, whether such substances are of one genus or of more than one; for example, some thinkers posit the Forms and also the Mathematical Objects between the Forms and the sensible things. As I say, then, we must examine these, and (5) whether our investigation is concerned only with substances or also with the essential attributes of substances; and in addition, con- *20* cerning sameness and otherness and likeness and unlikeness and con- trariety, and with regard to priority and posteriority and all other such, about which the dialecticians are trying to inquire, conducting their inquiry from accepted opinions only, to what science does it belong to *25* investigate all these? To these we must also add their own essential attributes, for we must inquire not only what each of these is, but also whether there is only one contrary to a contrary. And (6) are the prin- ciples and the elements the genera or the constituents into which a thing is divisible? And (7) if the genera, are they those which are proxi- mately predicated of the individuals or ultimately; for example, is it 'an *30* animal' or 'a man' that is a principle of, and exists to a higher degree than, an individual man? Also, (8) we must inquire and discuss most of all whether there is, besides matter, something which is a cause in virtue of itself or not, and whether this is separable or not, and whether it is one in number or more than one; and whether there is something apart from the *composite* or not (by "a *composite*" we mean what exists, *35* when something is predicated of matter), or in some cases there is but not in others, and in what sort of things there is. Again, (9) we must *996a* inquire whether the principles are definite in number or in kind, both in the formulae and in the underlying subject; and (10) whether the principles are the same in both indestructible and destructible things, or distinct, and whether all principles are indestructible, or those of de- structible things are destructible. Again, (11) there is the most difficult *5* and most perplexing problem, whether the *One* or *Being*, as the Pythag- oreans and Plato used to say, is not some other thing but is itself the *substance* of things, or this is not so but the underlying subject is some- thing else, for example, *Friendship*, as Empedocles says, or *Fire*, or *Water*, or *Air*, as others say. Again, (12) we may inquire whether the principles are universal or like individual things; and (13) whether they *10* exist potentially or *actually*, and further, whether they exist in some other manner or with respect to motion, for these problems might cause much *difficulty*. Moreover, (14) are numbers and lines and figures and points substances in any sense or not, and if substances, are they *15* separate from sensible things or are they constituents of them?

Concerning all these problems, not only is it difficult to arrive at the truth, but it is not even easy to discuss the problems well.

BOOK IV (= Γ)

1

1003a   There is a science which investigates being qua being and what belongs essentially to it. This science is not the same as any of the so-called
"special sciences"; for none of those sciences examines universally being
25   qua being, but, cutting off some part of it, each of them investigates the
attributes of that part, as in the case of the mathematical sciences. Now
since we are seeking the principles and the highest causes, clearly these
must belong to some nature in virtue of itself. If, then, also those who
were seeking the elements of things were seeking these principles, these
30   elements too must be elements of being, not accidentally, but qua
being. Accordingly, it is of being qua being that we, too, must find the
first causes.

2

    The term "being" is used in many senses, yet not equivocally, but all
of these are related to something which is one and a single nature. It
35   is like everything that is called "healthy", which is related to health by
preserving health, or by producing health, or by being a sign of health,
1003b   or by being receptive of health. And what is called "medical" is similarly
related to the medical art; for it is so called by possessing the medical
art, or by being naturally adapted for it, or by being something done
by it. And we can find other terms which are used in the same way as
5   "healthy" and "medical". Thus, also "being" is used in many senses, but
all of these are related to one principle, for some are called "being" in
view of the fact that they are substances, others by being *attributes*
of substances, others by being on their way to becoming substances, or
else by being destructions or privations or qualities of substances, or
productive or generative either of substances or of whatever is related
10   to substances, or negations of any of these or of substances. On account
of this, we even say that nonbeing *is* nonbeing.
    Now, just as there is one science of all that is healthy, so it is with the
others. For not only does the investigation of objects which are named
according to one nature belong to one science, but also of objects
which are named in relation to one nature; for the latter, too, are in some
15   sense named according to one nature. Clearly, then, the investigation
of all things qua things belongs to one science. Now in every case a
science is concerned mainly with that which is first, both as that on

which the others depend, and as that through which the others are named. Accordingly, if this is a substance, it is of substances that the philosopher should possess the principles and the causes.

For each genus of things there is both one power of sensation and one   *20*
science; grammar, for example, which is one science, investigates all kinds of speech. Accordingly, it belongs to one generic science to investigate all the kinds of being, and it belongs also to one specific science to investigate each kind of being.

If, now, being and unity are the same and are one nature in the sense that they follow each other in the same way in which a principle and a cause do, but not in the sense that they are signified by one formula (however, it makes no difference even if we were to believe the latter;   *25*
in fact, it would be even more suitable),   seeing that *one man* and *being a man* and *a man* are the same and that the added word in "one man exists" does not make it signify something other than what "a man exists" does (this is clear from the fact that unity and being are not separated in generation or in destruction),   and similarly with "unity", then it is   *30*
evident that the same thing is indicated by the addition of any one of these, and what is one is not distinct   from what is a being. Moreover, the *substance* of each individual   is one not by accident, and similarly it is essentially   a being; so that there are as many kinds of being as there are of unity. And the investigation of the whatness of these belongs   *35*
to the same generic science; I mean, for example, the investigation of sameness and likeness   and the others of this sort as well as of their opposites. And nearly all the contraries are referred to this principle.   *1004a*
Let us regard these as having been investigated in the *Collection of Contraries.*   And there are as many parts of philosophy as there are substances,   so that there must be among them a first   and one which follows; for there are immediate genera which have being and unity.   *5*
Therefore, the corresponding sciences will follow these genera. For the philosopher is like the so-called mathematician, for also mathematics has parts, and in it there is a first and a second science and others which follow.

Since it belongs to one science to investigate opposites, and plurality   *10*
is opposed to unity, and since it belongs to one science to investigate also denial and privation because unity is investigated in both ways, that is, with respect to its denial as well as to its privation   (for we say that something does not exist either without qualification or in some genus; thus, in the former case, from the denial of unity no   differentia is added to it, for the denial of it   is its absence; but in privation there   *15*
is also an underlying nature of which the privation is asserted);   to repeat, since plurality is opposed to unity, it belongs to the same science

to know also the opposites of the kinds of unity which we mentioned,
for example, otherness and unlikeness and inequality   and all the others
which are named either according to these or according to plurality
20   and unity. One of them is contrariety, for contrariety is a kind of difference, and difference is a kind of otherness.   Since, then, "unity" has
many senses, all these will also have many senses,   yet it belongs to one
science to know them all; for terms belong to different sciences not if
they just have many meanings, but if neither are they asserted of one
25   nature nor have their formulae reference to one nature. Now since all
things are referred to that which is primary, as for example all things
which are called "one" are referred to what is primarily one, we must
say that the case is similar with sameness and otherness and the contraries; so that after distinguishing the various senses of each, we must
give a similar account of how the others are related to that which is
30   primary in each category; for some are referred to what is primary in
the sense that they possess it, others in the sense that they produce it,
and others in other such ways.

It is evident, then, that it belongs to one science to discuss these things
as well as substance   (this was one of the problems we listed);[27] and so,
1004b   it is the philosopher's task to be able to investigate all of them. For if it
is not the philosopher, then who will examine whether Socrates and
sitting Socrates are the same, or if a given contrary has only one contrary to it, or what is a contrary, or the various senses of the term "contrary"? And similarly with all other such questions.
5   Since, then, these are essential *attributes* of unity qua unity and of
being qua being, but not qua numbers or qua lines or qua fire, clearly
it belongs to this science also to know both the whatness of these and
their attributes. And those who inquire into these matters err not in the
sense that they do not philosophize, but in not considering substances,
10   of which they comprehend nothing, as prior   to attributes. For just as
there are proper *attributes* of numbers qua numbers, such as oddness
and evenness, commensurability and equality, excess and deficiency,
whether these belong to numbers essentially or in relation to one
another,   and likewise other proper *attributes* belonging to solids,
whether motionless or in motion, and whether without weight or with
15   weight,   so there are proper *attributes* belonging to being qua being,
and it is the task of the philosopher to examine the truth about these. A
sign of this is the following: dialecticians and sophists put on the same
appearance as the philosopher (for sophistry only appears to be wisdom,
20   and dialecticians discuss everything) since being is common to all. But
clearly they discuss all things because these are *proper* to philosophy.
Now sophistry and dialectics busy themselves with the same genus

of things as philosophy, but philosophy differs from dialectic in the manner of its capacity, and from sophistry in the kind of life *chosen*. 25 Dialectics is tentative concerning things which philosophy knows, sophistry makes the appearance of knowing without knowing.

Again, one of the two columns of contraries is a privation, and all objects are referred to being and not-being, and to unity and plurality; for example, rest is referred to unity, motion to plurality. Now almost 30 all thinkers agree that things and substances are composed of contraries; at any rate, all say that the principles are contraries, some positing the *Odd* and the *Even*,[28] others the *Hot* and *Cold*,[29] others the *Limit* and the *Unlimited*,[30] others *Friendship* and *Strife*.[31] All the other objects, too, appear to be referred to unity and plurality (let us assume this refer- 1005a ence), and the principles posited by the other thinkers fall indeed entirely under these as if these were their genera. So it is evident also from this discussion that it belongs to one science to investigate being qua being; for all these objects are either contraries or composed of contraries, and the principles of contraries are unity and plurality. And 5 these belong to one science, whether they are named according to one nature or not; perhaps the truth is that they are not so named. But even if "unity" has many meanings, the other meanings are stated by being referred to the primary meaning, and likewise for the contraries of these; and even if being or unity is not universal and the same or not separable when applied to all things (as perhaps it is not), still some things are 10 referred to one primary object and the others to those which follow the primary. Because of this, it is not the task of the geometer to investigate what a contrary is, or completeness, or being, or unity, or sameness, or otherness, except by hypothesis.

It is clear, then, that it belongs to one science to investigate being qua being and whatever belongs to it qua being, and that the same science investigates not only substances, but also whatever belongs 15 to substances, both the attributes mentioned and also priority and posteriority, genus and species, whole and part, and the others of this sort.[32]

3

We must state whether it belongs to one or to a distinct science to inquire into what in mathematics are called "axioms" and into sub- 20 stances. It is evident that the inquiry into these belongs to one science and to the science of philosophy; for the axioms belong to all things and are not proper to some one genus apart from the others. And all men use them, since they belong to being qua being, and each genus is a being. However, they use them only to the extent that they need them, that is, as 25 far as the genus extends, in which [genus] they use demonstrations. So, since it is clear that the axioms belong to all beings qua beings (for this is common to them), the investigation of these axioms belongs also to him who is to know being qua being. On account of this, no one who

30 examines only a part of being, such as the geometer or the arithmetician, tries to say anything about them, whether they are true or not, except for some physicists who have done so for a good reason; for these thought that they alone were inquiring about the whole of nature or about being. But since there is a scientist who is yet above the physicist

35 (for nature is only one genus of being), the inquiry into these axioms, too, should belong to him who investigates universally and about first

1005b substances. Physics, too, is a kind of wisdom, but not the primary one.

The attempts of some[33] of those who state how truth should be received

5 show a lack of training in analytics; for they should have this *knowledge* before coming to the present inquiry and not inquire while learning it.

Clearly, then, it is the task of the philosopher, that is, of the one who investigates all substances insofar as they by nature come under his science, to examine also the principles of the syllogism. Now, it is fitting for him who is to have knowledge in the highest degree con-

10 cerning each genus to be able to state the most certain principles of things in that genus, so that he who is to have such knowledge of being qua being, too, must be able to state the most certain principles of all things. This is the philosopher, and the most certain principle of all is that about which it is impossible to think falsely; for such a principle must be most known (for all men may be mistaken about things which

15 they do not know) and be also non-hypothetical. For a principle which one must have if he is to *understand* anything is not an hypothesis; and that which one must know if he is to know anything must be in his possession for every occasion.

Clearly, then, such a principle is the most certain of all; and what this principle is we proceed to state. It is: "The same thing cannot at the

20 same time both belong and not belong to the same object and in the same respect"; and all other specifications that might be made, let them be added to meet logical objections. Indeed, this is the most certain of all principles; for it has the specification stated above. For it is impossible for anyone to believe the same thing to be and not to be,

25 as some think Heraclitus says; for one does not necessarily believe what he says. If, then, contraries cannot at the same time belong to the same subject (and let the usual specifications be added also to this premise), and if the contrary of an opinion is the negation of that

30 opinion, it is evident that the same person cannot at the same time be-

lieve the same object to be and not to be; for in being mistaken concerning this he would be having contrary opinions. It is because of this that all those who carry out demonstrations make reference to this as an ultimate doctrine. This is by nature a principle also of all the other axioms.

4

There are some who, as we said, say that it is possible for the same 35
thing to be and not to be and also to believe that this is so. Even many 1006a
physicists use this language. We, on the other hand, have just posited
that it is impossible to be and not to be at the same time, and through
this we have shown that it is the most certain of all principles. Some 5
thinkers demand a demonstration even of this principle, but they do so
because they lack education; for it is a lack of education not to know of
what things one should seek a demonstration and of what he should
not. For, as a whole, a demonstration of everything is impossible; for
the process would go on to infinity, so that even in this manner there
would be no demonstration. If, then, there are some things of which 10
one should not seek a demonstration, these thinkers could not say which
of the principles has more claim to be of this kind.

That the position of these thinkers is impossible can also be demonstrated by refutation, if only our opponent says something; and if he
says nothing, it is ridiculous to seek an argument against one who has
no argument insofar as he has no argument, for such a man qua such 15
is indeed like a plant. Demonstration by refutation, I may say, differs
from demonstration in this, that he who demonstrates might seem to
be begging the question, but if the other party is the cause of something posited, we would have a refutation but not a demonstration. The
principle for all such arguments is not to demand that our opponent
say that something is or is not (for one might believe this to be a 20
begging of the question), but that what he says should at least mean
something to him as well as to another; for this is necessary, if indeed
he is to say anything. For if what he says means nothing, such a man
could not argue either by himself or with another. But if he grants
this, there will be a demonstration; for there will already be some- 25
thing definite. But he who is the cause of something granted is not he
who demonstrates but he who takes a stand; for while he denies argument he listens to argument. Besides, he who has granted this has
granted that something is true without a demonstration, so that not
everything can be so and not so.

First, then, at least this is clearly true, that each of the expressions
30   "to be" and "not to be" has a definite meaning; so that not everything
can be both so and not so.   Again, if "a man" has one meaning, let this
be a two-footed animal. By "has one meaning" I mean this: if "a man"
means X, then, if something is a man, to be a man would be to be X. It
makes no difference even if one says that "a man" has many meanings,
1006b   provided that they are definite in number; for he might use a distinct
name for each formula—for example, if he were to say that "a man" does
not have one meaning but many, one of which would have the formula
"a two-footed animal", and that there are also other formulae, but defi-
5   nite in number; for he could then posit a distinct name for each of these
formulae. And if he did not so posit but were to say that the meanings
of "a man" are infinite in number, it is evident that there would be no
formula. For not to signify one thing is to signify nothing, and if names
have no meanings, then discussion with one another, and indeed even
10   with oneself, is eliminated; for it is not possible for anyone to conceive
of anything if he does not conceive of one thing,   and if it is possible,
he could then posit one name for this one thing.

Let a name, then, as stated in the beginning, mean something and
have one meaning. Then it is not possible for "to be a man" to have the
very same meaning as "not to be a man", if "a man" not only signifies
15   something predicable of one thing but also has one meaning; for we
do not use "having one meaning" in the sense of "predicated of one
thing", since in such a sense "the musical" and "the white" and "the
man" would also have one meaning, and so all of them would be
one, for they would be synonymous.   And "to be" and "not to be" will
not be the same except by equivocation, just as what we call "a man"
20   others would call "not a man."   But the problem is not whether the
same thing can at the same time be a man and not be a man in name, but
whether he can be and not be so in fact. Now if the meanings of "a
man" and "not a man" are not distinct, clearly, neither will those of "to
be a man" and "to be not a man" be distinct; and so to be a man will be
25   to be not a man, for they will be one.   (For "to be one" means, as in the
case of "a garment" and "a coat", that their formula is one.) And if they
are one, "to be a man" and "to be not a man" will have one meaning.
But it was shown that they signify distinct things. Accordingly, if it is
30   true to say "X is a man", it is necessary for X to be a biped animal, for
this was what "a man" was posited as signifying; and if this is necessary,
it is not possible for X not to be a biped animal (for "to be necessarily
a man" means this, namely, to be impossible not to be a man). Hence it
is not possible at the same time to truly say of a thing that it is a man
1007a   and that it is not a man. The same argument applies to being a not-

man; for "to be a man" and "to be a not-man" have distinct meanings, if indeed also "being white" and "being a man" have distinct meanings, for the former two terms are much more opposed, so that they must have distinct meanings. And if one were to say that "white" and "a 5 man" signify one and the same thing, we shall again say just what we said earlier, that not only the opposites but all things will be one. And if this cannot be, what follows is what we have stated, if our opponent answers our question. But if, when asked a single question, he adds also the denials, he is not answering the question. For nothing prevents 10 the same thing from being a man and white and a great many other things; yet when asked if it is true or not true to say that X is a man, he should give an answer with one meaning, but he should not add that X is also white and great. Besides, it is impossible to list an infinite number of accidents anyway; so, he should either list them all or none. Sim- 15 ilarly, even if X is a countless number of times a man and not a man, one should not, when answering the question "Is X a man?", say that X is at the same time not a man, unless he lists also all the other accidents which belong or do not belong to X. But if he were to do this, he would 20 not be arguing.

In general, those who say this eliminate substances and essences. For they must say that all things are attributes, and that the essence of being just a man or an animal does not exist. For if something is to be an essence of just a man, this will not be the essence of not-man or will not be not the essence of a man, and these are indeed the negations of 25 "the essence of a man"; for what this signified was one thing, and this was the *substance* of something. But to signify the *substance* of some- thing is to signify that its essence is not something else. And if the essence of being just a man were to be the essence of just being a not- man or just being not a man, it would be something else. And so these thinkers must say that there can be no such formula of anything but that 30 everything is an attribute of a thing, for it is in this way that the *substance* of a thing is distinguished from attribute of it; for example, white- ness is an accident of a man, in view of the fact that he is white, but he is not just whiteness. If every thing were an attribute of something, there would be no first subject of which something would be attributively a predicate (that is, if "an attribute" always signifies that something is 35 attributively a predicate of a subject). Such predication, then, must go 1007*b* on to infinity. But this is impossible, since not even more than two terms are combined in accidental predication. For an accident is not an accident of an accident unless both are accidents of the same thing. I mean, for example, that the white is musical, and the musical is white, and this is so in view of the fact that both are accidents of a man. But 5

Socrates is accidentally musical not in the sense that both Socrates and the musical are accidents of some other thing. So, since some things are said to be accidents in the latter sense and others in the former sense, those in the latter sense (like the white in Socrates) cannot be infinite in
10   the upward direction; for example, there can be no other accident to white Socrates, for no unity is formed out of all of them. Nor can the white have some other accident, such as the musical; for the latter is no more an accident of the former than the former of the latter, and we have already made the distinction that some are accidents in this sense and others in the sense in which the musical is an accident of Socrates. In
15   this last sense, the accident is not an accident of an accident, but in the other sense it is, and so it is not in every case that something will be an accident of an accident. So there will be something which signifies a substance. And if this is so, we have shown that contradictories cannot be predicates at the same time.
        Again, if all contradictories are true at the same time about the same
20   thing, clearly all things will be one. For the same thing will be a trireme and a wall and a man, if of anything one may truly affirm or truly deny anything, and this necessarily follows for those who use the argument of Protagoras. For if it seems to someone that a man is not a trireme, it is clear that he is not a trireme; but then he is also a trireme, if indeed
25   the contradictory is also true. And then what results is the doctrine of Anaxagoras, "All things are together"; and so no thing truly exists. Accordingly, they seem to be speaking of the indeterminate, and although they think that they are speaking of being, they speak of not-being; for the indeterminate is potential being and not actual being. But
30   of any thing they must assert the affirmation or the denial of every thing; for it is absurd if the denial of a thing belongs to that thing but the denial of something else not belonging to the thing does not belong to it. For example, if it is true to say of a man that he is not a man, clearly it is also true to say of him that he is not a trireme. Accordingly, if the
35   affirmation "he is a trireme" belongs to him, so must the denial. If, however, that affirmation does not belong to him, then the denial of it will
1008a   belong to him at least more than his own denial belongs to him. So, if his own denial also belongs to him, the denial "he is not a trireme" will also belong to him; and if this belongs to him, so does the affirmation "he is a trireme".
        These [absurdities] then follow for those who maintain this doctrine, and it also follows that it is not necessary either to affirm or to deny
5   something. For if it is true that X is a man and not a man, it is clear that X will neither be a man nor not a man; for the latter two are the denials

of the former. And if the former two are combined into one, the latter two would also be combined into one as opposed to the other.

Again, either the doctrine applies to all cases, and any X is both white and is not white and also a being and not a being, and likewise with the other assertions and denials, or it does not apply to all but it does to some and not to others. And if it does not apply to all, they should have stated which are the exceptions. But if it applies to all, again either (1) the denial is true if the assertion is true, and the assertion is true if the denial is true, or (2) the denial is true if the assertion is, but the asser- 15 tion is not always true if the denial is. And if (2) is the case, there will be some definite and permanent nonbeing, and the doctrine concerning it will be certain; and if nonbeing is something certain and known, the opposite assertion will be more known. But (1) if the assertion is like- wise true whenever the denial is true, then it is necessary that either (a) each is true when separately stated (for example, "X is white" is true, 20 and again "X is not white" is true), or (b) this is not the case. And if (b) it is not true to state each separately, he who is saying these things is also not saying them, and also nothing exists. But how can nonbeing talk or think? Also, all things will be one, as we said before, and the same thing will be a man and God and a trireme and the denials of these. 25 For if all assertions and denials are truly predicated alike of each thing, one thing will not differ from another. For if it does differ, to say this will be true and peculiar in this case. Similarly, (b) if each can be true whenever it can be stated separately, what we have said still follows. In addition, everyone will be speaking truly and also falsely, and the same man will admit that he is speaking falsely. It is evident at the same 30 time that to question him is to inquire about nothing, since he is not say- ing anything. For he says neither that it is so [definitely], nor that it is not so [definitely], but that it is both so and not so; and again he denies both by saying that it is neither so nor not so, for otherwise there would be something definite.

Again, if the denial is false whenever the assertion is true, and the 35 affirmation is false whenever the denial is true, it would not be possible truly to assert and deny the same thing at the same time. But perhaps 1008*b* they would say that this is just what they posit at the start.

Again, if anyone believes that something is so, or that it is not so, does he believe falsely, but he who believes both does so truly? If the latter believes truly, what does it mean to say that such is the nature of things? If he does not believe truly, but he believes more truly than 5 he who believes that something is so, or that it is not so, then things in some sense do possess something; and it would be true to say that this is so,   but it is not at the same time true to say that it is not so. But if one says that all speak alike falsely and truly, then such a man can neither speak nor mean anything; for he says that this is so and not so at the same time. If he has no belief of anything but is equally thinking and not thinking, how would he differ from a plant?

It is most evident that no one of those who posit this doctrine, or anyone else, is disposed in his actions in the same way.   For why does a man walk to Megara and not stay where he is with the thought that he is walking to Megara? And why does he not walk straight into a well or over a precipice, if such happens to be in his way, but appear to guard himself against it, with the thought that it is not equally good and not good to fall in? Clearly, then, he believes one course of action to be better and the opposite not better. And if this is so, then he must also believe one thing to be a man and another not a man, one thing to be sweet and another not sweet. For, when he thinks that it is better to drink water and see a man and then makes inquiries about them, he does not equally seek and believe everything; yet he should, if the same thing were alike a man and not a man. But as we said, no one who appears to guard himself against some but not against other things believes or acts according to such doctrine. Thus, as it seems, all men have beliefs in one way, if not about all things, at least about what is better and what is worse. And if it is not *knowledge* but opinion that they have, they should be all the more concerned about the truth, just as those who are sick are more concerned to be healthy than those who are healthy; for compared to a man with *knowledge*, a man with opinion, too, is not healthily disposed towards the truth.

Again, however much things may be so and not so, at least the more and the less are still present in the nature of things; for we should not say that both two and three are alike even, nor that both he who regards four to be five and he who regards one thousand to be five are alike mistaken. And if they are not alike mistaken, it is clear that the first man is less mistaken and so thinks more truly. Accordingly, if that which has more of something is nearer to it, there should be a truth to which the more true is nearer.   And even if there is not,   still there exists at least something which is more certain and more true, and this would free us from the unconditional doctrine which prevents a thing from being made definite by *thought*.

5

The saying of Protagoras, too, comes from the same doctrine, and both he and they are alike in positing that a thing must both be and not be. For if all opinions and all appearances are true, all of them must be both true and false at the same time. For many men have contrary beliefs, and they regard those whose opinions are contrary to theirs as mistaken; consequently, the same thing must both be and not be. And if this is so, all opinions must be true; for those who are mistaken and those who think truly have opposite opinions, and if this is the way things are, then all men think truly.

It is clear, then, that both doctrines come from the same *thinking*. But the manner of dealing with them is not the same for all these thinkers; for some need persuasion by *thought* while others by verbal arguments. Those who came to such belief from the *difficulties* they have raised can easily be cured of their ignorance; for our reply will be directed not to their vocal statements but to their *thought*. But those who state such a doctrine for its own sake can be cured by a refutation of that doctrine as expressed in speech and in words.

To those who have reflected on the *difficulties*, the doctrine came from the sensation of things. (1) The belief that contradictions and contraries belong to the same thing at the same time arises from observing that contraries are generated from the same thing. Accordingly, if nonbeing cannot become being, the thing was alike with both contraries earlier, just as Anaxagoras says that everything is blended in everything, and also Democritus; for he too says that the *Void* and the *Full* exist alike in every part, although he says that the *Full* is being and the *Void* is nonbeing. To those, then, whose belief comes from these sensations we shall say that in one sense they speak rightly but in another sense they are mistaken. For "being" has two senses, so that in one way something can be generated from nonbeing but in another it cannot, and the same thing can be at the same time both a being and a nonbeing, but not in the same respect; for the same thing can be potentially both contraries at the same time, but it cannot be so in actuality. Moreover, we shall also require them to believe that among things some other substance exists to which neither motion nor destruction nor generation belongs at all.

(2) The truth concerning appearances, too, came to some thinkers in a similar way from sensible things. For they think that truth should not be *judged* by the majority or the minority; the same thing seems sweet to some who taste it but bitter to others, so that if all men were sick or insane, except two or three who were healthy or sane, the latter would seem to be sick or insane and not the others. Again, they say that many animals have of the same things appearances which are contrary to ours, and that even to the same person the same things do not always seem to be the same with respect to sensation. Thus, it is not clear which of these appearances are true and which are false; for the ones are no

10

15

20

25

30

35

1009*b*

5

10

more true than the others, but both are alike true. It is at least on account of this that Democritus says that either nothing is true, or that truth, to us at least, is not clear.

   In general, then, it is because these thinkers believe thought to be sensation, and sensation to be alteration, that they say that what appears according to sensation must be true; for it is from these arguments that also Empedocles and Democritus and, one might say, each of the others came to possess such doctrines. For Empedocles, too, says that as the habits of men change, so do their thoughts:

   For thought in men increases with what is before them.

And elsewhere he says:

          And thought in them always alters as much as does their nature.

And Parmenides expresses himself in the same manner:

          For, as each is formed of many-jointed limbs,
          So is the mind of men; for that which
          Thinks in each and every man is but the
          Nature of his limbs; and what is more of
          This is also more of thought.

And Anaxagoras is reported to have expressed to some of his companions that things to them would be such as they would believe them to be. And they say that Homer, too, appeared to have had this doctrine, in view of the fact that he made Hector, when the latter was lying stunned by the blow, think other thoughts, the implication being that even the deranged are thinking, but not the same things. So it is clear that if both these are instances of thought, then things, too, are both so and not so at the same time. What results from all this, however, is most distressing. For if those who most of all have observed what the truth may be (and these are the ones who seek and cherish it most) have such doctrines and say these things about the truth, should we not expect beginners in philosophy to lose interest in it? For to seek the truth would be but to chase birds in the air.

   These thinkers came to this doctrine because of the fact that, though seeking the truth about things, they believed that only sensible things exist; and it is in these that the nature of the indeterminate and of being, in the sense in which we have stated, exists to a great extent. And so what they say does seem to be the case, but it is not true; for it is more fitting to state it this way than the way Epicharmus did about Xenophanes. Moreover, observing that all this nature is in motion, and thinking that nothing is true of that which changes, they came to the belief that nothing indeed may be truly said of that which changes altogether

and in every way. Now it was from this belief that blossomed the most   10
extreme of the doctrines we have mentioned, namely, that of the followers of Heraclitus, and also such doctrine as was held by Cratylus,
who finally thought that nothing should be spoken but only moved his
finger, and who criticized even Heraclitus for saying that one cannot
step into the same river twice, for he himself thought that one could   15
not do so even once.

   However, our reply to this argument, too, will be that when the
changing thing changes, there is some reason for these thinkers to truly
think that the changing thing is not. Yet even this is disputable; for
that which is losing an attribute still retains something of that which is
being lost, and some part of that which the changing thing becomes is
already there. And in general, while something is being destroyed,   20
there exists yet something; and if something is being generated, there
must be something out of which it is being generated and something
by which it is being generated, and the process in each case cannot go
on to infinity. But leaving these arguments aside, we maintain that to
change with respect to quantity is not the same as to change with respect
to quality. Let us grant that the object does not remain the same with
respect to quantity; still it is with respect to form that we know each   25
thing. Moreover, those who have such beliefs deserve criticism also
in view of the fact that from their observation of sensible things, small
in number, they have expressed themselves similarly about the entire
heaven. For it is only in the place of sensible things around us that
destructions and generations constantly occur, but this place is, in a   30
manner of speaking, not even a part of the whole universe; so that it
would be more just to reject the sensible things in this place for the sake
of the things in the rest of the universe than to condemn the latter for the
sake of the former. Moreover, it is clear that our reply to them, too,
will be the same as that made earlier to the others; for we shall have
to show and convince them that some immovable nature exists. More-   35
over, in saying that things both are and are not, these thinkers are even
faced with the consequence that all things are at rest rather than in motion; for there is nothing to which they can change, since everything
already belongs to every thing.   1010b

   Concerning the truth regarding the fact that not every appearance
is true, first, it is a fact that no sensation of its proper sensible is false;
but appearance is not the same as sensation. Then we are justly surprised if these thinkers raise the question whether the size of the mag-   5
nitudes and the kinds of colors are such as they appear to those at a distance or to those who are near, whether things are such as they appear to
the sick or to the healthy, whether those things are heavy which so
appear to the weak or to the strong, and whether those things are true

which appear to those who are asleep or to those who are awake. For it
10   is evident that they themselves do not think so; at least no one in Libya,
believing at night that he is in Athens, starts walking to the Odeum.
Again, with regard to the future, as Plato too says, the opinion of a
doctor and that of an ignorant man are indeed not equally reliable, that
is, as to whether the sick will get well or not. Again, with regard to the
15   powers of sensation themselves, the power of the non-proper object is
not so reliable as the power of the proper object, or, that of the object
nearby is not so reliable as that of its own object;   but in the case of
colors it is sight that *judges* and not taste, and in the case of flavors it is
taste and not sight. And no power of sensation ever says about its proper
object that it is so and not so at the same time.   But not even at an-
20   other time does it doubt about that affection, but it may doubt about
the thing to which the affection belongs. For example, the same wine,
either due to its own change or due to a change of one's body, might
seem sweet at one time but not at another; but at least sweetness, such as
25   it is when it exists, never changes, and one always thinks truly of it
as such, and that which will be sweet will of necessity be of this kind.
Yet all these doctrines do away with this; and just as they deny the existence of a *substance* of anything, so they deny that anything exists
of necessity; for the necessary cannot be now this and now that, and
30   so if something exists of necessity, it will not be so and not so.
    In general, if indeed only what is sensible exists, nothing would exist if
things with a soul did not exist, for then there would be no power of
sensation.   For one thing, it is equally true that the sensibles   and the
effects of the sensibles would not exist (for the latter are affections of
that which senses), but for another, it is impossible that the underlying
subjects which cause the sensations should not exist, even if there is no
35   sensation of them. For a sensation is surely not a sensation of itself, but
there is also something else besides that sensation which must be prior
1011a   to the sensation;   for that which moves is by nature prior to that which
is moved. And even if the two are spoken of in relation to each other,
this is no less true.

BOOK VI (= E)

1

1025b   We are seeking the principles and causes of things, but clearly, qua
things. For there is a cause of health and of good physical condition,

and there are principles and elements and causes of mathematical   5
objects, and in general, every science which proceeds by *thinking*
or which participates in *thought* to some extent is concerned with
causes and principles, whether these are very accurate or rather simplified. But all these sciences, marking off some being or some genus,
conduct their investigations into this part of being, although not into
unqualified being nor into their part of being qua being, and they say   10
nothing concerning whatness; but starting from the whatness of their
subject, which [whatness] in some sciences is made clear by sensation
but in others is laid down by hypothesis, they thus proceed to demonstrate more or less rigorously the essential attributes of their genus.
Consequently, it is evident by such induction from these sciences that
there is no demonstration of *substance* or of whatness but that these   15
are made known in some other way. Similarly, they say nothing as to
the existence or non-existence of the genus they investigate, and this is
because it belongs to the same power of *thought* to make known both
the whatness and the existence of a genus.

Now physical science, too, happens to be concerned with some genus
of being (for it is concerned with such a substance which has in itself   20
a principle of motion and of rest), and it is clear that this science is
neither practical nor productive. For in productive sciences the principle of a thing produced is in that which produces, whether this is
intellect or art or some power, and in practical sciences the principle
of *action* is in the doer, and this is *choice;* for that which is done and
that which is *chosen* are the same thing. Thus, if every *thought* is   25
practical or productive or theoretical,   physics would be a theoretical
science, and theoretical about such being as can be moved,   and about
substances which according to formula are for the most part non-
separable   only.

We must not fail to notice how the essence and the formula of an
object of physics exists, for inquiry without this leads nowhere. Now of   30
things defined and of the whatness of things, some are considered in the
manner in which snubness exists, others in the manner in which concavity exists. These differ by the fact that "snubness" is *understood* with
matter (for a snub is a concave nose) but "concavity" without sensible
matter. If, then, all physical things are named in a manner like the snub   1026a
(as for example a nose, an eye, a face, flesh, bone, and in general an
animal, and also a leaf, a root, a bark, and in general a plant; for what
is signified by the formula of each of these is not without motion but
always has matter), it is clear how we must seek and define the whatness
in physical things and why it belongs to the physicist to investigate even   5
some part of the soul, namely, that which does not exist without mat-

ter. From what has been said, then, it is evident that physics is a theoretical science.

Mathematics, too, is a theoretical science; but whether its objects are immovable and separate is not at present clear. It is clear, however, that some mathematical sciences investigate their objects qua immovable
10   and qua separate. But if there is something which is eternal and immovable and separate, the knowledge of it evidently belongs to a theoretical science, not however to physics (for physics is concerned with certain movable things) nor to mathematics, but to a science which is prior to both. For physics is concerned with separable but not
15   immovable things, and mathematics is concerned with some immovable things although perhaps not separable but as in matter. The first science, however, is concerned with things which are both separate and immovable. Now all causes must be eternal, and these most of all; for these are the causes of what is visible among things divine.[34] Hence, there should be three theoretical philosophies, mathematics, physics,
20   and theology. For it is clear that if the divine is present anywhere, it would be present in a nature of this sort, and the most honorable science should be concerned with the most honorable genus of things. So, the theoretical sciences are to be preferred over the other sciences, but theology is to be preferred over the other theoretical sciences.

One might raise the question whether first philosophy is in any way
25   universal or is concerned merely with some genus and some one nature. In the case of the mathematical sciences, their objects are not all treated in the same manner; geometry and astronomy are concerned with some nature, but universal mathematics is common to all. Accordingly, if there were no substances other than those formed by nature, physics would be the first science; but if there is an immovable
30   substance, this would be prior, and the science of it would be first philosophy and would be universal in this manner, in view of the fact that it is first. And it would be the concern of this science, too, to investigate being qua being, both what being is and what belongs to it qua being.

2

But since the unspecified term "being" has many senses,[35] one of which
35   is being by accident, another is that which is true (and nonbeing is that which is false), and besides these senses there are the various categories (for example, whatness, quality, quantity, whereness, whenness, and
1026b similarly any other meaning which the term may have), and in addition

to these there is potential being and also *actual* being—since "being", then, has many senses, we must first speak of accidental being, in view of the fact that there can be no investigation of it.

A sign of this is the fact that no science, be it practical or productive 5 or theoretical, takes the trouble to consider it. For the builder who is building a house is not producing at the same time the attributes which are accidental to the house when built, for these are infinite; for nothing prevents the house built from being pleasant to some men, harmful to some others, useful to still others, and distinct so to speak from any other thing, but the art of building produces none of these attributes. 10 In the same way, the geometer does not investigate the attributes which are in this manner accidental to figures, nor the problem whether a triangle is distinct from a triangle whose angles are equal to two right angles. And this happens with good reason; for an accident is a mere name, as it were. And so in a sense Plato[36] was not wrong when he ranked 15 sophistry as being concerned with nonbeing. For the discussions of the sophists deal most of all with what is accidental, so to speak; for example, whether the musical and the grammatical are the same or distinct, and likewise for musical Coriscus and Coriscus, and whether everything which exists, but not always, has come to be, so that if he who was musical became grammatical, then also he who was gram- 20 matical became musical, and all other such arguments. For accidental being appears to be somewhat close to nonbeing. This is also clear from such arguments as the following: of things which exist in another manner, there is generation and destruction, but of accidental being there is no generation or destruction. Nevertheless, concerning accidental being we must state, as much as can be stated, what its nature 25 is and through what cause it exists; for perhaps it will be at the same time clear also why there is no science of it.

Now since, among things, some exist always in a certain way and of necessity so (by "necessity" we do not mean the one according to force, but the impossibility of being otherwise), while others exist neither 30 of necessity nor always but for the most part, this latter existence is the principle and the cause of the existence by accident; for that which exists neither always nor for the most part we call "an accident". For example, if in the dog-days we have storm and cold weather, this we say is an accident, but not if we have sultry heat, in view of the fact that the latter occurs always or for the most part, but the former does not. 35 And a man is pale by accident (for he is neither always so nor for the most part), but he is an animal not by accident. And the builder produces health by accident, in view of the fact that it is by nature a 1027a doctor and not a builder who produces health, but it is an accident that the builder is a doctor. And a cook, who aims at making tasty food, may make something which produces health,   but he does so not in virtue of the art of cooking; so, we say that this occurred by accident,

5   and in a qualified sense the cook produces health, but in an unqualified sense he does not. For in some of the cases of things which happen always or for the most part there exist productive capacities,   but in the case of accidents there is no art and no definite capacity at all; for of things which exist or are generated by accident the cause is accidental too. Thus, since not all things are or are generated of necessity or always,

10   but most of them are so for the most part, accidental being must exist. For example, it is neither always nor for the most part that the pale is musical, but since this occurs sometimes, it is an accident; if such things never occur, all things will exist of necessity. So, matter is an acciden-tal cause, capable of being otherwise than for the most part.

15   We must begin, then, by raising the problem whether there is noth-ing besides what exists either always or for the most part, or is this impossible? Since this is impossible,   there is something besides what exists either always or for the most part, and this is what exists by chance or by accident. Again, do things exist for the most part without anything existing always at all, or are there things which exist eter-nally?   We must examine this later.[37] However, it is evident that there is

20   no science of accidental being; for every science is of that which is always or for the most part. For how else will one be instructed or instruct another; for it must be definitely stated that this is so either always or for the most part, for example, that for the most part honey-water is beneficial to a patient with fever. But science cannot state the

25   exception to what occurs for the most part; for example, it cannot say "this benefit will not occur on the day of the new moon", for then the non-occurrence of benefit on the day of the new moon will itself be a thing which is either always or for the most part, and an accident is something other than what is always or for the most part.   We have stated, then, what an accident is, through what cause it exists, and that there is no science of it.

BOOK VII (= Z)

1

1028a10   The term "being" is used in several senses, as we pointed out previ-ously[38] in our account of the various senses of terms. In one sense, it signifies whatness and a *this;* in another, it signifies a quality or a quan-tity or one of the others which are predicated in this way. Although

"being" is used in so many senses, it is evident that of these the primary
sense is whatness, and used in this sense it signifies a substance. For   *15*
when we state that this has some quality, we say that it is good or bad
but not that it is three cubits long or a man; but when we state what
it is, we say that it is a man or a God but not white or hot or three
cubits long. The others are called "beings" in view of the fact that they
are quantities of being which is spoken of in this primary sense, or
qualities of it, or affections of it, or something else of this kind. Because   *20*
of this, one might even raise the problem whether walking, being
healthy, sitting, and the others of this kind are beings or not beings;
for by nature each of these does not exist by itself and cannot be separated from a substance, but rather, if anything, it is that which walks or   *25*
that which sits or that which is healthy that is a being. These latter
appear to be beings to a higher degree, because there is something
definite in each of them, namely, the underlying subject; and this is
the substance and the individual, which is indicated in the corresponding predication, for we do not use the terms "the good" and "that which
sits" without including the substance. It is clear, then, that each of   *30*
the others exists because substances exist. Thus, being in the primary
sense, not in a qualified sense but without qualification, would be a
substance.

Now the term "primary" [or "first", or "prior to all others"] is used
in many senses, yet a substance is primary in every sense: in formula,
in knowledge, and in time. For of the other categories no one is separable, but only substance. And in formula, too, substance is primary;   *35*
for in the formula of each of the other categories the formula of a
substance must be present. And we think we understand each thing
to the highest degree when we know, for example, what a man is or
what fire is, rather than their quality or their quantity or their where-   *1028b*
ness,   and even of these latter, we understand each when we know
what a quantity is or what a quality is.   And indeed the inquiry or
perplexity concerning what being is, in early times and now and always,
is just this: What is a substance? For it is this that some assert to be
one,[39] others more than one,   and some say that it is finite,[40] while others   *5*
that it is infinite.[41] And so we, too, must speculate most of all, and first
of all, and exclusively, so to say, concerning being which is spoken of
in this sense. What is being?

2

Substance is thought to belong most evidently to bodies; and so we
say that animals and plants and their parts are substances, and also   *10*

the natural bodies, such as fire and water and earth and each one of this sort, and also parts of these, and composites of these (either of parts or of all of them), such as the heavens and its parts, the stars and the Moon and the Sun. We must inquire whether these alone are sub-
15   stances or also others, or some of these and some others, or none of these but some others.

Some thinkers[42] are of the opinion that the limits of bodies are substances, such as surfaces and lines and points and units, and that they are substances to a higher degree than bodies or solids. Moreover, some think that no such as the ones just mentioned exist, but only sensible objects; but others think that such do exist, and that they are many and are eternal and are beings to a higher degree, as in the case
20   of Plato, who posits two [kinds of] substances, the Forms and the Mathematical Objects, and also the sensible bodies as the third kind. Speusippus spoke of yet a greater number [of kinds] of substances, and of distinct principles for each kind; he starts from the *One* as a principle for numbers, posits another principle for magnitudes, still another for soul, and in this manner he extends the kinds of substances. Still
25   others[43] say that the Forms and the Numbers have the same nature, and that from these follow all the others, such as the lines, the planes, and so on, all the way down to the substances of the universe and the sensible substances.

Concerning these matters we must examine what is stated well and what is not, which are the substances, whether there are other sub-
30   stances besides the sensible or not and how these exist, whether there exist separate substances other than sensible substances or not, and if yes, then why such exist and how. But first, we must sketch out what a substance is.

3

The term "substance" is spoken of, if not in more, still in four main senses; for the essence is thought to be the substance of an individual,
35   and the universal, and the genus, and fourthly the underlying subject. The subject is that of which the others are said, but the subject itself
1029a   is not said of anything else. And so we must describe first the subject; for the primary subject is thought to be a substance in the highest degree.

In one sense, the subject is said to be the matter; in another sense, it is said to be the *form*; in a third, it is said to be the composite of these. By "matter" I mean, for instance, bronze; by "*form*", the shape of

its outward appearance; and by "the composite of these", the statue as 5
a *composite*. Thus, if the form is prior to matter and is a being to a
higher degree than matter, for the same reason it will be prior to the
composite of form and matter.

We have now stated sketchily what a substance is, that it is that which
is not said of a subject but of which the others are said. But we must
not state it only in this manner, as this is not enough. The statement 10
itself is not clear, and further, matter becomes a substance. For if this
is not a substance, we are at a loss as to what else is a substance. If the
others are taken off, nothing appears to remain. For, of the others, some
are affections and actions and potencies of bodies, while length and
width and depth are quantities and not substances (for a quantity is 15
not a substance), but that to which as first these belong is a substance
to a higher degree. Yet if length and width and depth are removed, we
observe nothing left, unless there is something bounded by these; so
matter alone must appear to be a substance, if we inquire in this
manner. By "matter" I mean that which in itself is not stated as being 20
the whatness of something, nor a quantity, nor any of the other senses
of "being". For there is something of which each of these is a predicate,
whose being is other than that of each of the predicates; for all the
others are predicates of a substance, while a substance is a predicate[11] of matter. Thus, this last is in itself neither a whatness nor a
quantity nor any of the others; and it is not a denial of any of these, 25
for even a denial belongs to something accidentally.

From what has been said, it follows that matter is a substance. But
this is impossible; for to be separable and a *this* is thought to belong
most of all to a substance. Accordingly, the form or the *composite*
would seem to be a substance to a higher degree than matter. The 30
composite substance, that is, the composite of matter and *shape*, may
be laid aside; for it is posterior and clear. Matter, too, is in a sense
evident. But we must examine the third, for this is the most perplexing.

It is agreed that there exist substances among the sensibles, so we
must first inquire into the sensibles. For, it is useful to proceed from the 1029*b*3
less to the more known. Instruction is acquired by all in this manner:
through the less known by nature to the more known by nature; and 5
just as in *actions*, in which the purpose is to start from what is good
to each individual and make good to each individual that which is
good in general, so here, the purpose is to start from what is more
known to the individual and proceed to make known to the individual
what is known by nature. Now what is known and first to each individual
is often known slightly and has little or no being. Nevertheless, from 10
what is poorly knowable but knowable to oneself one must make an

effort to know what is generally knowable, proceeding, as we stated, from what is knowable to oneself.

4

1   Since we have specified in the beginning[44] the number of ways in
2   which the term "substance" is used, and one of these was thought to
13   be the essence, we must investigate this. And first let us make some
logical remarks about it. The essence of each thing is what the thing
15   is said to be in virtue of itself. The essence of you is not the essence
of a musician; for, it is not in virtue of yourself that you are a musician.
Your essence, then, is what you are in virtue of yourself; but not in every
sense of the expression "in virtue of yourself", for, it is not in this sense
that a surface is white in virtue of itself, since to be a surface is not to
be white. Moreover, the essence of a surface is not the essence of both,
that is, of a white surface. Why not? Because "surface" reappears in
20   the expression of its own essence. In the expression of the essence of a
thing, in other words, the term signifying the thing must not appear
as a part. Thus, if to be a white surface is to be a smooth surface, then
to be white and to be smooth are one and the same.
    Since composites exist also with respect to the other categories (for
there is some underlying subject in each case, as in quality, quantity,
25   whenness, whereness, and in motion), we must inquire whether there
is a formula of the essence for each of them and whether essence belongs
to them; for example, whether to a white man belongs an essence of a
white man. Let the term "a cloak" signify a white man. What is the
essence of a cloak? But "a cloak" does not signify something which is
30   said to be in virtue of itself. Perhaps "not in virtue of itself" has two
senses, one by addition, the other not by addition. In the first sense,
that which is being defined is stated by being attached to something
else, for example, if, in defining the essence of white, one were to state
the formula of a white man; in the second sense, if to something something else is attached, for example, if "a cloak" were to signify a white
1030a man, and one were to define a cloak as white. Now a white man is
white, indeed, yet his essence is not the essence of white.
    But is to be a cloak an instance of an essence at all, or not? But an
essence is just a *this*, whereas if something is said of   something else
we do not have just a *this*; for example, a white man is not just a *this*,
5   if a *this* belongs only to substances. Thus, there is an essence only of
those things whose formula is a definition. However, there is a definition,
not if a name and its formula merely have the same meaning (for then

all formulae will be definitions, since there can be a name having the
same meaning as any given formula, and so even the *Iliad*   would be
a definition), but if the name and its formula signify something pri-   *10*
mary;   and in the formula of such a primary being it is not the case
that something is said of   something else. Essence, then, will belong
to nothing which is not a species of a genus, but only to a species   of
a genus; for it is these that are thought to be stated neither in virtue
of participation, nor with an attribute, nor with an accident.   As for
the others, if there is a name for each of them, there will be a formula   *15*
signifying that this belongs to that, or instead of a simplified formula
one that is more accurate;   but there will be no definition and no
essence.

Or else, the term "definition" like the term "whatness" has many
senses; for in one sense the term "whatness" signifies a substance and
a *this*, in another it signifies each of the other categories, a quantity,   *20*
a quality, and the like. For, just as existence belongs to all although
not similarly, but to some   primarily and to others   secondarily, so
whatness belongs to substances in the full sense but to the others in a
qualified way. We might even ask of a quality "What is it?", so that a
quality, too, is an instance of whatness, although not in the full sense   ,   *25*
but just as, in the case of nonbeing, some[45] use the verbal expression
"nonbeing is", not that nonbeing simply exists but that nonbeing is
nonbeing, so with the whatness of a quality.

Thus, we must also consider how we should express ourselves on
each point, but we must not allow our expression to go beyond the
facts.   And so now, since what we have said is evident, in a similar
manner an essence will belong primarily and in the full sense to a   *30*
substance; and it will belong also to the others, just as the whatness
will, not as an essence in the full sense, but as an essence of a quality,
or of a quantity, or etc. For we must say that these latter are beings
either by equivocation, or by adding and subtracting (as when we say
that the unknowable is knowable),[46] although it is in a way right to
call them "beings" neither equivocally nor in the same sense, seeing   *35*
that they are like what we call "medical", which are neither one and
the same thing nor called "medical" equivocally, but are called so in   *1030b*
view of the fact that they are related to one and the same thing; for
the materials and the operation and the instrument are called "medical"
neither equivocally nor with one meaning, but in relation to one thing.

Anyway, it makes no difference whichever way one wishes to speak
about these things; what is evident is the fact that definitions and   *5*
essences, in the primary and unqualified sense, are of substances alone.
There are also definitions and essences of the others   in a similar man-

ner, but not in the primary sense. If we posit this, it is not necessary
that there be a definition of a term if the term and its formula have the
same meaning, unless the formula is of a certain kind, namely, a formula
which signifies one thing,   not one by continuity as in the case of the
10   *Iliad*   or of things which are bound together,   but one in any of the
main senses of "one". The senses of "one" correspond to those of "being", and "being" signifies a *this,* or a quantity, or a quality.   And so
there will be a formula and a definition even of a white man, but in a
sense distinct from that of whiteness and that of a substance.

5

If one denies that a formula by addition is a definition, a *difficulty*
15   arises as to whether there can be a definition of anything which is not
simple but is a combination, for this must be indicated by an additional
term. What I mean, for example, is this: there is a nose and concavity,
and also snubness, which is stated in terms of the two, since one of
them is in the other, and concavity or snubness is an *attribute* of a
20   nose not by accident but essentially; and it is in the nose not as whiteness is in Callias or in a man (by the fact that Callias is white, to whom
the essence of man happens to belong), but as the male is in the animal
and as the equal is in quantity and as all the attributes are in things to
which they are said to belong essentially. And each of these *attributes*
(a) has in its formula the formula or the name of the subject of which
it is the *attribute* and (b) cannot be signified apart from that subject.
For example, whiteness can be signified apart from the man, but the
25   female cannot be signified apart from the animal. Thus, either there
is no essence and no definition of any of these *attributes,* or if there is,
it is in another way, as we said.[47]
But there is also another *difficulty* concerning such *attributes.* For if a
snub nose and a concave nose are the same, snubness and concavity
30   will be the same; but if the latter two are not the same (because one
cannot speak of snubness apart from the thing of which it is an essential
attribute, for snubness is concavity in the nose), then either one should
not say "a snub nose" or he will be saying the same thing twice, namely,
"a concave nose nose"; for "a snub nose" will be "a concave nose nose".
35   And so it is absurd that such things should have an essence; otherwise,
1031a   there is an infinite regress, for in "a snub nose nose" there will be still another "nose".
Clearly, then, only of a substance is there a definition. For if there
is a definition of the other categories also, it must be by addition, as in

the case of a quality or oddness; for oddness cannot be defined without a number, nor a female without an animal. In saying "by addition", I mean an expression in which the same term is stated twice, as in the examples cited. And if this is true, neither can there be a definition of a combined pair, such as an odd number. Yet we fail to see that the formulae are not stated accurately. But if there are definitions of these, too, then either they are definitions in another sense, or, as we stated,[48] we should say that "a definition" and "an essence" have many senses. Thus, in one sense, a definition and an essence can belong to nothing but substances, but in another sense, they can belong also to other things.

It is clear, then, that a definition is a formula of an essence, and that there are essences either of substances alone, or of substances in the highest sense and primarily and in the full sense.

6

We should inquire whether each thing and its essence are the same or distinct. This is useful for our inquiry into *substance;* for each thing is thought to be nothing else but its own *substance,* and the essence is said to be the *substance* of each thing.

Now of a thing which is stated accidentally, it would seem that the thing is distinct from its essence, for example, a white man is distinct from the essence of a white man; for if these were the same, the essence of a man and the essence of a white man would be the same, for a man and a white man are the same, as people say, and so the essence of a white man would be the same as the essence of a man. Or, it is not necessary for accidental being to be the same as its essence. For it is not in such a way that the outer terms become the same, since what would perhaps happen is this, namely, that the outer terms which are accidental to the same term would be the same; for example, the essence of white and the essence of musical would be the same, and this seems not to be the case.

As for things which are stated by themselves, is it necessary for them to be the same as their essences? For example, this would be the case if some substances exist, like the Ideas posited by some thinkers, prior to which no other *substances* or natures exist. For if Good Itself were distinct from the essence of Good, Animal Itself from the essence of Animal, and Being from the essence of Being, then besides the ones posited there would be other substances and natures and 'Ideas', and these latter would be also prior to the former, that is, if an *essence* is a

substance. And if the two kinds were severed from each other, there would be no science of the former, and the latter would not be be-
5   ings. (By "being severed" I mean this, that neither the essence of Good belongs to Good Itself, nor Good Itself to the essence of Good).
For there is a science of each thing only when we know its essence. And as it is with the Good, so it is with the others. So if the essence of Good were not Good, neither would the essence of Being be Being, nor would the essence of *One* be *One*.
10   Now all essences exist alike in this manner, or else none of them does so exist; so that if the essence of being is not a being, neither will any of the others be in the same way. Moreover, if the essence of good does not belong to something, this will not be good. Consequently, the good and the essence of good must be one, the beautiful and the essence of beautiful must be one, and so with all others which are stated not of something else but by themselves and are pri-
15   mary. For if this is so, it is also adequate, even if no Forms exist; and perhaps more so even if Forms do exist. At the same time it is clear that if indeed there exist Ideas such as some assert, the underlying subject will not be a substance; for these would of necessity be substances but could not be predicated of a subject; otherwise, they would exist by being participated in.
From these arguments it is clear that each thing and its essence are
20   one and the same but not by accident, and that to *know* each thing is to *know* its essence, and so even by exhibiting particular instances, it is clear that a thing and its essence must be one.
As for the thing which is stated accidentally, such as the musical and the white, since the terms "the musical" and "the white" have double meanings, it is not true to say that the thing and its essence are the same;
25   for both the subject to which the attribute belongs and the attribute itself are called "white", so in one sense the thing and its essence are the same, but in another sense they are not the same; for the essence of white is not the same as the man or the white man, but it is the same as the attribute white.
The absurdity would be apparent also if one were to use a name for
30   each essence; for there would be an essence also of an essence, for example, there would be an essence also of the essence of a horse. If so, why should not some things be their essences from the start, if indeed an essence is a *substance?* Moreover, not only a thing and its essence
1032a   are one, but also the formula of each is the same, as is clear also from what has been said; for it is not by accident that the essence of unity and unity are one. Further, if unity and the essence of unity were distinct, the process would go on to infinity; for, there would be the

essence of unity and also unity, so that according to the same argument there would again be the essence of the essence of unity and also the essence of unity, etc.

Of things which are primary and are stated by themselves, then, it 5
is clear that each of them and its essence are one and the same. Evidently, the sophistical refutations of this position and the problem whether Socrates and the essence of Socrates are the same are solved in the same way; for in solving a problem successfully, it makes no difference whether one is answering another's questions or is using the argu- 10
ments for the solution of that problem. We have stated, then, how each thing and its essence are the same and how they are not the same.

13

Since our inquiry is about substance, let us return to it once more. 1038b
Just as the underlying subject is called "a substance", and also the essence and the *composite* of the two, so too is the universal. We have discussed two of them, the essence[49] and the underlying subject;[50] and a 5
subject may underlie in two ways, (a) either by being a *this*, as an animal underlies its attributes, (b) or as matter underlies actuality.[51] The universal, too, is thought by some to be a cause in the highest degree and to be a principle, so let us discuss also the universal; for it seems that it is impossible for any of the so-called "universals" to be a substance.

First, the *substance* of a thing is peculiar to it and does not belong 10
to another thing, but a universal is common; for by "a universal" we mean that whose nature is such that it may belong to many. Of which of these, then, will the universal be the *substance?* Either of all or of none. But it cannot be the *substance* of all. And if it is of one of them, this one will also be the others; for things whose *substance* is one have also one essence and are themselves one. 15

Again, that which is called "a substance" is not said of a subject, but a universal is always said of some subject. But while a universal cannot be a *substance* in the manner in which an essence is, can it not be present in a substance as 'animal' is in a man and a horse? But clearly there is a formula of a universal. And it makes no difference even if there is no formula of everything that is in the *substance;* for 20
this will none the less be the *substance* of something, as 'man' is the *substance* of a man in whom it is present. If so, then again the same result will arise; for it will be, as 'animal' for example, the *substance* of that in which it is present as something peculiar to it. Moreover, it is impossible and absurd that what is a *this* and a substance, if composed of parts, should not be composed of substances or of *this-es* 25

but of a quality, for a non-substance or a quality would be prior to a substance and to a *this*. This is indeed impossible; for neither in formula nor in time nor in generation can the *attributes* of a substance be prior to that substance, since otherwise they would be separable. Further, to Socrates, who is a substance, another substance will be
30   present, and so a substance will exist in two things.

In general, if 'man' or any other thing spoken of in this manner is a substance, it follows that neither is any part of its formula a *substance* of anything nor does it exist apart from it or in something else; I mean, for example, that neither does 'animal' exist apart from individual animals, nor does any other part of the formula so exist.

35   From these theoretical considerations, then, it is evident that none
1039a of the things that belong universally is a substance, and that none of the common predicates signifies a *this,* but only a *such.* Otherwise, many difficulties follow, and also the *third man.*[52]

Again, this is clear also from the following. No substance is composed
5   of substances which exist in actuality; for two objects which exist thus in actuality are never one in actuality, but if they are two potentially, they can be one. For example, the double line is composed of two halves, but these latter exist potentially; for the actuality of each would make them separate. Thus, if a substance is one, it cannot consist of substances which are present in it. And in this sense Democritus
10   speaks rightly; for, he says, it is impossible for one thing to consist of two things or for one thing to become two things (for, he takes the position that substances are indivisible magnitudes). It is clear, then, that the situation with numbers is similar, if indeed a number is a composite of units, as is said by some[53]; for, either the number two is not one thing, or no unit in the number two exists in actuality.

15   But there is a *difficulty* in this result. For, if no substance can be composed of universals because a universal indicates a *such* but not a *this,* and if no substance can be a composite of substances which exist in actuality, every substance would be incomposite, and so there could be no formula of any substance. But it is the opinion of all and
20   it has been stated earlier[54] that either of a substance alone is there a definition, or of a substance most of all; and now, even of the latter there seems to be no definition. If so, then there can be no definition of anything; or else, in a sense there can be, and in a sense there cannot. This statement will be clearer from what will be said later.[55]

16

1040b5 It is also evident that most of what are regarded as substances are potentialities. These are the parts of animals (for none of them exists

separately, and when separated, even then, they all exist as matter),
and earth, and fire, and air; for none of them is one, but they exist like
a heap until they are transformed and a unity is produced out of them.   *10*
One might be led to believe that, most of all, the parts of living things
and those which are near the soul exist both actually and potentially,
in view of the fact that they have their principles of motion somewhere
in their joints; and on account of this, some animals continue living
after they are divided. Yet, when the animal is one and is continuous   *15*
by nature, and not by force or even by being grown together, every
part exists potentially; for that which is one by force or by being grown
together is abnormal.

Since the term "unity" is used like the term "being", and the *substance*
of what is one is one, and things whose *substance* is one numerically
are numerically one, it is evident that neither unity nor being can be
the *substance* of things, just as neither the essence of an element nor
that of a principle can be that *substance;* but we ask "What is the prin-   *20*
ciple of the thing?" in order to go back to something more known. Of
these, however, being and unity would be *substances* to a higher degree than a principle or an element or a cause, but even unity and
being are not *substances,* if indeed nothing else that is common is a
substance; for a *substance* belongs to nothing but to itself or to that
which has it   (of which it is the *substance*). Moreover, what is one   *25*
cannot exist in many ways   at the same time, but what is common
can exist in many ways at the same time; hence, it is clear that no universal exists apart from the individuals.   But those who posit the
existence of Forms are in one respect right, that is, by separating them,
if these are indeed substances, but in another respect they are not right,
that is, when they posit one Form as the form of many things.   The   *30*
cause of this is the fact that they cannot say what such indestructible
substances are which exist apart from individual and sensible substances. Accordingly, they posit them as being the same in kind as the
destructible substances   (for these we do know); for example, they
posit Man Himself and Horse Itself, adding the word "Itself" to the
names of sensible things. Yet, even if we had not seen the stars, I should   *1041a*
think that eternal substances would none the less exist apart from the
substances we would know. So now, too, if we cannot say what they
are, it is just as necessary that some eternal substances exist.

It is clear, then, that none of the so-called "universals" is a substance,
and that no substance is composed of substances.   *5*

17

Let us again continue the discussion from another starting-point, so
to say, and state what should be called "a substance" and what kind of

thing it is; for perhaps from this also the substance which is separate from sensible substances will be clear to us.

10   Since a substance, then, is a principle and a cause, let us proceed from here. Now the *why* is always sought in this manner: "Why does something belong to something else?" For to inquire why a musical man is a musical man is either to inquire into the fact already stated, namely, why a musical man is a musical man, or into something else.

15   But to ask why something is itself is to inquire into nothing, for the fact or the existence of something must be clear; for example, the fact that the moon is eclipsed must be clear. Thus, *the fact that something is itself,* this is the one *answer* and the one cause in all cases, as, for example, in the questions "Why is a man a man?" and "Why is the musical musical?", unless one were to answer that each thing is indivisible from itself, since to be one for each thing is to be indivisible from itself.

20   But this is common to all things and a short answer for all of them. On the other hand, we might ask why a man is an animal of such-and-such a kind. Here, however, it is clear that we are not asking why he who is a man is a man. We are asking, then, why something belongs to something else. That it does belong, this must be evident; otherwise,

25   the inquiry is about nothing. For example, "Why does it thunder?", that is, "Why is sound generated in the clouds?" In such an inquiry something is said of something else. And why are these things (for example, bricks and stones) a house? It is evident, then, that we are seeking the cause (logically speaking, this is the essence), which is in some cases the final cause (as perhaps in the case of a house or a

30   bed) and in others the first mover (for this too is a cause); but while we seek the latter kind of cause in generations and destructions, we seek the former kind also in cases of existence.

The object now sought escapes notice especially when the question

1041b raised is not properly expressed, as in the question "What is a man?", and this is because it is expressed simply and does not specify that something belongs to something else. But we should articulate the question properly before raising it, otherwise, it will be on the borderline between an inquiry into something and about nothing. Since, then, something must have something else and the existence must be as-

5   sumed, clearly the question is "Why is the matter some one thing?"; for example, "Why are these materials a house?" Because to them belongs this, which is the essence of a house; and because a man is this, or, this body has this. Thus, we are seeking the cause (and this is the form) through which the matter is a thing; and this cause is the *substance* of the thing. Concerning that which is simple, however, it is

10   evident that there is no inquiry and no teaching, but there is another manner of inquiring about such a thing.

Now since that which is composed of something exists in such a way as to be one in its totality, not like a heap but like a syllable (the syllable is not the letters, and so "*b*a" is not the same as "*b*" and "*a*", nor is the flesh the same as fire and earth; for after disintegration the flesh and the syllable no longer exist, but their elements, which are the letters *15* for the latter and fire and earth for the former, do exist), the syllable is not only its letters (the vowel and the consonant) but something else besides,   and the flesh is not only fire and earth or the hot and the cold but something else besides. If, further, that additional something must also be (a) an element or (b) a composite of elements, (a) in case it is *20* an element, the same argument will apply again, for flesh will then be composed of this element and of fire and of earth and of something else yet, and in this way the process will go on to infinity;   (b) but in case it is composed of elements, clearly it is composed not of one element (for we will have the previous case) but of many, so that again the same argument will apply to the result, whether in the case of flesh *25* or of the syllable.   It would seem, however, that this additional something is not an element but something else, and that it is the cause through which this is flesh and that is a syllable; and similarly in all other cases. And this is the *substance* of each thing; for this is the first cause   of the thing's existence. Since some objects are not *substances* of things, but those that are substances   are formed according to nature or by nature, the *substance* of these would appear to be this *30* nature, which is not an element but a principle.   As for an element, it is that which is present as matter in a thing and into which the thing is divisible, as the syllable "*b*a" is divisible into "*a*" and "*b*".

BOOK VIII (= H)

1

From what has been said we must draw conclusions, and, after sum- *1042a* ming these up, we must bring our inquiry to a close. We have said that it is of substances that we seek the causes and principles and elements.[56] *5* As to what objects are substances, some are agreed upon by all thinkers, but also certain others are advocated by some thinkers. Those agreed upon are physical substances, such as fire, earth, water, air, and the other simple bodies, and next, plants and their parts, and animals and *10* parts of animals, and finally, the heavens and its parts, but some thinkers say that also the Forms and the Mathematical Objects are substances.[57] From certain arguments it turns out that the essence and the underlying subject are also substances. Moreover, from other arguments the genus is to a higher degree a substance than the species,

15   and the universal is to a higher degree a substance than the individual;[58] and to the universal and the genus we may attach also the Ideas, for these are thought to be substances according to the same argument.

Since the essence is a substance, and the formula of this is a definition, for this reason we have given a description of a definition and of that which exists in virtue of itself.[59] Since a definition is a formula, and

20   a formula has parts, it was also necessary with respect to parts to examine what sort of objects are parts of *substances* and what are not, and also if to a part of a *substance* there is a corresponding part in the definition of the *substance*.[60] Moreover, we have shown that neither a universal nor a genus is a substance;[61] as for the Ideas and the Mathematical Objects, we must examine them later,[62] for some thinkers say that these exist in addition to the sensible substances.

Let us now proceed to discuss those which are agreed upon as being

25   substances. These are the sensible substances, and all sensible substances have matter. Now a substance is an underlying subject; and in one sense, this is matter (by "matter" I mean that which is not a *this* in *actuality* but is potentially a *this*); in another sense, it is the formula or the *form*, which is a *this* and separable in formula; in a third sense,

30   it is the composite of the two, of which alone there is generation and destruction, and which is separate without qualification, for of substances according to formula some are separable   but others are not.

It is clear that also matter is a substance, for in all opposite changes there is some subject which underlies the changes; for example, with

35   respect to place there is something which is now here but after elsewhere; with respect to increase   there is something which is now of a certain quantity but after less or greater; with respect to alteration there

1042b   is something which is now healthy but later sick; and similarly with respect to substance, there is something which is now in generation but later in destruction, and something which is now a subject as a *this* but later a subject with respect to a privation.   And the other changes follow this change   [with respect to substance], but one or two of the

5   other changes is not followed by this change; for if something has matter which can change with respect to place, it is not necessary for it to have matter which can change with respect to generation or destruction.   The difference between unqualified and qualified generation has been stated in the *Physics*.[63]

6

Returning to the *difficulty* stated earlier[64] concerning definitions and   *1045a*
numbers, we may ask: What causes each of them to be one? For in
anything which has many parts and whose totality is not just a heap but   *10*
is some whole besides just the parts, there is some cause, inasmuch as
in bodies, too, the cause of unity is in some cases contact, in others
viscosity, or some other such affection. Now a definition is one formula
not by the placing of things together, as in the *Iliad*, but by being a
formula of one thing. What is it, then, that makes a man one, and
why is he one and not many, such as an animal and also a biped, if   *15*
indeed there exists, as some say, Animal Itself and Biped Itself. For
why are these two not Man, so that men may exist by participating
not in Man or one Idea but in two, Animal and Biped? And, in general,
a man would then be not one but more than one, an animal and a   *20*
biped. It is evident, then, if we proceed in this manner, as these thinkers
are accustomed to define and speak, we cannot answer or solve the
difficulty. But if, as we maintain, the one is matter and the other *form*,
and the former exists potentially but the latter as *actuality*, what we
seek no longer seems to be a *difficulty*. For this is the same *difficulty*   *25*
as the one which would arise if the definition of a *cloak* were to be "a
round bronze"; for the name would be a sign of this formula, so that
we would be inquiring into the cause of the unity of roundness and
bronze. The difficulty indeed no longer appears, in view of the fact
that the one is matter and the other form. What causes that which   *30*
exists potentially to be in *actuality*, then, aside from that which acts
in the case of things which are generated? Doubtless, nothing else
causes that which is potentially a sphere to be a sphere in actuality, but
this is the essence in each.

Of matter, some is intelligible and some sensible, and in a formula
it is always the case that one part is matter and one part is *actuality;*   *35*
for example, in the case of a circle, "a plane figure." But of the things
which have no matter, whether intelligible or sensible, each is immediately just a unity as well as just a being, such as a *this*, or a quality, or *1045b*
a quantity. And so in their definitions, too, neither "being" nor "one"
is present, and the essence of each is immediately a unity as well as a
being. Consequently, nothing else is the cause of oneness or of being   *5*
in each of them;   for each is immediately a being and a unity, not in the
sense that "being" and "unity" are their genera, nor in the sense that
they exist apart from individuals.

It is because of this *difficulty* that some thinkers speak of participation but are perplexed as to what causes participation and what it is

10   to participate, and others speak of communion with the soul, as when
      Lycophron says that *knowledge* is the communion of *knowing* with the
      soul, and still others call life a composition or connection of soul with
      body. However, the same argument applies to all; for being healthy,
      too, will be a communion or a connection or a composition of soul and
      health, and the being of a triangular bronze   will be a composition of
15   bronze and a triangle, and being white will be a composition of surface
      and whiteness. They are speaking in this manner because they are
      seeking a unifying formula of, and a difference between, potentiality
      and actuality. But, as we have stated,[65] the last matter and the *form* are
      one and the same; the one exists potentially, the other as *actuality*. Thus,
20   it is like asking what the cause of unity is and what causes something
      to be one; for each thing is a kind of unity, and potentiality and
      actuality taken together exist somehow as one. So there is no other
      cause, unless it be the mover which causes the motion from potency
      to *actuality*. But all things which have no matter are without qualifica-
      tion just unities of one kind or another.

BOOK IX (= Θ)

1

1045b   We have discussed primary being,[66] which is substance, and to which
       the other categories of being are referred. For it is in virtue of the
30   formula of substance that each of the others, such as quantities and
       qualities and the like, is called "a being"; for all of these will have the
       formula of substance, as we said in the beginning of our discussion.[67]
       Now since "being" means whatness or quality or quantity, but it is also
       used with respect to potentiality and actuality and function, let us
35   also describe potentiality and actuality. And first, let us take up what
       is called "potentiality" [or "potency", or "power", or "capacity", or "ca-
       pability"] in the most proper sense of that term, although it is not useful
1046a for our present purpose. For "potentiality" and *"actuality"* are predi-
       cates of more objects than those in which there is motion. But after
       discussing this sense of "potentiality", we shall also make clear the
       other senses when we describe *actuality*.
5   We have explained elsewhere[68] the various senses of "potentiality" and
       "to be capable". Of these, we may dismiss the ones which are called
       "potencies" by equivocation; for some are called so by some similarity,
       as in geometry when we say that certain things are or are not powers
       by being or not being so and so in some way or other. As for the so-

called "potencies" which are related to the same kind, they are all prin- 10
ciples of one sort or another and are related to the primary one, and
this is a principle of change in another thing or in the thing itself qua
other. For one of them is a potency of being acted upon, and this is in
the thing which is acted upon and is a principle of change by being
acted upon by another or by itself qua other. Another is a habit of not
being acted upon for the worse or to destruction by a principle of
change in another thing or in the thing itself qua other. Now in all these 15
definitions there is the formula of the primary potency. Again, these
are said to be potencies either by merely acting or by merely being acted
upon, or by acting or being acted upon well, and so even in the formulae
of the latter the formulae of the former potencies are somehow present.

It is evident, then, that in a sense the potency of acting and of 20
being acted upon is one (for a thing is capable either if it itself has the
potency of being acted upon or if something else can be acted upon
by it), but in another sense it is a distinct potency. For one potency is
in that which is acted upon; for it is because this thing has some
principle, and also because matter is a principle, that the thing is acted
upon, or one thing is acted upon by another. For that which is oily can 25
be burned, and that which yields in a certain way is malleable, and
similarly with the others. But another potency is in that which acts, as
heat and the art of building, the former being in that which can heat,
the latter in that which can build. Hence, insofar as something is by
nature united, it is never acted upon by itself; for it is one and not
another thing. Also, incapability or the incapable is a privation which 30
is the contrary of a potency of this sort, and so to every potency there is
a contrary potency in the same subject and with respect to the same
thing. But "privation" has many senses; for a thing is said to be
deprived (1) if it does not have something, or (2) if it does not have
what it should by nature have, either (a) not at all, or (b) not when
by nature it should have it, whether in a certain way (for example, if it
lacks it entirely) or in any way at all. In some cases, we say that things 35
are deprived if by nature they would have something but by force they
do not have it.

2

Since of such principles some are present in inanimate things, but
others are present in living things and in the soul and also in that part 1046b
of the soul which has reason, it is clear that of the potencies, too, some
will be nonrational but others will be with reason. Hence, all the arts or

the productive sciences are potencies; for they are principles which can cause a change in another thing or in the artist himself qua other. And
5 every potency with reason is capable of causing both contraries, but every nonrational potency can cause only one; for example, heat can cause only heating, but the medical art can cause sickness as well as health. The cause of this is the fact that *knowledge* is reason, and the same reason makes known both the thing and its privation, although not in the same way; and in a sense it is a reason of both, but in another
10 sense it is a reason of the thing rather than its privation. And so such sciences must be potencies of both contraries, yet they are essentially of the thing but not essentially of the privation of that thing; for reason, too, is essentially of the thing but in a sense accidentally of its privation. **For, it is by denial and removal that the formula makes known the**
15 **contrary; for a contrary is the primary privation, and this privation is the removal of the other contrary.**

Since contraries cannot exist at the same time in the same thing, but science is a potency by having reason, and the soul has a principle of motion, then whereas the healthy produces only health and that which can heat produces only heat and that which can cool produces only
20 cold, the scientist can produce both. For reason is of both, although not in the same way, and it is in the soul which has a principle of motion; and so the scientist can produce both contraries from the same principle of motion by connecting it to the same thing. Hence, things which are capable with respect to reason produce contraries in things without reason; for the contraries are included in a single principle, in reason.
25 It is also evident that the potency of merely acting or being acted upon follows from that of acting or being acted upon well, but that the latter does not always follow from the former; for he who acts well necessarily acts, but he who merely acts does not necessarily act well.

3

There are some, such as the thinkers of the Megarian school, who say
30 that a thing has a potency only when it is active, but that when it is not active it has no potency for that activity; for example, he who is not building is not able to build, but he can build only when he is building, and similarly with the others. It is not difficult to perceive the absurdities which follow from these statements; for it is clear from this that if a man is not building then he will not be a builder, since to be a builder
35 is to be able to build, and similarly with the other arts. If, then, it is impossible for a man to have such arts without learning them and having

acquired them at some time, and also impossible for him not to have
them without having lost them at some time (either through forget-   1047a
fulness or through some affection or through lapse of time; for certainly
the objects cannot have been destroyed, since they always exist), when
the builder ceases to build, he will no longer have the art; and when he
will immediately start building again, how will he have acquired the
art? And similarly with regard to lifeless things. For no thing will have   5
the potency of being cold or hot or sweet or, in general, of being sensed
unless it is being sensed; and so these thinkers would turn out to be
asserting the doctrine of Protagoras.[69] What is more, nothing will have
the power of sensation if it is not sensing or active. Accordingly, if a
blind man is one who has no sight, although it is his nature to have sight
and to have it at that time of his existence, the same people will be blind   10
many times during the day, and likewise deaf.

Again, if that which is deprived of potency is incapable, that which
is not now in the process of generation will be incapable of being
generated; but he who says of that which was incapable of generation
that it now exists or that it will exist would be speaking falsely (for this
was the meaning of "incapability"). Thus the statements of these
thinkers eliminate both motion and generation. For that which is   15
standing will always stand and that which is sitting will always sit;
for that which sits will not get up, since it will be impossible for it to
get up if it does not have the power to get up. If, then, the statements
of these thinkers cannot be true, it is evident that potentiality and
actuality are distinct; but their statements make potentiality and
actuality the same, and so it is no small matter that they are seeking to   20
eliminate. Consequently, a thing may be capable of being something
else and yet not be it, or, it may be capable of not being something
else and yet be it; and similarly in the other categories, a thing may
be capable of walking and yet not be walking, and capable of not
walking and yet be walking. What is capable of something, then, is such
that nothing will be impossible if to it will belong the *actuality* of that of   25
which it is said to have the potency. I mean, for example, if a thing is
capable of sitting and may   sit, if sitting will belong to it there will be
nothing impossible;   and similarly in the case of a thing capable of being
moved or of moving, of standing or of making something else stand, of
existing or of becoming, of not existing or of not coming to be.

The term *"actuality"*, which is placed along with the term "actuality",   30
has been extended to other things from motions,   where it was mostly
used; for *actuality* is thought to be motion most of all. And this is why
people do not attribute motion to what does not exist but some other
predicates; for example, they say that nonbeings are thinkable or

35 *desirable,* but not that they are in motion. And this is in view of the
fact that, while they do not exist in *actuality,* they may exist in
1047b *actuality.* For some nonbeings exist potentially; but they do not exist,
in the sense that they do not exist actually.

4

If the possible is what we have stated it to be[70] and what follows from
5 it, evidently one cannot truly say "so-and-so is possible, but it will
not be" in a way so as to eliminate the impossible. I mean, for example,
one might say, without taking into account the impossible, that it is possible for the diagonal and the side of a square to be measured by the
same unit, but that it will not be measured, seeing that nothing prevents
what is possible to be or to become from not being or not coming to be.
10 But it follows from what we laid down, if we were to assume also that
what is possible, though not existing, exists or has become, that nothing
will be impossible; yet in this case something will be impossible, for it
will be impossible for a common unit to measure both the diagonal and
the side. Indeed, the false and the impossible are not the same; for
although it is false that you are now standing, nevertheless it is not
impossible.
15 At the same time it is clear that, if it is necessary for B to exist when
A exists, then it is also necessary for B to be possible when A is possible.
For if it is not necessary for B to be possible, nothing prevents B from
being not possible. Now let A be possible. Then when A is possible,
20 nothing impossible results if we lay down A as existing; and then it is
necessary for B to exist. But B was taken as impossible. So let it be
impossible; then, if B is impossible, so must A be. But A was taken as
possible; so, B also must be possible. If, then, A is possible, B also will
be possible, if indeed they were so related that, if A exists, it is necessary
for B to exist. If, then, A and B being laid down as related in this way,
25 B is not possible in this way, neither will A and B be related as laid
down. Also, if, when A is possible, it is necessary for B to be possible,
then, if A exists, it is necessary for B to exist also. For, the statement "If
A is possible, it is necessary for B to be possible" means this: if A exists
at the time when and in the manner in which it is possible for it to
30 exist, it is necessary also for B to exist then and in that manner.

5

As all potencies are either innate, like the senses, or come by practice,
like that of flute-playing, or by study, like those of the arts, one acquires

potencies by practice or by discourse from previous activity, but this is   35
not necessary in the case of potencies which are not of this sort and
which are potencies over that which is acted upon.

Since that which is capable is capable of something and at some time   *1048a*
and in a certain manner (and all the other specifications must be added
to make this definite), and some things can cause motion according to
formula and their potencies include a formula while other things are
nonrational and their potencies are without reason, and since the former
potencies must be in living things but the latter may be in both, then,   5
in the case of the latter potencies, when the agent and the patient ap-
proach each other, the former must act and the latter must be acted
upon, each in the manner in which it is capable, but in the case of the
former potencies this is not necessary. For each of the nonrational
potencies can produce only one effect, while each of the rational potencies can produce contrary effects. Will the latter, then, produce contraries at the same time? But this is impossible. So in the case of the   10
rational potencies there must be something else which decides, and by
this I mean desire or *choice*. For whichever of two things an animal
desires by decision, this it will bring about when it has the potency to
do so and approaches that which can be acted upon. Thus, every thing
which is capable according to formula must act on that which it desires,
whenever it desires that of which it has the capability and in the
manner in which it has that capability. And it has the capability of so   15
acting when the patient is present and is disposed in a certain manner;
otherwise, the agent will not be able to act. And to add the further specification "if nothing external prevents" is no longer needed; for the
agent has the potency in the manner in which this is a potency of acting,
and the potency is such not in any way whatsoever but in a certain way
which also takes care of the external hindrances, since these are barred   20
by some of the specifications present. And so, even if one wishes or
desires to do two things or contrary things at the same time, he cannot
do them; for it is not in this manner that he has the potency of doing
them, nor is it a potency of doing them at the same time, since he can
do things only in the manner in which he has the potency.

6

Since we have discussed[71] what is called "a potency" with respect to   25
motion, let us explain what *actuality* is and what sort of object it is.
For if this is distinguished, the potential [or capable], too, will be at the
same time clear in view of the fact that by "potential" we mean not only

that whose nature is to move another or to be moved by another
30 (whether without qualification or in some manner), but also something
else; and it is because of our inquiry into the latter sense of "potential"
that we have discussed the former senses.

Now *actuality* is the existence of a thing, not in the way in which we
say that something exists potentially. For example, we say that Hermes
is potentially in the wood and that the half-line is in the whole line,
in view of the fact that in each case what exists potentially can be
separated from the whole; and we say that a man is a scientist even if
he is not in the process of investigating something, provided that he is
35 capable of doing this; but Hermes and the line when separated, and the
scientist in the process of investigation, these exist in *actuality*. What we
mean is clear by induction from individual cases, and we should not
seek a definition of everything but should also perceive an object by
1048b means of an analogy; thus, as that which builds is to that which is
capable of building, so is that which is awake to that which is asleep,
or that which is seeing to that which has its eyes shut but has the power
to see, or that which is separated from matter to matter itself, or the
5   finished product to the raw material. Let the term *"actuality"* signify
the first part of each of these differences and "the potential" signify the
second part.

Things which are said to be in *actuality* are not all called so in the
same manner but by analogy, that is, as A is in B or is related to B, so C
is in D or is related to D; for, in some cases, *actuality* is to the potential
as motion is to the power to move, in others, as a *substance* to some
10   matter. But the infinite and the void and all other such objects are said
to exist potentially and in *actuality* in a sense distinct from many other
things, such as that which sees or walks or is seen. For the latter may
sometimes be truly stated as existing so even without qualification, for
of a thing we say that it is seen sometimes if it is actually being seen
and sometimes if it is capable of being seen; but the infinite is potential
15   not in such a way that it will be separate in *actuality*, but it is potential
in knowledge. For, to a never-ending process of division we attribute
an *actuality* which exists potentially, but not a separate existence to
the infinite.

Since of the actions which have a limit none is an end but each is
for the sake of an end, as in the process of losing weight, whose end is
20   thinness, and since that which loses weight while in motion does not
have that for the sake of which its motion exists, such an action is not an
action, or at least it is not complete, for it is not an end. But the end and
action belong to that other kind. For example, we are seeing and at
the same time we have seen, we are engaged in acts of prudence and

have been so engaged, we are thinking and have thought;   but it is
not a fact that we are learning and have learned or that we are being   25
cured and have been cured. Also, we live well and at the same time
have lived well, and we are happy and have been happy.   If not, the
action should have come to an end sometime, as in the process of losing
weight; but in these cases it is not so, since we are living and have lived.
Of these, the former should be called "motions," the latter "*actualities*".
For every motion is incomplete, as in losing weight, learning, walking,
and building. These, then, are motions, and they are incomplete; for one   30
is not walking and at the same time has walked, nor is he building and
has built, nor is a thing being generated and has been generated, nor is it
being moved and has moved, but they are distinct; and moving another
thing is distinct from having moved another thing. On the other hand,
the same thing has seen and is seeing at the same time,   and likewise
it is thinking and has thought. I call each of the latter "an *actuality*", but   35
each of the former "a motion". From these and other similar statements
it is clear what an *actuality* is and what kind   of an object it is.

7

We must now specify when something is potentially another thing
and when it is not; for it is not potentially another at any time. For   *1049a*
example, is earth potentially a man? No, but rather when it has already
become a seed, and perhaps not even then.   This is similar to being
healed, since not everything can be healed by the medical art or by
luck,   but only something which has this capability, and it is this thing
which is potentially healthy. A definition of that which becomes actual   5
by *thought* from existing potentially is this, that it becomes actual when
thought wishes it and nothing external prevents this, and, in the case of
that which is being healed, when nothing in it   prevents the healing.
Similarly with that which is potentially a house; if nothing in its parts,
which are its matter, prevents them from becoming a house, and if   10
nothing need be added or be taken away or be changed,   then this is
potentially a house. It is likewise with the others if the principle of
generation is external,   or even if this principle is in that which is
potential and nothing external obstructs it from becoming by itself
what it can be. For example, the seed is not yet potentially a man; for
it must be placed in something else and change. And when it is already   15
such that it can be moved by its own principle, it is then potentially a
man; but prior to this it has need of another principle.   It is like the
earth, which is not yet potentially a statue, for it needs to be changed
and become bronze.

It seems that in naming something after its material principle we say
not that it is a *this* but that it is a *that-en;* for example, the box is not
20   wood but wooden, the wood is not earth by earthen, and again, earth is
likewise not *that* (if this is its material principle) but *that-en;* and that
from which the derivative name comes is always potentially and without
qualification the object from which the thing generated is derivatively
named. For example, the box is neither earthen nor earth, but wooden;
for it is wood that is potentially a box or the matter of the box, wood
universally taken of a box universally taken, and this individual wood
25   of this individual box. If there is something first which is in no way
called "that-en" according to something else, then this is primary matter, for example, if earth is airy, and air is not fire but fiery, then fire is
primary matter; but if this last is a *this,* then it is a substance. For
the universal and the underlying subject differ in this, that the latter is
a *this* and the former is not; for example, a man and a body and a soul
30   are subjects to which affections belong, and the musical and the pale
are affections. That which acquires music is called not "music" but
"musical", a man is called not "paleness" but "pale", and not "a walk"
or "a motion" but "walking" and "moving", and these are like the word
"that-en". And whenever such predicates are used, the ultimate subject
35   is a substance; but if a predicate is not of this sort but is a form or
a *this,* the ultimate underlying subject is matter and a material sub-
1049b stance. And it is indeed right that an object should be called "that-en"
according to its matter and its affections, for both are indefinite. We
have stated, then, when something should be called "potential" and
when not.

8

5   As we have distinguished earlier[72] the various senses of "prior", it is
evident that *actuality* is prior to potentiality. By "potentiality" I do not
mean only the specific one which is said to be a principle of change in
another thing or in the same thing qua other, but in general every principle of change or of rest. For nature, too, is in the same genus of poten-
10   tiality; for it is a moving principle, not in another thing, but in the same
thing qua itself. To every such potentiality, then, *actuality* is prior both
in formula and in substance [or *substance*]; and in one sense it is prior
in time, but in another sense it is not.
Clearly, it is prior in formula; for that which is primarily capable is
capable by virtue of the fact that it may be in *actuality;* for example,
15   the constructive is that which can construct, the able-to-see is that
which is capable of seeing, and the visible is that which can be seen.

The same thing may be said of the others, so that the formula or knowledge of that which is in *actuality* must be prior to the formula or knowledge of that which is potential.

Actuality is prior in time to potentiality in this sense, that there exists another thing of the same species, but not numerically the same as the thing in question, which is prior in time to the latter. What I mean is this, that prior in time to this individual man who now exists in *actuality* and to this corn and to this animal that sees, there was the matter and the seed and that which could see, and these were potentially this man and this corn and this seeing animal, but not yet in *actuality*; but prior in time to these potential things there existed in *actuality* other things from which these things were generated. For it is always by a thing in *actuality* that another thing becomes *actualized* from what it was potentially; for example, a man by a man and the musical by the musical, as there is always a first mover, and this mover already exists in *actuality*. We have stated in our discussion of substance[73] that everything which is being generated is being generated from something and by something, and the latter is the same in species as that which will be generated. This is why it is also thought that no builder can exist if he has not built anything or a lyre player if he has never played the lyre; for he who learns to play the lyre learns to play it by playing it, and similarly in all other cases. From cases like the latter arose a sophistical objection, namely, one which claims that a man who possesses no science will do that which is the object of science. Doubtless, a learner does not possess the science, but because of that which is being generated a part has been generated, and, in general, of that which is in motion a part has been moved (this is clear in our discussion of motion),[74] it would seem that the learner, too, must possess some part of the science. It is clear, then, that here, too, *actuality* in this sense is prior in generation and in time to potentiality.

But it is also prior in substance. First, things which are posterior in generation are prior in form or in substance; for example, an adult is prior to a child, and a man is prior to seed; for the former in each case already has the form, the latter does not. Also, everything which is being generated proceeds towards a principle and an end. For the final cause [or, that for the sake of which] is a principle, and generation is for the sake of an end; and the end is an *actuality*, and potentiality is viewed as being for the sake of this. Animals do not see in order to have sight, but they have sight in order to see. Likewise, men have the art of building in order to build, and men have the power of investigation in order to investigate, but they do not investigate in order to have the power of investigating, unless they are learning; yet these are not investigating

except in a qualified sense or in view of the fact that they are in no
need of speculating.

15   Further, matter exists potentially in view of the fact that it might
come to possess a form; and when it exists *actually,* then it exists in
a form.   And it is likewise with the other cases, even with those whose
end is motion.   And so just as teachers think that they have achieved
their end when they have exhibited their pupils at work, it is likewise
20   with nature.   For if this is not so, we shall be faced with Pauson's
Hermes; and as in this case, so with *knowledge* it is not clear whether
it is inside or outside. For performance is an end, and *actuality* is performance.   And so even the name *"actuality"* (ἐνέργεια) is derived from
the name "work" (ἔργον) and points to "actuality" (ἐντελέχεια).

Since in some cases the ultimate end is the use of something (such as
25   seeing in the case of sight, and sight has no other function besides
seeing) but in other cases something else is generated, such as (in
addition to the act of building) a house, which proceeds from the art
of building, nevertheless in the former case the use is the end and in
the latter it is an end to a higher degree than the potency.   For the act
of building is in the thing which is being built, and that act progresses
30   and has come to be simultaneously with the house. Accordingly, in
those cases where that which is generated is something other than the
use of the potency, the *actuality* of that potency is in the thing that is
being made; for example, the act of building is in the thing which is
being built, weaving is in the thing which is being woven, and similarly
in the other cases, and, in general, motion is in the thing that is in
35   motion.   But in those cases in which there is no other function besides
the *actuality,* the *actuality* exists in that which has it; for example,
seeing is in that which sees, investigating is in a man who investigates,
1050b   and life is in the soul, and so happiness, too, is in the soul (for happiness is a kind of life). And so it is evident that the *substance* or the form
is an *actuality.* According to this argument, then, it is evident that
5   *actuality* is prior in substance to potency; and as we said,[75] one *actuality*
always precedes another in time, until we come to the *actuality* of the
eternal prime mover.

What is more, *actuality* is prior in substance to potentiality in the
more dominant sense; for eternal things are prior in substance to
destructible things, but nothing which exists potentially is eternal. The
argument is as follows. Every potency is at the same time a potency for
the contradictories; for, while that which is not capable of existing could
10   not exist at all, anything which is capable of existing may not be in
actuality. Thus, that which is capable of existing may or may not exist;
and so the same thing is capable of existing and of not existing. And

that which has the capability of not existing may not be; and that which may not be is destructible, either without qualification, or with respect to that which it may not be; for example, if in the latter case, it is with   *15* respect to place or quantity or quality,   but if without qualification, it is with respect to substance.   Hence, no thing which is indestructible without qualification exists potentially without qualification; but nothing prevents such a thing from being potential in some respect, for example, with respect to quality or place.   Indestructible things, then, exist in *actuality*.   Nor can things which exist of necessity exist potentially; and these are indeed primary, for if they did not exist, nothing would exist.   Nor does motion exist potentially, if it exists eternally; nor   *20* is anything, which is in motion eternally, moved potentially except from place to place, and nothing prevents such things from having matter.
And so the Sun and the stars and the whole heaven are always active, and there is no fear that any of them will ever stop (although natural philosophers do fear this). Nor are they worn out by this activity, for their   *25* motion does not come from a potentiality of two contradictories, as in destructible things, so as to make the continuity of such motion subject to wear; for the cause of weariness is substance in the sense of matter or potency,   and not in the sense of *actuality*.
Indestructible things are imitated by changing things, such as fire and earth. For these, too, are always in activity; for they move in virtue   *30* of themselves and have motion in themselves.   The other potencies, which have been distinguished, are all potencies for contradictories; for that which can move something in a certain way can also move it not in that way, that is, if it is a potency according to formula,   but if it is a nonrational potency, the same one is a potency for contradictories by being, respectively, present with or absent from that which it can move.
If, then, there exist such natures or substances   as in various discussions   *35* are called "Ideas", there will be something much more scientific than Science Itself and also something much more in motion than Motion   *1051a* Itself; for the former in each case is an *actuality* to a higher degree than the latter, since the latter is only a potency for the former.

It is evident, then, that *actuality* is prior to potency and to every principle of change.

9

That a good *actuality* is better and more honorable than the potentiality for it is clear from what follows. If a thing is named according   *5* to its capability, the same thing is capable of both contraries; for example, that which is said to be capable of being healthy is at the same

time capable of being sick, for the potentiality of being healthy is the
same as that of being sick, and likewise for the potentiality of being
at rest and in motion, of building and of demolishing, and of being built
and of being demolished. Now the potentiality for both contraries is
present at the same time, but the contraries cannot be present at the
same time; and the *actualities* of those contraries cannot be present in
a thing at the same time, as for example being healthy and being sick.
Thus, one of the two *actualities* must be good, but the corresponding
potentiality is alike a potentiality for both *actualities* or for neither of
them. Hence, a good *actuality* is better than the potentiality for it. It
is also necessary that the end and the *actuality* of what is bad is worse
than the potentiality for it; for that which is capable of a bad *actuality*
is capable of both contraries.

From this it is also clear that the bad does not exist apart from things;
for the bad is by nature posterior to the potentiality for it. And so
nothing bad or defective or corrupt exists in the first principles and
eternal things; for corruption is a kind of badness.

Also, geometrical demonstrations are discovered in *actuality*; for it
is by dividing that we discover them. If the divisions were already
made, the theorems would be evident; as it is, they exist potentially.
Why are the angles of a triangle equal to two right angles? In view of
the fact that the angles about a point on a line are equal to two right
angles. If the line parallel to one side had already been drawn, to the

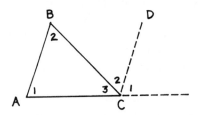 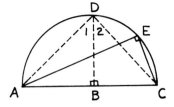

one who saw this the cause would be at once clear. Why is the angle
inscribed in a semicircle universally a right angle? Because if the three
lines are equal, two of them being the radii BA and BC from the center
B and forming the base AC, and the other being the perpendicular
BD, the theorem is clear to him who sees this and understands the
earlier theorem. Thus it is evident that potential things are discovered
by being brought to *actuality*. The cause of this is the fact that thinking
is an *actuality*. And so it is by *actuality* that the potential becomes
actual; and because of this we come to know by acting, for numerical
actuality is posterior in generation to its potentiality.

10

15

20

25

30

10

Since "being" and "nonbeing" have senses according to the types of categories and also according to the potentiality or *actuality* of these categories and their contraries, but being in the most proper sense is the true and the false, and this concerning things is in view of the fact that they are united or separated, so that a man thinks truly if he thinks that what is separated is separated and what is united is united, but falsely if his thought is contrary to the way in which things exist, we may raise this question: when does truth or falsity as expressed exist or not exist? Concerning this matter we must examine what our position is.

Now it is not because we think truly of your being white that you are white, but it is because you are white that we speak truly in saying that you are white. If, then, some things are always united and cannot be separated, others are always separate and cannot be united, and still others can have both contraries (and here *to be* is to be united and to be one, and *not to be* is not to be united but to be more than one), as regards those things which may have both contraries, the same opinion or the corresponding statement becomes false and true, and at one time it may be true but at another time false. But as regards things which cannot be otherwise, the same belief or the corresponding statement does not become true at one time and false at another time, but it is always true or always false.

Concerning things which are incomposite, what does "to be" or "not to be" or "truth" or "falsity" mean for them. Each of them is not a composite, like the white wood or the incommensurable diagonal, so as *to be* when two things are united and *not to be* when they are separated; nor can truth and falsity belong to them as they do in the previous cases. Or, just as truth about these is not the same, so *to be* is not the same for them; but truth about each of these is to apprehend it or to assert it (for affirmation and assertion are not the same), and ignorance of it is not to apprehend it. For it is not possible to be mistaken about the whatness of something except accidentally. Similar remarks may be made with regard to non-composite *substances*, for it is impossible to be mistaken about them. And all of them exist in *actuality*, not potentially, for otherwise they could be generated or destroyed; but as it is, being itself is neither generated nor destroyed, for it would have to be generated from something. Thus one cannot be mistaken concerning that which is just a being and in *actuality*, but either he conceives it or he does not. But we do inquire about the existence of them, namely, whether such things exist or not.

Concerning being as truth and nonbeing as falsity, being is true if
35   it is a united being but false if it is not united.   But in the case of what
1052a is one, if it is just a being, it exists in just this way, and if not in this
way, it does not exist;   and the truth about each such being is the
conception of it, and there is neither falsity nor mistake about it but
only ignorance, yet not the kind of ignorance which is like blindness,
for blindness exists as if one were to have no power to conceive of it
at all.

5   It is also evident, with regard to immovable things, that if anyone
believes [truly] that they are immovable, he cannot be mistaken with
respect to time. For example, if anyone thinks that a triangle does not
change, he will not think that at one time the sum of its angles is equal
to two right angles but at another time this is not so (for the triangle
would then change). However, it is possible to think that some instances
of an immovable thing have an attribute but others do not have it;
for example, one may think that no even number is prime, or that some
even numbers are prime but other even numbers are not prime. But it
10   is not possible to think thus in the case of what is numerically one,   for
one will no longer think that some instances have an attribute and others
do not have it, but he will think either truly or falsely that something
is always so.

BOOK XII (= Λ)

1

1069a   The subject of our investigation is substance; for it is of substances
that we are seeking the principles and causes. For even if the universe
were a kind of a whole, so to say, substance would be the first part;
and if it were a succession of parts, even then, substance would be first,
then quality, then quantity. At the same time the others which follow
are not even beings in an unqualified sense, so to speak, but are qualities
and motions; otherwise, even the not-white and the not-straight would
be beings (since we do say even of these that they exist, as for example
in "there exists a not-white"). Moreover, none of the others is separable.
25   Even the ancient philosophers would confirm this in view of what they
were doing; for they were seeking the principles and the elements and
the causes of substances. Now present-day thinkers[76] are more inclined
to posit the universals as substances; for the genera are universal, and
they say that these are principles and substances to a higher degree,
because they make logical inquiries into things. The early thinkers,

on the other hand, posited the individuals as substances, such as fire
and earth, but not what is common to them, 'body'.   *30*

There are three kinds of substances. One genus of substances is the
sensible, of which (1) one kind is eternal, and (2) the other is destructible (agreed upon by all thinkers), like plants and animals, and it is
of the latter that we must find the elements, whether these be one or
many. Another kind is (3) the immovable substances,   and certain
thinkers say that these are separate, some   dividing them into two
kinds, the Forms and the Mathematical Objects, others positing these   *35*
two as of one nature,   and others   positing only one of these, the
Mathematical Objects.[77] The sensible substances   are the subject of
physics, for they are in motion; but immovable substances are the sub-   *1069b*
ject of another science, if no principle is common to these and to sensible
substances.

Now sensible substances are changeable. If change proceeds from
opposites or from intermediates, and not from all kinds of opposites (for   *5*
also voice is non-white) but from contraries, there must be something
underlying which changes to contraries; for it is not the contraries that
change.

6

Since three kinds of substances were named,[78] two of them physical   *1071b*
and one immovable, we should discuss the latter, in view of the fact
that there must be some eternal substance which is immovable. For   *5*
substances are the first of all things, and if they are all destructible, all
things are destructible. But it is impossible for motion either to be generated or to be destroyed; for it always existed. The same applies to
time; for if there is no time, neither can there be a *before* and an *after*
in time. And so motion, too, is continuous in the same manner as time   *10*
is; for either motion and time are the same, or time is an *attribute* of
motion. But motion cannot be continuous except with respect to place,
and of this motion, only the one which is circular.

Moreover, if there is a thing which can move other things or can act
upon them but which will not *actually* do so, then there will be no motion; for that which has a potency may not be *actualizing* it. So there
is no gain even if we posit eternal substances, like those who posit the   *15*
Forms, unless there is in them a principle which can cause a change.
But even such a principle is not enough (nor is any substance other
than the Forms), for, if this principle will not be in activity, there
will be no motion. Moreover, if the substance of such a principle is a
potency, still this is not enough even if this principle is in activity, for
motion will not be eternal; for that which exists potentially may not be

20   existing [*actually*].   Hence, there must be a principle of such a kind
that its *substance* is *actuality*. Moreover, such substances must be without matter; for they must be eternal, if indeed something else is also
eternal.   They must exist, then, as *actualities*.

Yet there is a *difficulty*; for it seems that whatever exists in *actuality*
also has the potency for it, but that whatever has a potency need not
25   *actualize* it, and so potency seems to be prior   to *actuality*. But if this
is so, nothing will exist;   for something may have the potency to be
and still not be. And indeed, the same impossibility follows from the
statements of the theologians who generate the universe from *Night*,
or of the physicists who say that all things were together.[79] For how will
anything be moved if no cause exists in *actuality*?   Matter itself will
30   certainly not move itself, but carpentry   will move it; and neither the
menses nor the earth will move themselves, but the seeds   will act on
the earth and the semen on the menses.
This is why some thinkers, like Leucippus[80] and Plato,[81] posit eternal
activity; for they say that motion is eternal. But they do not state why
this exists nor which   it is, nor yet its manner   or the cause of it.   For
35   nothing is moved at random, but there must always be something, just
as it is at present with physical bodies which are moved in one way by
nature but in another by force or by the intellect or by something else.
Then again, which of them is first?   For this makes a great difference.
1072a   Plato cannot even state what it is that he sometimes considers to be the
principle, that is, that which moves itself,[82] for, as he himself says, the
soul came after,[83] and it is generated at the same time as the universe.
Now to regard potency as prior to *actuality* is in one sense right and
in another sense not right; and we have already stated[84] how this is so.
5   That *actuality* is prior is confirmed by Anaxagoras (for *Intelligence*
according to him exists in *actuality*), by Empedocles (who posits *Friendship* and *Strife*), and by others, such as Leucippus, who say that motion
always exists. If so, then *Chaos* or *Night* did not exist for an infinite
time, but the same things existed always, whether passing through
cycles or in some other way,   if indeed *actuality* is prior to potency. So
10   if the same things always take place in cycles, there must be something,
say A, which always remains and is in activity in the same way.   But
if there is to be generation and destruction, there must be something
else,[85] say B, which is always in activity now in one way and now in
another. So it is necessary for it to be active in one way according to
itself and in another according to something else; then the latter is either
still another thing, say C, or the first thing. Surely, it must be the first
15   thing; for otherwise C would still be its own cause and the cause of B.
So it is better to say that it is the first, for it is this that is the cause of

being in activity always in the same way, and it is something else that is the cause of being in activity in another way; and so it is evident that that which is always active in distinct ways requires two causes. And, in fact, it is in this way that motions take place. So why should we seek other principles?

7

Since the account given in this manner is possible, and if it were not, the universe would have been generated from *Night* or from the *to-*   20
getherness of all things or from nonbeing, the *difficulties* may be regarded as solved, and so there is something which is always moved with an unceasing motion, which is circular; and this is clear not only by arguments but also from the facts. So, the first heaven must be eternal; and further, there is also something which this moves. And since that which is moved and is a mover is thus an intermediate, there   25
is something which causes motion without being moved, and this is eternal, a substance, and an *actuality*. And this is the way in which the object of desire or the intelligible object moves, namely, without itself being moved. Of these, the primary objects are the same; for the object of *desire* is that which *appears* to be noble, and the primary object of wish is that which *is* noble. We desire because it seems rather that it seems because we desire; and thinking is the starting-point. Now   30
the intellect is moved by the intelligible, and things which are intelligible in virtue of themselves are in one of the two columns of opposites; and of these, substances are primary, and of substances, that which is simple and in *actuality* is primary. Oneness is not the same as the simple; for "one" signifies a measure, but "simple" signifies the manner in which something exists. Moreover, both the noble and that which   35
is chosen for its own sake are in the same column of opposites; and that which is primary is always the best, or by analogy so.   *1072b*

That the final cause exists in immovable things is clear by distinguishing the two meanings of "final cause". For the final cause may be (a) for some thing or (b) that for the sake of which, and of these the one may exist but the other may not; and it [the final cause] causes motion as something which is loved, and that which is moved moves the others. If, then, something is moved, it can be otherwise than as it is; so even   5
if the primary locomotion exists as an *actuality*, still that which is moved qua being moved can be otherwise with respect to place, even if not with respect to its *substance*. And since there is some mover which causes motion but is itself immovable and exists as *actuality*, this can

in no way be otherwise than as it is. Now of all changes locomotion is
10   primary, and of locomotions the circular is primary;   and it is this
motion which the immovable mover causes.   This mover, then, exists
of necessity; and if so, then nobly, and as such, it is a first principle. For
"necessity" has the following senses: (a) by force, which is contrary to
a thing's tendency, (b) that without which the good is impossible, and
(c) that which cannot be otherwise but exists without qualification.
Such, then, is the principle upon which depends the heaven and na-
15   ture. And its *activity* is like the best which we can have but for a little
while.   For it exists in this manner eternally (which is impossible for
us), since its *actuality* is also pleasure.   And it is because of this
[activity] that being awake, sensing, and thinking   are most pleasant,
and hopes and memories   are pleasant because of these. Now thinking
according to itself is of the best according to itself,   and thinking in
20   the highest degree is of that which is best in the highest degree. Thus,
in partaking of the intelligible, it is of Himself that the Intellect is thinking;   for by apprehending and thinking it is He Himself who becomes
intelligible, and so the Intellect and its intelligible object are the same.
For that which is capable of receiving the intelligible object and the
substance is the intellect,   and the latter is in *actuality* by possessing
the intelligible object;   so that the possession of the intelligible is more
divine than the potency of receiving it, and the contemplation of it is
25   the most pleasant and the best.   If, then, the manner of God's existence
is as good as ours sometimes is,   but eternally, then this is marvelous,
and if it is better,   this is still more marvelous; and it is the latter. And
life belongs to God, for the *actuality* of the intellect is life,   and He is
actuality; and His *actuality* is in virtue of itself a life which is the best
and is eternal. We say that God is a living being which is eternal and
30   the best; so life and continuous duration and eternity belong to God,
for this is God.
Those who believe, as the Pythagoreans [86] and Speusippus [87.] do, that the
most noble and the best are not in the principle, because the principles
of plants and of animals are also causes but nobility and completeness
35   are in what comes from them, do not think rightly. For the seed comes
1073a   from other things which are prior   and complete, and that which is first
is not the seed but the complete thing. One might say, for example,
that prior to the seed is the man, not the man who comes from this seed
but the man from whom this seed comes.
It is evident from what has been said that there exists a substance
5   which is eternal and immovable and separate from sensible things. It
has also been shown that this substance cannot have any magnitude
but is without parts and indivisible.   For it causes motion for an infinite

time, but no finite thing has infinite potency. Since every magnitude is either infinite or finite, this substance cannot have a finite magnitude because of what we said, and it cannot be infinite in view of the fact   *10* that there exists no infinite magnitude at all.   Moreover, it cannot be affected or altered; for all the other motions are posterior to locomotion.   It is clear, then, why these facts are so.

8

We should not neglect to consider whether we should posit one such substance or more than one, and if the latter, how many; but with regard   *15* to the statements made by other thinkers, we should mention the fact that concerning the number of such substances they said nothing that can be even *clearly* stated. The doctrine of Ideas does not inquire specifically into this problem, for those who speak of the Ideas speak of them as Numbers, and concerning Numbers they sometimes speak as if these were infinite but at other times as if they were limited to   *20* ten,[88] but as to why there should be so many Numbers, nothing is stated seriously enough to amount to a demonstration. We, however, should discuss this problem by starting with the assumptions and distinctions already made.

Now the principle and the first of beings is immovable, both in virtue of itself and accidentally, and it causes the primary motion, which is   *25* eternal and one. But since that which is moved must be moved by something, and the first mover is of necessity immovable in virtue of itself, and an eternal motion must be caused by an eternal being and one motion by one being, and since we also observe that, besides the simple locomotion of the universe which we say is caused by the first   *30* and immovable substance, there are other locomotions (those of the planets) which are eternal (for a body with a circular motion is eternal and is never at rest, and we have shown this in the *Physics*[89]), then each of these locomotions, too, must be caused by a substance which is in virtue of itself immovable and eternal. For a star is by its nature an eternal substance, and the mover is eternal and prior to that which is   *35* moved, and that which is prior to a substance must be a substance. So it is evident that there must be as many substances as there are locomotions and that in their nature they are eternal and immovable in virtue of themselves and without magnitude, and the cause of this   *1073b* has been stated earlier.[90]

It is evident, then, that the movers are substances, and that of these there is a first, a second, etc., according to the same order as the locomo-

tions of the stars. Now as regards the number of locomotions,   this
should be the concern of the mathematical science which is closest to
5   philosophy, and this is astronomy; for it is this science which is concerned with the investigation of sensible but eternal substances, while
the others, such as arithmetic and geometry, are not concerned with
any substances.   That there are many locomotions of heavenly bodies
is evident also to those who have studied the matter to some extent; for
10   each of the planets has more than one locomotion.   But as to the
number of these, we may for the present give an indication by quoting
what some mathematicians are saying, so that there may be in our
thought a belief in some definite number; as for the rest, we should
partly investigate ourselves and partly inquire from those who investi-
15   gate the subject, and if those who are investigating this subject have
opinions contrary to those just stated, we should respect both views
but accept the more accurate.

   Eudoxus held   that each of the locomotions of the Sun and of the
Moon is in three spheres, of which the first is that of the fixed stars,
20   the second along the circle which bisects the Zodiac, and the third
along the circle inclined across the breadth of the Zodiac, but the
circle along which the Moon moves is inclined at a greater angle than
that along which the Sun moves. The motion of each of the planets
is in four spheres, and of these the first and second are the same as
25   those in the previous case (for the locomotion of the sphere of the
fixed stars belongs to all the spheres, and that of the sphere next under
it which moves along the circle bisecting the Zodiac belongs to all),
the poles of the third sphere of each planet are in the circle bisecting
30   the Zodiac, and the locomotion of the fourth sphere is in the circle
inclined at an angle to the equator of the third; and the poles of the
third sphere are different for different planets, except for Venus and
Mercury which have the same poles.

   Callippus posited the same position of the spheres as that held by
Eudoxus, that is, with respect to the order of the intervals, but while
35   he assigned to Jupiter and Saturn the same number of spheres as Eudoxus did, he thought that two more spheres should be added to the
Sun and also to the Moon, if one is to account for the observed phenomena, and one more to each of the other planets.

1074a   But if all the spheres combined are to account for the observed phenomena, there must be other spheres for each planet, one less in number
than those assigned to it, which would counteract these and restore to
the same position the first sphere of the star which in each case is next
5   in order below; for only thus can the motion of the combined spheres
produce the motion of the planets. Since, then, the spheres in which the

planets are carried are eight for Jupiter and Saturn and twenty-five for
the others, and of these only those need not be counteracted in which
the lowest-situated planet is carried, the spheres which counteract
those of the first two planets will be six, those of the next four planets   *10*
will be sixteen, and the total number of spheres which includes both
those which carry the planets and the ones which counteract those
spheres will be fifty-five. If we are not to add to the Moon and to the
Sun the motions we mentioned,[91] all the spheres will be forty-seven.
Let, then, this be the number of spheres, and if so, it is reasonable to   *15*
believe that the immovable substances or principles are also as many.
As to what is necessarily the case, this may be left to more competent
thinkers.

If there can be no locomotion   which does not contribute to the
locomotion of a star, and if moreover every nature or substance   which
is unaffected and which in virtue of itself attains its best should be   *20*
regarded as an end, then there can be no other nature besides those
mentioned, but this must be the number of substances. For if there
were others, they would be movers as ends of locomotions; but there
can be no other locomotions besides those mentioned. And in view of
the heavenly bodies which are in locomotion, this is a reasonable
belief. For if each thing that carries   something does so by nature for   *25*
the sake of that which is carried,   and every locomotion is likewise
for the sake of something which is so moved, no locomotion can exist
for its own sake or for the sake of another locomotion, but each must
exist for the sake of a star. For if every locomotion exists for the sake
of another locomotion, the latter too will exist for the sake of a third;
and so, since it is impossible to proceed to infinity, the end of each   *30*
locomotion in the heavens must be some of the divine bodies which
are so moved there.

It is evident that there is only one heaven. For if there are more than
one,   like men, the principle   for each will be one in species but many
in number. But things   which are many in number have matter; for the
formula is one and the same for the many, as in the case of the formula   *35*
of a man, while Socrates is only one. But the primary essence   has no
matter, for it is actuality. Thus, the first immovable mover is one both
in formula and in number; and so, that which   is always and continuously in motion is only one. Hence, there is only one heaven.

The ancients of very early times bequeathed to posterity in the form   *1074b*
of a myth a tradition that the heavenly bodies are Gods and that the
divinity encompasses the whole of nature. The rest of the tradition has
been added later as a means of persuading the masses and as something   *5*
useful for the laws and for matters of expediency; for they say that

these Gods are like men in form and like some of the other animals, and also other things which follow from or are similar to those stated. But if one were to separate from the later additions the first point and attend to this alone (namely, that they thought the first substances to be Gods),
10 he might realize that this was divinely spoken and that, while probably every art and every philosophy has often reached a stage of development as far as it could and then again has perished, these doctrines about the Gods were saved like relics up to the present day. Anyway, the opinion of our forefathers and of the earliest thinkers is evident to us to just this extent.

9

15   Certain problems arise with regard to The Intellect [God]; for He seems to be the most divine of things manifest to us, yet there are certain difficulties as to how He can exist as such. For if He is not thinking of anything, why the veneration of Him? He is like a man who sleeps. And if He is thinking, but what decides this thinking is something else
20 (for the *substance* of that which decides thinking is not thinking, but a potency), then He cannot be the best substance. For it is because of [the act of] thinking that honor belongs to Him. Moreover, whether His *substance* is intellect or thinking, of what does He think? Either He thinks of Himself or of something else; and if something else, then either always of the same thing or sometimes of one thing and sometimes of another. But does it make any difference or not whether He is
25 thinking of that which is noble rather than of any chance thing? Would it not be absurd to be *thinking* of certain things? Clearly, then, He is thinking of that which is most divine and most honorable, and He is not changing; for change would be for the worse, and this change would then be a motion.

First, then, if He were not thinking but a potency, it is reasonable that the continuity of His thinking would be fatiguing Him. Moreover,
30 it is clear that something else would be more honorable than The Intellect, namely, the object of thought; for to think or thinking may belong even to that which thinks of the worst objects, so that if this is to be avoided (for there are even things which it is better not to see than to see), Thinking would not be the best of things. It is of Himself, then, that The Intellect is thinking, if He is the most excellent of things, and so Thinking is the thinking of Thinking.

35   But it appears that *knowledge* and sensation and opinion and *thought* are always of other objects, and only incidentally of themselves. Moreover, if thinking and being thought are distinct, in virtue of which of

these does goodness belong to The Intellect? For to be thinking and to
be an object of thought are not the same.   Or is it not that in some cases   *1075a*
knowledge and its object are the same?   In the productive sciences, this
object is the *substance* or the essence but without the matter, in the
theoretical sciences it is the formula and the thinking. Accordingly,
since the intellect and the object of thought are not distinct in things
which have no matter, the two will be the same, and so both thinking   5
and the object of thought will be one.

Further, there remains the problem whether the object of Thinking
is composite;   for if so, Thinking would be changing in passing from
one part of the whole to another part.   Is it not the case that what has
no matter is indivisible, like the human intellect,   or even that   which
is thinking of a composite object   in an interval of time? For it does
not possess goodness in this part or in that part but possesses the highest
good in the whole,   though it is distinct from it. It is in this manner   10
that Thinking is the thinking of Himself through all eternity.

10

We must also inquire in which of two ways the nature of the whole
has the good and the highest good, whether as something separate and
by itself,   or as the order of its parts. Or does it have it in both ways, as
in the case of an army? For in an army goodness exists both in the order
and in the general, and rather in the general; for it is not because of   15
the order that he exists, but the order exists because   of him. Now all
things are ordered in some way, water-animals and birds and plants, but
not similarly; and they do not exist without being related at all to one
another, but they are in some way related.   For all things are ordered
in relation to one thing. It is as in a household, in which the freemen are   20
least at liberty to act at random but all or most things are ordered,
while slaves and wild animals contribute little to the common good but
for the most part act at random;   for such is the principle of each of these,
which is their nature. I mean, for example, that all these must come
together if they are to be distinguished; and this is what happens in
other cases in which all the members participate in the whole.   25

We must not fail to notice how many impossible or absurd results
face those who speak otherwise, what sort of views are put forward by
subtler thinkers, and what sort of views are faced with the least difficulties. Now all thinkers posit all things as coming from contraries. But
neither "all things" nor "from contraries" is right.   Nor do these thinkers
say, of things to which contraries belong, how those things are composed   30
of contraries; for contraries cannot be acted upon by each other.   For

us, however, the problem is reasonably solved by the positing of a third object. But these thinkers posit one of the contraries as being matter, as in the case of those who posit the *Unequal* as the matter for the *Equal* or those who regard the *Many* as the matter for the *One*.[92] This difficulty, too, is solved in the same manner; for the matter, for us, is not

35 contrary to anything. Moreover, for these thinkers all things except the *One* will participate in badness; for *Bad Itself* is one of the two elements. As for the other thinkers,[93] they do not even regard the principles as being the *Good* and the *Bad;* yet in all things the good is in the highest degree a principle. Now the former thinkers rightly regard the

1075b *Good* as a principle, but they do not say how it is a principle, whether as an end or as a mover or as form.

Empedocles, too, speaks absurdly, for he posits *Friendship* as the good; and as a principle, it is posited both as a mover (for it brings things together), and as matter (for it is a part of the *Blend*). Indeed, even if the

5 same thing happens to be a principle both as matter and as a mover, nevertheless to be matter is not the same as to be a mover. In which sense, then, is *Friendship* a good? It is also absurd that *Strife* should be indestructible, since *Strife*, for him, is the nature of the bad. Anaxagoras posits the *Good* as a principle in the sense of a mover, since for him *Intelligence* moves things; but it moves for the sake of something, so that the *Good* should be something else (unless it is so

10 posited in another sense, as used by us; for, the medical art is in some sense health). It is also absurd that he should posit no contrary of the *Good* or of *Intelligence*. As a matter of fact, all those who posit contraries do not use them, unless we reshape their views into a system.

Again, no one states why some things are destructible but others are indestructible; for all things are posited by these thinkers as being com-

15 posed of the same principles. Again, some thinkers posit things as coming from nonbeing; others, to avoid this necessity, say that all things are one.

Again, no one states why there will always be generation and what is the cause of generation. And those who posit two principles need another principle which is more authoritative. And those who posit the Forms also need a more authoritative principle; for why did things

20 participate in the Forms or do so now? And for all other thinkers there must be something which is the contrary of wisdom or of the most honorable science; but for us this is not necessary, for there is nothing contrary to that which is first. For, in all cases, contraries have matter which is potentially these contraries, and ignorance, which is the contrary of knowledge, should be of the contrary object; but there is nothing contrary to what is first. Again, if there were nothing besides the

25 sensible things, there would be no principle or order or generation or

heavenly objects, but of a principle there would always be another principle, as all the theologians and the physicists say. And if the Forms or Numbers were to exist, they would not be the causes of anything; or if they were, at least not of motion. Again, how can magnitude or what is continuous come from things which have no magnitude? For no number, either as a mover or as a form, can make what is continuous. Moreover, no contrary is just a potency of acting or of moving,   *30* for it would then be possible for it not to exist, and besides, action is posterior to the potency of it; and if so, no things would be eternal. But there are such; so some of their premises must be rejected. We have stated how this should be done.[94]

Again, in virtue of what is a number one, or a soul, or a body, or in   *35* general, each form or thing? No one says anything at all; nor can any of them say anything, unless they do in the way we do, that it is the mover that makes each one. As for those who assert that Mathematical Numbers are first[95] and, following these, posit one kind of substances after another with distinct principles for each kind, they represent the   *1076a* substances of the universe as a plurality of unrelated parts (for substances of one kind, whether existing or not, contribute nothing to those of another kind) and with many principles; but things do not wish to be governed badly.

"*The rule of many is not good; let one the ruler be.*"[96]

BOOK XIII (= M)

3

Now, just as certain universal propositions in mathematics, which   *1077b* are about things not existing apart from magnitudes and numbers, are indeed about numbers and magnitudes but not qua such as having a   *20* magnitude or as being divisible, clearly, so there may be propositions and demonstrations about sensible magnitudes, not qua sensible but qua being of such-and-such a kind. For just as there are many propositions concerning sensible things but only qua moving, without reference to the whatness of each of these and the attributes that follow from it —and it is not necessary because of this that there should exist   *25* either a moving of a sort which is separate from the sensible thing or is some definite nature in the sensible thing —so also there will be propositions and sciences about things in motion, not qua in motion but only qua bodies, or only qua planes, or qua lengths, or qua divisible, or qua indivisible with position, or just qua indivisible.   *30*

Thus, since it is true to say, without specifying, that not only what is separate exists but also what is not separate (for example, that the moving exists), it is also true to say, without specifying, that the mathematical objects exist, and to be indeed such as mathematicians say they

35   are. And just as it is true to say, without specifying, that each of the other sciences is concerned with certain things—not with what is accidental to those things (for example, not with the white, if the healthy is white and if the science is concerned with the healthy) but only with

1078a those things qua such, that is, with the healthy qua healthy if it is the science of the healthy, and with a man qua man if it is the science of man—so it is with geometry. If the objects of the mathematical sciences also happen to be sensible but are not investigated qua sensible, this does not mean that those sciences will not be concerned with sensible

5   things, or that they will be concerned with other things separated from the sensibles.

If A belongs to a thing, many other essential attributes of A will also belong to that thing qua A. For example, proper *attributes* belong to the female animal qua female, or to the male animal qua male, although no female or male exists separate from animals. So, proper *attributes* belong also to sensible things qua having lengths or qua having surfaces.

10   And to the extent that we are investigating what is prior in formula and is simpler, to that extent the result will be more accurate, and by "accurate" I mean simple. Thus, the science which leaves out magnitude is more accurate than the one which includes it, and the science which leaves out motion as well as magniture is the most accurate of the three.   And if a science is concerned with motion, it is most accurate if it is concerned with the primary   motions; for these are the simplest, and of the primary motions the even motion is yet the simplest.   The

15   same statements apply to optics and harmonics; for they investigate sight and sound, respectively, no qua sight or qua sound, but qua lines and numbers, which, however, are *proper attributes* of sight and sound respectively.   Mechanics, too, proceeds in the same way. So, if one lays down as separate certain attributes and inquires into these qua what they are, he will not by so doing inquire into what is false, just as he

20   will not speak falsely when he draws a line on the ground and calls it a foot long when it is not a foot long; for this latter falsehood is not in the premises.

A thing can best be investigated if each attribute which is not separate from the thing is laid down as separate, and this is what the arithmetician and the geometrician do. Thus, a man qua a man is one and indivisible. The arithmetician lays down this: to be one is to be

25   indivisible, and then he investigates the attributes which belong to a man qua indivisible. On the other hand, the geometrician investigates a

man neither qua a man nor qua indivisible, but qua a solid. For it is clear that the attributes which would have belonged to him even if somehow he were not indivisible can still belong to him if he is indivisible. Because of this fact, geometers speak rightly, and what they discuss are beings, and these are beings; for "being" may be used in 30 two senses, as actuality and as matter.

Now since the good is distinct from the beautiful (for the good is always in *action* but the beautiful may also be in what is immovable), those[97] who assert that the mathematical sciences say nothing about the beautiful or the good speak falsely. For they do speak about and show these, and in the highest degree. The fact that they do not use 35 the names, while they do exhibit constructions and theorems about them, does not mean that they say nothing about them. Now the most important kinds of the beautiful are order, symmetry, and definiteness, 1078b and the mathematical sciences exhibit properties of these in the highest degree. And since these (that is, order and definiteness) appear to be causes of many things, it is clear that the mathematical sciences must be dealing in some way with such a cause, that is, the cause in the sense 5 of beauty.However, we shall speak about these matters at greater length elsewhere.[98]

10

Let us now turn to a point which presents some *difficulty* for both 1086b those who posit the Ideas and those who do not, and which has been 15 taken up at the beginning in the discussion of the *difficulties*.

If anyone does not posit the substances to be separate, and in the manner in which individual things are said to be separate, he will be eliminating substances in the sense which we mean by the term "substance". But if he posits substances to be separate, how will he posit 20 their elements and principles? If he posits them as individuals and not as universal, (1) there will be as many things as there are elements, (2) and the elements will not be *knowable*. For (1) let the syllables in speech be substances, and the letters of syllables be the elements of substances. Then there must be only one BA and only one of each of the 25 other syllables, if indeed these are not universal and the same in kind but each is to be numerically one and be a *this* and not have a common name (besides, each thing which exists as Itself is posited as being only one); and if this is so with the syllables, so is it also with the elements of which each syllable consists. Hence, there will not be more than one A and not more than one of each of the other letters, and this follows from the same argument by which no two syllables are the same. But 30 if this is so, there will be no other things besides the letters, but only the

letters. Moreover, (2) the elements will not be *knowable;* for they are not universal, but *knowledge* is of universals. This is clear from demonstra-
35 tions and definitions; for there is no syllogism of the fact that this triangle has its angles equal to two right angles unless every triangle has its angles equal to two right angles, nor of the fact that this man is an animal unless every man is an animal.

1087a   But if the principles are universal, or even if the substances composed of these are also universal, non-substances will be prior to substances; for the universal is not a substance, and the elements and the principles will be universal, but both the elements and the principles are prior to that of which they are the principles and elements.

5   All these, then, are reasonable consequences, when these thinkers posit the Ideas as out of elements and also claim that apart from the substances which have the same form there exists one Idea which is separate and unique.

Now if, as for example in the case of the elements of speech, nothing prevents the existence of many A's and B's even if there is no A-Itself
10 and B-Itself apart from the many A's and B's, then in view of this there can be an infinite number of similar syllables. Of the positions stated, the one, namely, "Since all *knowledge* is universal, the principles of things are necessarily universal and are not separated substances" contains a *difficulty* of the highest degree, but this statement is in one
15 sense true and in another not true. For *"knowledge"*, like *"knowing"*, has two meanings, one exists in potentiality and the other in *actuality.* Potentiality, like matter, being universal and indefinite, is concerned with the universal and the indefinite; but *actuality,* being definite and a *this*, is concerned with some definite thing and some *this.*   But it is
20 by accident that sight sees color universally, and this is in view of the fact that this color, which sight sees, is a color [universally taken];   and likewise, *this* A, which the grammarian investigates, is an A [universally taken]. For if the principles are of necessity universal, what comes from them must also be universal, as in demonstrations;   and if this is so, nothing can be separate or a substance. But it is clear that there
25 is a sense in which *knowledge* is universal and a sense in which it is not.

NICOMACHEAN ETHICS

CONTENTS

BOOK I

BOOK VI

1. Ethical virtue is a habit according to right reason (an intellectual virtue).

2. The estimative and the scientific parts of the soul.

3. The nature of science.

4. The nature of art.

5. The nature of prudence.

6. Intuition.

7. Wisdom.

8. Some remarks about prudence.

9. Deliberation and good deliberation.

10. Intelligence.

11. *Judgment* is right judgment by an equitable man.

12. How *judgment*, intelligence, prudence, and intuition are related.

13. How prudence and wisdom contribute to man's ultimate good.

BOOK VII

1. Discussion of continence and incontinence and the aim of BOOK VII.

2. Facts about continence and incontinence, and some difficulties which arise.

3. Both the continent and the incontinent man have good wishes but bad *desires* but differ as to which of these two desires overpowers the other.

4. Primary and secondary senses of the terms "continence" and "incontinence."

BOOK VIII

1. Friendship is necessary for a good life and noble in its perfect sense.

2. Problems about friendship and the three kinds of things we like.

BOOK X

NICOMACHEAN ETHICS

BOOK I

1

Every art and every *inquiry*, and similarly, every *action* and every   *1094a*
intention is thought to aim at some good; hence men have expressed
themselves well in declaring the good to be that at which all things
aim [1]. But there appears to be a difference among the ends; for some are
activities, others are products apart from the [activities which produce   *5*
them]. Whenever there are ends apart from the *actions* [which produce
them], the products are by nature better than the corresponding
activities.

Since there are many kinds of *actions* and arts and sciences, the corresponding ends are many also; for the end of the medical [science] is
health, that of shipbuilding is a ship, that of strategy is victory, and that of
economics is wealth. Whenever a number of such [sciences] come under   *10*
a single faculty (as bridle-making and all other arts concerned with the
equipment of horses come under horsemanship, and as this [science] and
every military *action* comes under strategy, and similarly in the case of
other [sciences] which come under another [science]), in every case the
end of the architectonic [science] is preferable to the ends of the sub-   *15*
ordinate [sciences], for the latter ends are pursued for the sake of the
former end. It makes no difference whether the ends of the *actions* are
the activities themselves or something other than those activities, as in
the case of the sciences just mentioned.

Now if of things we do there is an end which we wish for its own sake
whereas the other things we wish for the sake of this end, and if we do   *20*
not choose everything for the sake of something else (for in this manner
the process will go on to infinity and our desire will be empty and vain),
then clearly this end would be the good and the highest good. Will not
the knowledge of it, then, have a great influence on our way of life, and

would we not [as a consequence] be more likely to attain the desired end,
25   like archers who have a mark to aim at?   If so, then we should try to
grasp, in outline at least,   what that end is and to which of the sciences
or faculties it belongs. It would seem to belong to the one which is most
authoritative and most architectonic.   Now politics appears to be such;
1094b   for it is this which regulates what sciences are needed in a state and what
kind of sciences should be learned by each [kind of individuals] and to
what extent. The most honored faculties, too, e.g., strategy and economics
and rhetoric, are observed to come under this [faculty].   And since this
5   faculty uses the rest of the practical sciences and also legislates what men
should do and what they should abstain from doing, its end would include the ends of the other faculties; hence this is the end which would
be the good for mankind. For even if this end be the same for an individual as for the state, nevertheless the end of the state appears to be greater
and more complete   to attain and to preserve; for though this end is
10   dear also to a single individual, it appears to be more noble and more
divine to a race of men or to a state.
    Our *inquiry*, then, has as its aim these ends,   and it is a political
inquiry; and it would be adequately discussed if it is presented as clearly
as is proper to its subject-matter; for, as in hand-made articles, precision
should not be sought for alike in all discussions. Noble and just things,
15   with which politics is concerned, have so many differences and fluctuations that they are thought to exist only by custom and not by nature.
Good things,   too, have such fluctuations because harm has come from
them to many individuals; for some men even perished because of wealth,
20   others because of bravery. So in discussing such matters and in using
[premises] concerning them, we should be content to indicate the truth
roughly and in outline, and when we deal with things which occur for the
most part and use similar [premises] for them, [we should be content to
draw] conclusions of a similar nature. The listener, too, should accept
each of these statements in the same manner;   for it is the mark of an
25   educated man   to seek as much precision in things of a given genus as
their nature allows, for to accept persuasive arguments from a mathematician appears to be [as improper as] to demand demonstrations from
a rhetorician.
    Now a man judges well the things he knows [well], and it is of these
1095a   that he is a good judge; so a good judge in a subject is one who is educated

in that subject, and a good judge without qualification is one who is educated in every subject. In view of this, a young man is not a proper student of [lectures on] politics; for he is inexperienced in *actions* concerned with human life, and discussions proceed from [premises concerning those *actions*] and deal with [those *actions*].   Moreover, being disposed to follow his passions, he will listen in vain and without benefit, since the   5
end of such discussions is not knowledge but *action*.   (And it makes no difference whether he is young in age or youthful in character, for his deficiency arises not from lack of time but because he lives and pursues things according to passion). For knowledge about such matters in such a man, as in those who are incontinent, becomes unprofitable; but in those   10
who form their desires and *act* according to [right] reason,   it becomes very beneficial.

Let so much, then, be taken as a preface concerning (a) the kind of student, (b) the manner in which the discussion of the subject should be accepted, and (c) the subject of the *inquiry* which is before us.

2

To resume, since all knowledge and every intention desire some good, let   15
us discuss what is that which is aimed at by politics and what is the highest of all goods achievable by *action*. Most people are almost agreed as to its name; for both ordinary and cultivated people call it "happiness", and both regard living well and *acting* well as being the same as being happy. But there is disagreement as to what happiness is, and   20
the account of it given by ordinary people is not similar to that given by the wise. For some regard it as something obvious or apparent, such as pleasure or wealth or honor, while others regard it as something else; and often the same man changes his mind about it, for when suffering from disease he regards it as being health, when poor as being wealth,   25
and when he becomes conscious of his ignorance he admires those who discuss something great and beyond his comprehension. Again, some [the Platonists] held that besides these particular goods there exists something by itself [*Goodness*, as an Idea], and that it is this [Idea] which causes these particulars to be good.

To examine all the doctrines would perhaps be rather fruitless, but it is sufficient to examine only those which are most prevalent or are thought   30

to be based on some reason. Let us also not forget that arguments from principles differ from those which lead to principles. Plato, too, was right when he raised this problem and inquired whether the right way to pro-
1095b ceed is from the principles or towards the principles, [2] e.g., whether in a stadium the right procedure is from the judges to the goal or vice versa. One should begin, of course, from what is familiar; but things are familiar in two ways, for some are familiar relative to us while others are familiar without qualification. Probably we should begin from things which are familiar relative to us. Accordingly, he who is to listen effectively to
5 lectures concerning noble and just things and, in general, to subjects dealt with by politics should be brought up well in ethical habits; for the beginning [here] is the fact, and if this fact should appear to be adequate, there will be no further need of the why of it. Such a man either has or can easily get principles. As for him who lacks both, let him listen to the words of Hesiod:

10 That man's completely best who of himself
Thinks of all things, ... and he is also good
Who trusts a good advisor; but the man
Who neither for himself can think nor, listening,
Takes what he hears to heart, this man is useless.

                                   3

15 Let us continue the discussion from the point at which we digressed. It is not unreasonable that what men regard the good or happiness to be seems to come from their ways of living. Thus ordinary people or those who are most vulgar regard it as being pleasure, and in view of this they like a life of sensual pleasure. Now there are thee kinds of life which stand out most; the one just mentioned, the political, and thirdly the contemplative.
20 Ordinary people appear to be quite slavish in choosing deliberately a life of beastly pleasures, but their view has support because many men of means share the tastes of Sardanapalus. Men of culture and *action* seek a life of honor; for the end of political life is almost this. But this
25 good appears rather superficial to be what is sought; for it is thought to depend on those who bestow rather than on those who receive honor, whereas we have a strong inner sense that the good is something which belongs to the man who possesses it and cannot be taken away from him

easily. Further, men seem to pursue honor in order to assure themselves that they are good; at least, they seek to be honored (a) by men of prudence, and (b) among those who know them, and (c) on the basis of their virtue. Clearly, then, virtue, according to these, is superior to the other goods. And perhaps one might even regard this more than any other good to be the end of political life. But this too appears to be rather incomplete, for it seems that a man may have virtue even when he is asleep, or when he goes through life without *acting*, or, besides these, when one meets with the greatest sufferings and misfortunes; but no one would regard a man living in this manner as being happy, unless he wishes to uphold a paradox. But enough of this subject, for it has been sufficiently treated in periodicals. The third kind of life is the theoretical, which we shall examine later.[3]

As for the life of a money-maker, it is one of tension; and clearly the good sought is not wealth, for wealth is instrumental and is sought for the sake of something else. So one might rather regard as ends those mentioned above, for they are liked for their own sake. Yet they, too, do not appear to be the highest good, although many arguments have been used to support them. So let the discussion of these be left aside.

4

As for the universal *Good*, perhaps it is better to examine it and go over the difficulties arising from the way it is stated, although such an inquiry is made with reluctance because those who introduced the Forms are friends. Yet it would perhaps be thought better, and also our duty, to forsake even what is close to us in order to preserve the truth, especially as we are philosophers; for while both are dear, it is sacred to honor truth above friendship.

Now those who introduced this doctrine did not posit Ideas in which they assigned greater or less priority, and just for this reason neither did they set up an Idea of numbers. But what is called 'good' may be in the whatness [of a thing, i.e., in a substance], and also in a quality, and in a relation [etc.], and that which exists by itself and is a substance is prior by nature to a relation [and to the rest], for a relation is like an offshoot and an accident of being; so there could be no common idea for [all] these.

Further, since the term 'good' has as many senses as the term 'being'

25   (for it is predicated of whatness, as in the case of God and of the intellect, and of a quality, as in the case of the virtues, and of a quantity, as in the case of the right amount, and of a relation, as in the case of the useful, and of time, as in the case of right time, and of place, as in the case of the right location, and similarly with the other categories), clearly it cannot be a universal which is common and one, for it would not have been used in all the categories but only in one.

30   Again, since of things coming under one idea there is a single science, of all the goods, too, there would have to be a single science. But as it is, there are many sciences even of goods which come under one category. Under right time, for example, in war the science is strategy, but in disease it is medical science; and under the right amount, in nourishment it is medical science, but in exercise it is the science of gymnastics.

35   One might also raise this question: What in the world do they mean by
1096b   the term 'Thing Itself' if, for example, the definition of a man is one and the same whether applied to Man Himself or to an individual man? For insofar as they are just men, they will not differ at all; and if so, neither will *Good Itself* and a particular good differ insofar as each is good.

Further, if indeed a white thing which exists for a long time is not [necessarily] whiter than a white thing which exists for a day, neither will *Good Itself* by being eternal be more good than a particular good.

5   The Pythagoreans seem to have spoken more persuasively about the good when they placed the *One* in the column of goods; and Speusippus too seems to have followed closely their line of thought.   The discussion of these things, however, belongs elsewhere.[4]

An objection to what has been said [by us] appears to arise because the
10   arguments [of the Platonists] do not include all [kinds of] goods. Now one kind of things called 'good 'are those which are pursued and are liked for their own sake; but there are also things which somehow produce or pre- serve or prevent the contraries of the former kind, and these are called 'good' because the former are called 'good', but they are so called in an- other sense of the term. Clearly, then, things are called 'good' in two senses, some for their own sake,   others for the sake of these. So let us
15   separate those which are good for their own sake from those which are beneficial to other goods and consider whether the former are called 'good' according to one idea. What kind of things would one posit as being good for their own sake?   Are they not those which are pursued even just for

themselves, such as thinking wisely, seeing, certain pleasures, and honors? For even if we pursue these for the sake of something else, still one would posit them as being goods for their own sake.   But is it only the Idea   *20* [i.e., *Good Itself*, which is good in this sense] and none of the other things? If so, then the species [of goods] will exist in vain. And if these too are goods for their own sake,   the same definition [of good] should appear in all of them, like the definition of whiteness when whiteness is present in snow and in white lead.   But the definitions of honor and of thinking wisely and of pleasure are distinct and the things defined differ insofar as   *25* they are good. The good, then, cannot be something common in virtue of one idea.   But then, in what manner are these things called 'good'? They do not seem to be like those which have the same name by chance. Are they called 'good' by coming from one thing, or by contributing to one end, or rather by analogy?   By 'analogy' I mean, e.g., as vision is in the body, so is the intellect in the soul, and another thing in something else.

But perhaps we should leave these aside at present, for an accurate   *30* discussion concerning them belongs more properly to another philosophy; [5] and similarly with regard to the Idea [i.e., the *Good*].   For even if there is some one good which is commonly predicated [of certain things] or which is separate by itself, clearly it cannot be the object of *action* or of possession by a man; but it is such an object that we are seeking now.   *35*

Perhaps one might think that the knowledge of that separate good would be better for those goods which are objects of possession or of *action*, for   *1097a* by using it like a model we shall also know more the things which are good for us, and if we know them [more], we shall succeed [more] in attaining them. This argument is indeed somewhat persuasive, but it seems to clash with the sciences. For all of them aim at some good and   *5* seek what is lacking, and yet they leave out the knowledge of it; and it is unreasonable that all the artists should be ignorant of so great an aid and make no attempt at all to seek it out. Furthermore, one does not see how a weaver or a carpenter will benefit in the practice of his art by knowing *Good Itself*, or how one will be a better doctor or a better general by   *10* having contemplated that Idea [the *Good*]; for it appears that what a doctor examines is not health in this manner at all, but the health of man, or perhaps rather the health of an individual man, since what he cures is an individual [and not man in general].   So much, then, for the discussion of these.

5

15 Let us return to the good which we are seeking and inquire what it might be.
It appears to be different in different *actions* or arts; for in medical art it
is different from that in strategy and similarly from that in any of the rest
of the arts. What then is the good in each? Is it not that for the sake of
which the rest are done? This is health in the medical art, victory in
20 strategy, a house in architecture, something else in another art, and in
every *action* or intention it is the end; for it is for the sake of this that the
rest are done by all men. So if there is some one end of all the things that
are done, this would be the good achievable by *action*, but if there are
many ends, these would be the corresponding goods. Thus by taking a
25 different course the argument arrives at the same thing. But we must try
to state this more clearly.

Since the ends appear to be many, and since we choose some of them
(e.g., wealth, flutes, and instruments in general) for the sake of others, it
is clear that not all ends are complete; but the highest good appears to be
something which is complete. So if there is only one end which is complete,
30 this will be the good we are seeking, but if there are many, the most complete of these will be that good. Now what we maintain is this: that which
is pursued for its own sake is more complete than that which is pursued
for the sake of something else, and that which is chosen but never chosen
for the sake of something else is more complete than other things which,
though chosen for their own sake, are also chosen for the sake of this;
and that which is complete without any qualification is that which is
chosen always for its own sake and never for the sake of something else.
1097b Now happiness is thought to be such an end most of all, for it is this that
we choose always for its own sake and never for the sake of something else;
and as for honor and pleasure and intellect and every virtue, we choose
them for their own sake (for we might choose each of them when nothing
else resulted from them), but we also choose them for the sake of happiness,
5 believing that through these we shall be happy. But no one chooses happiness for the sake of these, nor, in general, for the sake of some other thing.

The result appears to be still the same if we proceed from self-sufficiency,
for the perfect good is thought to be self-sufficient. By 'self-sufficient' we
do not mean an individual who leads just a solitary life, but one with
10 parents and children and a wife and, in general, with friends and fellow-

citizens as well, since man is by nature political. Some limit, however, should be set to these, for if we extend them to include one's ancestors, descendants, and friends of friends, these will proceed to infinity; but we shall examine this later.[6] Now we posit the self-sufficient to be that which taken by itself makes one's way of life worthy of choice and lacking in nothing; and such we consider happiness to be. Moreover, we posit happiness to be of all things the most worthy of choice and not capable of being increased by the addition of some other good, since if it were capable of being increased by the addition even of the least of the goods, the result would clearly be more worthy of choice; for the result would exceed [the original, i.e., happiness], and the greater of two goods is always more worthy of choice. It appears, then, that happiness is something perfect and self-sufficient, and it is the end of things we do.

15

20

6

Perhaps to say that happiness is the highest good is something which appears to be agreed upon; what we miss, however, is a more explicit statement as to what it is. Perhaps this might be given if the function of man is taken into consideration. For just as in a flute-player or a statue-maker or any artist or, in general, in anyone who has a function or an *action* to perform the goodness or excellence lies in that function, so it would seem to be the case in a man, if indeed he has a function. But should we hold that, while a carpenter and a shoemaker have certain functions or *actions* to perform, a man has none at all but is by nature without a function? Is it not more reasonable to posit that, just as an eye and a hand and a foot and any part of the body in general appear to have certain functions, so a man has some function other than these? What then would this function be?

25

30

Now living appears to be common to plants as well as to men; but what we seek is proper to men alone. So let us leave aside the life of nutrition and of growth. Next there would be the life of sensation; but this, too, appears to be common also to a horse and an ox and all animals. There remains, then, the life of *action* of a being who has reason. Of that which has reason, (a) one part has reason in the sense that it may obey reason, (b) the other part has it in the sense that it possesses reason or in the sense that it is *thinking*. Since we speak of part (b), too, in two senses, let us

1098a

5

confine ourselves to the life with reason in activity [i.e., to the process of *thinking*], for it is this sense which is thought to be more important. Accordingly, if the function of a man is an activity of the soul according to reason or not without reason, and if the function of a man is generically the same as that of a good man, like that of a lyre-player and a good lyre-

10   player, and of all others without qualification, when excellence with respect to virtue is added to that function (for the function of a lyre-player is to play the lyre while that of a good lyre-player is to play it well, and if so, then we posit the function of a man to be a certain kind of life, namely, activity or *actions* of the soul with reason, and of a virtuous man we posit

15   these to be well and nobly done; so since each thing is performed well according to its proper virtue), then the good for a man turns out to be an activity of the soul according to virtue, and if the virtues are many, then according to the best and most complete virtue. And we should add 'in a complete life', for one swallow does not make a spring, nor does one

20   day; and so too one day or a short time does not make a man blessed or happy.

7

Let this, then, be the outline of the good [for a man], for perhaps we should first make a sketch and later fill in the details. When a good outline has been made, it would seem that anyone could go forward and articulate the parts, for time is a good discoverer and helper in such matters. It is in

25   this way that the arts advanced, for anyone can add what is lacking. We should also recall what has been stated previously: precision should not be sought alike in all cases, but in each case only as much as the subject-matter allows and as much as is proper to the *inquiry*. Thus a carpenter and

30   a geometer make inquiries concerning the right angle in different ways; for the first does it as much as is useful for his work, while the second inquires what it is or what kind of thing it is, since his aim is to contemplate the truth. We should proceed likewise in other situations and not allow side lines to dominate the main task. Again, we should not demand the

1098b   cause in all things alike, but in some cases it is sufficient to indicate the fact well, as is also the case with principles; and the fact is first and is a principle. Now some principles are perceived by induction, others are observed by sensation, others are acquired by some kind of habituation,

5   and others in some other way. So we should try to present each according

to its nature and should make a serious effort to describe them well, for they have a great influence on what follows; for a principle is thought to be more than half of the whole, and through it many of the things sought become apparent also.

8

We should consider this principle not only from the conclusion and from premises leading to its definition, but also from what men say about it; for all things which belong to it aie in harmony with a true [definition of it], but truth is soon bound to clash with a false [definition of it]. Now goods have been divided into three kinds: those which are called 'external', those of the soul, and those of the body; and we maintain that those of the soul are the most important and are goods in the highest sense, and *actions* and mental activities are activities of the soul. So our account must have been stated well, at least according to this doctrine, which is an old one and agreed upon by philosophers. It is also rightly said that the end is certain *actions* or activities; for it is in such a manner that the goods of the soul arise, and not from the external goods. The statement that the happy man lives well and *acts* well, too, is in harmony with the definition of happiness; for we have almost said that happiness is living well or *acting* well.

9

Again, all the things which men look for in happiness appear to belong to the definition given. For happiness is thought to be virtue by some, prudence by others, a sort of wisdom by others, or all of these or some of them, together with pleasure or not without pleasure by still others; and there are those who include also material prosperity. Of these opinions, some are held by ordinary men and by men of old, while others by the few and by men held in esteem; and it is reasonable that none of them should be altogether mistaken but should be right at least in one and even in most respects.

Our definition is in harmony with those who say that happiness is virtue or some sort of virtue; for the activity according to virtue is an activity of a virtue. It makes perhaps no small difference, however, whether we regard the highest good to be in possession or in use, or to exist as a disposition or as an activity according to that disposition. For a dis-

1099a   position may be present without producing any good at all, as in a man
who is asleep or inactive for some reason or other; but with the activity
this cannot be the case, for one will of necessity be *acting*, and *acting* well.
And as at the Olympic Games it is not the most beautiful or the strongest

5   who are crowned but those who compete (for it is some of these who
become victors), so in life it is those who *act* rightly who become the
winners of good and noble things. Moreover, these men lead the kind of
life which is by its nature pleasant. For to be pleased is something which
belongs to the soul, and the thing that pleases a man is that to which he
takes a liking, e.g., a horse pleases a man who likes horses, and a spectacle

10   pleases a man who likes spectacles, and similarly that which is just pleases
a man who likes what is just, and in general, virtuous things please a man
who likes things done according to virtue. Now things which give pleasure
to most men are in conflict with each other because they are not by nature
such. But things which give pleasure to those who like noble things are by
nature pleasant; and such are the *actions* according to virtue, and these are

15   both pleasant to such men and pleasant in virtue of their nature. Thus the
life of these men has no further need of pleasure as a sort of charm, to be
attached like an appendage, but has its pleasure in itself; for, besides what
we have said, no man is good who does not enjoy noble *actions*, nor would
anyone call a man 'just' who does not enjoy *acting* justly, or call a man

20   'generous' who does not enjoy generous *actions*, and similarly in all the
other cases. If this is so, then it is by their nature that *actions* according to
virtue would be pleasant. Moreover, they are also good or noble, and in
the highest degree so, if indeed a virtuous man judges them well; and he
judges them as we have stated. Happiness, then, is the highest good, and

25   the most noble, and the most pleasant, and these [three attributes] are not
separate, as the inscription at Delos claims:

That which is most just most noble is;
Health is best; by nature to obtain
What one desires is the pleasantest.

30   For all of these belong to the best activities; and these activities, or one of
them – the very best – we maintain to be happiness.
  But happiness appears also to require external goods, as we have mentioned;[9] for it is impossible or not easy to *act* nobly if one is not furnished

1099b   with external goods. For many *actions* are done through friends or wealth

or political power, as if by means of instruments; but the lack of some
things, such as high lineage, good children, and beauty, mars blessedness;
for one who is utterly ugly, or of low lineage, or lonesome and without
children is not altogether happy, and perhaps even less so if he were to   5
have very bad children or friends, or if these were good but perished.
As we have said, then, a man seems to need also such favorable conditions;
and in view of this, some [go as far as to] identify happiness with good
fortune, but others with virtue.

10

It is in view of these opinions that the problem also arises whether happiness
is acquired by learning or by habit or by some other form of training, or   10
whether it comes to us by some divine providence or even by luck. Now
if there are any other gifts at all which men receive from gods, it is reasonable that happiness, too, should be god-given, especially as it is the best of
goods for men. But perhaps this problem would be more proper to another inquiry; anyway, even if happiness is not god-sent but comes to us   15
through virtue or some sort of learning or training, it appears to be the
most divine [of goods for men], for the prize and the end of virtue appears
to be the highest good and something godlike and blessed. It might also
be shared by many men; for it can belong, through some kind of learning
and diligence, to all those who have not been incapacitated for virtue.
So if it is better that we should be living happily in this manner rather than   20
by luck, then it is reasonable that such be the case, if indeed things which
exist by nature attain their noblest state in accordance with their nature.
The situation is similar also with things which exist or are produced according to art or any cause, especially the best. But to entrust the greatest and
noblest [of human goods] to luck would be very incongruous indeed.   25
     The answer to this inquiry becomes apparent also from the definition,
for we have stated[10] that happiness is a certain kind of activity of the soul
according to virtue. As for the remaining goods, some of them exist as
necessities, the others are by their nature helpful and useful as instruments
to happiness. These statements are in agreement also with what we said in
the beginning;[11] for we posited the end of politics to be the highest good,   30
and politics takes the greatest care in making the citizens of a certain
quality, i.e., good and disposed to noble *actions*. Accordingly, it is reason-

able that neither an ox nor a horse nor any other animal should be called
1100a   'happy', for none of them can partake of such activity. For the same *reason*,
too, a child cannot be happy, for it is not yet capable of such *actions* because of its age; but some of them are called 'blessed' because they are
expected to be happy in the future. For happiness requires, as we have
5   stated, both complete virtue and a complete life, since many changes and
all sorts of events caused by chance occur in a lifetime; and it is possible
for the most prosperous man to suffer great calamities in his old age, as is
told of Priam in the Trojan stories, and a man who has met such fortunes
and has come to a wretched end would not be considered happy by anyone.

11

10   Should we consider no one happy, then, while he is living but wait, as
Solon said, to see the end of his life? And if we posit also such a requirement, will it not be the case, too, that a man is happy when he is dead?
But is not this entirely absurd, especially since we have maintained that
15   happiness is some sort of an activity? Now if we do not mean to say that a
dead man is happy and if Solon did not intend to say this, but instead that
one might safely consider a man blessed only when that man is already
beyond the reach of evils and misfortunes, this too would be subject to
dispute; for it seems that something good as well as something bad may
20   come to a dead man, if indeed it does also to a living man when he is not
conscious, e.g., honors and dishonors, and also good *actions* and misfortunes of children and of descendants in general. But this too presents a
problem; for if a man has lived according to reason a blessed life till old
age and died as befitted him, many changes might occur in his descendants,
25   for some of them might turn out to be good and to attain the life they are
worthy of, while with others the contrary might be the case. It is clear, too,
that the distance in the relationship between these descendants and the man
might vary in all sorts of ways. It would thus be absurd if also the dead
men were to change along with his descendants and become at one time
happy and at another wretched; but it would be also absurd if the lives of
30   descendants contributed nothing at all, nor for some time, to the happiness
or unhappiness of their ancestors.
    But let us return to the first problem, for perhaps from its considera-
tion we might be able to perceive the latter problem also. Now if we are to

look to the end and only then consider a man as blessed, not as being then blessed but as having led a blessed life earlier, is it not absurd to say that when the man is happy it would not be true to regard him as happy, giving   *35* as the *reason* the fact that we do not wish to call a man happy because of   *1100b* (1) the possible future changes and (2) our belief (a) that happiness is something enduring and by no means easily changed but (b) that the fortunes of a man often take many turns? For it is clear that if we were to go along with one's fortunes, we would have to call the same man at one   *5* time 'happy' and at another 'wretched', representing a happy man as a sort of chameleon and with an unsound foundation. It would not be right at all, then, to base happiness on a man's fortunes. For goodness or badness in a man does not depend on these, although, as we have stated, human life needs them, too; but it is the activities in accordance with virtue which   *10* play the dominant role in happiness, while the contrary activities are dominant in the contrary of happiness.

    This statement is confirmed also by the difficulty we have just discussed. For in none of man's actions is there so much certainty as in his virtuous activities (which are more enduring than even scientific knowledge), and the most honorable of these are the most enduring because those who   *15* are blessed live according to them most of all and most continuously; for this seems to be the *reason* why we do not forget them. The attribute [i.e., permanence] in question, then, will belong to a happy man, and he will be such a man throughout his life; for he will be engaged always or most of all in *actions* and studies of things done according to virtue, and   *20* he will bear the fortunes of life most nobly and with propriety in every way like a man who is truly good and 'foursquare beyond reproach'. Now there are many events which happen by chance, some of great but others of small weight; and it is clear that [for a virtuous man] those which are of small weight, whether bringing good luck or its opposite, do not   *25* have [much] influence on life, while those which are great and numerous make life more blessed if they turn out well (for these, too, by their nature add to the order and beauty of life, and the use of them becomes noble and good), but they restrict or ruin the blessedness of a man if they turn out to be the opposite, for they bring along pain and impede many activities.   *30* Yet nobility shines out even here, when a man bears many and great misfortunes with calm and ease, not through insensibility to pain, but through nobility of character and highmindedness.

Thus if it is the activities that play a dominant role in life, as we have
35   said, [14] no blessed man can become wretched; for he will never do what is
1101a   hateful or bad. For we hold that a truly good and sensible man will bear
all fortunes of life with propriety and will always *act* most nobly under
whatever the given circumstances may be, like a good general, who uses a
5   given army most effectively, or a good shoemaker, who makes the best
shoes out of a given leather, and likewise with any artist. If so, no happy
man will ever become wretched; nor of course blessed, were he to meet
with fortunes such as those of Priam. Nor again will he be subject to
variations or easily changeable; for he will not be moved from his happi-
10   ness easily, nor by any chance mishaps but by those which are great and
numerous; and in the latter case he will not again become happy in a short
time, but, if at all, in a long and complete time, during which he will
attain great and noble things.

What should prevent us, then, from saying that a man is happy when he
15   acts in accordance with complete virtue and is sufficiently furnished with
external goods, not for some chance period but during his entire life?
Should we not also add "and who will continue to live in this manner and
die as befits him", since the future is not manifest to us and since we posit
happiness to be an end and perfect in every way? If such be the case, we
20   may call 'blessed' those among the living who possess and will possess the
things already mentioned, but [we shall call them] 'blessed' [in the manner
which befits them as] men. Let so much, then, be the limit of what we have
to say about these problems.

As for the fortunes that may befall a man's descendants and all his friends,
to regard them as not contributing anything at all appears very unwelcome
and contrary to the opinions of men. On the other hand, since they are
25   many and differ in various ways, some of them coming more close to him
while others less so, to discuss each of them individually appears to be a
long and endless task, but to speak of them taken as a whole and sketchily
may perhaps be sufficient. Now just as some of a man's mishaps have
some weight or influence on his life, while others seem to be rather light,
30   so the things that happen to all of a man's friends are similarly related. So
since the sufferings which affect the living differ from those which affect
the dead much more than the unlawful and terrible deeds which are *acted*
on the stage differ from those which are presupposed in a tragedy, this
35   difference too must be taken into acount, and perhaps more so in dis-

cussing the problem whether the dead share in any good or its opposite.   *1101b*
For, even if any good or its opposite penetrates to them, this seems, from
the remarks just made, to be weak or small, either without qualification or
to them, or else to be at least so much and of such a kind as not to make
happy those who are unhappy nor to deprive happy men of their blessed-   *5*
ness. Good *actions* of friends, then, and bad *actions* similarly, appear to
contribute something to the dead, but they do so to such a degree and
extent as not to change happy into unhappy men or to make some other
such change.

12

Having settled these problems, let us examine next whether happiness is   *10*
among the things which are praised or, rather, among those which are
honored; for it is at least clear that it is not one of the powers.[15] Now it
appears that whatever is praiseworthy is praised by being a certain quality
or by being somehow related to something else; for we praise a just man
and a brave man and, in general, a good man and virtue because of the   *15*
actions or the things which are done, and we praise a [naturally] strong
man and a [natural] runner and each of the others in view of the fact
that each of them has by nature a certain quality and is disposed in a
certain way towards something good or virtuous. This is clear also whenever the gods are praised, for they appear ridiculous when they are referred
to us, and this happens because praises are referred to something else, as   *20*
we said. So if praise is such a thing, it is clear that, of a thing which is a
highest good, there can be no praise except something greater or better;
and this appears to be the case, for what we say of gods is that they are
blessed or happy, and we call the most godlike of men 'blessed'. So, too,   *25*
with the goods; for no man praises happiness as he does that which is
just, but he calls it 'blessed', since it is something more godlike or better.
It seems that Eudoxus, too, was right in advocating pleasure in his
speeches concerning the things to be prized; for he thought that the fact
that pleasure, which is a good, is not praised indicates that it is superior to   *30*
the things which are praised, and that such are God and the good, for all
the others are referred to these. For praise belongs to virtue, since by
means of virtue one is disposed to perform noble *actions*, while encomia
belong to activities of the body and those of the soul in a similar manner.
Perhaps precision in these matters is more proper to treatises concerned   *35*

1102a with encomia, but to us it is clear from what has been said that happiness is among those things which are honored and are perfect. And such seems to be the case also because happiness is a principle, for it is for the sake of this that all *actions* are done by everyone; and our position is that the principle and the cause of good things is something worthy of honor and is divine.

13

5 Since happiness is an activity of the soul in accordance with complete virtue, we should examine virtue; for perhaps our investigation of happiness, too, would be better if it is pursued in this manner. The true statesman, too, is thought to have made the greatest effort in studying virtue, 10 for his wish is to make the citizens good and obedient to the laws. As examples of this we have the lawgivers of the Cretans and of the Spartans, and also some others who became such lawgivers. And if this concern belongs to politics, clearly our inquiry into virtue would be in accordance with our original intention. Clearly, it is human virtue that we should be 15 examining, for what we were seeking, too, was the good and happiness for man; and by 'human virtue' we mean not that of the body but that of the soul, for it is of the soul, too, that happiness is stated by us to be an activity. If such be the case, it is clear that a statesman should understand in some way the attributes of the soul, like the doctor who attends to 20 the eyes or the whole body, and to the degree that politics is more honorable and better than medical science. Now the cultivated among the doctors take the trouble to learn many things about the body. So the statesman, too, should be investigating attributes of the soul, both for the 25 sake of these and as much as is adequate to what is sought, for greater precision is perhaps rather burdensome in view of what he is aiming at.

Some things about the soul have been sufficiently stated also in public writings, and they should be used; e.g., one part of the soul is nonrational, the other has reason. It makes no difference for the present whether these 30 two parts are separable, like the parts of a body and of any other divisible whole, or just distinguishable in definition but inseparable by nature, like the convex and the concave in the circumference of a circle. Of the nonrational, one part is like that which is common and vegetative, i.e., that which is the cause of nutrition and of growth. For one would posit such 1102b a power of the soul in all things which take in nutriment and in embryos;

and he would posit the same [kind of power] also in complete beings, since it is more reasonable to posit this than to posit some other kind of power. Now the virtue of this power appears to be common to all things having this power and not just human, for this part of the soul or this power seems to function most in sleep, and good and evil men are least 5 distinguishable [as being such] during sleep; and from this arises the saying that happy and wretched men do not differ during half their lives. This, of course, occurs with good reason; for sleep is an inactivity of the soul insofar as the soul is said to be good or bad, except when some motions somehow make their way to the soul a little, in which case the dreams of 10 *good* men turn out to be better than those of ordinary men. But enough of this; and let us leave aside the nutritive part of the soul, since by its nature it does not partake of human virtue.

There seems to be also another nature of the soul which is nonrational but which participates in some way in reason. For we praise reason or that part of the soul which has reason in the continent and the incontinent 15 man, since it urges them rightly to do what is best; but it appears that these men have also another part which by its nature violates reason, and this part fights against or resists reason. For just as the paralyzed parts of the body when directed to move to the right [often] move contrariwise to the 20 left, so it is with the soul; for incontinent men have an impulse to move in the contrary direction. But while in the body we observe this motion in the contrary direction, in the soul we do not. Perhaps in the soul, too, we should grant no less the existence of something which violates reason, i.e., a part which goes contrary to it or resists it. How this part is distinct 25 from the part with reason does not concern us here. Now this part too appears to share in reason, as we said;[16] for at least in the continent man it obeys reason, while in the temperate or brave man, perhaps it is even more disposed to listen to reason, for it agrees with reason on all matters. So the term 'nonrational', too, appears to have two meanings. For the vegetative part in no way communicates with reason, while the appetitive 30 part and, in general, the part which desires shares [in reason] in some way, namely, insofar as it listens to or obeys it; and this is the manner in which a man has reason when we speak of him as listening to or obeying his father or his friends, and not in the manner in which he has reason in mathematics. That the nonrational part is in some way persuaded by reason is indicated also by advice or by any censure or urging. And if one *1103a* should say that this part, too, has reason, then also the expression 'that which has reason' would have two senses: (a) that which has reason in itself, this being the principal sense, and (b) that which listens to reason, like a child listening to a father.

Virtues too are distinguished according to this difference, for we call some of them 'intellectual', e.g., wisdom and intelligence and prudence, but others 'ethical', e.g., generosity and temperance. Thus, when we speak of the character of a man, we say that he is good-tempered or temperate, not wise or intelligent, but we praise also the wise man in virtue of his disposition; and we call "virtues" those dispositions which are praise-worthy.

BOOK II

1

1103a14   Since virtues are of two kinds, intellectual and ethical, an intellectual virtue originates and grows mostly by teaching, and in view of this it requires experience and time, whereas an ethical virtue is acquired by habituation (ethos), as is indicated by the name 'ethical', which varies slightly from the name 'ethos'. From this fact it is also clear that none of the ethical virtues arises in us by nature [at birth], for no thing which exists by nature can be changed into something else by habituation; e.g., no stone, which moves downwards by nature, can be changed by being habituated to move upwards, even if one were to keep on throwing it up countless of times, nor can fire be similarly made to move downwards, nor can anything else with some other attribute existing by nature be made to change that attri-bute by habituation. Hence virtues arise in us neither by nature nor con-trary to nature; but by our nature we can receive them and perfect them by habituation.

Again, of things which come to us by nature, we first bring along the powers and later exhibit the corresponding activities. This indeed is clear in the case of sensations; for it is not by seeing often or hearing often that we acquired the corresponding power of sensation, but conversely: we used the power after we possessed it, we did not come to possess it after using it. In the case of the virtues, on the other hand, we acquire them as a result of prior activities; and this is like the case of the arts, for that which we are to perform by art after learning, we first learn by performing,

e.g., we become builders by building and lyre-players by playing the lyre. *1103b*
Similarly, we become just by doing what is just, temperate by doing what
is temperate, and brave by doing brave deeds. This is confirmed also by
what happens in states. For it is by making citizens acquire certain habits
that legislators make them good, and this is what every legislator wishes, 5
but legislators who do not do this well are making a mistake; and good
government differs from bad government in this respect.

Again, it is from the same *actions* and because of the same *actions* that
every virtue comes into being or is destroyed, and similarly with every art;
for it is by playing the lyre well or badly that men become good or bad lyre
players, respectively. In the case of architects and all the rest, too, the 10
situation is analogous; for men become good architects by building houses
well, and bad architects by building houses badly. For if such were not the
case, there would have been no need for a teacher, but all would have
become good or bad artists.

Such indeed is the case with virtues also; for it is by our *actions* with
other men in transactions that we are in the process of becoming just or 15
unjust, and it is by our *actions* in dangerous situations in which we are in
the process of acquiring the habit of being courageous or afraid that we
become brave or cowardly, respectively. It is likewise with *desires* and
with anger; for, by behaving in one way or in the contrary way in corresponding situations, some men become temperate or intemperate,
good-tempered or irascible. In short, it is by similar activities that habits 20
are developed in men; and in view of this, the activities in which men are
engaged should be of [the right] quality, for the kinds of habits which
develop follow the corresponding differences in those activities. So in
acquiring a habit it makes no small difference whether we are *acting* in
one way or in the contrary way right from our early youth; it makes a great 25
difference, or rather all the difference.

2

Since our present study is not for the sake of contemplation, like the other
theoretical inquiries – for we are inquiring what virtue is, not in order
[just] to know it, but in order to become good, since otherwise there would
be no benefit from that inquiry – we should examine certain things
about *actions*, namely, how they should be done, for these are the principal 30
[causes] also of the formation of the kinds of habits, as we have already
stated. Now to *act* according to right reason is commonly accepted, and
let it be assumed here; later there will be a discussion concerning right

reason,[17] both as to what it is and how it is related to the other virtues. But

1104a first, let us agree on that other matter, namely, that all statements concerning matters of *action* should be made sketchily and not with precision, for, as we said at first, our demands of statements should be in accordance with the subject-matter of those statements; in matters concerning *action*

5 and expediency, as in those of health, there is no uniformity. And if such is the universal statement, a statement concerning particulars will be even less precise; for these do not come under any art or precept, but those who are to *act* must always consider what is proper to the occasion, as in

10 medical art and in navigation. Yet even though our present statement is of such a nature, we should try to be of some help.

First, then, let us perceive this, that it is the nature of such things [ethical virtues] to be destroyed by deficiency as well as by excess, as we observe in the case of strength and of health (for we should use as evidence

15 what is apparent for the sake of what is obscure), for both excess and deficiency in exercise destroy strength; and similarly, when too much or too little drink or food is taken, it destroys health, but when the amount is proportionate, it produces or increases or preserves health. Such is the

20 case also with temperance and bravery and the other [ethical] virtues; for a man who flees from and fears everything and never stands his ground becomes a coward, but he who fears nothing at all but proceeds against all dangers becomes rash, and, similarly, a man who indulges in all [bodily] pleasures and abstains from none becomes intemperate, but he who avoids

25 them all, like a boor, becomes a sort of insensible man; for temperance and bravery are destroyed by excess as well as by deficiency, but they are preserved by moderation (or the mean).

Furthermore, not only is each virtue generated, or grows, or is destroyed from the same and by the same [kind of *actions*], but also the activities [according to each virtue] will depend on that same [virtue], for such is

30 the case with other things which are more apparent, as with strength; for not only does strength come into being by taking much nourishment and undergoing many exertions, but it is also the strong man who is most able to do such things. Such too is the case with the virtues; for by abstaining

35 from [excessive bodily] pleasures we become temperate, and, in turn, when we have become temperate we are most able to abstain from such pleasures.

1104b And similarly with bravery; for by becoming habituated to show contempt for and endure what is fearful we become brave, and when we have become brave we are most able to endure what is fearful.

As a sign of what habits are we may consider the pleasures and pains

5 which accompany our actions; for a man who abstains from [excessive] bodily pleasures and enjoys doing so is temperate, but a man who is

oppressed by so doing is intemperate, and he who faces danger and enjoys it or at least is not pained by so doing is brave, but he who is pained by so doing is a coward. Thus ethical virtue is concerned with pleasures and pains; for we do what is bad for the sake of pleasure, and we abstain from doing what is noble because of pain. In view of this, we should be brought up from our early youth in such a way as to enjoy and be pained by the things we should, as Plato says,[18] for this is the right education. 10

Again, since virtues are concerned with *actions* and passions, and since every *action* and every passion is accompanied by pleasure or pain, then for this *reason*, too, virtues would be concerned with pleasures and pains. This is indicated also by punishment, which is inflicted by means of pains; for punishment is a sort of cure, and cures by their nature are effected by means of contraries. Again, as we said before,[19] every habit of the soul has a nature which is related to and is concerned with those things by which it becomes by nature worse or better; but a habit becomes bad because of pleasures and pains, that is, by pursuing or avoiding pleasures or pains either when one should not, or at a time when he should not, or in the manner in which he should not, or in some other way contrary to that specified by [right] reason. It is in view of this that some thinkers even define the virtues as being certain states without feeling or as states of rest; but they do not define them well, for they define them in an un-qualified way and do not specify them by adding "in the manner in which they should or should not, or at the time when they should" or whatever other qualifications are needed. We assume, then, that such virtue is concerned with pleasures and pains and disposes us to do what is best, while vice disposes us to do the contrary. 15 20 25

That virtues and vices are concerned with the same things [pleasures and pains] may become apparent to us also from the following. There are three objects which we choose, the noble, the expedient, and the pleasant, and there are three contrary objects which we avoid, the disgraceful, the harmful, and the painful; and a good man is apt to *succeed* in all of these, while a bad man is apt to be mistaken, especially about pleasure, for pleasure is common to animals also and accompanies all objects of choice, for also the noble and the expedient appear to be pleasant. Again, pleasure has been from infancy with us all; so it is difficult to rub off this feeling, ingrained as it is in our life. We also regulate our *actions*, some of us more and others less, by pleasure and pain. Because of this, then, it is necessary for our whole study to be concerned with pleasures and pains; for to enjoy or be pained rightly or wrongly has no small effect on our *actions*. Again, as Heraclitus says, it is more difficult to fight against pleasure than to fight against temper, and of that which is more difficult 30 35 1105a 5

10   one can always acquire an art or a virtue; for excellence, too, is better in that which is more difficult to achieve.   So because of this, too, the whole study of virtue or of politics is concerned with pleasures and pains; for he who uses these well will become good, but he who uses them badly will become bad.

Let it be affirmed, then, that virtue is concerned with pleasures and pains, that it grows by those *actions* by which it is in the process of coming into

15   being but is destroyed if those *actions* are not done in this manner, and that its activity is concerned with the same *actions* as those from which it came to be.

3

One might raise this question: How can we say that men should do what is just in order to become just, and *act* temperately in order to become

20   temperate? For if they do what is just or temperate, they are already just or temperate, just as if they do what is grammatical or musical, they are already grammarians or musicians, respectively.

But this is not the case even with the arts. For it is possible for one to write something which is grammatical by luck also or when someone else suggests it.   Accordingly, a man is a grammarian precisely when he does

25   something grammatical and does it in a grammatical manner, that is, in accordance with the grammatical knowledge which he possesses. Furthermore, the case of the virtues is not even similar to that of the arts.   For the things produced by the arts have their excellence in themselves, so it is enough that, when produced, they should be of a certain kind; things done

30   according to virtue, on the other hand, are done justly or temperately not [only] if (1) they themselves are of a certain kind, but also if (2) the agent who *acts* is of a certain disposition, namely, (a) when he knows what he does, (b) when he intends to do what he does and intends to do it for its own sake, and (c) when he *acts* with certainty and firmness.   Now with the

1105b   exception of (a) knowledge, these [(b) and (c)] are not taken into account as requirements in the possession of the various arts; but in the possession of the virtues, knowledge has little or no weight, while the others [(b) and (c)] count for not a little but for everything, for it is indeed by doing many

5   times what is just and temperate that we acquire justice and temperance. Thus while things are just or temperate if they are such as a just or temperate man would do, a just or temperate man is not one who [just] does these, but one who also does them as a just or a temperate man

10   would.   So it is well said that it is by doing what is just or temperate that a man becomes just or temperate, respectively; and no one who is

to become good will become good unless he does good things. Yet most men do not do these; instead, they resort to merely talking about them and think that they are philosophizing and that by so doing they will become virtuous, thus behaving somewhat like patients who listen to their *15* doctors attentively but do none of the things they are ordered to do. And just as these patients will not cure their body by behaving in this way, so those who philosophize in such a manner will not better their soul.

4

Next we must inquire what virtue is. Since there are three things in the *20* soul, and these are feelings [or passions], powers, and habits, virtue would be one of these. By 'feelings' I mean, for example, *desire*, anger, fear, envy, courage, gladness, friendly feeling, hatred, longing, emulation, pity, and, in general, whatever is accompanied by pleasure or pain; by 'powers' I mean those qualities in virtue of which we are disposed to be affected by the above feelings, for example, those in virtue of which we are *25* capable of being angry or pained or feeling pity; and by 'habits' I mean those qualities in virtue of which we are well or badly disposed with reference to the corresponding feelings, e.g., with reference to being angry we are badly disposed if we are angry too violently or too weakly but well disposed if we are angry moderately, and similarly with the others.

Now neither the virtues nor the vices are feelings; for we are said to be *30* good or bad not with respect to feelings but with respect to virtues or vices, and we are praised or blamed not for our feelings (for he who is simply afraid or angry is not praised, nor is he who is simply angry the one *1106a* who is blamed but he who is angry in a certain manner) but for our virtues and vices. Furthermore, we are angry or afraid without deliberate choice, while virtues are intentions of some kind or [are acquired] not without deliberate choice. Finally, with respect to our feelings we are said to be *5* moved, while with respect to virtues and vices we are said not to be moved but to be disposed in a certain manner.

For the above *reasons* neither the virtues nor the vices are powers; for by being simply capable of feeling we are not said to be either good or bad, nor are we praised or blamed. And besides, it is by nature that we possess powers, but it is not by nature that we become good or bad; and we spoke *10* of this previously.[20]

So if the virtues are neither feelings nor powers, what remains is that they are habits. We have discussed, then, what virtue is as far as its genus goes.

5

Concerning virtue we should state not only this, that it is a habit, but also
15   the kind of habit it is. It should be noted that every virtue (a) makes that
of which it is the virtue be well disposed and (b) makes it perform its
function well; e.g., the virtue of an eye both makes the eye a good eye and
makes it perform its function well, for it is by the virtue of the eye that we
20   see well. Similarly, the virtue of a horse makes (a) the horse a good horse
and also (b) good at running and carrying its rider and facing the enemy.
So if such is the case in every instance, the virtue of a man, too, would be
the habit from which he becomes good and performs his function well.
How this can be done has already been stated,[21] but it may become evident
also if we view the kind of nature possessed by virtue. Now in everything
which is continuous and divisible it is possible to take an amount which is
greater than or less than or equal to the amount required, and the amounts
taken may be so related either with respect to the thing itself or in relation
to us; and the equal is a mean between excess and deficiency. By 'the mean',
30   in the case of the thing itself, I mean that which lies at equal intervals from
the extremes, and this mean is just one thing and is the same for everyone;
but, when related to us, it neither exceeds nor falls short [of what is
proper to each of us], and this is neither just one thing nor the same for
everyone. For example, if ten is many and two is few, then six is taken as
35   the mean with respect to the thing itself, for six exceeds two and is exceeded
by ten by equal amounts; and this is the mean according to an arithmetic
proportion. But the mean relative to us should not be taken in this
1106b   manner; for if ten pounds are too much and two pounds are too little for
someone to eat, the trainer will not [necessarily] order six pounds, since
this is perhaps too much or too little for the one who is to take it; for
Milo[22] it is too little, but for a beginner in athletics it is too much. It is
5   likewise in running and wrestling. And this is the way in which every
scientist avoids excess and deficiency but seeks and chooses the mean,
not the mean with respect to the thing itself but the one in relation to a
given person.

If, then, this is the manner in which every science performs its function
well, namely, by keeping an eye on the mean and working towards it
10   (whence arises the usual remark concerning excellent works, that nothing
can be subtracted from or added to them, since both excess and deficiency
destroy the excellence in them while the mean preserves it), and if, as is our
manner of saying, it is with an eye on this that good artists do their work,
15   and if virtue, like nature, is more precise and better than any art, then
virtue would be aiming at the mean. I am speaking here of ethical virtue,

for it is this which is concerned with feelings and *actions*, in which there is excess, deficiency, and moderation. For example, we may have the feelings of fear, courage, *desire*, anger, pity, and any pleasure or pain in general either more or less than we should, and in both cases this is not a good thing; but to have these feelings at the right times and for the right things and towards the right men and for the right purpose and in the right manner, this is the mean and the best, and it is precisely this which belongs to virtue. In *actions*, too, there is excess, deficiency, and moderation in a similar manner. Now an [ethical] virtue is concerned with feelings and *actions*, in which excess and deficiency are errors and   are blamed, while moderation is a *success* and is praised; and both *success* and praise belong to virtue. Virtue, then, is a kind of moderation, at least having the mean as its aim.   Also, a man may make an error in many ways (for evil, as the Pythagoreans conjectured, belongs to the infinite, while goodness belongs to the finite),   but he may *succeed* in one way only; and in view of this, one of them is easy but the other hard. It is easy to miss the mark but hard to hit it. So it is because of these, too, that excess and deficiency belong to vice, but moderation to virtue. 20 25 30

For men are good in one way, bad in many. 35

6

[Ethical] virtue, then, is a habit, disposed toward *action* by deliberate choice, being at the mean relative to us, and defined by reason and as a prudent man would define it. It is a mean between two vices, one by excess and the other by deficiency; and while some of the vices exceed while the others are deficient in what is right in feelings and *actions*, virtue finds and chooses the mean.   Thus, according to its *substance* or the definition stating its essence, virtue is a mean [of a certain kind], but with respect to the highest good and to excellence, it is an extreme. *1107a* 5

Not every *action* nor every feeling, however, admits of the mean, for some of them have names which directly include badness, e.g., such feelings as malicious gladness, shamelessness, and envy, and, in the case of *actions*, adultery, theft, and murder; for all of these and others like them are blamed for being bad, not [just] their excesses or deficiencies. Accordingly, one is never right in performing these but is always mistaken; and there is no problem of whether it is good or not to do them, e.g., whether to commit adultery with the right woman, at the right time, in the right manner, etc., for to perform any of these is without qualification to be mistaken. If this were not so, we would be maintaining that in *acting* unjustly or in a co- 10 15

20 wardly way or intemperately, too, there is moderation and excess and deficiency; for according to such a view there would be also a moderation of
excess and of deficiency, an excess of excess, and a deficiency of deficiency.
But just as there is no excess or deficiency of temperance or of bravery, because the mean is in a certain way an extreme, so, too, there is no
moderation or excess or deficiency in the vices mentioned above but only a

25 mistake, regardless of the manner in which one *acts*; for, universally,
there is no moderation of excess or of deficiency, nor an excess or a
deficiency of moderation.

7

We must not only state this universally, however, but also apply it to

30 particular cases; for, among statements about *actions*, those which are
[more] universal are rather empty while those which are [more] particular
tend to be more true; for *actions* deal with particulars, and it is with
these that our statements should be in harmony. So let us consider each
of these virtues and vices from our table.

1107b With regard to fear and courage, the mean is bravery. He who exceeds
in not fearing has no name (many virtues and vices have no names),
but he who exceeds in courage is rash; and he who exceeds in fear and is
deficient in courage is a coward.

5 With regard to pleasures and pains – not all of them [but mainly of the
bodily senses], and less with regard to pains than with regard to pleasures –
the mean is temperance while the excess is intemperance. Men deficient
with regard to pleasures hardly exist, and for this reason such men happen
to have no name; but let them be called 'insensible'.

With regard to giving and taking property, the mean is generosity,

10 while the excess and deficiency are, respectively, wastefulness and stinginess. Excess and deficiency in these two vices are present in contrary ways;
for the wasteful man exceeds in giving away and is deficient in taking,
while the stingy man exceeds in taking but is deficient in giving away.

15 (At present we are giving a sketchy and summary account of these, and this
is sufficient; later[23] we shall specify them more precisely). With regard to
property there are also certain other dispositions. The mean is munificence,
for a munificent man differs from a generous man in that he deals with
large amounts, while a generous man deals with small amounts [also].

The excess in large donations is extravagance or conspicuous consump-

20 tion, and the deficiency is meanness; but these vices differ from the vices
opposed to generosity, and the manner in which they differ will be stated
later.[24]

With regard to honor and dishonor, the mean is high-mindedness, the excess is said to be a sort of vanity, and the deficiency is low-mindedness. And just as generosity was said to be related to munificence by being *25* concerned with smaller amounts, so too there is a virtue which is concerned with smaller honors and is similarly related to high-mindedness, which is concerned with great honors; for it is possible to desire honor as one should, or more than one should, or less than one should. Now he who exceeds in his desires is called 'ambitious', he who is deficient is called 'unambitious', but he who desires honor in moderation has no name. *30* The dispositions too are nameless, except for that of the ambitious man, which is called 'ambition'. It is in view of this lack of name that those who are at the extremes claim to be in the middle position; and we, too, sometimes call the moderate man 'ambitious' but sometimes 'unambitious', and sometimes we praise the ambitious man but sometimes the un- *1108a* ambitious. The *reason* why we do this will be stated later;[25] for the present, let us continue with the other habits in the manner already proposed.

With regard to anger, too, there is excess, deficiency, and moderation. *5* These habits are almost nameless, but since we say that the moderate man is good-tempered, let us call the mean 'good temper'. As for the extremes, let the man who exceeds be called 'irascible' and the corresponding vice 'irascibility', and let the man who is deficient be called 'inirascible' and the corresponding deficiency 'inirascibility'.

There are three other moderations which have some likeness towards *10* each other yet differ from each other; for all of them are concerned with associations among men as they speak or *act* but differ in that one is concerned with truth about oneself while the other two are concerned with what is pleasurable, and of these two, one is exhibited in amusement while the other in all situations of life. So we should consider these, too, in order to observe better that moderation is praiseworthy in all cases *15* while the extremes are neither right nor praiseworthy but worthy of blame. Now most of these habits, too, have no names, but we should try, as in the other cases, to introduce names ourselves in order to make our point clear and easy to follow.

With regard to truth, then, the moderate man is a sort of truthful man *20* and the mean may be called 'truthfulness'; but pretense which exaggerates is boastfulness and the possessor of it is boastful, while pretense which understates is self-depreciation and the possessor of it is self-depreciatory.

With regard to what is pleasant in amusing others, the moderate man is witty and the corresponding disposition is wit, but the disposition which tends to exceed is buffoonery and the possessor of it is a buffoon, while he *25* he who is deficient is a sort of boor and the corresponding habit is boorishness.

With regard to what is pleasant in the other manner, the one found in [all] situations of life, the man who is pleasant as he should be is friendly and the mean is friendliness; but he who behaves excessively is complaisant, if he does this not for the sake of anything else, but is a flatterer, if he

30   does it for his personal benefit, while he who is deficient and is unpleasant in all situations is a quarrelsome sort of man or a man hard to get along with.

There are moderations in feelings, too, and in what concerns feelings. Thus a sense of shame is not a virtue, but a man with a sense of shame is praised also; for here, too, one man is said to be moderate, i.e., he who has a sense of shame, another behaves excessively, like the abashed man

35   who is ashamed of everything, and a third is deficient or is not ashamed at all, and he is called 'shameless'.

1108b   As for righteous indignation, it is a mean between envy and malicious gladness. These dispositions are concerned with pain and pleasure felt at the fortunes of others; for a man with righteous indignation is pained by the undeserved good fortune of others, an envious man, who exceeds, is

5   pained by the good fortune of all others, and a man who is maliciously glad is so deficient in being pained as to be even joyful at the good fortunes of others. These will be discussed elsewhere at the proper time.[26]

As for justice, since the term 'justice' does not have only one meaning, we shall, after discussing the other habits, distinguish those meanings and state the manner in which each of them is a mean[27]; and in a similar manner

10   we shall discuss also the rational virtues.[28]

8

Since the kinds of habits are three, and since two of them are vices, one with respect to excess but the other with respect to deficiency, while the third is a virtue, which is a mean, each of them is opposed to each of the others in some manner; for the extremes [the vices] are contrary both to

15   the mean and to each other, while the mean is contrary to the extremes; for just as the equal is greater when related to the less but less when related to the greater, so in both feelings and *actions* the middle habits [the moderations] exceed when related to the deficiencies but are deficient when related to the excesses. For the brave man appears rash to the coward

20   but a coward to the rash man. Similarly, the temperate man appears intemperate to the insensible man but insensible to the intemperate; and a generous man appears wasteful to a stingy man but stingy to the wasteful. Hence each man at each extreme regards the one at the middle as being

25   near the other extreme, and the coward calls the brave man 'rash' while

the rash man calls him 'a coward'; and the case with the others is analogous.

Since the three kinds of habits are opposed to one another in such a manner, the contrariety of the extremes to each other is greater than that to the mean, for they are further from each other than from the middle just as the great is further from the small and the small from the great 30 than each of them is from the equal. Again, in some cases one of the extremes appears to be similar to the mean, like rashness in relation to bravery and wastefulness in relation to generosity; but it is the extremes which are most dissimilar to each other. Now contraries are defined as things which are furthest from each other; so it is things which are further 35 apart which are more contrary to each other.

In some cases the mean is opposed by the deficiency more than by the 1109a excess, in others it is opposed by the excess more than by the deficiency. For example, it is not rashness, which is an excess, but cowardice, which is a deficiency, that is more opposed to bravery; on the other hand, it is not insensibility, which is a deficiency, but intemperance, which is an excess, 5 that is more opposed to temperance. This happens to be the case for two *reasons*. One of them comes from the thing itself. For since it is one of the extremes that is nearer to and more like the mean, it is not this but the other extreme that we oppose to the mean. For example, since it is rashness rather than cowardice that is thought to be more like and nearer to 10 bravery, it is cowardice rather than rashness that is more opposed to bravery; for it is the thing which is further from the middle that is thought to be more contrary to the middle. So this is one *reason*, and it arises from the thing itself. The other *reason* arises from ourselves; for the vice to which we are in some way naturally more drawn appears to be more contrary to the mean. For example, we are naturally drawn to [bodily] 15 pleasures more than to insensibility, and so we are more easily drawn to intemperance than to propriety. Thus we say that the vice to which we yield more readily is more contrary to the mean than the contrary vice is; and for this *reason* it is intemperance, which is an excess, and not insensibility that is more contrary to temperance.

9

We have sufficiently discussed the following: that ethical virtue is a mean; 20 the manner in which it is a mean; that it is a mean between two vices, one with respect to excess and the other with respect to deficiency; and that it is such a mean because it aims at what is moderate in feelings and *actions*.

In view of what has been said, it is a difficult task to become a virtuous man, for in each case it is a difficult task to attain the mean; for example, 25

not everyone can find the mean [the center] of a circle but only he who
knows geometry. So, too, anyone can get angry or give money or spend it,
and it is easy. But to give to the right person, the right amount, at the
right time, for the right purpose, and in the right manner, this is not something that anyone can do nor is it easy to do; and it is in view of this that
30   excellence is rare and praiseworthy and noble. Accordingly, he who aims at
the mean should first keep himself away from that vice which is more contrary to the mean, as Calypso recommends also: "keep the ship away from
the surf and spray"[29]; for one of the two extremes is more subject to mistake,
while the other is less so. So since it is difficult to attain the mean exactly,
35   we should choose as a second best, as the saying goes, that which has the
1109b least of what is bad; and this will most likely be effected in the manner stated.

We should take into consideration also the vices to which we are easily
drawn, for some of us are by nature inclined towards some of them, others
towards others; and we come to know these by our pains and pleasures.
We should then drag ourselves towards the contrary extreme, for by
5   drawing ourselves well away from our disposition to error, we shall be
more likely to arrive at the mean, like those who straighten warped sticks
by bending them in the contrary direction.

On every occasion, what we should guard against most is the pleasurable
or pleasure, for we do not judge pleasure impartially. Thus towards
pleasure we should feel just as the elders of the people felt towards Helen,
10   and we should repeat their saying[30] on every occasion; for by getting rid of
pleasure in this manner we are less likely to be mistaken. To sum up, then,
if we do all these things, we shall best be able to attain the mean.

Perhaps all this is difficult, and especially in individual cases, for it is
15   not easy to specify, for example, how and with whom and on what kinds of
provocations and how long a man should be angry; for we do sometimes
praise those who are deficient and call them 'good-tempered' but at other
times speak of those who are harsh as being manly. Nevertheless, the man
who is blamed is not he who deviates from goodness only a little, whether
towards excess or deficiency, but he who deviates much, for the latter does
20   not escape our notice. Nor is it easy to specify by a formula the limits beyond
which one becomes blameworthy and the extent to which one should be
blamed, for this is not easy for any sensible object; such specifications
depend on individual situations, and judgement depends on the sensation
of these. So much, then, is clear, that the intermediate habit is in all cases
praiseworthy, and that we should lean sometimes in the direction of excess
25   and sometimes in the direction of deficiency, for by so doing we shall most
easily attain the mean and goodness.

BOOK III

1

Since virtue is concerned with feelings and *actions*, and since feelings and   30 1109b
actions which are voluntary are praised or blamed, while those which are
involuntary are pardoned and sometimes even pitied, it is (a) likewise
necessary for those who examine virtue to specify what is voluntary and
what is involuntary, and also (b) useful for legislators in bestowing   35
honors and inflicting punishments.

It is thought that involuntary things are those which are done by force   *1110a*
or through ignorance; and that is said to be done by force whose [moving]
principle is external and is such that the agent who *acts* or the patient who
is *acted* upon contributes nothing, as in the case of a strong wind which
carries a ship off course or the case of men who have us in their power. As
for *actions* done through fear of greater evils or for the sake of some noble   5
deed (e.g., a tyrant who has a man's parents and children in his power may
order him to do something disgraceful, threatening to kill them if the man
does not obey but to spare them if he obeys), there is disagreement as to
whether they are involuntary or voluntary. Something of this sort happens
also when goods are thrown overboard during a storm; for no one would
voluntarily just throw goods away, but for one's safety and that of the   10
passengers every sane person would.

Such *actions*, then, are mixed, but they are more like voluntary than like
involuntary; for at the time they are done they are subject to choice, and
the end of the *action* depends on the right moment. So when a man *acts*,
both what is voluntary and what is involuntary should be mentioned. Now   15
in such *actions* he *acts* voluntarily, for the [moving] principle of setting the
parts of his body in motion is also in him; and if that principle is in him,
it is up to him to *act* or not to *act*. Such *actions*, then, are voluntary, but if
they are regarded without any qualification, they are perhaps involuntary;
for no one would choose any of them taken by itself. Sometimes men are   20
even praised for such *actions*, whenever they endure something disgraceful or painful in return for something great or noble; but they are blamed

whenever they take the contrary course, for to endure what is most
disgraceful for what is not noble or for mediocre ends is the mark of a bad
man. On some occasions a man is not praised but pardoned, whenever he
25 does things he should not do for *reasons* which are too strong for human
nature and which no one would endure. Perhaps there are some things
which one cannot be forced to do but would rather die than suffer the most
terrible things; and as for the things which compelled Euripides' Alcmaeon
to slay his mother, they appear ridiculous. Sometimes, however, it is
30 difficult for one to decide which of two alternatives he should choose and
which he should endure, and it is even more difficult to abide by his
decision; for the most part, what men anticipate is painful but what they
are compelled to do is disgraceful, and in virtue of these [i.e., the painful
1110b or disgraceful]they are praised or blamed according as they are compelled
to do something or not.

What sort of *actions*, then, should we say are done by force? Are they not
those whose [moving] cause is without qualification external and the
agent contributes nothing? But concerning those which taken by themselves are involuntary but which, when qualified, are chosen in the face of
the alternative consequences, if the principle of such choice is in the agent,
5 they are involuntary when taken by themselves but, when qualified, are
voluntary in the face of the alternative consequences. And in the latter
case they are more like the voluntary than the involuntary; for *actions*
depend on particular situations, and in such cases they are voluntary.
It is not easy, however, to state definitely which of the alternatives should
be chosen, for many differences arise in individual cases.

Now if one were to say that things which are pleasant and noble are
10 done by force – for, being external, they compel us – then in this way all
things would be done by force, for it is for the sake of these [pleasant or
noble] things that all men do whatever they do; but those who *act* by
force or unwillingly do so painfully, while those who *act* because of
pleasure or what is noble do so with pleasure. So it is ridiculous for a
man (a) to assign the [moving] cause to external things and not accept the
responsibility himself for being easily caught by such things but (b) to
15 regard himself responsible for what is noble while making the pleasant
[which is external] responsible for what is disgraceful. It seems, then, that
what forces a man is that whose [moving] principle is external,   without
the man who is forced contributing anything.

2

Everything done through ignorance is not voluntary, but if it causes pain and regret, it is involuntary; for he who through ignorance did something, *20* whatever this may be, but is not displeased at all by that *action*, though he did not *act* voluntarily, as he did not know what he was doing, neither did he *act* involuntarily if he is not pained. So of a thing done through ignorance, if the agent regrets it, he is thought to have *acted* involuntarily, but if he does not regret it, since he is different, let him be called 'nonvoluntary'; for since he differs, it is better for him to have a special name.

Again, *acting* through ignorance seems to be different from acting in *25* ignorance; for he who is drunk or angry is not thought to be *acting* through ignorance but through one of the causes stated, not knowing his *act* but in ignorance of it. Thus every evil man is in ignorance of what he should do and what he should abstain from doing, and it is through such error that men become unjust and in general bad. *30*

Now the term 'involuntary' tends to be used not whenever a man is ignorant of what is expedient, for ignorance in intention of what should be done is a cause not of what is involuntary but of evil; and [involuntariness] is not universal ignorance (for through universal ignorance men are blamed), but ignorance with respect to particulars in which *action* exists and with *1111a* which *action* is concerned. For it is on these particulars that both pity and pardon depend, since a man who is ignorant of some of these *acts* involuntarily.

It is perhaps better, then, to specify what these particulars are and how many there are, that is, who the agent is, what he does, on what occasion or on what object he *acts*, and sometimes with what (e.g., with an instru- *5* ment), and for the sake of what (e.g., for safety) or how he *acts* (e.g., gently or violently). Now no one would be ignorant of all of these, unless he were mad, and clearly he would not be ignorant of the agent; for indeed how can one be ignorant of himself? But one may be ignorant of what he is doing, e.g., as when one says that a word came out without realizing it, or that he did not know it was secret, as Aeschylus said after revealing the Mysteries, *10* or that he only wished to show how it worked but discharged it, e.g., the catapult. One might also mistake his son for an enemy, as Merope did, or a pointed spear as having a button on it, or some other kind of stone for a pumice stone; and one might strike something to save a man but

15   kill him instead, or one might wish to tap a man but might knock him out,
as in boxing. Since there may be ignorance of any one of these things in
which *action* is involved, he who was ignorant of some of them, especially
of the most important, is thought to have *acted* involuntarily; and by
'most important' we mean those things in which *action* is involved or on
which the outcome depends. In addition, an *action* done involuntarily in
20   virtue of such ignorance should be followed by pain and regret.

3

Since that which is involuntary is done by force or through ignorance, the
voluntary would seem to be that whose [moving] principle is the agent
who knows the particulars on which the *action* depends. For surely it is
25   not well to say, as some do, that whatever is done through temper or
desire is involuntary. For first, none of the other animals would then do
anything voluntarily, not even children. Then again, do we perform no
action through *desire* or temper voluntarily, or do we perform noble *actions*
voluntarily but disgraceful *actions* involuntarily? But is not the latter
alternative ridiculous, when the cause is [only] one person? It would be
30   equally absurd to say that things which we should desire are involuntary.
On the contrary, we should be angry with certain people and we should
desire certain things, such as health and learning; and involuntary *actions*
are thought to be painful, while those according to *desire* are thought to
be pleasant. Furthermore, what is the difference, in being involuntary,
between errors with respect to judgement and those with respect to temper?
1111b   For both should be avoided; and it seems that passions, which are nonrational, are not less human, and so are those *actions* which proceed from
temper and *desire*. It would be absurd, then, to posit them as being
involuntary.

4

5   Having specified what is voluntary and what is involuntary, we shall next
discuss intention (or deliberate choice); for intention is thought to be
most proper to virtue and to reveal character more than *actions* do.
Now intention appears to be volition but is not the same as volition,
since the latter is wider; for children and other animals share in volition,
10   too, but not in intention, and things done on the spur of the moment are

said to be voluntary but not according to intention. Those who say that
intention is *desire* or temper or wish or opinion of some sort do not
speak rightly. For intention does not belong to non-rational beings as well,
but *desire* and temper do; and the incontinent man *acts* by *desire* and
not by intention, while the continent man on the contrary *acts* by inten-   15
tion and not by *desire*. Again, *desire* may be contrary to intention but not
to *desire*. Moreover, *desire* is of the pleasant or of the painful, but intention is neither of the painful nor of the pleasant. Also, intention is temper
even less than it is *desire*; for it is thought that things done through temper
are least done according to intention. Again, intention is not even a wish,
though it appears to be close to it. For there can be no intention of what is   20
impossible, and if one were to say that he intends to do something impossible he would be thought to be a fool; but there can be a wish of what is
impossible, e.g., of immortality. Further, a wish can be also of things
which might be done not by the man who wishes them, like the wish that a
certain actor or athlete be the victor; but no one intends things such as   25
these, except those which he thinks he can bring about by his own effoits.
Also, a wish is of the end rather than of the means, while intention is of
the means relative to the end; e.g., we wish to be healthy but we choose
after deliberation the means through which we may become healthy, and
we wish to be happy and speak of this, but it does not befit us to say that
we choose after deliberation to be happy, and, in general, intention seems   30
to be concerned with things which can be brought about by us.

Again, intention could not be opinion. For opinion can be of everything,
of eternal and impossible things no less than of those which are up to us
to do;   and it is subdivided by being false or true and not by being bad or
good, while intention is subdivided rather by these, i.e., by being bad or
good. In general, then, perhaps no one would say that intention is the same   1112a
as opinion, not even the same as some opinions; for we are of a certain
kind of character by having good or bad intentions and not by having
opinions. And what we intend is to attain or to avoid something or to do
some such thing, but what we have an opinion of is, what a thing is, or to
whom it is expedient, or how it is expedient, but not at all of attaining   5
or of avoiding something.   And intention is praised for being concerned
with a right   end rather than for being right [about any given end], while
opinion is praised by being true. And we deliberately choose what we
most know to be good, but we may have opinion of what we do not quite

know. And we think that those who have the best intentions and those
10   who form the best opinions are not the same,   but that some persons
form rather good opinions, and yet, because of their vice, choose not what
they should. Whether opinion precedes or follows intention makes no
difference; for what we are considering is not this but whether or not some
opinions are the same [in nature] as intentions.

What, then, or what kind of thing is intention,   if indeed it is none of the
things mentioned? It appears that the object of intention is voluntary, but
15   not all voluntary things are objects of intention.   Is it not something
which has already been deliberated upon? For intention [is formed] with
reason or *thought*, and the name [προαιρετόν] itself seems to suggest that
it is something chosen before other things.

5

Do we deliberate about everything, and are all things objects of deliberation, or is deliberation impossible about some objects? Perhaps we should
20   call 'an object of deliberation' not that which a fool or a madman might
deliberate about, but that which a sane man would.

Now no one deliberates (a) about eternal things, e.g., about the universe
or the fact that the diagonal of a square is incommensurable with the side,
or (b) about moving things which occur always in the same way, whether
25   necessarily or by nature or through some other cause,   e.g., about the solstices and the daily sunrise, or (c) about things which [fairly regularly] occur now in one way and now in another, e.g., about droughts and rains,
or (d) about things occurring by luck, e.g., about the finding of a treasure.
Nor do we deliberate about all human affairs, e.g., no Spartan deliberates
30   about how the Scythians would best govern themselves, for things such as
this cannot occur through us.

We deliberate, then, about things which can be done by us, and these are
the things which are left; for [moving] causes are thought to be nature,
necessity, luck, and also intellect and every other cause through man.
Now each man deliberates about the things which he can do by himself.
1112b   And about sciences which are accurate and self-sufficient there is no
deliberation, e.g., about the writing of the letters of the alphabet (for we
do not hesitate as to how we should write them); but we do deliberate about
things which can occur through us though not always in the same manner,

e.g., about things which can occur according to medical science or the
science of money-making, and about navigation more than about gym-   5
nastics, to the extent that navigation is less precise, and also about the
rest in a similar manner, and about the arts more than about the sciences
since we are more uncertain about the arts. Thus we deliberate about things
(a) which are possible or occur for the most part, (b) whose outcome is not
clear, and (c) in which there is something indeterminate; and we call in   10
advisers on matters of importance when we are not convinced that we are
adequately informed to make a good diagnosis.

Now we deliberate not about ends but about the means to ends. For
neither does a doctor deliberate whether he should make people healthy,
nor an orator whether he should persuade, nor a statesman whether he
should enact good laws and enforce them, nor anyone else about whatever the end may be, but positing an end, each of them considers how and   15
by what means that end can be brought about; and if it appears that the
end can be brought about by a number of means, he examines further which
of these is the easiest and best, but if by one means only, he examines how
the end can be achieved by this means, and this by what further means,
and so on, until he arrives at the first cause, which is the last element in
the order of discovery. For the man who deliberates resembles the man   20
who inquires and analyzes, in the manner stated, as in the case of a geometrical diagram.

It appears, however, that not all inquiry is a process of deliberation,
e.g., mathematical inquiry is not a process of deliberation; but every
process of deliberation is inquiry, and the last step in the analysis is the
first step in the coming to be of an end. And if after a process of deliberation we arrive at something which is impossible, we give up our inquiry,   25
e.g., if money is required but this cannot be supplied; but if we arrive at
what appears possible, we undertake to *act*. By 'possible' we mean what
may be brought about by us; for what may be brought about by our
friends is in a way what may be brought about by us, since the [moving]
principle in this case is in us. Sometimes what we seek may be instru-   30
ments, at other times the use of instruments; and similarly in the other
cases, it may be the means through which, or the manner in which, or the
agent through whom the end may be brought about.

As already stated, then, it seems that man is the [moving] principle of
actions; and deliberation is about things to be *acted* upon by the man who

deliberates, and those *actions* are for the sake of other things. The object
of deliberation, then, is not an end but the means to an end; nor is it an
1113a   existing particular, such as whether this is bread or whether it has been
baked as it should, for these are objects of sensation.   Finally, if one were
to be always deliberating, he would keep on doing so to infinity.

The object of deliberation is [generically] the same as that of intention;
but the object of intention is distinguished from the other objects of
deliberation by being judged, after deliberation, to be the one to *act* on.
5   For every one ceases to inquire how he shall *act* when he brings the
[moving] principle back to himself and to the ruling part of himself;   for
the object to be *acted* on is the object of his intention. This is clear also
from the ancient constitutions portrayed by Homer; for under them the
kings announced to the people the things they had deliberately chosen to do.
10   Since the object of intention is the object which is deliberately desired
and which is in our power to attain, intention too would be a deliberate
desire of things which are in our power to bring about;   for having decided
on an alternative after deliberation, we desire that alternative in accordance
with that deliberation.

Sketchily, then, let this be our statement concerning intention, both as to
the kind of things it is concerned with and the fact that these are means
relative to ends.

6

15   We have already stated that a wish is for an end; but for some thinkers a
wish is thought to be for a good, while for others   it is thought to be for
an apparent good. Now those who say that the object of wish is a good
are faced with the consequence that the object wished by a man who does
not choose rightly is not an object of wish (for if it were an object of wish,
20   it would also be good, but, as stated, it turns out to be bad).   Again, those
who say that the object of wish is the apparent good are faced with the
consequence that there can be nothing which by its nature is an object of
wish but only what seems to each man to be good; and since things
appear different to different people, the objects of wish may also turn out
to be contrary.   If these consequences are not satisfactory, should we
then not say that the object of wish, taken without qualification and
according to truth, is the good, while to each person it is the apparent
25   good?   If so, then to a virtuous man the object of wish is the truly good,

while to a bad man it is any chance thing; and such is the case with human bodies, for if they are in a good physical condition, what is healthy for them is what is truly healthy, but if they are sickly, different things are healthy for them, and similarly for what is bitter or sweet or hot or heavy, and so on. For a virtuous man judges things rightly, and in each case what 30 appears to him to be the case is what is truly the case; for there are noble and pleasant things which are proper to each disposition, and perhaps a virtuous man differs from others most by perceiving the truth in each case, being like a standard or a measure of them. For the majority of people, on the other hand, deception seems to arise because of pleasure; for pleasure appears to be a good but is not. Accordingly, they choose what is pleasant 1113b as being good and avoid pain as being bad.

7

Since the object of wish is an end while the objects of deliberation and of intention are the means to an end, *actions* concerning the means would be 5 in accordance with intention and voluntary. But the activities of virtues are concerned with these. So virtue, too, is in our power, and also vice for a similar reason. For where it is in our power to *act*, it is also in our power not to *act*, and where it is in our power not to *act*, it is also in our power to *act*; so if to *act*, when it is noble, is in our power, then also not to *act*, which would then be disgraceful, would be in our power, and if not to *act*, when it is noble, is in our power, then also to *act*, which would then 10 be disgraceful, would be in our power. If it is in our power, then, to do what is noble or disgraceful, and likewise not to do what is noble or disgraceful, and to *act* or not to *act* nobly or disgracefully, as stated earlier, is to be good or bad, then it is in our power to be *good* or bad men. The saying "No one is willingly wicked nor unwillingly 15 blessed" seems to be partly false and partly true. For none is unwillingly blessed, but evil is voluntary; or else, we should dispute the statements just made and say that a man is not the [moving] principle or originator of his *actions* as he is of his children. But if those statements are evident and we have no [moving] principles, other than those which 20 exist in us, to which to refer our *actions*, then *actions* whose [moving] principles exist in us are also in our power to perform and are voluntary.

These statements seem to be confirmed by individuals in private life as

well as by legislators; for they punish or take vengeance on those who
commit evil *acts* (unless these are done by force or through ignorance
25   caused not by the doers themselves), but honor those who perform noble
actions, and they do this in order to exhort the latter but deter the former.
But no one exhorts us to do whatever is neither in our power nor voluntary, as it would be useless for one to try to persuade us, for example, not
to be feverish or pained or hungry or affected in any other such manner,
30   for we will be affected by these none the less. Even a man who is responsible for his ignorance is punished, if he is thought to be the cause of his
ignorance, as in the case of a drunkard on whom a double penalty is
imposed; for the [moving] principle exists in him, since he has the power
of avoiding drunkenness, which is the cause of his ignorance while drunk.
Men are punished also for being ignorant of certain legal matters which
1114a   are not difficult to learn and should be known; and likewise whenever they
are thought to be ignorant through negligence since it is up to them not to
be ignorant, for they have the power of exercizing care. But perhaps they
are of such a kind as not to exercise care. Still it is they themselves who,
5   by living without restraint, are responsible for having become men of
such a kind, e.g., unjust or intemperate, whether by being malevolent or
by spending their time in drinking bouts and the like; for it is particular
activities [of a certain sort] which produce men of a certain kind. This is
clear in the case of those who train themselves for any contest or *action*;
10   for they are constantly active. So to be ignorant of the fact that habits are
acquired by the corresponding activities is the mark of an utterly insensible man.

Moreover, it is unreasonable to think that he who *acts* unjustly does
not wish to be unjust or that he who lives intemperately does not wish to
be intemperate. So if a man without being ignorant does things from which
he will become unjust, he will be voluntarily unjust; but by mere wishing
15   he will not stop being unjust and become just, for neither will a sick
man become healthy by merely wishing to become healthy. And if it
happens that he became sick in this manner [i.e., not unknowingly],
by leading a life of incontinence and disobeying his doctors, then he is
voluntarily sick. Earlier it was certainly up to him not to become sick,
but now when his condition is far gone it is no longer up to him; and
this is like a man who cannot recall a stone he has already thrown off,
though it was in his power earlier not to have let it fall or to have thrown

it because the moving principle existed in him. Likewise, in the case
of an unjust and an intemperate man, it was up to them at first not   *20*
to become such, and so they are voluntarily such; but having become
such, it is no longer up to them not to be such now.

Not only are the vices of the soul voluntary, but for some men, whom
we censure, those of the body also; for no one censures those who are
ugly because of their nature, but we do censure those who are ugly because of lack of exercise or because of negligence. So too in the case of   *25*
physical weakness or injury; for one would never reproach a man who is
blind from birth or by disease or from a blow, but he would rather pity
him; but everyone would censure a man for being blind from habitual
drunkenness or from some other kind of intemperance. Of the bodily defects,
then, those which are in our power to induce are censured, but those which
are not in our power to induce are not censured. If so, then the other vices   *30*
[i.e., of the soul] which are censured are in our power to form also.

One might say that all men aim at the apparent good but cannot control
what appears to them to be good, and that the end appears to each man to   *1114b*
be of such a kind as to correspond to the kind of man he is. Now if each
man is in some way the [moving] cause of his own habit, he is also in some
way the cause of what appears to him. But if not, then no one is the cause
of his doing what is bad but each man does these through ignorance of the
end, thinking that by doing them he will attain the highest good for him-   *5*
self, and the aiming at an end is not self-chosen but one must be born with
a power, as he is with vision, by which he will judge well and will choose
what is truly good; and so a man is gifted if he is from birth well endowed
with this power, for that which is greatest is also noblest, and that which
can neither be received nor learned from another but is disposed to func-   *10*
tion in the manner which corresponds to its quality from birth, if it be well
and nobly endowed, will be by nature a perfect and true gift.

If these remarks are true, then, why should virtue rather than vice be
voluntary? For, to both good and bad men alike, the end will be apparent
and fixed by nature or in whatever way it may be, and it is by reference to   *15*
this end that they will do all the rest, whatever their *actions* be. So whether
it is not by its nature that the end appears to each man such as it does but
depends on him somewhat, or whether the end is natural but virtue is
voluntary by the fact that a good man does all else voluntarily, vice too
would nonetheless be voluntary; for in the case of a bad man, too, his   *20*

actions will likewise be caused by him even if the end is not. If, then, as it is said, the virtues are voluntary (for we ourselves are somehow partly responsible for our habits, and it is by being persons of a certain kind that we posit the end as being of a certain kind), the vices too will be

25 voluntary for a similar reason.

BOOK V

1

1129a3 With regard to justice and injustice, we should consider (1) what kind of
5 *actions* they are concerned with, (2) what kind of a mean justice is, and (3) between what extremes the just is a mean. We shall examine these according to the same method as that used in the discussions which preceded.

We observe that all men, when speaking of justice, have in mind that kind of disposition by which one is disposed to do what is just and from
10 which one *acts* justly and wishes what is just; and similarly with injustice, they have in mind that kind of disposition from which one *acts* unjustly and wishes what is unjust. So let us, too, first make these sketchy assumptions; for the manner of dealing with sciences and faculties is not the same as that with dispositions. For it is the same faculty or the same science which is thought to deal with contraries, but a disposition which is one of two contraries does not tend to *actions* which are contraries;
15 e.g., from health only healthy things are done and not both contraries [health and disease], for we say that a man walks in a healthy manner when he walks as a healthy man would.

At times a disposition comes to be known from its contrary disposition, but at times dispositions come to be known from the subjects to which they are referred; for (a) if good physical condition is evident, bad
20 physical condition becomes evident also, and (b) good physical condition comes to be known from things which are related to good physical condition, and those things come to be known from good physical condition. For if good physical condition is firmness of flesh, it is necessary both for bad physical condition to be flabbiness of flesh and for a wholesome object to cause firmness of flesh. For the most part, if one contrary
25 term has many meanings, the other contrary has many meanings also; e.g., if 'the just' has many meanings, 'the unjust' has many meanings also.

2

Now it seems that 'justice' (and also 'injustice') has many meanings, but because of the closeness of these meanings the equivocation of the term escapes notice and is not so clear as it is in cases in which the meanings are far apart, e.g., as in the equivocal term κλείς, which means the collar-   *30*
bone of an animal but also an instrument with which one locks the door, for the observed difference here is great. Let us then consider the various meanings of 'an unjust man'. The unjust man is thought to be (a) the lawbreaker, but he is also thought to be (b) the grasping or unfair man; so clearly the just man will be the law-abiding man or the fair man. Hence 'the just' means that which is lawful or that which is fair, while   *1129b*
'the unjust' means that which is unlawful or that which is unfair.

Since the unjust man may also be the grasping man, he would as such be concerned with goods, not all goods, but those which may come by good or bad luck and which are always good if taken without qualification but not always good for a particular person. Now men pray for and pursue these goods, but they should not; what they should pray for is that the   *5*
unqualified goods be goods for themselves also, but they should choose those which are good for themselves. The unjust man does not always choose what is greater, but also what is less, as in the case of unqualified bad things; but since what is less bad, too, is thought to be a good in some sense, and since grasping is of that which is a good, for these *reasons* he is thought to be grasping. Of course, he is unfair; for unfairness is in-   *10*
clusive and is common to both.

3

As stated before, since the lawbreaker too is unjust whereas the law-abiding man is just, it is clear that all lawful things are in some sense just; for the things specified by the legislative art are lawful, and we say that each of them is just. Now the laws deal with all matters which aim at what   *15*
is commonly expedient, either to all or to the best or to those in authority, whether with respect to virtue or with respect to some other such thing [e.g., honor]; so in one way we call 'just' those things which produce or preserve happiness or its parts in a political community. Thus the law orders us to perform the *actions* of a brave man (e.g., not to desert our   *20*

post, nor take to flight, nor throw away our arms), and those of a temperate man (e.g., not to commit adultery, nor abuse anyone), and those of a
good-tempered man (e.g., not to strike, nor to speak abusively), and
similarly with respect to the other virtues and evil habits, commanding us
25   to do certain things and forbidding us to do others; and it does so rightly
if it is rightly framed, but less well if hastily framed.

This kind of justice, then, is complete virtue, but in relation to another
person and not in an unqualified way. And, because of this, justice
is often thought to be the best of the virtues, and "neither evening nor
30   morning star" is so wonderful; and, to use a proverb, "in justice is
included every virtue". And it is a virtue in the most complete sense,
since the use of it is that of complete virtue; and it is complete, since he
who possesses it can use it also towards another and not only for himself,
for many men can use virtues whose effect applies only to their own house-
1130a hold but cannot use those virtues which affect others. And it is because
of this that the saying of Bias is thought to be well put: "the way a man
rules will show him up"; for a ruler affects others and he is a ruler in a
community. And for the same *reason* justice alone of the virtues, by
5   affecting others, is thought to be another's good[32]; for the just man *acts*
for what is expedient for someone else, whether for a ruler or a member
of the community. The worst man, then, is the one whose evil habit
affects both himself and his friends, while the best man is one whose virtue
is directed not to himself but to others, for this is a difficult task. Accordingly, this kind of justice is not a part of virtue but the whole virtue,
10   and injustice, which is its contrary, is not a part of vice but the whole
vice.

What the difference is between virtue and this kind of justice, then, is
clear from what we said; for [numerically] they are the same, but their essences are not the same. Insofar as the disposition is defined in relation
to something else, it is justice, but insofar as it is such-and-such a
disposition, it is a virtue without qualification.

4

But we are inquiring about that kind of justice which is a part of virtue,
15   for there exists such a kind of justice, as we said; and similarly with
regard to injustice as a part of [vice]. A sign of the existence of these

kinds is the fact that a man who *acts* according to the other evil habits does so unjustly but is not grasping at all (e.g., like the man who throws away his shield through cowardice or uses abusive language because of his harsh temper or fails to help another with money because of stinginess), while a man who *acts* graspingly often does so neither according to   20
any of these evil habits nor according to any other form but according to some sort of wickedness (for we blame him) and injustice. So there is another kind of injustice, which is a part of injustice taken as a whole vice, and also a kind of unjust thing as a part of what is unjust as a whole and in violation of the law. Again, if one commits adultery for gain and receives money for it, while another does it through *desire* but pays for it   25
and loses money, the latter would be regarded as intemperate rather than as grasping, whereas the former would be regarded as unjust and not as intemperate and so clearly as *acting* for the sake of gain. Again, each of the other forms of an unjust effect is always attributed to some form of evil habit, e.g., to intemperance if one commits adultery, to cowardice if   30
one deserts his comrade in battle, and to anger if one strikes; but if a man makes [undeserved] gain, this is attributed to injustice but to no [other] evil habit. So it is evident that, besides injustice taken as a whole, there is another kind of injustice which is specific, and it has the same name, for its definition falls within the same genus; for both have the force [of   1130b
being defined] in relation to some other person, but the narrow one is concerned with honor or property or safety or something (if we had a single name) which includes all these and has as its aim the pleasure which comes from gain, while the other [the wide one] is concerned with all the things with which a virtuous man is concerned.   5

5

It is clear, then, that there are many kinds of justice, and that, besides the one which is the whole of virtue, there is also another. So let us find out what it is and what kind of thing it is.

The unjust has been distinguished into the unlawful and the unfair, and the just into the lawful and the fair. Now injustice with respect to what is   10
unlawful is the one we considered earlier. But since the unfair and the unlawful are not the same but different and are related as a part to a whole (for whatever is unfair is unlawful but not everything unlawful is unfair),

the unjust and injustice in the narrow sense likewise are not the same but
different from those in the wide sense and are related to them as parts to
15   wholes; for injustice as unfair is a part of injustice as a whole, and justice
as a part is similarly related to justice as a whole. So we should also discuss justice and injustice as parts, and, in a similar manner, also that which
is just and that which is unjust.

We may leave aside the discussion of justice and injustice with respect to
the whole of virtue, the first [i.e., justice] being used as the whole of virtue
20   in relation to another person and the second [i.e., injustice] as the corresponding whole of vice. It is also evident how the just and the unjust which
exist or are done according to these [justice and injustice] will be defined; for perhaps most lawful things are those done by the whole of
virtue, since the law orders us to live in accordance with each of the virtues
25   and prohibits us from living according to each of the evil habits. Other
lawful things are those which have been enacted and produce the whole
of virtue, and they are concerned with education for the common good.
As for each individual's education, in virtue of which a man becomes
good without qualification, we must determine later[33] whether it belongs
to politics or to another inquiry; for perhaps to be a good man is not the
same as to be a good citizen in every case.

30   One kind of justice in the narrow sense, and of what is just according to
this justice, concerns itself with the distributions of honor or property or the
other things which are to be shared by the members of the state (for it is
these who may be so related that some possess a fair share and others an
1131a   unfair share). Another kind is that whose aim is to correct the wrongs done
in exchanges, and it has two parts; for of exchanges some are voluntary
but others are involuntary. Voluntary exchanges are such things as sale,
purchase, loan, security, use of property loaned, deposit, and hiring; and
5   they are said to be voluntary, since they are initiated voluntarily. Of involuntary exchanges, (a) some are clandestine, such as theft, adultery,
poisoning, procuring, enticing slaves away from their masters, assassina-
tion, and false witness, but (b) others are violent, such as assault, im-
prisonment, murder, seizure, injury, defamation, and besmirching.

6

10   Since an unjust man is unfair and whatever is unjust is unfair, it is clear

that there is also a mean between two unfair extremes, and this is the fair;
for in any kind of *action* in which there is the greater and the less, there is
also the equal. So if the unjust is unfair, the just must be fair; and this
indeed is thought to be the case by all, even apart from argument. So
since the fair is a mean, the just would be a mean of some sort. Now the
fair depends on   at least two things. Accordingly, the just must be a   15
mean, and fair, and in relation to something, and for certain persons. As
a mean, it lies between certain things (and these are the greater and the
less); as fair, it is in respect of two things; and as just, it is in relation to
certain persons. The just, then, must depend on at least four things; for
the persons to which it happens to be just are [at least] two, and the things   20
are distributed into [at least] two parts. And it is the same equality which
exists with respect to the persons and with respect to the things, for as the
latter are related, so are the former, for if the former are not equal, they
will not have equal parts. Quarrels and accusations arise, then, when
those who are equal possess or are given unequal parts or when those who
are unequal possess or are given equal parts.   Again, this is clear from
what happens with respect to merit. All men agree that what is just in   25
distribution should be according to merit of some sort, but not all men
agree as to what that merit should be; those who advocate mob rule assert
that this is freedom,   oligarchs that it is wealth, others that it is high
lineage, and aristocrats   that it is virtue.

What is just, then, is something in a proportion of some kind, for a   30
proportion is a property not merely of numbers with units as elements,
but of all kinds of numbers; for it is an equality of ratios, and it exists in at
least four terms.   Clearly, then, a discrete   proportion exists in four terms.
But a continuous proportion   too exists in four terms; for it uses one term
as two and mentions it twice. For example, the term B in $A:B::B:C$ is   1131b
mentioned twice; so if B is posited twice, the terms of the proportion will
be four.

That which is just, too, exists in at least four terms, and the two pairs
have the same ratio; for they are divided in a similar manner, as persons   5
and as things.   Accordingly, as the term A is to the term B, so will the
term C be to the term D;   and by alternation, $A:C::B:D$.   Hence the
whole $(A+C)$, too, will be similarly related to the whole $(B+D)$, and
this indeed is what the distribution combines;   and if the combination is
effected in this manner, the distribution is done justly.

7

10   The conjunction of *A* and *C* and of *B* and *D* is, then, what is just in a distribution, and what is just in the proportion here is a mean; for the proportion is a mean, and what is just is this proportion. Mathematicians call such a proportion geometrical; for in a geometrical proportion it also follows that the whole is to the whole as each term is to the corresponding

15   term. But this kind of proportion is not continuous; for in it no one term which is numerically one can be both the person to whom the portion is given and that portion.

    That which is just, then, is that which is proportional as stated, and that which is unjust is that which violates that which is proportional in this manner. Thus one ratio may become greater but the other less. And this indeed is what actually happens; for he who *acts* unjustly gets the greater

20   portion of a good, while he who is treated unjustly gets the smaller portion. It is the reverse in the case of what is bad, since that which is less bad relative to that which is greater comes under the definition of a good; for what is less bad is preferable to what is greater, that which is chosen is a good, and that which is preferable [i.e., chosen more than another] is a greater good. This, then, is one kind of what is just, namely, the proportional as stated.

25   The remaining kind of what is just is the corrective, and it occurs in exchanges, both voluntary and involuntary. This form of the just is different from the previous form. For what is distributively just in things which are common exists always in accordance with the proportion stated above

30   (for even if the distribution is made from common earnings, it will be made according to the same ratio as that of the funds put into the business by the partners); and the unjust which is opposed to the distributively just is in violation of this proportion. But in exchanges, though that which is

1132a just is something which is fair (and the unjust is unfair), it exists not according to that [i.e., the geometrical] proportion but according to an arithmetical proportion. For it makes no difference, here, whether it is a *good* man who deprived a bad man of something or the reverse, nor whether it is a *good* or a bad man who committed adultery; if one man

5   *acts* unjustly while the other is treated unjustly, or if one man does harm while the other is harmed, the law attends only to the amount of harm and treats both parties as equals. So it is this sort of what is unjust which,

being unfair, the judge tries to equalize; for when one man receives and the other inflicts a wound, or when one man kills and the other is killed, the suffering and the *action* are distinguished as unequals, but the judge tries to equalize the two by means of a penalty which removes the gain of the assailant. Of course, the terms 'gain' and 'loss' as applied to the assailant and the victim, respectively, are used here in an unqualified sort of way, even if they are not appropriate in some cases; but when a measured value is assigned to the suffering, the terms 'gain' and 'loss' are appropriately used. Thus the fair is the mean between the greater and the less, and the gain and the loss are, respectively, the greater and the less in contrary ways, the gain being the greater good or the lesser of what is bad while the loss is the contrary; and the mean between these two was stated to be fair, which we call 'just'. That which is correctively just, then, would be the mean between the loss and the gain. It is in view of this that those who dispute bring the matter before a judge; and to go to a judge is to go to what is just, for a judge tends to be something which is just and has a soul. And they look for a judge as an intermediate, and they call judges 'mediators', thus thinking that if they get what is intermediate they will get what is just. What is just, then, is a kind of a mean, if indeed a judge too is a sort of a mean.

Now the judge restores equality to unequals; and just as, in the case of a line which has been divided into two unequal segments, a geometer takes from the greater segment its excess over half the line and adds it to the smaller part to restore equality, so here. It is when the whole is divided into equal parts and each recipient receives an equal part that each of them is said to receive what belongs to him. Thus the equal [or fair] is the mean between the greater and the less according to an arithmetical proportion. And it is because of this that it is called 'just', for it is a division into halves, as if one were to call it 'divided into halves' and to call a judge 'a divider into halves.' For if a part is subtracted from one of two equal lines and is added to the other, the latter will exceed the former by two such parts (for if the subtracted part were not added to the latter line, this line would exceed the former line only by one such part). Accordingly, the latter line will exceed the intermediate [or equal line] by one such part, and the intermediate line will exceed the diminished line also by one such part. It is by this part, then, that we shall know what to subtract from the greater line and what to add to the smaller line; for the part by which the

5   intermediate [or equal] line exceeds the smaller line must be added to the
latter, and the part by which the intermediate [or equal line] is exceeded
by the greater line must be subtracted from the greater line. Thus let AX,
BY, and CZ be equal to one another; and let AE be removed from AX
and be placed next to CZ

$$A\underline{\qquad \overset{E}{\qquad}\qquad}X$$
$$B\underline{\qquad\qquad\qquad}Y$$
$$D\underline{\quad\overset{C}{\quad}\ \overset{F}{\quad}\qquad}Z$$

as DC. Then the whole line DCZ exceeds EX by $DC + CF$ [where $CF =$
$= AE$], and hence it exceeds BY by DC.

10   The terms 'loss' and 'gain' here have come from voluntary exchange,
where to have more than one's own is called 'to gain' but to have less than
15 the original amount is called 'to lose', as in buying and selling and in all
other exchanges which the law has allowed. But when two parties have
neither more nor less but just what they start out with, then they are said
to have what belongs to each of them and neither lose nor gain. So the
just is a mean between a gain and a loss in exchanges which violate what
20 is voluntary, and it is the possession of equal amounts before and after the
exchange.

8

Some think that what is just without qualification is reciprocity, as the
Pythagoreans said; for they were defining the unqualified just as reciprocal treatment by another. But reciprocity does not fit either what is
25 distributively just or what is correctively just, yet this is the kind of
just which was meant by Rhadamanthus in:

For when the doer suffers what he's done,
At once there's justice.

For in many cases this opinion conflicts with what is commonly believed.
To take an example, if a magistrate strikes another, he should not be
struck in return, but if someone strikes a magistrate, he should not only be
30 struck in return but also be punished. Furthermore, there is a great difference between what is done voluntarily and what is done involuntarily.
     Moreover, in associations for exchange, the kind of what is reciprocally

just which holds men together is not the one based on equality but the one based on proportion; for it is by an action which is reciprocally proportional that a state continues to hold together. For what men seek is either to return something bad – otherwise they consider their position as one *1133a* of slavery – or a good, failing of which there can be no give-and-take; and it is by give-and-take that men hold together. And it is in view of this that men give a prominent place to the Temple of the Graces, so that men may return a service, for a proper mark of grace is this: to return a service to one who has shown grace, and later to take the initiative in showing 5 grace.

Now a proportionate exchange is produced when the diagonal terms are combined. For example, let *A* be an architect, *B* a shoemaker, *C* a house, and *D* a shoe. Then the architect must receive from the shoemaker the latter's work and must himself

give him in return his own work. First, then, if the proportion is an equali- 10 ty and reciprocity takes place, what will be done is what we have called 'just'. If not, reciprocal give-and-take will not be equal and what is done will not be just; for nothing prevents the product of one artist from being better than that of another, and these should be equalized. This is the case with the other arts also, for they would be destroyed if what is given as a 15 combination of quality and quantity is not what is received as a combination of quantity and quality. For an association for exchange is not formed by two doctors but by a doctor and a farmer, and, in general, by artists who are different and unequal and who require equal exchanges.

It is in view of this that things which are to be exchanged should in some way be comparable. To effect this comparison, a coin came into 20 existence, and this somehow functions as an intermediate or a mean; for it measures all goods exchanged and hence both excess and deficiency (e.g., it measures the number of shoes required to equal a house or a given amount of food). Accordingly, as an architect is to a shoemaker, so should the number of shoes be to one house; for if this were not so, there would be neither exchange nor association. But this proportion would be 25 impossible if the goods exchanged were not somehow equal. All goods

to be exchanged, then, should be measurable by some standard coin or measure, as stated before. In reality, this measure is the need which holds all things together; for if man had no needs at all or no needs of a similar nature, there would be no exchange or not this kind of exchange. So a coin is a sort of substitute (or representative) for need and came into
30   being by convention; and it is because of this that its name is 'coin' ($=$ νόμισμα), for it exists by regulation ($=$ νόμῳ) and not by nature, and it is up to us to change a given coin or make it useless.

There will be a reciprocity, then, when the equalization in the exchange becomes such that a farmer is to a shoemaker as the product of the shoe-
1133b   maker is to that of the farmer.   We should use this form of proportion, however, not after the exchange (otherwise, one of the upper terms will have both excesses) but when both parties have their own products and are thus equal and capable of association and can then effect this equality [i.e., the exchange according to proportion]. Thus let A be a farmer, C be
5   food, B be a shoemaker, and D be his product, which has been equalized to C. If reciprocity could not be made in this manner, there would be no association of the parties.

That need holds these together as a single thing is clear from the fact that if the two parties, whether both or only one, do not need each other, they do not make the exchange, whereas if what each has the other needs,
10   there may be exchange, as in the exportation of corn for wine, which should then be equalized. If one does not now need something but might need it later, then money serves as a security to make a future exchange; for by bringing money later he should get what he needs.

Now this money, too, is subject to the same fluctuation in need, for its worth does not always remain the same, but it has a greater tendency to
15   remain the same. In view of this, all things should have a price on them; for in this way an exchange is always possible, and if so, also an association of men. A coin, then, like a measure, by making goods measurable by the same unit, makes their equalization possible; for neither would an association of men be possible without exchange, nor exchange without equalization, nor equalization without measurement by the same unit. It is true that goods whose difference is great cannot be measured by the
20   same unit, but when referred to the needs of men they become sufficiently measurable. There must, then, be some one unit which men posit as a standard measure; and in view of this, it is called 'a coin', for this makes

all goods comparable since all of them are then measured by that coin.
Let *A* be a house, *B* ten minae,   and *C* a bed. If the house is worth five
minae or equal to it, then *A* is worth or equal to half of *B*; and let the bed
C be one-tenth part of *B*. It is clear, then, how many beds are equal to one   *25*
house, namely, five. Clearly, then, it is in this manner that exchange took
place before money came to existence; for it makes no difference whether
a house is exchanged for five beds or for the value in coin of five beds.

9

We have stated, then, what the unjust and the just are. These having been   *30*
specified, it is clear that a just *action* is a mean between *acting* unjustly and
being treated unjustly; for to *act* unjustly is to get more than what one
deserves while to be treated unjustly is to get less than what one deserves.
Thus justice is a mean not in the same manner as the virtues already considered, but by being of an intermediate; and injustice is of the extremes. *1134a*
And justice is a disposition in virtue of which the just man is said to be
disposed by intention to do what is just and to make a distribution, either
between himself and another or between others, not so as to get more of
what is choiceworthy for himself and to give less of it to another, nor to   *5*
take less of what is harmful and to give more of it to another (and similarly if the distribution is between others), but in such a way that the parties
receive what is proportionally equal. As for injustice, which is the contrary of justice, it is of what is unjust;   and this, which is in violation of
what is proportional, is an excess or deficiency of what is beneficial or
harmful, respectively. In view of this, injustice is excess and deficiency,
since it is of that which is in excess and of that which is deficient; for one-   *10*
self, it is an excess of what is beneficial without qualification or a deficiency
of what is harmful, while towards others, it is (a) the whole [i.e., deficiency
of what is beneficial or excess of what is harmful] in a similar manner and
(b) a violation of the proportionally equal [if the distribution is between
others], regardless of which [party gets the excess of what is beneficial or
the deficiency of what is harmful]. In an unjust effect, to receive less of
a good is to be treated unjustly, and to get more of a good is to *act* unjustly.

Let such be our discussion of justice and injustice, and similarly of what   *15*
is just and what is unjust in general.

10

Since it is possible to *act* unjustly and still not be unjust, what kind of unjust effects must one bring about to be unjust with respect to each kind of injustice, e.g., must one be a thief, or an adulterer, or a bandit? Is it not the case that the question, raised in this manner, does not show the differ-
20 ence? For a man may commit adultery with a woman whom he knows, but he may do so because of passion and not because of intention. Accordingly, he *acts* unjustly but he is not unjust. And just as a man stole without being a thief, so he committed adultery without being an adulterer, and similarly in the other cases.

  We have stated previously how reciprocity is related to what is just;[34]
25 but we must not forget that what we are seeking is what is just without qualification as well as politically. This exists among men who share their life for the sake of self-sufficiency and who are free and equal, whether proportionately or numerically. So what applies to those who do not possess these attributes is not what is politically just but only what is just in
30 a qualified way or in virtue of some likeness; for what is just [without qualification] belongs to those who come under the law also, and the law applies to situations where there may be injustice, for a verdict is a judgement of what is just or unjust [in this sense].

  Now where there is injustice, there one finds unjust *actions* also, but injustice does not exist in every unjust *action*; and unjust *actions* occur when one takes for himself not the equal but the greater share of un-
35 qualified goods or the lesser share of what is unqualifiedly bad. It is in view of this that we do not allow a man to rule but a written document,
1134b since a man tends to do this [i.e., to take more] for himself or to become a tyrant. The ruler [by law], on the other hand, is a guardian of what is just, and, if so, then he is also a preserver of what is fair. And since he is not thought to have more for himself (for he does not take for himself more of the unqualified goods, unless these are proportionally [equal, even if
5 numerically greater], and in view of this he is regarded as acting for others; and it is because of this that justice is said to be another's good, as stated previously),[35] if indeed he is just, some reward should be given to him, such as honor or privilege. Those who regard such rewards insufficient, on the other hand, become tyrants.

  What is just for a master or a father, on the other hand, is not the same

as what is just for citizens but is similar to it; for there can be no unquali- *10*
fied injustice towards what belongs to oneself since a man's possession or
child (till it reaches the age when it becomes separate) is like a part of
himself, and no one intends to harm himself. In view of this, there can be
no injustice towards oneself. Hence what is just or unjust for a master or
a father is not political; for the politically just or unjust was stated to be
according to law   and to exist among those who by nature live according
to law, and these were stated to be equal in ruling and in being ruled. *15*
Hence what is just applies to one's wife more than to one's children or
possessions, for this is what is just in a household; but this, too, is
distinct from what is politically just.

   That which is politically just may be natural or legal. It is natural if it
has the same power everywhere   and is not subject to what one thinks *20*
of it or not; it is legal if originally it makes no difference whether it takes
one form or another but, after a form is posited, it does make a difference,
e.g., the specification that a prisoner's ransom shall be one mina, or that
a goat shall be sacrificed and not two sheep, and in addition, all laws
passed for individual cases, like that concerning a sacrifice in honor of
Brasydas [a Spartan general] or any particular decree.

   There are some who think that all kinds of justice are such as these [i.e., *25*
legal], in view of the fact that what exists by nature is unchangeable and
has the same power everywhere, like fire, which burns here as well as in
Persia, but that things which are just are observed to be subject to change.
Such is not the case, however, although there is a sense in which this is
true. Perhaps among the gods, at least, this is not the case at all,   but
among us there is something which is just by nature, even if all of what is
just is subject to change. Nevertheless, some of what is just exists by *30*
nature and some not by nature.   Now of things which can be otherwise,
what kind exist by nature also and what kind exist not by nature but by
law or convention, if indeed they are alike in being both subject to change,
is clear from the examples which follow; and the same distinction applies
to the other cases. The right hand is by nature stronger, although it is possible for some men to become ambidextrous. As for the things which are *35*
just by convention or expediency, they are like standard measures; for *1135a*
measures of wine or of corn are not everywhere equal but larger in whole-
sale and smaller in retail markets. Similarly, what is just according to men
and not by nature is not the same everywhere, since forms of government,

5   too, are not all the same; nevertheless, there is only one form of government which is by nature the best everywhere.
    Of that which is just and according to law [universally taken], each is
related to the individuals under it in a universal manner; for the things
which are done are [numerically] many, while each of the former, being a
universal, is one.   There is also a difference between an unjust effect and
what is unjust, and between a restitution and what is just; for that which
10   is unjust exists by nature or by enactment,   but when that thing is done,
it is an unjust effect, whereas prior to being done it is not yet so but is
unjust.   So, too, with a restitution; but the common term is rather 'a just
effect', while the correction of an unjust effect is called 'a restitution'.
    Each of these should be examined later[37] with respect to the nature and
15   number of the species under it and the kind of things each species is concerned with.
    Just and unjust things being those which we have stated, a man *acts* un-
justly or justly when he does these things voluntarily; but when he does
them involuntarily, he *acts* neither unjustly nor justly, except by accident,
for it is by accident that what he does is unjust or just. Thus an unjust and
20   a just effect are distinguished by being voluntary and [not] involuntary;
for when that which is unjust is done voluntarily, the man is blamed, and
at the same time the thing done is an unjust effect. Hence there are some
unjust things which are not yet unjust effects, namely, when voluntariness
is not present in them. By 'voluntary', as stated earlier,[38]   I mean that
which, being in a man's power to do, he does knowingly and not in ig-
25   norance of the person *acted* upon or of the means used or of the purpose
of his action, e.g., not in ignorance of whom he strikes and with what and
why, if he does each of these [striking a man, using an instrument, having
a purpose] not by accident nor by force (as when *A* uses by force *B*'s hand
to strike *C*, in which case *B*'s act is not voluntary since it was not in his
power to act so). Thus the man struck may be the striker's father, but the
30   striker may know that he is striking a man or one of those present and
still not know that it is his father; and a similar distinction may be made
with regard to the purpose and the whole *action*. That which is done
through ignorance, then, or is done not through ignorance but either (a)
when it is not in the power of the doer to *act* or not *act* or (b) when it is
done under compulsion, is involuntary; for even of things existing by
1135*b*   nature there are many which we know and do or which affect us, but

which are neither voluntary nor involuntary, e.g., getting old or dying. What is done by accident, too, applies alike to what is unjust and to what is just. For a man might return a deposit unwillingly and because he is   5 afraid, in which case we should not say that he does what is just or that he *acts* justly, unless it be by accident; and, in a similar way, a man who is forced unwillingly not to return a deposit should not be considered as *acting* unjustly or as doing what is unjust, except by accident.

Of voluntary *actions*, some we perform by intention, others not by intention; we perform by intention those about which we have previously   10 deliberated, and we perform not by intention those about which we have not previously deliberated. Thus there are three kinds of harm which arise in associations among men. Those done with [i.e., in] ignorance result from error, and they are done when the person *acted* upon or the instrument used or the outcome of the *action* is not what the agent supposed it to be; for he may have thought that he was not striking, or not with this instrument, or not this man, or not for the sake of this [i.e., what actually occurred], but what happened is not what he thought would happen   15 (e.g., he struck not to wound the man but to urge him on, or he struck but not him, or he struck but not in the way he thought). Accordingly, (1) when the harm done is contrary to calculation, it is a mishap; (2) when it is not contrary to calculation yet without vice, it results from error, for one is mistaken when the source which causes the harm is in him, but he meets with a mishap when the source is outside of him; (3) when a man   20 *acts* knowingly but (a) without previous deliberation, the harm is an unjust effect (e.g., like those through anger or other passions which are compelling or natural to men), for although men *act* unjustly when they cause harm and are mistaken, and the effect is unjust, still they are not yet unjust or wicked because of these *actions*, since the harm done results not through an evil habit; but (b) when a man acts by intention, he is unjust   25 and evil. Hence *actions* proceeding from anger are rightly judged as done not by forethought; for it is not the man in anger who first starts to act but the man who provokes him to anger. Moreover, the dispute here is not whether the angry man *acted* or not but whether his *action* was just or not; for anger is caused by what appears to be an *act* of injustice. For the dispute is not about the occurrence of the act (as it is in exchanges in which   30 one of the parties is of necessity evil, if the dispute is not caused by forgetfulness);   both parties agree as to what has occurred but disagree as to whether it was just (whereas in exchanges, the man who plots against a second man is not ignorant of it), so while one of them, the second, thinks

1136a   he is being treated unjustly, the first does not so think. So if a man causes harm by intention, he *acts* unjustly;   and it is precisely in virtue of such unjust effects,   which are in violation of what is proportional or fair, that the man who *acts* unjustly is unjust. Similarly, a man is just when he *acts*

5   justly by intention; and he *acts* justly if he *acts* only voluntarily.

Of involuntary *acts*, some are pardonable but others not; for the errors which men make not merely in ignorance but because of ignorance are pardonable,   while those which are made not because of ignorance, but in ignorance and yet because of a passion which is neither physical nor such that men are likely to do,   are not pardonable.

11

10   One may wonder whether to be treated unjustly and to *act* unjustly have been adequately specified.   (1) If it is possible to say truly, as Euripides expressed it in a strange manner,

"I killed my mother, the tale is briefly told."
"Were you both willing, or unwilling both?",

15   is it truly possible for a man to be willingly treated unjustly, or is a man always unwilling to be treated unjustly, just as *acting* unjustly is always voluntary? Is a man, then, treated unjustly always in this manner [involuntarily], or always in that manner [voluntarily], as in the case of *acting* unjustly, or sometimes voluntarily and sometimes involuntarily? And (2) similarly, when one is treated justly; for it is always voluntarily

20   that one *acts* justly, so it is reasonable that there should be a similar opposition in being treated unjustly and in being treated justly and that each of these should be either [always] voluntary or [always] involuntary. But it would also seem strange if being treated justly, too, were posited as being always voluntary; for some people are treated justly but unwillingly.

One might raise also a second problem, whether everyone who suffers what is unjust is treated unjustly, or is the case of suffering what is unjust

25   like that of doing what is unjust? For in both cases it is possible to partake of what is just by accident, and clearly the situation is similar in

partaking of what is unjust; for to do what is unjust is not the same as to *act* unjustly, and to suffer what is unjust is not the same as to be treated unjustly. It is likewise with *acting* justly and being treated justly; for it is impossible for a man to be treated unjustly if another man does not *act* unjustly, or for a man to be treated justly if another man does not *act* 30 justly. But if to *act* unjustly without qualification is to harm someone voluntarily, and if 'voluntarily' means knowing the thing one does and also the person *acted* upon and the instrument used and the manner in which he *acts*, and if the incontinent man voluntarily harms himself, then he would voluntarily be treated unjustly, and so it would be possible for one to *act* unjustly towards himself. But this, too, is one of the problems, *1136b* namely, whether it is possible for a man to *act* unjustly towards himself. In addition, a man, because of his incontinence, might voluntarily be harmed by another man who *acts* voluntarily, and so it would [seem to] be possible for a man to be voluntarily treated unjustly.

But is our specification right? If not, we should add to "harming another with knowledge of the man harmed and of the instrument used and of the manner" the expression "against his wish". Accordingly, a man 5 may voluntarily be harmed or suffer what is unjust, but no one is voluntarily treated unjustly, for no one wishes to be treated unjustly, not even the incontinent man, although the latter may do something which is against his own wish; for no one wishes what he considers not to be good, and it is the incontinent man himself who does what he thinks he should not do. As for the man who gives what is his own, as Homer tells of Glaucon's 10 having given Diomedes

Armour of gold for brazen, worth the price of
A hundred beeves for nine, [39]

he is not unjustly treated; for it is up to him to give, while it is not up to him to be treated unjustly since this would require another man to *act* unjustly. With regard to being treated unjustly, then, it is clear that it is not voluntary.

12

Of the problems which we intended to discuss, there still remain two: the 15 third is, whether the man who *acts* unjustly is (a) the distributor who assigns to another more than the latter deserves or (b) the latter who receives more than he deserves, and the fourth is, whether it is possible for a man to *act* unjustly towards himself or not.

Now if, in the third problem, alternative (a) is possible and it is the giver who *acts* unjustly and not he who receives more, then he who
20 knowingly and voluntarily gives another more than he gives himself *acts* unjustly towards himself. This indeed is what moderate men are thought to do; for a *good* man tends to take less than he deserves. But is not this an unqualified statement? For a *good* man gets more than his share of some other good, e.g., more reputation or, simply stated, more of what is noble. Moreover, the problem is also solved in view of the definition of *acting* unjustly; for one does not suffer contrary to his own wish, and so
25 he is not being treated unjustly through his *act* of giving another more, but, if at all, he is only harmed. It is also evident that it is the distributor who *acts* unjustly, but not always he who ends up having more; for he who *acts* unjustly is not he who ends up having what is unjust, but he who voluntarily does this, and that which acts here is the source which begins the *action*, and this is in the person who makes the distribution and
30 not in the person who receives. Again, since 'to act' has many senses, and since there is a sense in which that which kills may be something lifeless, or a hand, or a servant who is ordered to do so, these do not *act* unjustly, although what they do is unjust. Again, if one gave a judgement in ignorance [of all the relevant particulars], neither does he *act* unjustly according to what is legally just nor is his judgement unjust, except in a certain sense; for what is legally just is distinct from the first kind of what
1137a is just. But if it is with knowledge that he gives a judgement which is unjust, then he too gets more, whether this be a favor or vengeance. Accordingly, as in the case of a man who takes for himself the greater part of an unjust effect, so here a man who judges unjustly because of any of these [favor or revenge] gets more; for if, for example, the unjust gain which results from his judgement is a plot of land, he still gets money from the gainer if not a share of the land.

13

5 Men think that it is in their power to *act* unjustly, and hence that it is easy to be just also. But such is not the case; for to commit adultery or strike a neighbor or deliver a bribe is easy and in our power, but to do these by

being disposed in a certain way is neither easy nor in our power. Likewise, men think that one needs no wisdom to know what is just and what 10 is unjust, since it is not hard to understand what the laws state. It is not these [to have the power and to understand the laws], however, that are just, except indirectly, but the manner in which just things are done or distributed, and to do just things in a certain manner is a greater task than to know what produces health (though even here it is easy to know that honey and wine and hellebore and cautery and surgery produce 15 health, but to know how to use these, and for whom, and when, etc., in bringing about health, is such a task that only a doctor can succeed).

For this very *reason*, too, men think that it is in the power of the just man to *act* unjustly no less than in the power of the unjust man, since the just man is not less but even more able to do each of these unjust things; for he is able to commit adultery or to strike a neighbor, and a brave man 20 can throw away his shield and turn to flight in this or that direction. Yet to *act* in a cowardly way or unjustly is not simply to do these things, except accidentally, but to do so by being disposed in a certain manner, just as to practice medicine or to heal is not just to use or not to use a knife, nor 25 just to give or not to give medicine, but to do so in such-and-such a manner.

What is just exists among those who participate in unqualified goods and who may have them in excess or in deficiency. For some beings (e.g., perhaps the gods) can have no excess of these goods; others (the incurably bad) get no benefit from any part of them but always harm, still others 30 are benefited up to a point. For this *reason*, justice and injustice belong only to men.

14

Next we shall consider equity and the equitable (or *good*) and discuss how equity is related to justice, and how the equitable is related to what is just, for upon examination they appear to be neither the same in an unqualified way nor different in genus; and while sometimes we 35 praise what is equitable and the equitable man (and in such a way that even in other instances of praise we use the term 'equitable' instead of the 1137*b* term 'good', and by 'a more equitable thing' we mean a thing which is better), at other times it appears absurd, if we are to follow reason, that what is equitable, though in violation of what is just, is nevertheless

praiseworthy. For either (a) what is just is not good, or (b) what is equi-
5   table is not just, if what is equitable is different from what is just, or else
(c) they are the same if both of them are good.

The problem regarding what is equitable, then, arises mainly because
of the above arguments, all of which are in some sense right and in no way
contrary to each other; for the equitable is just although it is better than
one kind of what is just, and it is better than that kind of what is just not
10   by coming under another genus. So the just and the equitable are the
same [generically], and though both of them are good, the equitable is
superior.

What causes the problem is the fact that the equitable is just not according to law but as something which is a correction of what is legally
just. The *reason* for being better than, or a correction of, the legally just
is the fact that all laws are universal in statement but about some things it
is not possible for a universal statement to be right. So in certain cases,
15   in which a universal statement is necessary but no universal statement can
be [completely] right, the law accepts what is mostly or in the majority
of cases right without being ignorant that there is error in so doing. And in
doing this, it is nonetheless right, for the error lies neither in the statement
of the law nor in the lawgiver, but in the nature of the subject; for from
the start the subject matter of *actions* which are done is of such a nature.
20   So when the law makes a universal statement about a subject but an instance of that subject is not rightly covered by that statement, then it is
right to correct the omission made by the legislator when he left some error in his unqualified [i.e., universal] statement; for the legislator himself
would have made that correction had he been present, or he would have
legislated accordingly if he had known.

Thus the equitable is just; and it is better than a certain kind of what is
25   just, not the unqualified just but that which has error because it is stated
in an unqualified manner [i.e., universally]. And this is the nature of the
equitable, namely, a correction of the law insofar as the law errs because
it is or must be stated universally. And the *reason* why not all things come
under the law is this, that it is impossible to lay down the law for some
things, and so a decree is needed. For of that which is indefinite, the rule
too is indefinite, like the leaden rule used in Lesbian construction;   for
30   the rule here is not rigid but adapts itself to the shape of the stone, and so
does the decree when applied to its [variable] subject matter.

It is clear, then, what the equitable is: it is what is just, and it is better
than one kind of what is just. It is also evident from this who the equitable
man is; for he who is disposed and intends to do equitable things and is not   35
overly just in insisting that his neighbor get less but is content to take less,   *1138a*
although he has the law on his side, is an equitable man, and the corresponding disposition is equity, which is one kind of justice and not a disposition of a different genus.

15

Whether a man can *act* unjustly towards himself or not is evident from
what has been said. Now (1) just things of one kind are those done with   5
respect to every virtue laid down by the law, e.g., the law commands us not
to commit suicide, and it forbids us to do what it commands us not to do.
Furthermore, when a man voluntarily harms another not in retaliation
but in violation of the law, he *acts* unjustly, and in doing so voluntarily he
knows the person harmed and the instrument used, etc. But the man who
voluntarily kills himself through anger does so in violation of right reason,   10
and the law does not permit this; so he *acts* unjustly. But towards whom?
Surely towards the state and not towards himself; for he suffers voluntarily, but no one is voluntarily treated unjustly. And it is in view of
this that the state imposes a penalty by attaching a certain dishonor to
those who kill themselves and who thus *act* unjustly towards the state.

Again, a man who is unjust by only *acting* unjustly and is not wholly   15
bad cannot *act* unjustly towards himself (for this *action* is different from
the other; for there is a sense in which an unjust man is wicked like a
coward and not in the sense of being wholly wicked, and so he does not
act unjustly in virtue of this [whole wickedness]); for otherwise (a) he would
be subtracting and adding the same thing to the same person at the same
time, and this is impossible, since what is just or unjust requires more than   20
one person. Besides, (b) to *act* unjustly is voluntary or by intention and is
prior in time; for he who, because he has suffered, performs the same *act*
in return is not thought to be *acting* unjustly, while he who *acts* on himself
would be suffering and acting the same thing at the same time. Again, (c)
in *acting* unjustly towards himself he would be treated unjustly but
voluntarily.

Finally, no one *acts* unjustly without doing some specific thing which   25 is an unjust effect; but no one commits adultery with his own wife or breaks into his own house or steals his own property.

In general, the problem of whether it is possible for one to *act* unjustly towards himself or not is solved by the specification we made with regard to whether it is possible for one to voluntarily be treated unjustly.[40]

It is also evident that both are bad, i.e., to be treated unjustly and to *act*
30   unjustly; for the one is to have less and the other is to have more than the mean, which is like that which is healthy in medical science or that which causes a good physical condition in gymnastics. To *act* unjustly, however, is worse; for *acting* unjustly is done with vice and is blameworthy, and this vice is either complete or unqualified or close to it (for not all voluntary *acts* are done with injustice),   while he who is treated unjustly does not
35   [in being so treated] have vice or injustice.   In itself, then, being treated
1138b unjustly is less bad than *acting* unjustly, but nothing prevents it from being by accident a greater evil. Art, of course, is not concerned with accidents, and it states, for example, that pleurisy is a greater disease than a hurt caused by a stumble;   but the reverse might happen by accident, e.g., if a
5   soldier, by stumbling, happens to get caught by the enemy and be put to death.

Metaphorically or by similarity (a) what is just may arise between the parts of a man but not between the man [as a whole] and himself, and (b) between a master and a slave or between members of a household not every kind of what is just may arise;[41] for in such discussions   the rational part of the soul is distinguished from the nonrational part. It is indeed by
10   attending to these parts that people also think that a man may be unjust to himself, for these parts may suffer something contrary to their desires; so what is just between these, too, is like what is just between a man who rules and a man who is ruled.

Concerning justice and the other ethical virtues, then, let this be our account.

BOOK VI

1

18 1138b Since we have stated earlier that one should choose the mean and not
20   excess or deficiency, and since the mean is such as right reason   declares

it to be, let us go over this next. Now in each of the habits we have mentioned, as in all the other cases also [art, inquiry, *action*, intention], there
is an aim in view towards which a man who has reason intensifies or slows
down [his feelings or *actions*], and there is a definition of the mean which,
we maintain, lies between excess and deficiency and exists in accordance   25
with right reason. Such a statement is indeed true, but not at all clear; for
in other endeavors, too, of which there is a science, it is true to say that
we should exert ourselves or slacken neither more nor less but in moderation and as right reason states, but with this alone a man would not know   30
any more, e.g., [he would not know] what kind of medicine to apply to the
body if some one were to say "whatever medical science prescribes and as
the doctor orders". So with regards to the dispositions of the soul, too, one
should not only state this truth but also specify what right reason is and
what its definition is.

2

In distinguishing the virtues of the soul we stated that some are ethical   35
and the others intellectual.[42] We have already discussed the ethical virtues;   1139a
as for the others, we shall proceed as follows, after some preliminary
remarks about the soul.

We have stated previously that there are two parts of the soul, the one
which has reason and the other which is nonrational.[43] As we must now sub-   5
divide the part which has reason in the same manner, let it be assumed that
there are two parts which have reason: (a) that by which we perceive the
kinds of things whose principles cannot be other than they are [i.e., cannot
vary], and (b) that by which we investigate the kinds of things whose principles may be other than they are [i.e., can vary]; for corresponding to
distinct genera of things there are in the soul generically distinct parts,   10
each of which is by its nature concerned with its own genus of things, if
indeed it is in virtue of a certain likeness and kinship to each genus of
things that the knowledge of those things belongs to each of those parts.
So let one part of the soul be called 'scientific'; and let the other be called
'estimative', for to deliberate and to estimate are the same [generically],
and no one deliberates about the things which cannot be other than they
are. So the estimative part is one part of the soul which has reason. We   15
must consider, then, what is the best disposition with respect to each of
these parts, for that disposition would be the virtue of each part, and each
virtue is relative to its proper function.

There are three parts of the soul which have authority over *action* or
truth: sense [i.e., power of sensation], intellect (or intuition), and desire.

Of these, sense is not a principle   of any *action*; and this is clear from the
20   fact that brutes have sense but do not participate in *action*. Now what
affirmation and denial are to *thought*, pursuit and avoidance are to desire;
so since ethical virtue is a habit through intention while intention is
desire through deliberation, reason should, because of these, be true and
25   desire should be right, if indeed intention is to be good, and what reason
asserts desire should pursue. So this *thought* or truth is practical, while
goodness   or badness in *thought* which is theoretical but neither practical
nor productive is, respectively, truth or falsity; for this is the function of
the *thinking* part of the soul, while the function of the part which is both
30   practical and *thinking* is truth in agreement with right desire. Now the
principle of *action* is intention, but as a source of motion and not as a
purpose, whereas that of intention is desire and reason for the sake of
something; hence intention cannot exist without intuition and *thought*,
35   nor without ethical habit,   for goodness or its opposite in *action* cannot
exist without *thought* and character.   It is not *thought* as such that can
move anything, but *thought* which is for the sake of something and is
1139b   practical, for it is this that rules productive *thought* also; for he who
produces does so for the sake of something [a product], though a product
is not an end without qualification but is relative to something else and is
a qualified end.   But an object of *action* [is an end without qualification],
for a good *action* is [such] an end, and this is what we desire. Hence inten-
5   tion is either a desiring intellect or a *thinking* desire, and such a principle
is a man.
An object of intention cannot be a past event, e.g., no one intends the
destruction of Troy in the past, for no one deliberates about past events
but only about future events and what may or may not turn out to be the
case. Past events cannot be undone, and Agathon was right in saying,

10   Of this alone, you see, is God deprived,
To make undone whatever has been done.

The function of both thinking parts of the soul, then, is truth; so the
disposition according to which each part attains truth in the highest sense
is the virtue of that part.

3

15   Let us start our discussion, then, once more from the beginning. Let [us
posit that] the things by which the soul possesses truth when it affirms
or denies something are five in number: art, *knowledge* [or scientific

knowledge], prudence, wisdom, and intuition, for one may think falsely by belief or opinion, [so we leave these out].

What *knowledge* is, if we are to speak precisely and not follow metaphorical language, is evident from the following. We all believe that the *20* thing which we *know* cannot be other than it is; and as for the things which may be other than they are [i.e., may or may not be], when they are outside of our observation, we are not in a position to know whether they exist or not. Thus the object of *knowledge* exists of necessity, and hence it is eternal; for all things which exist of necessity without qualification are eternal, and what is eternal is ungenerable and indestructible. Further, it is thought that all *knowledge* can be taught and that all objects *25* of *knowledge* can be learned. Now all teaching proceeds from what is previously known, as we have already stated in the *Analytics*;[44] for it may proceed either by induction or by syllogism. But induction is a starting point and leads to the universal, while a syllogism proceeds from the universal. Hence there are principles from which a syllogism is formed *30* and of which there is no syllogism; so it is by induction that principles are acquired. Thus *knowledge* is a disposition acquired by way of demonstration, and to this may be added the other specifications given in the *Analytics*;[45] for it is when one is both convinced and is familiar with the principles in a certain manner that he has *knowledge*, since he will have *knowledge* only by accident if he is not convinced of the principles more *35* than of the conclusion.

Let *knowledge*, then, be specified in this manner.

4

That which may or may not be can be an object produced as well as an *1140a* object of *action*. Now production is distinct from *action* (and one may be convinced of this from public writings), and so practical dispositions with reason are distinct from productive dispositions with reason; and in view *5* of this, the two exclude each other, for no *action* is a production, and no production is an *action*. Since architecture is an art and is a species of a disposition with reason and ability to produce something, and since there is no art which is not a disposition with reason and ability to produce something and no disposition such as this which is not an art, art would *10* be the same [in essence or definition] as a disposition with true reason and with ability to produce something. Every art is concerned with bringing something into existence, and to think by art is to investigate how to generate something which may or may not exist and of which the

15

20

[moving] principle is in the producer and not in the thing produced; for art is not concerned with things which exist or come to be of necessity, nor with things which do so according to their nature, for these have the [moving] principle in themselves. So since production and *action* are different, art must be concerned with production and not with *action*. And in some sense both luck and art are concerned with the same things; as Agathon says, "art is fond of luck, and luck of art."

As we have stated, then, art is a disposition tending to produce with true reason something which may or may not be, while bad art, which is its contrary, is a disposition tending to produce with false reason something which may or may not be.

5

25

30

Concerning prudence, we might arrive at its nature by examining the nature of those whom we call 'prudent'. A prudent man is thought to be one who is able to deliberate well concerning what is good and expedient for himself, not with respect to a part, e.g., not the kinds of things which are good and useful for health or strength, but the kinds of things which are good and expedient for living well [in general]. A sign of this is the fact that even in some particular respect we call 'prudent' those who make good judgments about things for a particular good end of which there is no art. So a man who deliberates [well] might be prudent in a general way also.

35

1140b

5

10

Now no one deliberates about things which cannot vary, nor about those which he cannot himself do. Hence since scientific knowledge is acquired by means of demonstration, and since there can be no demonstration of things whose principles may vary (for all these things may vary, and it is not possible to deliberate about necessary things), prudence cannot be scientific knowledge or art; it cannot be scientific knowledge since the object of *action* may vary, and it cannot be art since the genus of *action* is different from that of production. What remains, then, is this: prudence is a disposition with true reason and ability for *actions* concerning what is good or bad for man; for the end of production is some other thing [i.e., a product], but in the case of *action* there is no other end (for a good *action* is itself the end). It is because of this that we consider Pericles and others like him to be prudent, for they are able to perceive what is good for themselves as well as for other men; and we regard also financial administrators and statesmen to be such. And it is from this disposition that the term 'temperance' (=σωφροσύνη) is named after

the term 'prudence' (=φρόνησις), as if indicating something which preserves prudence (=σώζουσα τὴν φρόνησιν). And temperance does preserve such a belief [i.e., prudence]; for it is not every kind of belief that
the pleasant and the painful corrupt or pervert, like the belief that the   *15*
triangle has or has not its angles equal to two right angles, but only those
concerned with objects of *action*. For the starting-point of an *action* is
the purpose of that *action*. But to him who is corrupted because of pleasure or pain the starting-point is not apparent, nor is it apparent that he
should choose and do everything for the sake of this and because of this
starting-point; for vice is destructive of the starting-point.   *20*

Prudence, then, must be a disposition with true reason and ability for
actions concerning human goods. Further, while there is virtue with
respect to art, there is no virtue with respect to prudence; and while in
art he who errs willingly is preferable, in the case of prudence he who does
so is the reverse, as in the case of virtues. So it is clear that prudence is a
virtue and not an art. And as there are in the soul two parts which have   *25*
reason, prudence would be a virtue in one of them, that which can form
opinions; for both opinion and prudence are about things which may or
may not be. Finally, prudence is not just a disposition with reason; and a
sign of this is the fact that a disposition with reason may be forgotten,
but prudence cannot.   *30*

6

Since scientific knowledge is belief of universal and necessary things, and
since there are principles of whatever is demonstrable and of all scientific
knowledge (for scientific knowledge is knowledge with the aid of reason),
a principle of what is scientifically known cannot be scientific knowledge
or art or prudence; for what is scientifically known is demonstrable, while   *35*
art and prudence are about things which may or may not be. Nor is   *1141a*
wisdom of [just] these principles; for it is possible for a wise man to give
some demonstrations. So if the [dispositions or principles] by which we
think truly and never think falsely concerning things which cannot vary
(or even those which can vary) may be scientific knowledge, prudence,   *5*
wisdom, and intuition, since they [the dispositions or principles] cannot
be three of them (prudence, scientific knowledge, wisdom), we are left
with intuition [as the disposition] of those principles.

7

In the arts, we attribute wisdom to men who are most accurate in their   *10*

field, e.g., we say that Phidias the sculptor is wise and Polyclitus the statue-
maker is wise, and by 'wisdom' here we mean nothing but the virtue of
an art. But we regard some men as being wise in general and not in a
particular field or in some other qualified way, as Homer says in *Margites*,

15   The Gods, then, did not make him wise at digging
      Nor plowing nor at any other thing.

So clearly wisdom would be the most accurate of the sciences. Thus the
wise man must not only know what follows from the principles, but also
possess truth about the principles.

    Wisdom, then, would be intuition and scientific knowledge of the most
20   honorable objects, as if it were scientific knowledge with its own leader;
for it would be absurd to regard politics or prudence as the best [disposi-
tion], if man is not the best of beings in the universe. If indeed what is
healthy or what is good is different for men and for fishes, while what is
white or what is straight is always the same, everyone would say that what
25   is wise is always the same while what is prudent may be different; for they
would say that a prudent creature is one which perceives well matters
which are for its own good and they would entrust those matters to that
creature. It is in view of this that people say that some brutes too are
prudent, namely, those which appear to have the power of foresight with
regard to their own way of life. It is also evident that wisdom and politics
30   are not the same. For if by 'wisdom' one were to mean the disposition
which is concerned with things which are to one's benefit, there would be
many kinds of wisdom; for there would be not one kind of wisdom concerned with the good of all kinds of animals but a different kind for each
species of animals, unless one were to go as far as to say that there is one
medical art for all the kinds of things also. And if one were to say that
man is the best of the animals, this too would make no difference; for
1141b there are also other things much more divine in their nature than man,
like the most visible objects of which the universe is composed.

    From what has been said, then, it is clear that wisdom is scientific
knowledge and intuition of the objects which are most honorable by their
nature. It is in view of this that Anaxagoras and Thales and others like
5   them, who are seen to ignore what is expedient to themselves, are called
'wise' but not 'prudent'; and they are said to have understanding of things
which are great and admirable and difficult to know and divine but which
are not instrumental for other things, for they do not seek human goods.

8

Prudence, on the other hand, is concerned with things which are human and objects of deliberation; for we maintain that the function of a prudent man is especially this, to deliberate well, and no one deliberates about in-   *10* variable things or about things not having an end which is a good attainable by *action*; and a man who deliberates well without qualification is one who, by judgment, can aim well at the things which are attainable by *action* and are best for man.

Now prudence is not limited to what is universal but must know also   *15* the particulars; for it is practical, and *action* is concerned with particulars. And it is in view of this that some men, without universal knowledge but with experience in other things, are more practical than those who have universal knowledge only; for if a man knew universally that light meats are digestible and healthy but did not know what kinds of meats are light, he would not produce health, but a man who knows that chicken   *20* is light and healthy is more likely to produce health. Now prudence is concerned with *actions*; so we should have both kinds of knowledge, or else the latter rather than the former, which is universal. Nevertheless, in this case too there should be one kind of knowledge which is architectonic.

Both politics and prudence are the same disposition, but in essence they are not the same. Of prudence concerned with the state, the one which is   *25* architectonic is legislative, while the other which is concerned with particulars has the common name 'political prudence'; and the latter is concerned with particular *actions* and deliberations, for a particular measure voted on is like an individual thing to be *acted* upon. In view of this, only those engaged in such *actions* are called 'public servants', for only these *act* like manual laborers.

Prudence is thought to be concerned most of all with matters relating to   *30* the person in whom it exists and with him only; and this disposition has the common name 'prudence'. Of the other kinds, one is financial management, another is law-giving, and a third is political, of which one part is deliberative and the other judicial.

9

One kind of prudence, then, would be knowing what is good for oneself, and this differs much from the others; and a man who knows and is en-   *1142a* gaged in matters which concern himself is thought to be prudent, while public servants are thought to busy themselves with other people's business. For this reason Euripides says,

But how might I be wise, who could, unbusied,
Listed as one among the army's mass,
Have had an equal share? ....
5   For those who do too much and are excessive ....

For these seek what is good for themselves and think that this is what they should be doing. And from this opinion arose the belief that only these are prudent, although perhaps one's own good cannot exist without
10 financial management nor without some form of government. Moreover, how one should manage his own household is not clear and needs consideration. A sign of what has been said is also the *reason* why young men become geometricians and mathematicians and wise in such [fields] but do not seem to become prudent. That *reason* is the fact that prudence
15 is concerned with particulars, which become familiar from experience; but a young man is not experienced, for experience requires much time. And if one were to inquire why it is possible for a boy to become a mathematician but not wise or a physicist, the answer is this: the objects of mathematics exist by abstraction while the principles of philosophy and of physics are acquired from experience; and young men have no convic-
20 tion of their principles but only use words, while the nature of the objects of physics and of wisdom is not unclear to physicists and wise men. Further, error in deliberation may be either about the universal or about the particular; for we may err either concerning the fact that all heavy water is bad or concerning the fact that this sample of water is heavy.

It is evident, then, that prudence is not scientific knowledge; for it is
25 concerned with the ultimate particular, as we said,[46] and such is the object of *action*. It is thus opposed to intuition; for intuition is of definitions, for which there is no reasoning, while prudence is of the ultimate particular, which is an object not of science but of sensation, not the sensation of proper sensibles, but like that by which we sense that the ultimate particular in mathematics is a triangle (for even in mathematics there is a stop in the direction of the particular). But this kind of sensation is
30 closer to sensation [in the main sense] than to prudence, while the sensation of the other [i.e., by prudence] is of another kind.

10

Inquiry differs from deliberation; for deliberation is a species of inquiry. We should also grasp the nature of good deliberation, whether it is scientific knowledge of some kind or opinion or discernment or a thing in some other genus. Now it is not scientific knowledge; for scientists do not inquire about the things they know, while good deliberation is a kind *1142b* of deliberation, and he who deliberates inquires and makes estimates. Again, it is not discernment, for discernment acts without the use of reason and quickly, while those who deliberate take much time, and people say that we should *act* quickly on the conclusions of deliberation *5* but we should deliberate slowly. Finally, acuteness is distinct from good deliberation; for acuteness is a species of discernment. Nor is good deliberation a kind of opinion. But since he who deliberates badly is in error *10* while he who deliberates well is right, it is clear that good deliberation is a kind of rightness, but neither of scientific knowledge nor of opinion. For there can be no rightness (nor error) of scientific knowledge, and rightness of opinion is its truth; and the objects of opinion have already been specified. Yet good deliberation does not exist without the use of reason. It remains, then, that it is [rightness] of *thinking*, for this [i.e., *thinking*] is not yet assertion; for opinion too is not inquiry but is already an assertion, while he who deliberates, whether well or badly, is in the process of *15* inquiring and estimating. But good deliberation is a kind of rightness of deliberation; so first, we should inquire what deliberation is and of what object.

Since "rightness" has many senses, clearly good deliberation is not rightness in every sense; for the incontinent or the bad man will, from his judgment, [usually] attain that which he sets out to do, and so he will have deliberated rightly, but what he has chosen is a great evil. Now to *20* deliberate well is thought to be a kind of good; for good deliberation is rightness of such deliberation which brings about a good. But it is possible to attain a good even by a false syllogism, i.e., to attain what needs be done by a false middle term and not through the true term; so this, too, is not yet good deliberation, for it is deliberation in virtue of which one *25* attains what he should but not through the middle term he should. Again, one man may attain an object after a long deliberation while another may attain it quickly. Still a good deliberation is not quite attained in this

manner; for it is rightness with respect to that which is beneficial as well as with respect to the proper object and the proper manner and the proper time [etc.]. Finally, one may deliberate well either in an unqualified way
30   or relative to a qualified end. Thus an unqualified good deliberation *succeeds* with reference to an unqualified end while a qualified good deliberation *succeeds* with reference to a qualified end. Accordingly, if to deliberate well is a mark of a prudent man, good deliberation would be rightness with respect to what is expedient in relation to an end   whose prudence is true belief.

11

1143a   Intelligence or good intelligence, in virtue of which men are said to be intelligent or of good intelligence, is neither altogether the same as scientific knowledge or as opinion (for all men would have been intelligent), nor is it the same as any scientific knowledge in particular, like medical knowledge, which is concerned with health, or like geometry, which is concerned with magnitudes; for intelligence is concerned neither with eternal
5   or immovable objects   nor with any kind of things which are in the process of becoming but with things about which one might raise questions and deliberate. Thus intelligence is concerned [generically] with the same kind of objects as prudence, but intelligence is not the same [in definition] as prudence. Prudence gives orders, for its end is what should or should
10   not be done, while intelligence only judges, for intelligence and good intelligence are the same, and so are men of intelligence and of good intelligence. Now intelligence is neither the possession nor the acquiring of prudence. But just as a learner is said to be intelligent when he uses scientific knowledge, so a man is said to be intelligent when he uses opinion in judging objects of prudence, when someone else speaks about
15   them, and does so excellently; for 'well' and 'excellently' are the same. And it is from this source that the name 'intelligence', according to which men are said to be of good intelligence, came into use, namely, from its use in learning; for 'learning' is often used to mean being intelligent.
      What we call '*judgment*', in virtue of which we say that a man is a good
20   *judge* or has *judgment*, is right judgment of an equitable man. A sign of this is the fact that we speak of the equitable man as being the most likely to forgive and of equity as showing forgiveness in certain cases. As for forgiveness, it is a species of right *judgment* of an equitable man; and it is right by being of that which is true.

12

Now all these dispositions are directed to the same things, and with good   *25*
reason. For when we speak of *judgment* and intelligence and prudence and
intuition, we regard the same men as having *judgment*, having intuition,
being prudent, and being intelligent, since all these are faculties dealing
with ultimates and particulars; and in having judgment about things with   *30*
which a prudent man is concerned, one is intelligent and has good *judgment* or is disposed to forgive, for equitable things are common to all good
men in their relation to other men. Now all objects of *action* are particulars and ultimates; for both a prudent man should know them, and also
intelligence and *judgment* are concerned with them, and these objects are   *35*
ultimates. And intuition, too, is of ultimates, and in both directions,   *1143b*
for of both the primary terms and the ultimate particulars there is intuition and not reasoning; and intuition with respect to demonstrations
is of immovable terms and of that which is primary, whereas in *practical*
[reasonings intuition] is of the ultimate and variable objects and of the
other [i.e., minor] premises, since these are principles of final cause; for
it is from particulars that we come to universals. Accordingly, we should   *5*
have sensation of these particulars, and this is intuition. And in view of
this, it is thought that these [powers] are natural and that, while no one is
by nature wise, one [by nature] has *judgment* and intelligence and intuition. A sign of this is the fact that these [powers] are thought to follow
certain stages of our life, e.g., that such-and-such an age possesses intuition or *judgment*, as if nature were the cause of it. Hence intuition is both   *10*
a beginning and an end; for demonstrations come from these and are
about these. Consequently, one should pay attention to the undemon-
strated assertions and opinions of experienced and older and prudent men
no less than to demonstrations; for they observe rightly because they gained
an eye from experience.
We have stated, then, what prudence and wisdom are, and with what   *15*
objects each is concerned, and that each of them is a virtue of a different
part of the soul.

13

One might raise certain problems concerning these virtues: Of what use
are they? Wisdom investigates none of the things which make a man
happy, for it is not concerned with any generation of objects; and though   *20*
prudence does this, for what purpose is it needed, if indeed prudence is

concerned with things which are just and noble and good for a man but
which will be done by a good man anyway, and if by merely knowing
25   them we are no more able to *act*, since the [ethical] virtues are habits,
just as we are no more able to perform, by knowing things which are
healthy or in good physical condition, those things which do not themselves produce but come to be from the corresponding habits (for we are
no more able to *act* in a healthy or well-conditioned manner by having
medical science or the science of gymnastics)? If, on the other hand, we
are to posit a prudent man to be not for the sake of these but for the sake
of coming to be virtuous, prudence would be of no use to those who are
30   already virtuous, nor to those who do not possess virtue, for it would
make no difference whether they possess prudence themselves or obey
those who possess it; and it would be enough for us if, in the case of
prudence, we use the same argument as we did in the case of health, for
although we wish to be healthy, still we do not learn medical science.
Again, it would seem strange that prudence, which is inferior to wisdom,
35   should be more authoritative than wisdom; for prudence, whose role is to
act, has a ruling and ordering function with respect to its objects. These
problems, then, should be discussed, for at present we have only raised them.
1144a   First, we maintain that these [wisdom and prudence] must be worthy of
choice for their own sake, at least since each of them is a virtue of the
corresponding part of the soul, even if neither of them produces anything.
But more than this, they do produce something, not as the medical art
produces health, but as health [as a habit produces a healthy activity], and
5   it is in this sense that wisdom produces happiness; for being a part of the
whole of virtue, wisdom produces happiness by its possession and its
exercise.
Again, a man's work is completed by prudence as well as by ethical
virtue; for while virtue makes the end in view right, prudence makes the
means towards it right. But of the fourth part of the soul, i.e., of the
10   nutritive part, there is no such virtue; for that part cannot *act* or refrain
from *acting*.
As for the argument that through prudence we are no more able to
perform noble and just *actions*, let us begin a little way back and use the
following principle. Just as we say that those who do what is just may not
15   yet be just, as in the case of those who perform what is ordained by the
law but do so unwillingly or through ignorance or for some other reason
but not for the sake of what is just (even if they do what they should and
whatever a virtuous man ought to do), so it seems that in order to be
good a man must be disposed in a certain way, that is, he must *act* by in-

tention and for the sake of the things done. Now that which makes the 20
intention right is virtue, but the things which are by their nature done
for the sake of [that intention] depend not on virtue but on another
power. Let us attend to these matters more clearly for a moment.

There is a power which is called 'shrewdness', and this is such as to
enable us to *act* successfully upon the means leading to an aim we set 25
before us. If the aim is noble, that power is praiseworthy, but if the aim is
bad, the power is called 'unscrupulousness'. It is in view of this that we
speak even of prudent men as being shrewd or unscrupulous. Now
prudence is not shrewdness itself, but neither can it exist without this
power. And this disposition [i.e., prudence] develops by means of this eye 30
of the soul, but not without virtue, as we have already stated and as is
clear; for the syllogisms of things to be *acted* upon have a starting point,
such as this: "since such is the end, which is the best", whatever this may
be; and for the sake of argument let any chance end which is the best be
taken. This end is not apparent to a man who is not good, for his evil
habit perverts him and causes him to be mistaken about the starting- 35
point of *action*. Hence it is evident that a man cannot be prudent if he
is not good. 1144b

Let us then examine also virtue once more; for virtue, too, has its
parallel, that is, as prudence is related to shrewdness (by being similar but
not the same), so natural virtue is related to virtue in the main sense. For
all men think that each part of one's character exists in him by nature in 5
some sense, since from the moment of birth we are in some sense just and
temperate and brave and the like; but we seek goodness taken in the
main sense as something which is distinct from natural goodness, and we
regard such [virtues as justice, temperance, and bravery] as existing in
another manner. For natural dispositions exist also in children and in
brutes, but without intellect they appear to be harmful. What seems to 10
be observed is thus much, that just as a strong body in motion but without
vision stumbles heavily because of its lack of vision, so it is in the case
we are considering; so if a man acquires intellect, there will be a difference
in his *action*, and it is only then that his disposition, though similar to the
corresponding natural disposition, will be a virtue in the main sense. So
just as there are two kinds of dispositions in the part of the soul which 15
forms opinions, shrewdness and prudence, so also in the ethical part of
the soul there are two dispositions, the one being natural virtue and the
other being virtue in the main sense, and of these the one in the main
sense cannot come into being without prudence.

In view of this, some thinkers assert that every virtue is a species of
prudence; and Socrates was in one sense right in his inquiries concerning
20 virtue but in another sense mistaken, for he was mistaken in regarding
every virtue to be prudence, but he spoke well in thinking that without
prudence virtues cannot exist.   A sign of this is the following: all men
who nowadays give a definition of a virtue, besides stating the objects to
which the virtue is directed, add also the expression "a disposition according to right reason"; and, of course, reason is right if it is in accordance with prudence. So it seems that all men somehow have a strong
25 inner sense that such a habit is a virtue in accordance with prudence. But
we must go a little further, for virtue is a habit not only according to right
reason, but also with right reason;   and right reason about such things
is prudence. Thus Socrates thought that virtues are [right] reasons (for he
30 thought that virtue was *knowledge*), but we say that they are with reason.
It is clear from what has been said, then, that a man cannot be good in
the main sense without prudence, nor can he be prudent without ethical
virtue.   This fact would also refute the argument by which one might
claim that the virtues are separable from each other; for [one might say
that] the same man may not be most gifted by nature for all the virtues,
35 and so he may have acquired some of them but not others. Now with
1145a respect to the natural virtues, this is possible;   but with respect to those
by which a man is called 'good' without qualification   it is not possible,
for when this one [virtue] exists, i.e., prudence,   all the others are present
also. It is also clear that, even if prudence were not practical, it would be
needed because it is a virtue of a part of the soul, and that there can be no
5 right intention without prudence or virtue; for the one   [i.e., virtue]
posits the end while the other [i.e., prudence] makes us do those things
which bring about that end. Moreover, prudence does not rule wisdom
or the best part of the soul, just as the medical art does not rule health;
for prudence does not use wisdom but sees to it that wisdom is acquired.
So prudence gives orders for the sake of wisdom but does not give orders
10 to wisdom.   Further, saying that prudence rules wisdom is like saying
that politics rules the gods since it gives orders about all matters that
belong to a state.

BOOK VII

1

Next, let us make another start and list the three kinds of things which   *1145a15*
should be avoided in regard to character, namely, vice, incontinence, and
brutality. The contraries of two of these are clear, for the first is called
'virtue' and the second 'continence'; as for the contrary of brutality, it
would be most fitting to say that it is a virtue above us, one that is heroic   *20*
and divine, as Homer made Priam say of Hector that he was exceptionally
good,

He seemed no son of mortal man, but of God.

So if, as they say, men become gods because they exceed in virtue, then
clearly the disposition opposed to that which is brutal would be one such   *25*
as this; for just as in a brute there can be neither vice nor virtue, so in a god,
but the disposition of a god would be more honorable than virtue, while
that of a brute would be generically different from vice.

Now as it is rarely that a divine man exists, if we are to use that expression of the Spartans whenever their admiration for a man is exceptionally
high (for they call him 'a divine man'), so too a brutal man among men   *30*
rarely exists. A brutal man is most likely to exist among barbarians, but
sometimes also because of disease or injury; and we apply such bad expression also to those among men who go beyond the limits of vice. Some
mention concerning such a disposition will be made later, and vice has al-   *35*
ready been discussed. We should now discuss incontinence, softness, and
effeteness, and also continence and endurance; for we should regard these   *1145b*
habits as being neither the same as the virtues or the vices nor generically
different. So as in other cases we should, after laying down the facts as
they appear and going over the difficulties, indicate as far as possible the
truth of all the accepted opinions concerning these affections, or if not,   *5*
the truth of most of those opinions or of the most important ones; for if
the difficulties that cause concern are refuted and the accepted opinions
are left standing, we shall have established our case sufficiently.

2

Now (1) both continence and endurance are thought to be among the things which are good and praiseworthy, but incontinence and softness
10   among the things which are bad and blameworthy; and it is the same man who is thought to be continent and disposed to abide by his judgement, or who is thought to be incontinent and disposed to depart from his judgement. And (2) it is thought that the incontinent man knows that to do certain things is bad but does them because of passion, and that the continent man knows that his *desires* are bad but does not follow them because of his reason. And (3) it is said that (a) a temperate man is conti-
15   nent and disposed to endure, and, according to some, every such man is temperate, but, according to others, this is not so, and that (b) according to some, an intemperate man is incontinent and an incontinent man is intemperate indiscriminately, but, according to others, the two are different. (4) As for the prudent man, sometimes people say that he cannot be incontinent, but at other times they say that some prudent and shrewd men are incontinent. Finally, (5) men are called 'incontinent' even with
20   respect to temper, or honor, or profit. These, then, are the things that are said.

3

One might raise the problem of how a man who has the right belief of how to *act* can *act* incontinently.
     Some say that if he has *knowledge* of how to *act* rightly, he cannot be
25   incontinent; for, as *Socrates* thought, it would be strange for a man to have *knowledge* and yet allow something else to rule him and drag him about like a slave. For *Socrates* was entirely opposed to this view and held that there is no such thing as incontinence; for he thought that no one with the right belief does what is contrary to the best, but if a man does so, it is through ignorance. Now this argument obviously disagrees with what appears to be the case; and if a man *acting* by passion does so through ignorance, we should look into the manner in which this igno-
30   rance arises. For it is evident that an incontinent man, before getting into a state of passion, does not think that he should do what he does when in passion.
     There are some thinkers who partly agree with this view but partly dis-

agree; for they admit that there is nothing stronger than *knowledge*, but they do not agree with the view that no man *acts* contrary to what in his opinion is the better course, and because of this view they say that when an incontinent man is ruled by pleasures he does not have *knowledge* but   35
opinion. But if it is opinion and not *knowledge*, and if the belief which resists the passion is not strong but weak, as in men who hesitate, we   *1146a*
should pardon those who fail to abide by that belief when they face a strong *desire*, though not those who are ruled by an evil habit or any of the other blameworthy habits.

Is it then prudence which resists *desire*? For this is the strongest of the   5
virtues. But it is absurd to think that prudence resists *desire*, for the same man would then be at the same time prudent and incontinent, and no one would maintain that a prudent man would willingly perform the worst of *actions*. Moreover, it has been shown earlier that a prudent man has a disposition for [right] *action*, for he is concerned with the ultimates [i.e., particular *actions* or things] and [already] possesses the other virtues.

Again, if to be continent one must have strong and bad *desires*, neither   10
will the temperate man be continent nor will the continent man be temperate; for it is not the mark of a temperate man to have excessive or bad *desires*. But the continent man must have such *desires*. For if his *desires* are for a good purpose, his disposition which prevents him from following them will be bad and so not all continence will be good; but if they are   15
weak and not bad, continence will not impress us, nor will there be anything great in continence if they are weak but bad.

Again, if continence disposes a man to abide by every opinion, it may be bad, e.g., like that of a man who abides by a false opinion also; and if incontinence disposes a man to abandon every opinion, it may be good, like that of Neoptolemus in the *Philoctetes* of Sophocles, for he is to be   20
praised for not abiding by what he was persuaded by Odysseus to do, because he is pained at telling a lie.

Again, the sophistic argument, which is false, presents a problem. For, because of the wish to refute what is contrary to accepted opinion in order that one may be regarded as shrewd when he succeeds, the syllogism which is formed gives rise to a difficulty; for *thought* is tied like a knot,   25
when it does not wish to rest because it dislikes the conclusion, and it cannot advance because it cannot refute the argument. There follows from a certain argument that imprudence, taken along with incontinence, is a

virtue; for a man does the contrary of what he believes because of in-
30   continence, but he believes that what is good is bad and hence that he
should not do it, so he will do what is good and not what is bad.

Again, a man who by conviction *acts* badly or pursues pleasurable
things or deliberately chooses them would be thought to be better than a
man who does any of these not through judgement but through incontinence; for the former is more disposed to being cured because he might
be persuaded to change his mind. But the incontinent man is open to the
35   proverbial charge "When water chokes, what should one take to wash it
1146b down with?"; for if he were persuaded of what he does, he might be
persuaded to change his mind and stop it, but as it is, although he is
persuaded to do what he should, he does something else nonetheless.

Finally, if incontinence and continence are concerned with every kind
of object, who is incontinent in an unqualified sense? For no one has
every kind of incontinence, but we speak of some men as being inconti-
5   nent in an unqualified sense.

4

The difficulties that arise are such as the ones stated, and we should refute
some of them but allow the others to stand; for the solution of a difficulty
is the discovery of a truth. We should consider, then, (a) whether incontinent men *act* knowingly or not, and, if knowingly, in what way; also (b)
10   the kinds of things which both continent and incontinent men are posited
to be concerned with, i.e., whether they are concerned with every kind of
pleasure and pain or with certain definite kinds; also (c) whether the
continent man and the man who endures are the same or different; and
similarly (d) the other problems which are closely related to this investigation.

15   The starting-point of our inquiry is (1) the problem of whether continent and incontinent men differ (a) in respect to the objects with which
they are concerned, or (b) in the manner in which they are disposed
towards the objects, that is, whether the incontinent man is incontinent
only with respect to such-and-such objects or with respect to his manner
[towards objects], or (c) with respect to both the objects and the manner.
Second, there is (2) the problem of whether incontinence and continence
are concerned with all kinds of objects or not. Now the incontinent man
20   in the unqualified sense is concerned not with all kinds of objects but only
with those with which the intemperate man is concerned, and he is incontinent by being disposed towards the objects not in any manner whatsoever (for then incontinence might be the same as intemperance), but in

a specified manner. For an intemperate man is led on to the objects by deliberate choice, thinking that he should always pursue pleasure as it comes, whereas an incontinent man thinks that he should not do so, and yet he does.

5

As to the view that it is true opinion and not *knowledge* against which a   25
man *acts* incontinently, this makes no difference to the argument; for some men who have opinions show no hesitation but think that they have accurate knowledge. So if one argues that it is because of the weakness of their convictions that those who have opinions are more likely to *act* against their belief than those who have *knowledge*, we answer that there may be no difference between [having] *knowledge* and [having] opinion; for some men are no less convinced of their opinions about things than   30
others of the things they *know*, as is clear in Heraclitus. But since we use the term "to *know*" in two senses (for both the man who has *knowledge* but is not using it and he who is using it are said to *know*), there will be a difference between having without exercising one's *knowledge* as to what one should do, and having but also exercising that *knowledge*; for it is the   35
latter which is thought to be strange and not when one does not exercise that *knowledge*.

Again, since there are two ways in which premises exist, nothing pre-   1147a
vents a man from having both premises but *acting* contrary to *knowledge*, although he is using the universal but not the particular; for things to be *acted* upon are particulars. There is also a difference in the case of the universal, for it may apply to the agent or it may apply to the thing, as in   5
(a) the premises "dry food benefits every man" and "*X* is a man", or in (b) "such-and-such food is dry", but as to "*Y* is such-and-such", either the agent does not possess it or he is not exercising it. Thus there will be such a great difference between these ways of knowing, that to know in one way would not seem absurd but to know in the other way would seem strange.   10

Again, the possession of *knowledge* may belong to a man in a manner distinct from those just stated; for in having but not using that *knowledge* we observe such a difference in his disposition that in one sense he has but in another he does not have that *knowledge*, as in the case of a man who is asleep or mad or drunk. Now such is the disposition of those who are under the influence of passions; for fits of anger and sexual *desires* and   15
other such passions clearly disturb even the body, and in some men they also cause madness. So it is clear that incontinent men must be said to

be disposed like these. The fact that such men make scientific statements
when so disposed is no sign that they know what they are saying; for even
20 those under the influence of passions [i.e., drunkards, madmen] recite
demonstrations and verses of Empedocles, and also beginners [in science]
string together statements [which prove a conclusion], but they do not
quite understand what they are saying, for these expressions must sink in,
and this requires time. So incontinent men must be regarded as using
language in the way actors do on the stage.

25   Again, the cause may be observed also from physical considerations.
Now one premise is a universal opinion, but the other premise is concerned with a particular, and sensation has authority over particulars.
And when from these two premises a unity is formed, then, in one case,
the soul must assert the conclusion, but where action is required, it must
act immediately.   For example, if the premises are "everything sweet
30 should be tasted" and "X (which is one of the particulars) is sweet", then
the man who is able to *act* and is not prevented from *acting* must at the
same time *act* on this [i.e., on the conclusion]. Accordingly, if there is in
the soul a universal belief which forbids us to taste sweets and another
belief, namely, "everything sweet is pleasant", and if there is also before us
a particular X which is sweet (and this is used) and a *desire* in us to taste
what is sweet, then the former belief tells us to avoid tasting X but *desire*
35 bids us to taste X, for each of these parts [of the soul, i.e., wish and *desire*]
1147b can move us;   so what turns out is that we become incontinent somehow
by argument or opinion, not one which is contrary to itself except in virtue
of an accident,   for it is *desire* and not opinion which is contrary to right
reason. For this *reason*, too, brutes are not incontinent, for they have no
5   universal beliefs but only appearance and memory of particulars.

As to how an incontinent man is freed from ignorance and regains
knowledge, the argument is the same as that for a man who is drunk or
asleep, and it is not peculiar to this passion, and we should learn it from
the physiologists.   Now since it is the last [i.e., the minor] premise which
10 is an opinion about a sensible object and has authority over our *actions*,
the man in passion either does not possess this *knowledge* or his possession of it, as we said, is not [actually] *knowing* but a mere verbal expression of it, like that of a drunkard who utters verses of Empedocles. And
because of the fact that the last term is not universal or scientific nor is
15 thought to be similar to the universal, what Socrates sought to show also
seems to follow; for it is not in the presence of what is thought to be *knowledge* in the main sense that the passion arises, nor is it *knowledge* which is
dragged about through the passion, but [only the knowledge] of sensibles.

Concerning the man who does or does not know, then, and how he can knowingly be incontinent, let this be our account.

BOOK VIII

1

After what has just been said, a discussion of friendship would follow, for friendship is a virtue or something with virtue, and, besides, it is most necessary to life; for no one would choose to live without friends, though he were to have all the other goods. Also those who possess wealth or have acquired authority or power are thought to need friends most of all; for of what benefit is the possession of such goods without the opportunity of beneficence, which is most exercised towards friends and most praised when so exercised, or how can such goods be guarded and be preserved without friends? For the greater these goods, the more insecure they are. In poverty and other misfortunes, too, we regard our friends as our only refuge. Friends help the young in guarding them from error, and they help the old who, because of their weakness, need attention or additional support for their *actions*, and they help those in their prime of life to do noble *actions*, as in the saying: "And the two are coming together",[47] for with friends men are more able to think and to *act*.

Again, it seems that by nature parents show a friendly feeling towards their offspring, and the offspring towards their parents, and this is the case not only among men but also among birds and most animals; and the same feeling is shown among members of the same race towards one another, and especially among men, in view of which we praise those who are friendly towards other men. In travels, too, one may observe how close and dear every man is to another man. Friendship seems to hold a state together, too, and lawgivers seem to pay more attention to friendship than to justice; for concord seems to be somewhat akin to friendship, and this they aim at most of all and try their utmost to drive out faction, which is inimical to the state. And when men are friends, they have no need of justice at all, but when they are just, they still need friendship; and a thing which is most just is thought to be done in a friendly way.

Friendship is not only necessary, but also noble. For we praise those

30   who like their friends, and to have many friends is considered as one of the
noble things in life; and some men regard good men and friends to be
the same.

2

The disagreements concerning friendship are not few. Some posit friendship as being a likeness of some sort and friends to be men who are alike;
35   hence the sayings 'like as like', 'birds of a feather flock together', and
other such. Others take the contrary position and say 'two of a trade
1155b   never agree'. Still others seek causes for these things which are higher and
more physical, like Euripides, who says, "parched earth loves rain, and
lofty heaven filled with rain loves to fall to earth", and Heraclitus, who
5   says "it is opposites that help each other", and "sweetest harmonies from
different tones arise", and "all things from *Strife* arise"; and contrary
to these are others and also Empedocles, who says, "like aims at like".
Now problems which belong to physics may be left aside (for they are
not proper to the present inquiry); so we shall examine just those which
10   pertain to men and are proper to character and feelings, e.g., whether
friendship can be formed between any two men or whether those who are
evil cannot be friends, and whether there is only one kind of friendship or
many. For those who think that there is only one, using as a reason the
fact that friendship admits of degree, have based their conviction on in-
15   sufficient evidence; for things which differ in kind, too, admit of degree.
This has already been discussed.
Perhaps these matters will become evident after we come to know what
the likeable object is;   for it seems that not every object is liked but only
the likeable, and this is the good or the pleasant or the useful.   But it
20   would seem that the useful is that through which some good   or pleasure
is produced; so what is likeable as an end would be the good or the
pleasurable. But do men like the good [without qualification] or that
which is good for themselves? Sometimes these kinds of goods clash; and
the same applies to the pleasurable. Now it is thought that each man
likes what is good for himself, and that, although the likeable is the good
25   without qualification, what each man likes is what is good for himself. Yet
each man likes not what is good for himself but what appears to him to be
good for himself. But it makes no difference, for what is likeable will be
what appears to be so.

There are three kinds of things because of which one may like something, but when one likes an inanimate object, men do not call this 'friendship'; for the object liked does not like in return, and [a man or animal] does not wish that object's good (for it would perhaps be ridiculous for a man to wish the wine's good, though he might, if at all, wish that it be preserved 30 so as to be available to himself). In speaking of a friend, on the other hand, we say that we should wish the things that are good for his own sake. But we call 'well-disposed' those who wish in this manner someone's good, if the latter does not also return the same wish; for there is friendship when good will is reciprocal. Should we not, then, add also 'provided that good will does not escape their notice'? For many people are well- 35 disposed towards those whom they have not seen but whom they regard as *good* or useful to others, and one of these might have the same reci-   1156a procal feeling. Two such persons, then, appear to be well-disposed towards each other; but how could one call them friends if they are unaware of each other's dispositions? To be friends, then, two men should be well-disposed towards each other and wish each other's good without being unaware of this, and for one of the *reasons*   already stated.   5

3

Now these *reasons* differ in kind; so the likings and the friendships, too, differ in kind. Hence there are three kinds of friendship, equal in number to the kinds of likeable things; for with respect to each kind there is a reciprocal liking of which both parties are not unaware. Now those who like each other wish each other's good exactly in the respect in which they 10 like each other. So those who like each other because of their usefulness to each other do so not for the sake of the person liked but insofar as some good may be obtained from each other. It is likewise with those who like each other for the sake of pleasure; for men like the witty not for their character but for the pleasure received. Thus he who likes another for the sake of usefulness or of pleasure does so, respectively, for the sake of 15 what is good or pleasurable for himself, and so he likes another not for what the latter is but insofar as the latter is useful or can give pleasure to him. These kinds of friendship, then, exist in virtue of an attribute, for a man is liked not in virtue of what he is but insofar as he gives some good or pleasure. Accordingly, such friendships are easily dissolved, since the 20 parties do not long continue to be similarly disposed; for if they are no longer pleasant or useful to each other, they stop liking each other.

Now the useful does not persist long but changes from time to time. So when the cause of men's friendship is broken, their friendship too is dissolved, since friendship exists in relation to that cause. Such friendship
25   is thought to occur especially between old people – for men at that age tend to pursue what is beneficial and not what is pleasurable – and to occur between those who are young or in their prime of life but who tend to pursue what is expedient. Such friends do not live together much, for sometimes they are not even pleasant to each other; nor indeed do they have a need for such social relation unless they are beneficial to each
30   other, for they are pleasant to each other only as long as they expect some good from each other. Under such friendships come also those between hosts and guests.

Friendship between young men is thought to exist for the sake of receiving pleasure, for they live by their passions and pursue mostly what is pleasurable to themselves and what exists at the moment; but with increasing age what is pleasant to them changes also. Hence young men
35   become friends quickly and stop being friends quickly; for friendship
1156b   changes along with that which is pleasurable, and such pleasure changes quickly. Young men are also amorous, for the greater part of amorous friendship occurs by passion and for the sake of pleasure; and it is in view of this that they become friendly and soon end that friendship, and
5   often do these the same day. But they do wish to spend their days and live together, for what friendship means to them is living in this manner.

4

Perfect friendship exists between men who are good and are alike with respect to virtue; for, insofar as they are good, it is in a similar manner
10   that they wish each other's goods, and such men are good in themselves. Now those who wish the good of their friends for the sake of their friends are friends in the highest degree; for they are so disposed because of what they are and not in virtue of an attribute. Accordingly, their friendship lasts as long as they are good, and virtue is something stable. And each friend is good without qualification and also good to his friend; for good

men are good without qualification as well as beneficial to each other. And they are likewise pleasant, since good men are pleasant without 15 qualification and also pleasant to each other; for a man's own *actions* and the *actions* which are similar to them are pleasant to himself, and the *actions* of good men are the same or similar. And there is good reason for such a friendship to be stable, for in it all the things that should belong to friends come together. For all friendship is for the sake of good or of 20 pleasure, whether without qualification or for the one who feels friendly, and it exists in virtue of a similarity; and all the things named belong to this kind of friendship in virtue of each such friend, for in that friendship the other things are similar also, and the unqualified good is pleasurable without qualification also. Now it is these that are liked most, and in these both the friendly feeling and friendship exist in the highest degree and are best. Such friendships are likely to be rare indeed, for few men 25 can be such friends. Further, such friendships require time and familiarity; for, as the proverb says, it is impossible for men to know each other well until 'they have consumed together much salt', nor can they accept each other and be friends till each has shown himself dear and trustworthy to the other. Those who quickly show the marks of friendship towards 30 each other wish to be friends indeed but are not, unless both are dear to each other and also have come to know this; for while a wish for friendship may arise quickly, friendship itself is not formed quickly.

5

This kind of friendship, then, is perfect both in duration and in the other respects, and in all respects each gets from the other the same or similar 35 goods, those which should indeed belong to friends. As to the friendship for the sake of pleasure, it bears some likeness to this, for good men are *1157a* also pleasant to each other; and it is likewise with the one for the sake of usefulness, for good men are also such [i.e., useful] to each other. Among friendships for pleasure or the useful, too, those are most enduring in which friends continue to get the same thing from each other, e.g., pleasure, and not only thus but also in which they get pleasure of the same 5 kind, as between two witty persons and not as between a lover and his beloved. For the latter are not pleased by the same thing, but the lover is pleased by beholding his beloved, and the beloved is pleased by receiving

attention from the lover; and when the prime of youth fades away, sometimes this friendship fades away, too, for the view of the beloved is not
10 pleasant to the lover and so the beloved gets no attention. Many of these
who are alike in character, on the other hand, retain their friendship, if
familiarity makes them satisfied with each other's character. But those
who exchange not what is pleasant but what is useful in their love-affairs
are friends to a lesser extent and their friendship is less enduring. And
those who are friends for the sake of usefulness stop being friends when
15 the exchange of what is expedient terminates; for what they came to like
in their friendship was not each other but what was profitable. Accordingly, for the sake of pleasure or of usefulness even bad men may be friends
to each other, or one of them may be *good* and the other bad, or one of
them may be neither good nor bad and the other may be anyone [bad or
good or neither]; but it is clear that only good men can be friends for the
20 sake of each other, for bad men do not enjoy each other's company unless
some benefit is exchanged.

Again, only the friendship of good men cannot be harmed by slander;
for it is not easy for a good man to believe what anyone says about his
good friend who has stood the test of time. And it is among good men
that trust and unwillingness to *act* unjustly and whatever else belongs
to true friendship are expected without question, while in the other
25 kinds of friendship nothing prevents the contraries of these from taking
place.

Now since men call 'friends' also those who associate with each other
for the sake of usefulness, as states do (for the alliances between states are
thought to be formed for the sake of expediency), and also those who like
each other for the sake of pleasure, as boys do, perhaps we too should call
30 these 'friends' but add that there are many kinds of friendship. But
friendship in the primary and principal sense will be that between good
men just because they are good, while those between the rest will be in
virtue of some similarity; for men in the latter friendships will be friends
insofar as they exchange only a part of what is good or is similar to it, for
the pleasurable too is a part of what is good in the case of those who are
friends because they like the pleasurable. These friendships, however, do
not often go together, nor is it often that men become friends for the sake
35 of both the useful and the pleasurable; for it is not often that accidents
are joined together.

6

These being the kinds into which friendship is divided, bad men will be   *1157b*
friends for the sake of pleasure or what is useful, as this is the way in
which they are similar, while good men will be friends for the sake of
each other, for they will be friends just because they are good. The latter,
then, will be friends without qualification, while the former will be friends
in virtue of some attribute and by resemblance to these.   *5*

Just as in the case of virtues some men are called 'good' in virtue of
their habits while others in virtue of their activities, so too in the case of
friendship; for some enjoy living with each other and giving goods to each
other, while those who are asleep or are separated by distances, though
not actually present with each other, are so disposed as to *act* as friends   *10*
towards each other when they meet, for distances do not break up a friendship entirely but only the exercise of it. But if friends are apart from each
other for a long time, this seems to make them forget their friendship;
hence the saying

Lack of discourse has broken many a friendship.

Neither old nor sour men appear disposed to make friends, for they are   *15*
disposed to give but little pleasure; and no one is inclined to spend his
days with one who causes pain or gives no pleasure, for nature   appears
to avoid pain most of all and to aim at pleasure.

Those who accept each other but are not living together appear to be
well-disposed men rather than friends; for nothing stands out among
friends so much as living together. For while the needy desire benefits, the   *20*
blessed desire to spend their days with others also, for solitude befits these
least of all. But it is impossible for men to pass the time together unless
they are pleasant and enjoy the same things, and comrades are thought
to have these attributes.

7

Friendship in the highest degree exists between good men, as we have often   *25*
stated.[48] For it is the good or pleasurable without qualification which is
thought to be likeable and choiceworthy, while it is that which is good or
pleasant to each man that is thought to be such [i.e., likeable and choice-
worthy] by him; and a good man [is likeable and choiceworthy] by a good
man for both these *reasons*. Now liking resembles a feeling, while friend-

30 ship resembles a disposition. For liking is directed no less towards inanimate things; but to like in return requires intention, and intention
proceeds from a disposition. Again, good men wish what is good for
those whom they like for the latter's sake, not by feeling but by disposition. And in liking a friend, they like what is good for themselves; for a
good man, in becoming a friend, becomes a good thing to his friend. Ac-
35 cordingly, each of two such friends both likes what is good for himself
and returns as much as he receives in [good] wishes and in pleasure; for,
1158a as is said, 'friendship is equality', and indeed these [liking and returning]
belong to good men most of all.

Among sour and older men, on the other hand, friendship is less likely
to be formed, and this to the extent that they are harder to get along with
and enjoy less being in company with others, for these things [getting
along easily and enjoying company] most of all are thought to be marks
5 and causes of friendship. It is in view of this that young men become
friends quickly; but not so in the case of old men, for these do not become
friends with those whose company they do not enjoy, and similarly with
sour people. But such men may still be well disposed towards each other;
for they want good things and meet each others's needs, but they are
hardly friends because they neither spend their days together nor enjoy
10 each other's company, and these things most of all are thought to be
marks of friendship.

It is impossible to be a friend to many men in a perfect friendship, just
as it is impossible to be in love with many persons at the same time; for
love is like an excess, and such excess is by its nature felt towards one
person only, and it is not easy for many people to satisfy very much the
same person at the same time, or perhaps for many persons to be good
15 at the same time. Besides, one must also acquire experience and become
familiar with many persons, and this is extremely difficult. But it is possible to satisfy many persons by means of what is useful or pleasurable,
for there are many such who seek the useful or the pleasurable, and the
services required take little time. Of these two friendships, the one for
the sake of what is pleasurable seems to be a friendship to a higher
degree, whenever both parties receive the same things and enjoy each
20 other or the same things, like the friendships of the young; for in these
generosity is shown to a higher degree, whereas friendship for the sake of
what is useful belongs to the commercially-minded.

As for the prosperous, they have no need of the useful, but they do need what is pleasurable; for they wish to live with others, and though they can bear what is painful for a short time, no one can endure it continuously, not even if this be the *Good Itself,* if it were painful to him. So they seek friends who are pleasant; and perhaps these should be also good, and good for them too, for thus they will have all that friends should have. As for those in positions of authority, they appear to use different kinds of friends separately; for some friends are useful and others are pleasant, and the same men are not frequently both useful and pleasant. For men in authority in general do not seek pleasant friends who are also virtuous, nor useful men who have noble ends; they seek witty friends if they aim at pleasure, and shrewd friends to carry out orders, and these [i.e., wit and shrewdness] are not frequently found in the same man. We have already stated that a virtuous man is at the same time pleasant and useful,[49] but such a man does not become a friend of a superior man unless he, in turn, is superior to him in virtue, otherwise there is no proportional equality when he is surpassed. But such men rarely become friends.

8

Now the friendships which have been discussed depend on equality of exchange. For friends receive the same things from each other and wish the same things for each other; or else one thing is exchanged for a different thing, e.g., pleasure for benefit. But these are friendships to a lesser degree and are less permanent, as already stated.[50] And they are thought to be and not to be friendships because of likeness and unlikeness, respectively, to the same thing (e.g., pleasure, or usefulness); for, on the one hand, they appear to be friendships on account of their likeness to the friendship according to virtue (for one friend has pleasure as an end while the other has usefulness, and these ends belong to the friendship according to virtue also), but, on the other, they appear not to be friendships because of their unlikeness to the friendship according to virtue, for this friendship is unshaken by outside slander and is enduring, while the others are quickly dissolved and differ in many other respects.

There is another kind of friendship in which one of the parties is superior, e.g., that of a father to his son and, in general, of an elder to a younger person, as well as that of a husband to his wife and of every ruler to his

15 subject. These friendships differ also from each other; for that between parents and children is not the same as that between rulers and subjects, nor is that of a father towards his son the same as that of a son towards his father, or that of a husband towards his wife the same as that of a wife towards her husband. For the virtue and function of a friend in each of these friendships is different, and the *reasons* why friends like each other in each of them are different also. Accordingly, both the affections of these
20 friends for each other and their friendships are different. Certainly, each such friend neither receives from the other the same as he gives to the other, nor should he seek to do so; but when children give to their parents what they should to those who brought them into the world, and when parents give to their children what should be given to one's offspring, the friendship of such persons will be enduring and *good*. So, too, the feeling of affection in all friendships which exist according to superiority
25 should be proportional, e.g., the better party should be liked more than he likes, and so should the party which bestows greater benefits; and similarly in each of the other cases. For whenever the feeling of affection is shown according to merit, then in a certain sense there arises an equality, which is indeed regarded as belonging to a friendship.

9

30 Equality in what is just does not appear to be similar to equality in friendship; for the equal in what is just is primarily according to merit but secondarily according to quantity, while in friendship the equal according to quantity is primary but that according to merit is secondary. This becomes clear if there is a great interval between the virtues or vices or wealth or whatever else exists in the parties to an association; for then
35 they are no longer friends, nor do they expect to be. And this is most evident in the case of the gods; for their superiority in all the goods is the
1159a greatest. This is also clear in the case of kings, for those who are far inferior to them do not expect to be their friends; nor do those of no account expect to be friends with the best or wisest of men. In such cases, of course, an accurate definition cannot be given of the extent to which men can
5 differ and still become friends; for the differences between friends may be widened but their friendship may still remain, but if the interval is great, as between a man and God, there can be no friendship at all.

It is in view of this that the problem arises whether men wish for their friends the greatest of goods, e.g., that of being gods, for then these will be neither friends to them any longer nor goods to them; for a friend is a good to his friend. So if it was well stated that a man wishes good for his friend for the latter's sake,[51] the latter will have to remain such as he is; and   *10* the former will wish the greatest goods for the sake of the latter while the latter is still a man, though perhaps not all the greatest goods, for a man wishes the goods for himself most of all.

Most people, because of their ambition, seem to wish to be liked rather than to like, and in view of this most people like flatterers; for a flatterer is a friend in an inferior position, or a man who pretends to be such a friend and to like rather than to be liked. But being liked by someone is   *15* thought to be close to being honored by him, and indeed this is what most people aim at. And they seem to choose honor not for its own sake but for something else; for most people enjoy being honored by men of means because of expectation, since they think that they will obtain from   *20* them whatever they might need, and so they enjoy honor as a sign of future favors. As for those who desire honor from *good* men or from men of knowledge, their aim is to assure their own high opinion of themselves; and so, basing their conviction on the judgment of those men, they enjoy thinking that they are good men. But it is for its own sake that people   *25* enjoy being liked; so it would seem that being liked is better than being honored and that friendship is chosen for its own sake. On the other hand, friendship is thought to depend on liking more than on being liked. A sign of this is the fact that mothers enjoy loving their children more than being loved by them; for some of them who give their children to others to bring them up love and know their children but do not seek to be loved   *30* in return (whenever both are not possible) but are satisfied in seeing them do well, and they love their children even if the children, because of ignorance, give back nothing that is due to their mothers.

10

Since friendship depends more on loving than on being loved, and since it is those who love their friends who are praised, loving rather than being   *35* loved seems to be the virtue of a friend, and so it is those showing this [feeling or disposition] according to merit who endure as friends and who   *1159b* have an enduring friendship. And such is the manner in which unequals can be friends in the highest degree, for in this way they can be equalized.

But it is equality and likeness that is more conducive to friendship, and especially likeness in virtue. For the virtuous, being steadfast in them-
5 selves [in view of their virtue], remain steadfast towards each other also, and they neither ask others to do what is bad nor do they themselves do such things for others, but one might say that they even prevent such things from being done; for good men as such neither err nor allow their friends to fall into error. Wicked men, on the other hand, have nothing to be certain about, for they do not even remain alike [in their feelings
10 and *actions*]; they become friends but for a short time, enjoying each other's evil habits.

As for those who are useful or pleasant, they remain friends for a longer time, that is, for as long as they give each other pleasures or benefits. Friendship for the sake of usefulness seems to arise mostly between men with contrary needs, e.g., between the poor and the rich or between the ignorant and the learned, for a man aims at something which he happens
15 to need, offering something else in exchange; and we might bring in under this the lover and his beloved and also the beautiful and the ugly. And it is in view of this that lovers sometimes appear ridiculous when they demand to be loved as they themselves love; if indeed they are just as lovable, perhaps their claim is reasonable, but if they are not such at all,
20 it is ridiculous. But perhaps a contrary as such does not even aim at the other contrary, except indirectly, since desire is for the intermediate; for this is what is good, e.g., for that which is dry it is to arrive at the intermediate state and not to become wet, and similarly for that which is hot and the others. But let us leave these problems aside, for they are rather foreign to the present inquiry.

11

25 As stated at the start of this discussion,[52] both friendship and what is just seem to be concerned with the same things and to belong to the same persons; for in every association there seems to be both something which is just and also a friendship. At least, men address their fellow-voyagers and fellow-soldiers as friends also, and similarly with those in any of the
30 other associations. Friendship goes as far as the members associate with

each other; for what is just extends as far also. And it has been rightly said, "to friends all things are common"; for friendship exists in an association. Now brothers and comrades have all things in common, but other people have only certain things in common, some more, some fewer; for of friendships, too, some are to a higher degree but others to a lower degree. Just things, too, differ; for the things that are just for parents towards their children are not the same as those between brothers, nor are those between comrades the same as those between citizens, and similarly with the other kinds of friendships. Accordingly, unjust things towards men are different also; and they become more unjust by being directed towards the more friendly, e.g., it is more abominable to defraud a comrade than a citizen, or to refuse help to a brother than to a stranger, or to strike a father than any one else. What is just, too, increases by nature along with friendship, since they depend on the same kind of things and extend equally to them.

Now all other kinds of associations are like parts of the political association; for people come together for the sake of something expedient and bring along something which contributes to their life. The political association itself is thought to have originated and to continue to exist for the sake of expediency; for the lawgivers, too, are aiming at this and say that what is commonly expedient is just. Each of the other associations, then, is aiming at some part of what is expedient; e.g., sailors undertake a voyage for the sake of making money or some other such thing, fellow-soldiers go to war for the sake of spoils or victory or capturing a city, and similarly for the members of a tribe or of a town. Again, some associations seem to be formed for the sake of pleasure, e.g., religious associations and social clubs, for these are formed for the sake of sacrifice and company, respectively. All these, however, seem to come under the political association, for the aim of a political association seems not to be limited to the expediency of the moment but to extend to life as a whole; and they make sacrifices and arrange gatherings for these, pay honours to the gods, or provide pleasant relaxations for their members. For the ancient sacrifices and gatherings appear to have occurred after the harvest as a sort of first-fruits, since it is at that time that men had most leisure.

All other associations, then, appear to be parts of the political association; and the kinds of friendships will correspond to the kinds of associations.

35
1160a

5

10

15

20

25

30

12

There are three forms of government; and the corresponding deviations
from these, being as it were corruptions, are equal in number. Two of them
are kingdom and aristocracy; and the third, which it seems proper to call
35   'timocracy', is based on property qualification but is usually called by
1160b most people 'democracy'. The best of these is kingdom, the worst is timocracy. The deviation from kingdom is tyranny, since both are monarchies
and differ most; for a tyrant looks for what is expedient for himself while
the king looks for what is expedient for his subjects. For a ruler is not a
king unless he is self-sufficient and superior to his subjects in all good
5   things, and if he is such, he has no need of anything; accordingly, he would
look not for his own benefit but for that of his subjects, for if he were not
such, he would be a king by ballot.

Tyranny is the contrary of kingdom, for a tyrant pursues what is good
for himself. And it is more evident that tyranny is the worst deviation;
and the contrary of the best is the worst.

10   Kingdom passes over into tyranny; for tyranny is a bad monarchy and
an evil king becomes a tyrant. Aristocracy passes over into oligarchy by
the badness of the rulers, who distribute the goods of the state in violation
of merit, taking most or all of the goods for themselves, keeping the posi-
15   tions of authority always for themselves, and paying attention to wealth
most of all. Accordingly, these rulers are few and evil, instead of being the
most equitable. Timocracy passes over into mob rule; for these border
each other, since timocracy too tends to be the rule of the many and
since all those who have the property qualification in it count as equals.

20   Of the forms of government which deviate, that of mob rule is the least
evil, for this kind of state deviates only to a slight extent.

It is in this manner, then, that forms of government change most frequently, for it is in this manner that the transitions are smallest and
easiest.

One may observe similarities and in a way examples of these forms of
government in households also. The association of a father with his
25   children has the appearance of a kingdom, for a father is concerned with
the care of his children. It is in view of this that Homer, too, addresses
Zeus as 'father', for kingdom tends to be a paternal rule. In Persia, on the
other hand, the rule of fathers is tyrannical, for they use their children as

slaves. The rule of a master over his slaves, too, is tyrannical; for in it *30* things are done for what is expedient to the master. Now this rule appears to be right, but the rule of a father in Persia is in error; for the rule over different kinds of subjects should be different. The rule of a husband over his wife appears aristocratic, for a husband rules in virtue of merit and is concerned with things that befit a husband; and he assigns to his wife those matters which befit a wife. But if a husband rules over every- *35* thing, his rule becomes oligarchical; for then he does this in violation of *1161a* merit and not to the extent that he is superior. Sometimes it is the wives who, having become heiresses, rule their husbands; and then they rule not according to virtue but because of wealth or power, as in oligarchies. As for the association of brothers, it resembles a timocracy, for brothers are equal, except for their differences in age; hence if they differ much in age, *5* their friendship is no longer fraternal. Mob rule exists mostly in a communal arrangement where there is no master (for here all men are equal), and also in a communal arrangement in which the ruler is weak and each member has the power to do what he pleases.

13

In each form of government friendship exists to the extent that what is just *10* exists. In the friendship of a king towards his subjects there is a superiority of good services for his subjects, for a king makes his subjects good, if indeed by being good he sees to it that they *act* well, as a shepherd does for his sheep; whence Homer called Agamemnon 'shepherd of people'. Such *15* too is the friendship of a father towards his children, although it differs in the magnitude of good services; for he is the cause of their existence, which is thought to be the greatest good, and also of their nurture and education. These things apply to ancestors also, for the relation of a father to his sons or of ancestors to descendants or of a king to his subjects is by nature that of a ruler to one who is ruled. And these are friendships *20* by virtue of superiority; hence parents are also honored. Accordingly, also what is just in those friendships is not the same for the two parties but is according to merit; for friendship, too, exists in this manner. The friendship of a husband towards his wife, too, is the same as that which depends on aristocratic superiority. For it is in accordance with virtue, and the greater good should go to the superior party, and to each party

25   should go what befits that party; for what is just, too, exists in this manner. The friendship of brothers, however, is like that of comrades; for they are equal and of about the same age, and such persons are for the most part alike in feelings and in character. Like this, too, is the friendship of the members in a timocracy, for its citizens tend to be equal and equitable; and indeed their rule exists by turns and on the basis of equality, and so

30   does their friendship.

      In forms of government which deviate, just as there is but little that is just, so too there is little friendship, and friendship exists least in the worst form of government; for in a tyranny there is no friendship at all or very little of it. For in relations in which there is nothing common to the ruler and to the ruled, there is no friendship, as there is nothing just. The rela-

35   tion is like that of an artist to his tool, or that of the soul to its body, or

1161b   that of a master to his slave, for in each of these the former is benefited by using the latter; and there is no friendship or anything just towards in-animate things. Nor is there friendship towards a horse or an ox or towards a slave as a slave, for there is nothing common to the two parties;

5   for a slave is a living tool, and a tool is a lifeless slave. Accordingly, there can be no friendship towards a slave as a slave, but there may be friend-ship towards him as a man; for there seems to be something just between every man and every one who can participate in an association where there is law or agreement, and hence in a friendship to the extent that each of them is a man. So in tyrannies, too, there are friendships and what is just, though to a small extent; but friendships in perverted constitutions

10   are most likely to exist where there is mob rule, for where men are equal, they have many things in common.

14

As we have stated,[53] then, every kind of friendship exists in an association; but one might mark off from the rest the friendships of kinsmen and of comrades. Friendships of fellow-citizens and of fellow-tribesmen and of fellow-voyagers and other such are more like friendships by [mere] asso-

15   ciation, for they appear to be based on a sort of [mere] agreement. To these we may add also the friendship between host and guest.

      Friendships between kinsmen, too, appear to be of many kinds, but all depend on paternal friendship; for parents love their children as if these

were parts of themselves, and children love their parents since their being
comes from their parents. Parents know that their offspring come from 20
them, however, more than the offspring know that they come from their
parents, and parents feel close to their offspring more than the latter do
to their parents; for that which comes from a person is that person's very
own, like a tooth or a hair or any of his possessions, but this is not at all
related to that person in this way, or is less so related. And as for the
length of time, parents love their children from the moment of their birth, 25
whereas children begin to love their parents years after birth, when they
have gained intelligence or sense. From these remarks it is also clear why
mothers love their children more than fathers do.

Parents, then, love their children as they love themselves (for what
comes from them is like other selves, being different by having been
separated), and children love their parents as being born of them; but 30
brothers love each other by having been born of the same parents, for
sameness in relation to the same parents produces sameness in relation to
each other (whence come the expressions 'the same blood' and 'the same
roots' and other such). Thus they are in a certain sense the same even if
they are separate persons. Being brought up together and being of about
the same age, too, contribute a great deal to their friendship; for, as the
saying goes, 'two of an age', and it is men familiar with each other who 35
become comrades; in view of this, the friendship of brothers, too, resembles that of comrades. As for cousins and all other kinsmen, their 1162a
closeness arises from these, for all of them come ultimately from the
same parents; and they are more close or less close to each other by being,
respectively, nearer or farther from their first ancestor.

The friendship of children towards parents, and of men towards gods, 5
is one towards something good and superior; for parents have done the
greatest of goods, since they are the causes of the existence and nurture of
their children and then of their education. And such friendship possesses
more pleasure and usefulness than that towards strangers, and to the
extent that their life has more in common. The friendship between
brothers has the good attributes present in that between comrades; and it 10
is a friendship to a higher degree for brothers who are *good*, and in
general for those who are alike, and to the extent that they are closer to
each other and are fond of each other from birth and that, born of the
same parents, they are alike in character and upbringing and have been

15 educated alike. And the test of time here has been the longest and most certain. Friendly relations between the rest of kinsmen, too, exist but in proportion to their closeness.

The friendship between husband and wife is thought to exist by nature; for men by nature tend to form couples more than to be political, and they do this to the extent that a household is prior and more necessary than a state and that reproduction is more common to animals. Accordingly,
20 associations in the other animals exist only to that extent, but men live together not only for the sake of reproduction but for other things in life as well; for the functions among men are divided from the start, and those of a husband are different from those of a wife, and so by contributing to the common stock whatever is proper to each they supply each other's needs. It is for these *reasons*, too, that this friendship is thought
25 to be both useful and pleasant; and if both are *good*, it may also be a friendship through virtue, for there is a virtue for each of them, and both would enjoy such a state of affairs. As for children, they seem to keep husband and wife together, and this is why childless marriages are more easily dissolved; for children are a common good to both of them, and what is common holds them together.
30 To ask how a husband and a wife, or any two friends in general, should live together appears to be none other than to ask how it is just for them to live; for what is just towards a friend does not appear to be the same as what is just towards a stranger, or a comrade, or a classmate.

15

35 Since there are three kinds of friendships, as we stated at first,[54] and since in each kind one may be a friend to another by virtue of equality or by virtue of superiority (for two men who become friends may be alike good
1162b or one may be superior to the other in goodness, and similarly if they are friends by being pleasant to each other or because they are useful to each other, whether the benefits received are equal or different), those who are equal should bring about equality by being equally disposed in their love for each other and in other respects, while those who are unequal should do so by being disposed in a manner proportionate to their superiority or inferiority.
5 There are good reasons why accusations and complaints occur exclu-

sively or most of all in friendships which are based on usefulness. For those who are friends through virtue are eager to treat each other well, since this is a mark of virtue and of friendship, and when both strive to do this, there can be neither accusations nor quarrels; for no one is displeased with a man who likes him and treats him well; on the contrary, if he is grateful, he requites the other by returning a good. And he who is superior in achieving what he aims at would not accuse his friend, for each of them aims at the other's good. In friendships for the sake of pleasure, too, complaints hardly arise; for both friends get what they desire, if they enjoy each other's company. And a man would appear ridiculous were he to accuse his friend of not receiving delight from him, when he can part company at will. Friendships for the sake of usefulness, on the other hand, give rise to accusations. For by using each other for their own benefit, each of them always wants more than he gives and thinks that he receives less than his due, and he complains of not receiving what he deserves and has asked for; and in conferring a benefit, each cannot supply as much as the other wants.

It seems that, just as there are two kinds of things which are just, one unwritten and the other according to law, so there are two kinds of friendship based on usefulness, one ethical and the other legal. Accordingly, accusations arise especially whenever exchanges are made not according to the same kind of friendship and the parties break off their friendship.

Now legal friendship is formed on specified terms; and it may be purely commercial and carried out immediately, or it may be more liberal with respect to time but agreed upon as to its terms. The debt in the latter case is clear and not subject to dispute, and the postponement has an element of friendship; and it is in view of this that some states allow no suits concerning those debts but think that men should accept the consequences regarding exchanges based on trust.

Ethical friendship, on the other hand, is not formed on specified terms; a gift or any other good is bestowed as to a friend. But the giver expects to receive as much, or more, as if what he gave were not a gift but something lent to be used; and if at the end of the exchange he is not as well off, he accuses the receiver. This happens because all or most people, though wishing what is noble, deliberately choose what is beneficial to themselves. Now to treat others well without seeking a return is noble, but to receive

10

15

20

25

30

35

1163a

the services of another is beneficial. So if the receiver is able, he should return the equivalent of what he received and do so voluntarily; for no one should be made an unwilling friend. It would really be as if one made a mistake at the start and received a good from a person from whom he should not have received it; for he received the good not from a friend,

5   nor from one whose *action* was for its own sake. Accordingly, he who has so received a service should dissolve the friendship as if it were made on specified terms. And he should grant that, if he could, he would return the equivalent of the service rendered, for if he could not, neither would the giver have expected to receive it; so if he can, he should return the service. But a man should first consider carefully (a) the person from whom he receives a service and (b) the terms on which he does this, so that with both these in mind he may accept or decline it.

10   There is disagreement as to whether a good which is to be returned should be measured by the receiver's benefit or by the giver's service. For the recipients belittle the goods received by saying that such goods meant little to the benefactors and could have been received from others; the

15   benefactors, on the other hand, claim that they have conferred the greatest of goods and those which could not have been conferred by others, and that they did this at a time of risk or some other such need.

Now if the friendship is one for the sake of usefulness, should not the measure be the benefit of the receiver? For it is he who wants the benefit, and the benefactor supplies this with the expectation of an equivalent return; accordingly, the assistance given is as great as the benefit which he

20   receives, and so what he should return is as much as he has been benefited, or even more, for this is more noble. But in friendships based on virtue accusations do not arise, and it is the intention of the giver which seems to be the measure; for the main principle in virtue and in character lies in intention.

16

Disagreements arise also in friendships in which one party is superior to

25   the other, for each claims to deserve more; and whenever this happens, the friendship is dissolved. For the better of the two parties thinks that he should by right have more, since he thinks that more should be given to a good man than to one who is less good. It is likewise with the man who is more beneficial to others, since it is said that those who are not useful to

others should not have as much as those who are useful; for it is said that
the association becomes a public service and not a friendship if the actions
in a friendship are not measured by what they are worth. For men think   *30*
that, just as in a business partnership those who contribute more money
should receive more, so it should be in a friendship. But the man who is
in need or is inferior takes the opposite view; for he thinks that a mark
of a good friend is to assist the needy. Where is the advantage, he asks, of
being a friend to a virtuous or powerful man if one is to gain nothing   *35*
from him?

It seems that each of these is right in his claim and that each of them   *1163b*
should get more than the other out of the friendship, not more of the same
thing, however, but the superior should get more honor and the needy
should get more gain; for the prize of virtue and of beneficence is honor,
but that which relieves a need is gain. In a state, too, this appears to be   *5*
the manner in which goods are distributed, since the man who is honored
is not he who contributes nothing to the common weal; for a common good
is bestowed upon the man who renders service to the public, and honor is
a common good. For one cannot expect to make money out of the public
and be honored at the same time, since no one puts up with getting less
in all respects. So they pay honor to the man who takes a loss in money   *10*
but give money to the man who wants money; for what effects equality and
preserves a friendship is what each gets according to merit, as already
stated.[55]

Among unequals, too, this should be the manner of their association;
the party who is benefited financially or towards virtue should repay in
honor, since this is what he can do. For friendship calls for what is pos-   *15*
sible, not something according to merit, since a return according to merit
does not even exist in all friendships, as in the case of honors paid to gods
or to parents; for here one could not ever return the equivalent of what
he has received, but he is thought to be *good* if in return he renders as much
service as he can. In view of this, it would even seem that it is not up to a
son to repudiate his father, although a father may disown his son; for a   *20*
son should repay what he owes, and there is nothing he can do which will
be the equivalent of what he has received, so he will always be in debt.
But a creditor may remit a debt owed by the debtor; and so can a father.
Still it seems that perhaps no one would ever disown a son who has not
gone too far in his evil habits; for apart from the natural affection of a

25 father for his son, it is human not to reject the help of a son. An evil son, on the other hand, will regard helping his father as something to be avoided or not eagerly pursued; for most people wish to be treated well but avoid doing so to others since there is no gain in it.

Concerning friendship, then, this account may be taken as sufficient.

BOOK X

1

1172a After what has been said, perhaps a discussion of pleasure comes next; for
20 pleasure is thought to be closely associated with human nature most of all, and this is the reason why we guide the education of the young by means of pleasure and pain. And it also seems that to enjoy the things we should and to hate the things we should contribute most to the formation of virtuous character, for these are present with us throughout our life and have
25 influence and power in forming virtue and making our life happy, since we deliberately choose what is pleasant and avoid what is painful. And it would seem that we should least of all omit the discussion of such matters, especially when there is much disagreement concerning them. For some thinkers say that the good is pleasure,[56] but others,[57] taking the contrary position, say that pleasure is altogether bad, and some of the latter are
30 perhaps convinced that such is actually the case, while others think that to represent pleasure as bad has a better effect on our way of life, even if this is not so, for they think that most men are inclined towards pleasures and are slaves of pleasures and hence should be led towards the contrary direction, since it is in this way that they will arrive at the mean.

But surely these thinkers are not stating the case well; for arguments
35 concerning passions and *actions* are less convincing than facts, and when arguments disagree with what is observed, they fall into contempt and
1172b discredit truth as well. For if a man speaks disapprovingly of pleasure and is sometimes seen to aim at it, his inclination towards it is thought to indicate that all pleasure is such that men aim at it; for most people are not given to making distinctions. So true arguments concerning
5 pleasure and pain seem to be most useful not only to knowledge, but to our way of life as well; for, being in harmony with the facts, they impart

conviction, and hence they exhort intelligent men to live according to them. But enough of such remarks; let us go over what is said about pleasure.

2

Eudoxus thought that the good is pleasure because he observed all ani- *10* mals, both rational and nonrational, aiming at it. He argued that since in everything the object of choice is *good* and the object mostly chosen is the best, and since the fact that all animals are drawn to the same thing indicates that this is the highest good for all of them (for each animal finds its own good just as it finds its own food), that which is good for all animals and at which all animals aim is the good. *15*

These arguments carried conviction more because of his virtuous character than because of themselves as arguments, for Eudoxus was regarded as being exceptionally temperate; so men thought that he was saying these things not as a friend of pleasure but as if such was the truth of the matter. He held that his doctrine was no less evident from arguments by the use of contraries, for he regarded pain in itself as being an object avoided by all and its contrary as being in a similar way an object *20* chosen by all. He maintained that a choiceworthy object in the highest sense is one which does not exist for the sake of another nor is chosen for the sake of another, and that pleasure is agreed upon as being such an object; for no one asks for what further reason one is pleased, so pleasure must be chosen for its own sake. And when pleasure is added to any good thing, e.g., to a just or a temperate *action*, he regarded the result as being *25* more choiceworthy than that thing and so goodness itself as being increased by additional goodness.

Now the above argument seems to show merely that pleasure is one of the goods, and not a higher good than another kind of good; for any kind of good whatever would thus be more worthy of choice when another good is added to it than when it is by itself. It is indeed by an argument such as this that Plato,[58] too, refutes the statement that the good is pleasure; for, according to him, a pleasant life is preferable with rather than *30* without prudence, and if the combination of the two is better, the good cannot be pleasure, for the good itself cannot become more choiceworthy by the addition of anything. It is clear, then, that neither can a thing, other than pleasure, be the good if the addition of what is good by itself makes the combination more choiceworthy. What thing, then, is such that we too can participate in? For it is a thing such as this that we are *35* looking for.

Those who object to the view that that at which all creatures aim is good
1173a   are talking nonsense. For that which is thought by all to be the case is said
to be the case, and he who rejects this conviction will hardly assert anything which is more convincing; for if only senseless creatures desired
certain things, there might be something in what they say, but if also
prudent creatures desire them, how could there be anything in what they
are saying? Perhaps even in bad creatures there is some natural good
5   which is better than they themselves are and which aims at its proper
good.

Nor does the argument which concerns the contrary of pleasure seem
to be stated well, for they   say that, if pain is bad, it does not follow that
pleasure is good; for evil may be opposed to evil, and both of them may
be opposed to what is neither of them, and in saying these they do not
speak badly, but these statements are not true of the things [pleasure and
10   pain] in question. For if both pleasure and pain were evil, both would
have been avoided, and if neither was evil, neither would have been
avoided or both would have been similarly related to us. But as it is, men
appear to avoid pain as an evil but to choose pleasure as a good; so this
is the manner in which pleasure and pain are opposed.

Again, the fact that pleasure is not a quality is not a reason for ex-
15   cluding it from being a good; for neither the activities of virtue nor
happiness is a quality, but they are goods.

Some thinkers say[59] that the good is definite, but that pleasure is indefinite since it admits of degree. Now if they judge this from the fact that
one is pleased, [for one may be pleased sometimes more and sometimes
less,] the same will be the case with justice and the other virtues, according
20   to which men are obviously said to be such-and-such and also to *act* to a
higher or to a lower degree; for men may be more just or more brave, and
they may *act* more justly or less justly, and more temperately or less
temperately.   But if they think that indefiniteness is present in the pleasures themselves, perhaps they are not stating the cause, [e.g.,] whether
some pleasures are unmixed but others are mixed. For what prevents
25   pleasure from being like health, which is definite yet admits of degree?
For proportion is not the same in all things which admit of it, nor does a
single proportion exist in the same thing always, but it may deviate up to
a point and still persist, and so it may vary in degree. So such may be the
case with pleasure.

Again, positing the good as being perfect but motions and generations as being imperfect,[60] they try to show that pleasure is a motion   *30*
or a generation. But they do not seem to speak well, nor is pleasure a
motion. For quickness and slowness are thought to be proper to every
motion, or if a motion by its nature is not [quicker or slower], as in the
case of the motion of the universe, still it is quicker or slower than other
motions; but quickness and slowness do not belong to pleasure.   For
though we may come to be pleased quickly as we may get angry quickly,   *1173b*
while we are being pleased we are not pleased quickly, not even in relation
to something else, but we can walk or grow, or the like, quickly. So
while we may change into a state of pleasure quickly or slowly, we cannot
be in activity with respect to pleasure in a quick or slow way, i.e., our
state of being pleased is not quick or slow.

Again, how can pleasure be a generation? For a thing generated is not   *5*
thought to be generated from any chance thing, but it is generated from
that into which it may be dissolved, and of that whose generation is
pleasure the destruction would be pain.

They say,[61] too, that pain is the lack of that which exists according to
nature, but that pleasure is the replenishment of it. Now these [i.e., lack
and replenishment] are attributes of the body. So if pleasure is the replenishment of that which exists according to nature, then also that in   *10*
which there is replenishment would be that which is pleased. Hence this
would be the body. But this is not thought to be the case; so neither can
pleasure be replenishment, but one is pleased when replenishment is
taking place, and he is pained when he is being operated on.

This doctrine [that pleasure is replenishment] seems to have originated
from the fact that pains and pleasures are associated with food; for men
in pain because of the need of food are pleased while taking in food. But   *15*
this does not happen with regard to all kinds of pleasures; for the pleasures of learning and, with respect to sensation, those through smell and
many sounds and sights, and also those of memories and expectations
are not preceded by pain. These pleasures, then, would be the generations
of what objects? There has been no lack of anything of which these could   *20*
be the replenishment.

Against those who bring forward the pleasures which deserve reproach
one might reply that these are not pleasant; for [he might argue that] if
they are pleasures to those who are badly disposed, one should not regard

them as pleasures except to those who are so disposed, just as we do not
regard things which are wholesome or sweet or bitter to sick people as
25   being such to healthy people, or things which appear white to those
suffering from a disease of the eye as being such to those with healthy
eyes.   Or, one might reply that pleasures are worthy of choice but not
those which deserve reproach, just as wealth is worthy of choice but not
at the cost of betraying one's country, or as health is worthy of choice but
not at the cost of eating any chance food. Or else, one might reply that
pleasures differ in kind; for those which come from noble *actions* are different from those which come from disgraceful *actions*, and one cannot get
30   the kind of pleasure of a just man without being himself just, nor the
pleasure of a musical man without being himself musical, and similarly
with the others. The difference between a friend and a flatterer, too, seems
to bring out the point that pleasure is not a good or that pleasures differ
in kind; for a friend's company is regarded as being for the sake of what
is good whereas that of a flatterer is for the sake of giving pleasure, and a
1174a   flatterer is reproached whereas a friend is praised, and this fact indicates
that the ends of the two associations are different. Further, no one would
choose to live all his life with the *thoughts* of a child and with the greatest
pleasures a child is capable of, or to enjoy doing something which is most
disgraceful, even if he were to suffer no pain at all.   There are many
5   things, too, we would make an effort in doing even if they were to bring
us no pleasure at all, such as seeing, remembering, knowing, and having
virtues; and it makes no difference if pleasures follow these activities of
necessity, for we would choose them even if no pleasure were to come from
them.   It seems clear, then, that neither is pleasure the good,   nor is
10   every pleasure worthy of choice, and that some pleasures are worthy of
choice in virtue of their nature and differ in kind or by the fact that they
come from different sources.

Let the above, then, suffice as an account of the things that are said
about pleasure and pain.

3

What pleasure is or what kind of thing it is might become more evident if
we take up the discussion by starting from a principle.
15   Now seeing is thought to be complete at any interval of time; for it
needs no thing which, when it comes into being later, will complete the

form of seeing. Pleasure, too, resembles a thing such as seeing; for it is a whole, and no pleasure at an interval of time can be taken whose form will be completed by pleasure at a later interval.

In view of this, pleasure is not a motion, for every motion takes time and   *20* is for the sake of an end; e.g., the process of building is complete when that which is aimed at [e.g., a house] is made. So this motion is complete either in the whole interval of time or at the moment when the house is completed. But within every part of the time which is required for the whole motion, the corresponding partial motion is incomplete, and the partial motions are different from each other and from the whole motion, for the fitting of the stones is different in kind from the fluting of the columns, and these are different from the construction of the [whole] temple; and the construction of the temple is complete (for nothing is   *25* missing from the end proposed), whereas the construction of the founda- tion or of the triglyph is incomplete (for each is a motion of a part of the temple). So they differ in kind, and it is not possible to find in any interval of time a motion which is complete in form, but, if at all, only in the whole interval of time. It is likewise with walking and the rest of the motions. For since locomotion is a motion from one place to another,   *30* and of locomotion there are different species (flying, walking, jumping, and the like), differences arise not only in this manner, but also in, let us say, walking itself; for the starting point and the goal are not the same in the whole racecourse and in a part of it, nor are they the same in tra- versing two different parts of it, (for one goes over not just a line but a line   *1174b* which is in place, and the place of one line is different from that of another. We have discussed motion with accuracy elsewhere).[62] So it seems that motions are not complete within every interval of time; but most of them are incomplete and differ in kind, if indeed their starting point and end   *5* also cause a difference in those motions.

The form of pleasure, on the other hand, is complete in every interval of time during which one is pleased. So it is clear that pleasure and motion would be [generically] different, and that pleasure would be among the things which are wholes and which are complete within any interval. This would seem to be the case also from the fact that it is not possible for a thing to move except in time, but it is possible to be pleased [not in time]; for [to be pleased] in a moment is a whole. From these remarks it is also clear that those who call pleasure 'a motion' or 'a generation' do not   *10*

speak well, for these are predicated not of all things but of things which
are divisible into parts and also of things which are not wholes. For there
is no generation of seeing or of a point or of a unit, nor is any of these a
motion or a generation; and so neither is there a generation of pleasure,
for this is a whole.

4

Since every faculty of sensation, when active, is directed towards a sen-
15   sible object, and since such a faculty when in excellent condition acts per-
fectly on the noblest sensible object coming under it (for perfect activity in
the highest sense seems to be an activity such as this, and it makes no
difference whether we regard the faculty itself as acting or the organ in
which that faculty resides), it follows that the best activity of each faculty
is the activity which is best disposed towards the best object coming under
20   that faculty. This activity would be the most perfect and most pleasant;
for there is pleasure with respect to every faculty of sensation, and likewise with *thought* and contemplation, and the most pleasant activity is the
most perfect, and the most perfect is that of a [faculty or organ] which is
excellently disposed towards the best object coming under it. Now it is
pleasure that makes the activity perfect. But pleasure does not perfect the
25   activity in the same way as the sensible object or sensation does, although
both of them are *good*, just as health and the doctor are not alike causes
of being healthy.

It is clear that pleasure arises with respect to each faculty of sensation,
for we speak of sights and of things heard as being pleasant. It is also clear
that these activities are most pleasant whenever both the faculty is at its
best and its activity is directed towards its best corresponding object; and
30   if both the object sensed and he who senses it are such, there will always
be pleasure provided both the agent and that which is acted upon   are
present. But pleasure perfects the activity not as a disposition which
resides in the agent   but as an end which supervenes like the bloom of
manhood to those in their prime of life; so while the object which is being
thought or sensed and that which thinks or judges it continue to be as they
1175a   should, there will be pleasure in the activity, for when both the agent and
the object acted upon remain in a similar condition and are related to
each other in the same manner, the result produced is by nature the same.

How is it, then, that no one is continuously pleased? But do we not

become weary? For human activities cannot continue indefinitely; so   *5*
neither can pleasure, for it accompanies such activities. For the same
reason, some things delight us when they are new but later fail to do so
in a similar way; for at first *thought* is attracted and its activity towards
them is intense, as in the case of vision when men look intently at a thing,
but afterwards the activity does not have the same quality but loses its   *10*
force, and hence its pleasure too fades away.

One might think that all men desire pleasure, since they all aim at
living. Now life is a kind of activity, and a man directs his activities to the
things and with the things which he loves most; for example, the musician
uses the faculty of hearing to listen to tunes, and he who loves learning
uses his *thought* on theoretical objects, and similarly in each case. But   *15*
pleasure perfects the activities, and also living, which men desire. It is with
good reason, then, that men desire also pleasure; for this makes living
perfect for each man, and this is worthy of choice. Whether we choose
living for the sake of pleasure or pleasure for the sake of living may be
left aside for the present. For living and pleasure appear to go together   *20*
and not to admit separation; for there can be no pleasure without activity,
and pleasure perfects every activity.

5

It is in view of this that pleasures, too, are thought to differ in kind, for
we think that things which are different in kind are perfected by different
things. For this is the way in which both natural things and those coming
under art appear to be perfected, e.g., animals and trees, and also paintings, statues, houses, and furniture; and, in a similar way, also activities   *25*
which differ in kind appear to be perfected by things which differ in kind.
Now the activities of *thought* differ in kind from those with respect to
sensation, and those within each genus [i.e., those with respect to *thought*,
or those with respect to sensation] differ in kind within themselves; so the
corresponding pleasures which complete these activities, too, will be
different. This might appear to be the case also from the fact that each of
the pleasures resides in the activity which is perfected by that pleasure.   *30*
For an activity is increased along with the pleasure which is proper to it;
for those who engage in activity with pleasure judge things better or *think*
them out more accurately than those who take little or no pleasure in

those activities, e.g., those who become geometricians and think out each
geometrical object better are those who enjoy geometrical thinking, and,
35   similarly, it is by enjoying their activity that those who love music or
constructing a building, etc., make progress in their proper field. What
causes each of them to advance further in his own field is pleasure, and
1175b   that which causes such advance is proper to that field; and attributes
proper to subjects which are different in kind are themselves different in
kind.

This becomes even more apparent from the fact that activities are obstructed by the pleasures of other activities; e.g., those who love to hear
flute-playing are unable to attend to an argument when they hear atten-
5   tively someone playing the flute, for they enjoy listening to the flute more
than the activity of attending to the argument, and so the pleasure of
hearing flute-playing destroys the activity connected with the argument.
It is likewise in all other cases in which a man is engaged in two things at
the same time; for the more pleasant activity pushes the other activity
back, and if the former activity is much more pleasant, it pushes the latter
10   activity even further back so that the man cannot even attend to the latter
activity. For this reason, when we enjoy anything very much we do
nothing else at all; and when we lose interest in something, we do other
things, e.g., those who eat sweets in theaters do so most when actors are
bad.

Now since the pleasure which is proper to the activities of a given kind
15   makes those activities more accurate, more enduring, and better, while
alien pleasures impair them, it is clear that proper and alien pleasures are
much different; for alien pleasures have almost the effect which proper
pains have, since proper pains destroy those activities. For example, if
writing or counting numbers is unpleasant and painful to a man, he does
20   not write or does not count since these activities are painful. But the
effects of an activity arising from its proper pleasures and its proper
pains are contrary – and proper pleasures and pains are said to be those
which supervene on an activity in virtue of its own nature – while alien
pleasures, as already stated, have an effect which is just about the same as
[proper] pains have, for they too destroy that activity, though not in the
same manner.
25   Since activities differ by being *good* or bad, and since some should be
chosen, others should be avoided, and others are neutral with respect to

choice or avoidance, pleasures, too, differ in a similar way; for corresponding to each activity there is a proper pleasure. Accordingly, the pleasure proper to a good activity is *good*, while that proper to a bad activity is evil; for of *desires*, too, those of noble activities are praised while those of disgraceful activities are blamed. But the pleasures in activities are more proper to them than the corresponding desires; for the desires are distinct from the activities both in time and in nature, while the proper pleasures are quite close to them and are so indistinguishable from them that men disagree as to whether activities and pleasures are the same or not. Still, pleasure does not seem to be the same as *thought* or sensation, for this would be strange, but they appear to some to be the same because they are not separated. Just as activities are distinct, then, so are the corresponding pleasures. Now vision differs from touch in purity, and so do hearing and smell from taste. So the corresponding pleasures, too, differ in a similar way, and those of *thought* differ from these, and within each of the two [genera, i.e., of sensation and of *thought*] there are differences.

Each animal is thought to have a proper pleasure, just as it has a proper function; for a given pleasure is proper to its corresponding activity. This would appear to be so if each species of animals is considered also; for the pleasures of a horse, of a dog, and of a man are different; and as Heraclitus says, "Donkeys would choose sweepings rather than gold", for food is more pleasant to them than gold. So the pleasures of different animals are themselves different in kind, and it is reasonable to think that the pleasures within each species do not differ. But in the case of men, at least, the pleasures vary to no small extent; for the same things delight some men but pain others, and they are painful or hateful to some but pleasant or lovable to others. This happens in the case of sweet things, too; for they do not seem the same to those who have fever and to those who are healthy, nor hot both to a sickly man and to one in good physical condition, and similarly in other cases. In all such cases, then, what is thought to be the case is what appears to a virtuous man. And if this is well stated (as is thought to be) and the measure of each thing is virtue or a good man as such [i.e., as virtuous], those things, too, will be pleasures which appear to him to be pleasures and those things will be pleasurable which a good man enjoys. And if the things which distress him appear pleasant to some persons, there is nothing surprising about this (for men

30

35

1176a

5

10

15

20

are ruined or impaired in various ways), and such things are not pleasurable but only to these persons and to others who are disposed in such a manner. So it is clear that we should not speak of those pleasures which are generally regarded to be disgraceful as being really pleasures, except to those who are corrupt.   But of pleasures which are thought to be *good*,
25   what kind or which should be said to belong to a man? Are they not clear from [a consideration of] the corresponding activities? For it is these activities that the pleasures accompany. So whether there is one or more than one activity that belongs to a perfect and blessed man, it is the pleasures which perfect those activities that would primarily be called the 'pleasures' belonging to a man, and the others would be called 'pleasures' in a secondary sense or to a small degree, like the corresponding activities.

6

30   After a discussion of the virtues and friendship and pleasures, what remains is a sketchy discussion of happiness, since this is what we posited as the end of whatever is human. Our discussion will be shorter if we review what has already been stated.
       We have said[63] that happiness is not a disposition; for otherwise it might
35   belong also to a man who sleeps all his life and so lives like a plant, or to a
1176b man who suffers the greatest of misfortunes. So since this is not satisfactory but happiness should be posited as being rather an activity of some sort, as we have stated earlier,[64] and since some activities are necessary and are chosen for the sake of something else while others [are chosen just] for their own sake, it is clear that happiness should be posited
5   as chosen for its own sake and not for the sake of something else, for happiness has no need of anything else but is self-sufficient.
       Activities which are chosen for their own sake are those from which nothing else is sought beyond them. Now such are thought to be the *actions* in accordance with virtue, for doing what is noble or good is something chosen for its own sake. And such, too, are thought to be the amuse-
10   ments, which are pleasant, since they are chosen not for the sake of something else; for men are harmed rather than benefited by them, when they neglect their bodies and the acquisition of property. Most people who are regarded as happy resort to pastimes such as these; and this is the
15   reason why witty men are highly favored by tyrants, for they offer the

kind of pleasure which tyrants aim at, and tyrants need such men. So these pastimes are thought to contribute to happiness because it is in these that men in despotic positions spend their time.

But perhaps the apparent happiness of such men is no sign that they are really happy, for virtue and thought, from which good activities arise, do not depend on despotic power; and the fact that such men, who have never tasted pure and liberal pleasure, resort to bodily pleasures is no *reason* for regarding these pleasures as being more choiceworthy, for children too regard the things they value as being the best. It is with good reason, then, that just as different things appear to be of value to children and to men, so different things appear to be of value to bad men and to *good* men. Accordingly, as we have often stated,[65] things which are both valuable and pleasant are those which appear such to a good man. The activity most choiceworthy to each man, then, is the one in accordance with his own disposition, and so the activity most choiceworthy to a virtuous man would be the one which proceeds according to virtue. Consequently, happiness is not found in amusement, for it would be also absurd to maintain that the end of man is amusement and that men work and suffer all their life for the sake of amusement. For, in short, we choose everything for the sake of something else, except happiness, since happiness is the end of a man. So to be serious and work hard for the sake of amusement appears foolish and very childish, but to amuse oneself for the sake of serious work seems, as Anarchasis put it, to be right; for amusement is like relaxation, and we need relaxation since we cannot keep on working hard continuously. Thus amusement is not the end, for it is chosen for the sake of serious activity.

A happy life, on the other hand, is thought to be a life according to virtue; and it proceeds with seriousness but does not exist in amusement. And we speak of serious things as being better than those which are humorous or amusing, and we speak of the activity of the better part of a man or of a better man as being always better; and the activity of what is better is superior and so makes one more happy. Any man, even one with a slavish nature, can indulge in the bodily pleasures no less than the best man, but no one would attribute happiness to a man with a slavish nature, unless he attributes to him also a way of life which is human; for happiness is not found in such pastimes but in activities according to virtue, as we have already stated.[66]

20

25

30

35
1177a

5

10

7

Since happiness is an activity according to virtue, it is reasonable that it should be an activity according to the highest virtue; and this would be an activity of the best part of man. So whether this be intellect or something
15 else which is thought to rule and guide us by its nature and to have comprehension of noble and divine objects, being itself divine or else the most divine part in us, its activity according to its proper virtue would be perfect happiness. That this activity is contemplative has already been mentioned;[67] and this would seem to be in agreement both with our previous remarks[68] and with the truth.

20 (1) This activity is the highest of all since the intellect (a) is the best of the parts in us and (b) is concerned with the best of the known objects.

(2) It is the most continuous of our activities; for (a) we are more able to be engaged continuously in theoretical activity than to perform any *action* continuously, and (b) we think that pleasure should be intermingled with happiness; and it is agreed that the most pleasant of our virtuous
25 activities is the one in accordance with wisdom. Indeed, philosophy is regarded as possessing pleasures which are wonderful in purity as well as in certainty, and it is reasonable for men who have understanding to pass their time more pleasantly than those who [merely] inquire.

(3) What goes by the name 'self-sufficiency', too, would apply to theoretical activity most of all; for although wise men and just men and all the
30 rest have need of the necessities of life, when they are all sufficiently provided with them, a just man needs others towards whom and with whom he will *act* justly, and similarly in the case of a temperate man, a brave man, and each of the others, while a wise man is able to theorize even if he were alone, and the wiser he is, the more he can do so by him-
1177b self. Perhaps it is better for him to have colleagues; but still, he is the most self-sufficient of all.

(4) This activity alone is thought to be loved for its own sake; for nothing results from it except contemplation itself, while from practical activities we gain for ourselves, either more or less, other things besides the *action* itself.

5 (5) Happiness is thought to depend on leisure; for we toil for the sake of leisurely activity, and we are at war for the sake of peaceful activity. Now the activities of the practical virtues are concerned with political or

military matters, and the *actions* concerning these matters are thought to be toilsome. Military *actions* are altogether toilsome; for no reasonable man chooses to wage a war for its own sake or to prepare for a war for its own sake; for if a man were to make enemies of his friends for the sake of fighting or killing, he would be regarded as utterly bloodthirsty. The activity of a man in politics, too, is toilsome and aims at something other than itself, namely, power or honor or, at any rate, at one's own or the citizens' happiness, which is different from the political [*action* itself] and is clearly sought as an activity which is different.

So if political and military *actions* among virtuous *actions* stand out in fineness and greatness and, being toilsome, are aimed at some other end but are not chosen for their own sake, whereas the activity of the intellect, being theoretical, is thought to be superior in seriousness and to aim at no other end besides itself but to have its own pleasure which increases that activity, then also self-sufficiency and leisure and freedom from weariness (as much as are possible for man) and all the other things which are attributed to a blessed man appear to exist in this activity. This, then, would be the perfect happiness for man, if extended to the full length of life, for none of the attributes of happiness is incomplete.

Such a life, of course, would be above that of a man, for a man will live in this manner not insofar as he is a man, but insofar as he has something divine in him; and the activity of this divine part of the soul is as much superior to that of the other kind of virtue as that divine part is superior to the composite soul of a man. So since the intellect is divine relative to a man, the life according to this intellect, too, will be divine relative to human life. Thus we should not follow the recommendation of thinkers who say that those who are men should think only of human things and that mortals should think only of mortal things, but we should try as far as possible to partake of immortality and to make every effort to live according to the best part of the soul in us; for even if this part be of small measure, it surpasses all the others by far in power and worth. It would seem, too, that each man is this part, if indeed this is the dominant part and is better than the other parts; so it would be strange if a man did not choose the life proper to himself but that proper to another. And what was stated earlier[69] is appropriate here also: that which is by nature proper to each thing is the best and most pleasant for that thing. So for a man, too, the life according to his intellect is the best and most pleasant, if indeed a man in the highest sense is his intellect. Hence this life, too, is the happiest.

8

The life according to the other kind of virtue is happy in a secondary
10   way, since the activities according to that virtue are concerned with human affairs; for it is according to the virtues which relate one man to another that we perform just and brave and other *actions* relating to contracts and needs and all other sorts, observing in each case what is fitting with regard to our passions. All these appear to be concerned with human affairs.
15   Some of them are thought to result even from the body, and the virtue of character is thought to be in many ways closely associated with the passions.

Prudence, too, is bound up with ethical virtue, and ethical virtue is bound up with prudence, if indeed the principles of prudence are in accordance with ethical virtues and the rightness of the ethical virtues is in accordance with prudence. Since these ethical virtues are connected with
20   the passions also, they would be concerned with the composite nature of man; and the virtues of that composite are concerned with human affairs. So the life and happiness in accordance with these virtues, too, would be human.

The virtue of the intellect, on the other hand, is separated [from the passions]; and let this much be said about this virtue, for detailed accuracy about it would take us beyond our present purpose. We might add, too, that this virtue would seem to require external resources only to a
25   small extent, or less than ethical virtue does; for if granting that both kinds of virtue require the necessities of life equally, even if a statesman's effort concerning the body and other such things is greater than that of the theoretical thinker (for there would be little difference here), still there will be much difference in what their activities require. For a gener-
30   ous man will need property for his generous *actions*, and so will a just man if he is to reciprocate for the services done to him (for wishes are not clearly seen, and even unjust men pretend that they wish to *act* justly); and a brave man will need power, if he is to perform an *action* according to virtue, while a temperate man will need the means, for how else can he manifest himself as being a temperate man rather than one of the others [i.e., stingy or wasteful]?

Disagreement arises as to whether the more important part of virtue   35
is intention or the corresponding *actions*, since virtue depends on both.
Clearly, perfection of virtue depends on both. As for *actions*, they require   1178b
many things, and more of these are required if the *actions* are greater and
nobler. A theoretical thinker, on the other hand, requires none of such
things, at least for his activity, and one might say that these even obstruct
theoretical activity; but insofar as he is a man and lives with many   5
others, he will choose to *act* according to [ethical] virtue, so he will need
such things to live as a man.

That perfect happiness is contemplative activity would be evident also
from the following. We regard the gods as being most blessed and happy;
but what kind of *actions* must we attribute to them? Are they just *actions*?   10
Will they not appear ridiculous if they are regarded as making contracts
and returning deposits and all other such things? Are they brave *actions*?
Are they to be regarded as facing dangers and risking their lives for something noble? Are they generous *actions*? But whom will they give gifts to?
It would be absurd, too, if they are regarded as using money or some   15
such thing. And what would their temperate *actions* be? Is it not vulgar
to praise them for not having had *desires*? If we were to go through all of
these ethical virtues, all praises or honors concerning the corresponding
actions would appear trivial and unworthy of the gods. Yet all believe
that the gods are living and in activity, for surely we cannot regard them
as being asleep like Endymion. So if *action*, and production even more   20
so, are omitted from their lives, is not contemplation the only activity
left?

The activity of a god, then, which surpasses all other activites in blessedness, would be contemplative. Consequently, of human activities, too,
that which is closest in kind to this would be the happiest. A sign of this is
the fact that none of the other animals share in happiness but are com-   25
pletely deprived of such activity; for while the entire life of the gods is
blessed, the life of men exists as a sort of likeness of such [blessed]
activity, but none of the other animals is happy since none of them shares
in contemplation. So while contemplation endures, happiness does so
also, and those who are more contemplative are more happy also, not   30
in virtue of some other attribute but in virtue of contemplation, for contemplation is by its nature honorable.   Happiness, then, would be a kind
of contemplation.

9

Being human, however, a man will need external resources also; for his
nature is not self-sufficient for contemplation but he needs a healthy body
and nourishment and other services. Still, we must not think that the man
who is to be happy will need many and great external goods if he cannot
be blessed without them; for self-sufficiency and *action* do not depend on
the excess of them, and one can do noble things even if he is not a ruler
of land and sea since he can *act* according to virtue even with moderate
means. This can be plainly seen from the fact that private citizens are
thought to do *good* deeds no less than those in power, but even more. So
it is enough if one has as much as that [i.e., moderate means], for the life
of a man whose activity proceeds according to virtue will be happy.

Perhaps Solon, too, expressed it well when he spoke of happy men as
being those who were moderately supplied with external means but who
have performed the noblest *actions* – so he thought – and have lived a
temperate life; for it is possible for one to *act* as he should with moderate
possessions. Anaxagoras, too, seems to have regarded the happy man to
be neither wealthy nor in a position of power, when he said that he would
not be surprised if a happy man appeared strange to most men, for they
judge a man by externals since these are the only things they perceive. The
opinions of the wise, then, seem to be in harmony with our arguments.
But while these opinions, too, carry some conviction, still the truth concerning practical matters is judged by what men do and how they live, for
it is these that carry authority. So we should examine the statements which
we have already made by referring them to the deeds and the lives of
men, and we should accept them as true if they harmonize with the facts
but should regard them merely as arguments if they clash with those facts.

Now he who proceeds in his activities according to his intellect and
cultivates his intellect seems to be best disposed and most dear to the gods;
for if the gods had any care for human matters, as they are thought to
have, it would be also reasonable that they should take joy in what is best
and most akin to themselves (this would be man's intellect) and should
reward those who love and honor this most, as if they cared for their
friends and were *acting* rightly and nobly. Clearly, all these attributes
belong to the wise man most of all; so it is he who would be most dear to
the gods, and it is also reasonable that he would be the most happy of

men. Thus if we view the matter in this manner, it is again the wise man
who would be the most happy of men.

10

If we have sufficiently discussed in a sketchy manner these matters and the
virtues, and also friendship and pleasure, should we think that we   35
achieved what we have intended to do, or, as the saying goes, is the end
in practical matters not speculation and knowledge but rather *action*?   1179b
With regard to virtue, to be sure, it is not enough to know what it is, but
we should try to acquire and use it or try to become good in some other
way. Now if arguments alone were enough to make us *good*, they would   5
with justice, according to Theognis, have brought us many and great rewards, and we should have obtained these. As a matter of fact, however,
while arguments appear to have an effect in exhorting and stimulating the
liberally-minded among young men and might cause the character of
those who come from high lineage and are truly lovers of what is noble
to be possessed of virtue, they cannot exhort ordinary men to do good   10
and noble deeds, for it is the nature of these men to obey not a sense of
shame but fear, and to abstain from what is bad not because this is disgraceful but because of the penalties which they would receive, since by
leading a life of passion such men pursue the corresponding pleasures and
the means to them but avoid the opposite pains, having no conception of   15
what is noble and truly pleasant as they have never tasted it. What argument, then, would reform these men? It is not possible or not easy to remove by argument the long-standing habits which are deeply rooted in
one's character. So when all the means through which we can become
good are available, perhaps we should be content if we were to get some
share of virtue.   20
   Some think that men become good by nature, others think that they do
so by habituation, still others, by teaching. Now it is clear that nature's
part is not in our power to do anything about but is present in those who
are truly fortunate through some divine cause. Perhaps argument and
teaching, too, cannot reach all men, but the soul of the listener, like the 25
earth which is to nourish the seed, should first be cultivated by habit to
enjoy or hate things properly; for he who lives according to passion would
neither listen to an argument which dissuades him nor understand it, and

if he is disposed in this manner, how can he be persuaded to change? In general, passion seems to yield not to argument but to force. So one's

30 character must be somehow predisposed towards virtue, liking what is noble and disliking what is disgraceful.

But it is difficult for one to be guided rightly towards virtue from an early age unless he is brought up under such [i.e., right] laws; for a life of temperance and endurance is not pleasant to most people, especially to

35 the young. For this reason the nurture and pursuits of the young should be regulated by laws, for when they become habitual they are not painful.

1180a Getting the right nurture and care while young, however, is perhaps not sufficient; but since young men should pursue and be habituated to these also when they have become adults, laws would be needed for these too, and, in general, laws would be needed for man's entire life, for most

5 people obey necessity rather than argument, and penalties rather than what is noble. In view of this, some think[70] that legislators (a) should urge men to pursue virtue and should exhort them to act for the sake of what is noble, expecting those who are well on their way in their habits of acting well to follow the advice, (b) should impose punishments and penalties on those who disobey and are of inferior nature, and (c) should

10 banish permanently those who are incurable[71]; for they think that a man who is *good* and lives with a view to what is noble will obey reason, while a bad man who desires [just bodily] pleasures should be punished by pain like a beast of burden. And for this reason they also say that the pains inflicted should be those which are most contrary to the pleasures these

15 men love. So if, as already stated,[72] the man who is to be good should be well nurtured and acquire the proper habits so that he may live in *good* pursuits and neither willingly nor unwillingly do what is bad, these [proper habits] would be attained by those who live according to intellect and an order which is right and has effective strength. Now paternal com-

20 mand possesses neither strength nor necessity, nor in general does that of a single man, unless he be a king or some such person; but the law has compelling power and is an expression issuing from a sort of prudence and intellect. And while we are hostile to those who oppose our impulses, even if these men are right, we do not feel oppressed by the law when it ordains us to do what is *good*. . .

Since our predecessors left the subject of lawgiving without scrutiny, perhaps it is better if we make a greater effort to examine it, and especially the subject concerning constitutions in general, so that we may complete 15 as best as we can the philosophy concerning human affairs. First, then, let us try to go over those parts which have been stated well by our predecessors, then from the constitutions we have collected let us investigate what kinds of things tend to preserve or destroy the states or each of the forms of government and why some states are well while others are badly 20 administered; for, after having investigated these matters, perhaps we would also be in a better position to perceive what form of government is best, how each form of government should be ordered, and what laws and customs each should use. So let us start to discuss these.

POLITICS

CONTENTS

BOOK I

POLITICS

BOOK I

1

We observe that every state is a sort of association, and that every association is formed for the sake of some good (for all men always *act* in order to attain what they think to be good). So it is clear that, while all associations aim at some good, the association which aims in the highest degree and at the supreme good is the one which is the most authoritative and includes all the others. Now this is called "a state," and it is a political association.

Those who think[1] that a statesman, a king, a ruler of a household, and a master of slaves are all the same do not speak well, for they hold that these [rulers] differ not in kind but with respect to the number of their subjects. Thus they regard a master as a ruler of few, a householder as a ruler of a somewhat greater number, and a statesman or a king as a ruler of a still greater number, as if there were no difference between a large household and a small state; and [they distinguish] a king from a statesman [only] in this, that the first is the sole authority of the state but the second rules and is ruled in turn according to the truths of political science.

Now these views are not true, and this will be clear if we examine what has just been said according to our usual method of inquiry. For, just as in every other discipline it is necessary to analyze a composite subject into its elements, which are the smallest parts of the whole, so by looking closely at the elements of a state, we will be better placed to observe how these elements differ from one another and, if possible, to grasp something about each of the above-mentioned arts [royal art, political art, etc.].

2

If one were to look at the growth of things from their beginning, one would also be, as in other disciplines, in the best position to speculate on these matters. First, there must be a union of those who cannot exist without each other, that is, a union of male and female for the sake of procreation (and the tendency in men, as in the other animals and in plants, to leave behind their own kind is natural and not the result of deliberate choice). Second, there must be a union of that which

1252a

5

10

15

20

25

30

by nature can rule and that which [by nature should be] ruled, for the sake of their preservation; for that which can foresee by *thought* is by nature a ruler or by nature a master, whereas that which [cannot foresee by *thought* but] can carry out the orders with the body is by nature a subject or a slave. In view of this, the master and the slave have the same interest [i.e., preservation].

1252*b*   Now there is a distinction by nature between the female and the slave. For nature is never niggardly like the smiths who make the Delphian knife: she makes a thing to serve only one thing, for an in-
5   strument can best accomplish its task by serving one and not many functions. Yet among the barbarians the female and the slave are placed in the same rank; and the *reason* for this is the fact that they do not have rulers by nature but their association consists of slaves, both male and female. It is in view of this that poets say,

"It is meet that Greeks should rule barbarians,"

implying that a barbarian and a slave are the same by nature. Out of
10   these two associations [male-female, master-slave] a household is formed first, and Hesiod was right when he said,

"First a house and a wife and an ox for the plough,"

for a poor man uses an ox instead of a house slave. An association formed by nature for the daily needs of life, then, is a household, and its members are called by Charondas   "companions of the hearth,"
15   and by Epimenides the Cretan "companions of the manger." But the first association formed from many households for other than daily needs   is the village, and the most natural form of a village seems to be a colony of a household, comprised of the children and grandchildren, those who are called by some "suckled with the same milk"; and it is in view of this that the first states were at first ruled by kings, (and nations are still so governed nowadays), for they were formed of per-
20   sons [already] governed by kings. For every household is ruled royally by the eldest, so the [early] colonies, too, were similarly ruled because of their kinship.   And this is Homer's meaning [concerning the Cyclopes] when he says,[2] "each of them rules over children and wife," for they lived in scattered groups, as in ancient times. And it is
25   because of this, too, that all men say that the Gods are ruled by kings, for men were ruled by kings in ancient days, and are still so ruled now; just as the forms of the Gods were thought to resemble those of men, so were the living habits of the Gods.
    Finally, a complete association composed of many villages is a state, an association which (a) has reached the limit of every self-sufficiency,
30   so to speak, (b) was formed for the sake of living, but (c) exists for the

sake of living well. For this reason, every state exists by nature, if indeed the first associations too existed by nature; for the latter associations have the state as their end, and nature is the end [of becoming]. For the kind of thing which a subject becomes at the end of a generation is said to be the nature of that subject, as in the case of a man or a horse or a house. Besides, the final cause or the end is the best, and the self-sufficiency [of an association] is the end and the best.

1253*a*

From the above remarks, then, it is evident that a state exists by nature and that man is by nature a political animal; but [he] who exists outside a state because of [his] nature and not by luck is either [bad] or superior to man: [he] is like the man denounced by Homer[3] as being "tribeless, lawless, hearthless." In addition, such a [man] by [his] nature *desires* war inasmuch as [he] is solitary, like an isolated piece in a game of draughts. It is clear, then, why man is more of a political animal   than a bee or any other gregarious animal; for nature, as we say, does nothing in vain, and man alone of all animals has the power of reason.[4]

5

10

Voice, of course, serves as a sign of the painful and the pleasurable, and for this reason it belongs to other animals also; for the nature of these advances only up to the point of sensing the painful and the pleasurable and of communicating these to one another. But speech serves to make known what is beneficial or harmful, and so what is just or unjust;   for what is proper to man compared to the other animals is this: he alone has the sense of what is good or evil, just or unjust, and the like, and it is an association of beings with this sense which makes possible a household and a state.   Further, a state is prior by nature to a household or each man, since the whole is of necessity prior to each of its parts.   For if the whole [man] ceases to exist, his foot or hand will exist only equivocally, and such a hand will then be like a hand made of stone. Indeed every part, such as [a hand or a foot], is defined by its function or power, so if the [power and the function] are lacking, one should not say that what remains is the same as a hand unless one uses the term "hand" equivocally.

15

20

25

It is clear, then, that a state exists by nature and is prior to each [of its parts]; for if each man is not self-sufficient when existing apart from a state, he will be like a part when separated from the whole; and one who cannot associate with others or does not need association with others because of self-sufficiency is no part of a state but is either a brute or a God.

Now there is a natural tendency in all men to form such an association [i.e., a state], and he who was the first to do so was the cause of the greatest good; for just as man when perfected is the best of all animals, so he is the worst of all when separated from law and judgement. For the most cruel injustice is the one which has weapons to carry it out;

30

and a man, born with weapons [e.g., speech, hands, ability to reason,
35 etc.] to be used with prudence and virtue, can misuse these [weapons
through folly and vice] for contrary ends most of all. For this reason, a
man without virtue can be the most unholy, the most savage, and the
worst [of animals] for lust and gluttony. Justice, on the other hand, is
political [i.e., belongs to the state]; for judgment about matters requiring justice, that is, the discernment of what is just, is the principle of
ordering in a political association.

3

1253b   Since it is evident of what parts a state is composed, we must discuss
household management first, for every state is made up of households. The parts of a household are those of which a household is in
turn composed, and a complete household is composed of freemen
5   and slaves; and since our inquiry should begin with the smallest parts,
which are master and slave, husband and wife, and parent and children, we should consider what each of these three [associations] is and
what kind of thing it should be; the three are: the master-slave associ-
10 ation, the marital association (the union of *man* and woman has no
name), and thirdly the parent-child association (for this association,
too, has no special name). So let these three be the associations of a
household. There is another part which is thought by some to be
household management, and by others to be the main part of that
management. I am speaking of the so-called "art of finance". What the
truth of the matter is needs examination.
15   Let our discussion begin with a master and a slave, so we may get a
view of those things which contribute to the indispensable needs and
might also learn something which is better than what is nowadays accepted in understanding matters concerning a master and a slave. For
some are of the opinion that the rule of a master is a science and that,
as we stated at the outset,[5] it is the same [in kind] as the rule of a house-
20 hold or of a state, whether political or royal. Others, however, are of
the opinion that the rule of a master is contrary to nature; for [they
think that] it is by law that the one is a freeman and the other is a slave
but that by nature they do not differ, and that, in view of this, it is not
just to be a slave since one is forced to be so.

4

Now, then, possessions are a part of a household, and the art of acquisition is a part of [the art of] household management (for without
25 the necessities of life it is impossible to live or live well); just as in arts
with a definite end the appropriate instruments must exist if the corresponding function is to be achieved, so it is in the case of the art of
managing a household. Now of instruments some are inanimate and

others are animate. To the pilot, for example, the rudder is inanimate
but the lookout man is animate; for a servant is a kind of an instrument   30
in the arts. So, too, a possession is an instrument for living, and possessions [in general] are a multitude of instruments; and a slave is an animate possession, and every servant is like an instrument in charge of
other instruments. For if every instrument could perform its function,
whether by obeying another or by anticipating what to do, like the   35
[statues] of Daedalus in the story, or the tripods of Hephaestus, which,
as the poet says,[6]

"enter of their own accord the divine assembly,"

and likewise if every shuttle could by itself weave and every plectrum
by itself strike the lyre, a master-artist would need no servants and a   1254a
master would need no slaves. Now the instruments of which we are
speaking exist to produce something, but a possession exists just to be
used; for a shuttle is used to produce something else whereas a garment or a bed is just used. Further, since production differs in kind   5
from *action* and since both need instruments, instruments too must
possess a corresponding difference. But [man's] living [as an end in it-
self] is an *action* and not a production; hence a slave , too, is a servant
who attends to things to be *acted* upon [i.e., to be just used as ends by
the master].

Now we speak of a thing possessed as we speak of a part; but a part is
not only a part of another thing [i.e., of a whole] but also belongs whol-   10
ly to that thing, and so does a thing possessed. In view of this, whereas a master is a master of a slave and does not belong to a slave, a slave
is not only a slave to a master but also belongs wholly to a master.

From the above discussion the nature and capacity of a slave are
now clear: a slave by nature is an individual who, being a man, is by his   15
nature not his own but belongs [wholly] to another [man]; and a man
is said to belong to another if, being a man, he is a thing possessed; and
as a possession he is an instrument which, existing separately, can be
used [by the master] for *action*.

5

Next, we should consider whether there exists by nature such a man
or not, and whether it is better and just for some to serve others or
rather that all slavery is contrary to nature.

It is not difficult to speculate on this problem by using reason and   20
also base our perception on the facts themselves. To rule and to be
ruled are not only necessary, but also beneficial. For immediately
after birth some are marked out to be ruled but others to rule. But
there are many kinds of rulers and subjects; and the rule over better   25

subjects is always better, e.g., over men than over brutes, for what is accomplished with better [subjects] is better. Now wherever there is that which rules and that which is ruled, some function is performed by them; for, whenever something common is performed by a thing
30 with parts, whether these be continuous or discrete, there appears to be in that thing that which rules and that which is ruled. And this fact, which arises in every case in the nature of things, exists in animate beings; in fact, even in inanimate beings there is a [ruling] principle, as, for example, in harmony. But perhaps the discussion of these matters lies rather outside our subject.
35   Anyway, an animal consists first of soul and body, of which the soul by nature rules but the body [by nature] is ruled; and we should observe what exists by nature not among animals which are defective but among those which act according to their nature. This fact will be clear if, as a consequence, we examine the man who is best disposed with respect to both his body and his soul; for one would think that
1254b among men who are vicious or disposed to vice it is the body that often rules the soul because such men are badly disposed and *act* contrary to nature.
    It is possible, then, in the manner we are speaking, to start by speculating on the despotic and the political rule in animals, for the rule of
5 the soul over the body is despotic, whereas the rule of the intellect over desire is political or royal; and it is evident from these examples that the rule over the body by the soul is according to nature and is beneficial, and so is the rule over the passionate [i.e., the *desiring*] part of the soul by the intellect and by the part which has reason, but that the rule by both parts alike or by the inferior part is harmful to all.
10 Again, similar remarks hold true among men and the other animals; for tame animals have a better nature than wild animals, and among tame animals the rule by men is better for their safety. Further, of the sexes, the male is by nature superior to the female, and [it is better for] the male to rule and the female to be ruled.
15   Among men as a whole, too, the same must be the case. Those differing from others as much as the body does from the soul or brutes do from men (they are so disposed that their best function is the use of
20 their bodies) are by their nature slaves, and it is better for them to be ruled despotically, as indeed it is for the inferiors in the cases already mentioned. For a slave by nature is a man who can belong to another (and for this reason he does belong to another) and who can participate in reason to the extent of apprehending it but not possessing it; for the animals other than men cannot apprehend reason but serve their passions. The use made of slaves, too, departs but little from that
25 made of other animals; for both slaves and tame animals contribute to the necessities of life with the aid of their bodies. Nature, too, tends

to make the bodies of freemen and of slaves different, making those of slaves strong for the necessities of life but those of freemen upright and useless for such services but useful for political life, whether for 30 war or peace. But often the contrary, too, happens, for some [slaves] have the bodies of freemen but some [freemen] have the souls [of slaves].   Anyway, it is evident that if men were made to differ in their 35 bodily forms alone as much as the bodily forms of Gods which are portraited by men, everyone would say that those who fall short in bodily form deserve to serve the others. So if this distinction is true with respect to the bodies of men, it would apply to the soul even more justly. But, of course, it is not so easy to perceive the beauty of the soul as it is to perceive the beauty of the body.

It is evident, then, that it is by nature that some men are slaves but 1255a others are freemen, and that it is just and to the benefit of the former to serve the latter.

6

It is not difficult to see that those who take the contrary views, too, are in a sense right; for each of the terms "slavery" and "slave" has two senses. [Besides a slave by nature], there is also a slave by law 5 who serves a master, for the law [in this case] is a certain agreement by which those who are conquered belong to the conquerors. It is indeed this sort of 'just *action*' which many jurists denounce, as they would a public speaker who brings forward an illegal measure, for they think that it is dreadful for a man who is stronger than another to 10 force the latter to become a slave or a subject. Now even among wise thinkers, some take this position, others the contrary.

The cause of this dispute and overlapping of opinions is the fact that, in some sense, virtue, when furnished with means, is also most capable of using force, and the one who is stronger always excels in 15 some good; and so it is thought that force cannot exist without virtue, but that the dispute is whether [slavery] is just [or not]. It is for this *reason* that some thinkers regard justice to be good will towards men, but others regard it to be the ability of the stronger to rule, for if these two views are separated from their common ground, then, in ei- 20 ther case [i.e., in the sense in which they do not overlap], these arguments would be neither cogent nor persuasive against the view that one who excels in virtue should rule or have slaves.

Some thinkers, however, adhering completely to something which they regard as just (for law is something which is just), hold that the slavery resulting from war is just; but at the same time they deny this. For a war may start unjustly [by a bad ruler, or for a bad purpose], and 25 no one would say that he who does not deserve to be a slave should be a slave; otherwise, those who come from the most noble families but

happen to be taken prisoners and sold into slavery should be regarded
as slaves or descendants of slaves. For this reason, what they really
mean to say is that the barbarians and not the Greeks should be called
30   "slaves." Yet, whenever they say this, they do nothing more than inquire who is a slave by nature, something we spoke of at the outset,[7]
for they must admit that some men are slaves wherever they are but
others are nowhere slaves.   The same must be said about noble birth;
for Greeks of noble birth are regarded as such not only in Greece but
35   everywhere, whereas barbarians are so regarded only in their own
country, and this implies that men who are of noble birth and free are
of two kinds, those without qualification and those who are qualifiedly
so, as Theodectes's *Helen* says:

"But who would dare to call me servant
When sprung from twofold stock divine?"

40   And whenever they say this, it is by virtue and vice that they distinguish a freeman and a slave, respectively, a man of noble birth and one
1255*b*   of low birth. For they claim that just as a man springs from a man and a
brute from a brute, so a good man springs from good parents. Now nature tends to bring this about, but frequently it cannot do so.
5   It is clear, then, that there is some reason for the dispute that slaves
or freemen [by custom] are not [necessarily] slaves or freemen by nature, respectively, that such distinction [i.e., between a slave by nature and a freeman by nature] exists, and that it is expedient and just
for such a slave to be ruled and for a master to exercise the kind of rule
which befits his nature, i.e., that of a master. To rule badly, on the
10   other hand, is harmful to both [master and slave by nature]; for what is
beneficial to a part is beneficial to the whole also, whether this be the
body or the soul or both, and a slave is a certain part of a master, so to
speak, an animate but separate part of the body [of the master]. For
this reason, the relation between master and slave, whenever they deserve by their nature to be called such, should be one of friendship
15   and of benefit to both;   but if their relation is not such but exists by
law or is forced, it leads to contrary results.

7

It is also evident from what has been said that the rule of a master
and the political rule are not the same, nor are all rules the same, as
some assert. For one kind of rule is that over freemen by nature, another is over slaves [by nature]; and the rule of a household is monar-
20   chical (for every house is ruled by one man), whereas the political rule
is over freemen and equals. A man is [truly] called "a master," then,
not by virtue of having scientific knowledge but by virtue of being a
man of a certain kind; and similarly if a man is [truly called] "a slave" or

"a freeman." There might, of course, be a science for a master and a science for a slave, the latter science being such as the one which a man was teaching in Syracuse; for the teacher there was paid to teach   25
boys the menial duties of a household. There might be instruction in additional tasks also, such as cooking and other such kinds of menial services. There are other such tasks, some of them somewhat honorable, others tending to mere necessities; as the proverb says,

"A slave over a slave, a master over a master."

Now all such sciences are servile; but the science of a master is con-   30
cerned with the use of slaves, for a master is concerned, not with acquiring slaves, but with the use of slaves. This science, however, is neither of great importance nor dignified; for a master should only *know* how to order the tasks which the slave should learn how to per-   35
form. For this reason, those who can afford not to be troubled with such tasks assign them to a steward to perform, while they themselves attend to political matters or to philosophy. As for the science of acquiring [slaves] justly, whether by war or by hunting, it differs from the [science of using slaves and the science of a steward].
    Let so much be said concerning the distinctions between a master   40
and a slave.

8

    Let us now investigate in general in the usual manner all kinds of   1256*a*
possessions and the art of finance, since a slave as such, too, was seen to be a part of one's possessions.
    First, one might pose the problem of whether the art of finance is the same as the art of household management, or a part of it, or subser-   5
vient to it, and if subservient to it, whether in the manner in which the art of making shuttles is to the art of weaving or in the manner in which the art of making bronze is to the art of making statues; for the art of making shuttles and that of making bronze are not subservient in the same way, but the former furnishes the tools whereas the other furnishes the matter. By "matter" I mean the underlying subject out of which a piece of work is made; e.g., for the weaver, wool is matter for cloth, for the statue-maker, bronze is matter for a statue.   10
    Now it is clear that the art of household management is not the same as the art of finance; for the function of the latter is to provide the matter, whereas the function of the former is to use the matter. For what other art will there be to use materials for a household if not the art of household management?
    There is a dispute, however, whether [the art of finance] is a part of [the art of household management] or an art of a different kind. For if   15
the function of the artist of finance is to investigate the sources from

which money and possessions are to be procured, but there are many
kinds of possessions or wealth, then, first, will the art of farming and,
in general, the arts of acquiring and of caring for food be parts of the
art of finance or different kinds of arts? Moreover, there are many
20 kinds of food, and so many ways in which animals or men live; for living without food is impossible, and the differences in food have produced different ways of living among animals. For some brutes are
gregarious, but others live apart from each other, depending on how
25 conveniently they get their food, because some are carnivorous, others are herbivorous, and still others are both; and so nature has distinguished their ways of life by their choice of food and the ease of acquiring it. And since it is not the same food that is pleasurable by its
nature to all but different kinds of food are pleasurable to different
brutes, among carnivorous or herbivorous brutes, too, the ways of living differ from each other.
30   The same applies to men also, for their ways of living differ. The
most inactive are shepherds, for those who lead an idle life get their
food from tame animals without effort; and since their herds must
wander from place to place in search of pasture, they too are com-
35 pelled to follow them, as if cultivating a living farm. Others get their
food by hunting, and in various ways: some from piracy, others from
fishing, i.e., those who live near lakes or marshes or rivers or the sea,
still others by hunting birds or wild animals. But most men live from
40 the land and by cultivating crops. So many, then, are roughly the ways
in which men live, at least those who produce their food themselves
1256b and do not obtain it by barter or by retail trade; they are the lives of
nomads, farmers, pirates, fishermen, and hunters. Some men live
pleasantly by combining these ways also, adding to their somewhat in-
5 adequate livelihoods that which is needed for self-sufficiency. For example, some nomads are also pirates, some farmers are also hunters,
others lead a life in a way similar to these, depending on what their
needs compel them to do.
    Possessions such as the above appear to be supplied to all [animals]
by nature herself; and just as this occurs immediately after they are
born, so it does when they have been perfected [i.e., reached
10 maturity]. For, even immediately after birth, some animals bring
forth their offspring together with enough food to last until these are
able to provide for themselves, as in the case of those animals which
produce larvae or eggs; and viviparous animals have in themselves
enough of the natural food called "milk" to feed their offspring for a
15 certain period. So clearly and in a similar way one should also suppose
that, among [living] things which have been generated, plants are for
the sake of animals, and animals [except men] are for the sake of men,
tame animals for use and for food, and wild animals, at least most if

not all, for food and for comfort, such as clothing and other instru-   20
ments. Accordingly, since nature makes nothing imperfect or in vain,
she must have made all other things for the sake of men. For this reason, the art of war, too, would be by nature an art of acquisition in
some sense. For the art [of acquisition] includes the art of hunting,
which should be used against brutes and those men who, born by na-   25
ture to be ruled, refuse to do so, inasmuch as this kind of war is by nature just.

   According to nature, then, one species of the art of acquisition is a
part of the art of household management; and this [part] should either
exist or be secured [by the household manager]. It is concerned with
the accumulation of goods which are necessary for and useful to life
and contribute to the political association or to the household. And   30
indeed true wealth seems to consist of things such as these; for self-
sufficiency of such possessions for a good life is not infinite, notwith-
standing Solon's remark,

"No bounds to wealth appears to be fixed for man";

but bounds here do exist, as they do also in the other arts. For no in-   35
strument of any art is infinite, whether in number or in magnitude,
and wealth is but a [finite] number of instruments for political and
household rulers.

   It is clear, then, that there exists according to nature an art of acquisition for household and political rulers, and it is also clear what the
reason for this is.

       9

   There is another genus of the art of acquisition which is by most   40
men called "the art of finance," and justly so, and for this *reason* it is
thought that there is no limit to wealth or possessions; and many men   1257a
regard this art to be one and the same as the art of acquisition just discussed because of its closeness to it. However, it is neither the same
nor far removed from it. The art of acquisition we spoke of before is
natural, whereas the art of finance is not natural but is acquired rather
by experience and art. Let us consider this art from the following   5
starting-point.

   Each possession may be used in two ways, both of which belong to
the thing itself but not in a similar way; for one of them is but the other
is not appropriate to the thing's [nature]. For example, a shoe may be
worn or it may be exchanged for something else, and both of these are   10
uses of the shoe; for even he who exchanges the shoe for currency or
food with a man who needs it uses the shoe as a shoe, but this is not the
appropriate use of the shoe, for the shoe was not [originally] made for

the sake of exchange. The same may be said of the other possessions,
15 for the art of exchange extends to all of them; and it first began from
what was done according to nature, when some men had more of what
they needed but others had less. From this fact it is clear that the art of
retail trade does not by nature belong to the art of finance; for barter
[at first] was necessary only to the extent that needs were satisfied.
20   Now it is evident that within the association at its first stage (I mean
the household) retail trade had no function at all; but it arose within a
higher association [i.e., the village], which has many parts. For, in the
former association, the members had all [possessions] in common; but
in the latter [i.e., the village], in which there were many separate
members [i.e., households], these had to get things which they needed by an exchange of different articles, a form of barter which is still
25 used among barbarian nations. For what is bartered by both parties
here is what is needed for use only and nothing more, e.g., wine for
corn, and the like. Now such an art of exchange is neither contrary to
30 nature nor a species of the art of finance, for it supplies what is needed
for natural self-sufficiency. But it is from such exchange that the
other [i.e., financial] exchange arose, and with good reason. For as the
distances from which needed articles had to be imported and to which
surplus had to be sent for exchange became greater, the introduction
of a medium of exchange (or coin) became necessary; for not all the
35 necessities of life are easily portable. Accordingly, for purposes of exchange, men introduced in their dealings with each other such a thing
which, being itself useful, was easy to handle for the purposes of life,
for example, iron or silver or some other thing of this sort. At first, the
medium of exchange (or coin) was specified by its size or weight; fi-
40 nally, a stamp was impressed upon it to save the trouble of weighing,
for the stamp indicated the quantitative value of the coin.
1257b   When the use of currency was well established as a result of barter
for the necesssities of life, the other kind of financial art came into existence, that of retail trade, proceeding at first perhaps in a simple
manner, but later becoming through experience more skillful by
knowing the sources and the manner of exchange which would yield
5   the greatest profit. For this reason, it is thought that the art of finance
is concerned with currency most of all and that its function is to be
able to discover the sources which will yield a great deal of money; for
this art is capable of producing money or wealth. Indeed, men often
regard wealth as being a quantity of currency, because the art of fi-
10 nance and that of retail trade are concerned with currency. Others,
again, are of the opinion that currency exists not by nature but is entirely a sham and a convention; for, when one currency is replaced by
another [as legal tender by the users of it], the first is worthless and of
no use to the necessities of life, and he who is rich in currency is often

in need of necessary food. But it is indeed absurd that a man, well sup- 15
plied with such 'wealth,' should perish with hunger, like Midas in the
fable whose insatiable prayer was that everything before him should
become gold.

It is for this reason that men inquire into the difference between
[the art of] wealth and the art of finance, and rightly so; for the art of finance is distinct from [the art of acquiring] natural wealth, and the lat- 20
ter comes under the art of household management whereas the art of
retail trade produces money, not in every way, but by exchange which
uses money. It is thought, too, that the art of retail trade is concerned
with currency, for coins are the elements of exchange and are the ultimate aim; and indeed, the acquisition of such wealth by this art of finance has no limit. For just as the medical art has no limit in producing 25
health and each of the other arts has no limit in achieving its end (for
each art wishes to achieve its end to the utmost degree), whereas the
means to an [actual] end are not unlimited (for the end of each [work
of art] has a limit), so there is no limit to the end of this art of finance,
for the end of this art is [limitless] wealth or a [limitless] acquisition of 30
money.

Now the art of household management, unlike the above art of finance, has a limit; for the function of the art of household management is not that of making money. For this reason, it appears that
there must be a limit to wealth in every case, but as a matter of fact we
observe that the opposite takes place; for all those who deal only with
currency keep on increasing it without limit. The cause of this is the 35
closeness [of the two arts of finance to each other]: the same thing [i.e.,
money] is used by the two arts [of finance] but for different ends; for
acquisition of money for use is made [by both arts], but not with respect to the same [end], since the end of [one of the arts of finance] is
the increase of it, whereas the end of [the art of finance   under the art
of household management] is something else. So some men are of the
opinion that the function of the art of household management is the
[increase of money], and they spend their time with the thought that
property in the form of money should be either preserved or in- 40
creased without limit. The cause of this disposition in men is that they
are zealous for [mere] living but not for living well; so since their *desires* for [mere] living are unlimited, their *desires* to produce the 1258a
means for such living, too, are unlimited. And some of those who are
eager to live well, too, seek the means to enjoy bodily pleasures. So
since [such enjoyment] appears to depend on the acquisition of pos- 5
sessions, too, they spend all their time making money; and it is because of this that the other art of finance came into being. For since
their *desire* for [bodily] enjoyments is excessive, they seek that which
can bring about such excessive enjoyments; and if they cannot acquire

those means by the art of finance, they try to do so in some other way
10   by using every possible means which is contrary to nature.   For instance, the function of bravery is to produce not money but courage,
and that of strategy or of the medical art is to bring victory or produce
health, respectively, but not money. These men, on the other hand,
regard all these arts as arts of making money, as if their end were
money, and they think that all else should be directed to that end.
15   We have discussed, then, the art of finance whose aim is not the necessities of life, both what it is and why it is used.   We have also discussed the other art [of finance] which, unlike the one which has no
limit, differs from it by having a limit, is according to its nature a part
of the art of household management, and deals with the provision of
food.

10

The solution to the problem raised at the start,[8] too, is now clear,
20   namely, whether the art of finance belongs to the manager of a household and to the statesman or not, but [possessions] should be presupposed as already existing. Now just as the political art does not make
men but takes them from nature and uses them, so nature provides
food and other things from the earth or the sea or the like; and it be-
25   longs to the household manager to dispose of these things as is proper.
For, the function of the art of weaving, to use an example, is not to
make wool but to use it and know what kind of wool is good and suitable or bad and unsuitable.
Yet one may inquire why it is that the art of finance is a part of
30   household management, but that the medical art is not a part, although the members of a household should have health just as they
should have life or something else which is indispensable. But since in
one sense it is the household manager or the ruler who should attend
to health, but in another it is not he but the doctor, so in one sense it is
the manager of a household who should attend to financial matters,
but in another sense it is not he but one who practices a subordinate
art; but most of all, as stated before, [the indispensable means]
35   should be by nature available. For it is the work of nature to furnish
food to that which is born, since every offspring has for food the residue of that from which it comes.
In view of the above, it is according to nature that the art of finance
which is concerned with crops and with animals belongs to men. As
40   we said, this art is of two kinds, the one about retail trade, and the
other about certain matters of household management. Of these, the
latter kind is concerned with what is necessary [for life] and is praised,
1258b   but the one dealing with [mere] exchange is justly blamed (for men
make gain not according to nature but from each other). Therefore it

is most reasonable for men to hate usury because acquisition is made from money itself and not by the use of money for the reason intended. For money was introduced for the sake of exchange [only], but the interest received increases its quantity, as the name τόκος (= "interest," also "offspring") suggests; for the offspring resembles its parent, and interest is money born of money and is therefore money acquired in the most unnatural way.

11

Having discussed adequately the things which are related to knowledge, let us now go over the things which are related to use. All such things [i.e., those discussed] may be freely treated from the theoretical point of view, but experience in them is necessary.

The useful parts of the art of finance are concerned with: (1) experience in possessions—what kinds are most profitable, where, and how—for example, possessions of horses or oxen or sheep, and similarly of other animals; for, by comparing them with each other, a man should be experienced in those possessions which are most profitable and in the localities where they are most profitable, for different breeds thrive in different places. Concerning agriculture, one should be experienced in arable land and orchards and also in the care of bees and fish and fowl, which may be of assistance. These, then, are the primary parts of the art of finance in its most appropriate form.

As for (2) the part [of the art of finance] which deals with exchange, the most important branch is concerned with (a) commerce, whose three branches are: transportation by sea, transportation by land, and direct marketing; and these differ from each other with respect to safety and profitability. The second branch is concerned with (b) the practice of usury, and the third with (c) wage earners, whether craftsmen or unskilled bodily labor.

There is (3) a third part of the art of finance which lies between the first and second, for a certain part of it is natural and a certain part is like exchange, [and it is an art dealing with] such things which come from the earth and what is produced from them; and these objects, although bearing no fruit, are useful. This part includes such arts as that of the cutting of timber and that of mining of every sort; for mining has many branches, since many kinds of metals are dug out of the earth.

We have given a general account of the parts [of the art of finance] at present, but a detailed and accurate description of each part, although useful in practice, is inappropriate and a waste of time here. The occupations which require art in the highest degree are those in which luck is least involved, the meanest occupations are those in which the body is abused the most, the most servile are those which use the body most, and those are most degrading which need virtue least.

40   There are works on these subjects by some writers. Chares the
1259a Parian and Apollodorus of Lemnos have written works on the two
forms of agriculture, arable land and orchards, and others have written similarly on other subjects. Those who are interested may study
these works. In addition, one should make a collection of scattered
5   stories of the methods which some individuals have used and happened to make a fortune, for all these are of benefit to those who value
the art of finance. For example, there is the story about the device
which Thales of Miletus used to make money. This device is attributed
to him because of his wisdom, but it happens to have universal
10 application. He was reproached for his poverty, which indicated that
philosophy was of no benefit to man. But, the story goes, from his
knowledge of astronomy he perceived, while it was still winter, the
coming of a great harvest of olives in the coming season, and, having
procured a small sum of money, he made a deposit for the use of all the
olive presses of Miletus and Chios, which he rented at a low price
15 since no one bid against him. When the harvest time came and there
was a sudden and simultaneous demand for the use of the presses, he
let these at whatever price he wished and made a fortune, thus pointing out that philosophers can easily become wealthy if they wish but
that wealth is not their main pursuit in life.
    This is the manner in which Thales is said to have given a display of
20 his wisdom, but, as we said, such device for making money has universal application and can be used by anyone who can create a monopoly.
It is in view of this fact that some states make use of this device whenever they are in need of money, for they set up a monopoly of provi-
sions.
    There was a man in Sicily who, with a sum of money deposited with
25 him, bought up all the iron from the iron shops; and, when merchants
from various markets came to buy, he was the only one who was selling iron. And, without much increase of the usual price, he still made
100 talents beyond the fifty he had invested. When King Dionysius
30 learned of this, he ordered the man to take his earnings and get out of
Syracuse, for he regarded this man's discovery of making money as
being against his own interests. This man's insight, of course, is the
same as that of Thales; for both used the art of creating a monopoly for
themselves. Statesmen, too, should know how to make use of these
devices. In fact, many states, like households, are in need of financial
35 resources and the means of acquiring them, and even more so; and it is
in view of this [need] that many men in public life devote all their time
to financial matters.

12

As already stated, the art of household management has three parts: (a) that of the rule of a master over slaves, already discussed, (b) that of the rule of a father over children, and (c) that of the rule of a husband over his wife. The ruler of a household, as a husband and a father, rules both his wife and his children, who are free, but he does 40 this not in the same manner; he rules politically over his wife but royally over his children. For the male is by nature more able to lead than the female, except in some cases where there is a departure from nature, and so is the elder and mature man compared to the younger and immature. But in most political states the citizens rule and are ruled 5 in turns, for it is the nature of such a state to aim at equality of its members and show no difference. On the other hand, whenever one citizen rules and another is ruled, we expect a difference in outward form and manner of address and honors, as illustrated by a speech of Amasis about his foot-pan.[9] The rule of the male over the female is of this 10 kind, and it is permanent; but his rule over children is royal; for a father rules [his children] by virtue of his affection and by right of his seniority, and this is indeed a form of royal rule. It is in view of this that Homer, in using the expression "father of both *men* and Gods," spoke well of Zeus, who is the king of them all. For a king, although of 15 the same race as his subjects, should be by nature superior to them; and such indeed is the relation of the elder to the younger and of a father to his child.

13

Concerning household management, then, it is evident that more attention should be paid to men than to inanimate possessions, more to the virtue of men than to the virtue of possessions, which we call 20 "wealth," and more to the virtue of freemen than to the virtue of slaves.

First, then, one might pose the problem of whether a slave can have a virtue which is more honorable than the instrumental virtues and those of menial tasks; e.g., whether he can have temperance or bravery or justice or any other such disposition, or whether he can have no 25 virtues other than those of bodily services. Difficulties arise regardless of the answer. For if he can have those other virtues, in what way will he differ from a freeman; and if he cannot have those virtues, will it not be absurd to say that there are men who do not share in reason? Almost the same problem may be posed about a wife and a child: whether these too can have those virtues, that is, whether or not a 30 wife should be temperate or brave or just, and whether or not a child can be intemperate or temperate. And, in general, one may inquire about a ruler by nature and a subject by nature, whether their virtues are the same or different. For if both of them should partake of what is noble and good, why should one always rule and the other always be 35

ruled? Nor can [one argue that] they differ in degree; for a ruler and a
subject differ in kind, and this difference is not one of degree at all.
Yet it is strange that one of them should have certain virtues but the
40   other should not have them. For if a ruler is not temperate or just, how
will he rule well, and if a subject is not temperate or just, how can he
1260a   be ruled well? If indeed [either of them] is intemperate or cowardly,
[he] will fail to do his duty.

Now it is evident that, although both a ruler and a subject must partake of virtue, the virtue of the subject must differ from that of the
ruler, just as subjects by nature differ in kind. This is immediately sug-
5   gested by the make-up of the soul, for in it there is by nature a part
which rules (i.e., that which has reason) and a part which is ruled (i.e.,
that which has no reason [but is irrational, i.e., the appetitive part of
the soul]) but the virtues of these two parts are distinct. Clearly, then,
a similar distinction exists in the other cases also, and so there are by
nature many [kinds of] things which rule and of things which are
10   ruled. Thus a freeman rules a slave in one way, the male rules the female in another, and a [mature] *man* rules a child in a third way; the
corresponding parts of the soul exist in all three cases, but in different
ways. The slave does not have the deliberative part of the soul at all;
the woman has it, but it has no authority; and the child has it, but it is
not fully developed. Accordingly, the corresponding ethical virtues
15   must be understood in a similar manner. So we should regard all as
partaking of virtue, not in the same way, but as much as is required by
each to perform his function.   In view of this, a ruler should have
complete ethical virtue (for his function is without qualification that
of a master-artist, and the ruling art is [true] reason), but each of the
others should have as much of virtue as is required to perform his
function.
20   It is thus evident that each of the above-mentioned can have ethical
virtue, and that temperance or bravery or justice is not, as *Socrates*
thought,[10] the same in a *man* as it is in a woman, but that there is a ruling
bravery and a serving bravery.   A similar distinction exists also in the
other virtues.   This becomes even clearer to those who examine the
25   matter in specific cases, for those who use general statements by saying that virtue is a right disposition of the soul or a right *action* or
something of this sort deceive themselves; for instead of using such
definitions, it is far better to enumerate the various virtues, as Gorgias
does.[11] In view of this, one should view each case as the poet did who,
30   speaking of a woman, said,

"Silence brings credit to a woman,"

for this does not apply to a *man*. And since a child is immature, it is
clear that his virtue, too, should be referred not to the child itself but

to [the virtue of] his guide, who is mature; and the same applies to the virtue of a slave in relation to his master.

We have laid down that a slave is useful for the necessities of life; so it is clear that he requires but little virtue, as much as is needed to prevent him from failing to perform his work because of intemperance or cowardice. If what we are saying is true, one might pose the problem whether artisans, too, require virtue; for they often fail to perform their work because they are intemperate. But is there not a great difference between an artisan and a slave? For the slave shares in [the master's] life; but the artisan is more distant, and the extent of his virtue depends on the extent to which he serves another. A craftsman has a definite service to perform; but some men are slaves by nature, whereas it is not by nature that a man becomes a shoemaker or any other craftsman. So it is evident that the cause of the slave's [ethical] virtue should be the master [as a master], but the cause of an artisan's skill is not the knowledge of the master qua master.[12] For this reason, those who say that a master should only give orders to slaves and not converse with them do not speak well, for slaves need admonition more than children. Let the discussion of these topics suffice here.

Concerning the virtue of a *man* and a woman and children and parents and their relation to each other, what is proper and what is improper and how each should pursue what is good and avoid what is evil, these matters must be treated later when we discuss the forms of government.[13] For since these associations are parts of a household and every household is a part of a state, and since the virtue of a part should be viewed in relation to the virtue of the whole, the education of children and women must be viewed as related to the virtue of the government of a state if indeed the virtue of children and of women makes a difference in the virtue of the state. Now it must make a difference; for half of the free persons in a state are women, and children eventually grow and participate in the government of a state. So since the above relations have been distinguished but what remains should be taken up later, let us consider the present discussion as ended and, making another start, examine first the received views concerning the best form of government.

BOOK III

1

In examining what each form of government is and what kind of a thing it is, perhaps one should first attend to a state and ask, "What is a

35

40

1260*b*

5

10

15

20

1274*b*

35 state?"; for nowadays disputes arise. Some say that it is the state that brought about a certain *action*; others, that it is the oligarchy or the tyrant and not the state. Now the whole concern of a statesman or lawgiver is the state, and a government is an arrangement of [certain] individuals who live in a state. And since a state, like any other whole

40 composed of many parts, is a composite of [elements], it is clear that the inquiry into [the nature of] a citizen should precede that into [the

1275*a* nature of] a state; for a state is a certain plurality of citizens, so one should be concerned as to who should be called "a citizen" and what a citizen is. Disputes often arise, too, as to who is a citizen, for not all thinkers agree that the same man is [without qualification] a citizen;

5 for he who is a citizen in a people's rule will often not be a citizen in an oligarchy.

Leaving aside those who happen to be called "citizens" in some other way, e.g., "naturalized citizens," we may say that a man is a citizen not [merely] by virtue of residing in a certain place (otherwise resident aliens and slaves who reside in the same place, too, would be citizens) nor by partaking of what is just to the extent of having the right

10 to sue and be sued (for this right belongs also to those who make agreements, since these, too, can sue and be sued). In fact, in many places, even those who are resident aliens do not completely have that right, for a sponsor must be assigned to them;   and for this reason they participate somehow incompletely in such a right, like children

15 who, because of age, are not registered, and also very old men who have been discharged of their duties. For these should be called "citizens" in a qualified and not in an altogether unqualified sense, that is, they are so called by adding that they are immature or past their prime or something of the sort; it makes no difference, since the meaning is clear. What we seek to know, however, is what a citizen in an unqualified sense is, not one who has a deficiency which requires

20 correction; for one may also discuss and answer difficulties concerning citizens who are deprived of privileges or who are exiles.

A citizen without any qualification is no other than he who shares in decisions or in offices.   Now of offices some are limited in time and

25 cannot be held more than once by the same person or can be held for specified times [only], others are indefinite in time, like those of a judge or a member of the assembly. Now one might say that such men are not rulers at all and that they do not share in rule because of their office. But it would be ridiculous to say that the most authoritative are

30 deprived of office. Anyway, it makes no difference, since this is a matter of a name; for there is no name which would be applicable to both a judge and a member of the assembly, so for the sake of specification let us use the term "indefinite office." So we posit as citizens to be [also] those who [actually] partake of such office. Comprehensively

taken, then, such is the definition which best fits all those who are called "citizens."

We should not forget that what is common to things whose subjects 35 differ in kind in such a way that there is a first, a second, and so on, either does not exist at all or exists tenuously insofar as those things are so related. Now we observe that governments differ in kind, and that some are prior to others, for those which are erroneous or deviant 1275*b* are of necessity posterior to those which are without error; the meaning of the term "deviant" will become evident later.[14] Consequently, a citizen under one form of government will differ from a citizen under another form. For this reason, the definition of a citizen as 5 given earlier is most applicable to a citizen under a people's rule, and it may be applied to citizens in the other forms of government, but not necessarily. For in some forms there are no common people as citizens and no regular but only special assemblies, and verdicts are given by special bodies of men. In Sparta, for example, different suits about contracts are decided by different Overseers, cases of homicide 10 are decided by the Council of Elders, and other cases are decided perhaps by other kinds of officials. Similarly, in Carthage[15] all lawsuits are decided by certain officials. So our previous specification of what a citizen is needs modification; for in forms of government [other than a people's rule] it is not the indefinite official who is an assemblyman or 15 a judge but a definite person with respect to each office. So the right to deliberate or decide some or all matters is assigned to these persons, whether to all or to some of them.

What a citizen is, then, becomes evident from the above discussion. A citizen of a state is said to be a man who has the right to participate in a legislative or judicial office of that state; and a state, speaking 20 simply, is a plurality of [citizens] large enough for a self-sufficient life.

2

For practical purposes, people define a citizen as a man whose parents are both citizens, not only his father or only his mother; others go further back and include grandparents or great grandparents or more distant ancestors. Some thinkers, however, have a difficulty in ac- 25 cepting such a political and hasty definition, for they ask, "How did one's grandparents or great grandparents, etc., come to be citizens?" (Gorgias of Leontini, perhaps partly because of this difficulty and partly in jest, said, "As mortars are made by mortar-makers, so Larissians are made by craftsmen," for some craftsmen are makers of 30 larissians [= kettles of a certain kind]). The difficulty here is simple; for if by [our] definition [the ancestors] participated in the government, they might be citizens, but born of a father or mother who was a

citizen ..." cannot be applied to the first inhabitants or founders of a
state.

35   But perhaps there is a greater difficulty in the case of those who
were made citizens after a change in government. For example, in
Athens, after the expulsion of the tyrants, Cleisthenes enrolled as
members of the tribe foreigners and slaves of foreign origin. But the
dispute with respect to these is not who is a citizen, but whether one is
justly or unjustly a citizen. And one might also raise a further difficul-
1276a ty, namely, whether he who is unjustly made a citizen is in fact a citizen, as if being unjustly a citizen amounts to being falsely a citizen.

Now since we observe also unjust officials whom we call "officials"
but who rule unjustly, and since a citizen has been specified by an of-
5   fice of a certain kind (for, as we said, a citizen is a man who shares in
such and such an office), it is clear that these men (i.e., those who are
made citizens unjustly), too, should be called "citizens" but that the
dispute which arose earlier has to do with whether they were made
citizens justly or unjustly.[16]

3

Some thinkers pose the problem of when the state is said to have
acted and when not, as in the case of a change from an oligarchy or a tyr-
10   anny to a people's rule; for then some men do not wish to fulfill their
contracts or many other such obligations, arguing that it was the tyrant
and not the state that made them and that some governments exist by
force and not for the common interest. Now if indeed popular states,
15   too, exist in the same manner [i.e., by force]), we should likewise say
that the *actions* attributed to the states with such governments, too, are
similar to *actions* attributed to oligarchies and to tyrannies. This argument seems to be closely related to this problem: Under what conditions should we say that a state remains the same or becomes different
[e.g., after a change in the form of government]?

20   The most superficial inquiry into this problem is the one which considers [only] the locality and the population [of the state]; for the locality and the men in it may be separated, and some men may live in one
place and others in another. This problem, however, is somewhat
easier to handle; for, since the term "state" has many senses, such in-
25   quiry is in some way easy to handle. Similarly, when should men who
live in the same place be regarded as forming one state? Not by the
walls which surround the alleged state, for surely Peloponnesus, too,
could be surrounded by one wall. Perhaps such is Babylon (which is
said to have been captured for three days without some of its inhabi-
30   tants being aware of it) or any other territory which may be described
as a nation rather than a state. The inquiry into this problem, however,
will be useful on another occasion;[17] for a statesman should not neglect

to consider the size of a state, both with respect to the number of its
inhabitants and whether it is to their benefit to be members of one
race or of many. Again, should we say that the state remains the same
while the same race of men inhabit the same place although always   35
some of them are dying while others are being born, as we usually
speak of rivers and fountains as being the same although running
water is always coming and going, or should we say that the men are   40
the same for such a *reason* [i.e., same race] but that the state is different [if its government changes]? For if a state as such is a sort of an as-   1276*b*
sociation whose members are citizens under a government, then,
whenever a government changes in form and becomes different, one
would think that also the state would not be the same, just as we speak
of a chorus as being different if it is at one time comic and at another   5
tragic, even if its members often remain the same. In a similar manner,
we speak of any other kind of association as being different whenever
the composition of its members differs, as in the case of a scale whose
mode is at one time Dorian and at another Phrygian even if the notes
are the same. If such is the case, it is evident that we should speak of a   10
state as being the same by referring it mainly to its form of
government; and one may or may not use the same name for the state
whether its inhabitants are the same or entirely different. As to
whether it is just to fulfill or not to fulfill one's obligations if a state
changes its form of government, this is another matter.   15

4

Following directly upon the above remarks is the consideration of
whether or not the virtue of a good *man* should be posited as being the
same as the virtue of a virtuous citizen. But certainly if our inquiry
into this problem is to succeed, we should first get a general idea of
what the virtue of a virtuous citizen is. Now just as a seaman is one of   20
the members of an association, so we speak of a citizen. But seamen do
not have similar capacities (for one of them is a rower, another a pilot,
a third a lookout, and each of the others has a name appropriate to his
capacity). So it is clear that while the most accurate specification of
each of them will be proper to his own virtue, in a similar way there   25
will be some specification which will be common and applicable to
them all; for the function of all of them is the safety of the voyage,
since this is desired by each of them. In a similar way citizens, although differing in their capacities, have as their function the safety of
their association, which is their government. For this reason, the vir-   30
tue of a citizen must be referred to the [form of] government [of which
he is a part]. Accordingly, since there are many forms of government,
it is clear that the perfect virtue of various citizens cannot be one in
kind. But we say that a *man* is good according to his perfect virtue. It is

35 evident, then, that a virtuous citizen does not necessarily possess the virtue of a virtuous *man*.

We may arrive at the same conclusion in another way if we discuss the problem with reference to the best form of government. Since a state cannot be composed only of [*men*] who are virtuous, and since each citizen should perform well his own proper function, which de-

40 pends on his proper virtue, and since it is impossible for all citizens to

1277*a* be alike, the virtue of a citizen and of a good *man* cannot be one [in kind]; for the virtue of a virtuous citizen should belong to each of the citizens (since it is in this way that the state must be the best), but the virtue of a good *man* cannot belong to all citizens since not all of them

5 can be good *men* in a virtuous state.

Again, a state consists of members who are not all similar. So just as an animal consists first of soul and body, and the soul [of a man consists] of the rational part and the appetitive part, and a household of a husband and a wife, and ownership of master and slave, so similarly a state consists of all of these and also of other parts which are dissimilar

10 in kind [e.g., ruler and ruled]. It follows, then, that the virtue of all the citizens cannot be one in kind, any more than the virtue of the leader of a chorus is the same as that of his followers. It is evident from the above arguments, then, that the virtue of a virtuous citizen is not the same unqualifiedly as the virtue of a virtuous *man*.

But will not the virtue of a virtuous citizen and of a virtuous *man* be

15 the same in some individual? Now we speak of a virtuous ruler as being a good [*man*] and also prudent, and we say that a statesman must be prudent. And some say that the education of a ruler is from the start of a different kind, like that of the sons of kings who are seen to be trained in riding and the art of war, and, as Euripides says,

"No showy arts for me, but what the state requires,"

20 which implies that there is a special education for a ruler. So if indeed the virtue of a good ruler is the same as that of a good *man*, then, since he who is ruled, too, is a citizen, the virtue of a good *man* is not the same as that of a good citizen [insofar as he is a citizen], but only of a certain citizen [or certain citizens]; for the virtue of a ruler is not the same as that of any citizen. And perhaps this is the *reason* why Jason [the tyrant of Pherae] said he felt hungry when he could not rule

25 tyrannically, meaning that he did not *know* how to live as a private citizen.

On the other hand, the ability to rule and to be ruled [well] is praised, and the virtue of an esteemed citizen is both to rule and to be ruled well. If, then, we posit the virtue of a good *man* to be that of ruling but the virtue of a citizen to be that of both ruling and being ruled,

30 the two virtues would not be alike praiseworthy. So since it is some-

times thought that the [virtue of the ruler and that of the subject] are distinct, that the ruler should not learn the same things which the subject should learn, and that a citizen [should] *know* both [how to rule and be ruled well] and [so] partake of both, one might discern from these [where the line of reasoning leads].

Now there is a despotic rule, which is said to be concerned with the performance of necessities [only], and the ruler need *know* not how to perform these but rather how to make [good] use of them;   for the   35
other task is servile, and by "other" I mean both the ability to perform and the performance of menial tasks. But we speak of servants as being many in kind, for there are many kinds of [menial] tasks. Some [servants] are manual laborers, and these are, as the word "manual" signifies, men who make a living by using their hands; and craftsman   1277*b*
are included among these. For this reason, in some places in the old days such public workmen did not partake of office, and it is only lately under the extreme popular form of government that they were so allowed.   So a good [*man*] or statesman or citizen should not learn to perform the tasks of such men who are ruled, except sometimes for his   5
own personal need   (in which case he does not become now a master and now a slave).

But there is another rule according to which one rules over those who are similar by birth   and free, and we call this "political rule," in which the ruler should learn by first learning how to be ruled. Such a   10
ruler is like a commander of a cavalry or of an army or of a squadron or of a company, for each of these should serve under the corresponding ruler for some time before rising to that post; and for this reason it is well said that he who has not been ruled   cannot rule well. Now the virtue of the ruler and that of the ruled in each of these are different; but a good citizen should *know* how and be able to both be ruled and rule, and his virtue is this, namely, to *know* the rule of a freeman in   15
both ways [i.e., to *know* how to rule   and how to be ruled well qua a citizen]. The virtue of a good *man*, too, is to *know* how and be able to do both, even if temperance or justice for a ruler differs from that of a subject;   for it is also clear that a virtue, such as justice, is not one in kind in a good freeman who is ruled, since there are many kinds of vir-   20
tues according to which one rules or is ruled, like temperance and bravery, which differ in a *man* and a woman.   A *man* would be thought to be a coward if he were brave like a woman, and a woman would be thought to be loquacious if her talk were as moderate as that of a good *man*; and good management of the household differs for a husband and a wife, for a husband's function is to acquire goods but a   25
wife's is to preserve them. As for [unqualified] prudence, it is a virtue proper to a ruler alone;   for it seems that the other [virtues] must be common to both rulers and ruled. Prudence [without qualification] is

certainly not a virtue of one who is ruled [qua ruled], but only true
opinion;   for one who is ruled is like a maker of flutes, whereas a ruler
30   is like a flute player who uses them.

From the above discussion it is evident whether the virtue of a good
man is the same as or different from that of a virtuous citizen, and in
what way it is the same and in what way different.

5

There still remains a problem concerning a citizen. Is one truly a
35   citizen who has the right to share in offices or should we posit also artisans as citizens? If we posit as citizens also those who have no share in
offices, then such virtue [i.e., of a true citizen] cannot belong to every
citizen, for then an artisan would be a citizen. But if no such man is a
citizen, in what class should he be placed? For he is neither a resident
1278a   alien nor a foreigner. Shall we say that, at any rate, nothing strange
follows because of this argument, since neither slaves nor freed men
belong to either of the classes mentioned?

The truth of the matter is that not all men who are indispensable to
the existence of a state should be posited as being citizens, for neither
5   are children citizens in the same way as [free] *men* are. But [free] *men*
are citizens without qualification, whereas children are citizens hypothetically;[18] for children [may be future] citizens but are now immature.
In some states long ago artisans and foreigners were slaves, and for
this reason many of them are slaves even nowadays. Now the best
state will not permit an artisan to be a citizen. But if he too is a citizen,
10   then the virtue of a citizen we spoke of earlier cannot belong to every
citizen, nor to [every] freeman, but only to those who are released
from performing the necessities of life; and those who perform such
necessary functions under one *man* would be slaves, while those who
do them for the community would be artisans or laborers. The situation about these matters becomes evident if examined a little further,
15   for the evidence itself will make clear what has been said.

Since there are many forms of government, the kinds of citizens
must be many also, especially those who are ruled. So under some
governments artisans and laborers must be citizens, but under others
this is impossible, as in the one which is called "aristocratic," if there
20   be such, in which honors are bestowed according to virtue and merit;
for one cannot pursue virtuous activities if he leads the life of an artisan or a laborer. In oligarchies a laborer cannot be a citizen, for participation in office depends on high taxable property, but an artisan
25   can, for many artisans are wealthy. In Thebes there was a law denying a man participation⁷ in office unless he had ceased trading for at
least ten years. But in many governments the law extends citizenship
even to foreigners, for in some popular governments a man is a citizen

if his mother is a citizen; and, similarly, in many states even illegiti-
mate children become citizens. It is indeed because of scarcity of le-   30
gitimate citizens that such persons are admitted to citizenship (for it is
because of a dearth of population that states use laws in this manner);
but as the population increases, first the children of a male or a female
slave are excluded from becoming citizens, then the children whose
mothers only are citizens, and finally only children both of whose parents are citizens become citizens.

It is evident from these remarks, then, that there are many kinds of   35
citizens, and that a citizen in the highest sense is said to be one who
shares in the honors of the state; and, as Homer wrote of someone, he
is treated "like an alien, without honor,"[19] for he who does not share in
the honors of the state is like a resident alien. But where the [right to
such honor] is concealed, it is for the sake of deceiving the fellow in-   40
habitants.

Whether we should posit the virtue of a good *man* to be the same as   1278*b*
or different from that of a virtuous citizen, then, is clear from what has
been said: in some states it is the same, in others it is different,[14] and
in the former case not every good citizen is a good *man*, but only a
statesman and one who has or can have authority, whether alone or
with others, to take good care of the public interest.   5

6

Having settled these things, let us consider next whether we should
posit only one or many forms of government, and if many, what they
are and how many there are, and what the differences among them
are.

A government is the arrangement of the various offices of a state,
and especially of the most authoritative of all the others, for the au-   10
thority over each of the others is the ruling body, and this is [the main
part of] the government. I mean, for example, that the authority in
popular governments is the common people, whereas in oligarchies it
is the few [wealthy]; so we speak of these two governments as being
different, and we may speak of the other forms of government in the   15
same way.

First, let us lay down the purpose for which a state has been formed
and also the kinds of rule which govern men and their social life. Now
we have stated also at the start of this treatise,[20] where we described
household management and the rule of a master, that men are by nature political animals, and for this reason, even when they have no   20
need of each other's help, they desire no less to live with each other;
and, moreover, common expediency brings them together to the extent that it contributes to the good life of each. In fact, the good life is
the end in the highest degree for all men taken together and for each

of them taken separately; and they come together for the sake of mere
25   living also (for perhaps there is in [mere] living itself something fine),
and they maintain their political association even for the sake of mere
living, as long as life's hardships are not excessive. Clearly, most men
cling to life at the cost of enduring many ills, which shows that there is
30   some contentment and a natural sweetness in mere living.

    It is easy, surely, to distinguish the various modes of rule, and we
have also described them often in *Public Writings*. The rule of the
master, although when truly exercised is to the interest of both the
35   slave by nature and the master by nature, is nevertheless primarily to
the interest of the master but indirectly to the interest of the slave; for
it cannot be preserved when the slave perishes. But the rule over a
wife and children and the entire household, also called "household
management," whether exercised for the sake of those ruled or for
40   the sake of something common to both the ruler and the ruled, is essentially for the sake of those ruled (for we observe this also in the
1279*a*   other arts, e.g., in the medical arts and in gymnastics) but indirectly it
might be for the sake of the rulers themselves (for nothing prevents
the game trainer of boys to be himself one of the trainees, just as in the
case of the pilot of a ship, who is always one of the sailors). The game
5   trainer or the pilot, then, is aiming at the good of those who are ruled,
and whenever he himself happens to become one of those he rules, he
shares in that benefit but indirectly; for the pilot in the first case, although a pilot, is one of those who are sailing, and the trainer in the
second case, although a trainer, is one of those who are trained. So in
10   the political rule, too, whenever the state consists of citizens in virtue
of their equality and similarity, the citizens expect to rule [and be
ruled] in turn. Formerly, as was natural, they expected someone, say
A, to take his turn in serving others and then again someone else, say
B, to look after A's good just as earlier A looked after B's interest.
Nowadays, however, because of the benefits received from public
15   revenues for holding office, those who rule wish to do so
continuously; it's as if rulers who were disposed to sickness happen
to be kept always healthy while in office, for perhaps this is the assumption on which they are seeking office.

    It is evident, then, that the forms of government which aim at the
common interest happen to be right with respect to what is just without qualification; but those forms which aim only at the interest of
20   the rulers are all erroneous and deviations from the right forms, for
they are despotic, whereas a state is an association of freemen.

      7

    Having settled these matters, we shall next examine the forms of
government, their number and what each of them is, starting first with
25   the right forms, for when these have been described, the deviations
from them, too, will become evident.

The terms "government" and "ruling body" are [generically] the same in meaning, the ruling body being the authoritative part of a state, and this part must be either one ruler or few or the majority; and whenever the ruling body, whether one or few or the majority, rules for the common interest, the corresponding form of government is necessarily right, but whenever the ruling body rules for its own in-   30
terest, whether it be one ruler or few or the majority, the correspond-
ing form of government is a deviation from the right form. For we should say that either those who do not partake [of benefits] are not citizens, or that they [as citizens] should get a share of those benefits.

We usually employ the name "kingship" for a monarchy which aims at the common interest, the name "aristocracy" for a government by   35
the few but more than one, either because the rulers are the best *men*, or because they aim at the best interest of the state or of those who participate in it, and the common name πολιτεία [i.e., "democracy"] for a government by the many if it governs for the common interest. And there is a good reason for this [use of language]; for it is possible for one *man* or a few to excel in virtue but very difficult for the majori-   40
ty to become perfect in every virtue, unless this be military virtue,   1279*b*
which is most likely to exist in the majority. It is in view of this that, in this form of government, the military men have the greatest authority and those who share in the government are those who possess arms.

Of governments which deviate from the right forms, tyranny is op-   5
posed to kingship, oligarchy is opposed to aristocracy, and people's rule is opposed to democracy. For tyranny is a monarchy which aims at the interest of the monarch [only], oligarchy aims at the interest of   10
the prosperous [only], people's rule aims at the interest of the poor [only], but none of them aims at the common interest.

8

But we should state what each of the above governments is at great-
er length, for there are some difficulties; and it is appropriate for one, who makes a philosophical inquiry into a subject but does not attend only to the practical side of it, not to overlook or omit anything but to   15
bring out the truth concerning each point.

As already stated, tyranny is a monarchy, and its rule is despotic over the political association; oligarchy is a government ruled by those who possess [much] property; people's rule, on the contrary, is a government ruled by those who do not possess much property but are needy.

Now the first difficulty is concerned with the specification [of these   20
forms of government]. For if [in deviant states] it is in a people's rule that the majority has authority but this majority were to be [not needy but] prosperous, and, similarly, if it is in an oligarchy that the few have authority but those few happen to be [not prosperous but] needy and   25
stronger, one would think that the definitions of the various govern-

ments have not been framed well. Moreover, if one classifies the
forms of government by combining fewness with prosperity and majority with need and describes an oligarchy as a government in which
30 the prosperous who are few hold the offices and a people's rule as a
government in which the needy who are the majority have them, another difficulty arises. For what name shall we give to the other two
governments we have just described, that is, that in which the ruling
majority are prosperous and that in which the ruling minority are
needy, if indeed there can be no form of government other than the
35 six we mentioned? So the argument seems to indicate that the number of those who rule, whether few or the majority, is an accident, and
that fewness and majority are not differentiae of an oligarchy and of a
people's rule, respectively, just because everywhere the prosperous
happen to be few and the needy happen to be a majority. The differ-
40 ence between people's rule and oligarchy is that between poverty and
1280a wealth. So the government in which few or the majority hold office
because of wealth must be an oligarchy, and that in which the poor,
whether few or many, hold office must be a people's rule, although it
happens [always or most of the time], as already stated, that the rulers
in an oligarchy are few whereas those in a people's rule are the major-
5 ity; for those who are prosperous are [usually] few, but sharing in freedom belongs to all, and it is because of prosperity and freedom that
disputes arise between the wealthy and the free as to the form of
government.
        9
    First, then, we must ascertain what definitions are given [by think-
ers] of an oligarchy and of a people's rule and what is [considered as]
10 just in the oligarchic and the popular sense; for all men have a notion
of what is just in some sense but up to a point and do not state entirely
what is just in the main sense. For example, it is thought by some men
that what is just is the equal; and it is the equal, but for persons who
are equal and not for everybody. Again, also the unequal is thought to
be just; and it is the unequal, but for those who are unequal and not for
everybody. But these thinkers judge badly, for they fail to include the
kind of men to whom the equal or the unequal applies; and the *reason*
15 is the fact that their judgment is partial to themselves, for most men
are bad judges when their own interests are involved.
    So since that which is just applies in the same way to persons as to
things, as discussed earlier in the *Nicomachean Ethics,*[21] these men
agree about the equality of things but disagree about the equality of
20 the persons involved, and for two *reasons*: (a) most of all because of
what we have just said (i.e., for being bad judges of their own interests), and (b) because of the fact that, whereas they are talking of what
is just in a qualified sense, they are in the habit of thinking that they
are talking about what is just in the full sense. For those who are un-

equal [i.e., better off] in one respect, e.g., in wealth, think that they are unequal in all respects, and those who are equal in another respect, e.g., in freedom, likewise think that they are equal in all respects. But both fail to state the most important point [i.e., the *reason* for their association]. For if men formed an association and came together for the sake of possessions, then they [should] share in the state in proportion to their possessions, so here one would think that the argument of the oligarchs prevails; for it is not just for a man who contributes one mina out of a hundred to have a share equal to that of the man who contributes the rest, whether the share be of the principal or of the profits.

Now a state is formed rather for the sake of a good life and not only for the sake of mere living (otherwise slaves and other animals, too, would form a state, but they do not, since they cannot partake of happiness or a life which requires choice after deliberation), nor for the sake of mere alliance to prevent unjust treatment,nor for the sake of trade alone or of other useful exchanges, otherwise the Tyrrhenians and the Carthaginians and all those who have agreements with one another would all be citizens of one state. In fact, they do have treaties about imports, and agreements to prevent unjust treatment from each other, and written articles of alliance. But no common offices are established to handle their dealings (for each state has its own ruling offices), nor are the citizens of one state concerned with what the ethical habits of the citizens of the other states should be, nor is there [an office] to see to it that none of the parties to a treaty will be unjust or vicious; there is only an [agreement] that the parties will not be unjust to each other. As for political virtue and vice, this is the concern of each state which cares for good laws. And from this it is evident that each state, in the true sense of the word and not in name only, should pay attention to its own virtue only, otherwise this association becomes a mere alliance differing from other alliances only in that its members are nearer each other, and its laws become a mere treaty and, as the sophist Lycophron remarked, a mere guarantee to the parties to treat each other justly instead of the sort of thing [designed] to make its citizens good and just.

It is evident, then, that the situation is such as stated. For even if one were to bring the territories of states in one place so that, for example, the walls of the Megarians and the Corinthians touched each other, yet the two states would not become one state, not even if their citizens intermarried with each other, even though intermarriage is one of the associations which are characteristic of states. Similarly, if certain men lived at a distance from one another yet not far enough to make their association difficult, and if there were laws among them not to treat each other unjustly in exchanges (for example, if one were a carpenter, another a farmer, a third a shoemaker, and so on, and

25

30

35

40

1280b

5

10

15

20

their number were 10,000) and to associate with one another in exchanges and alliances *and nothing else*, even then they would not come under one state. But why not? Certainly not because their association is at a distance from each other; for if they were to come close

25 and associate with each other in the same way—each of them using his household in his own way as if it were a state—and merely to help each other as if through a defensive alliance against those who would be unjust to them, even then those who speculate accurately on this matter would not think that these men are under a single state if indeed they associate with each other in a similar way, whether they are

30 close to each other or far apart. So it is evident that a state is not [merely] an association of persons in a common locality for the sake of exchange and of preventing unjust *actions* against each other.

Now if indeed there is to be a state, a common locality and exchanges and prevention of unjust *actions* by others are necessary, but all these taken together do not yet make a state; for a state is an association of households and family relations for living well and exists for the

35 sake of a perfect and self-sufficient life, which cannot be attained without a common locality and intermarriage among the members of that association. It is for this reason that in cities there arose family associations and clans and common sacrifices and other pleasant ways of being together, all such activities being ways of promoting friendship, for friendship is the deliberate choice of living together.

40 The end of a state, then, is the good life, and the associations and activities just mentioned are for the sake of that end. And a state is an as-

1281*a* sociation of families and villages for the sake of a perfect and self-sufficient life, which is, in our way of saying, a happy and noble life. We should posit, then, that a political association exists for the sake of noble *actions* and not for the sake of [merely] living together. It is in-

5 deed for this reason that those who contribute most to such an association are a greater part of the state than those who are equal or greater in freedom or birthright but inferior in political virtue, or than those who exceed in wealth but are exceeded in virtue.

It is evident from what has been said, then, that all those who dis-

10 agree about governments are speaking only of a part of what is just.

10

A problem arises, however, as to what part of the state should have authority. Should it be the multitude, or the wealthy, or the equitable, or the one best man, or the tyrant? There appears to be a difficulty regardless of which of these alternatives is taken.

15 If the poor because of their superior number distribute the property of the wealthy, would it not be unjust? "No, by Zeus," it will be answered, "for this would be justly decreed by the part which has authority." But if not this, what should we call the height of injustice? For if the majority of all citizens once more distribute among them-

selves the property of the minority, etc., it is evident that the state will
be eventually ruined. Moreover, virtue certainly does not destroy its
possessor, nor is that which is just destructive of the state; so it is clear   20
that this law, too, cannot be just. Further, all the *actions* of a tyrant,
too, would of necessity be just; for, being stronger, he coerces all the
others just as the majority coerce the wealthy. But then, is it just for
the few or the wealthy to rule? If they, too, plunder or confiscate the   25
possessions of the majority, is this just? If it is, so will it be in the previous cases. It is evident, then, that all of these *actions* are bad and not
just.

But should the equitable hold office and have authority over all
matters? Then all the others, not being honored by being excluded   30
from political rule, will live without honor; for we call the offices of
the state its "honors," and if the same men always rule, all the others
must be always without honor. Again, is it better for the most virtuous
man alone to hold office? But this will be even more oligarchical, for
those without honor will be even more numerous. Perhaps one might
say that, in general, it is bad for a man and not the law to have authori-   35
ty, seeing that a man is subject to the passions of the soul. But if the
law is oligarchical or popular in form, what difference will it make as
regards the problems just raised? For the difficulties faced will be
similar to those already indicated.   40

11

The other problems will be discussed later;[22] but that the majority
rather than the few who are best should rule might be thought to be a
solution in spite of some difficulty, and perhaps this might even be
true. For a majority, of whom each is not a *man* of virtue, may be bet-   1281*b*
ter than the few best, not as each taken separately but as all of them together, just as feasts to which many contribute are better than a dinner at one's private cost; for each of a multitude of men has a part of
virtue and prudence, and when they come together they are like one   5
man with many feet and hands and senses; [and perhaps] such is a multitude when becoming one with respect to its character and *thought*.
It is for this reason that many [when taken together] are better judges
of the works of music and of poetry [than one or the few]; for different
persons in the multitude judge different parts [of music or of poetry]
better, and all taken together judge all the parts better. It is indeed in   10
this respect that, when individually taken, *men* of virtue are superior
to the many, just as those who are said to be handsome are superior to
those who are not handsome, and that beautiful paintings are superior
to the real things they depict; for the beautiful parts which are scattered in real things are combined into one painting, even if, in one
case, the eye of a certain man is more beautiful than the painting of it,   15
and, in another case, another part of another man is more beautiful
than the painting of it.

Now it is not clear whether in every group of common people and every multitude of men this difference between the many and the best few can exist. [One might say], "but surely, by Zeus, it is clear that in some cases [of multitudes] this is impossible." For the same argu-
20 ment would apply to irrational animals also, and so one might ask, "What difference is there between some men and irrational animals?" Yet nothing prevents the above argument from being true in some multitudes of men. For this reason, one might solve, by using these arguments, the problem posed earlier[23] and the one that follows from it, namely, the problem concerning the kind of authority which freemen and the majority of citizens should have, such being those who are
25 neither wealthy nor have any claim to high virtue. For to have them share in the highest offices is not safe because through their injustice and folly they tend to *act* unjustly and commit errors; but to give them no voice nor any share in office is fearful, for whenever a state has many citizens who are poor and allowed no honor [in partaking of gov-
30 ernment], it must have many enemies within itself. What is left, then, is to allow them to have a share in [some] matters which require deliberation or judgment. It is for this reason that Solon[24] and certain other lawgivers give them power of electing officials of the state and holding these accountable, but they do not allow them to be officials by
35 themselves. For when they all meet together they perceive things adequately, and together with their betters they are beneficial to the state, just as impure food mixed with [a small amount of] pure food makes the result more useful than [just] the pure food does; but each of them by himself is imperfect when it comes to matters of [political] judgments.

The first difficulty with this kind of arrangement in government is
40 the following. One would think that it is the same kind of man who (1) can judge whether a sick person suffering from a given disease has been rightly treated by a person and (2) also heal and make healthy
1282*a* the sick person, and this man is the physician; and similarly with other kinds of experiences and arts. [If so], then just as a physician is accountable for his medical work to other physicians, so should any other artist be accountable for his work to his peers. But a man is called "a physician" in three different ways: (a) if he [just] practices according to the rules of medicine, (b) if he is a master-artist, [who *knows* the causes in medical science], and (c) if he has a good educa-
5 tion in the art of medicine; for in practically every art there are three such kinds of artists, and we attribute [good] judgment to those who are well-educated in an art no less than to those who have understanding of that art.[5]

Second, one would think that, in a similar way, the same would apply to the election of officials [as to medicine]; for [he would think that] to select [an expert in a field] rightly is a task proper to those who have knowledge of that field, e.g., that only geometricians can choose rightly a geometrician, and only pilots can choose rightly a man who can steer. For [he would think that] even if some laymen participate in choosing experts in some occupations and arts, certainly they cannot choose better than the experts. So according to this argument [he would say that] the multitude should not be given the authority to elect officials or call them to account.   10

But perhaps not all these arguments are well stated, both because of what we said earlier[25]—that is, if the many are not too servile (for each of them will be inferior in judgment to those who understand, but when all of them come together they will be better or not worse than those who understand)—and by the fact that in some cases of art, i.e., those in which the artistic works are known even by *men* who do not possess the art, the artist is neither the only nor the best judge. For example, knowledge of a house is not limited to the builder, for the user is even a better judge of it (for it is the household manager who uses it), and, similarly, the pilot is a better judge of a rudder than the carpenter, and the guest is a better judge of a dinner than the cook. So one would think that perhaps such solution of the difficulty would be adequate.   15   20

There is another difficulty. It is thought to be absurd that *men* of bad character rather than equitable *men* should have authority over matters of some importance, and the election and calling to account of officials are matters of the greatest importance. Yet in some governments, as already stated,   these matters are assigned to common people; for the assembly is the authority in all such matters, and *men* of any age and with small property qualification sit in the assembly and deliberate and make judgments, while those with high property qualification serve as treasurers and generals and assume authority over the highest offices. But one might also solve this difficulty in a similar way; for perhaps these regulations, too, are right, since it is not one judge or councillor or assemblyman who rules but the court and the council and the popular body of which each of the above-mentioned is only a part—by a "part" I mean one councillor or one assemblyman or one judge. So [perhaps] it is just that the many should have authority over matters of some importance, for the popular body consists of many parts, and so does the council, and the court; and the property qualification of the whole senate or assembly or court, too, is greater than that of one member or of a few of those who hold high office. But enough of this.   25   30   35   40

1282*b*

Now the difficulty first mentioned[26] makes evident no other thing than that the laws, when rightly laid down, should be the authority, and that the ruler, whether he be one or whether there be many, should have authority over matters about which laws cannot be stated with precision because it is not easy for laws, which are universally stated, to   5

take care of every particular.   What is not yet clear, however, is what
such laws which are rightly laid down should be; so the former difficulty still remains.[27] For, like governments, laws are of necessity good or
10   bad, just or unjust. At any rate, this is evident, that the laws of a state
should be adapted to its form of government; and if so, it is clear that
laws in accordance with right forms of government are of necessity just,
but those in accordance with deviant forms cannot be just.

12

15   In every science and every art the end aimed at is a good; and the supreme good and the good in the highest degree depends on the most
authoritative discipline, which is politics. The political good is that
which is just, this being that which is of common benefit to all. Now it
is thought by all men that the just is something equal, and at least to
20   some extent all men agree with the philosophical distinctions which
we laid down in the *Ethics*;[28] for that which is just is *something* and is
just to *certain persons*, and men do say that those who are equal
should have equal things. But we should not overlook the kinds of
things to which this equality and the corresponding inequality apply,
for we have a problem here which belongs to political philosophy.
     Perhaps one might say that the offices of the state should be un-
25   equally distributed according to every superior goodness of its citizens, if these citizens happen to differ in no other respects but are
alike; for what is just and according to merit should be different for
men who differ in goodness. But if this were true, then what is politically just for those who excel in complexion or height or any of the
30   other goods would be a greater share in the offices of the state. But is
this not obviously false? Evidently it is, if we turn to the other sciences
and disciplines. If a number of flutists are alike in their art, the better
flutes should not be given to those of nobler birth, for they will not
play any better; the better instruments should be given to those who
excel in their performance.
35   If what I am saying is still not clear, it will be made more evident as
we proceed. For if a man were to excel in flute-playing but be far inferior to other men in birth or beauty, he should be given the better
flutes even if each of the others (i.e., high birth, beauty) is a greater
40   good than flute-playing and excels flute-playing in a greater ratio than
1283*a*   the flute-player excels the other men in flute-playing; for if the other
men are to be given the better flutes, wealth and high birth should
contribute to flute-playing, but they contribute nothing at all.
     Moreover, according to the argument of these thinkers every good
would be comparable to every other good. For if a certain height had
5   more goodness [than some other attribute of a man has], then height in
general could be matched against wealth or freedom. Thus if A excels
B in height more than B excels A in virtue, and if height in general excels virtue [in general], all goods will be comparable; for if height P

surpasses virtue Q in goodness, then clearly some other height R is
equal to virtue Q in goodness. But since this is impossible, clearly it is   10
reasonable that, when it comes to political offices, men do not disagree with respect to every kind of inequality. For if one man is slow in
running but another is swift, the latter should not, because of this, partake of rule more than the former; it is in gymnastic races that he who
excels should receive the honor. Disputes concerning offices, then,
must be based on those things on which the state is constructed.   15

In view of the above, it is with good reason that those of high birth
and freemen and the wealthy contend with each other for honor; for
[those who partake of political honor] should be free and tax-payers,
since a state can be no more composed entirely of poor men than entirely of slaves. Further, if a state needs men of wealth and freemen, it
is clear that it needs also just men and men with political virtue; and   20
whereas without wealth and freedom a state cannot exist at all, without justice and political virtue it cannot be managed well.

13

It would seem that all or at least some of the above points are rightly
disputed, if they contribute only to the existence of a state; but, as
stated earlier also,[29] it would be especially just to argue about educa-   25
tion and virtue, which contribute to a good life. Now since those who
are equal in one respect only should not share equally in all respects
and those who are unequal in one respect only should not share un-
equally in all respects, such forms of government which violate this
principle are of necessity deviations. It was also stated earlier[30] that all   30
those who disagree do so justly in some way, but not in an unqualified
way. (1) The wealthy claim a greater share in rule (a) on the grounds
that they have more land, and land is something common, and also (b)
on the grounds that they are for the most part more trustworthy in
contracts. (2) The free and those of noble birth, as if akin to each
other, claim a greater share of rule (a) on the grounds that those who
are true to their nature are citizens to a higher degree than those who   35
are not, since noble birth in every state is regarded as a mark of honor
by its citizens, and also (b) because descendants of better men are
likely to be better, since noble birth is a virtue of race. In a similar
way, we will say that (3) virtue, too, has a just claim to a greater share;
for we maintain that justice is a social virtue [i.e., a virtue towards oth-
ers],[31] inasmuch as all the other virtues must follow justice.[32] Finally, (4)   40
the majority, too, have more claim to rule than the few; for, taken collectively, they are stronger and more wealthy and better than the
few.

Now if all the above groups—i.e., the good and the wealthy and the   1283*b*
highborn and some other political multitude—were to live together
in a state, would there be a dispute or not as to who should hold office?
No doubt arises in judging who should hold office in each of the forms

5   of government already mentioned, for their differences are characterized by those who have authority; that is, in one form the rule is by the
wealthy, in another it is by virtuous *men,* and similarly in the other
cases. But the concern here is to decide who should rule whenever all
10 the above groups exist in a state at the same time. If those with virtue
are very few, in what way should the matter be settled? Should we
consider their number in relation to the task to be performed and ask
if they are too few to manage the state or enough in number to constitute the state?

The problem which arises concerns all those who disagree about
15 political honors; for those who have a claim to rule because of wealth,
or similarly because of [noble] birth, are thought not to speak justly at
all. For it is clear that again, on the same principle of justice, if one of
them is more wealthy than each of the others, he should be the ruler
of all the others; and in a similar way, the one who surpasses in noble
20 birth all the other contenders on the basis of freedom should assume
the leadership of all the others. The same applies equally to aristocracy, which is based on virtue; for if, of the ruling body, one of them is
more virtuous than each of the other virtuous *men,* then, on the same
principle of justice, he [alone] should be the authority. And if the multitude should be the authority because they are [collectively] stronger
25 than the few, then, again, one (or a minority of them) who is (or are)
stronger than the rest should be the authority rather than the others.

All the above arguments seem to make it evident that none of the
above specifications, according to which men claim to rule but all the
30 rest to be ruled by them, are right. Indeed, even against those who
claim that they should be the authority in the ruling body because of
their virtue, or similarly because of their wealth, the majority might
justly use the argument that nothing prevents a majority, not singly
35 but collectively, from being better or wealthier than the minority. In
view of this, the problem which arises and is put forward, too, can be
met in the same manner; for, whenever the above happens [i.e.,
whenever the majority is collectively better], some pose the problem
of whether a lawgiver who wishes to lay down the most just laws
should posit laws for the benefit of the better or of the majority.
40   Now what is right should be taken as that which is equally so; and
the equally right is that which is beneficial to the whole state and to
what is common to the citizens. And what is common to citizens is to
1284a share in ruling and being ruled, although differently in different forms
of government; but under the best form of government a citizen is one
who is able and deliberately chooses to be governed and to govern so
that he may lead a life of virtue.

On the other hand, if there is one man (or few, yet not enough to
5   make up a complete state) so pre-eminent in virtue that the virtue
and political capacity of all the others cannot be compared to the vir-

tue and political capacity of that man (or of those few), then that man
(or those few) should not be regarded as a part of the state; for, being
far superior to the others in virtue and political capacity yet regarded   10
as equal (or equals), he (or they) will be treated unjustly.   Such a man
would be like a God among men; and from this it is also clear that laws
must be framed only for those who are equal in birth and capacity, for
no law exists for such a man—he is himself the law. It would, indeed,
be ridiculous for anyone to try to make laws for such a man; for he   15
would perhaps say what, in the fable of Antisthenes, the lions said to
the hares ["Where are your claws and teeth?"][33] when the hares were
making speeches and claiming equal rights for all.

It is for a *reason* such as the one just stated that states with a popular
form of government institute ostracism; for they pursue equality most
of all and so have ostracized or banished from the state for fixed peri-   20
ods of time   those whom they have considered as being far superior
in power because of having wealth or many friends or some other political capacity.   According to the legend, too, it is for such a *reason*
that the Argonauts left Heracles behind; for Argo [the ship that talked]
did not wish to take him along with the crew since he was far superior   25
to them. And it is in cases such as this that those who blame tyranny
and the advice given by Periander to Thrasybulus should not be
thought to be altogether right in their censure.   (Periander, according to the story, said nothing when asked for advice by the envoy but
simply was levelling off the corn field by cutting off the ears that stood   30
out among the rest; but Thrasybulus, when told of this event by the
envoy who did not get the point, understood that he should do away
with *men* of superior capacity). For this practice is to the interest not
of tyrants alone, and tyrants are not the only ones who use it; oligar-   35
chies and popular forms of government are alike in this respect, for ostracism has in a way the same effect as restraining or banishing those
who are prominent. The same thing is done by the ruling authorities
of other states or nations, as the Athenians did to the Samians, the
Chians, and the citizens of Lesbos;   for, as soon as the Athenians sta-   40
bilized superiority in power, they humbled these states in violation of
their treaties. The king of Persia, too, repeatedly crushed the Medes,   1284b
the Babylonians, and those whose spirits were stirred by memories of
their former greatness.

The problem is universal and concerns all forms of government,
even those which are right. For the deviant forms adopt the practice   5
just stated with a view to their own interest, but those which are concerned with the common good, too, act in a similar manner. This is
clear in the other arts and sciences also. For the painter would not
allow the animal in the painting to have its foot, however beautiful, be
disproportionally large in size; the shipbuilder would not make the   10
stern or any other part of the ship likewise large; and the master of a

chorus would not include in the chorus a man who sings louder and better than the rest of the members.   So because of this, nothing prevents monarchs from keeping harmony in their states, if by the use of
15   this practice their own rule is beneficial to the states. For this reason, the argument concerning ostracism has *some* political justice where there are acknowledged superiorities.

   It would be better, however, if at the start the lawgiver structures the government in such a way that a remedy of this sort becomes un-
20   necessary; and the next best thing, if need arises, is to try to make a correction such as the one mentioned. But this was not what was taking place in states; for [rulers] were not attending to what was beneficial to their own government but were using ostracism for the sake of faction. Now in deviant forms of government it is evident that this practice is [legally] just and of benefit to the individual [ruler or rul-
25   ers]; but it is equally evident, too, that it is just not in an unqualified way.   But in the best form of government there is a great problem, not with excesses in such goods as power, wealth, and possession of many friends, but with what to do if a *man* excels in virtue; for no [reasonable] person would say that such a *man* should be expelled or ex-
30   iled. Further, neither should such a *man* be ruled [at all], for this would be like the claim that Zeus should be ruled and share rule with others. What is left, then, is something which is by nature desirable: all others should gladly obey such a *man* and allow *men* such as this to be kings for life in their states.

BOOK IV

1

10   In all the arts and sciences, each of which is complete with respect
1288*b*   to some one genus but has not been acquired part by part, it is the concern of one and the same [faculty] to investigate whatever is suitable to each genus. For example, it is the concern of gymnastics to deal with (a) the kind of training which is beneficial to each kind of body, (b) the best training of the body which is by nature best and best supplied (for it is this kind of training which must be suitable to that
15   body), (c) the kind of training which is most suitable for most people when applied to all of them (for this training, too, is the concern of gymnastics), and further, (d) if one *desires* to acquire not the appropriate skill or science of exercising, it is nonetheless the function of the game trainer of boys or the gymnast to be able to furnish a suitable
20   training [under given circumstances]. Similarly, we observe that this happens to be the case with medical science, shipbuilding, dressmaking, and each of the other arts.

   It is clear, then, that it belongs to the same science to deal with the best form of government, both (1) the kind which would best fulfill men's aspirations if there are no external impediments, and (2) the

kind which is suitable to particular [kinds of men]; for perhaps the best   25
form [without qualification] in many cases is impossible, so the good
lawgiver or true statesman should not fail to notice not only the best
form without qualification but also the best form under given
circumstances. (3) The same science should be able to speculate on
any hypothetical form also; for it should be able to speculate about
any given kind, both as to how it might originate and, after being established, in what way it might be longest preserved. What I mean is   30
that a state which happens to be neither best governed, nor supplied
with the necessities of life, nor even the best possible under the circumstances, but is rather inferior. A political scientist should know,
besides these, (4)the form which is most suitable to all the states; for   35
most political writers, although they speak well about other points in
politics, fall into error when it comes to what is useful; for one should
speculate not only about the best form of government [without quali-
fication], but also about the form which is possible under given circumstances, and similarly about the form which is easier or more common to all states. Some modern thinkers seek only the form which is
highest and which would require a great amount of supplies; others,   40
while speaking about a more common form, reject the existing forms
of government and praise the one in Sparta or some other. Yet the   1289*a*
kind of arrangement to be introduced should be one which the citizens, starting from their existing form, will be easily convinced and
able to share, for it is no less of a task to correct a form of government
than to establish a new one, just as it is no less of a task to correct one's   5
bad learning than to learn from the start.

It is in view of the above that a statesman, as we stated before,[34]
should be able to be of service to existing forms of government as well
as to those we have mentioned; but he cannot do this if he does not
know how many forms there are. It is nowadays thought that there is
only one kind of people's rule and only one kind of oligarchy; but this   10
is not true. So one should not be unaware of the different kinds [forms
and their species] of government, both as to their number and the
number of ways in which they may be combined. And it is with the
same [political] prudence that one would perceive also the best laws
and those which are suitable to each kind of government, for laws
should be framed to suit the kind of government, and not conversely,
and all [lawgivers] do so frame them; for a government in a state is an   15
arrangement of offices distributed in a certain manner, has a certain
authoritative part, and has a certain purpose for each [kind of politi-
cal] association; but laws, being distinct from that which articulates
the kind of government, are rules according to which the rulers
should rule and protect the government against offenders. So it is   20
clear that a statesman must know the varieties of each form of government, their number, and their relevance to the laws posited for them;

for the same laws cannot be beneficial to all varieties of oligarchy or of
people's rule if indeed there are various species of oligarchies and of
25   popular governments and not only one of each.

1295a   11

25   We should now inquire what is the best form of government and the
best way of life for most states and most men, using as a principle of
judgment not virtue which is far above ordinary men, nor the kind of
education which requires a [gifted] nature and fortunate circumstances, nor yet a form of government held up as an ideal, but rather a way
30   of life in which most men can share and a form of government in which
most states can participate. For even the so-called "aristocracies"
which we have just discussed,[35] although beyond the reach of most
states from one point of view, are close to the so-called "democracy"
from another; and in view of this, these two forms should be discussed
35   as if they were one form. Indeed, in making judgments about all these
forms, we must use the same elements. For if what we said in our
Ethics[36] is well-stated (namely, that the happy life is the life according
to virtue and free from impediments, and that virtue is a mean between extremes), then the best life [for most people] must be the
mean of what is attainable by the individuals. If so, the same defini-
40   tions must apply also to the virtue and vice of states and of forms of
1295b   government; for a government is a sort of life of a state.
        Now in every state there are three parts: the very prosperous, the
very needy, and the middle class. So since it is agreed that the moder-
5   ate and the mean are the best, it is evident that the best possession of
goods which comes from fortune, too, is the one which is moderate,
for this is the easiest to deal with in a rational manner; for he who
greatly excels in beauty or strength or noble birth or wealth, or in the
contraries of these, i.e., in ugliness or weakness or low birth or poverty, finds it difficult to follow reason. The former tend to become inso-
10   lent or great criminals, but the latter rather mischievous and petty ras-
cals; for, of unjust treatments, some come about because of insolence,
others because of mischief. Again, these [the middle class] are least
given to an [inordinate] love of power or rule, both of which are harmful to states. In addition, those who excel in good fortune—those who
15   are strong and wealthy and have friends and the like—neither wish
nor *know* how to be ruled (and they are brought up in this way at home
during their childhood, for, living in luxury, they do not acquire the
habit of submitting to instruction), while those who lack excessively
these goods of fortune are too humble [either to wish or to *know* how
20   to rule]. So the latter *know* not how to rule but only how to be ruled
despotically, while the former *know* not how to be ruled at all but only
how to rule despotically. Accordingly, what results is not a state of
freemen but one of despots and of slaves, of envious and of contemptuous men. Such a 'state' is farthest removed from being a political

and a friendly association; for an association is characterized by friendliness, whereas enemies do not wish to share even the same path. 25

Anyway, a state aims at being an association of men who are equal and alike as far as possible, and such is an association composed of middle-class citizens most of all. So a state which is, as we maintain, by nature composed of such men will necessarily be best governed, and such citizens are the ones most secure in the state; for neither do 30 they, unlike poor men, *desire* what belongs to others, nor others *desire* what belongs to them, as poor men *desire* what belongs to the wealthy. And because of the fact that they neither plot against others nor others plot against them, they lead a life free from danger. It is for this *reason* that the prayer of Phocylides was well expressed when he said,

"Many things are best in the middle;
And there, in a state, I care to be."

It is clear, then, that the best political association, too, is the one 35 which consists of the middle class. And states in which the middle class is large can be well governed; and best so, if the middle class is stronger than those of the wealthy and the poor combined, but [less so], if the middle class is stronger than either one of the two classes, for, in the latter case, the addition of the middle class to one of the other two classes tips the scale and prevents the remaining extreme class from becoming dominant.

It is for this reason that the most fortunate state is that in which its 40 citizens have moderate and sufficient property. A state where some 1296*a* citizens have excessive property and the rest nothing at all becomes either an extreme people's rule or an impetuous oligarchy or a tyranny because both parts are extremes; for from an uncontrolled people's rule or an oligarchy there arises a tyranny, but from moderate forms of 5 government or those close to them this is much less likely to occur, and the *reasons* for these will be given when the changes of forms of government are discussed.[37]

Evidently, then, the moderate form of government is the best, since it alone is free from rebellion; for where the middle class is large, rebellions or factions in such a government are least likely to occur. Large states, too, tend to be rather free from rebellion, because there 10 is a large middle class; but in small states all the citizens—or almost all—can easily be distributed into two classes, the prosperous and the needy, with nothing left in the middle. Popular governments, too, are safer and last longer than oligarchies do because their middle class is larger and has a greater share of honors in the government; but [here, 15 too,] whenever the needy greatly exceed in number and there is no middle class, evil *actions* arise and the government soon comes to an end. Belief [in the superiority of the middle class] is confirmed also by

the fact that the best lawgivers came from the middle class; Solon was
20 one, as his poems indicate, Lycurgus was another, for he was not a
king, and so were Charondas and almost all the others.

From the above discussion it is also evident why most forms of government are either popular or oligarchic. For the middle class in them
is very often small, and, because of this, those who are dominant,
25 whether the property owners or the common people, bypass the middle class and get hold of the government, and so a people's rule or an
oligarchy is formed. In addition, because of the factions and struggles
between the two opposing parties (the common people and the pros-
30 perous) the party which turns out to be the stronger forms a government which is neither for the common interest nor fair to all but assumes supremacy of the government as the prize of victory, and the
common people set up a people's rule but the prosperous set up an oligarchy. Further, of those in each of the two states [Athens and Sparta]
who became leaders of Greece and favored their own form of government, one group established a people's rule in the states under them
while the other established an oligarchy, thus aiming not at the good
35 of those states but at the good of their own interests. So for these *reasons* the moderate form of government—democracy—either did not
exist at all or only occasionally and in few places. In fact, of the earlier
40 rulers of Greece, only one man   was persuaded to set up this arrangement [i.e., democracy] for the citizens; and it has now become a cus-
1296b tom among those in the states not to care about fairness but either to
seek to rule or, if subdued, to put up with being ruled.

It is evident from the above discussion, then, what the best form of
government is and why. As for the other forms, since we stated[38] that
5 there are many species of people's rule and of oligarchy,   it is not difficult to see, after having specified the best form, which should be
posited as the next best, then which should follow this, and so on from
what is better to what is worse; for that which is the next best should
be of necessity nearest to the best, but that which is further from the
mean [i.e., from the best] should be of necessity worse, if one is not to
10 judge them hypothetically [i.e., under special circumstances]. By "hypothetically" I mean that, for example, although one form is better
than another, it often happens that nothing prevents the worse rather
than the better form from being more beneficial to some people.

BOOK VII

1

A man who seeks to make the proper inquiry into the best form of
1323a 15 government must specify first what is the most choiceworthy way of
life; for if this kind of life is unclear, so must be the best form of government also.   For it is fitting for those who are best governed under

the existing circumstances to be *acting* best, unless something contrary to reason happens. For this reason, first, it should be agreed as
to what kind of life is most choiceworthy for all, so to say, and second,
whether the best kind of life common to all and to each citizen taken   20
separately is the same or not the same.

The subject concerning the best life is assumed to have been adequately treated in *Public Writings,* and it will be used here. It is true
that no one would dispute the fact that the three kinds into which   25
goods are divided—external, those of the body, and those of the
soul—should all belong to those who are blessed; for no one would
call a man blessed who has no particle of bravery or temperance or
justice or prudence, who fears the flies passing by, who would never   30
abstain from the meanest *actions* to gratify his hunger and thirst, who
would ruin his dearest friend for the sake of a dime, and who, similarly, is foolish and *thinks* falsely like a child or a madman.

Now almost all men would assent to the above truths; but they dif-   35
fer as to what is the right amount and which of the goods is superior.
For some think that the possession of virtue to whatever extent is sufficient, but when it comes to wealth and material goods and power
and reputation and the like they seek an unlimited excess of these.
Our reply to these men is that it is easy to gain conviction about such   40
matters by the things men do also; for we observe that virtues are acquired and preserved not by external goods, but that external goods
are acquired and preserved by virtue, and that living happily, wheth-   1323*b*
er this be through enjoyment or through virtue or through both, belongs more to those who have high character and a highly cultivated
thought but are moderate in their possession of external goods than to
those who possess an excess of external useful goods but are deficient   5
in character and *thought.*

The fact just stated is easily perceived when viewed according to
reason also. External goods, like an instrument, have a limit, and the
excess of every external useful thing is of necessity either harmful or
of no benefit to its possessors. But with respect to each good of the   10
soul, the greater its excess, the more useful it becomes, if it is proper
to what is noble in the soul to add also the term "useful." In general, it
is clear that the superiority of the best disposition of a thing A over the
corresponding best disposition of another thing B follows from the su-   15
periority of A over B. Accordingly, since the soul is indeed more
honorable than the body or external possessions, both without qualification and to us, the best disposition of the soul, too, is of necessity
analogously related to the best disposition of the body or of those
possessions. Further, external goods and those of the body are chosen by nature for the sake of the soul and should be so chosen by all   20
men of good judgment, but the soul is not chosen for the sake of those
goods. Now let us acknowledge that the extent to which we become

happy corresponds to the extent to which our virtues and prudence
and the *actions* according to these are present, and let us acknowledge
25 as a witness also God, who is happy and blessed not because of any external goods but because of Himself and His kind of nature. Then
good fortune, too, must differ from happiness because the possession
of an abundance of external goods differs from the goods of the soul;
for the causes of goods which are external to the soul are chance and
luck, but no one becomes just or temperate by being fortunate or because of good fortune.

30   What follows next and requires the same arguments is that the
happy state, too, is that which is best and which *acts* well. Now people
cannot *act* well if their *actions* are not noble, and no thing done by a
man or a state is noble without virtue and prudence; and the bravery
35 and justice and prudence of a state has the same power and *form* as the
corresponding virtue possessed by each man when we say that he is
brave and just and prudent. But let these remarks serve as an adequate introduction to the present task here, for neither can we afford
not to touch upon these issues, nor can we allow ourselves to go over
all their appropriate details, since their treatment belongs to another
40 study. At present, however, let us assume that the best way of life,
for each individual separately as well as for what is common to states,
1324*a* is the virtuous life which is supplied with as many external goods as to
make *actions* according to virtue possible. As for the objections of
those who disagree with us, we will not consider them here; but we
will go over them later for the sake of those who have not yet been
persuaded.

2

5   It remains to discuss whether the happiness of the state should be
taken as being the same as that of each man or not. But this, too, appears to be the case; for all agree that it is the same. Those who posit
that living well for an individual is living in wealth posit that the whole
10 state, too, is blessed when it is wealthy; and those who value the
tyrant's way of life most would say that the most happy state, too, is
the one which rules over the greatest number of men; and he who accepts as true that the happiest life of an individual is a life through virtue would also say that the more virtuous a state is, the happier it is.

    But here there are two questions which should be considered: (1)
15 which way of life is more choiceworthy, that of an individual who is a
citizen and shares in the affairs of the state or that of an individual who
is a stranger and is relieved of political ties, and (2) which form of
government and what kind of disposition of the state should be posited as the best, regardless of whether all choose to participate in the affairs of the state or some participate but most do not? But since the
20 task of political *thought* and speculation is not the first but the second
question and our intention here is to consider the latter, the second

question would be a subject coming under our *inquiry* while the first would be a side issue.

Evidently, the best form of government must be the one whose arrangement makes it possible for anyone to *act* best and live blessedly. But those who admit that the most choiceworthy way of life is the one according to virtue still disagree as to whether the desirable way of life is the political one and that of *action*, or rather the one relieved of external goods (i.e., the theoretical life), which is said by some to be the life of a philosopher alone. For these two ways of life are about the only ones which appear to be chosen by those who are the most zealous for virtue, in the past as well as nowadays—I mean the political life and that of the philosopher. The difference between these two kinds of life is indeed no small matter, whatever be the truth about them; for a man with good judgment must order his plans in accordance with the better end, and this applies to the state as a whole as well as to each citizen.

There are some who maintain that if the rule over neighbors is despotic, it is exercised with the greatest injustice, and if it is political, although not unjust, it is still an impediment to one's well-being. There are others, however, who happen to have in a way contrary opinions; they maintain that the only way of life fit for a *man* is political and that of *action*, for they think that *actions* according to each of the virtues are no more those of private individuals than those which are public and political. Others, again, suppose that the despotic or tyrannical way of governing alone provides the happy life. In fact, in some states the aim of the laws of their government, too, is to rule despotically over neighboring states. For this reason, even though in most [such] forms most legal ordinances are laid down haphazardly, so to say, still the aim of all of them is, if anything, to rule over others. Thus both the system of education and most laws in Sparta and in Crete are practically framed with a view to war.

Further, such is the aim which is held in esteem in all other nations which have the power to expand [at the expense of others], as in Scythia and Persia and Thrace and that of the Celts. For, in some of them, there are even laws which exhort [military] virtue, as in Carthage, where it is said that men are decorated with as many armlets as the number of campaigns they have served. In Macedonia, too, there was once a law compelling a *man* who had never killed an enemy to wear a halter; and, in Scythia, a *man* who had not killed an enemy was not allowed at certain feasts to drink from a cup which was passed around. In Iberia, a war-like nation, the number of obelisks affixed around a *man's* tomb is the same as the number of enemies he killed in war. Indeed, there exist many other such practices in other places, some established by law and others by custom.

Yet those who wish to examine all these would perhaps regard it as very strange that a statesman's function should be his ability to find

25 the means of ruling and dominating despotically neighboring states,
whether these wish it or not. For how could this function, which is not
even lawful, be that of a statesman or a lawgiver? Men rule other
states unlawfully not only when they do so unjustly, but also when
they do so justly; and conquering others may also be unjust. More-
30 over, this function is not observed even in the other sciences; for neither is the function of the physician to persuade or coerce his patients,
nor is that of the pilot to do this to the sailors. Yet most people think
that the despotic art is [the same as] the political art,   and they are not
ashamed to practice towards others what they say is neither just nor
35 beneficial to themselves; for they seek a rule which is just to themselves but do not care whether it is just to others.   And it is strange to
deny that it is by nature that some things should be ruled despotically
but others should not; so since this distinction exists, one should not
try to rule as a master all others but only those who [by nature] deserve to be despotically ruled, just as one should not hunt human ani-
40 mals for food or sacrifice but only those which are suitable for this
purpose, e.g., wild animals which are meant to be eaten. Moreover, a
1325a single state which is well governed might by itself be happy, if indeed
it is possible for a state to exist somewhere by itself and have virtuous
laws; and in that case its government would be framed not with a view
5 to making wars or conquering enemies, for no such need would arise
[in that state].
   It is clear then that, although all military pursuits may be assumed
to be noble, they are not the ultimate end of the state but only instrumental to [its happiness].   Thus the function of a virtuous lawgiver is
to have in view a state and a race of men in it and every other association and see how those men can partake of a good life and the happi-
10 ness that is possible for them. Some of the enacted legal ordinances, of
course, will vary; and if there are neighboring states, it is also the function of the lawgiver's art to be aware of which of those laws should be
used and how they should be properly used in dealing with each of
those states.   But the question raised here, namely, what the end
15 aimed at by the best government should be, belongs to a later
investigation.[39]

3

   Let us consider those who agree that the life of virtue is the most
choiceworthy but differ as to the manner in which it should be used.
There are (1) those who disapprove of holding office in a state, re-
20 garding the life of a freeman as being (a) distinct from political life and
(b) the most choiceworthy of all.   There are (2) others who regard the
political life as being the best; for they think that it is impossible to *act*
well without *acting* at all, and that happiness is the same as *acting*
well.   Our answer to both these two schools is that in one sense they
speak rightly, but in another sense they do not.

(1) Those who regard the life of a freeman as being better than the life of a despot speak in this respect truly; for there is no dignity at all in the use of slaves as such, since commanding others to perform the necessities of life partakes of nothing that is noble. Anyway, to regard every kind of rule as being despotic is not right; for the rule over freemen differs from that over slaves no less than men who are free by nature differ from men who are slaves by nature. We have specified these matters adequately at the start of this treatise.[40] To think that *inaction* is more praiseworthy than *action*, too, is not true; for happiness is an *action* [of a certain kind], and the *actions* of just and temperate men have many noble ends.

(2) With the above distinctions, perhaps one might come to believe that authority is the best of all, for it is in such a way [i.e., with authority] that one could perform the greatest number of the most noble *actions*. So a man who is able to rule should not give it up to a neighbor but rather take it away from him, and a father should not take into account his father or his children or any of his friends and pay special attention to any of them; for the best [life is] the most choiceworthy, and to *act* well is the best.

Now perhaps it is true for them to say this, if indeed the most choiceworthy thing can be attained by plunderers and men who use violence. But certainly this cannot be the case and is falsely assumed; for if the ruler is not as much superior to the one ruled as a *man* is to his wife or a father is to his children or a master is to his slaves, his *actions* may no longer be noble. So a transgressor might not *succeed* later in recouping as much as he has already lost by deviating from virtue; for, among peers, the noble and the just should be shared by turns, as this is fair and alike to all. But it is contrary to nature that unequals should be given to equals or things which are unlike should be given to peers; and nothing which is contrary to nature is noble. For this reason, too, if there be someone who is [far] superior in virtue and in ability to perform the best *actions*, it is noble that we should follow him and also just that we should obey him. And such a *man* should have not only virtue, but also the power to *act* according to virtue.

If the above things are well stated and if happiness should be posited as being *actions* well performed, then the best way of life for every state as well as for every citizen would be the practical life [i.e., a life of *action*]. But a practical man is not necessarily one whose *actions* are related to others, as some suppose; and practical *thoughts*, too, are not only those occurring for the sake of what follows from *acting*, but much more those which are complete in themselves and are speculations and acts of *thinking* for their own sake; for a good deed is an end in itself, and so it is a certain [kind of] *action*. Outward *actions* in the highest sense, too, are said to be mainly those which master-artists perform by *thoughts*. Moreover, states which are founded in isola-

25

30

35

40

1325*b*

5

10

15

20

25 tion from others and intend to remain so, too, are not necessarily devoid of *action*; for *actions* may occur among the parts of the state since
there are many associations between those parts. [2] This is similarly
true also with any individual man [who lives by himself], for if not,
God and the whole universe, whose *actions* are not outward but ap-
30 propriate to themselves, would not fare nobly.

It is evident, then, that the best way of life is of necessity the same
for both the state and for each individual.

4

With the introductory remarks on the subject above and the earlier
35 consideration of the other forms of government, let us now turn to
what remains and begin first with the kinds of assumptions which
should be made concerning the construction of what is to be an ideal
state; for the best form of government cannot be realized without the
external means appropriate to its existence. For this reason, we
should start with a number of assumptions which, though ideal, so to
40 say, are nevertheless not impossible of realization. I mean, for example, assumptions concerning the number of citizens and the [kind of]
territory for the state. For just as in other skilled professions the artist,
1326a such as a weaver or a shipbuilder, should have suitable materials to
work with (for the better the material which is prepared for his work,
the finer must be the work done by him), so also the statesman or law-
5 giver should have the appropriate materials suitable [to establish the
best state].

The first requirement for a state is the size of the population, both
as to the number of men and the sort of men they should be by nature,
and likewise for the territory, both as to its size and its quality.

Most people think that, to be happy, a state ought to be large; but, if
10 this is true, they do not know what kind of state is large and what kind
is small, for they judge the size of a state by the number of its inhabitants. But they should attend to its power rather than to the number of
its inhabitants,[3] for a state, too, has a function to perform, and so it
should be regarded as being the greatest if it can best fulfill its
15 function. For example, one would say that Hippocrates is greater
than an [ordinary] man with a greater bodily size not with respect to
size but as a doctor. Further, even if one is to judge the greatness of a
state by attending to the number of its inhabitants, still he should not
posit any chance number (for perhaps a state must also have numerous
20 slaves and resident aliens and foreigners) but only those who are
members of the state [i.e., citizens] and constitute the appropriate
parts of the state;[4] for it is the numerical superiority of these that is a
sign of a great state, whereas a state which produces a large number of
artisans but few soldiers cannot be great, for to be a great state is not
25 the same as to be a state with a great number of men.

Moreover, this is evident also from the fact that it is difficult, per-

haps even impossible, for a state with a very large population to be well managed. At any rate, of states which are thought to be well governed, none is observed to be indiscriminate in the size of its population. Conviction through arguments, too, makes this clear. For law is a   30
certain order, so good law must be a good order; but a very excessive multitude of men cannot partake of order, for to do so would be a task for divine power, which also holds together the universe, whereas the performance of what is noble [or beautiful] for men usually depends on a [limited] plurality or magnitude.[41] For this reason, it is necessary for the magnitude of the best state, too, to have the limit mentioned.   35
So a state does have [an ideal] moderate magnitude, just as all other things have, e.g., animals, plants, and instruments; for each of these, too, when very small or very large, will not have its [proper] power but will be sometimes entirely deprived of its nature and sometimes badly formed (for example, a boat will no longer be a boat if it is a foot   40
long or a quarter of a mile long, and it will function badly as a boat if it   1326*b*
deviates from its proper size by a certain magnitude in either direction). Similarly, an association is not self-sufficient (as a state should be) if it is composed of very few members; and if it is composed of very many members, although self-sufficient in the necessities of life, like a nation, it is still not a state, for in this case it is not easy for a   5
government to exist. For who will be the general of such an excessive multitude, or who will be the herald unless he has Stentor's voice?

In view of the above discussion, a state in the primary sense must be a political association which first becomes large enough to be self-sufficient for a good life. There may be a state even with a larger popu-   10
lation, but, as we stated, not without a limit. As for what that limit is, it can be easily seen from the facts. For the *actions* of the state are those of the rulers and those of the ruled, and the function of a ruler is to command and to judge. Now in judging what is just and distributing   15
offices according to merit, the citizens must know each other's characters; for, wherever this does not happen to occur, both the election to offices and the judgments of what is just, being done without adequate preparation and so unjustly, are necessarily bad (and evidently   20
such happens to be the case whenever populations are very large). Further, foreigners and resident aliens would easily be able to participate in the government;   for it is not difficult to do so without being detected because of an excess of population.

Clearly, then, the best [upper] limit of the population of a state is the greatest number which, being easily seen at a glance, suffices for a [good] life of its citizens. So concerning the size of a state, let the   25
above remarks be sufficient.

13

As for the form of government itself, let us discuss of what parts and what kinds of parts the state should be composed if it is to enjoy   25 blessedness and be well governed.

The goodness of an object which is coming to be depends on two things. The first is the positing of the right aim, which is the end of *actions*; the second is finding the *actions* which, as means, bring about

30   that end. These two—the end and the means—may harmonize or fail to harmonize with each other; for sometimes the aim is well posited but the *actions* taken to achieve it are erroneous, sometimes all the means taken succeed in achieving the end but the end which is posited is bad, and there are times when both the end and the means taken are erroneous. For example, sometimes a physician neither judges

35   well the quality which a healthy body should possess nor uses the right medicine to effect the end he posits. But in arts and sciences both these two—the end and the *actions* taken towards that end— should be mastered.

Now it is evident that the aim of all men is living well or happiness.

40   But, through luck or nature, some men have the requirements to at-

1332a   tain this aim, others do not; for to live well a man needs also external goods, fewer if he has a superior disposition but more if he has an inferior disposition. Some of those who have the requirements, however, seek happiness in the wrong way from the beginning. But since the

5   object is to keep in view the best form of government according to which a state would be best governed, and since a well-governed state is one according to which it is most capable of being happy, it is clear that we should not fail to know what happiness is.

We have stated in our *Ethics*,[42] if the arguments there are of some

10   value, that happiness is a perfect activity or use of virtue, taken without qualification and not hypothetically. By "hypothetically" here I mean [an activity concerning] necessities, and by "without qualification" I mean that which is nobly done. For example, to punish and penalize justly is to *act* justly, and these *actions* arise from virtue, but their goodness is a necessity (for it would be more desirable if neither

15   a *man* nor a state had any need for them); but *actions* which lead to honors and good deeds are best without qualification. The former *actions* are chosen to negate evils; the latter, on the contrary, are realizations of goods or productive of goods. For a virtuous *man* would bear

20   well in poverty and sickness or any bad luck; but he attains blessedness under conditions which are contrary to these evils (for in our ethical discussions we have also shown that a virtuous *man* is a *man* to whom, because of his virtue, good things are good without qualification).[43] It is clear, then, that the uses of goods [to such a *man*]

25   will of necessity be also good and noble without qualification. It is for this reason [i.e., that goods can be used well], too, that men are in the habit of thinking that external goods are the causes of happiness, as if one were to say that the lyre is the cause of playing brilliantly and well rather than the art of the performer.

It follows from the above discussion, then, that some goods must [already] be present [in the best state], but that the other goods must be furnished by the lawgiver. For this reason, we pray that the composition of the state be lucky enough to be supplied with the goods which depend on fortune, for we posit fortune as being sovereign over them. The virtue of the state, on the other hand, is the work not of fortune but of *knowledge* and intention. So to be a virtuous state is to be a state in which those citizens who share in the government are virtuous; and in the state we are now discussing, all citizens will share in the government. We should consider, then, how a *man* becomes virtuous. For even if all citizens [collectively] can be virtuous but not each of them individually, it is more desirable [if each of them is virtuous]; for if each is virtuous, all of them are [collectively], [but the converse does not necessarily follow].

Men become good or virtuous through three things: [good] nature, [good] habits, and [good] reason. First, he should be gifted by nature; e.g., he should be a man and not some other animal, and his body should be [by nature] of a certain quality, and so should his soul. Nature can be of no use to certain [dispositions] since changes into them are caused by habits; for certain [potentialities] by their nature are changed by habit in either of the two directions, towards the better or the worse. Now all other animals live by their nature most of all, but few of them live also by habit, and to a slight extent. Man alone lives by reason as well [as by his nature and by his habits], for he alone has reason. So these three [nature, habit, reason] should be in harmony with each other; for men do many things which violate their nature and habits, if they are persuaded by reason that it is better to do them.

We have already specified, then, the kind of nature men should have if they are to be easily turned [into good men and good citizens] by the lawgiver,[44] but the rest is the work of education; for we learn certain things by habit and others by hearing.

14

Since every political association is composed of rulers and those ruled, let us consider whether these should interchange or remain the same throughout life; for clearly it will follow that the education of citizens should differ according to each of the two alternatives.

Now if there were some citizens who surpassed the rest as much as Gods and heroes are believed to surpass ordinary men (first, being far superior to them in their bodies, and second, in their souls), and in a way that the superiority of the rulers over the subjects would be evident without dispute, it is clear that it would be decidedly better for the rulers and those ruled to be always the same. But since this is not easily attainable and kings do not surpass their subjects as much as, according to Scylax, the kings of India do their subjects, it is evident that

30

35

40

1332*b*

5

10

15

20

25

for many *reasons* all must alike share in government by ruling and
being ruled by turns. For "equality" means that similar people [should
have] the same; and it is difficult to maintain a government constitut-
ed contrary to justice, for all those in the country who wish a change
30   will join with those who are ruled, and then it will be quite impossible
for the ruling body to be stronger than those who oppose them.

On the other hand, it cannot be disputed that the rulers should be at
least superior to the ruled. So the lawgiver should attend to these mat-
35   ters and to the manner in which sharing [by all citizens] should take
place. But we have considered this problem earlier;[45] for nature herself has furnished us with the distinction by making within the same
species some members young but other members older, the former
meant to be ruled but the latter to rule. Now the young never resent
being ruled while young nor regard themselves as being better [rul-
40   ers] than their elders, especially when they expect that they will make
up for being ruled when they reach the proper age. So one should say
1333a   that in one sense the rulers and the ruled are the same, but in another
sense that they are different, and that their education must be in one
sense the same, but in another sense different; for, as it is said,[46] he
who is to rule well should first [learn to] be ruled.

As we stated at the beginning of this treatise,[47] one kind of rule is for
the sake of the rulers, another is for the sake of those who are ruled.
5   We call the first rule "despotic"; the second is a rule over freemen. So
some commands differ, not in the things which are to be done but in
the purpose for which they are to be done. For this reason, many duties which are thought to be menial are also duties which are noble for
the children of freemen to perform; for the nobility or lack of nobility
10   of *actions* does not consist so much in the *actions* themselves as in the
end or purpose [for which they are performed]. So since we maintain[48]
that [in the best state] the virtue of a citizen and of a ruler is the same
as that of the best *man*, and since the same *man* should become first
one who is ruled and later a ruler, the task of a lawgiver would be (a) to
15   see that *men* become good, (b) to find the appropriate means by which
this can be accomplished, and (c) to know what the end of the best life
is.

Now the soul of man is divisible into two parts, one of which has by
its nature reason [or, is the rational part], but the other has by its nature no reason, yet it can listen to reason; and, in our view, a *man* is
said to be good if he has in a certain way the corresponding virtues of
20   these two parts. For those who adopt our division of the soul it is not
unclear in which of those parts the end of man ought to be said to lie.
For that which is inferior exists always for the sake of that which is superior, and this is similarly evident in things according to art and in
things according to nature; and the part which has reason is better
[than the part which has no reason but can listen to reason]. But the ra-

tional part, too, is further divided into two parts in the manner in
which we usually employ the term "division"; for one of those parts is 25
practical, but the other is theoretical.[49]

Clearly, then, also the rational soul must be divisible into two parts.
So we must say that the *actions*, too, of the rational soul are analogously divisible into two parts, and that the *actions* of one of these
parts which is better by nature [i.e., the theoretical] should be more
choiceworthy to those who can succeed in all *actions* [nonrational,
practical, theoretical] or in both [nonrational and rational] *actions*, for
the most choiceworthy [*action*] for a man is always that of the highest 30
[part of the soul]. Life as a whole, too, is divided into instrumental activities and leisurely activities, into war and peace, and, of things to be
acted upon, into those which are necessary and useful and also those
which are noble; and the corresponding parts of the soul and their re-
spective *actions* must be the same: war for the sake of peace, instru- 35
mental activity for the sake of leisurely activity, and the necessary and
the useful for the sake of the noble.

A statesman, then, should lay down laws with a view to all these
with respect to both the parts and the *actions* of the soul, and more
so with a view to the ones which are better or are ends [rather than
means]. And he should do likewise with the kinds of lives and the vari- 40
ous things to be done; for [citizens] should be capable of doing what is
necessary and of engaging in war, but more so of living in time of 1333*b*
peace and of being engaged in leisurely activities, and they should
be capable of doing what is necessary or useful, but more so what is
noble. These, then, should be the aims of the education of children
and of those who require education at their later stages of life. 5

The Greek states which are nowadays thought to be best governed
and the lawgivers who set up their forms of government do not appear
to have framed their governments with a view to the better ends, nor
to have introduced laws and a system of education with a view to all
the virtues; instead, they have leaned vulgarly towards what they have 10
thought as being useful and rather profitable. Some of the later writers, too, have expressed almost the same views; for they have praised
the Spartan form of government and lauded the lawgiver for having
framed laws aiming solely at conquest and war. Their praises can easi- 15
ly be refuted by arguments and have now been refuted by the facts
themselves. For just as most men seek to be masters of many others
in order to acquire a large supply of fortune's goods, so Thibron and
each of the other writers on government appeared to admire the lawgiver of the Spartans who ruled an empire by being trained to meet 20
dangers.

At any rate, it is clear that the Spartans are not happy citizens, nor
was their lawgiver a good one, seeing that they are no longer rulers of
an empire. Furthermore, it is ridiculous to see that, although the

Spartans are steadfast in obedience to their laws and nothing impedes
25   the operation of these laws, they have given away a noble life. These
writers do not even make the right assumption as to the kind of rule
which a lawgiver should appear to value; for the rule over freemen is
nobler and more virtuous than the despotic rule. Further, training the
citizens to conquer neighboring states with a view to ruling them
30   should not be the *reason* for regarding a state happy and praising the
lawgiver, since doing so is bringing great harm to the state. For it is
clear that any citizen with the power to do this should also try to assume the ruling power of his own state—and it is indeed this that King
35   Pausanias was accused by the Spartans of having tried to do,[50] even
though he [already] held the honor [of being a king]. So no argument
or law such as this [concerning the aim of a state] is either statesman-
like and beneficial, or true; for the same things are best for both individuals and states, and the lawgiver should implant them into the souls
of men. As for military training, it should be pursued not with a view
40   to enslaving those who do not deserve to be enslaved, but (a) to avoid
1334a   being enslaved by others, (b) to seek to be leaders of others for the
benefit of these and not for total enslavement, and (c) to become masters over those who deserve to serve others.

The facts themselves confirm the arguments that the lawgiver
should rather see to it that both military and other legislation be or-
5   dered for the sake of leisurely activity and peace. Yet most military
states, though preserved while at war, perish after having established
an empire; for, like unused steel, they lose their temper in time of
peace. And the cause of this is the lawgiver who has not taught them
10   how to live in leisurely activity.

15

Since the end is evidently the same for men collectively and for
each individual, and since the thing aimed at is the same for both the
best *man* and the best government, it is evident that the virtues for lei-
15   surely activity should exist; for, as we have stated often, the end of
war is peace, and the end of instrumental activity is leisurely activity.
The virtues which are useful when one has leisure or is occupied are
those whose function is fulfilled when one has leisure or is engaged in
instrumental activities, respectively; for many necessities should
exist if there is to be leisurely activity. For this reason, it befits a state
20   to be temperate and brave and have fortitude; for, as the proverb says,
"leisurely activity is not a mark of slaves," and those who cannot face
danger bravely become slaves to aggressors. Accordingly, bravery
and fortitude are needed for instrumental activities, philosophy for
leisurely activities,' temperance and justice in times of peace as well
25   as in times of war, and more so in times of peace and for leisurely activities; for war compels men to be just and temperate, but the enjoyment of good fortune and an easy life in peace time tends to make men

rather insolent.[6] Those, then, who are thought to *act* best and enjoy all the blessings—like men, if such be, in the Island of the Blessed, as the poets say— will need philosophy and justice and temperance most of all; and the more leisure they have when in abundance of such goods, the more they will need these virtues.

It is evident, then, why a state which is to be happy and virtuous should share in the above virtues. It is indeed disgraceful not to be able to use the goods of life, and more so when at leisure, but rather to appear good in instrumental activities and wars and lead a servile life in time of peace and leisure. For this reason, a state should not practice virtue[51] in the way the Spartans do. For these, while agreeing with other men as to what the greatest goods are, differ from them by thinking that those goods are acquired rather by a particular virtue.[51] So it is evident from their beliefs that, since [they regard] those goods as greater than others and their enjoyment as greater than the enjoyment of virtues, [. . .] they do so because of that virtue.[51] But how those goods are acquired and through what [virtues as] means surely requires examination.

We have distinguished earlier nature and habit and reason as the things which *men* need [to become good][52]. The kind of nature which the citizens of a state should have has been specified earlier.[53] It remains now to consider which education of the citizens should come first, whether that of reason or that of habits. These two [kinds of education] should harmonize with each other, and the harmony should be of the best sort; for it is possible for reason to err in regard to the best hypothesis and for habit to be similarly led astray.

First, then, it is at least evident that, as in other things, the generation of a thing [e.g., of the birth of a man] starts from a principle, and the end of that thing comes from a principle which has another end. Now reason and intellect are for us the end of our nature. So the generation and the training of the [right] habits, too, should be a preparation for these [reason and intellect]. Second, just as the soul and the body of man are two [distinct principles as parts], so two parts are observed in the soul, the nonrational and that which has reason and also their corresponding dispositions, desire and thought. Now just as the body is prior in generation to the soul, so the nonrational part is prior in generation to the part which has reason. And this, too, is evident: temper and wish and *desire* exist in children soon after birth, but reason and intellect come later to them by their nature. In view of this,(a) the care of the body must precede the care of the soul, and (b) then the care of desire must follow; for the care of the body is for the sake of the soul, and the care of desire is for the sake of thought.

RHETORIC

CONTENTS

BOOK I

15. Gifts of fortune. The disposition of men of high birth.
16. The disposition of the wealthy.
17. The disposition of those in power.

RHETORIC

BOOK I

1

Rhetoric is the counterpart of dialectic; for both of them are concerned   1354a
with such things which are, in a way, open to all men to know and do not
come under any specific science. In view of this, all men can participate in
some way in both disciplines; for to a certain extent all men try to examine   5
the views of others and maintain their own, and to defend their own position
but attack that of others. Ordinary men do this either randomly or through
practice acquired from habit. So since both ways are possible, it is clear that
the subject matter [of rhetoric] can be systematized; for it is possible to
investigate the *reason* why some men meet with success, whether through   10
practice or by chance, and all men would now agree that such success is
without doubt the work of art.

The current authors who compiled works on rhetoric have contributed
but a small part of this art; for only persuasive techniques are subjects of the
art of rhetoric, while all other matters are merely accessories. But these
writers say nothing about enthymemes, which are indeed the framework of   15
persuasion; instead, they busy themselves with matters most of which lie
outside the subject. For such affections of the soul as pity, anger, and [that
aroused by] slander do not deal with the subject but are directed to the judge
[juries included]. So if all legal decisions were carried out as they are
nowadays in some states, particularly the best governed ones, these writers   20
would have nothing to say. For whereas all men think that the laws should
proclaim [impartial] rules, some men, such as the judges in the Court of
Areopagus [the Supreme Court of Athens], actually practice this and
prevent discussions of extraneous matters, and rightly so; for one should not

25   try to pervert the judge by arousing him to anger or envy or pity, since this
      would be similar to trying to distort a carpenter's rule before using it.
      Besides, it is evident that a party to a dispute need only show that his
      allegation is or is not a fact, or is something which actually happened or did
      not happen; but as to whether a deed is great or small or just or unjust, or
30   whatever the lawgiver did not specify, surely the judge himself should know
      and not learn from the litigants.
          Now laws which are rightly framed should, most of all, specify
      everything that is possible [universally taken] and leave as few matters as
      possible to the judges to decide. First, then, it is easier to find one man, or
1354b a few men, who judge rightly and are able to lay down [good] laws and be
      [good] judges in accordance with them. Second, laws are made after long
      reflection, whereas judgments in courts are made in a very short time;
      hence, it is difficult for judges of a case to hand down a just and expedient
 5 , decision. But most important of all is the fact that the judgment of the
      lawgiver is not about particular and present matters but about future and
      universal matters, whereas assemblymen and judges make decisions about
      particular and immediate matters before them, and they are often so
10   affected by feelings of likes and dislikes and self-interest that they cannot
      see the truth before them but allow their judgment to be clouded by
      personal pleasure or pain. Concerning [universal and future] things, then, as
      we said, the judges should be allowed to decide as few of them as possible;
      but as to whether [particulars] did or did not happen, will or will not occur,
15   do or do not exist, these must be left to the judges to decide, for it is not
      possible for the lawgiver to foresee them. So if this is the case, it is evident
      that those who are laying down rules such as what the introduction or
      narration or each of the other parts of speech should include are dealing
      with matters whose art lies outside the present art; for they are dealing with
20   matters aimed at putting the judge in a certain frame of mind without
      indicating the persuasive techniques from which one might acquire the art
      of using enthymemes. Now it belongs to the same systematic inquiry to deal
      both with deliberative and judicial techniques of persuasion, and
25   deliberative matters are nobler and more political than those which deal
      with exchanges [and the like]. But, because of [their aim to put the judge in
      a certain frame of mind], these writers state nothing about deliberative
      oratory but all of them try to make rules about forensic matters; for in
      deliberative matters nonessentials have little effect, and deliberative oratory
      is less malevolent and deals with wider issues than forensic oratory does. In
30   deliberative matters, the listener makes a judgment which affects his own
      interest, so the only need is to prove that the situation is such as the adviser
      states. In forensic matters, on the other hand, this is not enough; the speaker
      finds it useful to cater to the listeners. For the latter make judgments about
      the interest of others, and so thinking only of themselves and listening for

their own pleasure, they give in to the disputants without judging them   *1355a*
impartially. It is in view of this, too, as we stated earlier,[1] that in many places
the law forbids a speaker to bring in nonessentials in court; and there the
judges themselves guard sufficiently against this practice.

It is evident, then, that the present inquiry as an art is concerned with the
techniques of persuasion, which are kinds of demonstrations (for we are   5
most persuaded of a thing when we believe that a demonstration of it has
been given). Now a rhetorical demonstration is an enthymeme, and an
enthymeme, simply speaking, is the most authoritative kind of persuasion.
An enthymeme is a kind of syllogism. It is the concern of dialectic or a part   10
of it to consider alike all kinds of syllogisms. Clearly, then, he who is most
able to apprehend syllogisms, their elements, and how syllogisms are
formed will also be an expert in enthymemes if he adds to this a knowledge
of the kinds of things with which enthymemes are concerned and the
differences between enthymemes and logical syllogisms; for it belongs to
the same faculty to apprehend both the true and a likeness of the true, and   15
men have a natural affinity for the truth and usually succeed in hitting upon
it. For this reason, those who aim successfully at the truth will be similarly
disposed to generally accepted opinions.

That modern writers on rhetoric are dealing with the art of things which
are not essential to rhetoric is evident, and so is the *reason* why they are   20
inclined more towards the forensic part of rhetoric.

Rhetoric is useful (1) because things which are true and things which are
just are by nature stronger than their contraries. So if the decisions are not
made as they ought to be, the judges must fail because of themselves; and
this deserves reproach. Again, (2) it is not easy for a man to persuade some
people even if he uses the most accurate science, for scientific arguments are   25
for the sake of instruction, and some people cannot understand such
arguments; so one must use ordinary language to communicate with and
persuade them, as we stated in the *Topics*[2] when we spoke about
conversations with ordinary people. Again, (3) as in syllogisms, we should be
able to persuade others of either of two contraries, not for the sake of so   30
doing (for one should not persuade others of what is bad), but in order that
we may be aware of what the facts are and that, whenever others are using
arguments unfairly, we may be able to refute them. None of the other arts
is concerned with proving contraries; dialectic and rhetoric alone do this, for   35
both of them draw contrary conclusions in a similar way. On the other hand,
facts are not similarly related to contrary statements about them; and,
simply speaking, things which are true or better by nature are easier to
prove or more persuasive than their contraries. Finally, (4) it is absurd to
regard as shameful one's inability to help himself with his body but not with   *1355b*
his reason, seeing that reason is more proper to a man than his body is. And
if one were to object that a man who uses the power of reason unjustly might

do great harm, the reply would be that this is common to all goods except
5   virtue, especially to the most useful goods, such as strength, health, wealth,
and generalship; for one would confer the greatest benefits by using these
justly but also the greatest harm by using them unjustly.

It is evident, then, that rhetoric, like dialectic, is not limited to things
10   under one definite genus, that it is useful, and that its function is not to
persuade but to apprehend the available means of persuasion which one can
use in each case, just as all other arts do. For the art of medicine, too, is not
to produce health but to promote this as far as possible; for one might try
15   to treat well even those who are incurably ill. Further, it is the function of
the same art [i.e., of rhetoric] to apprehend what is persuasive and what
appears to be [but is not] persuasive, just as it is the function of dialectic to
apprehend a syllogism and what appears to be a syllogism [but is not]. For
a sophist [differs from a dialectician] not in possessing a different power but
in intending to use the same power differently [i.e., for a bad purpose]. So
20   just as a dialectician would use the dialectical means available scientifically
whereas the sophist would use them with the wrong intention, so here one
kind of rhetorician would use the persuasive means scientifically while the
other would use them with the wrong intention.

Let us now try to give an account of the *inquiry* before us, both as to the
manner and the materials to be used in enabling us to succeed in each issue
before us. So, making as it were a fresh start, let us first define rhetoric and
25   then proceed with the rest.

                        2

Rhetoric may be defined as the faculty which apprehends the possible
means of persuasion in any given case. This is not the function of any other
art; for the function of each of the other arts is to instruct or persuade
concerning its own particular subject; for example, the medical art is
30   concerned with what produces health or disease, geometry investigates the
attributes of magnitudes and arithmetic the *attributes* of [natural numbers],
and similarly with the other arts and sciences. Rhetoric, on the other hand,
is the faculty of apprehending the persuasive means which may be used on
any given subject, so to say; and it is for this reason that we speak of rhetoric
35   as having no element of art which is proper to any particular genus.

Of the techniques of persuasion some do not come under this art, but
others do. By the former I mean the techniques which are not supplied by
the rhetoricians but already exist, e.g., witnesses, evidence given under
torture, written documents, and the like; by the latter I mean those which
come under this art and those which can be devised by the rhetorician

himself. So some of the means are there to be used but the others to be   *1356a*
discovered.

Of the means of persuasion to be supplied by speech there are three kinds:
(a) those which depend on the character of the speaker, (b) those which
depend on causing the listener to be disposed in a certain manner, and (c)
those which depend on proof or apparent proof given through speech.

Persuasion depending on character occurs when the speech is so rendered   5
that it makes the speaker credible; for, simply speaking, we trust the word
of equitable men about all things more and quicker than the word of others,
and entirely so in matters which lack accuracy and opinions are divided.
This kind of persuasion, like the others, occurs because of the speech itself
and not because of prior opinions which we may have about the character   10
of the speaker; for, contrary to what some writers on rhetoric posit, i.e., that
the equity of the speaker contributes nothing to his credibility, the truth is
that character is perhaps the most effective means of persuasion.

Persuasion because of the listeners is brought about when their emotions
are aroused by the speech; for our judgments when we are pleased or   15
friendly are not like those when we are pained or hostile. We may add,
writers on rhetoric nowadays pay attention to this kind of persuasion alone.
We will treat this part of persuasion in detail when we discuss the
emotions.[3]

Persuasion through argument is effected when we prove a truth or what   20
appears to be a truth by means of persuasive arguments appropriate to each
issue.

Since persuasions are effected by the three techniques just listed, it is
evident that these [means] can be acquired by those who (a) have the ability
to form syllogisms, (b) can speculate about character and the virtues, and (c)
can speculate about emotions, what each of these is, what kind of a thing
each is, and by what means and how they are aroused. So it turns out that   25
rhetoric is a sort of offshoot of dialectic and of an *inquiry* into character and
may justly be called "political." And it is for this reason that rhetoric
masquerades in the guise of political science and rhetoricians regard
themselves as political scientists, whether because of lack of education or
boastfulness or some other human failings; for it is a part of dialectic and is 30
similar to it, as we said at the start,[4] and neither rhetoric nor dialectic is a
science of any definite subject, but both are faculties of supplying
arguments. Concerning these two faculties, then, and how they are related
to each other, the account just given is quite enough.   35

Of techniques by proof or what appears to be proof [but is not], just as in
dialectic one of them is induction and another is a syllogism or what appears *1356b*
to be a syllogism [but is not], so it is in rhetoric. For an example is [a species
of] an induction, and an enthymeme is [a species of] a syllogism. By "an

5   enthymeme" I mean a rhetorical syllogism, and by "an example" I mean a
     rhetorical induction. All rhetoricians who persuade men by means of proof
     use either examples or enthymemes and no other method. So if, in general,
     a dialectician must prove or induce something or to someone by syllogisms
10   or inductions (this is clear to us from *Analytics*[5]), so a rhetorician must use
     enthymemes or examples which are the same as syllogisms or inductions,
     respectively. The difference between an example and an enthymeme is
     evident from the *Topics*,[6] where syllogisms and inductions have been
     discussed. In the *Topics*, showing that A belongs to many things similar to
15   the one in question is using an induction, in rhetoric, it is an example; and
     showing that through certain statements something else follows, either
     universally or for the most part, by the fact that those statements are true,
     in the *Topics* this is called "a syllogism" but in rhetoric "an enthymeme."
     It is also evident that each kind of proof in rhetoric is good in its own way;
20   for, as already stated in the *Methodics*,[7] the situation in rhetoric is similar.
     Thus some rhetorical speeches are good in examples, others are good in
     enthymemes; and, similarly, some orators are good in the use of examples,
     others are good in the use of enthymemes. Speeches which are good by using
     examples are not less persuasive than speeches which are good by using
     enthymemes, but the latter kind are applauded much more than the former.
25   The causes of the kinds of speeches and the manner in which each kind
     should be used will be discussed later.[8] At present, let us specify them more
     clearly.
          That which is persuasive is persuasive to someone, and a statement is
     persuasive and credible either directly through itself or by being thought to
     have been proved [ultimately] through premises which are persuasive and
     credible directly through themselves. So since no art is concerned with an
30   individual as such (for instance, the medical art is concerned with what is
     healthy not to Socrates or to Callias but to an individual or individuals of
     such and such a kind, for the latter can be subjected to an art but individuals
     as such are indefinite and unknowable), also rhetoric, like dialectic, will
     investigate what is generally thought to be the case not by Socrates or
35   Hippias but by men of a certain kind. For just as dialectic forms syllogisms
     not out of any chance premises (for some absurdities are apparent even to
     silly people) but from premises which are required, so rhetoric [forms
1357a enthymemes] from premises which are usually taken after deliberation.
          Now the function of rhetoric is to deal with such matters upon which we
     deliberate without the aid of an art, and in the presence of such listeners
     who can neither take in at a glance a complicated argument nor draw a
5   conclusion from a long chain of premises. What we deliberate upon are such
     matters which appear to admit each of two alternatives [i.e., of existing and
     of not existing]; for nothing would be gained by discussing matters which
     one regards as incapable of having occurred or of occurring now or in the

future. Of course, one may collect materials by using syllogisms which have
already been formed at other times or by using statements which require   *10*
proof because they are not generally accepted; but the former are
necessarily not easy to follow because of their length (for the listener who
is to make a judgment is assumed to have no depth in thought), whereas the
latter are necessarily not persuasive because they do not follow from
premises which are agreed upon or are generally accepted. Enthymemes
and examples, then, must deal with things which are possible for the most   *15*
part but can also be otherwise, in which case an example will be an
induction and an enthymeme will be a syllogism; and enthymemes should
use few premises, and often fewer than [the number of indemonstable
premises], which are required by a primary syllogism, for what is familiar
need not be mentioned; the listener supplies it himself. For instance, in
showing that Dorieus was crowned by being a victor in the Olympics, it is   *20*
enough to say that Dorieus was a victor in the Olympics, without adding
that victors in the Olympics are crowned, a fact which everybody knows.

Of the premises from which rhetorical syllogisms are formed, only few
are necessarily true. Most inquiries and decisions are about things which
may or may not be, for *actions* are about things upon which we deliberate   *25*
or into which we inquire, and things done come under such a genus of [the
possible], and none of these things are, so to speak, necessary. Hence,
conclusions of things which occur for the most part or which may occur
must be proved from other premises of a similar kind, whereas necessary
conclusions must be proved from necessary premises (this is clear to us from *30*
the *Analytics*[9]). It is evident, then, that some enthymemes are formed from
necessary premises, but most of them are formed from premises about
things which occur for the most part; for enthymemes are formed from
probabilities and signs, and these are the same, respectively, as the materials
for the two kinds of enthymemes.

A probability is of that which occurs for the most part, not without   *35*
qualification, as some define it, but of things which may be otherwise; and
it is related to that of which it is a probability as a universal to a particular. *1357b*
Of signs, however, one kind is that which is related to a statement as a
particular to a universal, another is related to a statement as a universal is
to a particular. Of these two kinds, that which is necessary is [called] "a sure
sign," that which is not necessary has no name. By "necessary" I mean   *5*
[premises of what is necessarily so] from which a syllogism is formed, and
for this reason it is [called] "a sure sign"; for, when people think that they
cannot refute what is said, they then think that a sure sign has been brought
forward, as if the proof of the statements has come to an end; for the term
τέκμαρ as used by ancients has the same meaning as the term πέρας (=   *10*
"limit" or "end"). One kind of sign, then, is related [to a statement] as a
particular to a universal. Thus, if one were to say "a sign that wise men are

just is the fact that Socrates, who was wise, was just," he would be using a
sign; but even if the statement ["wise men are just"] be true, the argument
15 can be refuted, for the statement has not been proved. But if one were to
say "a sign that he is sick is the fact that he has fever" or "a sign that she
gave birth to a baby lately is the fact that she has milk," the conclusion
follows of necessity; and among signs, this alone is a sure sign; for, if true,
it is the only kind that cannot be refuted. The other kind of sign is that
which is related to a statement as a universal to a particular. For instance,
one might say "a sign that he has fever is the fact that he breathes fast."
20 Here, what is concluded can be refuted, even if it is true; for one may
breathe fast even if one has no fever.

   We have now stated the nature of a probability, a sign, a sure sign, and
their differences; but these become more evident in the [Prior] Analytics,[10]
25 where we gave also the *reasons* why some of these cannot be proved [by a
syllogism] whereas the others can.

   We have already stated (a) that an example is [a species of] an induction
and also (b) the kinds of things with which such induction is concerned. It
is related [to what it is used to prove] not as a part to a whole, nor as a whole
to a part, nor yet as a whole to a whole, but as a part to a similar part,
30 whenever both parts come under the same genus but [the example] is more
familiar than the statement it is used to prove. For instance, to prove that
Dionysius, in asking for a guard, was plotting to make himself a tyrant, one
may use as examples the following: Peisistratus earlier had asked for a guard
and had used this scheme to make himself a tyrant, and so had Theagenes
at Megara; and others, too, who are known to have done so are examples of
35 what is not yet known, namely, the *reason* why Dionysius is asking for a
guard. All these examples are instances coming under the following
universal: all those who are plotting to make themselves tyrants ask for a
guard.
1358a   We have given an account, then, of the demonstrative means which are
thought to effect persuasion.

   The greatest difference between enthymemes which has been overlooked
most by practically all writers is one which exists also between syllogisms in
5 dialectical *inquiry*; for some matters in rhetoric which come under the
inquiry [into enthymemes] are like some in dialectic which come under the
inquiry into syllogisms, although others come under other arts and faculties,
whether existing or not yet acquired. For this reason, writers fail to attend
to listeners, and more so when, shifting to [a particular art or faculty], they
10 depart from the dialectical or rhetorical art. This will become clearer if it
is stated in greater detail. By "dialectical and rhetorical syllogisms" I mean
the common arguments, with which the *Topics* is concerned, and these
apply equally to problems coming under justice, physics, politics and many
other faculties which differ from one another in kind. For instance, such is

the argument concerned with *the more and the less*; for syllogisms or   15
enthymemes based on this argument apply equally to things coming under
justice, physics, or any of the other faculties, regardless of their differences.
Proper arguments, on the other hand, are those which are based on
particular species or genera of propositions; e.g., no enthymeme or syllogism
from propositions in physics can be formed to apply to ethical matters, no   20
enthymeme or syllogism from propositions from disciplines other than
physics can be formed to apply to objects of physics, and this is universally
the case. Now common arguments will not make anyone a good judge of
things within a particular discipline, for they are not concerned with a
particular subject. On the other hand, the better selection one makes of
propositions within a particular discipline, the closer he will be, without
noticing it, to a science distinct from dialectics and rhetoric; and if he   25
chances upon principles [of a particular discipline], he will be no longer in
dialectic or in rhetoric but in the discipline to which those principles belong.
Most enthymemes are formed out of specific [propositions], also called
"particular" or "proper," and only few out of those which are common. As
already stated in the *Topics*,[11] here too we should distinguish the kinds of   30
enthymemes and the topics from which they should be taken. By "specific"
I mean propositions proper to each genus, and by "topics," propositions
common to all disciplines. Let us discuss the specific ones [before those
which are common]. But first, let us consider the genera of rhetoric so that,
having determined how many there are, we may proceed to grasp the   35
elements and propositions of each of them separately.

3

There are three species of rhetoric; for hearers, too, are of three kinds. For
a speech involves three elements: the speaker, the subject of the speech, and   *1358b*
the person to whom the speech is addressed; and the speech's end in view
is the person to whom the speech is addressed, i.e., the listener. Now a
listener must be either an observer or one who makes a decision, and the
latter decides either about things past or about future things. A man who
decides about future things would be, for example, a legislator; a man who   5
decides about past things would be, for example, a judge [or a juryman]; and
a man who decides the [speaker's] ability is the observer. So there must be
three kinds of rhetorical speeches: (1) deliberative, (2) forensic, and (3)
oratorical display.

A deliberative speech urges people either to do or not to do something;
for both private and public counsellors always try to persuade people to do   10
or not to do something. Forensic speeches either attack or defend people; for
a party to a suit in court must always do either the one or the other of these

two things. Oratorical speeches either praise or blame people. As to the time to which the speeches have reference: the counsellor is concerned with the future (for his advice is either for or against doing something in the future); the forensic speaker is concerned with the past (for the speaker always attacks or defends things already done); oratorical speakers are concerned chiefly with the present, for they praise or blame the existing state of affairs, but they often find it useful to recall past events or indicate future probabilities.

Each of the above speakers has a different end in view, so there are three distinct ends in view, one for each kind of speaker. The deliberative speaker, aiming at what is expedient and what is harmful, advises doing what is better but refraining from doing what is worse; and as for other things he may include, such as whether the thing to be done is just or unjust, noble or disgraceful, he refers them to those ends. Parties to a lawsuit aim at proving that something is just or unjust, and they adduce other things with reference to these ends. Those who praise or blame are aiming at what is noble or disgraceful and refer other things to these ends. A sign that the ends aimed at are the above-mentioned is the fact that speakers sometimes do not dispute other ends. For example, a party to a lawsuit will sometimes not dispute the occurrence of a fact or that he did harm; but he would never admit that he acted unjustly, otherwise there would be no need of a trial. Similarly, deliberative speakers will often make other concessions but would not admit that they recommend the pursuit of what is inexpedient or the avoidance of what is beneficial; and they do not give heed to the injustice of enslaving neighbors or those who are not unjust to others. Likewise, those who praise or blame a man do not consider whether his acts were expedient or harmful to himself, but often they even praise him for belittling his own interest in order to *act* nobly. Thus, they praise Achilles for helping his friend Patroclus, although he knew that he was facing death, when it was possible for him to remain alive; but such a death was to him nobler, although life was expedient.

It is evident from what has been said that the speaker must, first of all, have at his command propositions for the above three ends; for sure signs, probabilities, and signs [in general] are rhetorical propositions. For every syllogism is composed of premises, and an enthymeme is a syllogism composed of the above-mentioned propositions.

Since it is not the impossible but only the possible objects which are such as to have been done [by man] or to be done in the future, and since neither objects which did not occur nor those which will not occur are such as to have been done or to be done in the future, respectively, it is necessary for deliberative and forensic and oratorical speakers to possess propositions about the possible and the impossible, about that which did or that which did not occur, and about that which will or will not occur. Again, since all those who praise or blame others, who advise others to act or not to act, and who accuse others but defend themselves, try to prove not only the thing they aim at, but also that the thing is great or small, good or bad, noble or *20* disgraceful, just or unjust, whether in themselves or in relation to other things, it is clear that they should also have at their command propositions, both universal and of particulars, about greatness and smallness, and the greater and the lesser, e.g., propositions as to which of two things, both of *25* which are good, or unjust treatments, or restitutions, is the greater or the lesser. And similarly with the others.

We have stated, then, the necessity of acquiring propositions which speakers should have [if they are to achieve their aim]. We should consider next each part of rhetoric on its own, e.g., deliberative, oratorical display, and forensic, and the matters with which they are concerned . . .

BOOK II

1

We have now considered the materials from which one should proceed *1377b* to advise whether to *act* or not to *act*, to praise or blame, and to accuse or defend, and also the kinds of opinions and propositions which should be used to persuade listeners; for it is from these and about these materials that enthymemes for each species of speeches taken separately, so to say, are *20* formed.

Since the purpose of rhetoric is to influence decisions (for men decide on advice given, and a verdict too is a decision), the speaker must not only see to it that his argument is demonstrative and persuasive, but also that he is a man of good character and can put his listener into the right frame of mind. It makes a great difference to a speaker, especially in matters *25* requiring advice, but also in lawsuits, to appear a man of good character and to be regarded as having the right attitude towards his hearers, and, in addition, if these happen to be in the right frame of mind [towards him]. For the speaker to appear to be a man of character is particularly useful in *30* giving advice, but to have the hearer be in the right frame of mind is particularly useful in lawsuits. Things do not appear the same to people

1378a

when they feel friendly as when they feel hostile, when they are angry as when they are calm: they appear either entirely different or different in degree. For, when people feel friendly towards a man they are to judge, they regard him as having *acted* either not unjustly or unjustly but to a small degree; but if they feel hostile, they regard him in the contrary manner. Again, when people *desire* a pleasurable thing and have good hopes for

5 getting it, it appears to them that the thing will be not only pleasurable but also good; but when people are indifferent towards the thing or displeased by it, the contrary is the case.

There are three *reasons* why some speakers are trustworthy, for the things which cause us to be convinced are also three if demonstrations are excluded; they are: (a) prudence, (b) virtue, and (c) goodwill. Indeed, false

10 statements or bad advice given concerning things are caused by all or some of those three; for either men form wrong opinions through folly, or, because of evil habits, they do not say what they think in spite of their right opinions, or, although prudent and equitable, they are not well-disposed towards others and hence fail to give the best advice in spite of their

15 knowledge. There are no other causes of failure. It follows, then, that a speaker who is thought to have all three of qualities [prudence, virtue, goodwill] must inspire trust in his listeners. Accordingly, the qualities we should possess if we are to appear prudent and [ethically] good can be gathered from the various statements about the virtues that we distinguished;[12] for it is these same qualities which will make both the speaker and others such men. So let us now consider goodwill and

20 friendliness, whose discussion comes under that of emotions.

Emotions, which are accompanied by pain or pleasure, are things which so change men as to affect their judgments. Such are anger, pity, fear and the like, and the contraries of these. We should distinguish three things which are involved in each emotion: in anger, for example, (a) how angry

25 men are disposed, (b) with whom they usually get angry, and (c) what sort of things they get angry about; for if one or two were present in a man, but not all three, they could not arouse anger. Similar remarks apply to the other emotions. So just as we described the various propositions for the speaker

30 earlier, so we shall proceed in the same manner and distinguish them here.

2

Let anger be [defined as] a desire, accompanied by pain, to exact an apparent revenge because of what appears to be an unjustified belittling of what is due to a man or to those dear to him. If, indeed, this is anger, then

35 it must be felt always against some individual, e.g., not against man

[universally taken] but against Cleon, who did or was about to do something   *1378b*
affecting him or those dear to him; and every instance of anger is
accompanied by some pleasure which comes from the expectation of taking
revenge. For the thought of attaining what one aims at is pleasant, and an
angry man aims at what he himself can attain; but no one aims at things
apparently impossible for him to attain. Hence it has been well said about   5
wrath,

> Sweeter it is by far than the dripping of honey
> Which spreads through the hearts of men.[13]

For anger is accompanied by a certain pleasure both because of this [i.e.,
expectation of revenge] and because thought dwells in exacting revenge,
since the image aroused by so doing, like the images in dreams, give one
pleasure.

Since to belittle is to entertain the opinion that something appears to be   10
of no worth (for we think that good things as well as bad things, and even
things which tend to bring these about, are worthy of consideration), we
regard things of little goodness or badness or of none at all as being of no
worth at all. There are three species of belittling: contempt, spite, and insult.   15
(1) A contemptuous man belittles; for one is contemptuous of things which
he regards as of no worth, and things of no worth are belittled. (2) A spiteful
man, too, appears to be showing contempt. But spite is the obstruction of
another's wishes, not in order to get something for oneself but to prevent
another from getting what he wishes; and since one spites a man not in order
to get something for himself, he belittles him. For clearly, by so doing, he   20
thinks he will not be harmed by him, for if he feared him, he would not
belittle him; nor does he expect a benefit from him when he considers him
of no worth at all, for otherwise he might be anxious to make him a friend.
(3) Insult, too, is a species of contempt. To insult is to harm or cause pain
by doing things which bring shame to another, not in order to obtain
something other than what he did in fact obtain, but just for the pleasure of   25
it; for those who react do not insult but take revenge. The *reason* why a man
gets pleasure by insulting others is that, by ill-treating them he regards
himself as far superior to them. This is why the young and the rich are
insolent; for, by insulting others, they think they are superior to them. One
kind of insult is dishonoring; so he who dishonors others belittles them, for   30
that which is of no value at all, whether for good or evil, has no honor at all.
It is in view of this that Achilles says in anger:

> He hath dishonored me, taking away my prize for himself,[14]

and

> Like an alien, honored by none,[15]

meaning that this is the *reason* for his anger. Men think they ought to be
respected by their inferiors in birth, or power, or virtue, or, in general, in   35
anything in which they might be greatly superior. For example, in matters   *1379a*

of money, a wealthy man thinks he ought to be respected by a poor man, in speaking, a rhetorician by a man who cannot speak well, a ruler by a man who is ruled, and a man who thinks that he is worthy of ruling by a man whom he considers worthy of being ruled. Hence it has been said,

5   Great is the wrath of kings, whose father is Zeus almighty,[16]
and
       Yea, but his rancor abideth long afterward also,[17]

for they resent being ruled because of their superiority [to other men]. Again, a man thinks he ought to be respected by those who, he thinks, should treat him well; and these are those whom he himself, or those at his request, or those dear to him, have treated or are treating or wish to treat or wished to treat well.

From the above it is now evident how men are disposed when they get
10 angry, with whom they get angry, and for what *reasons*. They do so when they are pained. For a man who is pained intends to do something. So if someone else gets in his way, whether directly or indirectly, e.g., by preventing him from drinking when thirsty, he appears to act similarly in
15 both cases; or if someone else works against him or refuses to help him or annoys him in some other way when he is in such a frame of mind [i.e., pained and aiming to do something], he gets angry with all of them. For this reason, people who are sickly or poor or in love or thirsty or, in general, have *desires* but are unable to satisfy them, become easily angered or excited, especially against those who belittle their present condition. Thus a sick man gets angry against those who belittle his sickness, a poor man against those
20 who belittle his poverty, a warrior against those who belittle the risk of war, a lover against those who belittle his love, and similarly with the others, for in each case the existing affection paves the way for anger. Again, a man is angered if what happens is contrary to what he expects; for an unexpected great evil is more painful [than an expected one], just as a great wish, when
25 fulfilled unexpectedly, brings greater joy [than when it is fulfilled expectedly]. Hence it is evident from these facts what kinds of seasons or times or dispositions or periods of life make men easily prone to anger, and where or when, and that the more men are in these conditions, the more easily they are prone to anger.

Under such conditions, then, one is easily stirred to anger; he gets angry
30 at those who make fun of or mock or jeer at him, for these are insults, and he gets angry at those who do the sort of harm which is a mark of insult. Such kinds of slight are neither retaliatory nor beneficial to the doers, for they are caused directly from insult. Again, one gets angry at those who speak ill of or show contempt for the things he cares most, e.g., at those who
35 speak ill of or show contempt for his philosophy or personal appearance or the like, if these are highly prized by him; and much more so if he suspects

that he does not possess, whether not at all or not much or not as others think,   *1379b*
the things he prizes highly, for if he thinks strongly that he possesses these
things, he pays no attention. And he is even more angry if those who say or
do these things are his friends, for he thinks that he ought to be treated even
better. Again, he feels angry at those who have usually treated him with
honor or showed consideration, if they changed their attitude towards him;   *5*
for he thinks that they are now showing contempt, for otherwise they would
be behaving as they were behaving before. Again, he is angry at those who
do not return favors, whether not at all or to a lesser extent. Again, he is
angry at those who, although inferior, act in a contrary manner, for all such
persons appear to show contempt: they act as if he were inferior to
themselves or as if they have received kindness from inferiors. Again, he is   *10*
more angry at men of no consequence at all if they belittle him more than
others do; for anger is posited to be directed towards those who ought not
to belittle others, and inferiors ought not to belittle their superiors. Again,
he is angry at friends who do not speak of him or treat him well, and even
more angry if they do the contrary; and he is angry at them if they do not
sense his needs, as Plexippus is angry with Meleager in Antiphon's play, for   *15*
not sensing one's needs is a sign of belittling him, since we should be aware
of the needs of those for whom we care. Again, he is angry at those who
rejoice at his misfortunes or who, in general, keep on being cheerful in the
midst of his misfortunes; for their behavior is a sign of being inimical to him
or of belittling him. Again, he is angry at those who do not care if they cause   *20*
him pain; and it is for this reason that men get angry with those who bring
bad news. Again, he is angry at those who listen to stories about him or point
out his weaknesses, since they are like those who belittle or are inimical to
him; for friends share in his distress, and all men are distressed when they
think of their own weaknesses. Again, he is angry at those who belittle him
in the presence of the following: (a) his rivals, (b) those whom he admires,   *25*
(c) those whom he wishes to admire him, (d) those whom they revere, and
(e) those by whom they are revered; for, if belittled, he becomes more angry
in the presence of these than in the presence of others. Again, he is angry
at those who belittle such persons as his parents, children, wife, or subjects,
for it will be disgraceful for him not to come to their aid. Again, he is angry   *30*
at those who do not return a favor; for belittling is not doing what one should
do. Again, he is angry at those who speak ironically of what he considers
serious; for to speak ironically of what is serious is to show contempt [for it].
Again, he is angry at those who treat the others well, but not him; for to
regard all others worthy of those things but exclude him is to show contempt
for him. Forgetfulness, too, makes one angry, as of names, although a trivial   *35*
matter; since forgetfulness is thought to be a sign of belittling. For
forgetfulness of a thing occurs because of neglect; and if one neglects

something, he belittles it.

1380a　　We have now discussed the persons with whom one is angry, the frame
of mind of a person who is angry, and the *reasons* for one's anger. Clearly,
then, it is up to the speaker himself to present his speech in such a way as
to bring his hearers to a state of mind disposed to anger, to represent the
opposing party as being guilty of the charges about which they are angry
and as being the kind of person with whom the hearers get angry.

5

1382a　　Let fear be defined as a pain or disturbance arising from an image of an
impending evil, whether painful or destructive. Surely men are not afraid
of every evil, such as the prospect of someone being unjust or slow, but only
of those which can cause great pains or destructions and appear to be about
25　to occur in the near and not the distant future. Indeed, they do not fear
occurrences in the very distant future. For example, they all know that they
will die but are not troubled since this will not occur in the near future. If,
then, this is [the definition of] fear, such things must be fearful which appear
30　to have great power of destroying or causing harm and tend to inflict great
pain. For this reason, the signs of such fearful things, too, are fearful, for
then the fearful appears to be close at hand. Indeed, danger is just this,
namely, the nearness of what is fearful; for example, such is the enmity or
anger of those who can do something to us, for it is clear that they wish to
35　do so and are about to *act*. Injustice, too, is feared, when it has power; for
it is by deliberative choice that the unjust man is about to commit an unjust
1382b　act. This is also true for virtue when insulted, if it has power; for it is clear
that, whenever insulted, it always intends to retaliate, and it has just been
insulted and has the power to *act*. Again, this is also true for the fear felt by
those who have the power to do something about it; for such men must be
prepared to *act* when they fear impending danger.
5　　Since most men are bad and are bested by greed and are cowards in the
face of danger, it is for the most part fearful for a man to be at the mercy
of others; for when they are aware that he has done something terrible, he
fears that they will betray or desert him. And those who can *act* unjustly are
feared by those who can [easily] be treated unjustly; for men who have
10　power to *act* unjustly do so for the most part. And those who were or think
they were treated unjustly are feared; for they are waiting for the
opportunity [to retaliate]. And those who have *acted* unjustly and possess
power are fearful, since they are afraid of retaliation; for we have already
assumed[18] that this is fearful.
　　And rivals for the same thing are feared, when they cannot all possess it;
15　for they compete against each other. And those who are feared by men

stronger than someone, are feared by him, for if they are feared by the stronger, they can harm the less strong even more; and those who are feared by others who are stronger are feared by him also, and for the same reason. And those who have destroyed others who are stronger than a man are feared by him. And those who have attacked others stronger than he is are feared by him; for they are either to be [simply] feared or to be feared when they have become stronger. Enemies or rivals who have been unjustly treated are to be feared, not the hot-tempered or outspoken but those who are calm or dissembling or unscrupulous; for it is not clear when they are about to [retaliate] and so it is never evident that one is safe for some time. All fearful things are even more fearful if, once done, they cannot be corrected, whether not at all or not by one who fears them but by those who are against him; and so are those things which cannot be helped or not easily helped. Simply speaking, those things are fearful which, when done or about to be done by others, cause a man to feel pity. Roughly speaking, then, the greatest things which are fearful and cause men to fear are the ones just stated.

    We may now state the dispositions which cause men to be afraid of things. If fear is indeed an affection which makes one expect that something destructive is about to happen, it is evident that no one fears whatever he thinks will not [adversely] affect him, whether these be things which he thinks will not affect him, or men who he thinks will not affect him, or the times when he thinks they will not affect him. Accordingly, one must be afraid of whatever he thinks will affect him, whether they be things or men or whether it be at a certain time. Now those who are or think they are very prosperous do not think that they will be [adversely] affected, and in view of this they are insulting or belittling or rash (it is wealth, physical strength, abundance of friends, and power that make them such); neither do those who are already used to the sufferings of all sorts of terrible things and have grown callous about the future, like those who have been beaten to the point of being insensitive. So there should lurk some expectation of safety if men are to feel the pain while struggling for escape. A sign of this is the fact that fear causes men to deliberate, and nobody deliberates when there is no hope. Hence, when it is better for an audience to be in fear, the speaker should use the means to make them such as to feel the danger, indicating that this happened even to others who were stronger than they were, or is happening or has happened to others like them, at the hands of those they did not expect or the things or at times they did not expect.

    Since it is evident what fear is, what things are fearful, and how various men become disposed to being afraid, it is also evident from these what confidence [or courage] is, about what things men are confident, and how [various] men become disposed to be confident; for confidence is contrary to fear, and that which causes confidence is contrary to that which causes

20

25

30

35

1383a

5

10

15

fear. Hence confidence is the expectation arising from an image of safety as being near and of fearful things as being absent or remote.

20 Things which cause confidence are (a) those which are terrible but remote, or (b) those which are near and expected as safe, or (c) remedies for danger or aids to confidence, whether many or great or both, or (d) the absence in the past of unjust treatments by others and unjust *acts* towards others, or (e) the absence of any rivals or of rivals who are not strong, or of rivals who are strong but friendly or have treated others well or have been 25 treated well or (f) the presence of many or more powerful or both who have identical interests.

Men themselves are disposed to being confident if they think that they have succeeded many times and suffered no reverses; or, if they have met terrible things many times but escaped them successfully. For men become unaffected when facing terrible things for two reasons, lack of experience 30 and help when it is available, as in dangers at sea during a storm, for both the inexperienced and those who have the means to deal with it because of their experience are confident of safety. Again, men are disposed to being confident (a) whenever terrible things did not affect others who are like them or even weaker or those who they think are weaker than themselves; and they so think if they have conquered those who are weaker or whom they 35 consider stronger than or as strong as themselves, and (b) if they think they 1383b are superior to others in the number and greatness of things (e.g., property, physical strength, friends, territory, weapons), whether in all or in the most important, and (c) if they have *acted* unjustly to none, or not to many, or 5 not to those whom they fear, and (d) in general, if their relations to the gods are right, with respect to signs and oracles and other such things, for anger makes men courageous, and not *acting* unjustly but being treated unjustly causes anger, and divine beings are believed to help those who are unjustly treated. Finally, men are disposed to being courageous whenever they think 10 that, by trying, they could not or will not fail or they will succeed.

8

1385b Let pity be defined as pain in a man caused by what appears to be a destructive or painful evil which befalls another who does not deserve it, 15 and which the man would think that he himself or someone close to him might be the victim of the same evil in the near future. For it is clear that a man who will pity someone must be such as to think that he himself or someone close to him might be the victim of an evil such as the one stated in the definition or similar or close to it. For this reason, neither those who 20 have been completely ruined feel pity (for, having suffered the worst, they think that no further evil can befall them), nor do those who think that they are happy beyond all bounds (on the contrary, these are insulting; for if they think that they possess all the good things, they also think that no evil can befall them, since the absence of evil, too, is one of the good things).

Men who would feel pity, then, are those who think that evil [as stated above] might befall them; and those who have been victims of it; and those 25 who have escaped it; and the elderly, because they think rightly or by experience; and those who tend to be cowardly; and those who are educated, for they are reasonable; and those who, being any of the above, have parents living, or children, or wives, for these are close to them and might be victims of such evil; and those who have no strong feelings such as anger or courage 30 (for these take no account of the future) nor an insulting disposition (for these, too, take no account of any suffering) but are between these two; and also those who have no great fear (for panic-stricken men do not feel pity because they are too involved with their own plight); and those who think 35 that some men are equitable (for those who think no such men exist would think that all men deserve to suffer evil); and, in general, one who is so *1386a* disposed as to recall such evils which befell him or those close to him or to expect that such evils will befall him or those close to him. We have stated, then, how men are disposed when they feel pity.

As for the things for which men feel pity, they are clear from the definition. Painful and grievous things which are destructive are all pitiful; 5 and so are those which tend to deprive [men of what they hold dear]; and those great evils which are caused by chance. Great evils which are grievous or destructive are, for example, death, bodily injury, affliction, old age, disease, lack of food; evils whose cause is chance are, for example, friendlessness, scarcity of friends (and in view of this, it is pitiful to be torn 10 away from friends and companions), deformity, weakness, mutilation, evil from an *action* whose source ought to have ended in something good; and the frequent repetition of the above. Also, the coming of a good when a great evil has already occurred is pitiful, e.g., the arrival of the king's gifts for Diopeithes after his death. Again, the nonoccurrence of any good for a 15 man, or the occurrence of it without its enjoyment. The things, then, which cause men to pity others are these and others like them.

Those whom men pity are: those they are familiar with but are not very closely related to them, and they pity them as if they themselves are about to suffer great evils. And for this reason Amasis, it is said, did not weep when 20 his son was being led to his death but did weep when his friend was begging [to die instead of his son]. For the latter was pitiful, the former terrible, and the terrible differs from the pitiful; it tends to drive it out and is often useful in bringing about the contrary [of pity]. Again, men feel pity when a terrible thing is near themselves. And a man pities those of about the same age or 25 character or habits or rank or race, for great evil which might befall him appears [to him] to have befallen these more than others who differ in age or any of the other traits; for, in general, here too one should understand that the things which one fears are those which arouse his pity when they happen to others.[19]

    Now since the sufferings of others are pitiful when they appear close to
30 us, while those which happened a hundred centuries ago are not remembered and those which will happen a hundred centuries from now are not expected and, in general, do not arouse pity or do but not in the same way, it follows that speakers who use to perfection gestures, tones, dress, and dramatic action in general are in a better position to arouse pity in the audience; for they make it appear before their eyes that a [great] evil will
1386b soon occur or has just occurred. For the same reason, great evils tend to be more pitiful if they have just happened or are about to happen soon, and so are signs of them and *actions* related to them, e.g., garments and the like of those who have suffered, and speeches and the like of those who are
5 suffering and are, e.g., about to die; and they are most pitiful at such times when sufferers were or are men of virtue, for all of these, by appearing near to the audience, arouse greater pity and make it appear before the eyes that the suffering was or is undeserved.

12

1388b   After what has been said, let us go over the types of character with respect to the emotions and habits of persons differing in age and fortune. By "emotions" I mean anger, *desire*, and the like, which have been already
35 discussed, and by "habits" I mean the virtues and vices, and these too have already been discussed;[20] and to these we added, for each type of person, the kinds of *intentions* they have and the kinds of *actions* they perform. By
1389a "ages" I mean youth, the prime of life, and old age. By "fortune" I mean good birth, wealth, power, and their opposites; or, in general, good fortune and ill fortune.

    Young men are of such a character as to have [strong] *desires*, and as such they tend to satisfy their *desires*. Of the bodily *desires*, they pursue sex most
5 of all and are incontinent about it. They are changeable and fickle in their *desires*, which are strong but end quickly. Their wishes are intense but shallow, like those of sick people who are thirsty or hungry. They are
10 quick-tempered and hot-tempered and tend to give vent to their temper; and their temper gets the better of them, for, because of their love of honor, they cannot bear being belittled but are indignant if they think they are unjustly treated. They love honor, but they love victory even more; for youth *desires* superiority over others, and victory is a form of superiority.
15 They love honor and victory more than money; in fact, they love money least because they have not yet experienced a lack of it — this is the

meaning of the remark made by Pittacus about Amphiaraus. They are not
malicious but well-meaning, because they have not witnessed many
instances of wickedness. They tend to trust others because they have not
often been deceived. They are hopeful; for, like intoxicated persons, they
are warm-blooded by nature and, also, because they have not yet failed   20
often. Their life is filled with expectation; for expectation is of future things
whereas memory is of things past, and youth has a long future before it but
a short past behind it: on the first day one has no past to remember but   25
everything to expect in the future. They are easily deceived for the *reason*
given above, for they are easily given to expect things. They are more brave
than persons of other ages, since hot temper and hopefulness makes them
fearless and courageous; for no angry person is in fear, and the expectation
of something good makes one courageous. They tend to be bashful, for they
have been educated under the existing customs alone and have as yet no   30
beliefs of other noble ways. They are high-minded, for they have not yet
been humbled by life and have no experience of the necessities of life; and,
being hopeful, they regard themselves as fit for great things, i.e., they are
high-minded. And they choose to do what is noble rather than what is
expedient, since they live by habit more than by practical thinking; for   35
practical thought aims at what is expedient whereas virtue aims at what is
noble. And at their age, more than at any other, they are fond of friends and
companions, because they enjoy living with others and are not yet judges of 1389b
anything — not even of friends — which contributes to what is expedient.
And they err by doing things in excess or more intensely, as Chilon
remarked, for they overdo everything: they love too much, they hate too   5
much, and likewise with all other things. And they think they know
everything and are quite sure about it; and indeed this is the *reason* for
overdoing everything. And they *act* unjustly for the sake of insult and not
for the sake of harm. And they are disposed to pity others because they
regard them as kind and better [than what they actually are]; for they
measure their neighbors by their own unwillingness to harm others and   10
hence regard them as not deserving to suffer. And they are fond of laughing
and so are witty; for wit is a cultivated insult.
  Such, then, is the character of the young.

13

  The character of elderly men or men who are past their prime is formed
mostly of traits which are contrary to those of the young. Old men have
lived many years, have been deceived many times, and have made mistakes   15
many times, and most events have turned out to be bad; and because of
these, they are not sure of anything and do by far less than they should. And

they have suppositions about things, but they never [claim to] know. And, hesitating to take a stand, they always use words such as "perhaps" or "probably," and this is the way they speak of all things and never positively.

20 And they are badly disposed, for such disposition is a belief that things are worse than they actually are; moreover, they are suspicious of evil because of their distrust, which came to them through experience. And for these *reasons*, they neither love intensely nor hate intensely but, as Bias hinted, they love as if they will hate later and hate as if they will love later. And they

25 are low-minded because they have been humbled by life; for they have no desire for anything great or remarkable but only for what will keep them living. And they are stingy, for material goods are one of the necessities of life and, in addition, they know by experience that it is difficult to acquire but easy to lose such necessities. And, being disposed in a way contrary to

30 that of the young, they are cowardly and tend to anticipate danger; for their zest has been chilled, while the young are warm-blooded. Thus old age has paved the way to cowardice; for fear is a form of chill. And they love living, especially during their last days, because they *desire* that which is

35 departing, and they particularly *desire* that which they lack most. And they love themselves more than they should, for this too is a form of low-mindedness. And they live by attending to what is expedient, not to what is noble, and they do so more than they should because they love

1390a themselves [more than they should]; for that which is expedient is a good to oneself, but that which is noble is a good without qualification. And they are shameless more than they have a sense of shame; for they hardly pay attention to what others think of them, and this is because they do not care for what is noble as much as they do for what is expedient. And, because of their experience, they are not hopeful of the future; for [they think that]

5 most things turn out bad, or, at any rate, worse [than expected], and one may add their cowardice as a cause. And they dwell in their memories rather than in expectations; for the life left to them is short while their past is long, and expectation is of the future while memory is of the past. And this indeed

10 is the *reason* why they are garrulous: they spend their time talking of the past, for they take pleasure in recalling past events. And their tempers are sudden but weak; and some of their *desires* are gone while others are weak, and so they are not disposed to *desire* anything or to *act* according to *desire*, unless it be for [material] gain. For this reason, men of such an age even

15 appear to be temperate; but in fact their *desires* have slackened and they have become slaves to gain. And they live not according to [moral] character but by thinking pragmatically; for pragmatic thought aims at that which is expedient, while [moral] character is related to ethical virtue. And they *act* unjustly not to insult but to harm others. And old men are disposed to pity

20 others, but not for the same *reason* as the young do: the young are so disposed because of kindness; but old men do so because of weakness, for

they consider all suffering to be close to that of their own kind, and such suffering, as stated earlier, tends to arouse pity. Hence they are disposed to complain, and neither are they witty nor do they love to laugh; for the disposition to complain is contrary to the love of laughter.

Such, then, are the characters of young men and of elderly men. So since 25 all men welcome speeches which are agreeable to and resemble their own character, it is clear how such speeches and the speakers who use them will appear [to the kinds of audiences].

14

It is evident that the character of men in their prime would be between that of the young and that of elderly men: it would be free from both 30 excesses. Thus such men have neither excessive courage (for such courage would be rashness), nor very much timidity but courage which is properly related to the two extremes; they neither trust nor distrust everybody but judge others more according to the truth; they lead a life which aims neither at what is noble alone nor at what is expedient alone but at a mixture of the 1390b two; and they are neither niggardly nor prodigal but aim at what is proper. Their attitude towards temper and *desire* is similar. They are temperate and also brave, or brave and also temperate, for these two [temperance and bravery] do not both exist in the young or the elderly: the young are brave 5 but intemperate, the elderly are temperate but cowardly. Generally speaking, men in their prime have both the [qualities] which are of benefit to the young and those which are of benefit to the old; and relative to the excesses and deficiencies in the young, which exist as deficiencies and excesses in elderly men, respectively, men in their prime pursue a career which is moderate and fitting. Man's body is at its prime from age thirty to 10 age thirty-five, but man's soul, at about age forty-nine.

Concerning the various types of character possessed by young men, elderly men, and men in their prime, then, let the above discussion suffice.

15

Let us next speak of the goods which men possess or acquire by luck and see how they affect the characters of men. The character of men of high 15 birth is to be ambitious; for every man who possesses some good tends to accumulate more of it, and high birth is a sort of honor acquired from one's ancestors. Such a man will be contemptuous even of others like him, because 20 what is honorable [seems to be] more honorable or something to boast about

if it is remote than if it is near. Being of high birth is having the virtue of high lineage; being excellent, on the other hand, is not departing from one's nature, something which for the most part does not occur in men of high
25 birth, for most of them are of little consequence. For there is a change in the descendants of men, as there is in the yield of crops from the [same] territory: a race of men is sometimes good, and their descendants continue to be eminent for some time; but then they again fail and go backwards. A race of noble nature tends to degenerate into one with a rather mad character, like the descendants of Alcibiades and those of the Elder
30 Dionysius, and a race of firm character tends to degenerate into one of stupid and sluggish character, like the descendants of Cimon, Pericles, and Socrates.

16

The character which follows wealth is evident to all. Men of wealth are insulting and conceited, being affected by the possession of property and
1391a riches; for they are disposed as if they possess all the goods in life. For wealth to them is a sort of standard of the value of all other things, and for this reason it appears to them that all those things can be bought by wealth. They are luxurious and ostentatious; luxurious, because of their luxury and display
5   that they are happy, ostentatious and ill-mannered, because since all men are accustomed to spend their time on what they love and admire, they think that others are zealous for the things they themselves love and admire. And it is also reasonable that they should be affected in that way; for there are many people who are in need of what they themselves possess. Hence the saying of Simonides about wise and wealthy men, when he was asked
10 by Hiero's wife whether it is better to become wealthy or wise: "wealthy, of course," he said, "for I see the wise spending their time at the doors of wealthy men." Wealthy men think also that they deserve to rule others; for they think that they possess the things which qualify them to rule. In short,
15 wealth belongs to the character of a happy fool. The newly rich, however, differ in character from those who have been wealthy for a long time: all the bad qualities already mentioned belong to the former to a higher degree and to a greater extent, for being newly rich is like being uneducated in wealth. Their unjust acts on others, e.g., assault and adultery, are not malicious but insulting and incontinent.

17

20 Similarly, ethical habits of those in power, too, are for the most part about as evident as those of the wealthy, for some of them are the same as those

of the wealthy but others are better; for men in power are more ambitious and more manly than the wealthy because they aim to do the things which their power permits them to accomplish. And, being compelled to attend to things which require power, they are more serious because they are in 25 charge. And they have more dignity and more depth [than the wealthy]; for their position makes them more visible to the public, and for this reason they tend to be moderate — dignity being a mild and becoming form of depth. And when they *act* unjustly, they do so not on a small but on a large scale.

The character of men of good fortune partakes of the character of those 30 above [men of good birth, wealth, and power]; for good fortunes which are thought to be the greatest tend to be those already treated; and we may add to good fortune also good children and the bodily goods. Now good fortune 1391b makes men rather conceited and unreasonable, but the one best thing which accompanies the character of these men is piety and a certain disposition towards the divine, and this is caused by the good fortune which befell them.

We have given an account, then, of the character of men according to age 5 and fortune; for the character of those who are contrary to the ones mentioned, i.e., of the poor or of the unfortunate or of those without power, is contrary, respectively, to that already described.

644

POETICS

CONTENTS

Chapter

POETICS

1

Concerning the art of poetry, both itself and its species, let us 1447*a*
speak about (a) the effect which each has, (b) how plots should be
constructed if the making of poems is to be done well, (c) how many 10
and what kinds of parts a poem [of each species should have], and
similarly (d) about any other things which belong to this *inquiry*; and
let us begin first with the things which are first according to nature.

Productions of epic and of tragedy and, moreover, of comedy and
dithyrambs and of most works for the flute and the lyre all turn out to 15
be, each of them taken as a whole, [poetic] imitations. These [imita-
tions] differ from one another in three respects, for they imitate either (a) by different means or (b) different objects or (c) in a
different and not in the same manner.

Now just as some imitate many things by making likenesses of them
with colors and figures, either by art or by habit, while others do 20
so by their nature, so, too, each of the above–mentioned [poetic]
arts produces its imitation in rhythm or language or harmony, using
these [means] either separately or in combination. For example, arts
which use only harmony and rhythm are those of the flute and the
lyre and any others which might happen to have a similar power, e.g., 25
the art of the Panpipe; an art which may use rhythm without harmony,
on the other hand, is that of the dancers, for these artists, too, imitate
character and feelings and *actions* by means of rhythmical gestures.

The art that uses only language, whether in prose or in verse (and if 1447*b*
in verse, [by] combining different meters with one another or using
only one kind of meter), turns out to be nameless up to now; for we
have no common name for the mimes of Sophron and Xenarchus and 10
for the Socratic dialogues, nor for any imitation by means of
trimeters or elegiacs or some other such meter that one might use.
Men, however, adding the word "making" to the meter employed,
use the terms "elegiac–makers" and "epic–makers" and so call such
writers "poets," doing so not with respect to their imitation of objects
but with respect to the name common to the meter. For even if what 15
is produced is a work on medicine or physics written in meters, they
are accustomed to speak of it in this way. But there is nothing common

to Homer and Empedocles except the meter; and so the one should
justly be called "a poet" whereas the other should be called "a natural
20   philosopher" rather than "a poet."   In like manner, if one were to
produce an imitation by combining all the meters (as Chaeremon did
in his *Centaur*, a rhapsody combined from all the meters), he should
be called "a poet" [in virtue of his imitation alone].

Let the distinctions about these matters, then, be made in this way.
There are, however, some [poets] who use all the three means men-
25   tioned above, that is, rhythm and song and meter, as indeed we find in
the making of (a) dithyrambs and nomes, and of (b) tragedies and
comedies; but they differ in this respect: the former use all the means
simultaneously, the latter use them in turn.

Among the arts, then, I say these are the different means by which
those artists produce their imitation.

2

1448*a*   Since those who engage in [poetic] imitation imitate [men] in *ac-*
tion, who must therefore be either virtuous or vicious (for character
is almost always attributed to these two kinds of men alone, inasmuch
as all men differ with respect to character in virtue and vice and so are
5   either better than average or worse than average or about average),
just as painters do (for Polygnotus made likenesses of better men,
Pauson of worse men, and Dionysius of men about average), it is clear
that each of the [three kinds of] imitations mentioned will also differ
from the other [kinds] by imitating in the same way men of one kind
[of character] only.   These dissimilarities may occur even in dancing
10   and flute–playing and lyre–playing, and the same may be said also of
prose and verse without harmony.   Thus Homer imitates better men,
Cleophon imitates average men, but Hegemon of Thasos, the first to
write parodies, imitates worse men, and so does Nicochares, the au-
15   thor of the *Deiliad*.   And this applies similarly to dithyrambs and to
nomes. One might imitate men as   ..., and as Timotheus and
Philoxenus did in their *Cyclopes*. Likewise, tragedy and comedy are
distinguished by the same kinds of differences; for comedy sets out to
imitate men who are worse than average, and tragedy men who are
better than average.

3

Imitations may differ in yet a third way: the manner in which one might imitate the objects [in each art]. For it is possible to imitate the   20
same objects with the same means: (1) by narration, either (a) when the narrator speaks in his own person at one time but assumes the role of someone else at another time, as Homer does, or (b) when the narrator speaks in his own person without changing, or (2) when the performers dramatize in the poem all the agents who are engaged in *action* or in other kinds of activity.

As we said at the beginning, then, the differences in imitation are   25
three: the *means*, the *objects*, and the *manner*. So, in one respect, Sophocles would be the same kind of imitator as Homer, for both produce imitations of virtuous men; in another respect, he would be the same in kind as Aristophanes, for both produce imitations of agents in *action* portrayed dramatically. It is in view of this fact that some say that these [i.e., tragedy and comedy] are also called "dramas" [= "*dramata*"] inasmuch as performers in them dramatize [= *drondas*] agents in the poems. For this reason, the Dorians claim the discov-   30
ery of both tragedy and comedy. For (1) the Megarians claim comedy: (a) those here in the mainland of Greece on the grounds that it arose in the time of their popular rule and (b) those from Sicily, for the poet Epicharmus came from there and lived much earlier than Chionides and Magnes;   and (2) some of the Peloponnesians claim   35
tragedy by pointing to the names "drama" and "comedy" as a sign of their claim. For the Dorians say that they call the suburbs "*comae*," whereas the Athenians call them "*demes*," and from this fact the Dorians argue that the word "*comodoi*" (= "comedians") came not from the verb "*comazein*" (= "to revel") but from the wandering of the comedians among the *comae*, since they were held in low esteem and were driven out of the city. The Dorians say also that for the word   1448*b*
"*poein*" (= "doing") they use the word "*dran*," whereas the Athenians use the word "*prattein*" (= "acting").

Concerning imitations with respect to the number and nature of their differences, then, let the above suffice.

4

It is reasonable to think that the art of poetry in general was brought into being by two kinds of causes, both of them natural; for (1) imitat-   5 ing is innate in men from childhood, and in this respect men differ from the other animals by being the most imitative of animals and learning first by imitating, and (2) all men enjoy works of imitation.

10 A sign of the second cause is what happens when we observe works [of art]; for, although we are pained while observing certain objects, we nevertheless enjoy beholding their likenesses if these have been carefully worked out with special accuracy, e.g., likenesses of the forms of the lowest animals and of corpses. And the *reason* for this enjoyment is that learning is pleasant—indeed most pleasant— not only for philosophers, but similarly for other men also, although the latter par-

15 take of such pleasure only to some extent. That is why men enjoy observing likenesses: as they behold them, they learn and infer what each likeness portrays, e.g., that this is a likeness of that [man]; and if one happens not to have observed earlier the object imitated, pleasure will still come, not because the work is an imitation, but because of the workmanship or the coloring or some other such *reason*.

20 Since imitating and also using harmony and rhythm come to us according to our nature (for it is evident that meters are parts of rhythm), those who at first had the greatest gifts for these, by gradually improving on them, gave birth to the making of poetry out of improvisations. But this activity went forward in two directions in ac-

25 cordance with the character [of each imitator]; for the more dignified poets were imitating noble *actions* or the *actions* of noble men, whereas the less worthy poets were imitating the *actions* of inferior men, first making invectives just as the others were making hymns and encomia. Now of the poets before Homer we can cite no poems of this [lampooning] sort, though it is likely that there were many such

30 poets; but starting from Homer we can give examples, e.g., his *Margites* and other such poems, in which the fitting meter, the iambic, came into use; and it was for this reason that these poems are now called "iambics," since in this meter the poets lampooned one another. Thus some of the ancient poets became makers of heroic poems, others of iambics, i.e., of lampooning poems.

35 Now just as Homer as a poet excelled in serious subjects (for he was unique not only in making his imitations well, but in making them dramatic also), so, too, he was the first to indicate by example the forms of comedy, dramatizing not invective but the ludicrous. There is indeed an analogy: as the *Iliad* and the *Odyssey* are to tragedies, so the

1449a *Margites* is to comedies. Once tragedy and comedy appeared on the scene, of those who pursued each of these two species of poetry in accordance with their special nature, some became comic instead of

5 iambic poets, others became tragedians instead of epic poets, be-

cause the forms of comedy and tragedy were grander and more esteemed than those of iambic and epic, respectively.

To examine whether or not tragedy is at present adequate in its
kinds, judged both with respect to its nature as such and in relation
to the theater, is another matter. In any case, tragedy and comedy
started from improvisations, tragedy from those who introduced the 10
dithyramb, comedy from those who introduced the phallic perfor-
mances which still, even now, remain the custom in many states. Then
[tragedy] grew gradually as the poets made advancements by adding
what appeared to be appropriate to it, and, having undergone many
changes, it ceased to change when it attained its nature. Aeschylus 15
was the first to raise the number of performers from one to two, to
lessen the role of the chorus, and to give speech the leading role;
Sophocles added a third performer and scenery. Furthermore, after a
period of short plots and ludicrous diction, which were characteristic 20
of early tragedy because of its change from satyric form, the size of
tragic plots after a long time achieved dignity, and the meter likewise
changed from [trochaic] tetrameter to iambic [trimeter]; for at first
[tragic] poets used the [trochaic] tetrameter because poetry then was
satyric and more associated with dance, but when diction [like that of
ordinary speech] came in, nature herself found the appropriate
meter, for the iambic meter is the most characteristic of conversation. 25
A sign of this is the fact that we use mostly iambs in our conversation
with one another, but we seldom speak in hexameters, and when we
do, we depart from the spoken intonation which characterizes [ordi-
nary] speech. Furthermore, as to how the number of episodes has
changed and how each of the other [parts of the tragedy] are said to
have been enhanced, let it be enough for us to have mentioned them, 30
for it would perhaps be a big task to go through them individually.

5

Comedy, as we have said, is an imitation of men worse than average, not with respect to every kind of vice but with respect to the ludicrous part of the ugly; for the ludicrous part is a kind of error or 35
ugliness that is neither distressing nor destructive, such as, to take an
obvious example, the comic mask, which is in some sense ugly and
distorted but causes no distress.

Now the changes in tragedy and those who made them have not
gone unnoticed. Comedy, on the other hand, has gone unnoticed 1449*b*
from the beginning because it was not taken seriously; for the archon
authorized a chorus of comic performers at quite a late date, but until

then there were only volunteers. It was when comedy had already
taken on certain forms that those who were called "comic poets" were
[first] recorded. But we do not know who it was who provided it with
5   masks or prologues or a number of performers or other such things.
Plots were first produced by Epicharmus and Phormis, who came [to
Athens] from Sicily, while of the comic poets of Athens, Crates was
the first to drop the lampooning kind of comedy and use language and
plots of a universal nature.

10   Epic poetry and tragedy are alike insofar as both imitate serious
[matters] in grand meter and language; but (a) epic poetry differs
from tragedy in using one [kind of] meter and in being narrative in
manner. Furthermore, it differs in length; for tragedy attempts as far
as possible to be complete within one revolution of the sun, or to
vary from this time period only by a little; but epic poetry has no definite limits in time, and in this respect it differs from tragedy, although
15   at first the poets set no definite limits of time in tragedies as well as in
epics. As for the parts, some are the same for both, whereas others
are proper to tragedy. In view of this, whoever understands good and
bad tragedy also understands good and bad epic poetry, for the parts
of epic poetry are present in tragedy, but not all the parts of tragedy
20   are present in epic poetry.

6

Concerning imitative poetry in hexameters and comedy we shall
speak later. Let us now speak of tragedy, taking out from what has
been said so far about it those parts which give rise to the definition of
its essence.

25   Tragedy, then, is (1) an imitation of an *action* which is serious and
complete and has a [proper] magnitude, (2) [expressed] in speech
with forms of enhancements appropriate to each of its parts and used
separately, (3) [presented] by performers in a dramatic and not a narrative manner, and (4) ending through pity and fear in a catharsis of
such emotions.

30   By "speech with forms of enhancements" I mean speech which has
rhythm or intonation or song; by "appropriate to each of its parts" I
mean that the poet achieves some of his ends through meter alone
and others through song [...].

Since it is by *action* that [performers] produce their imitation, first
the enhancement by spectacle would necessarily be a part of tragedy,
and then the use of song and diction; for it is by means of these that
[tragic performers] produce their imitation. By "diction" here I mean,

[for example], the combination of the parts; by "use of song" I mean,   35
that whose effect is evident to everybody.

Since imitation [in tragedy] is of an *action*, and since *actions* are
willed by men, who must have certain qualities, namely, character
and *thought* (for it is because of these that *actions*, too, are said to be   1450a
of a certain kind), there are by nature two causes of *actions*, namely,
thought and character; and it is in virtue of these that all men succeed
or fail. Now the imitation of the *action* is the plot, for by "plot" here I
mean the combination of the events; by "character" I mean that in vir-   5
tue of which we say that men in *action* are of a certain quality; and by
"*thought*" I mean that quality by means of which men say when they
argue for or against something or express a *judgment*.

Every tragedy, then, must use six parts in virtue of which it is a tragedy of a certain quality. These are plot, character, diction, *thought*,   10
spectacle, and song. Of these, two parts are the means of imitation,
one is the manner of imitation, three are the objects of imitation, and
there are no others. No small number of [dramatists], one might say,
have used these kinds [of parts], for all dramas are alike in having spectacle and character and plot and diction and song and *thought*.

Now the most important of these parts is the composition of the   15
events. For tragedy is an imitation not of men but of *action* and a way
of life and happiness or unhappiness; for happiness and unhappiness,
too, exist in *action*, and the end of man is a kind of *action* and not a
quality. Thus men are of a certain quality by virtue of their character, but they are happy or its contrary by virtue of their *actions*.   20
Hence performers *act* not in order to imitate character; they take on
character for the sake of [imitating] *actions*. Accordingly, the events
and the plot are the end in tragedy, and [in general] the end in each
thing is the most important [part]. Besides, without *action* tragedy
would not exist, but it would exist without character. In fact, the   25
tragedies of most young poets are deficient in character, and in general many poets are of this kind. Such is the case, too, with painters,
e.g., Zeuxis in comparison with Polygnotus; for Polygnotus is a good
portrayer of character, but the painting of Zeuxis has no character at
all. Moreover, if someone were to set down in a drama a succession of
dramatic speeches which reveal [mainly] character and are well expressed in diction and *thought*, he would not perform what was stated   30
to be the function of tragedy; but a tragedy which, although employ-
ing these in a somewhat deficient way, has a plot and a composition of
events will achieve [the function of tragedy] far better. In addition,
the greatest [elements] by which tragedy moves the soul—reversals
and recognitions—are parts of the plot. Another sign of this point is   35

the fact that those who attempt to write tragedy are able to be accurate in diction and in the portrayal of character before they are able to construct the events [well],   and such was the case with almost all the early poets.

    The plot, then, is the principle and, as it were, the soul of tragedy; character comes second.   In fact, there is a parallel even in painting; if some artist were to lay on the finest colors without order, he would not delight the viewer as well as the artist who sketches a likeness of an object in black and white.   Tragedy, after all, is an imitation of *action*; and it is an imitation of agents for the sake of that *action* most of all.

    Third [in order of importance] is *thought*, that is, the ability to express what there is to be said and what is fitting, and to speak in this manner is the function of politics and rhetoric.   In fact, the early poets made their agents speak like statesmen, whereas the poets nowadays make them speak like rhetoricians. Now character in speech is the kind of quality which makes clear the speaker's intention; and in general, for just this reason, speeches which do not reveal whether the speaker intends to pursue or avoid doing something have no character.   *Thought*, on the other hand, is found in those speeches in which speakers (a) argue that something is or is not the case, or (b) express something universally.

    Fourth is diction in language; by "diction," as mentioned before,   I mean the manner in which meaning is expressed in words;   and this part has the same effect whether in verse or in prose. Of the remaining parts, the fifth, which is the use of song, is the most pleasing accessory. As for [the sixth part], the spectacle, although it moves the soul, it is of all the parts the least a matter of art and has the least to do with the art of poetry; for the effect of [a good] tragedy is possible even without performance or performers. Besides, the working out of the spectacle comes under stagecraft more than under the art of the poet.

7

    These matters having been specified, let us next discuss the kind of structure which the events should have, since this is the first and most important part of tragedy. We have posited that tragedy is an imitation of *action* that is complete and a whole and has a certain magnitude; for a thing may be a whole even if it has no magnitude. Now that which has a beginning and a middle and an end is a whole. A beginning is that which may come but not of necessity after another thing, but another thing comes by its nature into existence or is generated after it;   an end, on the contrary, is that which by its nature comes after another thing, either of necessity or for the most part, but no other thing comes after it; and a middle is that which [by its nature] comes after something else and precedes another thing. Well–structured plots, therefore, should not begin at any chance [event] nor end at any chance [event] but should use the ideas just stated.

Furthermore, that which is beautiful, whether an animal or any other thing which is composed of a number of parts, should have not   35
only these parts [properly] ordered but also a magnitude, and not any chance magnitude. Indeed, beauty exists in magnitude as well as in order; for this reason, neither could a tiny animal become beautiful (for our view of it, which takes place in an almost imperceptible interval of time, becomes blurred), nor could an animal of very large size   1451a
(for the visual grasp of it and of its parts does not take place simultaneously, so its unity and wholeness are lost for the viewer, e.g., if there were to be an animal a thousand miles long). Hence, just as the magnitude of an inanimate body or of an animal should be such as to be easily visible [as a whole], so the length of a plot should be such as can be   5
easily retained in memory. As for the proper limit of a plot's length, if related to the performance at dramatic competitions and to [the audience's] perception, it does not come under the dramatic art; for if a hundred tragedies had to compete, they would have to be timed by water–clocks, as is said to have occurred at one time. The proper limit of a [good tragedy or plot] according to its own nature is this: the   10
greater the length up to the limit of being grasped as a whole, the more beautiful it is with respect to its magnitude. Simply specified, however, an adequate limit to the magnitude of the thing [i.e., the plot] is such that, if the events occur in a sequence which is either probable or necessary, a change takes place [in the protagonist] from misfortune to good fortune or from good fortune to misfortune.   15

8

A plot has unity not [simply], as some suppose, if it is concerned with a single [man]; for many or an indefinite number of generically distinct things may happen [to a man], yet from some of them no unity can be made. So, too, a man may perform many *actions* from which no unity results. For this reason, all those poets who wrote a *Heracleid*, a   20
Theseid, and other such poems seem to have been mistaken. Such poets think that, since Heracles was one *man*, the plot, too, must have unity. But just as Homer excelled in other respects, either because of his art or because of his nature, so, too, he seems to have grasped this point well; for in composing the *Odyssey*, [to take an example], he did   25
not include everything that had happened to Odysseus: Odysseus had been wounded on Mount Parnassus and also had feigned madness at

the mustering of [Agamemnon's] army, but the latter event did not
follow from the former, whether of necessity or with [high]
probability. He composed the *Odyssey* as a unified *action* of the kind
30   we have described, and he did likewise with the *Iliad*. Just as in the
other imitative arts, then, a single imitation should be of a unified object, so the plot, too, being an imitation of *action*, should be an imitation of one *action* which is a whole, with events as parts so constructed
that the transposition or removal of any part will make the whole dif-
35   ferent or perturb it; for if the presence or absence of a thing [in a
whole] produces no distinguishable difference, that thing is not a part
of that whole.

9

It is also evident from what has been said that the task of the poet is
to state, not what has [actually] occurred, but the kinds of things
which might [be expected to] occur, and these are possible by virtue
1451*b*   of their probability or their necessity. In fact, the historian differs
from the poet not by stating things without rather than with meters—
the writings of Herodotus would be no less a history if they were produced with meter rather than without meter—but by speaking of
what has actually occurred, whereas the poet speaks of the kinds of
5   things which are likely to occur. In view of this, poetry is both more
philosophical and more serious than history; for poetry speaks rather
of what is universally the case, whereas history speaks of particular
events which actually occurred. The kinds of things that a certain
kind of man happens to say or do in accordance with probability or
10   necessity are universal, and poetry aims at such things, albeit it attaches names [to individuals]; what Alcibiades actually did or suffered, on the other hand, is a particular.
Now this practice has already become clear in comedy; for having
constructed the plot in accordance with what is probable, the comic
poets then proceed to assign chance names, unlike the lampooning
15   poets, who make their poems about a particular man. In tragedy, however, the poets stick to historic names; and the *reason* for this is that it
is the possible which is persuasive. We are somehow not convinced
that things which have not occurred are possible; but it is evident
that what has occurred is possible, for it would not have occurred had
20   it been impossible. And yet, even in some tragedies only one or two
names of individuals are familiar to the audiences and the rest are
made up; and in other tragedies not even one name of an actual individual is well known, e.g., in the *Antheus* of Agathon, for in this play
both the events and the names of the agents are made up, and yet the

play delights us none the less. So one must not seek in every case to stick to traditional plots, with which [most] tragedies are concerned; 25 indeed, to seek to do so would be ridiculous, seeing that even [the names of] eminent men [in the past] are [nowadays] familiar only to a few, and yet those tragedies delight everyone.

It is clear from these statements, then, that the poet should be a maker of plots rather than of meters, inasmuch as he is a poet by vir- tue of imitation and imitates *actions*. So even if he happens to use 30 things that actually occurred, he is no less a poet; for nothing prevents some past occurrences which he uses as a poet from being the kinds of things that are probable and could happen again.

Without qualification, of plots and *actions* the episodic are the worst. By "episodic plot" I mean a plot in which it is neither probable 35 nor necessary for the episodes to follow one after the other. Such plots are produced by bad poets because of their own [lack of art], by good poets because of the performers; for by making pieces for show and by stretching the plot beyond its capability, [good poets] are often 1452a compelled to distort the [necessary or probable] sequence of events.

Now a tragic imitation is not only of a complete *action*, but also of events which arouse fear and pity, and these events come about best—and do so more when they occur unexpectedly—if they occur because of each other. For they are more wonderful if they occur in 5 this manner rather than if they occur by *chance* or by luck. And even those which occur by luck are thought to be most wonderful if they appear to occur as though by design, as in the case of the statue of Mitys at Argos: while the man who caused the death of Mitys was looking at the statue, it fell and killed him. Events such as these seem to occur not without plan, and so plots [with such events] are of neces- 10 sity finer [than plots with events which occur just by chance].

10

Of plots, some are simple and the others are complex; for the *ac- tions* which plots imitate, too, are such to begin with. By "simple ac- tion" I mean one in which, being continuous and having unity, as 15 already specified, a change of fortune occurs without reversal or rec- ognition; by "complex *action*" I mean one in which a change of for- tune occurs with reversal or recognition or both. These [changes] should come about from the very structure of the plot and so turn out to be either necessary or probable consequences of the preceding 20 events; for what occurs *because* of preceding events is far different from what occurs [merely] *after* preceding events.

11

A reversal, as has been mentioned, is a change of things being done
to a contrary [from what is expected], and this [change], as we have
been saying, [should come about] in accordance with what is probable
or necessary. Thus in the *Oedipus [Rex*, the messenger] who came to
cheer up Oedipus and to rid him of his fear about his relation with his
mother produced the contrary effect when he revealed who Oedipus
really was; and in the *Lynceus*, when Lynceus was led away to die and
Danaus followed in order to kill him, it turned out, as a consequence
of what had been done, that Danaus died and Lynceus was saved.

Recognition, as the name itself signifies, is a change from ignorance
to knowledge resulting in either friendship or enmity towards those
who are marked for good fortune or misfortune; and the finest recognition is the one which occurs at the same time as the reversal, like the
one in the *Oedipus [Rex]*. But recognitions may be of other kinds
also; for recognition of someone may occur through an inanimate or
an animate chance [cause], as just stated, or through the fact that
someone did or did not do something. But the kind of recognition
most [proper] to the plot and to the *action* is the one first mentioned:
it is the kind which, along with a reversal, will arouse either pity or
fear; for tragedy, as imitation, has been posited as being of *actions*
which arouse pity or fear. Besides, bad or good fortune will follow in
such cases. Now since this recognition occurs between men, in some
cases only one of them is recognized by the other, and this occurs
whenever the identity of the latter is already known; in other cases
each must recognize the other, e.g., Iphigenia was recognized by
Orestes from the letter that was sent, but a second recognition, in
which Orestes is made known to Iphigenia, was needed.

Two parts of [a complex] plot, then, are reversal and recognition; a
third part is suffering. Of these, the first two have been discussed. As
for suffering, it is an *action* which tends to lead to destruction or distress, e.g., to death on stage, agony, wounds, and the like.

12

We have discussed previously the parts which give a tragedy its
quality, but the separate parts into which a tragedy as a quantity is divided are as follows: prologue, episode, exode, and choral song, the
parts of the last being the parode and the stasimon. Now these [parts]
are common to every [tragedy], but certain other parts are proper to
some [tragedies], namely, the [songs] from the stage and the
commoi. The prologue is the whole part of a tragedy which precedes
the parode, [i.e., the entrance of the chorus]; the episode is the whole
part of a tragedy that comes between [two] whole choral songs; the

exode is the whole part of a tragedy after which there is no choral song. As for the choral parts, the parode is the first utterance, taken as a whole, of the chorus; then the stasimon is a choral song without anapests or trochees; finally, the *commos* is a lamentation sung in common by the chorus and the performers from the stage. 25

The parts which a tragedy should use, then, are those [i.e., the qualitative] which were discussed earlier and the quantitative, which have just been stated.

13

After what has been said, we should discuss next those things at which tragic poets should aim and those which they should guard against in constructing their plots, and also the things from which the 30 tragic function will be achieved.

Now the construction of the finest tragedy should be complex and not simple, and such tragedy should imitate *actions* which arouse fear and pity (for this is the proper function of such imitation). It clearly follows, then, that (1) neither should fair–minded *men* be 35 shown changing from good fortune to misfortune, for this change arouses neither fear nor pity but is repugnant; (2) nor should wicked *men* be shown changing from bad fortune to good fortune, for this change is the most untragic of all, inasmuch as it has none of the effects it should have, since it arouses no compassion and neither pity 1453a nor fear; and (3) nor should an utterly worthless *man* undergo a fall from good fortune to misfortune, for a tragedy thus constructed might arouse compassion but neither pity nor fear, inasmuch as pity is aroused by the misfortune of one who does not deserve it and fear by 5 the misfortune of one who is like us, in which case the outcome of such construction will arouse neither pity nor fear. The remaining type, then, lies between these two; and such is the *man* who, not differing [from us] in virtue and in justice, and being one of those who have a great reputation and good fortune, changes to misfortune not 10 because of vice or wickedness but because of some error, as in the case of Oedipus and Thyestes and other famous *men* from families of this sort.

It is necessary, then, that a good plot be not double, as some say, but rather single [in its outcome] and change not from misfortune to good fortune but, on the contrary, from good fortune to misfortune, 15 not because of wickedness but because of some grave error committed either by the sort of *man* we have cited or by one who is better than average rather than worse. A sign of this is what has happened [in the history of the theater]; for at first the poets would recount any story that came their way, but now the finest tragedies are composed

20 about a few families, e.g., those of Alcmaeon, Oedipus, Orestes, Meleager, Thyestes, Telephus, and others who have happened to do or suffer terrible things. The finest tragedy according to the poetic art, then, arises from a construction of this kind; and it is for this reason that those who criticize severely Euripides for using this [princi-

25 ple] and ending many of his tragedies in misfortune are mistaken, for this [type of ending] is, as we have said, the right one. But the best sign of this fact is the following: if such tragedies are rightly executed on the stage and in [dramatic] competitions, they turn out to be the most tragic;   and Euripides, even if he does not manage other things

30 well,   still appears to be the most tragic of the poets.

  In second rank is the kind of composition which some say comes first, namely, that which has a double construction, like the *Odyssey*, and has contrary endings for the better and for the worse agents.   Such tragedy is thought to be first in rank because of the weakness of audiences, for

35 the poets go along with the desires of the spectators.   This pleasure is not tragic   but rather appropriate to comedy; for, in a comedy, the bitterest enemies in the plot, such as Orestes and Aegisthus, go off as friends at the end and nobody is killed by anybody.

14

1453*b* Now it is possible that what arouses fear and pity come from the spectacle, but it is also possible that these feelings come from the very structure of the events;   and indeed this is a better   imitation and a mark of a better poet. For the plot should be so constructed as to

5 make the one hearing the events shudder   and feel pity as a result of what happens, even without seeing the tragedy performed. Such indeed is what anyone would feel on hearing the plot of the *Oedipus [Rex]*. To produce this effect by means of spectacle is less a matter of

10 art and requires extraneous apparatus.   As for those who, by means of spectacle, produce not a fearful sight but only a monstrous one, they are not dealing with tragedy; for one should seek to arouse from tragedy not every kind of pleasure but only that which is appropriate to it. So, since the poet should produce through imitation the kind of pleasure that comes from pity and fear, it is evident that he must do so by

15 means of the events themselves. Let us, then, take up what sort of encounters appear terrible or grievous.

  Such *actions* must be directed towards those who are either friends or enemies or neither. Now if someone kills or is about to kill an enemy, [the *action*], whether performed or about to be performed, does not arouse pity, except for the suffering itself; and this is the case

20 even if [the agent] is neither a friend nor an enemy of the victim. But whenever the sufferings occur among friends, e.g., if a brother kills or

is about to kill or do some other such thing to his brother, or a son his
father, or a mother her son, or a son his mother, these are what the
tragic poet should look for. The tragic poet, then, need not disturb
the traditional stories (I mean, for example, the death of
Clytaemnestra at the hand of Orestes and that of Eriphyle at the hand
of Alcmaeon), but he should devise incidents and handle the tradi-   25
tional material well. Let us state more clearly what we mean by the
term "well."

It is possible to make the *action* occur as the older poets did, that is,
by making the agents know what they are doing and to whom they are
doing it, e.g., as Euripides does in making Medea kill her children. It
is also possible to have the agents *act* but be ignorant of the terrible   30
deed done and later recognize the kinship, as Sophocles does in his
Oedipus [Rex]. Here the deed occurs outside the drama; but the deed
may be in the tragedy itself, e.g., the *act* of Alcmaeon in Astydamas'
tragedy or of Telegonus in *The Wounded Odysseus*. There is also a
third way, one in which the agent, being about to perform an irrepara-   35
ble deed not knowing the true identity of the intended victim, recognizes him before he does it. There are no other possible ways; for the
agent must either *act* or not *act*, and he either knows or does not know
toward whom he is about to *act*.

The worst of these possibilities is the one in which the agent is
about to *act* knowing toward whom he is to *act* but fails to *act*; for this
action is repugnant and, being devoid of suffering, has no tragic effect. For this reason, no one uses this possibility or one does so rarely,   1454a
as in *Antigone*, in which Haemon [threatens to kill his father Creon,
but does not]. The second possibility is one in which the agent [knows
and] *acts*. There is a [third and] better way, one in which the agent *acts*
in ignorance and then recognizes what he has done, for there is nothing repugnant here and the recognition is striking. The best of all is   5
the remaining.   In the *Cresphontes*, for example, Merope is about to
kill her son but, recognizing him, does not do so;   in the *Iphigenia*,
the sister recognizes her brother and does not kill him;   and in the
Helle, the son, about to hand over his mother [to the enemy], recognizes her [and does not do so].   It is for this *reason*, as stated earlier,
that the [existing] tragedies are concerned with only a few families;   10
for the [earlier] poets, in looking for [tragic material], discovered by
luck and not by art [the way to] produce such [a tragic effect] in their
plots,   and [even now] poets [still] find it necessary to have recourse
to those [few] houses in which such sufferings occurred.

Concerning the structure of events and the kinds of plots which
tragedies should have, then, enough has been said.   15

15

Concerning character, there are four things at which the poet should aim. (1) The foremost is that it should be cogent. Now an agent will have [cogent] character if, as stated previously, his words and *actions* make evident his intentions; so his character will not be cogent if his intentions are not made evident but will be cogent if his
20   intentions are made evident. But [cogency of character] depends on the role of the agent. A woman and a slave, too, may be [portrayed] cogently, [but in a different manner]; for perhaps a woman is inferior to a *man*, whereas a slave is of no account at all. (2) The character should fit the agent; for [a *man*] may be [portrayed as] manly in character, but it is not fitting to portray a woman as being manly or shrewd. (3) The character should be similar [to those we find in life];
25   for this is distinct from making character cogent or fitting as we have just described. (4) The character should be consistent; and even if the character is portrayed as being inconsistent, it should nevertheless be portrayed as being *consistently* inconsistent.

An example of baseness of character which is not necessary is that
30   of Menelaus in the *Orestes*; of what is improper and unfitting [examples are] Odysseus' lamentation in the *Scylla* and Melanippe's speech; and of inconsistency [an example is] the character in *Iphigenia at Aulis*, for Iphigenia the suppliant in no way resembles her later self.

In portraying character, too, as in constructing the events, the poet
35   should always look for what is either necessary or probable, so as to have a given agent speak or *act* either necessarily or probably, and [hence] to have one event occur after another either necessarily or probably. It is evident, then, that the resolutions of the plots, too,
1454*b* should come about from the plot itself and not by the use of *deus ex machina*, as in the *Medea*, or in the stampede of the Greeks in the *Iliad*. This device should be used [if at all] for events outside the drama, either those in the past which cannot be known by man, or those in the
5   future which require foretelling and reporting; for it is to the gods that we attribute the power of seeing all things. Again, there should be nothing unreasonable in the events, or, if there is, it should be outside the tragedy, as in the case of the *Oedipus [Rex]* of Sophocles.

Since a tragedy is an imitation of men who are better than average, tragic poets should follow the example of good portrait
10   painters; for, in painting men, they represent them more beautifully than they are but still retain the likeness of their visible form. So, too, when the poet imitates men who are quick or slow to anger or who have other such [defects of] character, he should render them as ex-

amples of fair–minded or indignant men, as Agathon and Homer made Achilles.

The poet, then, should keep in mind these points and, in addition,   15
the stage effects on the audience which must conform to the poetic art; for it is often possible to make mistakes here also.   But these matters have been sufficiently discussed in our published treatises.

16

What recognition is has been stated earlier; let us turn to its kinds.   20
Recognitions of the first kind are those through signs, and these are the most inartistic but most often used by poets because of their lack of resourcefulness. Some signs are congenital, as in "the lance which the earthborn bear on their [bodies]" or the kind of 'stars' used in the *Thyestes* by Carcinus. Other signs are acquired after birth; and of   25
these, some are bodily, like scars, others are external tokens, such as necklaces or the little boat which led to the recognition in the *Tyro*. And it is possible to use these in a better or worse way; for example, Odysseus was recognized by his scar in one way by his nurse, in another way by his swineherds. Recognitions which use signs for the sake of convincing others—indeed all such recognitions—are rather inartistic; those which arise from reversal are better, like the one in   30
the Bath Scene [in the *Odyssey*].

Of the second kind are those devised by the poet; and for this reason they are inartistic. One example is the manner in which Orestes reveals himself in *Iphigenia in Tauris*: he recognizes his sister by the letter, then he reveals himself by saying what the poet wants him to say and not what the plot requires. For this reason the mistake [in the   35
poetic art] is somewhat similar to that mentioned above, for Orestes could just as well have brought some [tokens]. The Voice of the Shuttle in the *Tereus* of Sophocles is another example.

Third is the recognition through memory, when at the sight of an   1455a
object one is affected in some way; in the *Cyprians* of Dicaeogenes, for example, a man bursts into tears at the sight of a picture. And in The Tale of Alcinous we have another example: Odysseus, hearing the minstrel play the lyre and remembering the past, weeps and, as a result, is recognized.

Fourth is the recognition from inference. For example, in the *Choephoroi* we have the following: "Someone resembling me has   5
come; nobody resembles me except Orestes; therefore it is Orestes who has come." We have another example [proposed] by the sophist Polyidus for *Iphigenia*: it would be probable for Orestes to reason thus, "My sister was sacrificed at the altar, and now I, too, am to be

sacrificed." So, too, in the *Tydeus* of Theodectes, the father says, "I
10   came to find my son, and I am to perish myself." Again, the women
in the *Phineidae,* having seen the place, inferred their destiny:
"Here we are destined to die, for here we were cast forth." There is
also a composite recognition arising from false reasoning on the part
of the audience, as in *Odysseus the False Messenger*; for [Odysseus]
15   says that he will know the bow (which he actually had not seen), but
the listener commits the fallacy of thinking that he will be recognized
[by that statement].
     The best of all recognitions is that which arises from the events
themselves, when the striking effect comes through probabilities, such
as that which we find in the *Oedipus [Rex]* of Sophocles; another appears in *Iphigenia [in Tauris]*, (725–803), for it is probable that
Iphigenia should wish to be sending letters home. Such recognitions
20   are the only ones that occur without the use of contrived signs or amu-
lets. The next best are the recognitions which arise from inference.

17

     In constructing the plot and in working out the diction to go with it,
the poet should make it his special effort to set the scene as vividly as
possible before his eyes; for in this way, visualizing as distinctly as
25   possible the events just as if he were a spectator of the performers in
action, he would discover what is proper and so be least likely to overlook incongruities. A sign of this is [the mistake] for which Carcinus
was censured. [The plot requires that] Amphiaraus [be seen] returning from the temple; but his return, not seen [on stage], was not evident to the audience, and the play failed in performance, since the
spectators were displeased by this [oversight].
     Further, the poet should work out the plot by making the appropriate
30   gestures himself as far as possible. Men are most persuasive whose sufferings are brought about naturally; for those who show agitation or
anger most truly are those who are actually agitated or angry. It is in
view of this that the poetic art belongs to those who are naturally gifted
or who have a touch of madness; for the former easily mold themselves
to any emotion, whereas the latter are prone to ecstatic [empathy].
1455b   As for the story, whether the poet takes it as handed down or makes
it up himself, he should make an outline of it, and then on this basis
make up episodes and fill in details. What I mean by "an outline," to
take *Iphigenia [in Tauris]* as an example, is the following: a certain
maiden, being offered up in sacrifice, disappears mysteriously from
the presence of those who are sacrificing her; being settled in another
5   country, in which it was the custom to sacrifice strangers to the god-

dess [Artemis], she is made the priestess. Sometime later, the brother [Orestes] of the priestess happens to come to this country (the fact that the god for some *reason* told him through an oracle to go there and what he commanded him to do is entirely outside the plot). Upon his arrival he is seized; and, as he is about to be sacrificed, he is recog-   10
nized, whether as Euripides brings it about or as Polyidus does by making him say, as it was probable that he would, "So not only my sister but I, too, must be sacrificed." As a result, he is saved. Once the names of the agents have been assigned, the poet should then make up the episodes and see to it that they are appropriate. In the case of Orestes, for example, one such episode is Orestes' fit of madness which led to his capture, another is the rite of purification which led   15
to his salvation.

Now the episodes in a drama are short; an epic poem, however, is lengthened by longer episodes, yet its outline is not long, as in the *Odyssey*: a certain man has been away from home for many years, kept that way by Poseidon, and he ends up being alone. Meanwhile, his affairs at home are in such a state that his wife's suitors are squandering   20
his property and are plotting against his son. Tempest–tossed, he arrives home; he reveals himself to some; he attacks and destroys his enemies and is saved. That is the essence of the *Odyssey*; the rest is made up of episodes.

18

One part of every tragedy is complication, the other is resolution. Events outside [the drama], and often some of those within it, consti-   25
tute the complication, while the remaining part constitutes the resolution. By "complication" I mean the part from the beginning until the last part after which a change from good fortune to bad ... fortune occurs; and by "resolution" I mean the part from the beginning of this change until the end. Thus, in the *Lynceus* of Theodectes,   30
the complication consists of the events that occurred before [the tragedy starts], the seizure of the child, ... [and also that of the parents]; the resolution is the part from the accusation of murder until the end.

There are four species [or kinds] of tragedy, for, as mentioned previously, there are as many parts: (1) the complex tragedy, the whole of it consisting of reversal and recognition; (2) the tragedy of suffering, such as those that deal with Ajax and Ixion; (3) the tragedy of charac-   1456a
ter, e.g., the *Phthiotides* and *Peleus*; and (4) ... [...], such as the *Phorcides* and the *Prometheus* and those which are about Hades.

Now the poet should do his utmost to work out well all the [parts], or at least most of them and the most important ones, especially nowa-   5

days when critics carp at poets. In the past, each part was well worked
out by some poets, but nowadays a poet is expected to surpass each of
the older poets at his special excellence.

It is also just to speak of tragedies as being the same or different
with respect to the plot more than to any other part; and by "having
the same plot" we mean tragedies whose involvements and resolu-
10   tions are the same. Yet many poets work out the involvement well but
the resolution poorly; but both should always be mastered.

Again, one must keep in mind what has often been said and not try
to make a tragedy out of an epic structure (and by "epic structure"
here I mean one with many plots), e.g., not to make a tragic plot out of
the whole of the *Iliad*. In epic, the parts assume a suitable magnitude
15   because of the epic's length, but in drama, [the use of episodes suitable for one epic] goes far beyond what is expected. A sign of this is
that the poets who have made a tragedy by using the whole capture of
Troy instead of a part of it, as did Euripides, or the whole story of
Niobe instead of a part of it, as did Aeschylus, either failed or showed
up badly in the competitions; and even Agathon failed once in this re-
20   spect. In reversals and in simple events,   however, [these poets] succeed remarkably well in achieving what they wish. For the effect
produced is tragic or else it arouses a feeling of compassion, as in the
case of a clever rogue like Sisyphus, who is outwitted, or of a brave
but unjust man who is defeated.   As Agathon says, an event of this
kind has a probability of occurring, since [according to him] improba-
25   ble things, too, have a [mathematical] probability of occurring.

The chorus, too, should be regarded as one of the performers, as a
part of the whole and as sharing in the *action*, that is, not in the manner of Euripides, but in that of Sophocles.   As for the choral songs [of
the later poets], they are no more parts of the plots [of their tragedies]
than [of the plot] of any other tragedy; and for this reason they are
30   [nowadays] sung as interludes—a practice first introduced by
Agathon. But, one may ask, what difference is there between singing
choral parts as interludes and fitting a speech or a whole episode from
one tragedy into another?

19

Now that [plot and character] have been discussed, it remains to
take up diction and *thought*.
35   Concerning *thought*, let the discussion of it in the *Rhetoric* be assumed here, for this topic is more proper to that *inquiry*. The things
concerned with *thought* [in tragedy] are all those matters which

should be rendered by speech; and the parts of these are (a) demonstrating and refuting, (b) rendering the feelings, such as pity, fear, 1456*b* anger, and the like, and also (c) maximizing or minimizing what is to be said. In dealing with events [occurring on stage], too, it is clear that the poet should use the same devices as those he uses for *thought* in presenting those events as pitiful or terrible or important or probable [or etc.], but with this difference: whereas things spoken 5 should be presented by or follow from the speaker's choice, [actual events on stage] should be apparent without any verbal exposition. For what else would the speaker add to those events if they were to appear [on stage] as they should without any verbal exposition?

Of the [parts] concerned with diction, one kind of inquiry deals with the forms of diction, such as what an injunction is, a prayer, a 10 narration, a threat, a question, an answer, and others like them, and understanding of these comes under the [science] of delivery or under one who has the architectonic [science] which includes the [science] of delivery. No serious censure, then, should be directed to one's [poetic] art for his knowledge or ignorance about these matters. For example, why would anyone regard as a [poetic] mistake that 15 which Protagoras censures: that Homer, meaning to pray, used a command when he said "Sing, Goddess, the wrath ...?" For Protagoras says that telling someone to do or not to do something is a command. For this reason, let us pass over this study as belonging not to poetics but to another [science].

20

The [material] parts of diction in general are as follows: letters, syl- 20 lables, connectives, nouns, verbs, joints, inflections, and speech.

Now a letter is an indivisible vocal sound, not any such sound but one from whose nature, as a part, a composite vocal sound can be formed; for brutes, too, can make indivisible vocal sounds, but I do not call any of these "a letter." The kinds of letters are the vowel, the 25 semivowel, and the mute. A vowel, such as "a" and "o," is a letter having an audible vocal sound without the application [of the tongue or lips or teeth to the various parts of the mouth]. A semivowel, such as "s" and "r," is a letter having an audible vocal sound made with the application [of the tongue or lips or teeth, etc.]. A mute, such as "g" and "d," is a letter formed with the application [of the tongue or lips or teeth, etc.] and has no vocal sound by itself; but, when combined 30 with letters having vocal sound, it becomes audible. Letters differ with respect to the shapes assumed by the mouth and with respect to the places [at which they are formed], and they are (a) aspirated or unaspirated, (b) long or short, and (c) acute or grave or intermediate [in pitch]. Each of these comes under the [science] that is concerned with metrical matters.

35   A syllable is a non–significant vocal sound composed of a mute and a letter having vocal sound; thus "gr" without the vowel "a" is a sylla- ble, and so is "gra," which has the vowel "a." But the discussion of these distinctions, too, belongs to [the science of] metrics.

1457a   A connective is (a) a non–significant vocal sound which by its nature neither prevents nor produces a unity of a significant vocal sound com- posed of many vocal sounds, and which can be placed at either end or in the middle of a sentence unless its nature is such as it is not fitting to be placed at the beginning of a sentence, e.g., μέν, ἤ, τοι, δέ; or (b) a

5   non–significant vocal sound which by its nature produces a unified sig- nificant vocal sound out of more than one significant vocal sound.

A joint is (a) a non–significant vocal sound which makes clear the be- ginning or end or dividing–point of a sentence, e.g., ["around"] or ["about"] and other such words; or, it is (b) a non–significant vocal sound which neither prevents nor produces a unified significant vocal sound (i.e., a vocal sound composed of more than one vocal sound) and

10   by its nature can be placed at either end or in the middle of a sentence.

A noun is a composite vocal sound with meaning which does not in- clude time, and no part of it by itself has meaning. In [some] double nouns, too, each part considered not by itself but as a part has no meaning; e.g., in the name "Fairbanks" the parts "Fair" and "banks" have no meaning [as parts].

A verb is a composite vocal sound having meaning which also in-

15   cludes time; and, just as with nouns, no part of it by itself has mean- ing. For the nouns "man" and "white" do not include time in their meaning; but the verbs "walks" and "walked" include in their mean- ings present and past time, respectively, [in addition to the meaning of the noun "walk."]

An inflection is a modification of a noun or a verb and signifies: (a) a

20   genitive or dative or some other such [case], as in "of a house" or "to a house," respectively; or (b) a singular or a plural, as in "man" and "men," respectively; or (c) a form of delivery, as in a question raised or a command given, for "Walked?" and "Walk!" are inflections of a verb in accordance with these two kinds of mood.

Speech is a composite significant sound some parts of which, taken

25   by themselves, signify something. But not every speech consists of nouns and verbs; for speech may have no verb, as in the definition of man.   In any case, speech will always have a part which, taken by it- self, signifies something;   e.g., the part "Cleon" in "Cleon walks" sig-

nifies something. Speech has unity in two ways: (a) if it signifies something which is a unity, or (b) if it signifies a unity made by connecting many [speeches each of which has unity]. For example, the *Iliad* has unity by connection, whereas the definition of man has unity by signifying just one thing.

21

Of the kinds of names, some are simple (and by "simple" I mean a name consisting of parts no one of which is significant, such as the noun "hug"), others are double; and some double names consist of two parts, one significant and the other non–significant, but others consist of [two] significant parts. There may also exist names which are triple or quadruple or any other multiple, as we find many of them in grandiloquent language, e.g., such as "megalomaniacology."

Every name is either standard or foreign or metaphorical or ornamental or newly–coined or lengthened or shortened or altered.

By "standard" I mean a name that a group of men ordinarily use; by "foreign" I mean one that is ordinarily used by other groups. So it is evident that the same name may be both foreign and standard, but not to the same group; for "*sigynon*" [= "lance"] is standard among the Cyprians but foreign to us [the Athenians].

A metaphor is a name belonging to one thing but applied to another thing, and it replaces (a) a genus of it, or (b) a species of it, or (c) another species [under the same genus], or (d) a thing analogous to it.

An example of (a) is "There stood my ship," for "lying at anchor" is a species of "standing." An example of (b) is "Truly Odysseus has done ten thousand noble deeds," for "ten thousand" is a species of "many" and is used here instead of "many." Examples of (c) are "drawing off the soul with a bronze weapon" and "cutting away the blood with unyielding bronze"; for here the poet has used "drawing off" for "cutting away" in the first example and "cutting away" for "drawing off" in the second, and these two are species of "taking away."

By "analogy" I mean a similarity of relations in which A is to B as C is to D. Here (a) the poet will use C instead of A or A instead of C; and sometimes (b) the poet adds something related to the term used. I mean, for example, that (a) the cup [A] is to Dionysus [B] as the shield [C] is to Ares [D]; accordingly, the poet will call the cup "the shield of Dionysus" and the shield "the cup of Ares." Or, again, old age is to life as evening is to day; accordingly, the poet will speak of evening as "the old age of day," and of old age as the "evening of life" or (as Empedocles puts it) "the sunset of life." In some analogies, there is no single name to signify one of the terms, but one may nevertheless

speak analogously. For example, the scattering of seed [by man] is
called "sowing," but there is no name for the emission of flame [by the
sun]; still, this emission of flame is to the sun as sowing the seed is to
man, and for this reason, (b) the poet, [speaking of the sun], said "sow-
30   ing the God–created flame." There is yet another way of using this
kind of metaphor: (c) the poet, in calling an object by a name belonging to another object, may then deny a predicate which is appropriate
to the name he uses; for example, he may call the shield not "the cup
of Ares" but "the wineless cup [of Ares]."

A newly–coined name is one that is not used at all by any group of
men but is introduced by the poet himself; and some names are
35   thought to be of this sort, e.g., "sprouters" for "horns" and
"supplicator" for "priest."

1458*a*   A name may be either lengthened or shortened: it is said to be lengthened if a vowel longer than the appropriate vowel is used or if a syllable is
inserted, e.g., if "*polēos*" is used for "*poléos*" or "*Pelēiadeo*" for
5   "*Pelēidou*"; it is said to be shortened if something is taken away, e.g., if
"*kri*" is used [instead of "*krithe*" (= "barley")] or "*dō*" [instead of "*dōma*"
(= "house" or "chamber")], or "*ops*" [instead of "*opsis*" (= "vision")], as
in "*mia ginetai amphoteron ops*" (= "a single vision sees both").

A name is said to be altered whenever one part of the original is left
unchanged but another part is made up, e.g., the poet uses "*dexiteron*"
instead of "*dexion*" (= "to the right") in "*dexiteron kata mazon*".

Some nouns are masculine, some feminine, and some in between
[i.e., neuter]. Masculine nouns end in ν or ρ or ς [in English, "n" or "r"
10   or "s"] or in letters which include ς [="s"]; there are two of these, ψ [=
"ps"] and ξ [= "ks"]. Feminine nouns end in vowels which are always
long, i.e., in η̄ (= "e") and ω̄ (= "o") and in long ᾱ (= "ā"); thus the
feminine endings are as many in number as the masculine, for the
masculine endings ψ and ξ are really endings in "s." No noun ends in a
15   mute or a short vowel. Only three nouns end in ι (= "i"): "*meli*" (=
"honey"), "*kommi*" (= "gum"), and "*peperi*" (= "pepper"), and only
five end in υ (= "y"), "*pōy*," "*nāpy*," "*gony*," "*dory*," and "*asty*," and
neuter nouns end in these and in "n" or "s."

22

It is a virtue of diction to be lucid without being commonplace.
Now the most lucid kind of diction is the one that uses only standard
20   names, but such diction is commonplace; and examples of it are the
poetry of Cleophon and of Sthenelus. Diction which uses strange [as
well as standard] names, however, has dignity and avoids ordinary
language; and by "strange names" I mean names which are foreign or

metaphorical or lengthened or any of those which are not standard.
But if one were to use only names such as those, the result would be
enigmatic or barbaric, enigmatic if the diction consists of metaphors,   25
barbaric if it consists of foreign names. An enigmatic diction takes the
form of a combination of expressions signifying [literally] an impossible connection of [things or facts]. A combination of [standard] names
cannot achieve this, but metaphors can, as in "I saw a man sticking
bronze on another man with fire" and the like. If, on the other hand,   30
one uses [only] foreign names, the result becomes a barbarism.

[Poetic diction,] then, should use [an appropriate combination of]
the above [two kinds, standard and strange names]; for foreign names
and metaphors and ornaments and the other forms will prevent diction from becoming ordinary or commonplace, whereas the use of
standard names will produce lucidity. Not the least part contributing
to [poetic] diction that is lucid without being ordinary is the one   1458b
which uses expansions and contractions and alterations of [standard]
names; for, by deviating from what is standard and thus going beyond
what is customary, diction avoids becoming ordinary, but by partak-   5
ing of the customary, it becomes lucid.

Critics, then, who object to a style such as the above and ridicule a poet
for using it are not right. Euclid the Elder, for example, was not right in
maintaining that it is easy to write poetry if one is allowed to lengthen
names at will; and he caricatured such style in the following lines:

'Επιχάρην εἶδον Μαραθῶνάδε βαδίζοντα   10
Epicharus I/saw on his/way going/Mar–a/–thon/ward.
and
οὐκ ἄν γ' ἐράμενος τὸν ἐκείνου ἐλλέβορον
not loving his hellebore.

Now the ostentatious use of such devices is ludicrous, but their
moderate use is appropriate to every part of diction; in fact the inappropriate and deliberate use of metaphors and foreign names and of
the other forms of diction would produce the same ludicrous effect.   15
But consider how much difference the use of what is fitting makes in
the epics if different names are inserted in verse; if one substitutes
standard names for foreign names or metaphors or any other form of
diction, one would realize the truth of what we are saying. For example, Aeschylus and Euripides produced the same iambic line; but   20
Euripides changed only one word, using a foreign instead of the usual
standard name, and his line appears beautiful, that of Aeschylus commonplace. Aeschylus wrote in the *Philoctetes*,

φαγέδαινα ἤ μου σάρκας ἐσθίει ποδός
= cancer, which eats the flesh of the foot,

but Euripides replaces ἐσθίει (= "eats") with θοινᾶται (= "feasts on").
25   On the other hand,   in the line

νῦν δέ μ' ἐὼν ὀλίγος τε καὶ οὐτιδανὸς καὶ ἀεικής
= Now I, being paltry and frail and unseemly,

one might use standard names and say,

νῦν δέ μ ἐὼν μικρός τε καὶ ἀσθενικὸς καὶ ἀειδής
= Now I, being small and weak and ugly,

or in

δίφρον ἀεικέλιον καταθεὶς ὀλίγην τε τράπεζαν
= Having set an unseemly chair and a paltry table,

one might do likewise and say,

30   δίφρον μοχθηρὸν καταθεὶς μικράν τε τράπεζαν
= Having set a bad chair and a small table.

Again, one might change ἠιόνες βοόωσιν (= "the sea–coasts roar")
to ἠιόνες κράζουσιν (= "the sea–coasts scream").
   Ariphrades, too, ridiculed the tragedians for using expressions that
no one would use in conversation, e.g., δωμάτων ἄπο (= "from the
houses away") instead of ἀπὸ δωμάτων ("away from the houses"), and
σέθεν "of thine" instead of "your"), and ἐγὼ δέ νιν (= "and I her"),
1459a   and Ἀχιλλέως πέρι (= "Achilles about") instead of περὶ Ἀχιλλέως (=
"about Achilles"), and other such expressions. It is indeed because all
such expressions are not standard that they produce a diction which is
not ordinary; but Ariphrades was not aware of this fact.
5   The proper use of each of the devices mentioned as well as of double and foreign names is important, but by far the most important is
the use of metaphors. Indeed [the ability for metaphor] alone [of the
above devices] cannot be acquired from others but is a sign of a gift
endowed by nature;   for to make metaphors well is to perceive similarities in things.
   Double names are most fitting for dithyrambs;   foreign names for
heroic poems; and metaphors for iambic poems. Also, all [the forms of
10   diction] mentioned above are useful for heroic poems; but for iambic
poems whose diction is the most imitative, those names are fitting

which one might also use in conversation, and such are standard and
metaphorical and ornamental names.

Concerning tragedy or imitative *action* [on the stage], then, let the 15
above discussion be sufficient.

23

As for narrative which imitates in meter, it is clear that it should
have its plots constructed dramatically, just as in tragedies, and it
should be concerned with a single *action* which is a whole and complete, with a beginning and a middle and an end, like a single animal, 20
which is a whole, in order to produce its appropriate pleasure; and
its compositions should not be similar to the usual historical accounts,
each of which must present not a single *action* but all the chance and
unrelated events involving one or more men during a single period.
For just as the sea–battle at Salamis and the battle with the 25
Carthaginians in Sicily occurred at the same time without being related to the same end, so too sometimes events succeed one another
but have no single end. Yet, in constructing their plots, a good many
poets do what historians do. 30

As we have stated earlier, in this respect, too, Homer would appear
to have been divinely inspired in comparison with the other poets: he
did not attempt to make a poem out of the whole Trojan War even
though that war had a beginning and an end, for the plot would have
become too big to be easily grasped as a whole; or, even if it were
moderated in length, it would have become too complex in its variety
of events. What he did was to select one part of the whole and use 35
many episodes taken from the other parts, e.g., the Catalogue of
Ships and other episodes which he interspersed in the poem. But
other poets produce epics about one man or one period or one *action* 1459*b*
with a multitude of parts, as did the authors of the *Cypria* and of *The
Little Iliad*. So, whereas only one or two tragedies can be made out of
the *Iliad* or the *Odyssey*, many can be made out of the *Cypria* and
more than eight out of *The Little Iliad*, i.e., *The Awarding of Arms*, 5
Philoctetes, *Neoptolemus*, *Eurypylus*, *The Beggary*, *the Laconian
Women*, *The Sack of Troy*, *The Departure of the Fleet*, and one may add
Sinon and *The Trojan Women*.

24

Furthermore, epic poetry should have the same species as tragedy,
for there may be a simple epic, or a complex epic, or an epic of character, or an epic of suffering. Its parts, except for song and spectacle, 10

should also be the same; for epic, too, should make use of reversals and recognitions and sufferings. Again, the *thought* and diction in an epic should be of beautiful quality. Homer was the first to use all of these and to do so adequately; for, of his [two] poems, the *Iliad* is sim-
15 ple in structure and portrays suffering, while the *Odyssey*, using recognitions throughout and portraying character, is complex. In addition, he has surpassed all epic poets in diction and *thought*.

Epic poetry differs from tragedy in the length of its composition and in meter. Now with respect to its length, the limitation stated earlier is adequate, for one should be able to grasp as a whole both
20 the beginning and the end; and this will be possible if epic compositions are shorter than those of the early poets and the length of each amounts to that of a number of tragedies presented for one hearing. With respect to extending its length, however, epic poetry has a special advantage, and there is a *reason* for this: tragedy does not admit
25 of imitating many parts [i.e., episodes] which take place at the same time but only that part which takes place on stage with the performers; but epic poetry, being narrative, can be made to represent simultaneously many parts which, if appropriately related, can lengthen the poem. So this virtue of epic poetry contributes to its grandeur and
30 pleases the audience by varying their interest and representing a diversity of episodes; for monotony of events soon produces boredom and causes tragedies to fail.

The heroic meter [i.e., the hexameter] was found by trial and error to be [most] fitting. If one were to produce a narrative imitation in any other meter, or in several meters, it would appear unsuitable; for the
35 heroic is the most stately and most impressive of the meters, and for this reason it admits most readily foreign names and metaphors, and thereby narrative imitation surpasses other kinds. The iambic
1460a [trimeter] and the [trochaic] tetrameter, on the other hand, are appropriate for motion, the latter for the dance, the former for *action*. Furthermore, it would be rather absurd if anyone were to combine these meters, as Chaeremon did. And in fact, no one else has ever produced a long poetic composition in any meter other than the heroic, for, as we have already stated, nature herself teaches poets to choose the fitting meter.
5   Homer, who is worthy of praise for many other things, is also the only poet who is not ignorant of what part he should play in his own poems. For an epic poet should speak in his own person as little as possible, otherwise he fails to imitate to the extent that he fails to impersonate [the agents in the poem]. The other poets put themselves forward throughout [their poems] and imitate but little and seldom.

Homer, on the other hand, after a brief introduction, immediately   10
brings on a *man* or a woman or some other agent having character and
not just a speaker devoid of character.

Now poets should produce an effect of wonder in their tragedies;
but it is the epic that admits most readily what defies reason. It is in
this way that epic achieves the effect of wonder, because the reader
does not actually see the man performing the *action*. For example, the   15
passage recounting the pursuit of Hector, in which the Greeks stand
still and do not pursue while Achilles shakes his head to keep them
away, would certainly appear ludicrous on stage, but this absurdity escapes notice in epic poems. Of course, what arouses wonder gives
pleasure; and a sign of this is that everyone, when reporting events,
adds something of his own with a mind to please the audience.

It was Homer, most of all, who also taught other poets how false-
hoods should be expressed [artistically], namely, by the use of falla-   20
cies. For, if A's existence or occurrence implies B's existence or
occurrence, respectively, men suppose that, conversely, B's existence
or occurrence implies A's existence or occurrence. This inference, of
course, is false. Now if A's truth implies B's truth, but A happens to be
false while B is true, one might falsely infer that A is true also; and it is
because of knowing the truth of B's existence that our mind commits   25
the fallacy of thinking that A, too, exists.   There is an example of this
fallacy in the Bath Scene of the *Odyssey*.

Again, plausible impossibilities should be preferred to unpersua-
sive possibilities. Still [plots] should be constructed not of unreasonable parts but at best of parts which include nothing unreasonable. If
this cannot be done, the unreasonable parts should be outside of the
actual plot, as is Oedipus' not knowing how Laius died, and not within   30
the drama, as is the messengers' account of the Pythian Games in the
Electra or, in *The Mysians*, the man who came from Tegea to Mysia
without saying a word. To argue that the plot would have been spoiled
[without these incidents] is ridiculous, for such plots should not have
been constructed that way in the first place. If, however, the poet introduces something but makes it appear more reasonable than it re-   35
ally is, it should be allowed, even if it is an absurdity. For example, the
unreasonable episode in the *Odyssey*, in which Odysseus is landed on
the shores [of Ithaca], would clearly be intolerable if it had been writ-   1460*b*
ten by an inferior poet. As it is, the poet [Homer] hides the absurdity
by rendering it pleasing with his other good artistic touches.

The poet should elaborate the diction of his poem in the parts in
which there is no *action* but not in those which manifest character or
thought, for highly brilliant diction conceals both character and *thought*.   5

25

Concerning the number and nature of the types of problems that might arise [in evaluating poetry] and the [*reasons* the poet might offer for their] solutions, these become evident if viewed from the following perspectives.

10 Since the poet is an imitator, like a painter or any other maker of likenesses, he must always imitate one of three [kinds of] objects: (a) things such as they were or are, or (b) objects such as they are said or thought [to be or to have been], or (c) objects such as they should be.

All these objects are communicated in diction, in which there are foreign names and metaphors and many other features of diction that we grant the poet to use.

Furthermore, what is right in the poetic art is not the same as in the
15 political or any other art. Mistakes within the poetic art itself are of two kinds: (a) essential and (b) accidental. If the poet has chosen to imitate something but failed through lack of [artistic] ability, the mistake violates the [poetic] art itself [i.e., it is essential]; but if he chose incorrectly by imitating, for example, a horse with both right legs thrown forward or made a mistake or portrayed something impossible
20 in any of the other arts, e.g., in medicine or some other art, the mistake is not essential [but accidental].

Those who examine censures which arise from problems [in poems], then, should resolve them by using the above [principles].

(1) If the poet introduces an object which is impossible with respect to his own art, he makes a mistake. But he is right in doing so, provided
25 that the end of the art be served; for the end is enhanced if such use of the impossible makes the corresponding part or some other part of the poem more striking. An example is the pursuit of Hector. If, however, the end could have been served just as well or better without violation of the principles of any of the arts, the mistake is not justifiable; for, if possible, a poet should make no mistake at all.
30 (2) Furthermore, what kind of mistake is it: one that violates the [poetic] art or one that is accidental to that art? For it is a lesser mistake if the poet does not know that the female deer has no horns than if he has imitated her badly.

(3) If a poet is censured for not representing things truly, he may [with justice] reply, "Well, I have represented them as they should be." For example, Sophocles said that he imitated men as they should
35 be but that Euripides imitated them as they are.

(4) If a poet is censured for imitating things neither as they are nor as they should be, he may [with justice] reply, "This is the way men speak of things," as in matters concerning the gods. For perhaps it is

better [to imitate them] neither in this manner [i.e., as they should be] nor truly, but rather, as Xenophanes remarked, "But people do not speak [of them truly or as they should be]." 1461a

(5) In other cases, the poet may reply, "It is not better, [things being what they are nowadays], but such was the case with the objects in the past," as in the passage concerning arms, [where Homer says], "The spears stood upright, their butt–spikes in the ground," for such was the custom in those days, just as it is even now among the Illyrians.

(6) As to whether something was well or not well expressed or done, one should investigate the problem by attending not only to whether the thing done or said was [itself] good or bad, but also to the man who performed the deed or spoke, or the man this man spoke to or *acted* upon, or to the time he did so, or to the instrument he used, or to his purpose in doing so (e.g., in order to bring about a greater good or to avoid a greater evil). 5

(7) Criticism concerning diction should be answered by attending to the language used, e.g., whether the poet has used a foreign word in the line "First [he slew] the *oureas*," for perhaps by the word "*oureas*" the poet meant not the mules but the guards. And when Homer said of Dolon, "He was deformed," perhaps he meant not that his body was badly proportioned, but that his face was ugly, for the Cretans call a handsome face "well–formed." And in the line "Mix the drink *zoroteron*," Homer meant by "*zoroteron*" not stronger [as one mixes it for drunkards] but more quickly. 10 15

(8) Things expressed metaphorically have been discussed. For example, Homer says "All the gods and men slept the whole night long," but at the same time he also adds, "Whenever he [Agamemnon] gazed at the field of Troy, [he marveled] at the din of flutes and pipes." Here, the word "all" is used metaphorically instead of the word "many," for "all" is a species of "many." And in the line "She alone partakes not [in the baths of Ocean"] the word "alone" is used metaphorically, for the term "the most widely known" is a species of the term "alone." 20

(9) With respect to pronunciation, one may solve problems as Hippias of Thasos did in the phrase δίδομεν δέ οἱ (= "We give him"), [where he changes the accent and makes the words mean "We give to him," not "Give to him,"] and in the phrase τὸ μὲν οὗ καταπύθεται ὄμβρῳ (= "A part of it is not rotted by rain"), [where he substituted οὐ (= "not") for οὗ (= "of which") and made the line read "A part is not rotted" instead of "A part of which is rotted"].

(10) Some problems can be solved by division [i.e., grouping the words differently], as in Empedocles' line

25 αἶψα δὲ θνήτ᾽ ἐφύοντο τὰ πρὶν μάθον ἀθάνατα
ζωρά τε πρὶν κέκρητο

Suddenly things grew mortal that before had learned to be
immortal, and things unmixed before mixed,

|where the final clause may be punctuated in two ways: (a) "things un-
mixed, before mixed" or (b) "things unmixed before, mixed"].
   (11) Some problems can be solved by clarifying the ambiguity, as in
the line

παρῴχηκεν δὲ πλέω νύξ [τῶν δύο μοιράων, τριτάτη δ᾽
ἔτι μοῖρα λέλειπται]

= More [of the two parts of the] night had passed, [a third
part was still left.]

The word πλέω (= "more") is ambiguous.
   (12) Some problems can be solved by appealing to customary
usage. Wine mixed with water is still called "wine," and by the same
principle Homer was correct when he wrote

κνημὶς νεοτεύκτου κασσιτέροιο
= A greave of newly–wrought tin,

[for the word "tin" here means an alloy of tin and copper]; and workers of iron are called χαλκέας (= "bronze–workers"), and by the same
30 principle Homer calls Ganymede "Zeus's wine–server," although the
gods do not drink wine [but only nectar].   This last example might
also be taken as a metaphor. Also, whenever a name is thought to give
rise to an inconsistency, one should examine how many senses it
might have in the passage. For example, in the passage

τῇ ῥ᾽ ἔσχετο χάλκεον ἔγχος
= There the bronze spear was held,

among the possible meanings of "being checked there," one might
35 best avoid the mistake by taking the meaning opposed to the one as-
1461b sumed by the critics.   Or else, as Glaucon says, some critics make unreasonable presuppositions about the meaning of a name used by a
poet and proceed to draw conclusions based on those meanings; and if
they think that an inconsistency arises from these conclusions, they

censure the poet as if he actually said what it seems to them that he said. This is the treatment given to the passage about Icarius; for the critics suppose him to be a Spartan, and so they suppose it to be ab- 5
surd that Telemachus did not meet him when he went to Sparta. But perhaps the truth is just as the Cephallenians claim, for they say that Odysseus took a Cephallenian wife and that her father's name was "Icadius," not "Icarius"; so it is likely that the problem arose because of a mistake.

In general, the use of the impossible in poetry should be referred to 10
(a) the making of poetry, or to (b) what is better [than what actually exists], or to (c) what is generally accepted.   For (a) with respect to the making of poetry, [one may reply that] a plausible impossibility is preferable to an implausible possibility;   (b) [as to the impossibility of people being] such as Zeuxis painted them, [one may reply that] it is better to paint them in this manner, for the ideal should be [regarded as] superior to the real;   and (c) as to that which is asserted to be unreasonable, [one may reply that] this is [what men say] or that there are times when it is not regarded as unreasonable, for even the 15
improbable has a [mathematical] probability of occurring.

We should consider inconsistencies in poetic expressions in the same way as we consider refutations in arguments, i.e., we should ascertain whether by an expression the poet means the same thing, or the thing in relation to the same thing, or the thing in the same manner, and hence [whether he is inconsistent] with what he himself says or with what a prudent man would be assumed to say.

It is right to censure a poet for using without any necessity what is un- 20
reasonable or in bad taste, like the unreasonable appearance of Aegeus [in the *Medea*] of Euripides or the baseness of Menelaus in the *Orestes*.

Critics, then, advance five kinds of censure; for the poet may use what is (1) impossible, or (2) unreasonable, or (3) harmful, or (4) inconsistent, or (5) contrary to correctness in accord with art. And the [kinds of] responses to these criticisms must be sought among the 25
above—mentioned kinds, and there are twelve of these.

26

One might pose the problem whether the epic or the tragic form of imitation is better. For if the less vulgar [poem] is the better form, and if such a form is always addressed to the better class of spectators, it is quite clear that the one which imitates all [kinds of objects] is in bad taste. [Some performers], thinking that the audience will not perceive what is going on unless they add something themselves, indulge 30
in a great deal of movement [i.e., stage—business], like bad flute—

players who whirl about when they are imitating a discus–throw or pull at the chorus leader when they are performing the Scylla. Accordingly, for some thinkers tragedy [is thought to be] a form of this kind, like the new school of performers in the opinion of the old

35   school; thus Mynniscus used to call Callippides "the ape" for his highly exaggerated manner of performing, and such, too, was the

1462a opinion held about Pindar. [According to these thinkers, then,] the whole tragic art is to the epic art as the later performers are to the earlier performers; and they say that the epic art is addressed to cultivated spectators, who have no need of posturing, whereas the tragic art is addressed to vulgar spectators. So it is clear, [they conclude], that the tragic art, being in bad taste, would be inferior to the epic art.

5   (1) The charge, however, applies not to the art of poetry, but to the art of performing, since it is possible even for a rhapsodist to overdo his gestures, which is just what Sosistratus used to do, and so too may a singer in a contest, which is just what Mnasitheus the Opuntian used to do.

(2) Not every kind of movement should be rejected—any more than every kind of dancing—but only the movements of bad performers, which is precisely the censure made of Callippides and of other per-

10   formers nowadays who imitate [free women] as if they were vulgar.

(3) Tragedy, like epic poetry, produces its effect even without movements of performers, because its quality is evident even from reading it. So if it is superior to epic poetry in all other respects, one may say that at least this [i.e., imitation through movements of performers] is not a necessary attribute of tragedy.

(4) Now, [tragedy excels epic poetry] because it has all [the essen-

15   tial parts] that epic poetry has, and it can even use meter. In addition, no small parts of it are music and spectacle, whereby pleasures are most vividly produced.

(5) Tragedy produces vivid impressions when read as well as when performed.

(6) Tragedy excels epic by achieving the end of imitation in a

1462b shorter length of time; for what is more concentrated is more pleasant than what is diluted over a long period of time. For example, what effect would the *Oedipus [Rex]* of Sophocles produce if it were to be stretched into as many epic lines as the *Iliad* has?

(7) Epic imitation has less unity than does tragic, and a sign of this is

5   the fact that more than one tragedy can be made out of one epic. So (a) if only one plot is used by an epic poet, the epic must appear either

(i) truncated, if briefly presented, or (ii) diluted, if stretched to the usual length in this meter; but (b) if many [plots are used], that is, if epic consists of many *actions*, [the imitation] will be not a unity but like the *Iliad* and the *Odyssey*, which have many such parts each with a considerable magnitude of its own, although each of these poems is   10 constructed as well as it can be and is, as far as possible, an imitation of a single *action*.

Since, then, tragedy excels epic poetry in all the above [four] respects and also in performing the function proper to the poetic art (for [tragedy and epic] should produce not any chance pleasure but the one stated earlier), it is evident that, by achieving the function of the poetic art to a higher degree, tragedy is superior to epic poetry.   15

Concerning tragedy and epic poetry, with respect to each of them in general, their species and their parts, their number and differences, the *reasons* for their being well or badly constructed, the censures made of them by critics and the responses to those censures, let the above discussion suffice.

REFERENCES AND NOTES

REFERENCES TO ARISTOTLE'S WORKS

The references to Aristotle's Works given in the REFERENCES AND
NOTES and in the GLOSSARY are to the standard pages (sections) and
lines according to the Bekker's edition of Aristotle's Works (Berlin, 1831).
The Bekker pages covering each Work will be given now.

Abbreviations

Cat. = Categories
Prop. = On Propositions
Pr. Anal. = Prior Analytics
Post. An. = Posterior Analytics
Top. = Topics
Soph. Ref. = Sophistical Refu-
    tations
Phys. = Physics
G. D. = Generation And Destruc-
    tion
Soul = On The Soul (De Anima)
H. A. = History of Animals
P.O.A. = Parts of Animals

G. A. = Generation Of Animals
Met. = Metaphysics
N. Eth. = Nicomachean Ethics
Pol. = Politics
Rhet. = Rhetoric
Poet. = Poetics
Od. = Odyssey
Rep. = Plato's Republic
Ch., Chs. = Chapter, Chapters
VI (3,8) = Book 6, Chapters 3 and
    8, and similarly for others.

Categories: 1a1-15b33.
On Propositions (De Interpretatione): 16a1-24b9.
Prior Analytics: 24a10-70b38.
Posterior Analytics: 71a1-100b17.
Topics: 100a18-164b19.
Sophistical Refutations: 164a20-184b8.
Physics: 184a10-267b26.
On The Heavens: 268a1-313b23.
On Generation And Destruction: 314a1-338b19.
Meteorology: 338a20-390b22.
On The Universe, To Alexander: 391a1-401b29.
On The Soul: 402a1-435b25.
On Sensation And Sensibles: 436a1-449a31.
On Memory And Recollection: 449b1-453b11.
On Sleep And Wakefulness: 453b11-458a32.
On Dreams: 458a33-462b11.
On Divination From Dreams: 462b12-464b18.
On Longevity And Shortness Of Life: 464b19-467b9.

On Youth, Old Age, Life, And Death: 467b10-470b5.
On Respiration: 470b6-480b30.
On Breath: 481a1-486b4.
A Treatise On Animals: 486a5-638b37.
On Parts Of Animals: 639a1-697b30.
On Motion Of Animals: 698a1-704b3.
On Locomotion Of Animals: 704a4-714b23.
On Generation Of Animals: 715a1-789b20.
On Colors: 791a1-799b20.
On Objects Of Hearing: 800a1-804b39.
Physiognomy: 805a1-814b9.
On Plants: 815a10-830b4.
On Reported Marvels: 830a5-847b10.
Mechanics: 847a11-858b31.
Problems: 859a1-967b27.
On Indivisible Lines: 968a1-972b33.
Positions And Names Of Winds: 973a1-b25.
On Xenophanes, Zeno, And Gorgias: 974a1-980b21.
Metaphysics: 980a21-1093b29.
Nicomachean Ethics: 1094a1-1181b23.
Great Ethics: 1181a24-1213b30.
Eudemean Ethics: 1214a1-1249b25.
On Virtues And Vices: 1249a26-1251b37.
Politics: 1252a1-1342b34.
Household Management: 1343a1-1353b27.
Rhetoric: 1354a1-1420b4.
Rhetoric For Alexander: 1420a5-1447b7.
Poetics: 1447a8-1462b18.

CATEGORIES
1. 1a24-5. *2.* 1a6-7. *3.* 2a11-b22.

ON PROPOSITIONS
1. 16a22-27. *2. Poet.* 1456b11-13. *3.* 17b26-29. *4.* 17b29-37. *5.* 16a19-20, 30-33. *6. Pr. Anal.* 51b36-52a17. *7.* 17b38-18a1. *8. Top.* 160a17-34.

PRIOR ANALYTICS
1. Top. 100a27-b23, 104a8-15. *2. Post. An.* and *Top. 3.* 25a10-3,22-6. *4.* 25a7-13. *5.* 25a20-22. *6.* 25a14-17. *7.* 25a12-13. *8.* ch.13. *9. ch.46. 10. Post. An. 11.* 24b28-30. *12.* 24b28-30. *13.* 24b30. *14.* 26a2-4. *15.* 25b40-26a2. *16.*

27a21. *17.* 27b16-18. *18.* 27b20-23. *19.* 28a30. *20.*
25b19-24. *21. Post. An.* 75b21-36.

POSTERIOR ANALYTICS

1. Plato, *Meno* 80E. *2.* 78a22-79a16,93a1-b20. *3. Pr.
Anal.* I(25). *4. Pr. Anal.* II(5). *5. Pr. Anal.* II(5,6,7). *6.*
Plato, *Euthydemus* 277B. *7. Met.* 1053b25-1054a19. *8.*
76a4-25, 78b32-79a16. *9.* 75a38-b2, 76b11-22. *10. Pr.
Anal.* 24a22-b2. *11.* Perhaps Protagoras and followers. *12.*
100b5-17. *13.* 72b18-25, 84a29-b2. *14.* 90a35-92b38. *15.*
93a16-27. *16. Phys.* VI. *17. Pr. Anal.* II(5). *18.* I(2,7). *19.*
I(2). *20. Met.* 980b25-2a3.

SOPHISTICAL REFUTATIONS

1. 165a19-31. *2.* 183a27-36.

PHYSICS

1. 188a19-30. *2. Met.* 986a22-26. *3.* (a) The principles
are contraries, (b) contraries require a subject as a
principle. *4.* 187a12-17. *5. Met.* 1017b10-26,
1028b33-1029a34. *6.* 191b6-16. *7. Met.* 1017a35-b9. *8.*
The Platonists. *9.* Being comes, if not from being, then
from nonbeing. *10.* The privation. *11.* Plato, *Timaeus,*
50D-51. *12. Metaphysics.* *13. G.D.* I(3). *14.* A lost work.
15. Perhaps Democritus. *16.* Perhaps Democritus. *17.*
Perhaps Democritus. *18.* 197a36-198a13. *19.* Empedocles.
20. Anaxagoras. *21.* Empedocles, Fr. 62.4. *22.* 196b10-27.
23. VIII(5). *24.* Plato, *Timaeus,* 52E, 57E, 58A. *25.*
202a18-20. *26.* 201a9-15. *27.* 224b26-27. *28.* 227b3-229a6.
29. 225b10-226b17. *30.* 200b12-201b15. *31.* Plato,
Timaeus 38B. *32.* 250b11-2b6. *33.* ch.4. *34.* ch.5. *35.*
253a7-21. *36.* Locomotion. *37.* Locomotion. *38.* ch.1. *39.*
The planets. *40.* Any heavenly body. *41.* ch. 3. *42.* Plato,
Timaeus 59A, 79B,C,E, 80C.

GENERATION AND DESTRUCTION

1. Plato, *Timaeus* 51A. *2.* Plato, *Timaeus* 49D-50C. *3.*
Plato, *Timaeus* 530 ff. *4.* Plato, *Timaeus* 49A,52D. *5.*
Phys. 189a11-192b4. *6.* 329b30-2. *7. On Heavens,*
304b23-305a32. *8.* 323b1-324b24. *9. Phaedo* 96A-99C. *10.*
Phaedo 100B-101E. *11. Phys.* II(3,4,5,6,7). *12.* 335a32-b7.
13. Phys. VIII(7,8,9). *14.* The Sun. *15. Phys.*

260a21-261b26. *16.* 317b33 ff. *17.* The Sun's elliptic motion. *18.* 318a9 ff. *19.* *Met.* 1017a7-b9. *20.* *Phys.* 255b31-260a10. *21.* *Phys.* 217b29-224a17. *22.* i.e., towards effects. *23.* *Phys.* VIII(7,8,9).

ON THE SOUL

1. They are composites of body and soul. *2.* Frag. 109D. *3.* *Timaeus* 35A ff. *4.* The number 3. *5.* The number 4. *6.* 404b1-6. *7.* 434a22-435b25. *8.* 434a22-435b25. *9.* 412a6-9. *10.* 413a22-5. *11.* 413b32-3. *12.* III(12). *13.* III(3,11). *14.* III(12,13). *15.* III(4 to 8). *16.* 415b24. *17.* *G.D.* 323b18 ff. *18.* *Phys.* 201b31, 257b8. *19.* 416a29-b9. *20.* 417a12-20. *21.* 422b34 ff. *22.* 421b13-422a6. *23.* *Od.* xviii 136. *24.* 404b8-18. *25.* *N. Eth.* 1139b15 ff. *26.* *429a15-24.* *27.* Next chapter. *28.* 417b2-16, *Met.* 1048b29-30. *29.* 426b12-7a14. *30.* Plato, *Rep.* 435-441. *31.* *On Respiration, Sleep, Wakefulness.* *32.* *On Motion of Animals,* 704a4-714b23. *33.* 434b10-24. *34.* 434b24 ff.

PARTS OF ANIMALS

1. *Phys.* 199a35-200b10, *Met.* 1015a35-b16. *2.* *Met.* 1015a27-b16, *Post. An.* 94b37-5a3. *3.* Ch. 1, 639a27. *4.* Ch. 1, 639a18,27.

METAPHYSICS

1. Plato, *Gorgias* 448C, 462B,C. *2.* *N. Eth.* 1139b14-1141b8. *3.* *Phys.* II(3,7). *4.* Perhaps Plato included: *Cratylus* 402B, *Theatetus,* 152E, 162D, 180C. *5.* Homer, *Iliad* xiv. 201, 246. *6.* Homer, *Iliad,* ii. 755, xiv. 271, xv. 37. *7.* Thales, Anaximenes, Heraclitus. *8.* The Eleatics. *9.* Empedocles is one of them. *10.* 984a18-19. *11.* Anaxagoras. *12.* A work lost or not written. *13.* *Phys.* II(3-7). *14.* Plato, *Phaedo* 98B,C, *Laws* 967B,C,D. *15.* *On the Heavens* II(13). *16.* *Phys.* I(3). *17.* 984b15-19, b32-985a10. *18.* *Phys.* II(3 to 7). *19.* *On the Heavens* III(7). *20.* Plato, *Phaedo* 100C,D,E. *21.* He means Plato's School, of which Aristotle was a member. *22.* 991a20-22. *23.* Plato, *Rep.* vii. 531D, 533B to D. *24.* *Phys.* II(3 to 7). *25.* III(1). *26.* i.e., the definition of the infinite has a finite number of parts. *27.* 995b18-27. *28.* The Pythagoreans. *29.* Perhaps Parmenides. *30.* The Platonists. *31.* Empedocles. *32.* They are included in V. *33.* Perhaps Antisthenes is one of them. *34.* Perhaps the prime and other immaterial movers are meant. *35.* 1017a7-22. *36.* Plato, *Sophist* 237A, 254A. *37.* XII(6,7,8). *38.* 1017a7-b9. *39.* e.g., the Eleatics. *40.* e.g., the Pythagoreans and Empedocles. *41.* e.g., Anaxagoras. *42.* The Pythagoreans. *43.* Xenocrates and followers. *44.* 1017b10-26. *45.* Plato, *Sophist* 237,256 ff. *46.* It is known to be unknown. *47.* 1030a17-27. *48.* 1030a17-27. *49.* Chs. 4-6, 10-12. *50.* Ch. 3. *51.* 1029a2-3, 23-24. *52.* 990b17. *53.* Perhaps Thales. *54.* 1031a11-14. *55.* VII(15), VIII(6). *56.* VII(1). *57.* VII(2). *58.* Plato. *59.* VII(4-6, 12, 15). *60.* VII(10,11). *61.* VII(13,14,16), 1040b16-1041a5. *62.* XIII, XIV. *63. Phys.* 255a12-20, *G.D.* 317a17-31. *64.* VII(12), 1044a2-6. *65.* 1045a23-33. *66.* VII,VIII. *67.* VII(1). *68.* 1048a27-b6, V(12). *69.* IV(5,6). *70.* 1047a24-26. *71.* IX(1 to 5). *72.* 1018b9-1019a14. *73.* VII(7,8). *74. Phys.* VI(6). *75.* 1049b17-29. *76.* The Platonists. *77.* Plato, Xenocrates, Speusippus, respectively. *78.* 1069a30. *79.* Anaxagoras. *80. On the Heavens,* 300*b*8. *81. Timaeus* 30A. *82. Phaedrus* 245C, *Laws* 894E. *83. Timaeus* 34B. *84.* 1071b22-26. *85.* The Sun, by approaching and receding. *86.* 1075a36. *87.* 1028b21, 1091a34-6, 1092a11-15. *88. Phys.* 206b32-3. *89. Phys.* VIII(8,9), *On the Heavens,* I(2), II(3-8). *90.* 1073a5-11. *91.* 1073b35-1074a4. *92.* Plato's School. *93.* 1072b30-34. *94.* 1071b19-20. *95.* Speusippus, 1028b21, 1090b13-20. *96.* Homer, *Iliad* ii. 204. *97.* Aristippus, 996a32. *98.* A work either lost or never written.

NICOMACHEAN ETHICS

1. Perhaps Eudoxus, 1172b9. *2. Rep.* 511B. *3.* 1177a12-1178a8, 1178a22-1179a32. *4. Met.* 986a22-6, 1028b21-4, 1072b30-1073a3, 1091a29-1092a17. *5. Met.* 1003a32-b15. *6.* ch. 11. *7.* 1094b11-27. *8.* Plato, *Euthydemus* 279A,B, *Laws* 743E. *9.* 1098b26-9. *10.* 1098a16. *11.* 1094a27. *12.* 1098a16-18. *13.* 1099a31-b7. *14.* 1100a8-9. *15. Top.* 126b4-6. *16.* 1102b13-14. *17.* VI(13). *18. Rep.* 401E-402A, *Laws* 653A ff. *19.* 1104a27-b3. *20.* 1103a18-b2. *21.* 1104a11-27. *22.* A great wrestler. *23.* IV. *24.* 1122a20-29, b10-18. *25.* 1108b11-26, 25b4-18. *26.* III(9) to IV(15). *27.* V. *28.* VI. *29.* Homer, *Od.* xii 108, 219 ff. *30.* Homer, *Iliad* iii 156-60. *31.* 1111b26. *32.* Plato, *Rep.* 343C. *33. Pol.* 1276b16-1277b32, 1278a40-b5, 1288a32-

b2, 1333a11-16, 1337a11-14. *34.* 1132b21-1133b28. *35.*
1130a4. *36.* 1134a30. *37.* Lost or never written. *38.*
1109b35-1111a24. *39.* *Iliad,* vi 236. *40.* 1136a31-b5. *41.*
1134b15-17. *42.* 1103a3-7. *43.* 1102a26-28. *44. Post. An.*
71a1-11. *45. Post. An.* 71b9-23. *46.* 1141b14-22. *47.*
Homer, *Iliad* x. 224. *48.* 1156b7,23,33, 1157a30-b4. *49.*
1156b13-15, 1157a1-3. *50.* 1156a16-24, 1157a20-33. *51.*
1155b31. *52.* 1155a22-28. *53.* 1159b29-32. *54.* 1156a7. *55.*
1158b27,1159a35-b3, 1162a34-b4. *56.* Eudoxus, Aristippus. *57.* Speusippus. *58. Philebus* 60B to E. *59. Philebus*
24E-25A, 31A. *60. Philebus* 53C-54D. *61. Philebus*
31E-32B, 42C,D. *62. Phys.* III(1,2,3),VI. *63.*
1095b31-1096a2, 1098b31-1099a7. *64.* 1098a5-7. *65.*
1113a22-33. *66.* 1098a16. *67.* It follows from what has just
been said. *68.* 1097a25-b21, 1099a7-21, 1173b15-19,
1174b20-23, 1175b36-1176a3. *69.* 1169b33, 1176b26. *70.*
Plato, *Laws* 722D ff. *71.* Plato, *Protagoras* 325A. *72.*
1179b31-1180a5.

POLITICS

1. Plato, *Statesman* 258E-259D. *2. Od.,* ix 114, *N. Eth.*
1180a28-29. *3. Iliad,* ix. 63. *4.* 1332b4-5. *5.* 1252a7-16. *6.*
Homer, *Iliad* xviii. 376. *7.* ch. 5. *8.* 1256a3-7. Herodotus II
172. *10.* Plato, *Meno* 72A-73C. *11.* Plato, *Meno* 71E, 72A.
12. 1255b23, 31-35. *13.* Not discussed in the *Politics* as we
have it. *14.* 1279a19-20. *15.* 1273a21 ff. *16.* 1274b34. *17.*
1326a8-1327a3. *18.* They are potentially citizens. 19. *Iliad,*
ix. 648, xvi. 59. *20.* 1253a2-3. *21. N. Eth.* 1131a15. *22.* chs.
12-17, IV,VI. *23.* ch. 10. *24.* 1274a15-18. *25.* 1281a40-b21.
26. ch. 10. *27.* 1281a36. *28. N. Eth.* V. *29.* 1281a4. *30.*
1280a9 ff. *31.* 1253a37. *32. N. Eth.* 1129b25 ff. *33.* i.e.,
"where are your claws and teeth?." *34.* 1288b29. *35.*
1293b7-21, 1293b36-1294a25. *36. N. Eth.* 1098a16,
1153b10, 1177a22. *37.* 1308a18-24. *38.* 1289a8, b3,
1291b15-1293a10. *39.* 1333a11 ff. *40.* I(4-7). *41. Poet.*
1450b34-1451a3. *42.* 1328a37, *N. Eth.* 1098a16, 1176b4.
43. N. Eth. 1113a22-b1. *44.* 1327b36. *45.* 1329a2-17. *46.*
1277b9. *47.* 1277a33-b30, 1278b32-1279a8. *48.* III(4,5).
49. N. Eth. 1139a6. *50.* 1301b20, 1307a3. *51.* Military
virtue alone is meant. *52.* 1332a39-40. *53.* ch. 7.

RHETORIC

1. 1354a22. *2. Top.* 101a30-34. *3.* chs. 2 to 11. *4.* 1354a1.
5. Pr. Anal. I(1), II(23,24). *6. Top.* I(1,12). *7.* A lost work.
8. II(20-24). *9. Pr. Anal.* I(8, 12-14, 27). *10. Pr. Anal.*
II(27). *11. Top.* I(10,14), *Soph. Ref.* ch. 9 *12.* I(9). *13. Iliad*
xviii. 109. *14. Iliad*, i. 356. *15. Iliad*, ix. 648. *16. Iliad*, ii.
196. *17. Iliad*, i. 82. *18.* 1382a34. *19.* 1382b26,27. *20.*
I(9).

POETICS

1. 1448a17. *2.* ch. 23. *3.* A lost work. *4.* 1449b34. *5.* By
Theodectes. *6. Iphigenia Tauris.* *7.* ch. 6. *8. Modia* 1236.
9. Perhaps by Sophocles. *10.* Line 1231. *11.* By Euripides.
12. Author unknown. *13.* 1453a19. *14.* 1450b8. *15.* By
Timotheus. *16.* Euripides. *17.* Lines 1211 ff., 1368 ff. *18.*
Line 1317. *19.* ii. 155. *20. On Poets*, a lost dialogue. *21.*
1452a29. *22.* Author unknown. *23.* By Euripides. *24. Od.*,
xix. 386-475. *25. Od.*, xxi. 205-25. *26. Od.*, xix. 392. *27.*
Iphigenia in Tauris, 727 ff. *28. Iph. Taur.*, 800 ff. *29. Od.*,
viii.521 ff. *30.* Lines 168-234. *31.* Author unknown. *32.*
Iph. Taur., 582. *33. Iph. Taur.*, 281 ff. *34. Iph. Taur.*, 1163
ff. *35.* This does not agree with anything said before. *36.*
By Sophocles. *37.* By Aeschylus. *38.* Probaby by Aeschylus.
39. 1149b12, 1455b15. *40. Rhet.* 1356a1. *41. Od.*, i.185,
xxiv. 308. *42. Iliad*, ii.272. *43.* Empedocles. *44.* Timotheus.
45. Author unknown. *46. Iliad*, i.11. *47.* Empedocles. *48.*
Iliad, v. 393. *49.* See next paragraph, after Reference 77.
50. Od., ix. 515. *51. Od.*, xx. 259. *52. Iliad*, xvii. 265. *53.*
Soph. O.C., 986. *54.* 1451a23 ff. *54.* Both authors
unknown. *55.* 1451a3. *56. Centaur*, cf. 1447b21. *57.*
1449a24. *58. Iliad, xxii.205. 59. Od.*, xix. 164-260. *60.*
Sophocles, *El.* 660. *61.* Probably by Aeschylus. *62.* xiii.116
ff. *63.* 1452a4, 1454a4, 1455a17, 1460a11. *64. Iliad*, x.152.
65. Iliad, i.50. *66. Iliad*, x.316. *67. Iliad*, ix.202. *68. Iliad*,
x.1, ii.1. *69. Iliad*, x.11-13. *70. Iliad*, xviii.489. *71.*
Sophocles, *Electra* 166b1; *Iliad*, ii.15. *72. Iliad*, xxiii.327.
73. Iliad, x.251. *74. Iliad*, xxi.592. *75. Iliad*, xx.234. *76.*
Iliad, xx.267. *77.* Line 663.

49. Euclid's first example is here translated in the same metrical pattern as it appears in Greek, the dactylic hexameter, (–⌣⌣/–⌣⌣/–⌣⌣/–⌣⌣/–⌣⌣/––), with spondees substituted for dactyls in the second and fifth feet (a practice regular enough in Greek poetry). Unlike English poetry, Greek poetry achieves its meter by fitting long vowels and vowel-diphthongs to the stressed syllables in pre-established metrical arrangements. Occasionally, however, poets would make short syllables do the job of long syllables, and this is the 'lengthening' discussed in this context. The Greek practice of 'lengthening' would be analogous in English to what happens to the name "Epichares" in the translation, where the natural stress in English (Ĕp-ĭ-char / -ēs) must be altered in an unnatural way to make the syllables fit the dactylic pattern (Ep-ĭ-char / -ēs). The difference is that English poetry could never employ lengthening since its meters invariably depend upon natural stress, while Greek poets very frequently employed lengthening.

Because of textual difficulties, it is difficult to guess either the meaning of the second example or in what variation of the dactylic hexameter is should be read.

GLOSSARY

In the English-Greek Glossary, if an English term is used in many senses or has one or more synonyms, this is indicated. When convenient, we give the definition of a term, e.g., of the term "accident"; when not convenient, we often give the reference to page and lines according to the Bekker text, as in the case of the term "cause", or else we give examples or some sort of description. Some terms, especially those which are elementary or familiar, are not defined.

In the Greek-English Glossary, English synonyms used for the same Greek term are separated by a comma; for example, the translation of γένεσις is "generation" and "becoming", and the latter two terms are separated by a comma and so have the same meaning. But if the English terms are separated by a semi-colon, they are not synonyms but have different meanings. For example, the translations of σημεῖον are "sign" and "point", and the latter two terms have different meanings.

ENGLISH-GREEK

abstraction   ἀφαίρεσις   To abstract is to attend to a part (separable or inseparable) of a whole, thus leaving out the other part or parts. For example, a geometrician abstracts volumes from bodies, leaving out weight, color, etc., and studies them as such. 1061a28-b3, 1077b2-14.

abuse   Same as "insult".

accident   συμβεβηκός   B is an accident of A if B is an attribute belonging to A not always nor for the most part but occasionally. 1025a14-30.

accidentally   κατὰ συμβεβηκός   B belongs to A accidentally if it is an accident of A.

according to   κατά   Synonyms: "with respect to", "in virtue of", "by virtue of". 73a27-b24, 1022a14-35.

acted upon, be   πάσχειν   This is one of the categories. 1b25-7, 1017a24-7.

acting   ποιεῖν   This is one of the categories. 1b25-7.

acting unjustly   ἀδικεῖν   Doing willingly what is unjust. 1135a16-7, 1136a16-7.

action   ποίησις   1048b17.

action   πρᾶξις   An action *chosen* for its own sake with understanding and certainty and without hesitation. Synonym: "conduct". 1105a28-33. Any action of a living thing.

activity   ἐνέργεια   A term with wide meaning, having as species such things as action, thinking, sensing, awareness, and so on. Syn: "*actuality*". 1045b27-52a11.

actuality   ἐντελέχεια   It is opposed to potentiality. 412a3-28, 1047a17b2, 1050a15-23.

actuality   Same as "activity".

acuteness   ἀγχίνοια   Discernment which grasps the cause or *middle* in an imperceptible time. 89b10-20.

affected   Same as "acted upon, be".

affection   πάθος, πάθημα   An alterable quality or the actuality of it. 1022b15-21.

affirmation   κατάφασις   A statement signifying that something belongs to something else. 17a25.

affirmative demonstration   δεικτικὴ ἀπόδειξις, κατηγορικὴ ἀπόδειξις   A demonstration whose premises and conclusion are affirmative. 82a36-7, 86a31-b38.

air   ἀήρ   For the meaning of "air", see "water".

Air   ἀήρ   A material principle for Anaximenes and Diogenes. 984a5-7.

alleged fact or thing   See "fact".

alteration   ἀλλοίωσις   Motion with respect to quality; e.g., becoming sick. 226a26-9, 270a27-30, 319b10-4.

ambition   φιλοτιμία

analogy   ἀναλογία   Sameness of relation between two pairs; e.g., if A is to B as C is to D, then the first two terms in the order given are analogous to the last two terms in the order given. 74a17-25, 76a37-40, 98a20-3, 99a8-16.

anger   ὀργή, θυμός   (sometimes). 1378a31-3.

animal   ζῷον   The term includes man.

argument   λόγος   A statement or statements aimed at convincing someone that something is or is not the case.

aristocracy   ἀριστοκρατία   A form of government in which the virtuous rule.

art   τέχνη   Scientific knowledge and the corresponding skill of how to produce something in accordance with that knowledge. 1140a6-23.

art of acquisition   κτητική

art of finance   χρηματιστική

artisan   βάναυσος

assembly   ἐκκλησία

association   κοινωνία   A group of people coming together for the sake of some good.

assumption   Same as "belief" or "hypothesis".

at some time   ποτέ   This is one of the categories. 1b25-7.

attribute   συμβεβηκός   B is an attribute of A if it belongs to A as to a subject, whether necessarily or not, but is not in the essence or definition of A. 1025a14-24.

attribute   πάθημα, πάθος

authority   Same as "ruling body".

axiom   ἀξίωμα   A truth which one must have if he is to learn anything within a science. Axioms are necessarily true and are used not as principles in the sense of premises but as regulative principles, like the principle of contradiction. 72a16-8, 76a37-b2, 77a26-31.

be in a position   κεῖσθαι   This is one of the categories. 1b25-7.

be in a whole   ἐν ὅλῳ εἶναι   B is said to be in A as in a whole if A is predicable of every B. 24b26-8.

be present in   ἐν τινὶ εἶναι   A is said to be present in B if, not being the nature or a part of the nature of B or a material part of B, it is incapable of existing apart from B; e.g., color is present in a body. 1a24-5.

beautiful   καλός

because   διά   In "A is C because of B", B is the cause of the fact that A is C. Synonyms: "through", "by means of", "by".

because of itself   δι᾽ αὐτό   If in "A is B" the cause of B is A, then B belongs to A because of A itself and not through any other *middle*. Syn: "through itself".

become   Same as "generated, be".

beginning   Same as "principle".

being   ὄν   That which exists, whether potentially or actually. Synonyms: "thing", "fact". 1017a7-b9.

Being   ὄν   A principle for some thinkers; the only existing principle for Parmenides and some others.

belief   ὑπόληψις   The term is generic; it is an affection of *thought* about what is or is not the case. Its species are *"knowledge"*, "opinion", "prudence", and their contraries. 427b24-7.

belong   ὑπάρχειν   The term is wider in meaning than the term "be predicable". For example, maximum area for a given line on a plane belongs to a circle. 48a40-49a10.

beneficial   ὠφέλιμος

blend μῖγμα A union of bodies, readily adaptable in shape, which have acted upon and so altered each other; e.g., a union of coffee and cream, not of salt and pepper. 327a30-8b32.

Blend μῖγμα For Anaxagoras, this is a principle, the union of all things which existed at first as something motionless before *Intelligence* acted as a moving cause to separate the things. 250b24-6.

boundary ὅρος, πέρας 1022a4-13.

brutality θηριότης 1148b15-9a20.

brute θηρίον

by   See "because".

by its nature καθ᾽ αὑτό

by itself καθ᾽ αὑτό Something which exists separately from other things.

by means of   Same as "because".

by nature φύσει P is said to exist by nature if it has in itself a principle of motion or rest; e.g., animals and water and earth exist by nature. Sometimes, A is by nature B if B follows from the essence of A.

by virtue of   Same as "according to".

can   Same as "possible".

capability   Same as "potentiality".

case πτῶσις

category κατηγορία Any of the highest ten genera of things. 1b25-7, 103b20-3.

catharsis κάθαρσις

cause αἴτιον, αἰτία, διότι 983a24-32, 1013a24-4a25. Synonyms: *"why"*, *"reason"*.

center of universe μέσον

chance τύχη A moving cause which is accidental and hence variable or indefinite. 195b31-8a13.

chance αὐτόματον Chance which by nature has no capability of making a *choice*.

change μεταβολή This is a generic term, and its species are "generation", "destruction", and "motion". The kinds of motion are: locomotion, alteration, increase, and decrease. 225a1-b9.

character ἦθος The various habits of a person or any animal.

choice προαίρεσις A choice of one of the alternatives deliberated on. 1113a1-7.

circular (of a syllogism) κύκλῳ

citizen πολίτης A member of a state, usually one who partakes of rule.

coin νόμισμα

come to be   Same as "generated, be".

commensurable σύμμετρος Two quantities are commensurable if they can be measured by some unit, i.e., if their ratio is what we call "a rational number".

common κοινός

common people δῆμος The lower classes

commonly accepted opinion Same as "generally accepted opinion".

complete τέλειος (a) That of which no part is outside or missing. (b) That whose virtue within its genus cannot be exceeded, as a perfect doctor or flute-player. Syn: "perfect". 1021b12-2a3.

concept νόημα

conclude falsely παραλογίζεσθαι

concord ὁμόνοια Sameness of thought about practical and expedient matters of considerable importance; e.g., the thought by the people that the rulers should be just and virtuous. 1167a22-b16.

confidence Same as "courage".

consecutive ἐχόμενον A is said to be consecutive to B if A succeeds and touches B. 227a6-7, 1069a1-2.

contact Same as "touch".

contemplative Same as "theoretical".

contentious ἐριστικός A person is said to be contentious if he argues for the sake of winning an argument.

contiguous Same as "consecutive".

continence ἐγκράτεια A habit which disposes a man to have bad *desires* and to know it, but he does not yield to them because his reason or wish is stronger than his *desires*. 1145b8-52a33.

continuous συνεχής A and B are said to be continuous if their limits (not necessarily all) are one. A property of continuity is infinite divisibility. 227a10-7, 232b24-5, 268a6-7, 1069a5-9.

contradiction ἀντίφασις Two opposite statements or *thoughts*, one of which is the denial of the other. 17a25-37.

contrary ἐναντίον The primary meaning is: contraries are the most different under the same genus, e.g., whiteness and blackness, justice and injustice, oddness and evenness. For secondary meanings, see 1018a25-35, 1055a3-b29.

contrary to general opinion παράδοξον

contrary to reason παράλογον

convention νόμος, συνθήκη

correlatives πρός τι The two relatives in a relation. Either is said to be the correlative of the other; e.g., greater and less, master and slave.

council βουλή

councillor βουλευτής

courage θάρρος, θάρσος Bravery is good courage, rashness is bad courage. Thus courage is the material cause in bravery and rashness.

cowardice δειλία A vice in virtue of which one is disposed to avoid meeting dangers.

currency νόμισμα

custom ἔθος, νόμος (sometimes)

decide κρίνειν

decision κρίσις

declarative sentence Same as "proposition".

decrease μείωσις, φθίσις

definition ὅρος, λόγος, ὁρισμός An expression whose purpose is to signify analytically an object.

definition ὁρισμός A formula of the essence or whatness of a thing. 90b3-4, 94a11-4, 1031a11-4.

deliberate choice Same as *"choice"*.

deliberation βούλευσις Inquiry into the means needed to bring about a desired end, usually in practical matters, 1112a18-3a2.

democracy πολιτεία

demonstration ἀπόδειξις A syllogism through the cause of that which is necessarily true. 71b9-18. In a qualified sense, a syllogism of that which is necessarily true but not through the cause. 78a22-9a16.

denial ἀπόφασις A statement signifying that something does not belong to something else, i.e., any of the forms "A is no B", "some A is no B", "no A is B". 17a25-6, 72a13-4.

density βάρος

derivative name παρώνυμον A name somewhat changed in ending from the original name (with few exceptions) in order to indicate a certain difference in its meaning; e.g., "virtuous" is derived from "virtue". 1a12-5.

desire ὄρεξις It is a genus having as its species *desire*, wish, and temper.

desire ἐπιθυμία Desire of the pleasant or what seems to be pleasant (but is not). 146b36-7a4, 414b5-6.

despotic δεσποτικός Pertaining to a master

destruction φθορά Change from being to nonbeing. It is unqualified if it is with respect to substance, as when a man dies; it is qualified if it is with respect to quality or quantity or place. 225a12-20, 1067b21-5.

deterioration φθίσις

deviation Same as "perversion".

dialectic διαλεκτική A discipline dealing effectively with any problem, whether defending or attacking a thesis, starting from commonly accepted beliefs. 100a18-b23, 101a25-8, 1004b17-26.

difference διαφορά

differentia διαφορά If A and B are different but under the same genus, the parts in their essence which makes them distinct are said to be their differentiae.

direct demonstration ἀπόδειξις τοῦ δεικνῦναι A demonstration which uses only the premises which are posited, as against one which assumes the denial of the expected conclusion and leads to a contradiction. 85a13-9, 87a1-30.

discernment εὐστοχία 89b10-20.

discriminate κρίνειν Synonym: "distinguish".

discussion λόγος

disposition διάθεσις

distinguish Same as "discriminate".

doctrine δόξα A belief of great philosophic or scientific importance, true or false, and usually a principle or something given without proof. 987a32-4, 996b27-31.

doing Same as "action."

dyad δυάς The terms "dyad" and "two" are synonymously used.

Dyad δυάς This is Two, which is a Number as an Idea for Plato, and it is the first Number which is generated from the *Dyad* and *Unity*, which are the first two principles. It is also called "Dyad Itself" or "Two Itself".

Dyad δυάς For Plato, this is the material principle of all things generated. It also goes by the name "*Indefinite Dyad*".

earth γῆ For its meaning, see "water".

Earth γῆ

Earth γῆ A material principle for Empedocles. 984a8-11.

effect οὗ αἴτιον

element στοιχεῖον The primary constituent of a thing; and it is either indivisible or divisible into parts of the same kind as the whole. 1014a26-b15.

emotion πάθος

emulation ζῆλος

end τέλος The term is narrower in meaning than the term "limit". 1021b25-2a13.

ending πτῶσις

enthymeme ἐνθύμημα In rhetoric, a syllogism which proceeds from probabilities or signs. 70a10-b6.

epic ἔπος

episode ἐπεισόδιον

equity ἐπιείκεια A virtue by which one *acts* rightly towards others, either (1) justly (i.e., according to law), or (2) rightly when the law does not specify. 1137a31-8a3, 1374a26-b1. Syn: "fairness."

equivocal ὁμώνυμον Having or called by the same name. A and B are said to be equivocally named if the term which names them both does not have the same meaning for both; e.g., both George and his picture are equivocally named "George". 1a1-6.

eristic   Same as "contentious".

error   ἁμαρτία

especially   Same as "in the highest degree".

essence   τὶ ἦν εἶναι   (a) That which, being in a category, is in the thing and in virtue of which the thing remains the same and is univocally called by the same name, for example, of a statue, its form, and of a white thing, its whiteness insofar as the thing is white; (b) that in the soul as *knowledge* by which we know a thing's essence in sense (a). 1029b1-1030b13.

essential   καθ' αὑτό   A is said to belong essentially to B if as predicable or as an attribute of B it belongs to B as to a subject by being in the whatness of B (as animality or rationality is in a man) or by being demonstrable through B (as concurrence of altitudes is demonstrable through the triangle) or by being an attribute definable by means of B (as oddness by means of number). 73a28-b24, 1022a14-36.

ethical   ἠθικός

even (of numbers)   ἄρτιος

Even   ἄρτιος   For the Pythagoreans, a material principle of things. 986a15-21.

evil habit   μοχθηρία

example   παράδειγμα   68b38-9a19, 1356b4-5.

excess   ὑπερβολή, ὑπεροχή   A exceeds B if A is divisible into parts one of which is equal to B or if A has more of a certain quality as a principle than B has.

Excess   ὑπεροχή   Some thinkers posited *Excess* and *Deficiency* as the material principles of all things. 1087a17-8.

excessive weight   βάρος

exercise   Same as "activity".

exist   εἶναι, ὑπάρχειν

expectation   ἐλπίς

expedient   συμφέρον   That which is good to oneself is expedient to him or her. 1390a1, 1422a4-15.

experience   ἐμπειρία   Knowledge produced from many memories of the same thing; for example, knowledge that Socrates, suffering from disease X, recovers by taking medicine Y, if this happened repeatedly. 980b28-1a12.

expression   λόγος

fact   ὄν, πρᾶγμα, τὸ ὅτι   For example, a sick Socrates (if he is sick); the concurrence of the altitudes of a triangle. Alleged fact: πρᾶγμα   This may be a fact or nonbeing; so the Greek term is used in two senses, like a genus. For example, a sick Socrates, whether he is sick or well.

faculty   Same as power, but usually applied to living things.

fallacy   παραλογισμός   An argument in which that which is alleged to be a conclusion from certain premises does not follow from those premises.

false middle   ψευδές μέσον   A middle term so posited that both premises are false.

fear   φόβος   See *Rhetoric*, 1382a21-7.

figure   σχῆμα   (a) Syn: "shape". (b) In logic, it means any one of the three figures of a syllogism.

final cause   οὗ ἕνεκα   That for the sake of which something exists or is generated (the other tenses of time included). This is not limited to animals but extends to plants and to other things. 194b16-5b30, 983a24-b1, 1013a24-b28.

finite   πεπερασμένος   Syn: "limited".

Finite   πεπερασμένον   For the Pythagoreans, the *Infinite* as matter and the *Finite* as form were posited as the principles from which the other things (these being numbers) are generated. 987a13-9.

fire   πῦρ   This is a material element characterized by being hot and dry. See "water".

Fire   πῦρ   For Hippasus and Heraclitus, *Fire* is the only principle, a material principle, from which the other things are generated. 984a7-8.

first   Syn: "primary".

folly   ἀφροσύνη   The contrary of "prudence". See "prudence". Syn: "imprudence".

food   τροφή

for its own sake   δι' αὐτό

foreign name   γλῶττα

form   εἶδος, ἰδέα   (sometimes). Form is contrasted with matter, both being causes; for example, of a bronze statue, bronze is its matter and the shape is its form.

Form   εἶδος   For Plato, Forms are changeless, eternal, most real, and the causes of the existence of the Mathematical Objects and of sensible objects, whether destructible or not. Syn: "Idea". 987a29-b22.

form   μορφή   Syn: "*shape*". Perhaps the terms "form" and "*form*" are used synonymously.

form of government   Same as "government".

fortune   Same as "luck."

friendship   φιλία   1155b17-6b35.

Friendship   φιλία   For Empedocles, this is the principle which causes things to come together. 984b27-985a10.

700

generally accepted opinion ἔνδοξον Syn: "commonly accepted opinion".

generated, be γίγνεσθαι Synonyms: "become", "come to be". See "generation".

generation γένεσις A change from not-being to being. If the generation is of a substance, as of a baby born, it is called "simple generation", but if it is of an attribute, as of health from sickness, it is called "qualified generation". Syn: "becoming". 225a12-7, 1067b21-3.

generosity ἐλευθεριότης

genus γένος In the whatness or definition of a thing, the constituent as matter or subject, to which the addition of a differentia produces a species of that genus.

good ἀγαθόν That which is regarded or chosen by the intellect as an end in itself or as a means to such an end. 1096a19-29, 1362a21-1363b4.

good fortune εὐτυχία Usually, good luck of considerable magnitude. 197a25-7.

good luck εὐτυχία

good temper πραότης A virtue with respect to anger or temper. 1125b26-6b9.

good will εὔνοια

goodness εὖ

goods χρῆμα

growth αὔξησις

government πολιτεία The order or structure of a state.

habit ἕξις

happiness εὐδαιμονία Virtuous activity of the soul throughout life. 1102a5-6.

harmonic mode Same as "harmony".

harmonics ἁρμονική

harmony ἁρμονία, συμφωνία

hearing ἀκοή

heaven οὐρανός 278b9-21.

high birth (or lineage) εὐγένεια

high-mindedness μεγαλοψυχία A virtue according to which a man rightly regards himself as worthy of high honor and acts rightly according to such belief. 1123a34-5a35.

homogeneous ὁμοιομερής

honor τιμή 1101b10-2a4, 1361a27-b2.

hot, n. or adj. θερμόν 329b24-32, 378b10-26, 388a20-4, 1070b10-5.

Hot θερμόν For Parmenides, a principle of sensibles. 986b31-7a2.

household οἰκία

household management οἰκονομία

hypothesis ὑπόθεσις A statement or premise, which is posited as true without proof and which signifies that something is or is not the case. Syn: "assumption". 72a14-24.

idea ἰδέα

Idea ἰδέα The Ideas were posited by Plato as existing apart from sensible things, as being the causes of those things, as being changeless, and as being the objects of *knowledge*. Syn: "Form". 987a29-b22.

imagination φαντασία 427b27-429a9.

imitation μίμημα; μίμησις The first term signifies that which imitates another thing, like a picture of a man or a statue of Socrates; the second, the act of imitating. Syn: "work of imitation", of the first term.

immediate ἄμεσος Syn: "without a *middle*".

impression πάθημα

imprudence ἀφροσύνη The contrary of "prudence", "folly."

in a place ποῦ One of the ten categories. Syn: "somewhere", "whereness".

in a simplified way ἁπλῶς

in itself καθ' αὐτό 1022a14-36, 1029a21-2, 24-5.

in the highest degree or sense μάλιστα This term is used specifically for qualities which admit the more and the less, and analogically for other things, as when we seek to know the things which are substances most of all. Syn: "most of all".

in virtue of κατά A is said to belong to B, or to C in virtue of B, if it is in the whatness or follows from the whatness of B, or of C, or if it is defined in terms of B. Synonyms: "according to", "with respect to", "by virtue of". 73a27-b24, 1022a14-36.

in virtue of an attribute κατὰ συμβεβηκός Syn: "indirectly". For example, a man is white in virtue of the color of his skin and not in virtue of his essence or a part of it.

inasmuch as Same as "qua".

incommensurable ἄλογον

inconsistency ὑπεναντίωσις

incontinent ἀκρατής

increase αὔξησις

indicate σημαίνειν

indirectly Same as "in virtue of an attribute".

induction ἐπαγωγή 68b15-37.

infinite ἄπειρον Syn: "unlimited". 204a2-7, 1066a35-b1.

Infinite ἄπειρον The material principle for the Pythagoreans and Plato. It is the same as Plato's *Dyad* or *Indefinite Dyad*, or like the *Even* of the Pythagoreans.

injustice   ἀδικία   A habit by which one is disposed to do what is unjust. It is the contrary of "justice". 1134a1-7.

inquiry   μέθοδος   Systematic inquiry.

insofar as   Same as "qua".

instrument   ὄργανον

instrumental   Same as "useful".

insult   ὕβρις   Syn: "abuse". For definition, see *Rhet.* 1378b23-26.

intellect   νοῦς   The part of the soul which knows or *knows* the principles. 84b35-5a1, 100b5-17, 1140b31-1141a8, 1143a25-b17.

Intellect   νοῦς   For Aristotle, the prime mover or God.

intelligence   σύνεσις   Ability to use opinions in judging well objects of prudence, where someone else speaks about them. 1142b34-3a18.

Intelligence   νοῦς   For Anaxagoras, a moving principle and cause of things.

intelligible object   νοητόν   Syn: "object of thought".

intention   προαίρεσις   A choice of the apparently best of the alternatives deliberated upon. Syn: "deliberate choice", "*choice*". 1113a2-7.

interest   Same as "expedient".

intermediate   μέσον, μεταξύ

irascibility   ὀργιλότης

irony   ἀρωνεία   Syn: "self-depreciation".

irrational   The contrary of "rational".

judge, v.   κρίνειν

judge or think rightly   φρονεῖν

judging power or faculty   λογιστικόν   Usually, of what may or may not be.

judgment   κρίσις; λογισμός

judgment   γνώμη   Right judgment by an equitable man as such concerning particulars. 1143a19-35.

just thing   δίκαιον   Synonyms: "the just", "that which is just". 1131a9-2b20.

justice   δικαιοσύνη   A virtue by which one is disposed to do what is just. 1134a1-6.

kind   εἶδος

know   γνωρίζειν, γιγνώσκειν, εἰδέναι

knowledge   ἐπιστήμη   Knowledge of the causes of a thing which exists of necessity, whether this knowledge is demonstrable or not. Syn: "scientific knowledge", "science". 71b7-16.

laborer   θής

language   λέξις   Syn: "diction."

length   μῆκος   The term means what we usually call "a line" without reference to its being finite or not. 1020a11-4. Sometimes it means a line segment or finite line.

letter στοιχεῖον

life ζωή

like ὅμοιον Things are said to be like if their quality is the same. Syn: "similar". 1018a15-9, 1021a11-2, 1054b3-14.

limit πέρας 1022a4-13.

Limit πέρας For the Pythagoreans, the principle as form. Syn: *"Limited"*

limited πεπερασμένον

line γραμμή A limited length, or a one-dimensional limited continuous quantity. 1016b24-9, 1020a7-14.

live, v. ζῆν 413a22-b2.

logical λογικός

low-mindedness μικροψυχία A vice according to which a man regards himself as worthy of less honor than he is worthy and acts according to that belief. 1123b9-13.

luck τύχη Luck or what results from luck belongs to that which can deliberate, i.e., to men, but analogously to other things. Its genus is "chance". 195b31-8a13. Syn: "fortune".

major term μείζων ὅρος That which is taken as belonging or as not belonging to the middle term. Syn: "major".

make ποιεῖν

making ποίησις

man (both sexes) ἄνθρωπος

man ἀνήρ A male human being

manual laborer χερνίτης

many πολλά, πλῆθος The contrary of unity. Syn: "plurality". 1054a20-5a2.

Many πλῆθος A material principle posited by some thinkers, e.g., Speusippus.

marriage γαμική

mass ὄγκος

master δεσπότης It is opposed to "slave" as a relative to its correlative.

master-artist ἀρχιτέκτων

masterly Same as "despotic"

materials ὕλη Same as "matter".

mathematical objects μαθηματικά

Mathematical Objects μαθηματικά, τὰ μεταξύ For Plato, these are also called "Intermediate Objects" and lie between the Ideas and the sensible objects; they are immovable, eternal, and the objects of the mathematical sciences. For Speusippus, these are first in existence, eternal, and immovable, and the objects of the mathematical sciences; for Xenocrates, they are the same as the Ideas.

mathematical sciences μαθηματικαὶ ἐπιστῆμαι

704

mathematics μάθημα

matter ὕλη The term is generic. If physical, it may signify prime matter which underlies a form (192a22-34, 1029a20-6, 1042a27-8), or proximate matter like wood and nails in a chair which exist potentially or as parts in a chair but can exist separately (1044a15-32), or as something between. If nonphysical, it may be like the premises in a syllogism or the letters in a word, etc.

may be ἐνδέχεσθαι That which may be is that which, if posited as existing, does not lead to a contradiction. That which may be is possible, and conversely.

mean, n. μέσον It lies between two extremes. Syn: "moderation".

mean, v. σημαίνειν Syn: "to signify".

measure μέτρον That by which, as first or a principle, a given quantity is known. 1052b20-7, 1087b33-8a14. Syn: "unit".

mechanics μηχανική Its subject-matter is physical but the treatment of the subject is mathematical.

medium of exchange νόμισμα

menial διακονικός

metaphor μεταφορά

method μέθοδος

middle μέσου That which is between two parts or things.

middle μέσον A middle term as a cause in a demonstration, or the thing signified by that term.

middle term μέσον If A is predicated of B, and B of C, then B is the middle term (in the first figure). Similarly in other figures. The middle term does not appear in the conclusion.

misfortune δυστυχία Bad luck or fortune, usually of considerable magnitude.

mistake ἀπάτη

moderate μέτριον That which is neither excessive nor deficient but has the proper measure.

moderation Same as "mean".

money χρῆμα

more μᾶλλον A term which compares qualities. Sometimes it is used analogically. Synonyms: "to a higher degree", "rather".

most of all Same as "in the highest degree".

motion κίνησις The actuality of potential being qua potential. The kinds of motion are locomotion, alteration, increase, and decrease. 201a10-1, 1065b16,33, 1068a8-10.

must be Same as "necessary".

name ὄνομα Voice which is significant by convention and no part of which is significant. 16a19-20.

nation ἔθνος

natural φυσικός Syn: "physical".

natural gift εὐφυΐα

nature φύσις The form of a physical object; the matter of a physical object; the principle of motion present in a physical object. Sometimes, the essence of a thing in any category. 192b8-3b21, 1014b16-5a19.

necessary ἀναγκαῖον The primary meaning: that which cannot be otherwise, e.g., vertical angles are necessarily equal, and 16 is necessarily a square (natural) number.

negation ἀπόφασις The contradictory of an expression, whether this be a term or an affirmation.

negative στερητικός, ἀποφατικός

negative demonstration στερητικὴ ἀπόδειξις A demonstration whose conclusion is a denial. 82a36-b28.

noble καλόν That which exists or is *chosen* for its own sake and is praiseworthy, or, that which is good or pleasant. 1366a33-5.

nonbeing οὐκ ὄν, μὴ ὄν That which is impossible; that which does not exist but may exist or exists potentially. The latter is also called "not-being."

Nonbeing μὴ ὄν For some thinkers, a principle needed to generate the plurality of things.

nonrational ἄλογος

nonrational animal θηρίον

not-being   Same as "nonbeing".

noun ὄνομα

number ἀριθμός This is what we call "a natural number greater than 1".

Number ἀριθμός For Plato, a Number, such as Seven, is also an Idea, and it is generated ultimately from the two principles, the *One* and the *Dyad*. For Speusippus, Numbers are not Ideas but are first in existence and the objects of mathematics. 1075b37-6a4, 1084a3-7, 1090b13-9.

nutritive part of the soul θρεπτικόν

object of desire ὀρεκτόν

object of thought νοητόν Syn: "intelligible object".

ochlocracy δημοκρατία This is mob rule or rule by the masses or the people's rule, and usually, that of the poor.

odd (of a number) περιττόν

Odd περιττόν For the Pythagoreans, a principle as form of all things. Syn: "Finite" or "Limited".

one ἕν (a) That which is indivisible or undivided, whether numerically or in definition or in species or in genus or by analogy. (b) A unit or a measure. Synonyms: "the one", "oneness", "unity", "unit", "measure". 1015b16-7a3, 1052a15-4a19.

One ἕν For Plato and some others, the *One* is a principle as form from which other things are generated, such as Numbers and sensible objects. Synonyms: "the *One*", "*Unity*", "*Oneness*". 987a29-b22, 1084a3-7.

opinion δόξα A belief of what may or may not be, e.g., that Socrates is standing. 89a2-3, 100b5-7, 1039b31-40al, 1051b10-15.

opposite ἀντικείμενον The main kinds are: the contradictory, the contrary, the relative, and a privation. 11b16-9, 1018a20-b8.

optics ὀπτική

organ ὄργανον

pain λύπη

paradox θέσις A belief which is contrary to what is accepted by known philosophers; for example, the belief that contradiction is possible. 104b19-24.

paralogism Same as "fallacy".

particular demonstration ἀπόδειξις κατὰ μέρος A demonstration whose middle term states more than the cause; e.g., the demonstration that a penny sinks in the water because it is made of copper.

pattern παράδειγμα

peculiarity ἴδιον Same as "property".

people's rule Same as "ochlocracy."

perfect Same as "complete".

peripety περιπέτεια

persuade πείθειν

perversion παρέκβασις A perverted form of government is one which is ruled not for the interest of the citizens but for the interest of the ruler or rulers. Syn: "deviation".

philosophy φιλοσοφία A science of being qua being, i.e., of the highest principles and causes, which are most general or most noble.

physical Syn: "natural".

physical beauty κάλλος

physicist φυσικός

physics φυσική The science which treats of things which are movable qua being movable. 1025b18-21, 1061b28-30, 1064a15-6.

pity ἔλεος *Rhet*. 1385b13-16.

place τόπος The first inner motionless boundary of a containing body, e.g., the inner surface of a can of tomatoes. 212a20-1.

pleasure ἡδονή In general, it may be of thought or of action or of the senses; in a limited sense, it is of the senses. 1095b16-7, 1152a36-4b31, 1369b33-5.

plot μῦθος

plurality πλῆθος, πολλά Synonym: "many", as a noun. 1004b27-9, 1054a20-5a2.

Plurality πλῆθος For Speusippus, this is the material principle from which Numbers are generated. 1087b4-6.

poem ποίημα

poetics ποιητική

point στιγμή, σημεῖον

political πολιτικός

politics πολιτική

posit τίθεσθαι, ποιεῖν

position θέσις Something laid down as existing or true. 72a14-24.

possession ἕξις; κτῆμα

possession of property κτῆσις

possible δυνατόν Syn: "can".

potentiality δύναμις Capability of acting or of being acted upon; that which, as matter, can become something.

power δύναμις Ability to act

predicable, be κατηγορεῖσθαι

predicate, n. κατηγορούμενον That which is said about a subject.

predicate of, be a κατηγορεῖσθαι

predication κατηγορία The relation of the predicate to a subject.

premise πρότασις In a syllogism, an affirmation or a denial used as one of two statements from which a conclusion is to be drawn.

present in, be ἐν τινὶ εἶναι A is said to be present in B if, not being the nature or a part of the nature of B or a material part of B, it is incapable of existing apart from B; e.g., sickness is present in a living thing. 1a24-5.

primary πρῶτος Syn: "first".

principle ἀρχή The first thing from which something either is or is generated or becomes known. Syn: "beginning", "starting point", "source". 1012b34-3a23.

prior πρότερον P is prior to Q with respect to some principle X if P is nearer to X than Q is. For example, if X is existence, then an animal is prior in existence to a man; for if an animal exists, a man does not necessarily exist, but if a man exists, so does an animal. 14a26-b23, 1018b9-1019a14.

prior to us πρότερον ἡμῖν These are things as first known to us, usually through accidents and sensations and not through their nature or causes. 71b33-2a5, 72b25-32.

prior without qualification πρότερον ἁπλῶς These are things as known to us through their own nature or causes and, if definable, they are known through their definition. 71b33-2a5, 72b25-32. Syn: "prior by nature".

privation *στέρησις* (a) Not having; e.g., a sound is deprived of color, that is, it has no color. (b) Not having if by nature it should have; e.g., a blind man is deprived of sight. 1022b22-1023a7.

probability *εἰκός* A generally accepted opinion concerning that which exists or occurs, or fails to exist or to occur, for the most part.

produce *ποιεῖν* Syn: "make"

production *ποίησις* A change which starts at the end of the artist's thinking and ends when he has generated a work of his art. In a wider sense, any generation requiring some power or thought or art. 1032a27-8, b6-17.

property *ἴδιον* A property of a thing is an attribute of it which, not being the essence of that thing, belongs to it and to it alone; e.g., capability of learning science is a property of men. The term is also used in a qualified sense. 102a18-31.

property *κτῆμα* External materials or goods owned by man. Syn: "possessions".

proportion *ἀναλογία* Analogy with respect to quantity. See "analogy".

proposition *ἀποφαντικός λόγος* A statement or a combination of statements.

prove *συλλογίζεσθαι, δεικνύειν* To show or conclude truly.

prudence *φρόνησις* (a) Generically (for all animals), the ability to look after one's own good, 1141a20-8. (b) Specifically (for men), a habit by means of which one can deliberate truly concerning one's conduct for a good life. 1140a24-b30.

purging *κάθαρσις* Syn: "catharsis".

purpose *οὗ ἕνεκα* Usually, a final cause in living things. See "final cause".

qua *ἧ* An attribute of C is said to belong to C qua B if it belongs to B but to no genus of B. For example, capability of motion belongs to a man and to a chair qua physical bodies, and infinite divisibility belongs to a circle qua a magnitude. If B is the same as C, then the attribute is a property of B. Synonyms: "insofar as", "inasmuch as". 73b25-4a3.

quality *ποιόν, ποιότης* This is one of the categories. 8b25-11a38, 1020a33-b25.

quantity *ποσόν* This is a category whose primary species are numbers (i.e., natural numbers greater than 1) and magnitudes (i.e., lines and surfaces and solids). There are also indirect and derived quantities which depend on the primary quantities; e.g., time, place, motion, angles, and the like. 4b20-6a35, 1020a7-32.

race *γένος*

rather Same as "more".

ratio λόγος For example, 3:5 is a ratio, and so is 2:3:7 if the relation requires three elements, e.g., weights of water, of flour, and of sugar.

reason, n. λόγος

reason, v. λογίζεσθαι

reason, n. Same as "cause"

reasoning of the possible λογισμός

recognition ἀναγνώρησις In *Poetics*, it is a change from ignorance to becoming aware that those marked for good fortune or misfortune are friends, or enemies. 1452a29-32.

relative, relation πρός τι This is a category which involves two things, each of which may be a composite (e.g., if A is between B and C, the pair B and C is a composite). 6a36-8b24, 1020b26-1021b11.

reputation δόξα

restitution δικαίωμα Correction of unjust treatment. 1135a13.

rhetoric ῥητορική The art of persuasion, which is effected through logical arguments or the arousing of the emotions of the audience or the impression created of being trustworthy; and it is about things past or present or future.

riches Same as "wealth".

right, adj. ὀρθός A genus of "true" and of *"successful"*, the first species being a predicate of knowledge, the second, of good *actions*. 427b8-11.

right measure μέτριον

rule of a master δεσποτεία

ruling body πολίτευμα For example, kings or tyrants or those elected to run the state. 1278b10-1.

said of, be λέγεσθαι κατά A is said of B if A is a genus or a differentia or the essence or definition of B; for example, animal or rational or substance is said of man or an individual man. 1a20-b9.

science Same as *"knowledge"*

scientific knowledge Same as *"knowledge"*.

seed σπέρμα

self-depreciation εἰρωνία A disposition to think or speak of oneself as being less worthy than one actually is and to *act* accordingly. Syn: "irony". 1127a22-3, b22-3.

sensation αἴσθησις Actual sensing of an object.

sensation, power (or faculty) of αἴσθησις This is the ability to sense, whether one is actually sensing or not.

sense of hearing ἀκοή

sense of touch ἀφή

sentence λόγος A significant expression having parts each of which is significant. 16b26-33.

sentient part of the soul αἰσθητικόν The part of the soul of an animal which can sense.

servant δοῦλος

shape Same as "figure".

shape μορφή Syn: *"form"*

show δεικνύειν The term is more general than "prove".

shrewdness δεινότης Ability to act successfully upon the means leading to a practical end, whether the end is good or bad. 1144a23-8.

sign, n. σημεῖον A premise which, along with another premise not stated but understood, is put forward as necessitating demonstratively a conclusion or as being generally accepted to lead to a conclusion. 70a3-b6.

signify σημαίνειν A relation between a term or an expression and what the term or the expression stands for. Syn: "mean".

similar Same as "like".

slave δοῦλος

somewhere ποῦ This is one of the categories. 1b25-2a2. Syn: "whereness".

sophistry σοφιστική A discipline which is concerned with what appears to be wisdom or philosophy but is not. It has as its aim honor (by appearing to be philosophy) or making money or just winning an argument. The last kind is called "eristics". 165a21-3, 171b22-34, 1004b17-19.

soul ψυχή The form of a living thing. 412b4-25, 414a4-14.

sound ψόφος

source Same as "principle".

species εἶδος

spectacle ὄψις

speech λόγος

spirit Same as "temper".

spirited part of the soul θυμικόν

starting point Same as "principle".

state πόλις A group of citizens unified for the purpose of living well. 1275b20-1.

statement ἀπόφανσις An expression or thought which is true or false. It may be either an affirmation or a denial. 17a20-1, 72a11-2.

statesman πολιτικός

Strife νεῖκος For Empedocles, a principle which causes things to separate from each other. 984b27-5a10.

subject ὑποκείμενον This is relative to an attribute or to that which belongs to the subject. For example, color belongs to a body, sickness to an animal, and "P" is the grammatical subject in the statement "P is Q". An unqualified subject is a subject which cannot be an attribute of another subject; e.g., an individual man is such a subject.

substance   οὐσία   Substances are things in which all attributes are present, e.g., men and trees and chairs and the like; and they are separate from other things. 2a11-4b19.

substance   οὐσία   The substance of a thing is the nature or form of that thing, and it is applicable to all categories. For example, the substance of a man is his soul, and of a house it is its form. Syn: "essence".

succeed   κατορθοῦν   Succeed in doing what is right.

succession   ἑξῆς, ἐφεξῆς   P is said to succeed Q if, being further from a given principle than Q and being separate by itself in position or in kind or in some other way, there is no other thing in the same species as P and Q between it and Q. 226b34-7a6, 1068b31-9a1.

such (implying a quality)   τοιόνδε

sure sign   τεκμήριον   An irrefutable dialectical argument.

syllogism   συλλογισμός   An expression, verbal or written or in thought, in which a statement called "conclusion" follows necessarily from two other statements called "premises" which are posited as being so or true. 24b8-22, 100a25-7.

systematic inquiry   Same as *"inquiry"*.

temper   θυμός   The quality by which one shows courage or anger or the contraries.

temperance   σωφροσύνη   A virtue with regard to bodily pleasures, especially those of touch and taste. 1117b23-9b18.

tense   πτῶσις

term of a syllogism   ὅρος

theoretical   θεωρητικός   Synonym: "contemplative".

theory   λόγος

thesis   θέσις   An immediate syllogistic principle which cannot be proved or demonstrated, and as a premise in a syllogism it may be a statement or a definition. 72a14-21.

thing   Same as "being".

thing produced by art   ποίημα

think   νοεῖν   The term is generic and includes also "imagine" as one of its species.

think   διανοεῖν   In thought, to combine or divide or to affirm or deny, e.g., that 36 is a square number or that Socrates was not stupid.

thinking part of the soul   νοητικόν

thinking part of the soul   διανοητικόν

this, a   τόδε τι   An individual thing, usually a primary substance, which one can point to.

thought   νόημα

thought διάνοια

through   Same as "because".

through itself   δι' αὐτό

time   χρόνος   A number of motion with respect to before and after. Syn: "interval of time". 217b29-220a26.

timocracy   τιμοκρατία

to a higher degree   Same as "more".

topic   τόπος   A generally accepted kind of argument in dialectic, used to logically persuade others. It is a proposition common to all disciplines. 1358a32.

touch   ἀφή   The faculty of touching or touching itself.

truth   ἀληθές   A statement or *thought* which signifies what actually is or is not the case. 1011b25-7, 1051b3-5.

Two   δυάς   This is the first Number which is generated by Plato's principles, the *One* and the *Dyad*.

underlying subject   Same as "subject".

understand   εἰδέναι   In *Metaphysics* its primary meaning is knowing a thing through its causes. 981a21-30, 983a25-6. Elsewhere it seems to have a wider meaning.

understand   ξυνιέναι   To know or grasp the meaning of an expression.

unfortunate   δυστυχής   One to whom bad luck of considerable magnitude has befallen. 197a25-7.

unit   μονάς   That which is indivisible with respect to quantity and has no position. 1016b17-31. Sometimes it is used as a genus to include also points, which have position. 409b6.

Unit   μονάς   A unit of a Number. See "Number".

unity   Same as "one".

Unity   Same as *"One"*.

universal   καθόλου   That which by nature is predicable of or belongs to many. 17a39-40, 1038b11-2. For Plato, universals are Ideas.

universally   καθόλου, ὅλως

universal   καθόλου   An attribute A is said to belong *universally* to all of B if it is a property of B; and as a property, A belongs to B qua B. The term is also used for a demonstration which proves a property of a subject. 73b25-4a3.

universe   πᾶν, ὅλον

univocal   συνώνυμον   A and B are said to be univocally named by C if C has the same meaning when predicated of both A and B. For example, a horse and a dog are univocally named "animal". 1a6-12.

unjust thing   ἄδικον   1131a9-2b20.

unjustly treated, be   ἀδικεῖσθαι   To suffer unwillingly the unjust, 1136b1-13.

unjust treatment ἀδίκημα

unqualified ἁπλῶς Without qualifications or restrictions.

unreasonable ἄλογον

unscrupulous πανοῦργος

useful χρήσιμος Syn: "instrumental".

value τιμή

vanity χαυνότης A vice which disposes a man to regard himself as worthy of high honor when he is not so worthy and to speak or *act* according to that opinion.

verdict δίκη Judgment of what is just or unjust. 1134a31-2.

vice κακία A vice (usually ethical) which is contrary to virtue.

virtue ἀρετή An ethical or intellectual habit by the use of which, barring accidents, one leads a happy life. 1106b36-7a7. Occasionally, any excellence, e.g., of a good horse or of a violin, or of one who obeys the law.

virtuous σπουδαῖος Having virtue.

vision ὄψις The sense or faculty of seeing.

vocal sound φωνή Syn: "voice".

void κενόν A place in which there is no body at all, whether light or heavy. 208b25-7, 213a15-9, 214a2-17.

Void κενόν A principle of all things, posited by some thinkers.

volume ὄγκος

voluntary ἑκούσιον

water ὕδωρ As used by Aristotle, the term does not mean what we mean by "water" or "H₂O". For him, in terms of attributes, it means a body which is cold and moist and yields readily like water but is not gaseous. Similarly, "fire" means a gaseous body which is hot and dry, "air" means a gaseous body which is hot and moist, and "earth" means a hard body which is cold and dry. These are the four material elements from which the other sensible bodies (excluding the heavenly bodies) are composed. 330a30-b7, 382b13-5, 388a29-32.

Water ὕδωρ For Thales, the material principle of things; for Empedocles, one of the material principles of things. 983b20-4a9.

wealth πλοῦτος Syn: "riches".

weight βάρος

well εὖ

wellbeing εὖ

what a thing is τὶ ἔστι, τὸ A formula of what a thing is as expressed by a definition; it is primarily of substances and secondarily of the things in the other categories, and the existence of the thing is presupposed. 92b4-8, 93a16-20. Syn: "whatness".

whatness Same as "what a thing is".

whenness ποτέ This is one of the ten categories. Syn: "sometime", "at some time". 1b25-7.

whereness Same as "somewhere".

whole ὅλον (a) That from which no natural part is missing. (b) That which contains what is contained, either (i) actually many (as a universal contains the species or the individuals of which it is a predicate), or (ii) the parts which exist potentially. (c) That in which the position of the parts makes a difference, as a whole shoe. 1023b26-1024a10.

whole, be in a ἐν ὅλῳ εἶναι B is said to be in A as in a whole if A is predicable of every B. 24b26-8.

wisdom σοφία Intellect and science of the most honorable things (eternal and divine). Philosophy, then, would be wisdom. In a qualified sense, there is wisdom of some part of being, e.g., of the first principles and of some theorems of physics. 1005b1-2, 1141a9-b8.

wish βούλησις Desire of the good or the apparent good, but it is neither *desire*, which is limited to the pleasure of the senses, nor temper. The object of wish is an end, not a means to an end. 1113a13-b2, 1369a1-4.

with respect to κατά Synonyms: "in virtue of", "according to", "by virtue of". 73a27-b24, 1022a14-35.

without qualification Same as "unqualified".

work of imitation μίμημα For example, a painting of a man or a tree, a tragedy or comedy. It is not limited to what is or was or will be but extends to what might be.

wrongly οὐκ ὀρθῶς The contrary of "rightly".

GREEK-ENGLISH

ἀγαθόν good
ἀγχίνοια acuteness
ἀδικεῖν *acting* unjustly
ἀδικεῖσθαι be treated unjustly
ἀδίκημα unjust treatment
ἀδικία injustice
ἄδικον unjust thing, the unjust
ἀήρ air; *Air*
αἴσθησις sensation; faculty of sensation
αἰσθητικόν sentient; sentient part of soul
αἴτιον, αἰτία cause, *reason*
αἴτιον οὗ effect
ἀκοή hearing; sense of hearing
ἀκράτεια incontinence
ἀλλοίωσις alteration
ἄλογον nonrational; irrational; unreasonable; incommensurable
ἁμάρτημα what results from error
ἁμαρτία error
ἄμεσος immediate, without a *middle*
ἀναγκαῖον necessary, must be
ἀναγνώρησις recognition
ἀναλογία analogy; proportion
ἀνήρ *man* (male)
ἄνθρωπος man (either sex)
ἀντικείμενος opposite
ἀντίφασις contradiction
ἀξίωμα axiom
ἀπάτη mistake
ἄπειρον infinite, unlimited; *Infinite, Unlimited*
ἁπλῶς unqualified, without qualification; singly; in a simplified way
ἀπόδειξις demonstration
ἀπόδειξις, δεικτική affirmative demonstration
ἀπόδειξις, κατὰ μέρος *particular* demonstration
ἀπόδειξις, κατηγορική affirmative demonstration
ἀπόδειξις, στερητική negative demonstration
ἀπόδειξις τοῦ δεικνῦναι direct demonstration
ἀπόφανσις statement
ἀποφαντικός λόγος proposition, declarative statement
ἀπόφασις denial; negation
ἀρετή virtue

716

ἀριθμός   number (natural, greater than 1)
ἀριστοκρατία   aristocracy
ἁρμονία   harmony, harmonic mode
ἁρμονική   harmonics
ἄρτιον   even (of numbers); *Even*
ἀρχή   principle, beginning, source, starting point
αὔξησις   increase; growth
αὐτόματον   chance; *chance*
ἀφαίρεσις   abstraction
ἀφή   sense of touch; touch, contact
ἀφροσύνη   folly, imprudence
βάναυσος   artisan
βάρος   density; weight; excessive weight
βούλευσις   deliberation
βουλευτής   councillor
βουλή   council
βούλησις   wish
γαμική   marriage, matrimony
γένεσις   generation, becoming
γένος   genus; race
γῆ   earth; Earth; *Earth*
γίγνεσθαι   be generated, become, come to be
γιγνώσκειν   know
γλῶττα   foreign name
γνώμη   *judgment*
γνωρίζειν   know
δεικνύειν   prove; show
δειλία   cowardice
δεινότης   shrewdness
δεσποτεία   mastership, rule of a master
δεσπότης   master
δεσποτικός   despotic, masterly
δημοκρατία   people's rule, ochlocracy
δῆμος   common people, lower classes
διά   because, through, by means of, by (sometimes)
διάθεσις   disposition
διακονικός   menial
διαλεκτική   dialectic or dialectics
διανοητικόν   *thinking* part of the soul
διάνοια   *thought*
δι αὐτό   because of itself, through itself, for its own sake
διαφορά   difference, differentia
δίκαιον   just thing, the just

δικαιοσύνη   justice
δικαίωμα   restitution
δίκη   verdict
διότι   cause, *reason*
δόξα   opinion; doctrine; reputation
δοῦλος   slave; servant
δυάς   two, dyad; Two, Dyad; *Dyad*
δύναμις   potentiality; power; capability; faculty
δυνατόν   possible
ἐγκράτεια   continence
ἔθνος   nation
ἔθος   custom
εἰδέναι   know; understand
εἶδος   species; kind; form; Form (for Plato)
εἰκός   probability
εἰρωνία   self-depreciation, irony
ἐκκλησία   assembly
ἑκούσιον   voluntary
ἔλεος   pity
ἐλευθεριότης   generosity
ἐλπίς   expectation
ἐμπειρία   experience
ἕν   one, unity; unit, measure; the *One, Unity, Oneness*
ἐναντίον   contrary
ἐνδέχεσθαι   may be
ἔνδοξος   generally or commonly accepted opinion
ἕνεκα, οὗ   final cause; purpose
ἐνέργεια   *actuality*, activity, exercise
ἐνθύμημα   enthymeme
ἐν ὅλω εἶναι   be in a whole
ἐντελέχεια   actuality
ἐν τινὶ εἶναι   be present in
ἑξῆς   succession
ἕξις   habit, possession
ἐπαγωγή   induction
ἐπεισόδιον   episode
ἐπιείκεια   equity, fairness
ἐπιθυμία   *desire*
ἐπιστήμη   *knowledge*, scientific knowledge, science
ἔπος   epic
ἐριστικός   eristic, contentious
εὖ   well; wellbeing; goodness
εὐγένεια   high birth or lineage

εὐδαιμονία happiness
εὔνοια good will
εὐστοχία discernment
εὐτυχία good luck or fortune
εὐφυία natural gift
ἐφεξῆς succession
ἐχόμενος contiguous, consecutive
ζῆλος emulation
ζωή life
ζῶον animal (including man)
ζῆν live
ᾗ qua, insofar as, inasmuch as
ἡδονή pleasure
ἠθικός ethical
ἦθος character
θάρρος, θάρσος courage, confidence
θερμόν hot; *Hot*
θέσις position; thesis; paradox; *Position*
θεωρητικός theoretical, contemplative
θηρίον nonrational animal, brute
θηριότης brutality
θής laborer
θρεπτικόν nutritive part of soul
θυμικόν spirited part of soul (concerned with temper)
θυμός temper, spirit; anger (sometimes)
ἰδέα idea; form; Idea (for Plato)
ἴδιον property, peculiarity
κάθαρσις catharsis, purging
καθ' αὐτό essential, by its nature; by itself; in itself
καθόλου universal; *universal*
κακία vice (vs. virtue)
κάλλος physical beauty
καλόν noble; beautiful
κατά with respect to, according to, in virtue of, by virtue of
κατάφασις affirmation
κατηγορεῖσθαι be predicable of, be a predicate of
κατηγορία category; predication
κατηγορούμενον predicate, n.
κατορθοῦν *succeed*, succeed in what is right
κεῖσθαι be in a position
κενόν void; *Void*
κίνησις motion
κοινόν common

κοινωνία   association
κρίνειν   distinguish, discriminate; judge; decide
κρίσις   judgment; decision
κτῆμα   property, possession
κτῆσις   possession of property
κτητική   art of acquisition
κύκλῳ   circular (of a syllogism)
λέγεσθαι κατά   said of
λέξις   language, diction
λογίζεσθαι   to reason, especially of what is possible
λογικός   logical
λογισμός   reasoning of the possible, judgment
λογιστικόν   judging power
λόγος   sentence; speech; argument; reason; definition; discussion; ratio;
        expression; theory
λύπη   pain
μάθημα   mathematics
μαθηματικά   mathematical objects
μαθηματική   mathematical science
μάλιστα   most of all, especially, in the highest degree
μᾶλλον   more, rather, to a higher degree
μεγαλοψυχία   high-mindedness
μεῖζον ἄκρον   major term
μέθοδος   method; *inquiry*, systematic inquiry
μέσον   middle, intermediate, mean; Center of universe, *middle*
μέσον ψευδές   false *middle*
μεσότης   mean, moderation
μεταβολή   change
μεταφορά   metaphor
μέτοικος   alien resident
μέτριον   moderate, right measure
μέτρον   measure
μῆκος   length; line
μὴ ὄν   nonbeing, not-being
μηχανική   mechanics
μῖγμα   blend; *Blend*
μικροψυχία   low-mindedness
μίμημα   work of imitation
μίμησις   imitation
μονάς   unit; Unit
μορφή   *form, shape*
μοχθηρία   evil habit
μῦθος   plot

νεῖκος   strife; *Strife*
νοεῖν   think
νόημα   concept; thought
νοητικόν   thinking part of the soul
νοητόν   object of thought, intelligible object
νόμισμα   medium of exchange, currency; coin
νόμος   law; custom, convention
νοῦς   intellect; Intellect; *Intelligence*
ξυνιέναι   *understand*
ὄγκος   volume; mass
οἰκία   household
οἰκονομία   household management
ὅλον   whole; universe
ὁμοιομερής   homogeneous
ὅμοιος   similar, like
ὁμόνοια   concord
ὁμώνυμος   equivocal
ὄν   being, thing, fact; *Being*
ὄνομα   name; noun
ὀπτική   optics
ὄργανον   organ; instrument
ὀργή   anger
ὀργιλότης   irascibility
ὀρεκτόν   object of desire
ὄρεξις   desire
ὀρθός   right
ὀρθῶς, οὐκ   wrongly
ὁρισμός   *definition;* definition in *Met., Phys., Ethics*
ὅρος   definition; boundary; limit; term in a syllogism
ὅτι, τό   fact
οὐκ ὄν   nonbeing, not-being
οὐρανός   heaven
οὐσία   substance; *substance*
ὄψις   vision; spectacle
πάθημα   impression, affection; *attribute;* emotion
πάθος   affection; *attribute;* emotion
πᾶν, τό   universe
πανοῦργος   unscrupulous
παράδειγμα   pattern; example
παράδοξον   contrary to general opinion
παραλογίζεσθαι   conclude falsely
παραλογισμός   fallacy, paralogism
παράλογον   contrary to reason

παρέκβασις   deviation, perversion
παρώνυμος   derivative expression
πάσχειν   be acted upon, be affected, suffer
πείθειν   persuade
πεπερασμένος   finite, limited; *Finite, Limited*
πέρας   limit; boundary; *Limit*
περιπέτεια   peripety
περιττόν   odd (of a number); *Odd*
πλῆθος   plurality, many; *Plurality*
πλοῦτος   wealth, riches
ποιεῖν   act; make, produce; posit
ποίημα   poem; thing produced
ποίησις   making, production, action
ποιητική   poetics
ποιόν, ποιότης   quality
πόλις   state
πολιτεία   government; form of government; democracy
πολίτευμα   ruling body, authority
πολίτης   citizen
πολιτική   politics; political
πολιτικός   statesman
πολλά   many; *Many*
ποσόν   quantity
ποτέ   whenness, sometime, at some time
ποῦ   somewhere, whereness, in a place
πρᾶγμα   thing, fact; alleged fact or thing
πρᾶξις   *action*, doing
πραότης   good temper
προαίρεσις   intention, *choice*, deliberate choice
πρός τι   relation, relative; correlative; correlatives
πρότασις   premise; statement; proposition
πρότερον   prior
πρότερον ἁπλῶς   prior without qualification
πρότερον ἡμῖν   prior to us
πρῶτος   first, primary
πτῶσις   case; tense; ending
πῦρ   fire; *Fire*
ῥητορική   rhetoric
σημαίνειν   mean, signify; indicate
σημεῖον   sign; point
σοφία   wisdom
σοφιστική   sophistry
σπέρμα   seed

σπουδαῖος   virtuous
στέρησις   privation
στερητικός   negative
στιγμή   point
στοιχεῖον   element; letter
συλλογίζεσθαι   prove
συλλογισμός   syllogism
συμβεβηκός   accident; attribute
συμβεβηκός, κατὰ   accidentally; indirectly, in virtue of an attribute
σύμμετρος   commensurable
συμφέρον   expediency, interest
συμφωνία   harmony, as applied to voice or sounds
σύνεσις   intelligence
συνεχής   continuous
συνώνυμος   univocal
σχῆμα   figure, shape; *Shape*; figure (of a syllogism)
σωφροσύνη   temperance
τεκμήριον   sure sign
τέλειος   complete, perfect
τέλος   end
τέχνη   art
τὶ ἔστι, τὸ   whatness, what a thing is
τὶ ἦν εἶναι   essence
τιμή   honor; value
τιμοκρατία   timocracy
τόδε τι   a *this*
τοιόνδε   such (implying a quality)
τόπος   place; topic
τροφή   food
τύχη   luck; chance (sometimes); fortune
ὕβρις   insult, abuse
ὕδωρ   water; *Water*
ὕλη   matter, materials
ὑπάρχειν   belong; exist
ὑπεναντίωσις   inconsistency
ὑπερβολή   excess
ὑπεροχή   excess; *Excess*
ὑπόθεσις   hypothesis, assumption
ὑποκείμενον   subject, underlying subject
ὑπολαμβάνειν   believe, assume
φαντασία   imagination
φθίσις   decrease; deterioration
φθορά   destruction

φιλία   friendship; *Friendship*
φιλοσοφία   philosophy
φιλοτιμία   ambition
φόβος   fear
φρονεῖν   judge or think rightly
φρόνησις   prudence
φύσει   by nature
φυσική   physics
φυσικός   physical, natural; physicist
φύσις   nature
φωνή   voice, vocal sound
χαυνότης   vanity
χερνίτης   manual laborer
χρῆμα   goods, money
χρηματιστική   art of finance
χρήσιμος   useful, instrumental
χρόνος   time
ψόφος   sound
ψυχή   soul
ὠφέλιμος   beneficial